Benjamin Henry Latrobe

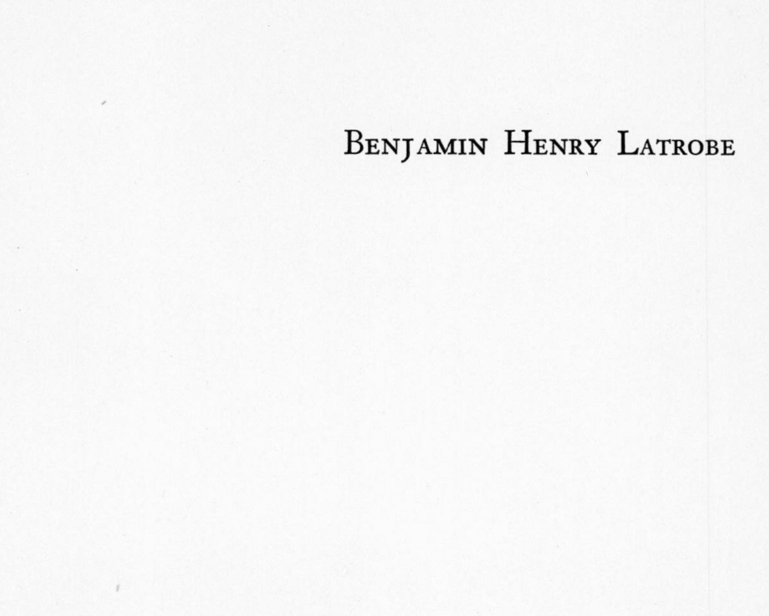

The Hermit and the Children. — Latrobe Sketchbooks

An Indian Mother Mourning Her Child: An illustration for *Ned Evans.* — Latrobe Sketchbooks

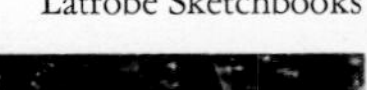

BENJAMIN HENRY

LATROBE

TALBOT HAMLIN

New York · OXFORD UNIVERSITY PRESS · 1955

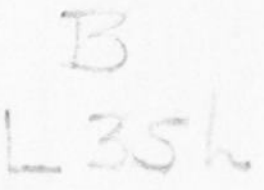

Library of Congress Catalogue Card Number: 55-8117

PRINTED IN THE UNITED STATES OF AMERICA

TO *Aileen Ford Latrobe*

FOREWORD

Of the importance of Benjamin Henry Latrobe to the future architecture of the United States my study of Greek Revival architecture in America made me continually more aware. It was my first attempts to express this conviction, through lectures and articles, that brought me the privilege of an acquaintance and eventual friendship with the late Ferdinand Claiborne Latrobe II (1889-1944), the architect's great-grandson. We shared an interest in the architecture, antiquities, and history of the young country, and little by little there grew up between us an informal understanding that someday I should write the biography of this pioneer American architect.

To know Ferdinand Latrobe was a delight. Definite and colorful, he was a man of wide curiosities. If you wanted to know where the best hunting in the Chesapeake was to be had, he could tell you; he could keep you enthralled for hours with early Chesapeake sailing ships and rigs, and he could give you the best way of cooking terrapin. But with equal pleasure he could cite you a reference in a Latrobe letter or give you the political background of Robert Goodloe Harper, and to him the devious patternings of the Nicholas Roosevelt–B. H. Latrobe finances were a simple riddle to read. His mind was saturated with the local history of the Virginia and Maryland countryside and with the political and economic history of Baltimore, of which his father, Ferdinand C. Latrobe I (1833-1911), had been mayor for seven terms. And all these varied interests were but facets of a personality of warm and unassuming charm, enlivened by a pungent vernacular wit. He wrote easily and with a definitely personal style; *Iron Men and Their Dogs* (Baltimore: Drechsler, 1941), commissioned as a history of the Bartlett-Hayward Company and its predecessors, shows how in dealing with such a subject his richly stored mind could make a book fascinating to read and could enhance its interesting story of the development of a great iron company with a wealth of anecdote and description to bring it all to vivid life. Among his other publications are *The Diamondback Terrapin; from The Epitome of the Chesapeake*

Bay (Baltimore: Twentieth Century Press, 1939) and *Chesapeake Bay Cook Book* (Baltimore: Horn-Shafer Co., 1940); several of his shorter pieces appeared in the magazine section of the Baltimore *Sunday Sun.*

Gradually I learned that Ferdinand himself, in association with Mr. Mark S. Watson, former editor of the Baltimore *Sunday Sun,* had prepared a manuscript entitled "The Writings of Benjamin Henry Latrobe," which was not published because he realized it was basically incomplete. But in the course of this work, as well as out of pure interest in his ancestor, Ferdinand had devoted years of whatever time he could seize from his many activities not only to the preservation, arrangement, and study of the priceless Latrobe papers and sketchbooks in the possession of the family but also to extensive delving in the widely distributed material elsewhere, and especially to investigating the political background of his great-grandfather's work. In this study he was continuing and broadening the efforts of his own grandfather, John H. B. Latrobe, who all through his life, by addresses and papers and by annotations on Latrobe drawings in the Library of Congress, had succeeded in keeping alive the memory of the architect's great contributions to the welfare and beautification of his adopted country.

In the course of this study Ferdinand had prepared a digest of the entire series of existing letter books, had indexed the notebooks and journals and the sketchbooks, and had begun a complete transcription of the letters. He had also made many notes on correlative material from Washington and Philadelphia newspapers and from other sources. All this material, together with the free use of the original documents themselves, he generously offered to me, and since his premature death his widow, Aileen Ford Latrobe, who herself has acquired a vast knowledge of the papers, has given me the most gracious and untrammeled co-operation.

At first my interest had been in Benjamin Henry Latrobe as an architect, but as I studied the material and talked further with Ferdinand I became more and more aware of the fascination of the architect's personality and the meaning behind the tragedy of his life. For besides being in touch with scores of the most noteworthy Americans of his time—Jefferson, Madison, Joel Barlow, and Robert Fulton among others—B. H. Latrobe had a definite place in the history of the country's industrial as well as architectural growth. The more deeply I dug into the large mass of available material the more important the task seemed to be. And the more difficult it appeared, too; not only the greatness of his architectural contribution had to be made clear, but in addition the quality of his character, the reasons for his successes and his failures, and the inevitability of the tragedy of the man "ahead of his time." The whole also had to be enriched with at least a modicum of the interesting sidelights which his letters and journals cast upon a time of struggle and transition. Without the work Ferdinand Latrobe had already accomplished, without the fruits of many conversations with a personality so rich in understanding, and especially without his encouragement and the inspiration which I received from his own enthusiasm, this work would have been, if not impossible, at least surrounded with almost insuperable difficulties. It is therefore to him first that I wish to set down my deepest gratitude—for his suggestion that I undertake the work, for his continuous assistance and co-operation, and for the inspiration his memory affords me.

Then, too, I am indebted to Mrs. Ferdinand C. Latrobe for her unstinted assistance—in arranging for me to have access to the material in her possession (often at great personal inconvenience and effort), in having transcriptions and photostats prepared, and in furnishing many valuable leads for further investigation—as well as for her continuing interest in the work.

And it is a pleasure to acknowledge the help I have received from other members of the family, especially two of the daughters of Mr. and Mrs. Ferdinand Latrobe: Mrs. John H. Heyrman, who with her husband photographed Latrobe and Hazlehurst tombs at Mount Holly, New Jersey, and did other research for me there; and Mrs. Samuel Wilson, Jr., who herself has an extensive knowledge of the contents of the Latrobe papers, transcribed many of them for me, and was of the greatest help in identifying elusive passages.

To Samuel Wilson, Jr., architect and historian, of New Orleans, I owe more than I can express for his continued and generous help in all matters regarding Latrobe in New Orleans, and for permission to use much material from Benjamin Henry Boneval Latrobe's *Impressions Respecting New Orleans* (New York: Columbia University Press, 1951), which he edited with an introduction and notes; I am grateful, too, to the Columbia University Press for its permission.

I cannot acknowledge in sufficiently appreciative words my debt to Miss Dorothy Stroud, Assistant Curator of Sir John Soane's Museum, London, for the amazingly productive research she accomplished in England at my behest. A large part of the sections dealing with Latrobe's life in London, and especially with his professional work there, is derived from her discoveries and from her photographs; her patience and assiduousness in discovering and documenting this material have achieved results of a richness I had not dreamed possible.

Professor Paul Norton, of Pennsylvania State University, had made a long and thorough study of Latrobe's work on the United States Capitol and had embodied this in a doctoral dissertation for Princeton University in 1950. This he generously put at my disposal, and I am happy to express my gratitude; many of the results of his study are necessarily included in the chapters on Latrobe's work for the United States government.

To Professor Louise Hall, of Duke University, I am also deeply grateful. In the course of her own research in the origins of the architectural and engineering professions in this country she had come across a wealth of material dealing with the life and work of Latrobe and the conditions surrounding it, and all that was pertinent to this book she placed at my disposal with unhesitating generosity. I am especially in her debt for a microfilm record of Latrobe's Washington lawsuits and of his bankruptcy proceedings, as well as for extensive illustrative material dealing with the Richmond penitentiary.

Mrs. George W. Emlen, of Ambler, Pennsylvania, and her son Mr. James Emlen, called to my attention and generously lent me the transcription of a two-year section of the diary of Thomas Cope, of Philadelphia, containing much valuable material dealing with the controversies surrounding the Philadelphia waterworks; I am grateful to them for the opportunity this give me of setting forth perhaps for the first time an adequate account of this struggle.

Mr. Charles E. Peterson, of the National Park Service, has been most helpful in calling my attention to many interesting Latrobe items and problems in connection with the Philadelphia region, and I am deeply indebted to his extraordinarily wide knowledge of the early architecture of this area.

But many other people have helped me, either by sending material that was directly pertinent or by calling my attention to sources I might otherwise have missed. Among them are: Mr. Jerome H. Abrams, Baltimore, for preparing excellent color photographs of many Latrobe sketches; Professor Nelson F. Adkins, of New York University, for calling my attention to Latrobe's contributions to the *Transactions of the American Philosophical Society;* Mr. Wayne Andrews, of the New-York Historical Society, for many valuable suggestions, and especially for calling my attention to items in the Livingston papers in the Society dealing with Latrobe, Roosevelt, and early steamboat affairs; Mrs. Truxtun Beale, Washington, for generously sending me photographs of the Latrobe drawings for the Decatur house, which she now owns, and permitting me to reproduce from them; Mrs. William F. Bevan, Ruxton, Maryland, for information regarding Latrobe's possible work on the Ringgold house in Hagerstown, and for an illustration of Latrobe's courthouse there; Mr. Nelson M. Blake, of the National Archives and Records Service, Washington, for assistance in tracing records and drawings of Latrobe; Mr. Louis H. Bolander, Librarian of the United States Naval Academy, Annapolis, Maryland; Mr. Richard Borneman, Assistant Curator of the Baltimore Museum of Art, for assistance with regard to Baltimore material of and about Latrobe, and for making available to me a large amount of material, including rare illustrations, concerning the Baltimore Exchange; Mr. Alan Burnham, architect, Greenwich, Connecticut, for permitting me to use his valuable notes and drawings of the Baltimore Exchange; Mr. J. N. Burr, Columbus, New Jersey, for a picture of Clover Hill in Mount Holly; and Mr. W. F. Burton, State Archivist of North Carolina, Raleigh, for generous help in sending me records of Latrobe's proposed employment as engineer of the state.

Also Mr. Courtney Campbell, New York, for valuable suggestions concerning Latrobe's relations with Gilbert Stuart; Mr. Milton H. Cantor, New York, who is preparing a book on Joel Barlow and sent me some Barlow material; Mrs. Ralph Catterall, Librarian of the Valentine Museum, Richmond, for valuable help in tracing many details concerning Latrobe's Virginia life and work; Mr. Randolph W. Church, Librarian of the Virginia State Library, Richmond, for help in investigating the Latrobe material in that library, and for permission to reproduce part of it; Mrs. Robert W. Claiborne, Director of the Valentine Museum, Richmond, for valuable assistance in many Virginia matters, and especially for her identification of Miss Susanna Catharine Spotswood; Mr. Meredith Colkett, of the National Archives and Records Service, Washington, and Director of the Columbia Historical Society, for valuable assistance in locating Latrobe material; Mr. H. P. Copland, Curator of Marine History, East India Marine Hall, Salem, Massachusetts, for assisting me in the effort to trace the history of the ship *Eliza;* Mr. Hubertis Cummings, Consultant of the Pennsylvania Historical and Museum Division of Public Records, Harrisburg, for sending me copies of the complete records of the Susquehanna survey made by Latrobe; Mr. C. Frank Dunn, Frankfort, Kentucky, for material concerning the arsenal in Frankfort; Mr. H. G. Dwight, New York, for making available to me a long letter from Latrobe to Dr. Scandella which was in his possession and which he later generously presented to the Avery Library of Columbia University; Mr. Harold Donaldson Eberlein, Philadelphia, for calling my attention to Latrobe material in the Ridgeway Branch of the Free Library of Philadelphia, as well as for sharing his deep knowledge of many phases of old Philadelphia; President William W. Edel, Dickinson College, Carlisle, Pennsylvania, for constant encouragement and assistance, and for calling my attention to the relation between Latrobe and Brackenridge; and Professor Cecil D. Elliott, of the School of Design, North Carolina State College, Raleigh, for calling my attention to Latrobe letters in the North Carolina state archives.

Also Professor Milton E. Flower, of Dickinson College, Carlisle, for valuable help concerning Latrobe's work at Dickinson, and for sending me photographs of the Latrobe drawings there, as well as for information with regard to Professor Cooper and the *Emporium;* Mr. James W. Foster, Director of the Maryland Historical Society, Baltimore, for continuing assistance in analyzing the rich stores of Latrobe material in the Maryland Historical Society, and for permission to reproduce some of it; Mr. W. Neil Franklin, of the National Archives and Records Service, Washington, for locating illustration material; Mr. Deoch Fulton, Assistant to the Director of the New York Public Library, for generously searching for Latrobe manuscripts in the library and for sending me a complete list of them; Bishop S. H. Gapp, Archivist of the Moravian Church, Bethlehem, Pennsylvania, for information with regard to the Moravian schools in Germany; Miss Bess Glenn, of the National Archives and Records Service, Washington, for generous assistance in locating the trial records of Latrobe's various legal adventures; the Reverend Dr. C. Leslie Glenn, Rector of St. John's Church, Washington, for his generous gift of a reproduction of Latrobe's rendering of St. John's Church; Mr. John S. Greenfeldt, Editor of the *Moravian,* for calling my attention to Moravian records in Bethlehem, Pennsylvania; Mr. Hugh J. Hazlehurst, Baltimore, for much valuable information with regard to the Hazlehurst family as well as Latrobe's Antes relatives; Professor Henry-Russell Hitchcock, Jr., of the Smith College Art Gallery, for important suggestions in respect to Latrobe as a painter; Mr. F. F. Holbrook, Librarian of the Historical Society of Western Pennsylvania, Pittsburgh, for suggestions concerning early Pittsburgh; Miss Hope K. Holdcamper, of the National Archives and Records Service, Washington, for locating plans of the Mississippi lighthouse; and Mr. Marion Johnson, of the National Archives and Records Service, Washington, for generous assistance in finding and reproducing the records of Latrobe trials.

Also Mr. Clay Lancaster, of Columbia University, for continual and generous assistance dealing with the Pope house, Ashland, and other Kentucky buildings designed by Latrobe, and for other pertinent Kentucky materials; the late Miss Mildred Latrobe-Bateman, Streatley, England, for the use of Latrobe family documents in her possession; the Reverend Mr. A. J. Lewis, Headmaster of Fulneck School, Yorkshire, for communicating important information regarding Latrobe's years in Fulneck; Miss Virginia E. Lewis, Curator of Exhibitions, University of Pittsburgh, for suggestions as to illustrations of early Pittsburgh; Mr. Alexander Mackay-Smith, President of the Clarke County Historical Society, Virginia, for valuable information including plans and photographs of Long Branch, designed by Latrobe; Professor Joseph Maurer, of Lehigh University, Bethlehem, for help in examining the Moravian background of Latrobe; Professor Doktor Georg Mayer, Rector of the University of Leipzig, East Germany, for examining the matriculation lists of the University; Professor Carroll L. V. Meeks, of Yale University, for information with regard to Latrobe's exhibits at the Academy of Fine Arts in Philadelphia; Dr. Isaac Mendelsohn, of Columbia University, for generously transcribing Latrobe's Hebrew script; Professor John O'Connor, Jr., Associate Director of the Department of Fine Arts, Carnegie Institute of Technology, for assistance in tracing early Pittsburgh material; Miss Alice Lee Parker, Acting Chief of the Prints and Photographs Division, Library of Congress, for her most co-operative assistance in connection with the Latrobe material in the library; Mr. Horace W. Peaslee, Washington architect, for assistance in connection with Christ Church and St. John's Church, Washington; Mr. James H. Rodenbaugh, of the Ohio State Museum and Ohio State Archaeological and Historical Society, Columbus, for information, plans, and photographs of Adena, in Chillicothe, designed by Latrobe; Mr. Nicholas G. Roosevelt, Philadelphia, for assistance in searching for material dealing with his ancestor Nicholas Roosevelt; and Miss Anna Wells Rutledge, Charleston, South Carolina, for a list of Latrobe's entries in the Academy of Fine Arts exhibitions in Philadelphia.

Also Miss Mary Wingfield Scott, Richmond, Virginia, for invaluable assistance in investigating the trail of Latrobe in Richmond, and for sharing her wide knowledge of the architecture and history of early Richmond; Professor H. L. Seaver, Lexington, Massachusetts, for sending me a copy of a Latrobe letter in his possession that dealt with glass for the United States Capitol; Professor Charles Coleman Sellers, of Dickinson College, for many valuable suggestions and for information with regard to the Peale family and the portraits of Latrobe; the Reverend Mr. C. H. Shawe, Chairman of the Provincial Board of the Moravian Church in Great Britain and Ireland, London, for assistance in searching Moravian records in England; Mrs. Roger Sherman, Williamsburg, Virginia, for fascinating material dealing with the Virginia theater and with West's troupe of players; Mr. Henry C. Shinn, Mount Holly, New Jersey, for sending me a history of the Hazlehurst estate, Clover Hill; Mr. Albert Simons, Charleston architect, for suggestions and assistance of many kinds; Professor Robert Smith, of the University of Pennsylvania, for valuable suggestions as to sources; Mr. John S. Still, Special Projects

Historian, Ohio State Archaeological and Historical Society, Columbus, for valuable information with regard to Adena, in Chillicothe, designed by Latrobe; Mr. Charles M. Stotz, Pittsburgh architect, for many valuable suggestions with regard to Latrobe's Pittsburgh work; Mr. Walter Knight Sturges, New York architect, for much assistance in connection with the Baltimore Cathedral, and for permission to use some illustrations of that building; Mr. John Summerson, Curator of Sir John Soane's Museum, London, for valuable suggestions regarding the English background of Latrobe; Mr. Howard Swiggett, Hewlett, Long Island, for interesting material concerning Gouverneur Morris and his relations with Latrobe; the Right Reverend Dr. H. St. George Tucker, Bishop of the Episcopal diocese of Virginia, who wrote me about the Latrobe water color of Mount Vernon which he owns and of which he generously sent me a photograph for reproduction; Mr. Carl Vitz, Director of the Cincinnati Public Library, for valuable information with regard to early steamboats on the Ohio River; the Reverend Mr. C. Preston Wiles, Rector of St. Mary's Church, Burlington, New Jersey, for assistance in tracing records of the Hazlehurst family; Mrs. George Windell, Assistant Librarian of the Historical Society of Delaware, Wilmington, for generous help in connection with Latrobe's survey and plan for Newcastle, and for sending me reproductions of it; and Mr. Joseph F. Winkler, of the National Archives and Records Service, Washington, for locating Latrobe's plans for Norfolk fortifications.

I wish also to thank the following for so generously responding to my published appeal for Latrobe material: Mrs. Leroy R. Dumsey, Allentown, Pennsylvania; the late Mr. James R. Edmunds, Past President of the American Institute of Architects, Baltimore; Mr. R. M. Harper, University, Alabama; Mr. T. Worth Jamieson, Baltimore; Mr. Stephen G. Rich, Verona, New Jersey; and Mr. William E. Rooney, Monroe, Louisiana.

Several of my Columbia University colleagues and friends have been most helpful, both through encouragement and through sharing with me their specialized knowledge. Especially I wish to thank Dean Leopold Arnaud of the School of Architecture for his continuing encouragement; Professor James Grote Van Derpool of the Avery Library for assistance in many matters concerning the background of Latrobe's architecture; and Professors Henry Steele Commager and John A. Krout of the History Department for help in historical matters and for constant and enthusiastic support. To Columbia University, too, I am deeply indebted for a generous grant from the Fund for Research in the Humanities (received through the recommendation of Vice-President and Provost John A. Krout) under which the foreign research was undertaken.

I have received the utmost in co-operation, also, from many libraries and historical societies. To them and their willing and skillful staffs I must express my warm gratitude. Among the libraries, which so often furnish the lifeblood of research, are the Avery Library of Columbia University, the Columbia University Library (chiefly its reference staff), the Library of Congress (especially its print, manuscript, and map divisions), the National Archives, the New York Public Library (particularly its print, map, manuscript, and local history rooms), the Ridgeway Branch of the Free Library of Philadelphia, and the Virginia State Library. The State Archive Departments of North Carolina and of Pennsylvania have also been most helpful. The societies whose facilities and holdings have been of the greatest value include the Boston Athenaeum, the Columbia Historical Society of Washington, the Historical Society of Pennsylvania, the Maryland Historical Society, the New-York Historical Society, and the Valentine Museum of Richmond, Virginia.

Last of all, I wish to set down my deep gratitude to my wife, Jessica Hamlin, for endless help of many kinds in putting this book into its final state, for preparing the index, and especially for her trained and sympathetic editorial eye which alone has saved me from numberless ambiguities and verbal infelicities.

TALBOT HAMLIN

Columbia University
June 30, 1954

PROLOGUE

If you had been walking down Second Street in Philadelphia on a fall Sunday afternoon in 1800, you might have seen ahead of you, turning into the street from Chestnut, a tall, dark-haired man, quietly but fashionably dressed, with his much younger wife on his arm. They had just come from Centre Square (where the City Hall now rears its ponderous hulk), and he had been showing her the progress on his latest building—the white-marble pump house of the waterworks—which, already well above the foundations, scaffold-surrounded, revealed through its doorway the deep pit within, where the awkward steam pump would eventually puff and wheeze. Now they were bound to his other great Philadelphia structure, the Bank of Pennsylvania; down the street its gleaming white walls and its Ionic portico formed an impressive contrast to the old rose and gray bricks of the usual Philadelphia streets.

The tall man—a good six feet two—was Benjamin Henry Latrobe, now at thirty-six in the flower of his young maturity; his wife, pretty, petite, slim in her fashionable Empire costume, had been Mary Elizabeth Hazlehurst of Mount Holly and Philadelphia before their marriage that May. As they approached the new bank, the purity of its simple walls, the graciousness of its proportions, the unaccustomed power and simplicity of its Greek Ionic capitals—the first that Philadelphia had ever seen—suddenly struck her with their beauty, as the drawings for them she had watched her husband making had never been able to do, and she stopped involuntarily, pressed her companion's arm, and looked admiringly up to him. As he felt the pressure he, too, turned to her, and his quiet, serious, almost somber face—with its strong rounded contours, the full artist's lips, and the eager eyes which alone gave a hint of the passion within—came suddenly to ardent, smiling life, and for the moment he seemed not only sensitive and strong but handsome; for he had been disciplined by long years of religious training, by years in England of gaiety, intellectual experiment, success, tragedy, and failure, and only imagination and emotion could break his usual control so that his countenance revealed the true depths behind.

Some seventeen years later, you might have seen the same man in Washington, striding along with almost the same eager tread, coming from a bankruptcy proceeding—his own. The face now has lost its earlier roundness; the cheeks are slightly hollowed, the chin sharper, the mouth drawn with greater determination. He is wearing steel-rimmed spectacles, and the eyes behind are sad; yet they are still the eyes of the dreamer and the maker, and they are still innocent and kind. He is going home through the chilly December gloom, almost forgetful of the half-frozen slush through which he walks, to the little house on the hills toward the northwest—home to tell his wife that the inevitable step has at last been taken and that soon, with whatever possessions the insolvency law allowed them to retain, they would be departing forever from the gangling city. Washington had seen for them so much of pain and of harassing attacks from professional and political opponents or rivals, so many lawsuits over the notes he had rashly endorsed for friends, so many growing claims from the shattered schemes that once had been bright dreams of financial security! Yet the expanding capital had brought them, too, tremendous professional successes; the finest new houses in the town were of his design, and the new interiors of the rebuilt Capitol—so much improved since the burning by the British in 1814—had a controlled richness, a power of space design, and a beauty and perfection of detail that were to win the admiration of later millions. In Washington they had also known their greatest social success; they had been intimate with presidents and cabinets, foreign ministers, clergymen and artists, and the best intellects in Washington had flocked to their doors. And now this—this insolvency—this mark of failure somewhere. Now, the Capitol commission resigned, they must move to Baltimore and try again to rebuild their lives.

Then another three years, and in a little house at the lower end of New Orleans you might have seen him lying dead—dead of the yellow fever that had earlier claimed his eldest son—and the distracted family planning how they might return again to the security of friends in Baltimore.

Latrobe's life, then, is a tale of rise, and of decline and fall. How did it happen that this man—this brilliant architect and engineer, this designer of so many of the country's most distinguished buildings, this single-minded creator of the architectural profession in the United States, this architect whose two pupils William Strickland and Robert Mills became in turn the country's most distinguished architects to carry forward the development of the profession—how did it come that Latrobe, apparently almost forgotten, was to die nearly penniless in New Orleans?

It is a long story, in which character and the conditions of life in the young country all had their part. It is the story of a man ahead of his time, a man with a vivid imagination that not only could create buildings of superb power and restraint but could also see (almost too clearly) the advantages that America—in those days spreading so rapidly into the west and in the east changing gradually from an agricultural to a commercial and industrial base—could gain from steam power and the development of machines. It is the story of how a country, then as alas occasionally now suspicious of the artist and fearful of beauty (or rather of the emotions beauty arouses), would give to Latrobe's intense aesthetic vision merely the most superficial and grudging admiration and would pay only grudgingly and under pressure a pittance for his professional services. It is the story of a man trained in England, where the architectural profession was already respected and secure, trying to bring the benefit of that system and the knowledge and talent his training had given him to a country where the old traditional builder-designer system still held almost complete sway and the "architect" was either an amateur or an ambitious carpenter or bricklayer. It is the tragedy of a man devoted to the ideals of imaginative planning in a country where mere improvisation was still the rule.

But, added to all this, it is the tale of an artist irresistibly drawn—almost by fate, it would seem, and by ambition, and later by the mere attempt to obtain a modicum of financial security—into business and speculation. Latrobe, almost at the beginning of his career, was plunged into a morass of debts, not his fault (except as his generous enthusiasm and lack of caution might be faults), losing thereby the capital he had brought with him from England; then, driven alike by his ambition and his imagination, he became engulfed in larger and larger schemes, each of which was intended to make the money to pay the debts which the preceding failure had entailed—until the whole structure crashed. In the story there is personal villainy on the part of more than one associate. Often there is merely the rather heartless business logic of men with more capital than he. Sometimes he is the victim of what can only be called the intervention of a cruel fate. And the irony of it is that all those schemes on which he labored (water systems, steam engines, steamboats, power looms) *were* good—but ten or fifteen years later. Out of them all, others did make successes and fortunes. But to Latrobe they brought only disaster, and the capital—so painfully obtained from his architectural practice—which he poured into them, drop by drop, all vanished into thin air or into the capacious pockets of other men. On his architectural earnings Latrobe could have lived not luxuriously, perhaps, but well. It was his optimistic business enterprises and his generous trust in others that spelled his ruin.

Today we can realize his enormous gifts to the country. Today every architect and every individual or corporation that has used and profited by architectural services may thank Latrobe, who almost single-handed created in this country the true professional attitude in the art of building. Now, when we walk through town after town in the East and the Middle West and see in the white houses the harmony that American genius has created by its imaginative use of Greek forms and Greek feeling, we may thank Latrobe again; for he, first in America, used Greek precedent and from it developed new and creative American expressions. And today, as hundreds of thousands of sightseers are guided through the Capitol, some at least will draw in their breath suddenly as the wide spaces of Statuary Hall (originally the House of Representatives) open to them; many will be thrilled at the purity and the grace that rules in what now is labeled the Old Supreme Court (originally the Senate Chamber); more will be delighted at the capitals Latrobe so deftly composed from the American corn and tobacco plants; a few will note the brilliance of the vaulting of the entrance stairs and of the room originally designed for the Supreme Court beneath the old Senate Chamber. They will carry back with them, these sightseers, however ignorant architecturally they may be, impressions of space and dignity, of richness and restraint, of fine and permanent materials beautifully used. These impressions, arising from the designs Latrobe made so long ago, continue a century and a quarter later to bear witness to his genius.

It is the tale of this architect, this artist, this engineer that the ensuing pages will tell; it is an evaluation of his work that this book attempts to give.

TABLE OF CONTENTS

Part IV: END OF THE ROAD

LIST OF PLATES

(Unless otherwise noted, the sketchbooks of B. H. Latrobe are in the possession of the Latrobe family.)

LIST OF TEXT ILLUSTRATIONS

(Unless otherwise noted, the journals, sketchbooks, and letter books of B. H. Latrobe are in the possession of the Latrobe family.)

PART I: LATROBE IN EUROPE

CHAPTER

I

Background and Youth

In the rolling country of mid-Yorkshire, halfway between the lush fields and streams of the East Riding and the wild and barren moors of the northwest, a little stream curves east and then north into the river Aire at Leeds. From the bend a rounded hill rises, breastlike, to a ridge where stands the ancient weavers' village of Pudsey. On this hill, midway down to the valley, a street of old buildings follows the contours around the slope; this is Fulneck.

Here, in the center of a great woolen-cloth weaving area, Fulneck was established some two centuries ago by the Moravians—the Unitas Fratrum (Unity of the Brethren, or United Brethren)—who had made many converts among the weavers in Pudsey and the villages near by. In due time there rose along the street a row of comely brick buildings: a school (still one of the distinguished boarding schools of England), a home for the director, a "sisters' house" and a "brothers' house" for the unmarried members of the community. As the advantages of the beautiful site and the rare combination it offered of country seclusion and nearness to Leeds and Bradford became plain, the Unitas Fratrum moved its London schools for boys and girls to Fulneck, which soon became the British educational center of the Moravian movement.

Today the immediate scene has changed but little, though Leeds in its industrial sprawl has reached out toward it. From the gracious, simple Georgian buildings one still looks down to the south and east over swelling vacant fields and, across the little river, to woods on the other side that are still, as they were a century ago, part of the park of an adjacent manor house. The little stream still flows down, curving out of sight to the north into a picturesque and rocky defile, and the schoolchildren still study and play in the rose-gray brick buildings and over the sloping, rounded fields.

There, in the schoolmaster's house, on May 1, 1764, a baby was born to Benjamin and Margaret Antes Latrobe, and on the next day he was baptized in the school chapel and christened Benjamin Henry Latrobe.[1]

The Latrobes were an exceptional family. At the time of the revocation of the Edict of Nantes, in 1685, the family of Boneval de La Trobe was divided, brother against brother, one a Protestant and the other a Roman Catholic. The Protestant, Count Jean Henri, fled the country with his wife and went to Holland, where he joined the army of the Prince of Orange. An uncle of his, a Catholic, later became famous (or at least notorious) in his own right; a wanderer, an eccentric, bored with France, he journeyed to Constantinople, embraced Mohammedanism, was created a Pasha by the Sultan, and had a luxurious palace complete with a large harem on the Bosphorus. Casanova visited him there in 1741 and later left in his *Memoires* an extensive if somewhat scandalous account of the visit. Long afterward the architect Benjamin Henry Latrobe, then in faraway America, remembered the legend and remarked in a letter (November 4, 1804) to his elder brother Christian in England, "From the days of our old grand uncle Count Boneval, Pacha of Belgrade, we have been an eccentric breed."

Nor was the life of the young Protestant count without adventure. He accompanied William III to England, then joined the Irish expedition, and was wounded at the Battle of the Boyne. Later he made Ireland his home and settled in Dublin, where he prospered; he was probably the John de La Trobe mentioned in old records as a founder and developer of the fine-linen industry in Dublin.[2] His son James (1702-52), who established a sailcloth business, dropped the Boneval and became simply James de La Trobe. A pillar of Protestant society there, James gave his son Benjamin (1726-86) the best possible education at the University of Glasgow and evidently on the Continent as well, including an intensive training in Germany, though the details are lacking. James married three times; Benjamin was the son of the first wife, Rebecca Adams,[3] but

---

1. Baptismal record and school journal.

2. David C. Agnew, *Protestant Exiles from France . . .* 3d ed. (London: for private circulation, 1886).

3. This is based on a genealogical table in the possession of the Latrobe family. Agnew (*op. cit.*) gives the mother's family name as Thornton, perhaps the name of James's second wife. A manuscript note signed "James Latrobe, Episcopus Fratrum, 26 July 1884," discovered in the papers of Miss Mildred La Trobe-Bateman by Miss Dorothy Stroud, contains the following passage: "A brief memoir of James Latrobe inserted in the Diary of

it was James's third wife with the good old Irish name of O'Toole that his grandson the architect came to know.

Benjamin had planned to enter the ministry as a Baptist and had formed a small group of some thirty enthusiastic young people to study theological problems. In 1746 they invited a Moravian missionary then in Dublin to preach to them, and Benjamin Latrobe was enthralled despite his Baptist upbringing; both the broad tolerance and the missionary zeal of the Moravian faith won his fervid support. Unhesitatingly he cast his lot with them—and was immediately disowned by his father, even though the Moravians made no claims of being a separate denomination. Actually they were declared, by an Act of Parliament in 1749, a valid part of the Church of England; their later sectarianism was forced upon them by the need for a definite organization not only to protect them from outside attacks but also to watch over their world-wide activities. Benjamin threw himself into the new movement with complete devotion. Some of the group later became Methodists, but he remained faithful to his Moravian associates. He began work with them on June 15, 1746, and in the same year accompanied Cennick on a missionary trip through Antrim. In 1750 the Dublin Moravians were formally instituted as a city congregation by Bishop Buehler.[4]

Unquestionably Benjamin Latrobe was a magnificent preacher; Holmes, the Moravian historian, writes of him, "We have never seen his equal in

---

the Dublin Moravian Congregation states 'that he was married to his first wife in 1721, by whom he had 13 children; she died in 1744.' " Another hand has inserted "Thornton" as this first wife's name.

The same manuscript, quoting one Peter Latrobe, remarks that Benjamin's father, James, had closed his doors on his son when Benjamin joined the Moravians; but he, too, was at last won over and joined them himself in 1750. Benjamin officiated at his father's first Moravian communion, and the father exclaimed, with tears, "My son, in my ignorance I drove thee from thy father's house, and now dost thou bring me the blessed bread."

The Latrobe family in America seems to have believed that Benjamin had been born in the colony of New York, to which his father James had emigrated and where he remained for a short time before returning to Ireland, and that it was on this ground that B. H. Latrobe claimed American citizenship from the time of his arrival in the country. In none of the English or Irish sources with which I am acquainted is there any mention of this American sojourn or of his father's birth in America. Furthermore, in a letter to Thomas Jefferson on July 4, 1807, he refers to his American descent in the *fourth* generation. This obviously has reference to his mother's family and to his mother's grandfather, Baron von Blume, the original Antes in Pennsylvania.

4. Rev. John Holmes, *History of the Protestant Church of the United Brethren* (London: the author, 1825).

our church." But he was a superb administrator as well, and a scholar and a man of means; the little Dublin congregation could not hold him. Soon he was sent to England, where he became head of the excellent Moravian school at Fulneck; in 1765 he was moved to London and placed in general charge of all the Moravian establishments in the British Isles, especially the schools. His title was merely "provincial helper," and despite his great services to the church he was never made a bishop.

His brilliance as a preacher, scholar, musician, and conversationalist won him entrée into all classes of society. He formed, says Holmes, "an extensive circle of acquaintances, especially in the higher ranks of society, who esteemed him as a man and a Christian, and honored him as a devoted servant of God." In London his close associates ranged from Sir Charles Middleton of the Navy to Dr. Burney and Dr. Johnson. Boswell, in commenting on the religious breadth and tolerance of the great lexicographer, cites his friendship for Benjamin Latrobe as an example. The Moravian leader was equally close to Dr. Burney and is said to have helped him translate most of the German musical authorities Burney used and cited in his various writings. This intimacy with the Burney family was to persist, after his death, among members of the younger generation.

But though Benjamin Latrobe was a friend of the great in society and in literature he seems to have been no less the friend of the lowly. Years later, his son, in America, set down at length a story that reveals the esteem in which he was held. While he was at Fulneck an illiterate cobbler of Leeds, one Thomas Rhodes, had come to know him well and to trust him like a father. Rhodes unexpectedly fell heir to a large fortune from a distant and childless relative, and went at once to Latrobe in London for advice. He wanted to be a gentleman, he said. And the story goes on to show how the Leeds cobbler, though unable to read and write, with the aid of Latrobe proceeded to Germany, bought a great estate in Silesia, married a fortune-seeking widow baronin, and himself became Baron von Rothe.

The background of the architect's mother was as romantic and as international as that of his father. Margaret Antes was born in Pennsylvania, where her father, Henry Antes, was a wealthy landowner who had become much attached to the Moravian missionaries there and had helped them in the purchase of the land where they built Bethlehem; in fact, in the early years of the settlement he was its titular owner. His own father—originally a German Baron von Blume, a religious-minded man and abbot of a monastery—somehow had become converted to Protestantism and had married an abbess, who like himself had become a Protestant; together they fled from Germany to the welcoming tolerance of Pennsylvania, where they started a new life and took the name of Anthos (the Greek word for flower, to correspond with the German *Blume*), which they later simplified to Antes.

Henry Antes had a large family. One of his sons, Frederick, became a noted colonel in the Revolutionary War and remained an important figure in Pennsylvania till his death. A daughter, Anna Catherine, was a leading figure in the settlement and building up of the two Moravian communities in North Carolina, Betharaba and Salem. But it was the life of his eldest daughter, Margaret, born in 1729, that showed most clearly the Antes devotion to the Moravian cause. In 1742 Count Zinzendorf, the acknowledged head of the Unitas Fratrum, visited America and made extended stays with Henry Antes between mission trips to the Indians and to New York. When he returned to Europe in 1743, Margaret, then a young girl of fourteen, accompanied him to be trained in the Moravian schools in England. There she remained, passing at graduation from the role of student to that of teacher in these schools. She was especially known as a teacher of music, and the Moravians set great store by music.[5] Later she became head of the girls' school in London, moving with it to Fulneck, and in 1756 she and Benjamin Latrobe, thrown into close association by their respective official responsibilities, were married.

It was to this extraordinary couple that Benjamin Henry Latrobe was born on the first of May in 1764. A French count become Irish Protestant, a German baron become Pennsylvania Dutch, and English, Scotch, and Irish strains all contributed to his inheritance, just as Moravian enthusiasm, Moravian unconventionality, and the tolerant cosmopolitanism of the Moravian ideal contributed to his education. From his mother he must have learned much about the primitive Pennsylvania that she had known as a child—the hearty hospitality of the Henry Antes home, as

5. See, for example, "Music in Wachovia, 1753-1800," by Maurer Maurer, *William and Mary Quarterly,* 3rd series, vol. 8, no. 2 (April 1951), pp. 214-27.

well as the idealism that governed it; the forests, the Indian missions, the hope of Indian conversion and friendship, and tales of occasional Indian hostility and cruelty. Though she had left America before the troubled days of the French and Indian war, she must have learned much of the pervading anxiety from her family and from the general Moravian talk; some of this she doubtless passed on to her children. To Benjamin Henry especially, one feels, America became a constant source of interest and curiosity. Later on he received through his mother large land holdings in Pennsylvania as his share in the Antes wealth, and these were to be incalculably helpful to him in time to come.

From his father the influences were no less important to his future; in him he could see the benefits of scholarship, of wide interests, of personal charm and vivacity, and through his father's wide social circle the son could not fail to realize the delights of social exchange with the great, the learned, the well born. Young Latrobe was in an ideal position—and that at an ideal time in the history of English culture—to react to the romantic background of his mother and to the intellectual and human richness of his father's personality. In this double heritage, whether a matter of genes or of relish in the environment so formed, lay the seeds of much of his character and personality.

The education Benjamin Henry Latrobe received was equally out of the ordinary. To understand it one must know something of the Moravian attitudes toward education as well as toward the family. Though their viewpoint was international, their educational objectives were individual. At this time, when the usual child-education aims in both England and America were concerned with "breaking the child's will" and rendering him a docile receptacle for rote learning, and when individual caprices were seen as works of the devil, the Moravian ideal was definitely "advanced" or, as we should call it, "progressive." The individual will was seen as an engine for God's work and *not* as an instrument of the devil. Much later, Jacob Smedley in Philadelphia expressed the Moravian ideal thus: "A great deal is said of the necessity of breaking a child's will. Why need a child's will be broken? He will have use for it all. The difference between strength of will and weakness of will is often the difference between efficiency and inefficiency. . . . Wide margin should be granted for the expansion of a child's own individuality, for his peculiar mental action and for the cultivation and the gratification of his tastes." [6]

But the international character of the Moravians was also a powerful factor in their educational aims. The Unitas Fratrum was not then British or American or German—it was all of them, and more. Its historic origins lay in Central Europe, but it had missions all over the world. Many of its greatest leaders—Zinzendorf, Nietschmann, Buehler, and others—came from Germany, and it remained a custom for the acknowledged leaders of the movement to obtain some of their education outside their own countries. Naturally the English and American groups turned toward Saxony, the home of their beloved leader. This meant that the brethren brought to the problems that faced them an attitude basically international.

Furthermore, the Moravians held the family per se in lighter esteem than did many other eighteenth-century Christians. It is significant that the early Moravian settlements in both England and America were communal in character, though their common holding of goods was always felt to be a temporary condition that was to yield to individual property and individual family living as soon as conditions became sufficiently stable. But the seed was sown; close family connections were long seen as perhaps a barrier to the freest, most efficient Christian living. Husbands and wives were seldom separated, it is true, but boarding-school education in a community and away from the family was considered the best type, even from the most tender ages. The results of this concept were various. In some instances it gave rise to a complete freedom from family ties, an attitude that to many seems cold or heartless; but in the case of more affectionate and sensitive natures (like that of Benjamin Henry, for example) it resulted in quite the reverse—a violently emotional need of a devoted family around, as if to make up for the earlier lack. Still another reaction—in which family living, when it was discovered, came as a complete surprise—is revealed in a letter from Fanny Burney to her sister Charlotte (December 7, 1784):

One of the Moravians was here again the other evening and was really entertaining enough by the singular simplicity of his conversation. He was brought

6. From *Hints for the Training of Youth: A Scrapbook for Mothers* (Philadelphia, 1875), quoted in Monica Kiefer's *American Children through Their Books, 1700-1835* (Philadelphia: University of Pennsylvania Press, 1948).

up in Germany and spent the greater part of his early youth in roving about from place to place, & country to country, for though he had his education in Germany, he is a native of Ireland & his father and mother reside chiefly in England.

"Not being used," said he, "to a family when I was a boy, I always hated it. They seemed to me only as so many wasps, for one told me I was too silent, another wished I would not speak so much & all of them find some fault or other. But now that I am come home to live, & am constrained to be with them, I enjoy it very much."

What must be the sect and where the travelling that shall un-Irish an Irishman?

Another of his confessions to me was this:—"Luckily for me," said he, "I have no occasion to speak till about 2 o'clock, when we dine, for that keeps me fresh. If I were to begin earlier, I should only be like skimmed milk the rest of the day."

As he came in between 5 & 6 o'clock, we were still at dinner. My father asked him if he would join, and do what we were doing. "No, Sir," answered he, very composedly, "I have done my tea at this hour." [7]

Both Benjamin Henry and his older brother were educated largely abroad and were much away from their parents. Although their father had been transferred to London the year after the future architect's birth and made his home there for the rest of his life, the younger son spent the greater part of his fourth to twelfth years at Fulneck, and it must have been early impressions of the Yorkshire hills, the lovely varied country around, and the rapidly growing cities of Leeds and Bradford that formed him rather than the London of his brief vacation periods. For a lad of ten, both these centers were within walking distance from Fulneck, and Leeds especially was undergoing at that time a phenomenal growth as the woolen trade expanded. That extraordinary Jacobean mansion, Temple Newsam, with its roof parapet formed into an inscription, was its great house, and on the banks of the Aire—rising in superb picturesqueness over the luxuriant trees and meadows of the river valley—were the ruins of Kirkstall Abbey (the finest of Cistercian Gothic abbeys), then much more extensive and better preserved than at present.

---

7. If, as is likely, this quotation refers to either Christian Ignatius or Benjamin Henry, for the young Latrobes had returned to England in the fall of 1784, Fanny Burney is inaccurate in calling her visitor a native of Ireland, for the two brothers were born in Fulneck. Probably the memory of their father's Dublin origin still held sway in her mind.

From *Fulneck Schools, 1753-1953*

FIGURE 1. North Terrace, Fulneck. School buildings at left.

B. H. Latrobe was a precocious artist and as a young child he loved to draw landscapes and buildings; his son John H. B. writes:

> There is now in the possession of the family [but it seems since to have disappeared] a drawing of Kirkstall Abbey, from nature, made by him in his twelfth year, the accuracy and force of which, in all its Gothic details, would do credit to any artist. Various other drawings, made about the same time prove him, at this early age, to have possessed a correctness of eye and a force and facility of delineation which are not easily attained until after years of practice.[8]

The Kirkstall drawing proves him not only an artist but a boy deeply interested in *buildings,* and here perhaps lay the seeds of his later professional passion.

Benjamin Henry remained at the Fulneck School till 1776, when he was twelve years old. By that time he must have received a good background in Latin and Greek, an introduction at least to geometry and algebra, and an extensive training in religion. His brilliance of mind

---

8. *The Journal of Latrobe,* with an introduction by J. H. B. Latrobe (New York: Appleton, 1905), p. viii.

must already have been evident to his parents and his teachers, and now he was ready for the next stage of his education, which by family habit would be on the Continent. Five years earlier, his brother Christian Ignatius (born February 12, 1758) had gone to Germany at the age of thirteen.

The school diary notes Benjamin Henry's departure in an entry toward the end of 1776:

Besides this we will mention the following changes and occurrences in our sphere. . . . In Sept. Four of our boys viz., John Hartley, Wm Okely, Benj. La Trobe and Frederick Landes set out for Germany with Br. and Sr. Okely to be brought up in the Pedagogium at Niesky.

On the day they left, September 17, 1776, we read:

In the morning we had a farewell Love Feast in our dining-room with our 4 Boys and Br. and Sr. Okely who will conduct them to Germany. Br. and Sr. Hauptmann were our guests. After the Children's meeting they set out for Leeds to take the coach to York. But as it rained we could not accompany them very far. Br. Nicholson and Lodge went with them as far as Leeds and Br. Bern Hartley as far as Hull.[9]

Evidently such departures were regular annual events and as such surrounded with a certain ceremony. The progression from Fulneck to Niesky was, in fact, a sort of Commencement—a passing from elementary school to one more advanced. That the new school was in Germany was merely incidental. In the introduction to *The Latrobe Journal,* John H. B. Latrobe suggests that this move was made because of the start of the Revolutionary War and the fact that the family had connections with the Revolutionary army through the architect's American mother; but in the light of the well-established Moravian custom it seems a dubious inference, especially since Christian was already in Germany. The basis for the claim is in a letter B. H. Latrobe himself wrote to a later associate, Samuel Blydensburg (September 1, 1810): "At the outbreak of the American war, my father ordered his children to be removed to Germany, & I completed my studies in the heart of the linen country in Saxony . . ." Here his memory was perhaps at fault; he may have misunderstood a remark of his father's that it was fortunate his two older

9. I owe this quotation to the Reverend Mr. A. J. Lewis, M.A., the present head of Fulneck School.

sons were then in Germany. Christian, in fact, had gone to Germany five years earlier.

Niesky, where he took up his studies, is a little city in German Silesia, about fifteen miles north of Görlitz. For over two centuries it has been an active Moravian center, and at least up to the Second World War the Paedegogium of the Unitas Fratrum has continued to operate. From here Latrobe passed on to the Moravian seminary at Barby, north of Halle in Saxony.

Young Latrobe was in Europe from 1776 to 1784, from the age of twelve to twenty, the most formative years. Unfortunately this important period is the least documented of his entire life; even in the voluminous notes about his earlier years which the architect, lonely in Richmond, wrote out in 1797 there are only a few indirect references to that time. There is, however, a family legend—set down by his son John H. B.—that in addition to the schooling at Niesky and Barby he spent three years in the University of Leipzig and that he served briefly as a "cornet" in the army of Frederick the Great, having enlisted almost as a lark with two English friends; that he was wounded in a skirmish and, when the wound was cured, resigned, and that after traveling extensively around Europe he returned to London "towards the end of 1786." Yet examination of the matriculation books at the University of Leipzig revealed not a trace of his name; [10] if he attended, it must have been informally or at public lectures only. The same doubts hang over his alleged military service. Nowhere in the extensive writings of B. H. Latrobe that have been explored is there a reference to a wound or any definite statement about his army service.[11]

There are nevertheless a few hints that might point to some military connection. The most important is a note that Latrobe added to his English translation of a popular German work on Frederick the Great which he published in London in 1788; it places him (if we may credit the

10. The rector of the University, in his letter answering my inquiry, adds that these records are so complete he can see no possibility of error.

11. Dr. William Thornton, however, in one of the numerous letters he wrote to the Washington *Federalist* attacking Latrobe's competence and personal rectitude, says that Latrobe had once told him that he had been in the Austrian army and had worn a green uniform. But the Austrian army was *not* the army of Frederick the Great, and Thornton's antics in controversy were at times strange indeed. His unsupported statement, therefore, confuses rather than clarifies the situation. I am grateful to Professor Paul Norton for bringing Thornton's letter to my attention.

statement) in 1782 in the "fortress of Silberberg, situated upon the ridge of mountains separating Silesia from Bohemia." He writes:

> I happened to be in Silberberg when the King arrived, and was close to his carriage. As soon as he alighted, the governor presented himself to his Majesty, and a conversation ensued which was almost verbally the following:— King. *Haas, have you finished your work, are all the fortifications complete?* Haas. *Indeed, Sire, they could not be finished.* King. *So! Is the moat compleated?* Haas. *Your Majesty will see that it was impossible.* King. *Arrest him immediately. . . .* The governor remained in arrest (I think) two months, but being an officer of merit, he was suffered to keep his post; but an inspector-general was appointed, who had the supreme direction under the King of all Silesian fortresses. I was afterwards informed by an officer of rank, that it was the opinion of the inspector-general, that the work could not have been completed in the time allowed.

We shall return to this book later; here the episode from it is quoted merely as evidence of Latrobe's military interests. Possibly his presence in Silberberg was somehow distorted into the notion that he was in the German army. Yet it is obvious that he had a vital interest in military affairs and especially in fortification; at one time, he wrote Jefferson (July 4, 1807), he had hoped to become a military engineer.[12] It seems likely, therefore, that it was in the capacity of a student of fortification rather than as an army officer that he visited Silberberg.

The wound he is said to have received is equally puzzling. The "Potato War," the last military episode of Frederick's reign, had ended in 1779, and Frederick's last years were years of complete peace; there were no skirmishes in which Latrobe could have been wounded. But in 1781—Latrobe states it was when he was seventeen—he did have a nervous and physical collapse (the first of a series of similar illnesses that were to occur periodically throughout his life), characterized by a blinding headache and accompanied by digestive disorders that left him exhausted and listless. In a note of 1806 he describes this first attack vividly; it was in some ways the worst of all, because it was coupled with a period of unconsciousness. Latrobe was on a mountain top, in Silesia, with two friends (perhaps the English friends of the army legend?) when suddenly he fainted; his friends carried him, still unconscious, to an inn in

---

12. ". . . I offer you the knowledge of fortification I acquired before I was 20 as a foundation of the profession of a military engineer I had adopted . . ."

the valley. There he recuperated, but for several days he was incapacitated by severe headaches and spells of violent indigestion. Could this sudden illness have been somehow transformed in his son's memory, long afterward, into the mythical wound?

But, although the question of army service and honorable wounds is still debatable, fortunately we do know a little about his Niesky period and something of his actual travels in these youthful years. It is clear, for example, that at Niesky he had a friend who watched over him and served, in a sense, *in loco parentis*—Baron Karl von Schachmann, an eminent Moravian who lived near by in his castle, Königshain. The baron was deeply religious, most understanding and kind, and a great scholar; he knew England well, was one of Zinzendorf's secretaries, and had been instrumental in the passage of the Act of 1749 by which Parliament accepted the Moravians as part of the English church. Latrobe notes that the baron's castle was his own "second home" and the place where he passed his happiest German hours.

And the baron was a classical expert, a collector, a connoisseur, and something of an artist as well. His collection of ancient coins and medals was famous, and in 1774 he had published a valuable catalogue of them; later they went to the ducal medal cabinet at Gotha. How Latrobe must have delighted in this collection; what a background in ancient history, what a training in sensitive taste it gave him as he pored over it! Baron von Schachmann was noted, too, for his talent in the painting of landscapes and of architecture. Here then, in Königshain, the growing youth found himself in affectionate association with an older man who could share his own enthusiasms, admire and criticize his precocious drawings, and perhaps even point the way to a different future from the Moravian ministry for which he seems to have been educated. The facts are uncertain, but the probability of the baron's influence in that direction is great. A nephew of Latrobe's, setting down his reminiscences of his father, Christian, states that the architect made the final decision about his profession "about 1783." Both Christian and Benjamin Henry were still in Germany then, and, if by that time the younger brother had acknowledged his hope of becoming an architect, surely the influence of the elderly baron—an enthusiast for architecture and presumably his most beloved German friend—can be inferred.

With that decision made, a trip around Europe became more than ever desirable, and to it a large part of the final year abroad was devoted. We do not know its itinerary, but fortunately we can place Latrobe definitely in certain localities. For instance, he knew Silesia well; he knew eastern Saxony, and Barby, and Leipzig; he knew the mountains along the Bohemian border. Farther south, he knew Paris, for later he used the anatomic theater of the Paris Hospital as an inspiration for the University of Pennsylvania Medical School. And, finally, an Italian stay is clearly indicated by the text he wrote in one of the two volumes he prepared for Susanna Catharine Spotswood, in Virginia, to help her to a knowledge of painting.[13] Here, in speaking of truth to nature, he tells the story of an artist he met on the Bay of Naples who refused to make sketches, but only looked; then, back in his house, the artist poured out generalized paintings of Vesuvius and a picturesque shore which he sold as paintings from nature. The value of the story is not in the fact that to Latrobe this practice seemed arrant dishonesty, but that the tale lends definite proof that Latrobe had visited Italy. In short, he had made almost the typical grand tour of the young Englishman, and it filled his mind with visions of architecture new and old which were to fertilize his genius later.

Latrobe returned to England in midsummer, 1784.[14] Still preserved is a letter from him on August 1, 1784 (from the Stamp Office, London, where he was working), to J. F. Fruauff, a professor at the seminary at Barby whom he calls the "foremost" of his German friends. The letter is full of Germanisms—almost as if written first in that language and then translated word by word—but from that time on his anglicization went on apace, and London for eleven years became his home.

Yet, if there is little dependable record of his whereabouts and activities from time to time in those eight critical years of his youth, his entire subsequent life was evidence of the breadth and depth of the education he achieved. First of all, he became an accomplished linguist. Besides German, his second tongue, he was fluent in French, was almost

---

13. "An Essay in Landscape, explained in tinted drawings," by Benjn Henry Latrobe Boneval, Engineer. Two illustrated manuscript volumes, 1798-1800, in the State Library of Virginia.

14. Latrobe seems to have made a second trip to the Continent in 1786. In his journal (May 22, 1797) he mentions having been a dinner guest of Sir William Hamilton's in Naples and notes that Mrs. Hart (later the famous and often painted Lady Hamilton) was present. Since she did not go out to Naples till early in 1786, this event could not have occurred till that year. It is this second visit from which, according to the family account, he returned in 1786.

equally so in Italian, and knew considerable Spanish. Of Greek and Latin he was a complete master; evidently he had read widely in both, and in his diary he cloaks some of the more intimate passages in one or the other of these languages. He had had a good Hebrew training as well and used that on occasion too. From childhood he was an excellent mathematician and possessed some knowledge of sidereal navigation to reinforce his skill as a surveyor.[15] Obviously he had read widely in philosophy, logic, and ethics. To cap it all, he was a musician with much more than an amateur's knowledge.

Much of this education would seem to indicate, as has been suggested, that Benjamin Henry was originally trained for the ministry. Unquestionably Christian was, and apparently their training was to a great degree parallel. But something in the mercurial, skeptical, inquiring nature of the younger brother evidently stepped in to make any such future for him unthinkable. If not the ministry, then what? He was at the mercy of the indecision that is the curse of many young people with multiple aptitudes. Certainly the Stamp Office job that he held on his return to London was only a stopgap; the civil service was not for him. Intellectually mature though he was, and far ahead of his contemporaries, emotionally he was still a boy—charming, vivacious, full of animal spirits, gay, impetuous, pert, and probably not a little vain when he came home to his father and mother. He was also amazingly gifted—and at the same time burdened with a nervous sensitiveness almost abnormal. But he had not yet found the niche he fitted or the work that could command his complete unbroken allegiance.

---

15. On September 11, 1804, he wrote to William Dubourg, Director of the College of St. Mary's in Baltimore: "I remember that getting hold of a few plain instructions at 8 years of age, I made myself a tolerable geometrician about that period; and at 12 I was almost master of the Mattheiis [sic] pura, having studied it from an irresistible propensity and with very little help . . ." Perhaps we should read "10 years of age" instead of "8" in consideration of the other errors in Latrobe's memory already referred to. But the "12" should probably stand, since that is the age at which he went on from Fulneck to Niesky.

CHAPTER

2

Latrobe in London

IN MIDSUMMER or the early autumn of 1784, then, Benjamin Henry Latrobe found himself back in London, living with his father and mother in a large, dignified old house in or close to Neville Court. The London political world was confused; vague projects for great reforms of all kinds were bubbling up all over and even exploding in bursts of oratory in Parliament. The social circles he entered were distinguished. Above the Latrobes lay the world of the nobility—confused, often frivolous, wealthy, powerful, and delighting in eccentricities. Around this roared the world of the businessmen of the city, rapidly growing in power and wealth and pushing up into politics and the nobility. And somewhere in between—extending feelers into both nobility and business and being fed from the large amorphous "mob" beneath—was the third world, the world of literature, art, and religion. It was a sort of Bohemia and, as the diaries of Fanny Burney and the Boswell papers show, it included scholars, artists, actors, dissenting clergymen, musicians, rogues, and all kinds of hangers-on. This was the freest of the London worlds; class stratifications tended to break down within it. It was vivid, creative, by turns pious or scandalous. It *produced,* despite the poverty of Grub Street and the uncertainties of patronage; from it came the great seminal ideas and the ferments that kept men's minds and ideals alive. It had many centers, but two of the most important were Dr. Johnson and Dr. Burney; with both of these the Latrobes were intimate.

One of the associates of the elder Latrobe was the eccentric general secretary of the Unitas Fratrum, John Hutton of Lindsey House, Chelsea.[1] This extraordinary man had sought the acquaintance of Dr. Burney in order to correct some of the musicologist's statements about German mu-

1. Fanny d'Arblay, *Memoir of Dr. Burney* . . . (London: Moxon, 1832), vol. 1, p. 251.

sic, and Hutton remained a good friend of the Burney family. It was probably through him that the Latrobes enjoyed a close association with the Burneys, and perhaps it was through Dr. Burney that Hutton and the elder Benjamin Latrobe became acquainted with Dr. Johnson, for Boswell brackets them together when he notes the friendship. Benjamin Henry Latrobe may well have met the great man, for Dr. Johnson did not die until December 13, 1784, and Latrobe returned to London in the summer of that year.

Thus the young architect-to-be found himself, on his return to this complex late-eighteenth-century metropolis, in the very midst of one of the city's most interesting and stimulating milieus. We see him, fresh from his continental experience and still strange and foreign in his ways, entering the Stamp Office as a clerk; evidently, with the Moravian ministry out of the question for him, he and the family had settled on the Civil Service, and his father's friendship with some highly placed individual had gained him a position at once. But we may imagine what boredom, what feelings of futility and frustration would creep over him, constituted as he was, at the routine work such a position entailed. For him—ebullient, mercurial, imaginative—a future of years of pen-pushing in the vague hope of achieving eventually a place of dull importance was completely unthinkable. How many months he remained there we do not know, but in all likelihood it was not long. What then?

In a note in Fanny Burney's *Early Diary,* the Latrobe brothers are referred to as "professional musicians." But Christian was already on the way to a career as a Moravian clergyman as well as a great collector of religious music and a learned hymnologist. Could it be that Benjamin Henry, for a time, played with the idea of using his musical knowledge as the basis of a career? There is a portrait of him from those early London days (now in the Maryland Historical Society) which shows a young man elegantly dressed, pert, even frivolous in expression; the face is still formless with the suave uncertainty of youth. We know he played the clarinet; perhaps for a while he may have toyed with the idea of becoming a professional musician, but that also was not his true vocation.

There are two glimpses of him slightly later from the pen of Charlotte Burney, who was his closest friend in the Burney household. Writing (now as Mrs. Francis) to her sister Fanny, probably from her home in Aylsham in Norfolk, where Benjamin Henry was visiting, she tells of a play and adds:

The overture was composed, or rather patched, borrow'd, stolen and flagrantly crib'd by Mr. Rivet, one of the band. . . . The most execrable composition I ever had the honor of hearing. At the end of one of the tunes, Benjamin La Trobe gave the signal, tho' it was in the middle of the overture, and set up a violent clap and encore! . . . [Then, two or three days later:] Sir William Jerningham call'd here last week and chatted with La T[robe] and me. . . . Saturday La T[robe] and the rest gave us a ball with twenty couple—a very merry one.[2]

If she dated the letters correctly, this must have been in 1788, and by then the shy foreign traveler had become a somewhat bumptious initiate in a gay society.

Years later Latrobe himself adds some amusing sidelights on this period in the course of a correspondence with Charlotte (then Mrs. Broome). She had been searching for evidence of the death in America of her former husband's brother, who was a trustee of some of the funds Dr. Francis had left her, and Latrobe by dint of a long and crooked search had at last found the evidence she needed and had forwarded it to her. In response to her reply he writes (August 13, 1816):

Thank you many times for your budget of news [with regard to Dr. Burney's death and Charlotte's disappointment that the sale of his extensive library had brought so little]. . . . That he miscalculated the value of his library was natural enough. There are not I suppose twenty men in England who would give a farthing for the most *rare,* the musical part, not even for Matheson's Musical rainbows, which I had such a fag at translating, & so much pleasure in seeing him laugh at them . . . [Mrs. Burney] was always very kind to me.—Dick was the naughty boy of your family, a character which those generally earn whose hearts & heads are both good, but whose susceptibility is a little morbid. What has become of Lady Bab Holderness? Mrs. Arthur Young, God bless her, has I hope taken her temper along with her to heaven. She has I hope repented of turning her husband's cattle into his Lucernefield, forgetting them there, and then making me get up at midnight to drive them out, as he was expected home next day. Had I broken my neck when I missed the gate and tumbled into the Haha she would have had still more to ask for. As it is, I must forgive her the pain of the rest of the night by having fallen into a forest of nettles and other *unpleasant* things at the bottom. Arthur Young's blindness is afflicting, & would be more so to a man of less genius & force of mind. With how many thousand pleasures & recollections

2. *The Early Diary of Frances Burney,* edited by Annie Ellis (London: Bell, 1889), vol. II, pp. 318-20.

would I not fill up my paper.—I could even commission *Dr. Munsey* [probably Dr. Monsey, the eccentric doctor of Chelsea Hospital, where Dr. Burney lived during his later years].—Your sister d'Arblay author has [?] of the Atlantic in Evelina, Cecilia, and Camila. In our simple life enough occurences of complication happen to make these novels intelligible [was he thinking, perhaps, as he wrote, of the strange romance of the marriage of his eldest daughter Lydia to Nicholas Roosevelt?], but the Wanderer is no favorite . . . After her her copyists Maria Edgeworth, Anna Seward borders on the Namby Pamby, & we'll go to sleep with her friend Hayley. As to my queer brother, he is gone to the Cape of Good Hope, so cheerful a Christian is not easy to be found . . .

The Arthur Young mentioned was a dear friend of the Burneys; Fanny d'Arblay in her *Memoirs of Dr. Burney* has a passage eloquent of their love and admiration for him. He was the great English agricultural scientist of his time and the author of agricultural writings that are said to have made over the face of England; hence the particular heinousness of his wife's error in turning the cows into his lucerne field! Mrs. Young's temper was also famous, winning mention even in the august pages of the Dictionary of National Biography. It produced continual friction and frequent crises in her relation to her husband, and they lived happiest apart. The episode of Latrobe's midnight wandering shows him in contact with another branch of this "fourth estate" of writers, artists, and scientists—an excellent social background for an alert and inquiring young man. And it may have been partly, at least, through Arthur Young that his interest was aroused in the natural sciences, an interest that plays so great a part in his early notes on Virginia.

If music, then, was not to be his life work, what about literature? Surely this field would offer opportunities for such a creative youth as Benjamin Henry Latrobe. And there was a family precedent: his father had published several translations as well as original works dealing with Moravian matters, had translated David Crantz's *History of the Moravian Church,* and had written a history of the Moravian missions in Labrador.[3] The son, in fact, out of his experience in Europe did produce two

3. David Crantz, *The Ancient and Modern History of the Brethren; or, A Succinct Narrative of the Protestant Church of the United Brethren, or Unitas Fratrum,* translated with additional notes by Benjamin Latrobe (London: Strahan, 1780). Benjamin Latrobe, *A Brief Account of the Mission Established among the Esquimaux Indians . . . by the Church of the Brethren, or Unitas Fratrum* (London: M. Lewis, 1774).

books, one published in 1788 and the other a year later. The first, *Characteristic Anecdotes . . . to Illustrate the Character of Frederick the Great,* was a translation of a book then popular in Germany, with the addition of a preface and various notes and stories about Latrobe's own experiences, one of which has already been cited. The second was *Authentic Elucidation of the History of Counts Struensee* [sic] *and Brandt and of the Revolution in Denmark in the Year 1772 . . . ,*[4] a translation of the amazing account of an eye witness usually identified as S. O. Falkenskiold, with an extensive introduction by Latrobe.

These two publications evidence how Latrobe's mind and personality had matured since the childlike letter to Dr. Fruauff only four years earlier; not only has he become a master of his native language, writing it in some passages with marked skill and effective design, but he also shows himself definitely interested in the great political disputes then tearing England in two. And the choice of the works he translated is significant; both of them deal with the essential problem of the relation of government to the popular welfare, and both show that Latrobe was already dedicated to the radical side of political and economic questions. To a young man brought up in the unselfish idealism of the Moravian brotherhood, the chasm between the mob and the aristocracy in the England of the 1780's must have been shockingly apparent; even if Latrobe had broken away from the dogmas of the Moravian faith, he was still the product of its somewhat egalitarian and communal thinking.

Not that this attitude would make him a revolutionary in the French sense of 1789; rather, it would make him want to do something about social reform and to make those in power do something about it. Thus in the first of these books he strove to give the English a truer picture of Frederick the Great; he shows him "doing something about it." He tells of the land banks, the tremendous expenditures for improving agriculture, the attempts—often so pitifully unsuccessful—to make the feudal landowners more conscious of their responsibilities as well as their rights. Yet he was puzzled, as so many had been, by the basic inconsistencies in Frederick's character—his rigidity, his refusal to change his mind even when confronted by irrefutable evidence that he was wrong—and,

---

4. London: printed for John Stockdale, opposite to Burlington House, Piccadilly, 1789. The original work was *Denkwürdigkeiten und hochstmerkwürdige Aufklärung Geschichte der Grafen Struansee und Brandt, aus dem französischen Manuscript eines Hohen ungenannten zum ersten mahl übersetzt und Gedruckt* (Geramien: Kempten, 1788).

on the other hand, surprised and pleased at the king's musical knowledge, his grasp of cultural as well as military affairs, and his personal understanding of common soldiers and uncouth peasants. One of the anecdotes he relates concerns a conversation between Frederick and an old peasant; here the king is speaking and, as Latrobe explains in a footnote, "The King of Prussia pronounced what the old man said in the broad provincial dialect of that country [Silesia]. I have attempted to imitate it, in the Yorkshire dialect":

Father! Can you tell me, why the two sovereigns quarrelled? "O dear-a-me, yea," replied the burgher, "that's what a can, th' top and bottom on 't. When ahr elector war a youngster, he larn'd at th' univarsity o' Utrecht, and thear wur th' King o' Sweden, tew, when he wur prince; and thear ye mun noa, they fratch'd, and wur ohlus at loggerheads: and nah a tell'd ye th' thing as 't is."

Then, too, as an Englishman—and this is the main evidence of Latrobe's complete acceptance of the Anglo-Saxon-Norman idealism of the English-speaking world—he was immensely bothered by the dichotomy of a despotism that *accomplished* things as contrasted with a free country that did nothing. Look not here, he warns the reader, for anything corresponding to English liberty; the basic liberties of Prussia of which so much has been written are not liberties in the English sense but merely the rights enjoyed by the Prussian nobility to be free from interference, to exploit their tenants to the last degree.[5]

---

5. "In a country, where neither the constitution, nor the wise and amiable character of the monarch, admits of the smallest idea of tyranny, every despotic act of a foreign unlimited prince, though authorized by the established laws of his dominions, may appear to be dictated by arbitrary or tyrannical motives. The sense of the natural rights of individuals, biases the mind too strongly, to suffer it for a moment to conceive an infringement of them, by the single will of one man, to be legal. But an exertion of power, which in this island would be looked upon as a most flagrant instance of oppression, might perhaps in Prussia, deserve the softer name of a beneficent exertion of royal authority in a case of necessity.

". . . —But whoever travels into Germany with English ideas of this jewel, who does not expect to find liberty in its pure and natural state, but hopes to see it as modified and curbed by the regulations of civilized society; may perhaps in most parts, be totally disappointed. . . .

"If TYRANNY can produce these effects, the meaning of that word is in general strangely misconceived. That they were produced by violent exertions of arbitrary power is certain, and that individuals often felt themselves hurt, and oppressed, is no less so. Every interest that stood in the way of the general good, was forcibly removed, and the dearest rights of

Thus the book is a puzzled book, just as it deals with a puzzling character in a changing and puzzling world. But in this very puzzlement there is something symptomatic of Latrobe's character. Theoretically he believed in English liberty to the uttermost. He was a passionate supporter of Charles James Fox. Personally he was always a hater of oppression, yet in practice he saw that democratic action had often resulted merely in schism and in futility, and he admired action and results. Evident in this book, therefore, are the foundations of a fundamental split in him—a split that at times of discouragement could result in an almost complete cynicism with regard to the effects of political action, yet a split that never resulted in his abandonment of his basically democratic ideals. It is only with this in mind that we can understand the complexities of his reactions to America later.

The second book—the tale of the Danish Revolution of 1772—is even more significant. The original is supposed to have been in French; the German translation appeared in 1788, and from this German edition Latrobe made his English version. The events described had excited wide English interest, for the queen who is the tragic protagonist was the sister of George III. The story of the scandals, the intrigues, and the use of the weakness of a half-crazed king to achieve unlimited national power is extraordinary and terrifying. The paradox of the great reforms, so sorely needed, for the realization of which the usurped power was used by Dr. Struansee and his friend Brandt; the bloody medieval horror of the collapse of the ill-fated, ill-born, but idealistic regime, and the execution and quartering of the two leaders—these together form one of the great tragic tales of history. Again it is a case of reform through imposition from above, but here another lesson is taught with almost the power of a Greek tragedy—the fact that ends *do not* justify means, that in the long run wickedness in the seizure of power works out inevitably to vitiate and to destroy the power created and the results achieved.

This story needed no embroidering by the translator; it told itself. But to it Latrobe added an extensive introduction which is worthy of some attention. It is both an apology for publishing the book and an explanation of why he considered it an important document; incidentally it sets forth Latrobe's own philosophy of historical writing and his criticism of

---

private persons were frequently trampled upon, to pave the road for some regulation, generally beneficent."

much of that in existence. In it he shows a basic skepticism, perhaps related to the critical attitude that prevented his becoming a Moravian minister. In all periods of the far past, Latrobe says, myth and legend necessarily confuse the reality of history; on the other hand, documents or accounts written at the time of actions are likely to be biased and partisan. The work he is translating he believes has "a degree of authenticity to which few similar works can lay claim" and "its youth is not so *tender* as to render its judgment partial or prejudiced, biassed by fear, or swayed by hope; nor its age so *decrepid* as to make its narrative fabulous, and to place it beyond the reach of enquiry and examination." And there is a touch of irony:

> But it is almost impossible to wish that the great historians, whose works carry us so smoothly and pleasantly along the current of time, had confined themselves to what is most probable or best authenticated. The defalcation would be too considerable: every pleasing *treatise* upon certain events would be bared of fancy and genius, and most of our elegant histories would shrink into dry chronicles; the greatest heroes would want the most brilliant motives for their actions; a victory, now ascribed to the superior valor of one general, would be found to be due to the greater cowardice or misconduct of his enemy; the *whim* of a courtezan would recover its merit, in bringing about a revolution, from the pretended wisdom of a statesman . . .

Latrobe was a true son of the Enlightenment, but he was going even farther along the critical road than most of the writers of his time.

The critical independence and idealism of this introduction characterized Latrobe's thinking all his life. A decade later there is confirmation of it in an early letter of his from Philadelphia (March 28, 1798) to Thomas Jefferson, whose writings he seems to have known and admired before he sailed from England. Remarking that he would like to be selected to design the proposed United States Arsenal at Harpers Ferry but that he had been told he had no chance, "for I am guilty of the crime of enjoying the friendship of many of the most independent & virtuous men in Virginia & even was seen at a dinner given by Mr. Monroe" (a reference to the Federalist hatred of himself that was already piling up), he goes on: "Since my arrival in America, it has been my very anxious wish to come to know you & to improve an old acquaintance with & admirer [sic] of your works, into a personal knowledge. If you will permit me, I will do myself the honor to wait upon you in your appartment tomorrow morning . . ."

In 1790 Latrobe was again involved with the writing and publishing world, when James Bruce finally brought out the first of the volumes describing his African travels and his researches in Abyssinia nearly two decades earlier. Referring to it long afterward in a letter to Jefferson at Monticello (August 12, 1817), Latrobe says that "the whole first volume [of Bruce's *Travels*], with the drawings . . . was published from my manuscript." He adds that the succeeding volumes "were, I believe, done into English by Fennel, the comedian. My uncle John Antes resided in Egypt 12 years . . . a favorite of Ali Bey . . . and connected with the Moravian Mission . . . he supplied [Bruce] with money" for the trip. From this it seems likely that Latrobe received the editorial job partly through the Antes family and partly through the Burneys, who had entertained Bruce with a grand party shortly after his return from Africa—as they entertained many lions of the time. Dr. Burney had been particularly interested in the harps and lyres that Bruce had found both in ancient Egyptian tombs and in use in Abyssinia; in her *Memoir* of her father Fanny d'Arblay tells of Dr. Burney's pride that it was in the pages of his history of music that these instruments were first published; then they appeared again in Latrobe's manuscript for Bruce's long-awaited and epoch-making work.

The style of the first volume of the *Travels* is straightforward and simple; Latrobe's work on it was apparently more than mere copy-editing. And in the case of the drawings the task must have been still greater; it was to take the sketches Bruce had made—though he was no mean delineator—and give them the precision and form, render them with the lights and shadows, that would be appropriate to the requirements of the skilled engravers of late-eighteenth-century England. Here again his job was not so much creative as interpretive, but much of the beauty and accuracy of the plates as published must be due to his sympathetic work. The view and, even more, the section of the Nile ship *Canja* display a touch that shows a technical skill of no common order; the views of Egyptian sculpture and wall decoration (containing the famous harp and lyre) are similarly skilled. These, if we may believe Latrobe's statement, may well be considered the earliest examples we possess of his professional work or at least of his technical skill.

The question of when Latrobe finally decided on an architectural career and of exactly what training he received is still unsolved. According to notes made by his nephew, as we have seen, his decision was made "about 1783," the year before his return to England from Germany. Family tradition has it that he received instruction from and worked with the famous engineer John Smeaton, who was a friend of the family, and then went into the office of S. P. Cockerell sometime between 1787 and 1789, working up rapidly to become the chief draftsman. Thus far it has been impossible to trace any pertinent records of either the Smeaton or the Cockerell offices, and few Cockerell drawings have been preserved. Fanny d'Arblay, voluble as she was, gives us for those early days only generalities; in the memoir of her father, however, there is a passage (vol. 1, p. 294) which though lacking in detailed information is at least eloquent testimony to the erudition and ability of the Latrobes and the esteem in which they were held by the Burneys: "The learned and venerable Mr. Latrobe, and his two sons, each of them men of genius, though of different characters, were frequent in their visits, and amongst the Doctor's warmest admirers; and, in the study of the German language and literature, amongst his most useful friends."

Facts that are definite seem to support the basic family tradition, particularly if we accept 1784 as the date of Latrobe's return to London and 1783 as the year when he decided to become an architect. Thus we may picture him as spending the last year of his sojourn abroad in travel, sketching, and technical study. On his return we may see him, after his short stay at the Stamp Office, studying informally with Smeaton for a year or two (or even three) and working for him as a draftsman.[6] Then, we are told, he entered the Cockerell offices "in 1787 or 88, it is not certain which."[7]

The Admiralty Building in Whitehall was built in 1787-8 from the designs of Samuel Pepys Cockerell, and we know from a Latrobe letter to Charles Middleton (after he had become Lord Barham) that he worked

6. Definite evidence of Latrobe's engineering work in England is contained in a letter to Joshua Gilpin (August 19, 1804) which deals with the Chesapeake and Delaware Canal: "The whole of the district of the Basingstoke Canal on which I was employed was let to Pinkerton at 6¢ a yard." This canal, built between 1791 and 1794, was under the general design and supervision of William Jessop; Latrobe was probably a divisional engineer. The canal is still in operation. He also mentions his work under Smeaton in a letter to Thomas More (January 20, 1811): ". . . having commenced my studies under Mr. Smeaton" by making a report for him on the "scouring works" which Smeaton had designed in the Lincolnshire and Cambridgeshire fens.

7. *The Journal of Latrobe,* with an introduction by J. H. B. Latrobe (New York: Appleton, 1905).

on that building; it is obvious, too, that one of Latrobe's early Philadelphia houses, the Burd residence, bears a close resemblance to it. This suggests a conjecture which may help to account for the young architect's rapid rise in Cockerell's office as well as for the fact that he was able to sidestep completely the long and expensive apprenticeship that was the usual means of entering the architectural profession. Admiral Sir Charles Middleton, an excellent executive, was then Controller of the Navy; later he became First Lord of the Admiralty. Lady Middleton and he, on trips in the West Indies while he was still a Navy captain, had been deeply shocked by the cruelty of West Indian slavery. Sir Charles, hearing that the Moravian missionaries were doing their best to alleviate the conditions of the slaves, called on Benjamin Latrobe and later became his intimate friend. So close, indeed, was this friendship that in 1786 the elder Benjamin, in his last illness, spent five months at the Middleton estate, Teston Hall; he died in the Teston vicarage.[8] Thus it seems altogether likely that in one way or another young Latrobe came to Cockerell through the influence of Middleton; he may even have made some drawings for the Admiralty Building earlier and brought them with him. Such an introduction would of course have given him a position of some standing in the Cockerell office and, combined with his own brilliance as designer and delineator, would have allowed him to rise to the position his talents justified without the benefit of the usual apprenticeship. Coming with such sponsorship, a man of his ability could not help rising rapidly; for, then as now, unfortunately perhaps, good connections had a vital influence on early success.

During part of this time Benjamin Henry and Christian were sharing a house. Their father had died in 1786, after a long illness. In 1788 the two brothers had bachelor quarters together on Great Tichfield Street, and the arrangement was a happy one on which the architect looked back with warm pleasure. On the ship *Eliza,* in mid-Atlantic on his voyage from England, he set down in his diary (February 12, 1796):

---

8. According to the Rev. C(hristian) I. Latrobe's *Letters to My Children, Written at Sea during a Voyage to the Cape of Good Hope, 1815,* with an introduction by the Rev. J. A. La Trobe, M.A., Incumbent of St. Thomas's Church (Kendal: privately printed, 1851), in the British Museum, he was laid up there for several weeks before his death. The authority for the residence in Teston Hall is a letter of B. H. Latrobe's to Isaac Hazlehurst on September 18, 1805.

This day I did not forget the birthday of my brother C. I. L. It has always been one of my most ardent wishes & sanguine hopes to be placed in a situation in which a constant intercourse might give me a full opportunity of receiving all the pleasure, happiness & instruction which the goodness of his heart & the brilliancy of his genius render inseparable from his society & conversation. The winter of 1788 during which we lived together will ever be memorable to me as almost the happiest of my life. Since then marriage and business have separated us, & whenever I have met him the regret arising from the scarcity of our interviews has almost overbalanced the pleasure they gave. We are now perhaps forever divided.

The marriage he speaks of was his own.

Perhaps through his brother, perhaps through the Middletons, he had made the acquaintance of the Sellon family. William Sellon was a famous clergyman—the "permanent Curate" of St. James, Clerkenwell—with considerable wealth and a prosperous living. Among the members of his large family was his daughter Lydia, three years Latrobe's senior and evidently a woman of charm and independence. The two young people fell in love, and Latrobe asked for her hand in the true eighteenth-century manner. The Reverend Dr. Sellon acquiesced at once, apparently with enthusiasm, but among the rest of the family there was much opposition. Years later in Richmond, Latrobe wrote out in 1797 a vivid account of the affair, with pungent character sketches of all the members of the Sellon group. It is obvious that Mrs. Sellon was more worldly than her husband and had hoped for a wealthy marriage for her daughter; eventually she was brought round to accept the one that was offered, to which even she could have no objections on any grounds of character, personality, or social charm. One married daughter was violently opposed, the other was favorable; similarly the sons were divided, and Latrobe notes that the family seemed split clean through the middle between those who were chiefly avaricious and worldly and those who like the father were idealistic and openhearted. But, finally, after various family meetings—at some of which Latrobe, to his great embarrassment, was forced to be present—the father won out and the marriage was at last approved.

Then came the question of a settlement. Lydia's father was generous; she had been his favorite daughter, and she was to be protected at all costs. Here he was adamant; the hostile children raged, without avail.

On Lydia therefore the Doctor settled a generous income during her lifetime, a small reversion to her husband, and a large reversion to her children after her death. It is ironic to find that after Lydia's death, when Latrobe (in 1795-6) and the children (in 1800) had come to America, all Latrobe's efforts to collect for his daughter and his son what was their due came to naught. The children's estate had been left in charge of their uncles, John and William Sellon, who never paid. Again and again, when Latrobe found himself faced with almost insoluble financial difficulties and his mind turned to this inheritance, he wrote to his brother Christian in London urging him to seek a settlement. He suggested that Christian call on John Sellon (which Christian did, without result) and later that the whole matter be put into the hands of John Silvester, the Latrobes' counsel, for handling. In one of these letters (May 7, 1804) Latrobe wrote:

> The conduct of the Sellons to me & my children, in not rendering an account of the money accumulating in their hands is unpardonable, and even dishonest, & the neglect of John Sellon in not returning your visit is ungentlemanly. William, I know, is no better than a bankrupt.—If justice were done, he should pay, principal & interest, to my children of at least £20,000.—But they will never get a penny.

Four years later he must have had news from his brother that perhaps some progress was being made, for he wrote to Christian (January 10, 1808) that he had drawn on him for £100 on account of the Sellon property. Christian paid, but protested. After three months Latrobe wrote again, apologizing for drawing on his brother inconveniently and saying that he thought the Sellons had paid the interest and that he would use the money to keep his son Henry another year in college. That hundred pounds is all that ever came to Latrobe and his family from the Sellon inheritance, and we do not even know whether the Sellons ever reimbursed Christian Latrobe. William Sellon's bankruptcy put a final quietus on any further hopes. Here the Sellon avarice had at last overreached itself, bringing ruin not only to William but to the other Sellons, whose assets like the Latrobes' were the basis of his speculations. But this unhappy finale came almost two decades after the settlement arranged by Dr. Sellon.

Lydia and B. H. Latrobe were married at her father's church on February 27, 1790. The house they took in Grafton Street—still standing—is bleakly simple, one of a long row typical of the speculative London houses of its day, three stories high, with an arched rusticated doorway. But it was not a mean house, and the area they chose to live in was an artistic center—the Chelsea or Greenwich Village of its time. Architects and artists were living all around; J. Bonomi, John Francis Rigaud, T. Scheemaecher, and Edward Burney, Fanny's artist cousin, were all near by, and other architects and artists were not far away.

The life these two lived was an extremely happy one. Lydia was gentle, sympathetic, and affectionate despite a quick temper, and for the first time Latrobe enjoyed the complete devotion and co-operation for which his soul, starved emotionally till then, so passionately yearned. We have many vivid pictures of their comradeship in his nostalgic notes of 1797 written in Richmond in a time of loneliness. There is, for instance, the story of Dr. William Sellon's death—an account worthy of the best late-eighteenth-century novelists. The contrast between the artificially inflated grief of the family at the deathbed and the angry recriminations at the reading of the will is vividly before us.[9]

Then a happier picture: Lydia, we learn, often accompanied her husband on his visits of inspection to his jobs; they would ride out together, and she would become almost as well acquainted with the various workmen as he was—she even wrote an elegy for one of the masons when he died. It is a picture that shows Lydia to have been independent as well as gentle, for it was not the custom then for women to be so close to the professional work of their husbands. And apparently in these first married years they lived a busy social life. Dining at Dr. Burney's apartment at Chelsea Hospital they met Fanny Burney, just on her return from a trip to the West of England to recover her broken health after five years' bondage as Lady of the Robes to Queen Charlotte. In connection with this dinner (in November, 1791) Fanny writes of Lydia and indicates that before her marriage Miss Sellon had been a visitor at one of those almost oppressively serious parties at Mrs. Montagu's—the queen of the bluestockings—held in the gorgeous salon that James Stuart had built for her (1777-82):

> The younger Latrobe and his wife have dined here. His wife seems a natural, cheerful, good character, rather unformed, though with very good and even sharp natural parts. [How much she sounds like a character from

9. See Appendix for excerpts.

a Jane Austen novel!] She told me she supposed I had forgotten her. I had never seen her, I answered. "O yes," she said, "before I was married I met you at Mrs. Montagu's. I was Miss Sellon. I should have known you again, because I took such good note of you, as Mrs. Montagu said you were an authoress, before you came in, which made me look at you."

Another scene still more amusing and personal comes from Latrobe's own notes. It seems that a bear cub had been caught when a survey was being made of his lands in Pennsylvania and then sent to him in London by some member of the Antes family. As a cub the bear had been a charming pet, but when it grew up and became ill-tempered and vicious a servant finally killed it. One day Benjamin Henry and Lydia were calling at Dr. Burney's—the indications point to the summer of 1792, for Lydia had a baby in arms at the time—and someone proposed they all write elegies to the bear, but recently dead. (Fanny apparently was not at home.) Latrobe's elegy is correct, rather pretentious, and uninspired; Lydia's is more real, occasionally witty, and satirical, though as verse rough and incorrect. The elderly Doctor, however, who was a rude versifier of considerable power, produced a quatrain so funny but so scatological as to put a quietus on the whole festival. As verse, his is the best of the three by far, and it reveals how an earlier, gustier, and less polite eighteenth-century manner persisted in some of the older folk well into this later, more "refined" period.

Yet the happiness and the well-rounded life of the pair were destined to be brief. From 1791 on, the French Revolution more and more occupied the front position in English policy. Latrobe was on the radical side in the English controversies, and he was one of those who like Hazlitt retained for many years his faith in the French Revolution. This position must have alienated some potential clients, and on February 1, 1793, the declaration of war against France brought almost all building to a standstill. The financial picture was no longer the rosy one that Latrobe's early successes and rapid rise had seemed to warrant. But worst of all was the purely personal tragedy. Lydia had borne her first child, Lydia Sellon Latrobe, on March 23, 1791; a second, Henry Sellon Latrobe, followed on July 19, 1792. Then, scarcely more than a year later, Fate struck and Lydia died in childbirth, along with her third child, in late November, 1793. Thus the same year saw the fall of the young architect's hopes, both personal and professional. One or the other alone, perhaps, he could have endured; with all his varied talents and with the love and co-operation of Lydia he could have been victorious over the slings and arrows of outrageous economic fortune, but without professional opportunities of any importance and with his sympathetic helpmate no longer at his side where could he turn?

One precious and poignant monument of their love remains; it is the "Ode to Solitude" which he composed sometime shortly after her death and wrote out again in Richmond in the lonely summer of 1797. Almost all his notebooks and diaries of that year are woven through with a violent longing for earlier days—the days of his settled social position in England—and the gold thread that dominates the weave is his passionate longing for and devotion to the memory of Lydia. The ode is not great or even good verse; but it is deeply sincere, and despite its outdated eighteenth-century conventions it rises at times to true poetic eloquence:

Ode to Solitude

written December 20, 1793

Oh solitude! though sung in fancy's glowing ode
Strewed by the pensive band with withery flowers,
Alas! to me how dreary seems the chill abode
How weighs the air in these thy silent bowers.—
Unnerved my mind starts from reflections forms,
Looks round! Ah me! is aught of guilt to fright?
Are these of lawless rage the embryo storms?
That tremble in my breast,—and sully reason's light?
Low on the horizon burns the evening gleam
Clouds thicken o'er the long-stretch'd radiant line
The dark fog glides on day's departing beam
Woods, streams and plains in misty tint combine.—

What sound hangs on the sighing blast
Quick let me fly!—Ah useless haste!
Thy wide dominion, Solitude, extends
Far as the low'ring welkin's circle bends:
Enthroned within my sick'ning soul
Thy baneful sceptre with'ring every budding smile
Each friendly phantom raised, my sorrows to beguile
Thou chas'st, kill'st all my infant joys, nor fearest controul.

Once—ah! how broken is the sullied trace
On mem'ry's tablet of that lovely face

Blotted by tears, worn by corroding woe!—
    The faint lines smile!—the pale cheeks' redd'ning glow!
Away! thou phantom.—To the dark vault they bore
    Her lovely corpse; those beauteous arms entwine
    Her pale cold boy,—my boy,—for she was mine.
Oh! break, my heart!—for she is mine no more!

    See where along the solitary way
To press their father to his dreary home
Clasp'd hand in hand, her orphan children come
    And ask him where,—oh heav'n,—his Lydia stay.

Go, go, ye wretched babes, why call your mother's name
    Why of your father's tears the dread occasion seek?
Why fan of fierce despair the madd'ning flame?
    And clasp his trembling knees, & kiss his fading cheek [?]

She's gone, she's gone! Did ye not hear the knell
    Nor see the sable hearse forsake the door
Weep, weep, poor babes,—your mother's passing bell
    Has toll'd,—she's gone, ah, to return no more.—

    But come, ye pledges of our spotless love,
    Where the young violet buds upon her sod
    Kneel by your father;—there the present God
    To calmer tears his burning eyes may move;
Pour balm upon his widow'd, wounded heart;—
And strengthen him to act a father's part.

Lydia's death was a stunning blow, and a pitiful end was drawn to this chapter of Latrobe's life. Though he remained two more years in England, trying vainly to rebuild his life there, his efforts seemed doomed to failure. Following a severe nervous breakdown he became listless, incapable of making decisions. A complete change of scene seemed essential.

CHAPTER

3

Architectural Background

LATROBE's education at Fulneck and in Germany and his architectural training and practice in London had obviously filled his mind with cogent architectural memories, yet at first sight his German experience during his formative years appears to have yielded little. Of the brilliant Early Renaissance which distinguishes the towns of Silesia—even Baron von Schachmann's castle, Königshain (Latrobe's second home), was Early Renaissance in style[1]—there seems in his work scarcely a trace. What today we admire in these Early Renaissance and Late Gothic towns and buildings probably seemed to him merely quaint or picturesque, and presumably as a late-eighteenth-century youth he found them without architectural significance.

In Germany at that time, however, there existed an architectural movement which must have excited him—the development of the new Prussian classicism. One of its important creators was a Silesian architect, Carl Gottfried Langhans (1733-98);[2] and it was precisely at the period of Latrobe's residence in Silesia that many new towns characterized by this new and quiet classicism were being built and important official buildings in the same vein were being added to older towns.[3] In both we can see clearly the rapid swing from Baroque and Rococo expressions to compositions ever more classic, some of them suggestive of the work of the Adam brothers in England. Among the new villages perhaps the

1. Hans Lutsch, *Verzeichnis der Kunstdenkmäler der Provinz Schlesien* (Breslau: Korn, 1886-92).

2. Walther T. Hinrichs, *Carl Gottfried Langhans, Schlesischer Baumeister* (Strassburg: Heitz & Mündel, 1909). See also Paul Mebes and Walter Curt Behrendt, *Um 1800 . . .* (Munich: Bruchmann, 1920).

3. Hans Joachim Helmigk, *Oberschlesische Landbaukunst* (Berlin: Verlag für Kunstwissenschaft, 1937).

most original was one that would have appealed especially to Latrobe—Gnadenfels, founded by the Moravian brethren. It was begun in 1780, from designs by M. Rietz, and completed in 1783. Surely Baron von Schachmann must have been impressed by this new colony and called it to the attention of his young protégé. It is interesting to note that the church-and-meetinghouse there resembles markedly the one that stands in Bethlehem, Pennsylvania, although in detail its restraint is characteristic of the new Prussian classicism. All of this new work, recently completed or under construction, filled Latrobe's mind with a vision of a new kind of restrained and dignified beauty.

With regard to what Latrobe gained specifically from his year of travel in Europe it is more difficult to be precise. Undoubtedly the brilliance of French architecture would have impressed him, probably more for its firmness of planning and the boldness of its construction than for its detail. The church of Ste Geneviève (later the Panthéon), by J. G. Soufflot, followed by Rondelet, was then under construction; could the daring of the light vaulting, added to the influences he later received from Soane, have helped to stimulate the love of vaults which is so evident in his American work? But it would have been the newer, simpler houses, like those of Ledoux, that interested him most, and he would have been delighted with the powerful geometry of Ledoux's new Barrières. For the rest, this tour seems to have served chiefly as a broadening, enriching experience generally, for in his work there is little trace of French Gothic or Italian Renaissance or Baroque influences. Undoubtedly the great Roman ruins impressed him and reinforced in his mind the importance of the inspiration to be gained from the ancient Greek and Roman forms. And surely the dome of the Roman Pantheon moved him profoundly, for its stepped base and relatively low outline appear constantly in his later work.

On his return to London Latrobe found English architecture in one of its most interesting stages—interesting because it was in rapid transition as English life was shifting from the world of *Tom Jones* to that of *Pride and Prejudice.* Three chief schools were active, all headed by important designers—Sir William Chambers, Robert Adam, and George Dance the younger, along with John Soane.

The first of these movements, and the oldest, was the school of Sir William Chambers. It stood for traditional Palladianism and owed much to the work of William Kent and the Earl of Burlington, but it was more thoughtful, more logical, in a way more strict. Chambers sought inspiration from other Italian Renaissance masters besides Palladio, and his own work was spiced with occasional exoticism. He had spent considerable time in Canton, China, where he was impressed by both the buildings and the gardens; the Pagoda which he designed for Kew Gardens remains as a telling monument to this influence. Chambers came of a merchant family; it is no accident that his style became the accepted model for the new *haute bourgeoisie* of England and that he was close to and admired by George III (of all the Georges the one most representative of waxing business influences), who appointed him Surveyor General and commissioned him to design Somerset House, the greatest governmental project of the time. It was begun in 1775, and the first block was complete by 1780; then the remaining blocks, including the river front, were built. When Latrobe returned to London in 1784 this was the most important edifice recently completed.

The second school, that of the Adam brothers, had just passed the height of its popularity but was still deeply influential. The members of this group seem to have worked chiefly for the wealthy Tory nobility, though they never enjoyed extensive royal patronage; yet their effect on the taste of England was incalculably great. Robert Adam's own personal style was definitely Roman in origin, though it had sprung from two different sources. The Palace of Diocletian at Spalato (Split), the measurements of which he took and then published in a book which John Summerson calls "one of the three most important architectural travel books of the century," taught him that in the time of Diocletian at least the "orders" held no such absolute sway in Roman architecture as the Palladian architects had believed. For example, in this palace there were hardly two orders alike, the proportions varied from slim to stumpy, and there was a riot of surface ornament which evidenced almost untrammeled imagination on the part of the designers and craftsmen. This freedom was bound to sap at the foundations of English Palladianism, and a similar variation of the orders in the architecture of Robert Adam ran directly contrary to the "correct" work of men like Chambers.

Another influence in the Adam designs was that of the wall and ceiling decorations in Nero's Golden House, which had been rediscovered and newly excavated in the eighteenth century. Robert Adam was in Rome in 1754, and it was precisely at this time that his compatriot Charles Cam-

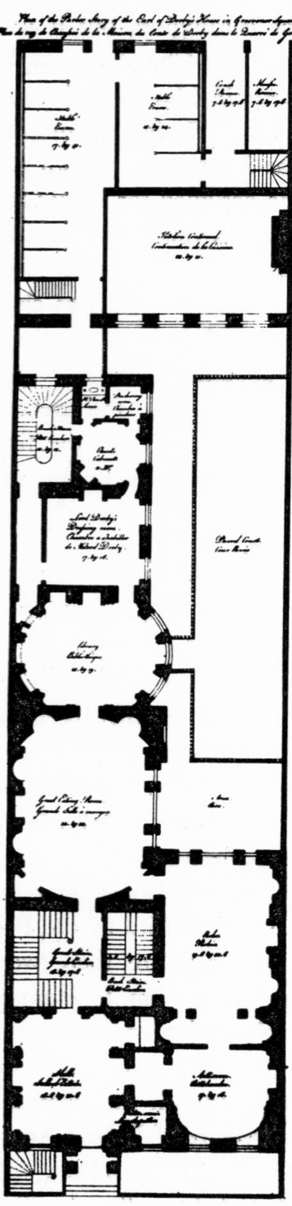

From *Works in Architecture of Robert and James Adam*
FIGURE 2. Earl of Derby's House, London. Plan. Robert Adam, architect.

eron (later the architect of Catherine the Great of Russia) was making careful explorations there. From those lavish decorations Adam drew the inspiration for the fans, the half and quarter fans, the swinging garlands, and the pictures framed in delicate moldings which characterized much Adam decoration. Yet Robert Adam used this ancient alphabet to write his own lyrics. His works, unlike those of some of his imitators, were in impeccable taste, with ornament concentrated in telling spots and bands on serene surfaces, with delicacy in just balance with monumentality, and with perfect clarity in over-all design.

Furthermore, the Adam brothers were superb planners; their work blends perfectly a grasp of functional requirements with the creation of varied and beautiful interior spaces. This is the mark of great planning, and it can be seen strikingly in the University of Edinburgh and in the plan for Lord Derby's London house, where the service needs are beautifully cared for and help to give form to the whole composition. The spirit of the Adams' planning is as Roman as the sources of their decoration. The varied vault shapes, the niches, the curve-ended rooms, and the columnar screens all come from Robert Adam's study of Roman plans.

A style of such vividness—with all the fresh appeal of a summer dawn—had tremendous effects on the architecture of its time, and influences from it affected men as different from Adam as James Paine, Henry Holland, and several of the

Wyatt family; even "Athenian" Stuart and the younger George Dance were influenced by it. And in the plan books of William Pain, such as the *British Palladio,* distant reflections of the Adam details were spread abroad in England and in the American colonies, to reappear, again transformed, in the later New England work of Asher Benjamin and Charles Bulfinch. Naturally work of such genius was bound to influence the young architect, and Latrobe's own love of niches and hemicycles, like his feeling for surface, may be traced at least in part to it, despite the fact that he felt the Adam decoration to be finicking and over-rich.

Latrobe belonged, rather, to the third of the schools, the work of which was characterized by simplicity, geometric power, and rationalism. This was sometimes called the "plain style." George Dance the younger, as Summerson has so brilliantly pointed out, was its English originator.[4] He had, during Latrobe's infancy, produced the surprising interior of All Hallows, London Wall (1765-7), the widely spaced engaged columns of which, like the plain walls and the clear patterning of the vaulted ceiling, set a new note. The same feeling affected men like Holland and later even John Nash. But it was in the work of Sir John Soane (1753-1837) that this movement achieved its greatest triumphs. Soane was a pupil and employee and the lifelong friend of the younger George Dance. As a student he had won the Royal Gold Medal, together with the chance to study in Rome, but it was only on his return that his true genius flowered, to give final authoritative expression to the new aims—simplicity, geometry, and rationalism.

This third movement was definitely Whig, even radical, in tone. Holland's great patron was the Prince Regent, later George IV, and the new manner appealed especially to those who were to follow Charles James Fox and show marked sympathy for the French Revolution. It was definitely a Francophile style and in many ways paralleled the revolutionary work of Ledoux, just as it found its sanction in the rationalist criticism of Laugier. This political orientation was not without importance in Latrobe's architectural development.

It was in the work of Soane that this style received its most perfect embodiment. In his published work his development can be readily seen,

---

4. For a description of the origin of this manner see John Summerson, "Soane: The Case History of a Personal Style," in *Journal of the R.I.B.A.,* January, 1951.

from the youthfully exuberant *Designs in Architecture*[5] through *Plans, Elevations, and Sections of Buildings . . .*[6] (often cantankerous, even eccentric, but at the opposite extreme from the style of either Chambers or Adam), to the dramatic *Sketches in Architecture . . .*[7] in which the orders are pulled out or pushed down, crowded together for decorative accent, and treated with what seems an almost angry disregard of classic canons.

Soane's master work is the Bank of England; as architect of this great project he had succeeded Sir Robert Taylor. In its famous "Tivoli Corner" he piled up a fantastic conglomeration of classic forms—a successful tour de force in which the dramatic value alone prevents a realization of its fundamental eccentricities—while within he shows himself magnificently the integrator of function, structure, and form. The daring vaults, pointed up with a new kind of incised and abstract decoration, bespeak his creative originality. In this interior he was inventing new kinds of volumes, lighted in a new way by lanterns and clerestories and decorated only to accent the volumes and the structure. Here indeed was precedent enough for all Latrobe's later inventions. Only one of these great halls was built during Latrobe's English years, but surely he must have watched it with admiration as it rose to completion in 1792. Like Soane, Latrobe retained a lifelong love of incised rather than raised plaster ornament. For instance, he wrote in a letter (October 24, 1805) to John Lenthall, his superintendent in Washington, with regard to the ornament in the entrance to the House of Representatives in the Capitol: "You will observe that in this room, as through all my designs, much of the plaister work is sunk below the surface . . . I am of the opinion that internally large projections are absurd in reason and exceedingly ugly in effect." This might almost have been written by Soane; elements in it seem taken from Laugier.[8] Latrobe obviously recognized and was proud of his "irregularities."[9] Nevertheless there appears to be no reference to Soane in the entire mass of the Latrobe papers.

---

5. London: Taylor, 1778.

6. London: Taylor, 1788.

7. London: Taylor, 1793.

8. Marc Antoine Laugier, *Essai sur l'architecture,* nouvelle edition (Paris: Duchesne, 1755), and *Observations sur l'architecture* (The Hague: Desaint, 1765).

9. For example, in a letter of September 22, 1817, he wrote to Mr. Shields, plasterer, at General Vanness': "I never, unless it is especially ordered, put up enriched mouldings in

Latrobe's active connection with architecture began with his association with Samuel Pepys Cockerell in 1787 in the design of the Admiralty Building. Of other work he did for Cockerell there is little evidence. To assess Cockerell's taste at the time is difficult. He seems to have been a busy architect, without perhaps too definite a creative personality, for it is only later (1803), in the extraordinary steeple of St. Anne's, Soho, that he produced a design of real originality. As in the case of many prosperous architects, his taste appears to have been conditioned by the job, by the taste of his clients, and by the particular skills of his office staff. To be in such an office would, for a young man like Latrobe, have afforded more valuable training than to be in the office of someone with a more rigid personal style—just as, on the other hand, a brilliantly imaginative designer like Latrobe would have been a priceless addition to Cockerell's office.

Thus Latrobe's eleven London years (1784-95) were a period in which the city was in a stage of exuberant growth, its rising or newly risen buildings an inspiring school to a promising young man just entering the profession. In the new Somerset House, for instance, what probably struck him most was the superb daring and the great scale of the bold arcaded warehouses on the Thames front rather than the pure Palladianism of the rest. Similarly he must have been conscious of a large amount of work in the Adam vein, and though he might have been inspired by its imaginative functional planning, he was probably bored by its lavish ornament. In the city he might have been depressed by the Mansion House by the elder George Dance, but the son's expressive Newgate Prison undoubtedly won his admiration, for here was power—the brute power of stone. Here was expression, the *architecture parlante* of which Ledoux wrote.[10] Farther west Latrobe would have seen Holland's Dover House at Whitehall; he would have been struck by the beauty of its Greek Ionic portico and moved by the dramatic contrast of the colonnade with the rusticated wall behind. Holland's Carleton House (1788-90) would also have delighted him because of the clear serenity and the dis-

---

plaister, because they are very expensive, because they are knocked off by the chambermaids sweeping down cobwebs, and they are ruined in their sharpness and beauty the first time they are whitewashed, unless soaked first in boiled oil, & then painted in water color . . ."

10. Claude-Nicolas Ledoux, *L'Architecture sous le rapport de l'art, des moeurs, et de la législation* (Paris, 1804).

tinguished classicism of its proportions.[11] Especially he would have been excited by the touches of Greek detail that were appearing here and there, for more than by any actual building he was undoubtedly overcome by the beautiful plates of Stuart and Revett's *Antiquities of Athens,* the new evangel of Greek purity. Just so, in the actual London architectural scene, what most impressed him was the new experimental work of the younger George Dance and of John Soane; here was inspiration indeed.

One of the elements that was sure to impress itself on any London observer at that time was the extensive building of homes to take care of the rapidly increasing population—row on row, on new streets and along new squares to the north, west, and south.[12] The houses were almost all of the simplest possible design, examples of a type that had taken form almost a century earlier and over which the changing fashions eddied, altering cornices, moldings, windows, and doors but making no essential modifications. Latrobe after his marriage lived in such a house near the end of a long row on Grafton Street (now Grafton Way). The house, which still stands, is undistinguished, obviously rented by him because of its neighborhood and its relative newness, and the general type probably buttressed his preference for the "plain style" and gave him another criterion by which to judge the houses of America later.

Latrobe opened his own office in 1791, shortly after his marriage. It was not altogether a propitious time; the French Revolution was already striking terror into the hearts of many an Englishman, and building was falling off. Nevertheless work did come in. Much was probably small commissions—alterations and the like—such as every beginning architect must undertake. Some of these alteration jobs we know—Teston Hall, Frimley, Sheffield Park, and Tanton Hall. The first was the home of the Charles Middletons; it became Barham Hall after Sir Charles had been created Lord Barham. It still remains, though much altered at various periods, and it is almost impossible to isolate Latrobe's work in it. The commission was a natural one because of the close association of Sir Charles with the Latrobe family. Frimley, too, is still standing—a large, classic pile of several dates, now used by the British Army. In this one may with more assurance pick out the young architect's work: the pedimented central pavilion. Here the arched recess enclosing a wreathed

---

11. Dorothy Stroud, *Henry Holland, 1745-1806* (London: Art and Technics, 1950).
12. See John Summerson, *Georgian London* (New York: Scribner's, 1946), p. 150.

opening above a Palladian window has a definitely personal quality and combines just those influences—a touch of Adam and a touch of the new simplicity—which one would expect to find in Latrobe's design of that time.[13]

Our knowledge of Sheffield Park, which is not mentioned in other lists of Latrobe's work, comes from letters written by a Lady Stanley of Alderly during her girlhood.[14] Writing to her friend Ann Firth (September 10, 1794) with regard to alterations at Sheffield Place, near Uckfield in Sussex, she says:

> What do you think of this house being once more in brick and mortar? The job now about, however, is I believe a necessary end, but I hope I have helped to stop another that was certainly not so. They are now pulling down the partition between Papa's bed-chamber and the dressing-room, which, being built of brick and without support, promised to descend speedily into the inferior regions. The superfluous is a project of Mr. Latrobe's, an architect employed by Mr. Fuller in the house he is building upon the Forest [Ashdown House], and brought here by him. It is to open a great window into the dressing room, and the Lord knows what vagaries besides.

A sympathetic client! Sheffield Park had originally been designed by James Wyatt, who was commonly famous—or infamous—for the cheap construction he often allowed. Whether or not Latrobe's "superfluous" alterations were made we may never know.

Tanton Hall (village and county unknown) cannot now be identified, but we have its record in Latrobe's own notes; it was commissioned for the "two Miss Hoissards." The story behind it is a fascinating one; Latrobe wrote it out later in America. John Silvester, the Latrobe family lawyer, had married the widow of an East Indian trader, a Mrs. Hoissard. Her brother, one George Livius, according to Latrobe, had cut quite a swathe in London as a dandy and man-about-town. Her two daughters lived with the new husband's family, and the younger one, Charlotte, was a gentle, retiring girl, timid though charming. One day she sud-

---

13. This entire section on Latrobe's English work is based on research by Miss Dorothy Stroud, who not only visited and photographed the buildings where they still existed and could be identified but also gave me the benefit of her wide knowledge of English architecture in that period.

14. *The Girlhood of Maria Josepha Holroyd (Lady Stanley of Alderly), Recorded in Letters of a Hundred Years Ago,* edited by J. H. Adeane (London: Longman's Green, 1896). This reference was given me by Miss Dorothy Stroud, Assistant Curator of the Soane Museum.

denly eloped with the family groom, a complete ne'er-do-well, and they were secretly married. The Latrobes and John Silvester sought them through London and soon ran them to earth, living in a slum, the girl crushed and horrified at the cruel behavior of her drunken husband. They rescued her, already pregnant, found the husband and had him sent abroad to Canada; Charlotte was sent into the country, where she had her child, who was "put out" for adoption. The family had succeeded in keeping the matter entirely private, and, in order to give time for all to blow over, John Silvester bought an old house—apparently far from London—and had Latrobe alter it into an elegant country house where Charlotte and her older sister could live a retired but fitting life as society spinsters. This was Tanton Hall. But the true irony of the story was yet to come, for, after a divorce had been quietly arranged for, Charlotte married a second groom! This one was in the service of the local duke and apparently was a fine, upright man, and generous John Silvester (by then Sir John) set them up with a good farm, where for all we know they lived happily ever after. Latrobe wonders why a beautiful, gentle girl, bred in the best society, with exquisite tastes and manners, should show such a penchant for grooms.

In addition to these alterations, two large and completely new houses by Latrobe still stand in England—Ashdown House and Hammerwood Lodge. Both are obviously the work of a young designer full of imagination and eager to try his wings. Ashdown House, the later of the two, is the more polished and more completely achieved, but Hammerwood Lodge is the more dynamic, full as it is of violently experimental forms.

Ashdown, of stone, is almost a square house, three bays wide and deep, entered through a semicircular porch of four Greek Ionic columns. The front is broken into three parts vertically, and this division is emphasized by carrying an attic story over the ends alone, with only a parapet above the central element. The center is stressed by framing the second-floor window with delicately projecting pilaster strips that carry up to the frieze, but there is no break in the frieze itself. The tall windows flanking the porch are set in recessed arches. Throughout, the influence of the "plain style" makes itself felt. The cornice is thin and delicate, the frieze an unbroken band; in the attic the base and cap are formed by mere projecting bands of stone. Within, too, the detail is of the simplest type, though the parlor doors are of rich mahogany.

The plan of Ashdown House is unusual; it is interesting to note that in many of its arrangements it is closely related to the plan of the Markoe house in Philadelphia which Latrobe designed some fifteen years later. It forms as a whole a home of modest size but definite distinction, and the interweaving of the square plan with the three-part façade is handled oddly but effectively. The whole promised well for the further development of its designer.

Hammerwood achieves importance as a monument in Latrobe's career when it is realized (if we can believe the architect's obituary in Ackermann's *Repository*[15]) that it was his first independent work. According to Ackermann:

> While pursuing his studies at home, he was visited by a friend, Mr. Sperling, who, finding him disengaged [apparently he had already resigned from the Cockerell firm], and admiring his growing talents, commissioned him to design and build for him a mansion near East Grinstead, to be called Hammerwood Lodge . . . This building obtained for him the further patronage of Mr. Trayton Fuller, for whom he designed a house at Ashdowne Park . . .

Today Hammerwood Lodge is chopped up into flats, and its interiors are wrecked; we can judge little of its original plan. But its exterior reveals a basic desire to tear open the usual conventions of eighteenth-century country-house design, to use new forms and old forms strangely, to create drama—almost wonder—for the observer. In places it harks back to the stark power of Vanbrugh; in others it looks forward to the Greek Revival. It has a great main body five bays wide, with heavy Doric pilasters for the central pavilion; between these the three central windows under recessed arches are crowded in with only hairline jambs. The frieze—again a plain band (except over the pilasters)—is much heavier than ancient precedent would suggest, as though its designer were after the colossal in scale even in a country house, and above rises an attic as quietly powerful as the rest. A slightly projecting band course separates the two lower floors, and the recessed arches are without architraves or moldings. The two wings that flank the central block are even more unusual in design. Here the lower floor consists of arcades of narrow arches, with a window in each, and is terminated at the end by a primitive Greek Doric temple porch carrying a pediment. The upper floor has simple rectangular windows, those over the arcade treated as a single band with recessed

15. 2nd series, vol. XI, January 1, 1821, pp. 30-33.

piers. It has been suggested[16] that the second floor of the wings is a later addition, but the simple flat frieze band and the thinness of the cornice might equally well suggest that they were original despite their awkward juncture with the main block; perhaps this incoherence is due merely to the youth and inexperience of the architect.

Thus Hammerwood Lodge is a strikingly interesting whole, full of awkwardness but of daring imagination as well; it is complicated in composition, but every detail has been reduced to the basic simplicity of the "plain style." Its virtues, like its faults, are those of youth, enthusiasm, and a violent search for originality. We may be astonished at the introduction of Greek Doric end pavilions at this date—that is unusual enough—but we also find something even rarer: Greek inspiration used with a surprising freedom. The capitals have the broad spread of the primitive Doric of Paestum or Sicily, and they have fluted neckings; but the entablature above combines frieze and architrave into one single broad band without triglyphs or metopes. It is Greek, but not Greek taken directly from the plates of Leroi or Stuart; it is Greek seen through the eyes of and interpreted with the taste one would expect from a Soane. The whole, in other words, is entirely Latrobe's—in its unconventional scale, its search for drama, its use of ancient inspiration in an original manner, and its basic drive toward simplification of details. It shows Latrobe already expressing, albeit in an unformed, youthful way, almost all the ideals that were his guiding principles in his mature design.

In London we know there was a small amount of official work, too, for Latrobe calls himself at various times Surveyor of the Police Offices or Surveyor of Public Offices.[17] Careful research has failed to disclose documentary evidence of his appointment, though this is not surprising since documents for those years are scarce; but what we learn tends to support the claim. It turns out that the two titles are one and the same, for police offices were often called simply public offices, just as the original Bow Street Police Station had been called the Public Office. Seven police sta-

16. By Miss Dorothy Stroud.

17. Family legend has it also that Latrobe was offered and refused the job of Surveyor General to the Crown at £1,000 a year. This is manifestly incorrect; it may have arisen through a confusion with regard to his Police Office work and his final dropping of it as described below. Not only did Sir William Chambers hold the position till 1796, the year after Latrobe's departure from London, but politically Latrobe as a friend of Fox would have been completely unacceptable. Moreover, the salary Chambers received was £500 a year, not £1,000.

tions were set up (in addition to the Bow Street central office) as a result of the Middlesex Justices Act of 1792. These were Queens Square, Hatton Garden, Worship Street, Whitechapel, Shadwell, Southwark, and Great Marlborough Street. Generally they were housed in existing buildings, so that architectural work in connection with them was limited to alteration, repair, and equipment. It is significant that Henry Dundas, the Home Secretary from 1791 to 1794, was a relative of the Latrobes' friend Sir Charles Middleton, and the probability is that it was through Sir Charles that Latrobe received the appointment. The position was not an easy one; all kinds of minor details had to be checked, and in the process of carrying out the task the young surveyor found himself confronted with the less estimable conditions that sometimes arose—even then—in connection with governmental work. Eventually, because he would not connive at polite graft, his position was rendered untenable, as may be seen from a letter (January 5, 1807) to his brother Christian, who in recent correspondence had mentioned Henry Dundas:

> But I am not equally an admirer of Henry Dundas, because as I owe to Ch. Fox thanks for distinguished politeness, so I owe to Old Harry an old grudge, for when I was Surveyor to the Public Offices, and managed the whole business in the absence of Mr. Reeves, the Receiver General, a proposal was made to me, sanctioned by a note from Mr. Dundas, thro & by a relation of his, for the supply of everything they wanted, which would have committed my honesty completely. I hesitated and refused. From that moment I found obstacles to all I attempted, & could not get a shilling from the Treasury. You remember the circumstance, no doubt . . .

One other monument remains of Latrobe's professional career in England: two of the drawings he made for the Chelmsford Canal.[18] This project was formally called the Chelmer-Blackwater Canal and was designed to connect Chelmsford with navigable salt water at the coast town of Malden. Rennie had proposed a canal that would follow the course of the Chelmer and Blackwater rivers and by-pass Malden completely, but Malden—then a busy port which owed its living to the traffic from the hinterland—naturally opposed the canal in general and the Rennie scheme in particular. As a result, Latrobe was commissioned to restudy the scheme, and in 1793 and 1794 he submitted his proposals. His plan,

18. These were discovered by Miss Dorothy Stroud in the Essex Record Office at Chelmsford.

based on deepening and straightening the Chelmer between Malden and the sea, took the canal through Malden, improved Malden harbor, and thus did much to obviate the Malden objections. The scheme was acceptable locally and was taken through Parliament as far as the committee stage, but it was then turned down; apparently in this period of national jitters arising from the French war local canals were considered luxuries. The Latrobe drawings consist of two maps showing the proposed improvement—the earlier dated November 11, 1793; the later, covering a larger area, dated September 30, 1794. They are exquisitely drawn, especially the earlier one, and beautifully lettered in a decorative eighteenth-century script. The second of the two schemes shows a different route for the canal above Malden, apparently designed to make it more direct and less expensive.

With these buildings and these drawings before us, we are now able to make a much better judgment of Latrobe's American career. We can see him already original, accomplished, and thoroughly prepared for larger and more demanding work. We can see him as an architect doing distinguished houses, and as an engineer sufficiently respected to have been commissioned to design an important local canal. In the face of this evidence, how stupid, how malicious, and above all how completely unfounded seem his Washington enemies' attacks upon him later as an untrained bungler!

CHAPTER

4

To America

AFTER the death of his wife, the architect faced in England a bleak and difficult future. His home was gone, destroyed almost in the twinkling of an eye. Building was in the dumps because of the French war; architectural commissions bid fair to be few and far between for an indefinite time to come. All the political ideals cherished by Latrobe were condemned and attacked; to seek and cherish sympathetic intellectual companionship might even be dangerous. And across the Atlantic, three thousand miles away, lay the United States, still to many Europeans a beacon light of freedom; there, too, lay his Pennsylvania lands. Is it strange that at this juncture his eyes turned longingly westward?

To have faced the English future successfully would have required the most active effort, clear-sighted and constant, and that was precisely what Latrobe in this moment could not achieve. He was emotionally and nervously broken, the center of his whole life now removed. He was suddenly alone—and, after three years of great happiness and emotional fulfillment, alone in a hostile world. His great need for affection, both to give and to take, was again without direction or object, and a dull lethargy for a while flooded over him.

Even his two children were taken away from him (though with his consent) under what must have been harrowing circumstances, for English common sense—or was it prudery?—was at work. Latrobe himself unveils the moving story in a letter (August 25, 1805) to his friend Eric Bollmann, who was himself in a somewhat similar predicament, though one that had a different and rather sordid end. Bollmann's wife had died and left him with two small children; as the daughter of the wealthy Philadelphia banker Nixon she had been a great catch, but her family had cut her off without a cent because of her marriage to the German-born adventurer. Bollmann consoled himself with the children's nurse, and she had a child by him; the resultant scandal rocked Philadelphia society and did not a little to make his business prospects even shakier than they were. In answer to a letter of Bollmann's bewailing the whole occurrence and attacking the Philadelphians for their narrow hypocrisy, Latrobe wrote him about his own experience:

> I have been exactly in your station, however,—as a widower, with two small children,—and have felt & experienced the difficulty of discretion in that case. Perhaps it was the lynx-eyes of the two maiden aunts that discovered *scandal,* where the cause did not *as yet* exist, & which alarmed my *discretion,* which otherwise I believe would have slept, *where it is said,* yours did. Those good ladies saved me from the precise course which you have *to all outward appearance* followed.—For my nursery maid was *very pretty,* & every moment distressed for me,—and very fond of the children, & often in tears, & still oftener in the room with none but the children as witnesses.—However I escaped: for my good sisters-in-law invited themselves to stay at my house and comfort me, & kept so jealous a watch over me & Isabella,—as to put the thing into my head which I really had not thought before, namely that the poor girl was violently in love with me.—Under these circumstances, I had discretion enough to break up housekeeping. My children went,—Lydia to my own sister, Henry to his maternal aunt White, and Isabella got an excellent place through her interest. [He goes on to state that, had it not been for the aunts, perhaps someone would have written to him in just the way he was now writing to Bollmann. He concludes,] for human nature under the influence of tenderness is very weak, especially when *pleasure* coaxes *sorrow* to be comforted.

Latrobe by the time he wrote this letter was again happily married, and time had given him the perspective to realize the worldly—perhaps even the personal—wisdom of the steps that had been taken in his case; there had been no scandal, and a potentially dangerous personal relationship had been killed in the bud. But, during the sad days of the waning year of 1793, this too must have bitten deeply into his soul, and in the chilly gloom of an English winter his loneliness must have been all the more devastating. Wife and children gone, what was there to work for?

The intellectual and political climate in England from 1793 to 1795 was also profoundly distasteful to him. Hazlitt has left us scores of glowing references to the heady inspiration, like the lighting of a sudden brilliant lamp in a dark room, which the French Revolution raised singing in the minds of many enthusiastic Englishmen, as in this from "The Feeling of Immortality in Youth":

> For my part, I set out in life with the French Revolution, and that event had considerable influence on my early feelings, as on those of others. Youth was then doubly such. It was the dawn of a new era, a new impulse had been given to men's minds, and the sun of Liberty rose upon the sun of Life in the same day, and both were proud to run their race together. Little did I dream, while my first hopes and wishes went hand in hand, that long before my eyes should close, that dawn would be overcast, and set once more in the night of despotism—"total eclipse"! Happy that I did not. I felt for years, and during the best part of my existence, *heart-whole* in that cause, and triumphed in the triumphs over the enemies of man! . . .

At the beginning, sympathy with the French Revolution was widespread in England, especially among the intelligentsia—precisely the group with which the Latrobes were in closest contact. Even the pious Fanny Burney once belonged to a "Revolutionary Club." In her diary letters to her sister Susan she remarks (in October, 1791):

> The respectable Mr. Bateman was there also, and we had much Windsor chattery. Miss Merry, too, was of the part; she is the sister of the "Liberty" Mr. Merry, who wrote the ode for our revolution club. . . . [Miss Merry talked about French affairs] which I would not have touched upon for the world, her brother's principles being notorious. However, she eagerly gave me to understand her own were the reverse . . . [Fanny goes on to inveigh against the tyranny of Mrs. Schwellenberg at Windsor and continues:] 'Tis dreadful that power often leads to every abuse!—I grow democrat at once on those occasions. Indeed, I always feel democrat where I think power abused, whether by the great or the little.

This is significant of the mixed emotions felt by thousands of liberal English people at the time, as well as of the tremendous effect that Burke's writings on the French Revolution had in turning England against it. As time passed, sympathy gave way to fear: what if the poverty-ridden mob of England were to rise? Then came the Terror, and fear was buttressed by violent moral passions. The French war of 1793 was the fruit of fear; its popular support was procured by appeals to a morality with which its basic cause had in reality little to do. This was not the first time—nor, alas, has it been the last—in which a basic power conflict has clothed itself in the shining armor of the crusader.

Everywhere friends of France and friends of the Revolution were suspect, and in 1794 came the final fruit of the hysteria—the repeal of the right of habeas corpus in cases of suspected political crime. And Latrobe was among the friends of Fox and of the French Revolution. Of his admiration for Fox he writes to his brother in the letter (January 5, 1807) already quoted in part in connection with Henry Dundas:

> Mr. Fox on one occasion paid me the highest compliment I ever received, for tho' only slightly introduced to him, he recognized me once in Pall Mall, took me into a coffee house & conversed with me on all sorts of things, and the next day, when the tax on bricks was proposed, sent for me and obtained from me, in a manner I shall never forget, all the information on the subject of bricks, and brick houses which I possessed.

And of his own revolutionary enthusiasm, in his later life in New Orleans (March 6, 1819) he set down sadly in his journal:

> I remember the time when I was over head & ears in love with *Man in a state of nature.*—By the bye, I never heard any fine theory spun together in behalf of *Woman in a state of nature. Social compacts* were my hobbies, the American revolution (I ask its pardon, for it deserves better company) was a sort of dawn of the golden age, and the French revolution the Golden Age itself. I should be ashamed to confess all this if I had not had a thousand companions in my Kalei[do]scopic amusement, & those generally men of ardent, benevolent & well informed minds, & excellent hearts. Alas! experience has destroyed the illusion, the Kallei[do]scope is broken, and all the tinsel of scenery that glittered so delightfully is tarnished & turned to raggedness. A dozen years of residence at the republican court of Washington has assisted wonderfully in the advance of riper years.[1]

To Latrobe's natural enthusiasm for the Revolution the Terror itself must have come as a stunning blow, even though it did not destroy his faith and hope. And this, too, must have increased the sadness of those last years in England. To be one of a passionately hated minority might offer a challenge, but to a man of Latrobe's affectionate and trusting nature it must have been torture as well. Can he then be blamed for having sought a different social and political scene, particularly when that scene was also the scene of that other revolution which seemed to

---

1. Benjamin Henry Boneval Latrobe, *Impressions Respecting New Orleans,* edited with an introduction and notes by Samuel Wilson, Jr. (New York: Columbia University Press, 1951).

him "the dawn of the golden age"? Besides, there loomed ahead the shadow of bankruptcy, of professional failure. We do not know what he lived on during his last two years in England, with Lydia's annuity forever stopped and even the stated reversion to him held back by the trustees. What and how much he may have received from his father's family may never be known, but it is not likely to have been a large amount. What he earned professionally during that period must have been only a pittance. If the Chelmsford Canal had gone ahead, that would have assured him a position for several years to come and brought with it other jobs. But with the failure of the canal scheme in Parliamentary committee—after so much eager anticipation—the gates of hope clanged shut.

There remained only the American land left to him by his mother. To realize on this in London at the time would have been difficult if not impossible. Apparently it was still a wilderness, unimproved and unexploited, and Latrobe was not the man to make a future out of land speculation in acres he had never seen. So far, its only revenue to him had been one bear cub and three elegies. But might it not bring him a fortune in America? And his memories of his mother's stories of the distant, romantic land, mixed with enthusiasm for the American Revolution and admiration for the new country where at last English ideals of liberty would be able to flower, far from Parliamentary chicanery and the influence of a greedy aristocracy, must have made America seem a promised land indeed.

Toward the end of 1795, therefore, he made his decision. He packed up and sent on ahead the greater part of his large library—about fifteen hundred books, he says later—and some of his precious instruments. He arranged for passage and at last, on November 25, 1795, was rowed out to board the American ship *Eliza* at Gravesend; a little later she set sail. Apparently he had left his affairs in England in confusion, for his name occurs in a list of bankruptcies in the *European Magazine* for July-December, 1795: "Latrobe, Benjamin, Gratton [Grafton] Street, December 5th." But now he had put this and other disappointments behind him. Before him stretched three thousand miles of winter sea—and a new world.

Benjamin Henry Latrobe's initiation into America—if an American ship can be called a part of America—was not propitious. The *Eliza* was a new vessel of moderate size—286 tons—and apparently fairly fast, but she was ill-provisioned, ill-equipped, and badly run. Her captain, Noble, was manifestly unqualified; he was a bad organizer, a loud talker, a careless navigator, and this was his first trip to Europe in command of a ship. The food and water aboard were so insufficient that only fortunate meetings with vessels better supplied enabled them to avoid actual famine and thirst, and for a week or more the rations were so scanty that the crew was unable to carry on the routine work with any efficiency.[2] This winter voyage westbound—the upwind passage—was undertaken with only one spare sail (a foretopsail) and gear already worn, and with insufficient repair material; instead of doing the necessary repairs in port and sailing with a shipshape vessel at the start, Captain Noble had "taken a chance," and no radical repairs were made until pieces of gear were literally falling off the spars. In the first severe weather the foremast was almost lost as a result of this carelessness.

The voyage was some fifteen weeks in length, but that was by no means exceptional then for a westward winter passage. The *Eliza* took the standard route: south to the Azores, then picking up the northeast trades and west across the ocean, and at last gradually north in the Gulf Stream to port. But many things combined to confuse the clear design of the passage. A possible voyage of this duration could have been foreseen and should have been provided for. The water shortage (the supply was even less than that called for by the American regulations) was emphasized by the fact that the most valuable part of the cargo was a shipment of horses. Latrobe reports (February 17, 1796):

On the 15th or 16th of December, the whole ship's company, passengers included, were put on an allowance of 2 quarts a day. We had then been out only three weeks. The allowance of the horses was stinted to a bucket a day . . . the deficiency [of water] p. man will be more than 65 gallons, and the whole deficiency nearly 20 casks . . . But of [the captain's] misconduct there is so much to be said that I sicken at the idea of dwelling upon it.

---

2. Latrobe's journal of his voyage to America exists in transcript only, in two versions, one slightly more extensive than the other. These two transcripts were in the hands of Gamble and Osmun Latrobe when they were collated and retranscribed by Ferdinand C. Latrobe II. It is this retranscription that has been used for quotation here. It is my surmise that the original was brought to this country by Charles Joseph Latrobe, Christian's son, the famous traveler and author; that it was transcribed during his visit here in 1832 and was taken back with him when he left the country. If the original still exists, it very probably is in Australia, where Charles spent many years; he was Lieutenant Governor of the state of Victoria from 1851 to 1854.

Except for a Mr. Taylor who was picked up at Deal, the passengers came on board at Gravesend and found the ship a shambles; even the cabin was filthy and in terrific disarray. Only after some two weeks of acute discomfort were they able, by taking things into their own hands, to produce some order out of the chaos and impose on the shiftless crew a sense of even ordinary cleanliness and decency. The cabin was too small for the comfortable housing of the cabin passengers; Latrobe, after trying an athwartship bunk, moved first to the floor and later to a hammock in the between-decks steerage, and Mr. Taylor's wife and her baby were transferred from the steerage into the first mate's stateroom, which was vacated for her.[3]

Starting with wild westerly winds, fog, rain, and sleet, the *Eliza* took two weeks—till December 9—to get out of the Channel, most of the time tacking back and forth with no precise idea of her position. Latrobe was horrified to discover that the captain had not the slightest knowledge of the Channel tides and shores and that no dead reckoning was kept of the ship's heading or the distance run; it was all a matter of wild guessing—of sailing so many hours south and then so many north. Latrobe himself made a tide table of the Channel for the captain, but because of the slipshod way in which the ship was sailed even that could be of little real help. And always there was the danger of French privateers. The captain's attitude did little to allay the passengers' sense of insecurity; on the night of November 30, after a grueling day of tacking or wearing ship

3. The passenger and crew list seems to have been as follows:

Cabin Passengers

- Mr. Brewster (who had an excellent library with him)
- Mr. Califf (an experienced sailor)
- Mr. Latrobe
- Mr. Martin ("a busy and good-natured man")
- Mr. and Mrs. Taylor and baby
- Mr. Tenney (an ex-butcher)
- Mr. Turner (a minister)
- Mr. Young (an American)

Steerage Passengers

- Mr. Christie (a Scotch farmer)
- Mr. Cotton (a painter and glazier)
- Two sons of Mr. Turner

Officers and Crew

- Captain Noble (lazy, incompetent)
- First Mate Shaw (the real hero of the voyage)
- Second Officer
- Cook
- Groom
- Cabin Boy, Dick
- Antonini, a Portuguese
- Joseph, a Frenchman
- Peter, a Negro
- Six others

This means that for a ship the *Eliza* was undercrewed as well as under supplied; there would have been but four men in each of the two watches.

every three hours under reefed courses only and in a wild sea, with nearly everyone sick, he said (as quoted by Latrobe):

"Why, I could make my fortune by going to Havre, & giving up the ship & cargo as English property. I don't say I should do so; but no man can answer for himself when strong temptation comes in his way." "If you will excuse my opinion, Captain [said Latrobe], I believe you incapable of the thing you suggest: & that you play with our feelings. But, if you could, for a moment, entertain it, you would deserve to be hung at your own yard arm." "Why," he replied, "I know such things have happened, & I can't [?] say that I should be sorry to have any such temptation, especially as some of you have left families in England, & therefore I would rather not go to Havre, but I do not think any man ought to answer for himself. Why, now, even the passengers' goods are worth something."

On the very brink of leaving the Channel they were delayed again by being hailed and stopped by British men-of-war who asked for their identification; but at last with a fresh and fair breeze they stood down the Channel, and under the influence of the more favorable weather Latrobe took the occasion to give a picture of the life aboard:

We are shamefully short of water, & the men already on an allowance of half a gallon a day. We are not allowed a drop to wash our hands & faces. For the most commonest calls of nature, in illness, no provision has been made. The cabin which is only 22 feet wide by 14 long is occupied by two sleeping places on each side and two others across over the lockers. A stove in which we seldom care to make a fire on account of the insufferable smoke & a filthy table occupy the remaining space. The floor is the receptacle of every species of filth, & the violent agitation of the ship so frequently overturns dishes, cups & glasses, that indifference is almost necessary . . . We have one tin coffee pot, & a tin tea kettle. Dick, our cabin boy, makes coffee for breakfast, & in the coffee pot water is boiled for tea. The coffee is not bad by any means, but the tea is the coarsest Bohea. We have a few pewter teaspoons that are never cleaned, & the deficiency is made up by pewter table spoons still blacker than the others. Our biscuits are good & the butter tolerable, but put upon the table in the nastiest manner imaginable . . . For supper we eat up the remains of dinner if any, cold cabbage, cold beef, all mixed up in the square tin pans in which they have been dressed. We have not a sufficient number of wine glasses to serve all, & we therefore assist each other. All tumblers are broken but three, & the last passes from the hand of the grog drinker to that of the porter drinker, contains brown sugar at tea, & serves as a slop basin at breakfast. If in the course of the several offices it gets one washing we are more than usually happy. Mr. Brewster [4] has a collection of books of the best sorts which, with great liberality he has given to the general use of us, & Mr. Taylor has many volumes of novels. We are extremely unsociable . . . The evenings are necessarily occupied in reading, in which we all crowd around a farthing candle swinging by a rope yarn in a lacquered candlestick . . . But to sit & read by a movable candle, holding fast to a rickety table, & remember what is read requires more genius than is ordinarily granted to mortals. Poor Martin [the ship's bore] alone finds comfort in listening to his own harangues upon law, religion, prolifixity (a noun derived from prolific) of rabbits and Scotswomen, the inspiration of Milton . . . the bundling of American inamorati, & the prophecies of Jeremiah. . . .

The ship is wholly navigated by the mate [Mr. Shaw].

Out of the Channel, the *Eliza,* instead of being sailed south to get across the Bay of Biscay as rapidly as possible, was driven toward the southwest, for the captain, Latrobe says, was afraid of getting "into the hands of the Algerines. Now, by the best accounts, peace has subsisted between the Algerines & America these 18 months, nor has a single vessel been captured during that time." Two or three days later, on December 12, an incident occurred which revealed startlingly the qualities of the captain's character and seamanship:

The captain who is not often on deck, excepting to look after dinner, has become a great reader. About 8 in the evening he had just finished "The Vicar of Wakefield," & was enquiring of me "whether I recollected how Goldsmith had disposed of Burchell," when I observed to him that I thought the vessel began to pitch more than usually. "I suppose," he said, "that the jib is set. I will order it down presently." Mr. Califf however, whose intrepidity saved the ship, ran upon deck, & before the captain could follow him the wind blew a hurricane. The mate had turned in, the second mate was frightened out of his wits, & the captain did not know what to do. Mr. Califf, however, got the ship before the wind, and every sail was shivered. All hands were soon on deck & the mate got up. For a long time it was doubtful whether we could save our masts. The ship was with difficulty kept large [off the wind, in modern usage "broad off"]. . . . With much exertion we got our courses, the main & mizzen topsail, as well handed as the violence of the wind would permit, & scudded under our foretopsail which threatened every moment to go. The foremast bent like a cane. In two or three hours the gale somewhat moderated. At 10, the captain went to bed, nor did he rise till the next morn-

4. This man's name is doubtful; it has been transcribed as "Bowker" and as "Brewsher," but my acquaintance with Latrobe's writing makes me venture that it is really Brewster.

ing after 7 o'clock. The mates & the crew were up all night, wet to the skin & hard at work. Towards morning the wind died. Though danger existed more in the unskillfulness of the captain, his entire neglect of precautions & his incurable laziness, than in the violence of the storm, we had for an hour, in the captain's opinion, no chance of saving the masts. To the exertions of Mr. Califf & the mate we owed our escape.

Monday, December 14:

As our beef becomes unpleasantly salt, we this day killed one of our sheep. The live stock we took on board was four sheep, four pigs & some dozen of fowls. The sheep have done very well. . . . The pigs are miserably poor, & two of them not likely to live. Of the fowls, we have lost one half & the others are not likely to be eaten, so wretchedly old & tough are they. Besides these live provisions, we have a cask or two of beef salted in London, five or six hams and a barrel or two of potatoes. This is all we have to look to for subsistence on a voyage one tenth part of which is not yet finished . . .

So they slogged down slowly, south and southwest, as the heavy westerly gales permitted. Mr. Shaw, the mate, only twenty-one years old, proved the one bright spot in a dreary succession of stormy days; always cheerful and a fine seaman, he supplied the knowledge and the energy which the captain so woefully lacked. On January 4 they considered that they had reached the latitude of Corvo, "the most northerly & westerly of the Azores Islands, but that they were considerably to the west of them." Yet two days later, January 6:

. . . we were all called on deck by the cry of "Land" to the northwest of us. Surprise took possession of all our sea folks from the captain to the cabin boy. For my part, I confess that the beauty of the morning and the grandeur of the scene, exhibiting three or four islands covered with clouds that were gilded by the rising sun gave me much more pleasure than I felt disappointment from the certainty we were much behind our hope and our reckoning. By degrees, the sun dispelling the clouds, showed the majesty of Pico de Azores half covered with snow the brilliant whiteness of which was equal to polished silver . . .

It took them two whole days to leave the land behind, but the captain refused to put into Fayal for supplies. On January 12:

The warmth of the weather has produced a general disposition to sauntering & idleness. I have read since we left the Downs—Hume's History of England, all Smollet's & Fielding's novels, which Mr. Taylor has, some parts of Voltaire's works & several other small volumes, & have now undertaken Gibbon's Decline & Fall of the Roman Empire. . . .

Generally the horse latitudes brought them only calms and severe squalls; they made little progress, until at last, on Thursday, January 21, almost two months out:

. . . the first breath of the tradewind blew from the NE & inspired us with new hopes. We immediately hoisted starboard & larboard . . . steering sails forward, & ran before it. A very heavy swell from the north made the ship roll exceedingly, & our rigging, tumbling about our ears rendered the deck dangerous.

On this day, too, Neptune was scheduled to come on board, to signalize not the crossing of the equator, as today, but the crossing of the Tropic of Cancer. The captain, who had refused to go farther south in his search for the trades, faked the latitude to make this possible.

Antoni[ni] impersonated Neptune, & Joseph, a french sailor on board, transformed himself into a species of priest with a rosary of blocks, a cross of hoops & a beard of rope yarn. How Neptune came to be transformed into an old Portuguese sailor & to be attended by a french priest cannot easily be explained, but it would be still more difficult to explain . . . his occupation as barber to the green sailors on board.

Unfortunately for the rite, most of the green sailors and passengers found a way of escaping from the 'tween decks in which they had been imprisoned preparatory to their initiation, and Neptune and his priest "were obliged to content themselves by lathering with slush tar & shaving with a harpoon our miserable negro Peter. All the rest escaped, & the elegant amusement which was to have rewarded Antonini's & Joseph's ingenuity at least with a gallon of grog ended in disappointment & ill humor." Even Neptune seemed cursed on the *Eliza!*

By failing to go farther south, the ship found itself again in the horse latitudes, slatting in calms and belabored by squalls. And every day the food and water situation got worse. On January 26:

. . . we must now be content to live upon maggoty bread for a week, & then descend to a few casks of completely rotten biscuit. . . . Our fate is miserable for food, but our apprehensions are worse. The sailors have already refused & are indeed unable to do anything but the commonest work of the ship, & famine must attack us in a fortnight, unless we are relieved or resolve to eat the horses. They, even, are upon a very short allowance & would furnish but a lean supply of beef . . .

Yet the surroundings of the vessel grew more and more interesting, and the weather stayed generally warm and pleasant. Latrobe notes the great number and the beauty of the flying fish. On February 4, the weather being perfectly calm, the captain permitted Latrobe and Mr. Taylor to launch the small boat, and with two sailors they rowed to a great patch of floating seaweed near by. (They were then in the Sargasso Sea area.) Latrobe was fascinated by the gulfweed and the eels and small crabs that made this floating island their home. Later he wrote a long, vivid description of the Portuguese man-of-war and commented on its beautiful color as well as its poisonous tentacles. He remarks: "This animal has a caustic quality when handled, & leaves a painful impression which lasts for some time upon the skin. The sailors play tricks with the green-hands by telling them it serves the purpose of soap for washing; & one or two of our people were taken in . . ."[5] But the evening of the same day brought more serious thoughts:

[It] called us to a consideration of bread & water; & the loss of time & the near approach of famine occurred to us when the last ten biscuits per man was delivered. The same quantity is reserved for us in the cabin & when they are consumed, nothing remains but ten or twelve casks that are absolutely rotten. [Mr. Taylor, who had been put in charge of the water rationing,] took such excellent care of the water that instead of a deficiency some quarts were saved. The captain succeeded him last week, & I am to take charge of our few remaining provisions for the ensuing week. Our last pig being now in tolerable case, but consuming more water than we can spare, I ordered him to be killed, in hope of relief before we shall eat him all up.

On Monday, February 8, their hopes for relief were raised by the sight of a sail to windward, but night was falling and although they got out the boat to pursue the distant ship it was all in vain. The next day, however, their hopes were rewarded. They had reached the general traffic

5. In these passages on nautical fauna and on the gulfweed, together with the sketchbook drawings that illustrate them, we get the first expression of one of Latrobe's controlling interests—biology. Where he picked up his extensive knowledge of the natural sciences is at present unknown, but, whatever the source, he had undoubtedly read widely, remembered what he had read, and applied it with more than amateur accuracy. Insects, plants, geological structure—these were all endlessly fascinating to his inquiring mind.

route between the United States and the Virgin Islands, and again they sighted a sloop:

We immediately hoisted our ensign at the mizzen peak, and she bore away for us. She was about 2 leagues distant. . . . Mr. Shaw with Mr. Califf left the ship with the small boat & reached her about a league from the ship, & we found when she came within hail that she could supply us with every article in the list sent on board. She came from Stonington, in the state of Connecticut, commanded & as it would seem owned by Captain Stanton. . . . The articles with which he supplied us were 4 dozen fowls, 2 turkies, 1 barrel of captain biscuits, ½ barrel excellent beef, 1 barrel of butter, a cask of potatoes, 6 pounds of sugar, all he could spare, 6 gallons of rum, a bag of white beans, 2 hams, a box of mould candles, & a quantity of tobacco. He offered to break his cargo to supply us with more biscuits, but Mr. Shaw, very properly, would not suffer it. Besides this he sent as a present to the cabin passengers two case bottles of brandy, & to Mrs. Taylor, whom he accidentally saw on deck, a cheese. His bill, which he offered to reduce . . . amounted to only 79½$, or £17, 19s., 9d. sterling. Being the market price in America. . . . The sloop was bound to the Swedish Island of St. Bartholomew. The contrast between the conduct of the two American captains before our eyes was infinitely advantageous to Captain Stanton. Upon his departure we gave him three rousing cheers. . . . His sloop was a beautiful little vessel of 60 tons . . .[6]

With good food again, everyone's spirits rose, although squalls and variable winds continued. But the new supplies, despite careful rationing, could not sustain twenty-nine people for long; again famine was not far away. On February 15 they hailed another ship:

She bore up & proved to be the Hermaphrodite brig *Sally* of New York, Captain Match, bound for Jamaica. She was in every respect the ugliest machine I ever saw, & though there was very little wind and scarce any swell, she rolled her chains in on each side and appeared as she bore down on us, ridiculously drunk. Mr. Shaw and Taylor went on board and found her captain in liquor, but sufficiently sober to sell us 2 barrels of seaman's biscuits at 7 dollars, a very big price. He had nothing else that we wanted & was very un-

---

6. The sloop was the *Olive Branch;* her name is given in the caption Latrobe wrote for an exquisite water-color sketch of her. According to data from the New London Custom House, the *Olive Branch* was 50 feet long and 17 broad. She was built in Stonington in 1795 by Zebulon Hancox and sold in June that year to Ebenezer Stanton (her captain) and Stephen Brown. She went through several ownerships in the next few years and is last listed in 1804. I owe this information to the Mystic (Connecticut) Marine Museum.

civil. She therefore rolled off without receiving the usual compliments of three cheers.

Two days later there were sails in sight all around the horizon. They hailed the beautiful brig *Sally,* of Philadelphia, bound for Havana. Unfortunately the only things they could get from her were some sugar, of which they had none, two kegs of "American biscuits called crackers" —an interesting note on the early use of this now common term—and a few apples. But there were also some American papers, the latest dated February 11. Captain Audlin of the *Sally* gave them his longitude as 71° west of London; their own reckoning had been 73°. They now hoped to make Norfolk on Sunday, but a heavy northwester dashed their hopes; they were driven south, and it was not till a week later that they succeeded in working back toward their desired course—and, Latrobe adds, "God knows how much to the eastward." But the color of the water had changed from deep blue to green and, although they could get no soundings at 80 fathom, they felt that land was not far away.

For the next week they worked slowly in toward the Chesapeake, speaking on the way the schooner *Telegraphe* of Baltimore, from which they obtained two casks of bread and some "tasteless oranges." A small Marblehead fishing schooner gave them the bearing and distance of Cape Henry thirty leagues away. They caught a brief glimpse of the low shore on March 4, but there they were becalmed. Again they had the good fortune of getting needed firewood and a bushel of potatoes from the ship *Birmingham* of Baltimore, which almost drifted afoul of them in the calm. She had had an even worse trip than theirs, for she had sailed on October 9, had been nearly wrecked by a gale in the Irish Channel, and was delayed in Kinsale two months for repairs.

Finally, on Monday, March 7, a fair southwest breeze came up. Every heart was raised:

Our hopes of safe arrival within the capes before eventide, the delicious weather, & a good fresh dinner, after so long a period of almost fasting and despair, raised sensations to which we had long been strangers. Seventeen vessels of different kinds were in sight steering the same course as ourselves, & every moment brought us nearer to the shore. . . . About 4 o'clock a pilot boat came alongside, but she had no Norfolk pilots on board, & the Potowmack & Baltimore pilots have no right in the navigation of the James River.[7]

---

7. It is interesting to note that this strict division of pilotage rights is still in force.

At eight o'clock a brisk southeast breeze sprang up:

Our joy was such as the deliverance from 15 weeks voyage in which everything that deserves the name of anxiety had been experienced could only occasion, the man in the chains sung "quarter less six" and the lighthouse was only a mile's distance, when all in a moment—all our prospects vanished, the wind chopped around to NE b E & began to blow a gale. No time was to be lost, & at 5 the light was discerned no more. It then began to snow & grew excessively cold. Our mainsail was shivered, & we were glad to come under close reefed main topsail and fore course. I had been up the greatest part of the night, & was perfectly seasick in the morning so violently was the vessel agitated.

The next day was no better:

The most dismal day we have yet experienced. The weather was so cold that the ropes were frozen in the blocks. The snow lay thick on the yards and the deck was covered with a sheet of ice. The gale continued with immense violence & we shipped many heavy seas. The agitation of the vessel would not permit us to light a fire in the cabin and we sat shivering though covered with heavy great coats. Our meals were eaten upon the floor; for the bars that had secured our plates and dishes on the table were destroyed on the day of our hopes. I was so ill that I neither ate nor drank the whole day. A beautiful mare in foal belonging to Col. Holmes fell down through weakness and could not rise for want of food. Our poor sailors were miserably cold and wet and quite dispirited. I went to bed at nine and put all the clothes I could get over me and slept tolerably but was frequently awakened by the convulsive kicking of the mare in the hold who died about four o'clock.

Wednesday, March 9, 1796. With this date but no entry the journal ends, the day after Latrobe's first devastating and disappointing experience of that all-too-common American phenomenon—the sudden bursting forth of a wild polar front. There is no record of the final arrival at port, but on March 14 the Norfolk *Herald* carried the following advertisement: "For freight or charter. To any part of the world. The American ship *Eliza.* A new vessel, 286 tons. She made one voyage to London. Apply to the subscriber at Mrs. Livingston's, who has been a constant trader to London. Samuel Chauncey. She will be ready to receive a cargo in ten days."[8] Thus it would appear that probably on March 9

8. Some four weeks later she was evidently still in Norfolk, for on April 11 she was advertised again: "For London. The American ship *Eliza.* Samuel Chauncey, Master. Has

the northerly had blown itself out and had left the ship perhaps a hundred miles out; then the breeze had veered south, as it usually does in such circumstances, and the *Eliza* could have docked late on March 11 or 12.[9]

The Virginia diaries of B. H. Latrobe begin on March 21 and indicate that he had been some days ashore; in all probability, therefore, by the evening of March 12 at least he had become a resident of the United States. One great section of his life had come to an end and another, more fruitful, was about to begin.

---

good [!] accommodations for passengers and is on her second voyage. Burthen 500 tons Tobacco; having the greater part of her cargo already engaged. For freight of the remainder, or passage, apply to the Master on board, or to Phineas Davis." Evidently Captain Noble's incompetence had been discovered, and the agent or owner—Chauncey—had finally decided to take over the command himself.

9. I owe this analysis to notes on the journal made by the late Ferdinand C. Latrobe II.

PART II: Latrobe Becomes an American

CHAPTER

5

Latrobe in Virginia: 1796-1798

By mid-March, despite occasional cold, spring had begun in Virginia, and some of its intoxication swept over Latrobe when he landed in Norfolk. There was, too, intense relief after the long and dangerous voyage, as well as the excitement of seeing a new country founded in revolution and dedicated to freedom. He became all ears, all eyes; insatiable curiosity intensified his perceptions and drove away for the time being any nostalgia for the England he had left. All through the notes in his journals, as in his sketches, during 1796 and early 1797 there is a breathless eagerness as he describes peculiarities of speech and manners and the special characteristics of the land itself—its flora and fauna, its rocks and soils and valleys. And he plunged almost at once into a flurry of professional work.

Latrobe's obituary in Ackermann's *Repository* [1]—perhaps founded largely on the architect's own notes—is our only authority for his earliest days in America. According to it, his ship had originally planned to land in Philadelphia and came to Norfolk only because of the stress of weather. This hardly seems likely, for in his journal of the voyage Norfolk is mentioned as the port to which they were sailing ten days before they raised Cape Henry. There are other reasons as well to suggest that Ackermann is in error on this point.[2] But the circumstances of his introduction to American society may well be those which Ackermann gives: "Here [in

1. 2nd series, vol. XI, January 1, 1821, pp. 30-33.

2. The late Ferdinand C. Latrobe II has pointed out, for instance, that the horses on board the *Eliza* were imported by a Colonel Hoomes and that a Colonel Hoomes of Bowling Green ran the stage from Richmond to Washington. These would hardly have been shipped on a vessel bound for Pennsylvania. The confusion might easily have arisen from a misinterpretation of a remark in Latrobe's notes that one of his reasons for going to America was to examine his Pennsylvania lands.

Norfolk], unknown to everyone, he accidentally accosted a gentleman, who proved to be a commissioner of customs, and who, interested in his amiable manners, invited him to his house, and shortly introduced him to Col. Bulstrode [sic] Washington." [3] Evidently, too, through the commissioner he soon met the intellectual aristocracy of Norfolk, for he writes (March 31) in his journal:

> The friends to whom I was recommended have been extremely kind to me, & I have loitered my time away at their Houses, doing odds & ends of little services for them; designing a staircase for Mr. Acheson's new house, a House and Offices for Captn Pennock,[4] tuning a pianoforte for Mr. Wheeler, scribbling doggerel for Mrs. Acheson, tragedy for her mother, & Italian songs for Mrs. Taylor. An excursion into the Dismal Swamp, opened a prospect for professional pursuits of more importance to me; I saw there too much to describe at random, & too little to describe at all without seeing more.

Norfolk, he found, was a rambling, straggling, unbeautiful town. It had only begun to rise again from the ashes left by the terrible fire set by the British bombardment in 1776. Latrobe observed that the town was ill-built and unhealthy. His sketches bear this out, and obviously the malaria from the surrounding swamps was endemic. Yet even in Norfolk he found at least one thing to interest him greatly—the way the wharves were built, of logs set layer on layer and left to sink into the mud by gravity at any angles they might take, then gradually straightened out to the horizontal by the adding of more logs and timbers as necessary, and back-filled with ballast stones and with

> Wharfwood (that is young fir trees of about 4 or 6 inches diameter) cut into lengths of 10 or 12 feet, and laid parallel across the ties. . . . These wooden wharfs are said to have been the invention of Mr. Owen, a Welshman. He was a drunk dog . . . but when sober his ingenuity and industry made up for lost time.

All these observations are prophetic. Not yet three weeks in America, Latrobe was already at home in the best society of Norfolk; his charm,

---

3. The misspelling "Bolstrode" for "Bushrod" is interesting and provides additional evidence that the Ackermann passage was composed from Latrobe's notes; the same misreading of the architect's handwriting occurs constantly in *The Journal of Latrobe,* with an introduction by J. H. B. Latrobe (New York: Appleton, 1905).

4. Captain Pennock was a commercial and not a Navy or Army captain; he was a shipowner and in the general export and import business.

his musical knowledge, and his literary abilities won him almost immediate welcome. But, more important, he had also designed his first American building (the house for Captain Pennock), he had entered the field of engineering in his trip to the Dismal Swamp, and he had become deeply interested in those new ways of building which ingenious American immigrants had devised to meet local conditions. Not only was he the cultivated gentleman bringing to the new country the riches of his unusual background; also, in less than a month, he became an American architect, an American engineer.

And gradually his mind became saturated with the historical background of his adopted country, its legends, its memorials, its pride. On March 29 he writes of the memories of the Revolution which still filled the hearts of many Americans. Ruined Norfolk itself was a reminder, but that was not all:

There are few stones in the country or I should have said *Nullum sine nomine saxum*. Many of [the mementos] are of a melancholy nature. In passing down the Elizabeth River, its eastern shore recalled the shocking remembrance of thousands of miserable negroes who had perished there with hunger or disease.—Many waggon loads of the bones of men, women & children, stripped of their flesh by Vultures & Hawks which abound here, covered the sand for a considerable length. Lord Dunmore, soon after the commencement of the War, offered liberty to all the slaves who would rise against, or escape from their *Rebel* masters. The hopes of getting on board the English fleet collected them at the mouth of Chesapeake bay,—they were left behind in thousands & perished.

Evidently the trip to the Dismal Swamp was at least semi-professional. The projected canal had been partly dug, but the company had run into all sorts of difficulties. As a result of his advice in this matter and because of his obvious technical knowledge, his new friends told him of the plans to improve the channels of the James River and its tributaries and impressed upon him both the urgency of the work and the likelihood of his being put in charge of it. This is the "prospect for professional pursuits of more importance to me" which he mentions. To further any such appointment a visit to Richmond, the capital of the state, was essential; on April 1, therefore, he set out, going via Williamsburg, and soon his circle of Norfolk friends was widened to include a large number of the most influential and interesting families in the tidewater area.

As he traveled, his journal was not overlooked. The eagerness with which he sought information, the keenness of his eyes and ears for local peculiarities, and his continual reference of these thronging new experiences to his wide background make his writings the most vivid and revealing of existing pictures of that somewhat unformed area, where family traditions and a sense of class were struggling with the new vision of liberty, where great gentlemen lived in log mansions in the wilderness, where beautiful houses were surrounded by fields still filled with tree stumps, and where backward agricultural methods were fighting already worn-out soil.

Latrobe crossed Hampton Roads on the mail boat (a schooner) and, landing in Hampton, he notes that the schooner's owner, Captain Loyal, was growing prosperous in this trade, for there was much coming and going between Norfolk and the north and the Hampton route was the quickest. The day was April 1, as indicated by a dated sketch of Craney's Island made from the mail boat. His route to Richmond led him through Williamsburg, which both interested and depressed him. It was, in 1796, almost deserted and rapidly falling into ruin; its one function—except for being the seat of William and Mary College—had disappeared when Richmond was made the state capital. Of it he paints a mournful picture:

> The principal street of Williamsburg is near a mile in length. At one end stands the Capitol, at the other the College. The Capitol is a heavy brick pile with a two story portico towards the street, the wooden pillars of which are stripped of their Mouldings & are twisted and forced out of their planes in all directions.[5] . . . A beautiful statue of Lord Bottetcourt, a popular governor of Virginia before the war, is deprived of its head & mutilated in many other respects. This is not the only proof of the decay of Williamsburg. The Court House which stands on the North side of the street, has lost all the columns of the Portico, & the Pediment sticks out like a Penthouse carried only by timbers that bind into the roof.[6] Many ruined & uninhabited houses disgrace the street . . .

And in his sketchbook he made a vivid sketch of the ruined hall of the Capitol and the mutilated statue, adding a carefully drawn detail of the exquisite pedestal—documents which have proved of great value to the

---

5. The original capitol had had no such portico, but one had been added later to bring the building "up to date" and in accord with the growing classicism of eighteenth-century fashion.

6. Evidently Latrobe thought that the courthouse had originally had its four columns. In the present restoration it still lacks them.

modern restorers. By April 5 he was at Richmond and was at once struck by its similarity to the Richmond he knew in England. On April 7 he writes:

The amphitheatre of hills covered partly with wood, partly with buildings, the opposite shore with the town of Manchester in front, & fields & woods in the rear,—are so like the hills on the South bank of the Thames, & the situation of Twickenham on the north, backed by the neighboring woody parks, that if a man could be imperceptibly & in an instant conveyed from one side of the Atlantic to the other he might hesitate for some minutes before he could discover the difference . .

He remained in Richmond till the beginning of June, except for a trip to Petersburg at the end of April. This Petersburg visit brought him his first taste of Virginia's passion for horses and for gambling. On April 21 he wrote from there to his new friend Colonel Thomas Blackburn of Rippon Lodge, the father of Mrs. Bushrod Washington:

I travelled hither with Col. Prior, Mr. Martin (who came with me from England) & a Mr. Thornton. The latter afforded me a good deal of entertainment. He seems to be a proper horse jockey,—what at Newmarket you would call,—*a knowing one*. . . . Religion & love have old claims to preference in producing [the] delightful sensation *enthusiasm,* but our friend Thornton in speaking of 50 different courses proved that horse racing is not behindhand with them. The woods rang to the clattering of Lamplighter's hoofs, and the dogwood shed its flowers to the shriek of applause bestowed on the haunches of *Daredevel*. . . .

We dined at Osbornes.—A most miserable dinner & six & threepence to pay for it.—It is an exception to my general observation of good & plentiful table, and moderate charges in this part of the World. After stopping an hour, & bestowing a few ninepences on a very clumsy sleight of hand man we jogged on, & got time enough to Petersburg, for me to find that I might as well have staid at home as to business, & for us all to see the horses entered for the race. The same scenes I find collect in every country the same sort of people & for the same purposes. Here was a *duodecimo* edition of a Newmarket horse race *in folio*. The contents on the first turning over the leaves were the same in every respect. Respectable gentlemen attending for amusement,—young puppies waiting to be pilfered,—sharpers ready to do their business, and whores all agog to drain the sharpers. . . . I cannot help thinking that Dame Nature's freaks & fun are the principal part of her employment,—& that if ever *Nature's self shall die,* as some mad poet expresses himself, she will be choked with a fit of laughter. *Rational beings* indeed!—

Things in leather breeches with a great four legged irrational being between their two legs jostling, & hustling, & pushing & grinning & made to pay the cash which should support their families in order to acquire a supposed interest in the fore & hind quarters of another man's horse. Just as I was going on in a train of reflections which might have ended in a compleat elucidation of the doctrine of the transmigration of the soul . . . a glass of punch washed away the whole fabric, & I betted a quarter of a Dollar or a drink of Grog upon the field against the Carolina horse with Capt. Howel Lewis. . . . [Later they returned to Armstead's tavern, where a roulette game was established and] . . . a *lusus artis* still remained behind, more dangerous to the morals & interests of your friends. With two Majors, one Colonel, a member of the House of Representatives of the state of Virginia, & a rich merchant . . . we just went *to take a touch*. . . . First then this said touch is a circular affair in the center of which is a whirligig. You may naturally suppose the whirligig whirls round. . . . Upon the edge of the said whirligig are 72 boxes marked with the letters A B C. The whirligig which I think you may call the wheel of Misfortune being set in motion a Ball is thrown into it which naturally must find its way into one or other of the 72 boxes. The ball runs round & round bobbing from box to box, while the anxious spectators' hearts bob about in their breasts, & the restless dollars in their pockets, till at last it settles in some one of the literary boxes, & those who have betted on A, B, or C pay or receive the stake. As the devil is in perpetual want of kitchen boys & turnspits to attend his fire, Nature has provided a number of Gentlemen, professed Gamblers, who by providing and attending his business here, qualify themselves for usefull and necessary situations hereafter. Messers Hayden, Harris, Overton, & Willis . . . are at present in due preparation in Petersburg.—"But what," you will ask,—"puts Latrobe into such a passion?" The loss, my dear Sir,—no, I can never acknowledge that the loss of *ten* Dollars has any share in it;—it is, to be sure, my zeal for the good of society, & my detestation of the vice of gambling.—Ah, had I but my ten dollars back!!!—Then might I gain credit for my sincerity in deploring that the *youth* of a country which once meant its *virtue,* now means only its *poverty, indolence,* and dissipation. . . .[7]

This letter is quoted at considerable length, for it so clearly expresses Latrobe as he was at that time; its denunciation of betting and gambling is sincere, but the whole is artificial and written with a definite aim for effect. It is a "stunt," the work of a man still very young despite the hardships and sorrows he had already undergone.

7. Manuscript journal, vol. 1, pp. 42-5.

In the town, crowded for the races, Latrobe had the greatest difficulty in finding accommodations. He was given one of six beds in a room in a private house, but when he found that he was to share it with a disgustingly drunken mulatto he fled back to the inn. This was little better. Kept awake by the sound of the colonels and majors carousing in the bar, but finally falling into a light slumber, he was wakened by their drunken arrival upstairs. Sleep was impossible and he arose early to seek the fresh air and quiet of the dawn. Such were the difficulties of travel in these early days!

Evidently Latrobe's letters of introduction had served him well and he was sent out in June to examine the navigational possibilities of the Appomattox River. In those days of few and bad roads, water transportation was vital. The inland parts of Virginia were growing rapidly, but communication between them and tidewater was difficult. Two water approaches were possible; the north area was tapped by the Potomac through the Shenandoah Valley (one of the chief reasons why Potomac canals were considered so vital at an early date), and the south by the Appomattox, which wandered down from the hills and fell into the James River in one of its then most populous reaches. The Appomattox was narrow and often shallow, with many rapids, but it wound through a region that was rapidly filling with plantations belonging to the first families of Virginia. If it could be made more navigable by flatboats and barges, tremendous benefits to the state would accrue, and Latrobe was asked to make a preliminary survey. After a busy period forming new acquaintances, visiting the courts to study American legislative and judicial ways, and laying the foundations of his friendship for the Bushrod Washingtons and the Randolphs, he left Richmond to make his investigation.

His general plan was to go by land to the headwaters, then descend the stream by boat or along the banks. It was a trip through wild land, still sparsely settled, and living conditions were often crude enough; but Latrobe seemed to have savored it all and eagerly taken the rough with the smooth—long rides through wilderness; hospitality that varied from luxury to indigence and from warm welcome to brusque rudeness; a wild shooting of rapids; life in a primitive flatboat. His journal contains vivid pictures of it all.[8] He finally arrived at the mouth of the James River

8. See *The Journal of Latrobe,* especially pp. 1-36.

on June 15 and in a leisurely fashion returned to Richmond. But more interesting than these bare facts are the striking vignettes he made of people and manners along the way.

Latrobe left Richmond early in June, going first to Colonel Skipwith's place in Cumberland County—well named Hors du Monde—where he expected but failed to meet two of the Navigation directors. From there, vainly seeking them, he proceeded southwest to Richard Randolph's plantation, Bizarre, where he found himself an accidental witness to the denouement of one of early America's most puzzling tragedies. On this distant and lonely estate, in a simple, rather crude house, lived Richard Randolph, his wife, their son, and her beautiful sister who much later was to become Mrs. Gouverneur Morris. Apparently Latrobe had heard nothing of the earlier scandal that had linked Richard Randolph with his sister-in-law Nancy and brought them both to trial for doing away with a newborn child; they had been acquitted.[9] Latrobe rode into Bizarre toward noon on June 10, planning to stay there overnight with the Randolphs and to press on the next day. He found Richard Randolph ill with some sort of digestive fever—very ill indeed and very weak—and he offered to go on at once. But Randolph would not hear of it and made it plain that for the architect to leave before he had intended would be considered a discourtesy; Latrobe therefore remained overnight, making himself as useful as he could to the distracted family. Evidently he was as fascinated by Nancy as many other men had been before and were to be later, for her looks haunted him and he made a sketch of her. In it her face is partially concealed by a bonnet; only her long classic nose and her strongly sculptured profile appear. Even the sketch has a disturbing quality.

The next morning a doctor came to examine the sick man and told Latrobe privately that he could see very little hope. The architect rode away grieving for the wife and her sister and totally unaware that a murder was possibly taking place before his eyes, for it has been universally believed that Richard Randolph was poisoned by either his wife or Nancy or by both. From Bizarre he returned to Hors du Monde and found the two directors, Venable and Epperson. They all proceeded to

---

9. Jay and Audrey Walz's *The Bizarre Sisters* (New York: Duell, Sloan & Pearce, 1950) is a fictionalized account of this strange ménage and of Nancy's further career. It offers, however, only one of several possible interpretations of the events. See also Howard Swiggett, *The Extraordinary Mr. Morris* (New York: Doubleday, 1952).

Captain Patterson's on the Appomattox, where they embarked on a bateau with an awning rigged over it as a protection against sun and rain, to float down to the mouth of the Appomattox and to map it and make studies of what could be done to improve its navigation.[10] It was the first time such a trip had been made. Latrobe arrived at the mouth on June 15, 1796, having enjoyed the trip and the hospitality he had everywhere received. As he wrote to Colonel Blackburn:

In Amelia I could have again fancied myself in a society of English Country Gentlemen,—(a character to which I attach everything that is desirable as to education, domestic comfort, manners and principles)—had not the shabbiness of their mansions undeceived me. Of the latter I do not mean to speak disrespectfully. It is a necessary consequence of the remoteness of the country [from places] where workmen assemble & can at all times be had. An unlucky boy breaks two or three squares of glass. The glazier lives fifty miles off. An old newspaper supplies their place in the *mean time*. Before the *mean time* is over the family gets used to the newspapers & think no more of the glazier.

On his return to Richmond he went to visit the Blackburn place on the Potomac—Rippon Lodge—which he sketched. It consisted of two two-story log cabins set some distance apart, apparently to leave between them space enough for a large future mansion. And it was from here that he made the memorable trip to Mount Vernon of which his journal and his sketches form a priceless record. With him he took a letter of introduction from Bushrod Washington, the President's nephew and the future owner of the estate, whom he calls his "particular friend." He realized the importance of the occasion, understood the extraordinary historical stature of his host, and in his journal took pains to write carefully, vividly, and at length. His approach to Mount Vernon had been through Colchester, ten miles away on the Occoquan, and he comments on the condition of the estate:

Good fences, clean grounds, and extensive cultivation strike the eye as something uncommon in this part of the world, but the road is bad enough. The house becomes visible between two groves of trees at about a mile's distance. It has no very striking appearance, though superior to every other house I have seen here. [A brief description follows.] Everything else is ex-

10. One night was spent at Clemen's Mill, another at Mr. Walk's house at Flat Creek, and a third at Watkin's Mill. The high state of the river hindered accurate determinations.

tremely good and neat, but by no means above what would be expected in a plain Englishman's country house of £500 or £600 a year.

He continues with a panegyric on the superb site, with its unsurpassed views up, down, and across the Potomac, and at last comes to the visit itself:

Having alighted at Mount Vernon, I sent in my letter of introduction, and walked into the portico next to the river. In about ten minutes the President came to me. He was attired in a plain blue coat, his hair dressed & powdered. There was a reserve but no hauteur in his manner. He shook me by the hand, and desired me to sit down. Having enquired after the family I had left [the Bushrod Washingtons], the conversation turned upon Bath [the Virginia Hot Springs], to which they were going. [The President deplored the growing dissipation there, and remarked that he planned never to go there again except from purely medical necessity.]

The conversation then turned upon the rivers of Virginia. He gave me a very minute account of all their directions, their natural advantages, and what he conceived might be done for their improvement by art. He then enquired whether I had seen the Dismal Swamp, and seemed particularly desirous of being informed upon the canal going forward there. He gave me a detailed account of the Dismal Swamp Canal Company and of their operations, of the injury they had received by the effects of the war, and still greater, which their inattention to their own concerns had done them. . . .

This conversation lasted above one hour, and, as he had at first told me that he was finishing some letters to go by the post . . . I got up to take my leave; but he desired me, in a manner very like Dr. [Samuel?] Johnson's, to "keep my chair," and then continued to talk to me about the great works going forward in England, and my own object in this country. I find him well acquainted with my mother's family in Pennsylvania. [The talk then turning upon mines and Latrobe having mentioned the discovery of silver ore at Rockette in Virginia, President Washington] made several minute inquiries concerning it, and then said that "it would give him real uneasiness should any silver or gold mines be discovered that would tempt considerable capital into the prosecution of that object, and that he heartily wished for his country that it might contain no mines but such as the plow could reach, excepting only coal & iron. . . ."

Washington then excused himself, after inviting the visitor to dinner, and Latrobe took the occasion to "prowl" about the lawn and make a few sketches. When he returned to the house he found Mrs. Washington and Miss Custis in the hall:

I introduced myself to Mrs. Washington as a friend of her nephew, and she immediately entered into conversation upon the prospect from the lawn, and presently gave me an account of her family in a good-humored free manner that was extremely pleasant & flattering. She retains strong remains of considerable beauty, seems to enjoy very good health, & to have a good humor. She has no affectation of superiority in the slightest degree, but acts completely in the character of the mistress of the house of a respectable & opulent country gentleman. Her granddaughter, Miss Eleanor Custis, the only one of four who is unmarried, has more perfection of form, of expression, of color, of softness, and of firmness of mind than I have ever seen before or conceived consistent with mortality. She is everything that the chisel of Phidias aimed at but could not reach, and the soul beaming through her countenance and glowing in her smile is as superior to her face as mind is to matter.

Young Lafayette with his tutor came down sometime before dinner. He is a young man about seventeen, of a mild, pleasant countenance, favorably impressing one at first sight. His figure is rather awkward. His manners are easy, & he has very little of the usual French air about him. He talked much, especially with Miss Custis, and seemed to possess wit & fluency. . . .

Dinner was served about half after three. It had been postponed a half-hour in hopes of Mr. Lear's arrival from Alexandria. [At dinner, Washington placed Latrobe at Mrs. Washington's left; Miss Custis sat at her right, and the President next her.] There was very little conversation at dinner. A few jokes passed between the President and young Lafayette, whom he treated more as a child than as a guest. I felt a little embarrassed at the silent, reserved air that prevailed. As I drank no wine, and the President drank only three glasses, the party soon returned to the portico. Mr. Lear, Mr. Dandridge [Bartholomew Dandridge, Martha Washington's nephew and one of Washington's secretaries], and Mr. Lear's three boys soon after arrived & helped out the conversation. The President retired in about three-quarters of an hour.

Again Latrobe made a motion to leave, and once more was restrained and urged to stay the night.

Coffee was brought about six o'clock. When it was removed the President, addressing himself to me, inquired about the state of the crops about Richmond. I told him all I had heard. A long conversation upon farming ensued, during which it grew dark [it was mid-July], and he then proposed going into the hall. He made me sit down by him & continued the conversation for above an hour. During that time he gave me a very minute account of the Hessian fly and its progress from Long Island, where it first appeared, through New York, Rhode Island, Connecticut, Delaware, part of Pennsylvania, & Maryland. It has not yet appeared in Virginia, but is daily dreaded.

[Washington went on to discuss Indian corn as a crop and its value as food, especially for the Negro farm laborers.] He conceived that should the Negroes be fed upon wheat or rye bread, they would, in order to be fit for the same labor, be obliged to have a considerable addition to their allowance of meat. But notwithstanding all this, he thought the balance of advantage to be against the Indian corn.

[They then discussed plows; the President had tried many and preferred the heavy Rotherham plow; next came the Berkshire iron plow. Latrobe promised to send him one of] Mr. Richardson's ploughs of Tuckahoe, which he accepted with pleasure.[11]

Mrs. Washington & Miss Custis had retired early, and the President left the company about eight o'clock. We soon after retired to bed. There was no hint of supper.

I rose with the sun & walked in the grounds near the house. The President came to the company in the sitting room about one-half hour past seven, where all the latest newspapers were laid out. He talked with Mr. Lear about the progress of the work at the great falls [of the Potomac, near Georgetown] and in the City of Washington. Breakfast was served up in the usual Virginia style. Tea, coffee, and cold broiled meat. It was soon over, and for an hour afterward he stood upon the steps of the west door talking to the company who were collected around him. The subject was chiefly the establishment of the University at the federal city. He mentioned the offer he had made of giving to it all the interests he had in the city on condition that it should go on in a given time, and complained that, though magnificent offers had been made by many speculators for the same purpose, there seemed to be no inclination to carry them into reality. He spoke as if he felt a little hurt upon the subject. . . .

Latrobe then, about ten o'clock, took his leave. The journal continues:

Washington had something uncommonly majestic & commanding in his walk, his address, his figure, and his countenance. His face is characterized, however, more by intense & powerful thought than by quick & fiery conception. There is a mildness about its expression, and an air of reserve in his manner lowers its tone still more. He is sixty-four, but appears some years younger, and has sufficient apparent vigor to last many years yet. He was frequently entirely silent for many minutes, during which time an awkwardness seemed to prevail in everyone present. His answers were often short and sometimes approached to moroseness. He did not at any time speak with very remarkable fluency; perhaps the extreme correctness of his language,

---

11. This promise was to arise and plague him later. See page 285.

which almost seemed studied, prevented that effect. He appeared to enjoy a humorous observation, and made several himself. He laughed heartily several times in a very good-humored manner. On the morning of my departure he treated me as if I had lived for many years in his house, with ease & attention, but I thought there was a slight air of moroseness about him as if something had vexed him.

For Washington, had Horace lived at the present age, he would have written his celebrated ode: it is impossible to have ever read it and not to recollect in the presence of this great man the *virum justum propositique tenacem,* etc.[12]

It is interesting to compare this account with his earlier letter to Blackburn. Here there is no artificiality, no writing for effect, no immature frivolity. Instead, the prose is simple, direct, and vivid.

But Latrobe did more than leave a striking word picture; he also drew a plan of Mount Vernon and sketched its river front, which looks out over the Potomac today much as it did then. And for good measure he made three sketches of the Washington household. One is a portrait of young Lafayette, the great French general's son, then living with the Washingtons while his father was imprisoned in Austria. Another—a beautiful group—shows Mrs. Washington, garbed in an old-fashioned gown and presiding at the tea table, with the statuesque Miss Custis—dressed in the latest Parisian classic fashion—posing with self-conscious grace against one of the portico pillars, like a famous Pompeiian painting of Medea; on the step below is a young boy, probably the child of Tobias Lear, Washington's secretary. This group he combined with his exterior sketch into a charming water color painted in Richmond soon afterward and apparently sent to the Bushrod Washingtons as a gift, for it has come down in their family.[13]

Back in Richmond, the architect took up more or less permanent residence there, charmed by its hospitality as well as its democratic spirit. And, though he made several extended visits away and two professional tours, Richmond was his real home till the end of 1798. It was here that in 1796 he probably met Volney[14] and Scandella, the French radical and

12. From the manuscript journal, vol. 1, pp. 58ff. Reprinted in *The Latrobe Journal,* pp. 50-63.

13. It is now the property of Bishop H. St. George Tucker of Virginia, a descendant.

14. See Gilbert Chinard, *Volney et l'Amérique, d'après des documents inédits . . .* (Baltimore: Johns Hopkins Press; Paris: Les Presses Universitaires de France, 1923).

the Italian physician-philosopher. Both men gave him a necessary intellectual and imaginative stimulus that few of the kind Virginians could furnish; both renewed his curiosities and sharpened his vision.

Constantin F. C. Volney apparently included many of Latrobe's observations in his *Tableau du climat et du sol des États-unis d'Amérique . . .* published in Paris in 1803, with an English translation, *View of the Climate and Soil of the United States of America,* the following year in London; in turn he fired Latrobe's interest in geology, and the architect's journals and notebooks are filled with geological observations. And Latrobe's first American published work was a "Memoir on the Sand Hills of Cape Henry," printed in 1799 in the *Transactions of the American Philosophical Society* (vol. 4, pp. 439-44).

His friendship with Scandella seems to have been more personal; Scandella's inquiries about and comments on American ways stimulated Latrobe's own questioning and quickened his analyses. Scandella described Niagara Falls to him; from this vivid description Latrobe made a forceful water color of the falls and wrote a verse on their grandeur. One evening he and Scandella discussed the question of hospitality; Scandella complained that the famed American hospitality was merely an inevitable accompaniment of small population, great distances, and primitive conditions. Latrobe sat down later and wrote a long, carefully thought-out essay on the whole matter "in the form of a discussion with Dr. Scandella." He shows the doctor that there is no reason for his criticism; that American hospitality, though a necessity, is also real; and that Dr. Scandella was wishing for the moon if he expected, stranger and foreigner as he was, to be taken instantly into the bosom of a family or if he hoped to get from planters and soldiers intellectual conversation like that of professional circles in Europe. Evidently the two carried on a fairly lively correspondence after Scandella left Richmond, and one letter (February 22, 1798) survives,[15] addressed to Dr. Scandella at 233 South Front Street, Philadelphia, shortly before Latrobe's first visit to that city. In this letter, which will be cited in another context later, there are a few passages of personal interest that are germane here. Latrobe remarks that all his practical interests suggest Philadelphia as the ideal location for him—

---

15. In the Avery Library, Columbia University.

In Maryland Historical Society

FIGURE 3. Strata in the Well, Penitentiary, Richmond. From the Latrobe journals.

. . . as the only situation in which I ought to reside,—if I reside in America;—and yet, by some enchantment I find myself unable to stir from this state.—To my own indolence I can give a very good account of this phaenomenon,—but not to the prudence or the little common sense I may happen to possess.—I have not even the excuse of *love* to plead, whatever you may suppose. . . .

You are, my dear friend, very eloquent upon the subject of the Lady who turned her back upon me.—She is going to be married immediately, & she therefore did *right.* You never saw, &, I believe, never heard of her. Is it not the very sensible, witty, & lively Miss J. R—whom you hint at?—I hope she will not use me so ill, should I ever conceive the idea of putting it into her power to mortify me.—But I assure you, that when I so loosely rallied your partialities I was not more serious, than when I exposed my own.—It is a subject on which I am not imprudent enough to be serious.—I have children, & may therefore with more propriety than you perhaps, say *"it is not for me to be in love."* I must weigh the matter first for *them* & then for *myself.* However you will be happy to hear that your three friends Miss McClurg, Miss J. Randolph, & Mrs. Washington are very well, & desire,—I am sure very sincerely,—that I should assure you of their kind remembrance. The two latter have been most seriously ill,—but are now recovered.—

With the greatest pleasure I will send to you my remarks upon slavery in Virginia as soon as I can transcribe them, & add whatever else occurs to me upon the subject. You will show your regard for me by not sparing me in anything in which I can at all afford you a pleasure. . . . [Postscript:] Could you give me a corner in your *cabaret philosophique* if I come to Philadelphia?

Unfortunately the notes on slavery in Virginia are lost.

Obviously Latrobe was conscious of his own basically lonely state. No man was less fitted to live a bachelor's life, and behind the light touch of the letter to Scandella there is an undoubted wistfulness. Who the lady was who turned her back on him we may never know, but early in 1798 he includes in his journal (January 17) a somewhat cryptic passage which may provide a clue. He was at the home of the actress Mrs. Green, for whom he had written a comedy (to be discussed later), when some expression on his face seemed to surprise and interest her. He writes:

Answer to Mrs. Green's question, Pray how am I to translate that look of yours?

Ingulph me, earth! crush me, ye skies!
My grieving soul is on the rack!
On John she's turned her beauteous eyes!
On me,—her back.

The name of the young lady whose cruelty could be the cause of the above expressive look is [veiled in Hebrew script,[16] Louise Nelson Black or Louise Black Nelson].

And there is evidence of other possible infatuations during this period. For Susanna Catharine Spotswood he prepared an elaborate two-volume book of water-color sketches with an extended text, in the guise of teaching her how to paint. The title page of the first volume is inscribed: "An Essay in Landscape Explained in Tinted Drawings by Benj. Henry Latrobe Boneval, Esquire. Richmond, Virginia, 1798." The second volume has no title page, but its charming postscript is dated from Philadelphia, April 7, 1799. In it he says, in part:

Although this little volume has travelled with me in all my excursions . . . & has been my favorite, & consoling companion in solitude . . . still I have been unable to compleat it as I wished. A few days of leisure at Orange Grove would add much to its neatness & perfection of detail, and were I not tempted to send it to you, by the hands of one of the best & dearest friends I possess . . . I should still trespass for a short time on your patience.—When it is gone, I shall miss it, as I should a child . . .

[He concludes:] I have promised you a little dissertation on perspective . . . It will have the additional value of giving me an opportunity of gratifying myself by following an employment, which, while it relaxes my own mind after the fatigue of business, has a chance of being acceptable & usefull to the friend most deserving of my respect.

Did only artistic enthusiasm fire the loving beauty of this work? [17]

---

16. Dr. Isaac Mendelsohn, of Columbia University, who transliterated the Hebrew, remarked that the lettering was a particularly elegant eighteenth-century script. The lady in question cannot be further identified.

17. Illustrated in part in *Virginia Cavalcade,* Autumn, 1951. Miss Susanna Catharine Spotswood was the daughter of Colonel John Spotswood and granddaughter of Governor Alexander Spotswood; she lived at the Spotswood plantation Orange Grove. Since she did not marry till 1801, she is probably not the person referred to in the letter to Scandella. Her husband was John B. Bott, M.D., a well-known doctor of the time, and in her later life, after her husband's death in 1824, she devoted her time to good works. She died in 1853, and in 1857 A. B. Van Zandt, D.D., published a memoir of her, *The Elect Lady, A Memoir of Susan Catharine Spotswood, of Petersburg, Virginia.* I owe this information to

Several fragments in the Latrobe papers contain evidence of his intimacy with the Randolphs of Tuckahoe and with the Bushrod Washingtons. In the journal he notes at length a conversation with Mrs. Randolph and Mrs. Washington, in which Mrs. Randolph had objected to some of Shakespeare's language as indecent; the discussion thus started spread to the question of modesty in language and dress, the general standards of morals and manners, and the effects of novel reading. Latrobe's position is one in favor of relative rather than absolute standards, and he supports it with all kinds of historical examples based largely on things that had happened within the preceding fifty years or so. It is a fascinating document.[18] In that congenial circle he also amused himself with considerable versifying. For example, he sends his excuses to Mrs. Washington for not dining with her on Sunday in a prolix poem, a few excerpts from which will suffice:

Dear Madam,

If ever hominy & hog
Stiff toddy & delightful grog
  Our buckskins set a longing,
If e'er the rattle of the dice
Our men of council did entice
  To Strass's * net to throng in,
If ever billiard ball did roll
The pride of legislator's soul
  Slap! into Radford's † pocket:—

. . . . .

If e'er Jack Willis ** took a card
Or Harry Banks †† drove bargains hard
  Or Edmund *** took a fee, Ma'am

and so on for several stanzas. Latrobe furnishes the notes:

* Strass, is a German who keeps a Farobank & presides over the gambling of Richmond. He is in great vogue & countenanced by men of the first character.

Mrs. Robert W. Claiborne (whose great-grandmother was a sister of Susanna Spotswood), Director of the Valentine Museum in Richmond, and to Mrs. Ralph Catterall, Librarian of the Museum.

18. See Appendix for the text.

† Radford keeps the Eagle Tavern, & plays billiards well & successfully at his own table.

** Jack Willis, a man of immense powers & size of body, & equal wit & good sense, the Falstaff of the age. He professes gambling.

†† Mr. Henry Banks well known for his wit, & sense, which contrary to the usual use of these qualities, have contributed extremely to his *worldly* interests.

*** Edmund Randolph, quondam Secretary of State, now a successful attorney at law.

In his poem he goes on to refer indirectly to the anger of the Dismal Swamp Canal directors that his own report was unfavorable to the work of a Mr. Capern, and finally:

Meanwhile time still stole slyly on,
Five long dull tedious days were gone,
And Sunday followed after
That day to Belvidere due,
To music, friendship, and to *you*
To chat & guiltless laughter . . .

In sum, he had been delayed on his trip by vile weather and mistaken roads and could not get to Belvidere at all. He also records various verses at Tuckahoe, the Thomas Mann Randolph place; among them this is perhaps the most palatable:

On Mrs. R[andolph] requesting each of the gentlemen present to mend her a pen

To mend a pen
Four able men
With might & main unite
No wonder why:—
It was to try
To make the Widow's write

The Widow fair
With gracious air
Smil'd while the pens were making
But each poor wight
Till she should write
Was in a desp'rate taking

With fav'ring look
The pen she took
  Which Arthur had made ready
Alas! how sad
The pen was bad
  And never could write freely.

That laid aside
The next she tried
  Was the pen which Steele did mend, Sir
She cried and spoke
At ev'ry stroke
  "Your pen's too soft, & bends, Sir

Latrobe's next came
To please the Dame
  He hoped with fond reliance
But she took tiff
Call'd it too stiff
  And bid the pen defiance

The bright'ning face
And jovial grace
  Of Bishop soon proclaimed it
That of four men
His well shap'd pen
  Had won the prize they aim'd at.

But it was not only these high-placed Virginians that intrigued Latrobe. In Richmond he came to know well the actors of West's troupe and gained the friendship of Thomas West himself; the journal shows him their close associate.[19] Most of them were English and not too long resident in America to fail to understand his own nostalgias and share his curiosities. They were an imaginative and literate group, with the beguiling vanities of their calling; for him they had a basic congeniality as artists.

The only theater in Richmond was an old and rather tumble-down building in the outskirts of the town, uncomfortable and architecturally uncouth, and above all ill-fitted for the elaborate scenery and the spec-

19. See Susanne K. Sherman, "Thomas Wade West, Theatrical Impresario, 1790-99," *William and Mary Quarterly,* vol. 9, no. 1 (January, 1952), pp. 10-28.

tacles West liked to present. West was ambitious; his performances were popular, but beyond that he wanted to build the drama into the center of Richmond life. Obviously for this a new building was necessary, and Latrobe—who knew the theaters of England and the Continent—was manifestly well qualified to be its architect. In his journal he says that he had begun the designs for the theater, hotel, and assembly rooms (in one building) on December 1, 1797, and completed them on January 6, 1798. Fortunately they are preserved and will be discussed later.

In the troupe was a singer and dancer whom he found especially congenial—the Mrs. Green (née Willems) whom he addressed in the quatrain referred to above. In an effort to express to her his appreciation and also to satisfy his delight in authorship, he wrote a comedy, *The Apology,* for her benefit performance in the current 1797-8 season. On January 17, soon after he had finished his theater designs, he writes:

> . . . began a Comedy the idea of which was suggested in Mr. Jones's phaeton on my trip with him to Hansen, but had lain dormant till my desire to serve Mrs. Green, the excellent comedian, & the more excellent man revived it.—(See the manuscript [lost, alas!]).—Though I finished it in 26 hours, the necessary trouble of making fair copies & writing out the parts was very great & this is my first free day, on which I could think of my old habits of journalizing. . . .

On Saturday evening (January 27, 1798) the play was performed and received a most varied response. The cast, in part, consisted of

Vaucamil	Turnbull
Bob Vaucamil	Tom West
Twoshoes	Sully (the American painter's father)
Simon Care	Lathy
Louisa	Mrs. J. West
Skunk, a newspaper editor	Mr. Green

Mrs. Green, Mrs. Turnbull, and Bignall also had parts, but they are not specified. The Prologue "(which was written but a few hours before the play went on) was spoken to great applause by Mr. Green," who also recited an "apology" at the end. The afterpiece was *Octavian*.

Apparently the performance was worse than indifferent; Latrobe was bitterly disappointed in it and in his journal suggests that the Wests' jealousy of the Greens may have had something to do with its flaws. Some of the actors did not know their parts and improvised absurdly. Several were wooden and stiff; some spoke their parts automatically without any apparent understanding of the words. In the last act Sully did not get his cue from Bignall, who had forgotten his part, and, writes Latrobe, "Sully, not receiving his cue, & being unused to act, & very bashful,—having moreover a cold which made him hoarse as a raven—was so embarrassed that not a word was spoken for so many minutes that the whole play ended there, nobody knew how or why.—In Simon Care's last speech Lathy was so hampered by the word *municipal* that the rest of his speech was drowned in the laughter caused by his embarrassment. Mrs. J. West in Louisa was very correct . . ."

On Monday, bad weather prevented any performance; on Tuesday, West played one of his most popular parts, Richard III; then, in the night, after the play, the old playhouse burned down and with it many of the costumes and much of the elaborate scenery belonging to the company—a disastrous loss to them. And for Latrobe there were unpleasant repercussions. *The Apology* was largely a satire on the Federalists, especially Hamilton and Cobbett, who were undoubtedly lampooned as "Vaucamil" and as "Skunk, a newspaper editor." Then, too, there was adultery in the plot and perhaps some rather outspoken language, though at the end sin was punished and virtue triumphed. But the political implications aroused the Richmond Federalists to a storm of objections, and a violent newspaper controversy followed. On January 31 came the first blast, a letter to the Richmond paper suggesting that the theater was burned by the wrath of God. In part, after expressing sympathy for the Wests' losses, it read:

> Yet, sir, if I could conceive that Omnipotent Heaven ever condescended to regard the ordinary activities of us poor mortals, I should be led to think it a judgment on the house for the prostitution committed on the stage a few evenings ago; for certain "The Apology" of Mrs. Green was not sufficient for the vile, low stuff contained in that of Mr. Thing 'um Bob, there with his one ey'd spectacle. Be that as it may, however . . .

The author goes on to suggest support of Mr. West in building a new theater, little realizing that if the new house was built it would be from the designs of the terrible "Mr. Thing 'um Bob" himself! This letter was answered by two others published on February 6, written, "I believe," says Latrobe, "the first by Mr. Bolling Robertson, the second by Mr. John Baker, two young gentlemen of great promise, who study the law under Mr. Warden." The controversy hurt the architect intensely;

he was puzzled as to what to do, but wise friends persuaded him that the best thing was to do nothing. So ended his first and only attempt at the drama.[20]

Yet, despite the social meetings with the great and the pleasant time spent with the actors and actresses of West's troupe, Latrobe's chief interests were, first, his professional work (to be considered in the next chapter), and, second, the continued study of the characteristics of America and Americans, to which his journals bear full witness. Flora and fauna, history, language, temper, costume, and manners—all are graphically portrayed; Latrobe had a keen ear and an almost phonographic as well as photographic memory, and he was continually on the search for the typical or the unfamiliar. He notes that beavers, though by his time already extinct in Virginia, had been extremely useful; some mill dams were built on old beaver dams. Beavers, he says (May 12, 1796), should have been preserved instead of exterminated. He finds that land once under cultivation is already deserted and going back into pine forest (unmixed with any deciduous trees). He comments on the falls in all the rivers, which so definitely divide the lower alluvial tidewater lands from the higher plateaus behind. And he was a keen observer of insects and natural life in general and of snakes and snake-bite antidotes (the "blood Wort" is the best, according to several anecdotes he cites); he makes note of the fact that Captain Murray at the siege of Yorktown found his hearing of the artillery entirely dependent on whether the weather was clear or cloudy. In Richmond he was fascinated by the Falls of the James and the ingenious weirs the fishermen had built to catch the "chad" (as he spells it), taking delight in their clever if primitive engineering; he makes numbers of rapid graphic sketches, and his pleasure carries over into the swift pen strokes of his drawings.

But it is the people especially who fascinate him, and particularly their differences from the English. Thus:

> I have formerly observed that better English is spoken by the common people, even by the Negroes in Virginia than by the lower orders in any county in England with which I am acquainted.—The little improprieties and peculiarities that occur seem equally divided between all classes of whites.—The only irregularity of pronunciation which I have noticed is the broad &

---

20. There is a legend that *The Apology* was later acted successfully in Philadelphia, but so far research has uncovered no evidence.

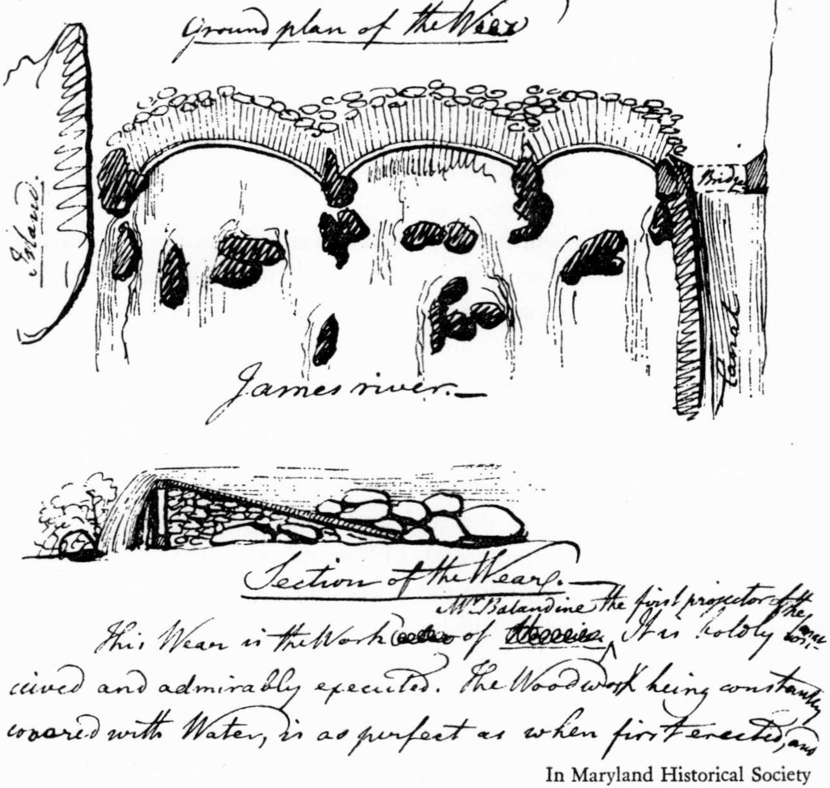

In Maryland Historical Society

FIGURE 4. Weir on the James River, Richmond. From the Latrobe journals.

drawling manner of articulating the vowel *i,* which is lengthened to a distinct *aw, e,* or *ai* as every other nation pronounce these vowels . . .

He goes on to give "A Virginia Conversation" as an example, underlining the following as Americanisms: *Old fellow,* as a term of endearment or intimacy. *I happened at Manchester. Sundown. Last evening. Mighty glad. Mightily opposed to it. He was raised. I'm right heartily glad to see you.* Then he adds:

N.B. A Virginian *mighty hearty welcome,* must be experienced to be understood. It includes everything the best heart can prompt, the most luxuriant country afford.—It is that which will oblige a stranger to stop his career to the *cautious prudent* Pennsylvanians, & force him to settle among men whom he experiences to be liberal, friendly, & sensible.

On his trip to the Appomattox he lost his way among various unmarked forest paths and at last found a Negro from whom he could obtain directions; he gives the passage between them at length as an example of the careful helpfulness he often received as well as of the peculiarities of American speech.[21] He notes a strange man who lives on nothing but tea and sugar yet has physical and procreative powers above the average. A few tragic vignettes of the poverty-struck and drink-ridden poor whites who somehow had failed to measure up to the challenge of the new country are included, and he comments on the fact that military titles—captain, major, and colonel—are as common in America, as proudly insisted on, and as meaningless for the most part as titles of nobility in Poland. He became interested in the Pocahontas legend and traced as well as he could all her immediate descendants; he found that there had been at least 362 of them—239 still then alive—and comments:

> It is somewhat singular that, though this family are rather proud of their royal Indian descent, not one of them should have preserved the names of their Ancestors in their own family excepting Robert Bolling, son of Colonel John Bolling . . . who named a son & a daughter Powhattan & Pochahontas.—He was a man of great wit & learning.

These notes he later expanded in a paper he read before the American Philosophical Society.[22] In his journal he also remarks on the extraordinary number of first-cousin marriages among the Virginia planters—a natural result, perhaps, of their strong class feeling and of the great distances between plantations. The Randolphs, especially, were famous for marrying Randolphs, and the eccentricities that occasionally appeared in the family have sometimes been attributed to this habit. Latrobe objects to such a system of close intermarriage among a few families, but not on genetic grounds; he says that experiments in cattle breeding seem to

---

21. See Appendix.

22. This paper he read to the Society on February 18, 1803, but it was not printed. The complete list of his published papers in the *Transactions* includes: vol. 4 (1799), "Memoir on the Sand Hills of Cape Henry in Virginia," pp. 439-44; vol. 5 (1802), "Drawing and Description of the Clupea Tyrannus and Oniscus Praegustata," pp. 77-81; vol. 6 (1809), "On Two Species of Sphex Inhabiting Virginia and Pennsylvania and Probably Extending through the United States," pp. 73-8; "First Report in Answer to the Enquiry Whether Any and What Improvements Have Been Made in the Construction of Steam Engines in America," pp. 89-99; "Account of the Freestone Quarries on the Potomac and Rappahannoc[k] Rivers," pp. 283-93; "Observations on the Correspondence Relative to the Principles and Practice of Building in India," pp. 384-91.

prove that close relationships between parents are no barrier to good children. Instead, his objections are political, for he sees the system developing closely organized and selfish cliques; for him, society should be like a coat of mail, interlocked from side to side and from top to bottom, and he believes that the happiest marriages are between people of quite divergent temperaments. In Richmond he visited the courts and comments on the different types of oratory offered by James Innes, Jack Stewart, Edmund Randolph, John Marshall, and Bushrod Washington. And he was surprised at the absence of wigs, though he notes that some of the older men preserve the picturesque ancient types of costume or hair dress. Of wigs, he writes as a true radical:

> We may therefore, very fairly, I think conclude, that wherever we see wigs decrease or vanish in any profession, bigotry & obscurity will lessen & cease, and good sense and liberal principles gain ground and become general in the same ratio.

And in the same radical vein, as a son of the Enlightenment and with the same analytical skepticism that probably kept him out of the Moravian ministry, he remarks, apropos of the hanging of a Negro, that it is dogmatic religions that are responsible for the worst possible barbarisms.

In 1797 the tone of the journals changes. The first flush of excitement in discovering a new country had passed. He had met the Virginians; they had come to know and to accept him. There was less entertaining on their part and less almost frenzied note taking on his. As he settled down to life in Richmond, despite an increase in his professional work he had more time on his hands. In early June he was sent again to the Dismal Swamp Canal to make an official report for the directors of the canal company; on his return he received, on June 25, a letter from the governor of the state announcing that Latrobe's plans for the penitentiary had been accepted and that he had been appointed to direct and supervise the construction. On June 30 he was at Lindsey's hotel in Norfolk (perhaps in connection with the building of the Pennock house) and while there had opportunities "of seeing and conversing with Commodore Barney [an officer in the French navy], who is, in the present uncertain state of politics, grown into an object of attention."

Subsequently Latrobe was sent to Norfolk to examine the fortifications there and to recommend improvements and additions,[23] and he also took

23. See page 255.

Maryland Historical Society

Benjamin Henry Latrobe as a young man.

British Museum

Benjamin Latrobe, the architect's father.

PLATE I

ırkstall Abbey, Leeds. From Latrobe's "An Essay in Landscape."

State Library of Virginia

Photograph Dorothy Stroud

Ashdown House. B. H. Latrobe, architect. General view.

Photograph Dorothy S

Ashdown House. The porch.

PLATE 2

Hammerwood Lodge. Detail.

Photograph Dorothy Stroud

Hammerwood Lodge. B. H. Latrobe, architect. G
eral view.

Photograph Dorothy S

Avery Library

Somerset House, London. Sir William Chambers, architect. River side.

Bank of England, London. Sir John Soane, architect. Bank Stock Hall.

Avery Library

PLATE 3

Old Newgate Prison, London. George Dance, Jr., architect.

Avery Library

Latrobe Sketchbooks

Sloop *Olive Branch,* of Stonington, Connecticut.

PLATE 4

View on the York River, Virginia.

Latrobe Sketchbooks

Latrobe Sketchbooks

onel Blackburn's House, Virginia.

PLATE 5

w on the Appomattox River, Virginia. From Latrobe's "An Essay in Landscape."

State Library of Virginia

PLATE 6

Courtesy Bishop H. St. George Tucker

Mount Vernon, Virginia. From a Latrobe water color.

Clifton, the Harris House, Richmond. Latrobe's perspective.

Library of Congress

PLATE 7

Library of Congress

Pennock House, Norfolk, Virginia.
Stair hall. Latrobe's perspective.

Proposed Tayloe House, Washington. Latrobe's section.

Library of Congress

Photographs Mr. and Mrs. John H. Heyrman

Juliana Latrobe's Tombstone, Mount Holly, New Jersey. B. H. Latrobe, architect. General view and detail.

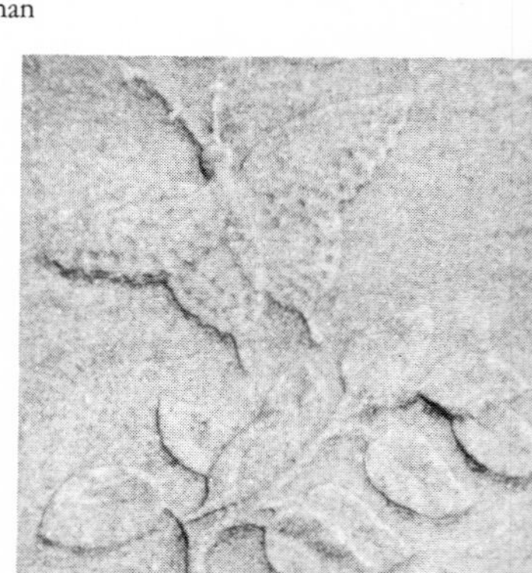

PLATE 8

Mrs. Claiborne's Tomb, New Orleans. B. H. Latrobe, architect; Giuseppe Franzoni, sculptor. General view and detail.

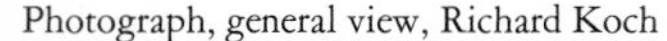

Photograph, general view, Richard Koch

Photograph, detail, Samuel Wilson,

the occasion to visit and sketch in the Yorktown area. He made one other visit to Hampton Roads in November, 1798, just before his final removal from Virginia, and notes that on November 2 he dined on board the frigate *Constellation* with Commodore Truxton after spending the day with a local builder, Miles Key, in connection with a proposed lighthouse at Old Point Comfort. Accordingly he and Miles Key combined to offer a joint bid of $3,000, but they were unsuccessful and the contract went to others. Sometime during this period, too, he met Jefferson for the first time, in Fredericksburg.

Yet, in spite of the increasing number of duties and the various short trips he took, Latrobe was becoming restless. He found himself bitterly lonely even in the midst of Virginian hospitality. And perhaps the lady who "turned her back" had moved him more deeply than he knew; her refusal or withdrawal may have drawn his mind back over the years to his life in England, to his dead wife and his two children there, for we have seen in his letter to Scandella how important they were to him. Now he spends his "journalizing" time not so much on notes of Virginian life as on reminiscences of his early days and fills his sketchbooks with strange and haunting visions or illustrations of Gothic tales.

For us, this interlude is valuable, because from these notes and memories, these anecdotes and verses, we gain much of the knowledge we have of his youth. He includes keen character sketches of all the members of the Sellon family; some of the sketches are savage, some admiring, all vivid. The scenes surrounding the death of his first wife's father, Dr. Sellon, have been mentioned earlier. He tells in prolix detail the story of Charlotte Hoissard (the young woman who ran away with her father's groom) and the extraordinary tale of the illiterate cobbler Tommy Rhodes who became the Baron de Rothe. His life in Germany with the learned and artistic Baron von Schachmann is described. He includes a number of verses that have already been cited and ends with the affecting Ode to Solitude written after his wife's death.

And it is the same with the sketchbooks. There is a "sketch for a portrait" of a graceful and handsome young woman. Is it a picture of his wife?—or does it represent one of the girls he had found lovely in Virginia? There is another pretty drawing of a man and a woman. The man seems to be intended for himself; the woman is probably his wife as he remembers her. And there is a whole series of fantastic sketches in which a storm of withheld or frustrated emotions is expressed: A ghostly woman on a rock in a turbulent stream—the ghost of his wife? An illustration of an Indian widow for *The History of Ned Evans* (attributed to Elizabeth Hervey and published in London in 1796)—again the haunting death sense. And finally an old bearded hermit gazing out of a cave; before him sweep by the ghosts of a young man and a young woman—an allegory of himself and his children? But, whatever the subjects, there plays over these drawings a spirit of tension, of tragedy, quite unlike the simple clarity that distinguishes his ordinary paintings, and the same spirit darkens the colors. They seem the works of a different man from the artist who in the same book sketches the Potomac or the James smiling in the sun.

For Latrobe had reached a turning point. Internal stresses were piling up. Virginia and Richmond came to have less and less meaning or appeal for him. He must seek other places, change his environment, get other work—if only to preserve his integrity and his peace of mind. He was at the end of a chapter and, whether he realized it or not, was now eager to begin the next.

CHAPTER

6

Architectural Work in Virginia and Some Other Houses

LATROBE'S first American building was the house for William Pennock in Norfolk. It was the result of a challenge: was it possible to design a house with a grand, well-lighted staircase at the front of the building and still preserve a regular elevation and a central doorway? Latrobe claimed that it was possible, and the Pennock house was the result. The drawings of it show how prophetic it was of the buildings its architect was to design later. And it shows as well that Latrobe was aware he was in a new country; for the house is not a London or even an English house but has instead the compactness of planning, the efficiency of circulation, and the economy of arrangement which American clients demanded. And yet it also differed markedly from the usual Virginia houses of the time; it was a true creation.

In 1796, or later, Latrobe made a beautiful perspective of the stair hall which had been the *raison d'être* for the whole design. The stair starts up at the right of the entrance door, in the middle of the hall, and rises toward the front wall, sweeping up in a lovely curve to the second-story landing; it is well lighted by the second-floor windows. The rear of the hall extends back into a segmental niche to give an unusual sense of space. Beyond the stair, on the right, a wall shuts off the service stair that occupies the far corner of the house and leads from basement to top. This is conveniently related to a rear door that gives easy communication to the slave quarters behind. Thus not only had a beautiful and inviting stair hall been formed in this relatively modest house, but complete privacy of service had also been achieved. And ever after privacy of service remained one of the architect's chief aims in house design.

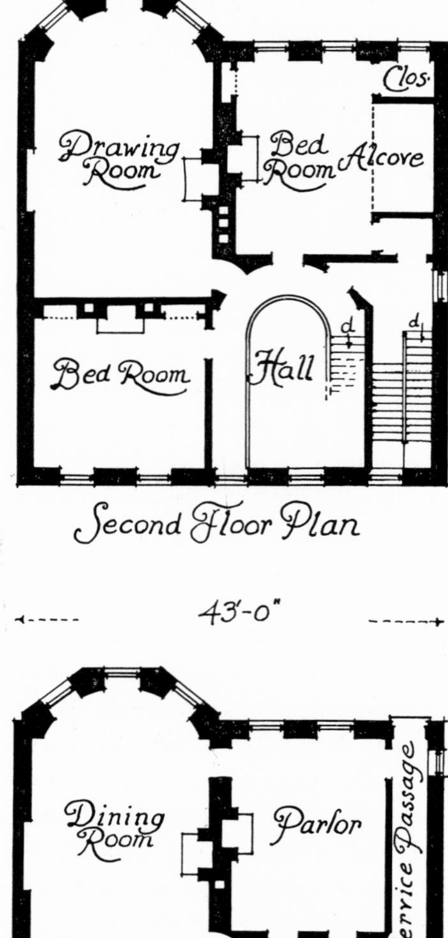

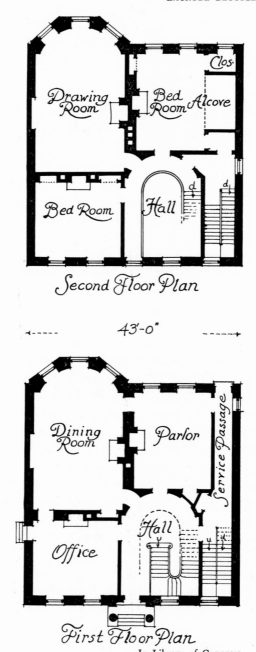

In Library of Congress

FIGURE 5. Pennock House, Norfolk. Plans. Redrawn from Latrobe's drawings.

The rest of the first floor contains three rooms. The two most important—a parlor and a dining room of beautiful proportions—look out over the garden and the Elizabeth River to the rear; the third, the owner's office, occupies the front corner of the building to the left of the hall. In style the house is less revolutionary, though obviously controlled by Latrobe's passion for simplicity and elegance. The façade is severely simple, the windows and door are beautifully proportioned punctuations in the plane of quiet brick, and the cornice is delicate and restrained. Inside, the hall perspective has a slightly Adam flavor, and the stair and handrail—with the step ends uncarved and plain slim vertical balusters—are not too unlike those in many other American houses of the time. But what is remarkable is the sense of space Latrobe has contrived by his treatment of the stair well, the walls, and the ceiling. Here, even in this first of his American houses, it is the sense of designed volume, of air, and of views up and around that give these relatively modest dimensions a kind of original and unforced monumental quality. Here is a mild prophecy of the kind of imaginative space design that was to govern so much of his work.

Latrobe dreamed, much later, of a full presentation of his architectural work, in rather a lavish style, to be published in London.[1] It is to this desire that we owe the preservation of a group of his drawings now in the Library of Congress. A number of them are gathered together under the title, "Designs of Buildings in Virginia," and he prepared a title page. Some of the drawings are apparently completed, ready for the engraver, and are rendered in water color and with careful and uniform border lines. There are also other drawings without borders, and some with no lettering whatsoever, preserved obviously in the same group for future redrawing or completion. A number can be identified; some seem

---

1. See Fiske Kimball, "Some Architectural Designs of Benjamin Henry Latrobe," in *The Library of Congress Journal of Current Acquisitions,* vol. III, no. 3 (May, 1946), pp. 8-13. With regard to the proposed publication of his work, Latrobe on May 11, 1816, wrote Eric Bollman, who was about to leave for England: "I wish exceedingly to publish some account, in rather a splendid form, of my works. There is in Holburn a man of the name of Taylor [one of the famous architectural publishers, A. & J. Taylor], who deals entirely in architectural works. You remember my view of the Capitol. . . . The companion to it shall be either the President's House, or the Baltimore Cathedral, or the Bank of Pennsylvania, or an internal view of the House of Representatives. I will send him over the drawings this year . . . Will you be so good as to endeavor to see him, & try to make some bargain for me?"

to be studies for buildings of which we have no other knowledge. The title page is dated September 8, 1799. Besides the lettering, various miniature vignettes (two below on a lightly indicated landscape, others above and partly hidden by clouds) decorate the page, and there is also an allegorical figure, bearing in her hand a model of the Bank of Pennsylvania. On the back is a descriptive note:

> The only two buildings which were executed from the drawings were Capt[n] Pennock's at Norfolk, and Colonel Harvie's at Richmond . . . The former stands on terra firma in the background to the left,—the latter on the hill in the middle ground. The wings of Col. Harvie's house were never built, & are following the other buildings in the sky. Higher up among the clouds, are the buildings which may be easily known from the following drawings. To the right hovers the figure of the architect's imagination, such as she is. With the model of the Bank of Pennsylvania in her hand, she is leaving the rocks of Richmond & taking her flight to Philadelphia.
>
> The idea of the figure is imitated from Flaxman, the famous sculptor.

It is all a quaint conceit, delicately rendered.

The strangest design, dated August, 1796, is for an enormous plantation house called Mill Hill. Despite its size, the house is disappointing. It has an inconvenient English plan, with the dining room far from the kitchen and its services, and one entire end of the house is occupied by a great stair hall that seems better fitted for a ducal mansion in the shires than for the residence of even a wealthy Virginia plantation owner. The exterior is equally unlike Latrobe's usual manner. It is grand—almost grandiose—in its bigness. Perhaps reminiscences of Hammerwood Lodge, his first independent work in England, were running through his mind; but this house lacks both the drama and the eccentricities of that extraordinary design. On the front Mill Hill is two stories high, but across the rear there is a colossal Ionic colonnade supported on the exposed arcaded basement wall, and back of the columns there is a large piazza or gallery.

This design is remarkable, therefore, not only for the monumental scale of its colonnade but also for its unusual character; it shows that its architect could create in more than one manner. The house may have been designed for one of the hills overlooking Richmond. It was never built—it may be seen in the clouds on his title page—but it is perhaps significant that several large Richmond hillside houses erected during the next three decades had porches carried by columns across the entire rear to take advantage of both the air and the view. With this local tradition it is possible that Latrobe's Mill Hill design may have had some connection.

Completely different is the next unrealized design, dated December, 1797—one of those without indication of owner or place. The perspective would seem to depict one of the Richmond promontories; it shows a river, probably the James, curving off into the distance below. This is a design for a small house of unusual plan. In the center of the main front there is a boldly projecting semi-octagonal bay enclosing an octagonal parlor 14 feet in diameter. The main entrance, at the right, leads directly into the stair hall in the right front corner. The large drawing room, directly behind the stair hall, sweeps out into a segmental bay; beyond this a garden wall is carried back to balance the end of the stair hall. The entire left-hand section of the building is the dining room, 18 by 26 feet. Thus the plan is essentially unsymmetrical, although the façade is symmetrical in mass and a large window under a recessed arch at the left of the octagonal bay balances the entrance door at the right. Obviously Latrobe was fond of this particular design, for he drew it up with special care and presented it in one of his most exquisite small renderings.

There is no indication as to the client for whom this small but delightful house was designed, yet perhaps a guess may be hazarded. In Richmond there was a small group of "octagon" houses. Before 1796, James Boyce had built himself, on East Leigh Street, a frame house with semi-octagonal ends which was later known as the MacFarlane house. Edmund Randolph, in 1800, had a rectangular house with semi-octagonal ends. Since the Edmund Randolphs were among Latrobe's close friends during his Virginia years, it would not have been strange for them to consult him about their building plans. Then, when they actually came to build, two years after Latrobe had left Richmond, the memory of that striking octagonal feature in his sketch may have led them to adopt the octagonal ends in the house they finally built. If this building was not then handled by Latrobe, we have a possible reason why the Randolph name does not appear on the sketch in question.

The collection also includes the design made in 1798 for Colonel John Harvie's Richmond house, later called Gamble Hill. It is a brilliantly planned formal residence with colonnaded one-story porches at the sides and long side wings. The wings were never built, and it may have been their omission that led to a quarrel between Harvie and Latrobe. Samuel Mordecai tells the story: "Col. Harvie wished to make some change in

Latrobe's plan, to which the architect would not accede. They parted, the house stood unfinished for some time, when it passed into the hands of Colonel Robert Gamble . . . The Colonel finished it and occupied it for many years until his death."[2] Actually the "some time" was about a year, for the house was occupied in 1799. Over a decade later, after Robert Gamble's death, his son, apparently wishing to make some further changes or perhaps to complete the whole according to the original scheme, wrote Latrobe for the drawings; on March 28, 1811, Latrobe answered him, offering to have copies made.

This Harvie-Gamble house, on Byrd Street between Third and Fourth and not far from the penitentiary, was on a hill that at the time commanded a superb view over the James River valley. The plan shows a monumental entrance hall culminating at each end in semicircular niches. Behind are three beautiful living rooms *en suite:* at the left the dining room, 17 by 20 feet; in the center a drawing room, 20 by 25 feet, with a segmental projecting bay; at the right a parlor of the same size as the dining room. The kitchen was originally designed to be placed in the left-hand wing; when the wings were omitted it was probably put in the basement beneath the dining room, with service through the stair hall. Above, on the second floor, are three large bedrooms above the three main rooms, a dressing room, and a "gallery or ladies' drawing room" above the entrance hall. The whole is organized with a deceptive simplicity of arrangement that gives rise to noble and elegant interior volumes.

On the exterior we find the expected simplicity. The building was designed to be of brick, stuccoed; a simple projecting band course marks the story divisions, and the upper windows, much shorter than the ones beneath, give a pleasant proportional harmony. There is a slight projection to express the entrance hall and create a central motif. The delicate cornice consists of a simple bracketed gutter, and the hipped roof is broken only by the pediment over the central pavilion. For this house Latrobe had designed a broad and welcoming porch, with primitive

---

2. In *Virginia, Especially Richmond, in By-Gone Days,* 2nd ed. (Richmond: West & Johnston, 1860), p. 97. See also Mary Wingfield Scott, *Old Richmond Neighborhoods* (Richmond: the author [c1950]). Latrobe had a continuing interest in this part of Richmond, for he had won a lot adjoining the Harvie land in the famous Byrd lottery of 1797. He held it for a decade; then in 1807, when he was in dire need of cash, he wrote Orris Paine in Richmond (March 17) to sell it. Eventually it was purchased from Latrobe by Colonel Gamble himself. For octagonal houses, see Mary Wingfield Scott, *Houses of Old Richmond* (Richmond: Valentine Museum, 1941), pp. 54f.

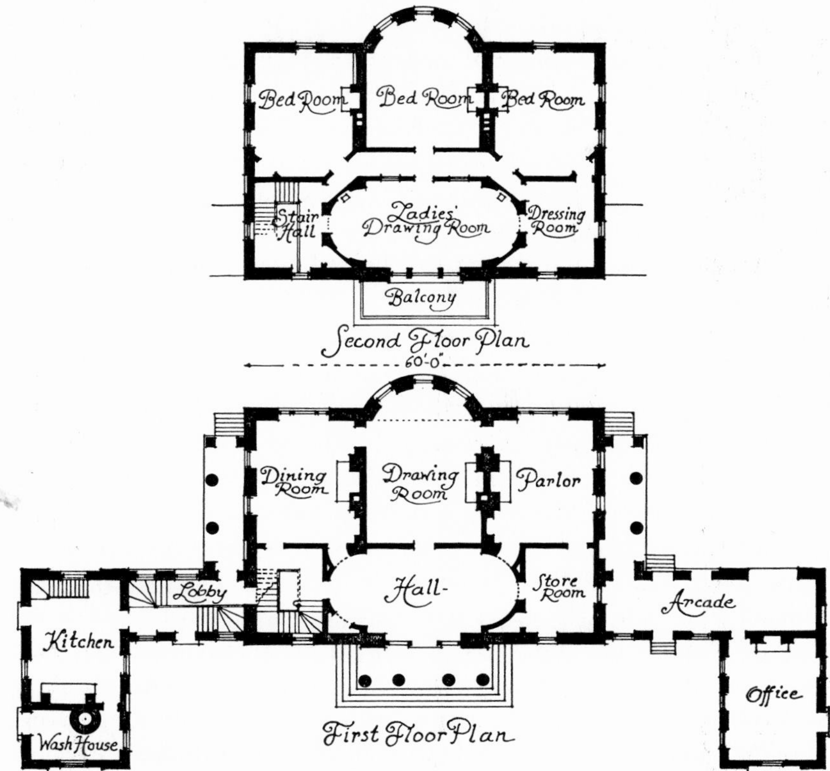

In Library of Congress

FIGURE 6. Harvie-Gamble House, Richmond. Plans. Redrawn from Latrobe's drawings.

Greek Doric columns—a favorite form with him which he used in Hammerwood Lodge and in all the porches for these earlier American houses.[3] Evidently that porch was never built; the actual porch shown in existing photographs, though of approximately equal breadth, was an undistinguished and characterless intrusion on the pure clarity of the architect's conception.

3. This favorite Doric order of Latrobe's seems to have been based originally on the "Temple" at Delos shown in volume III of James Stuart and Nicholas Revett's *Antiquities of Athens* originally published in 1794. It was also a favorite order of Revett in his few English works. Apparently it never occurred to either of these architects that the omission of the fluting on the greater part of the shaft was merely an indication that the work had never been completed.

In the collection is another study for a large, elaborate mansion which bears no date or identification. It shows a cross-shaped plan, one arm of which is a projecting semi-octagon containing a magnificent 30-foot octagonal salon; in another wing there is a tremendous monumental stairway that recalls the arrangement of Mill Hill, and in the center a dark niche-ended vestibule or hall. The other rooms on this floor—the dining room and parlors—are large and well planned, and upstairs the six bedrooms open on a central domed hall lighted from above. It is all very handsome and somewhat overwhelming.

Yet functionally the plan is hardly better than that of Mill Hill. The awkward entrance leading directly into the octagonal salon, the oversized grand stairs, and above all the inconvenient service arrangements all indicate it was an early design.

Also in the group and shown on the title page, in the clouds, with the other unbuilt projects, there is another design with a square plan and central lighting from above; it is labeled in faint pencil, "Mr. Tayloe's house in the Foederal City." It is interesting that at this time the architect made a design for such a rabid Federalist as Tayloe; perhaps it was because of their basic difference in political ideals that the scheme was never carried out. Instead, when the time for actual construction came, Tayloe turned to a fellow Federalist, Dr. William Thornton, the first architect of the United States Capitol. The result was the famous Octagon, still standing at the corner of New York Avenue and Seventeenth Street, N.W.—one of the most exquisite houses of its time and now the home of the American Institute of Architects.

Latrobe's design, for a larger mansion than the Thornton scheme, is one of great originality. It has been drawn and rendered with loving care, as though for inclusion in his proposed publication, and the drawings include studies for all four sides of the large dining room, showing the furniture, the pictures, the decorations, and the beautiful triple window at the end. At the four corners of the house, little square pavilions covered with curved roofs project. Between the two left-hand pavilions a service passage runs back to the garden and the service entrance; between the other two there is a Doric colonnade. The rear yard is treated with unusual care as a small garden with informal paths; on its axis is a three-arched, pedimented garden loggia which masks the stable wall; the stable door opens on the side street. There is one especially interesting feature—a water closet over the service passage and opening from the second-floor hall. That the design is a fairly early one we may deduce from the fact that, in addition to this facility, carefully arranged privies are included in the garden and stable buildings at the rear.

In the elevation the most unusual elements are the four projecting corner pavilions. Two later Philadelphia houses by Latrobe had such pavilions: Sedgeley, built in 1799; and the Waln house, 1805 to 1808. This repetition of a motif developed earlier is a common architectural habit of Latrobe's—again and again he used a single idea in different designs until he had discovered and utilized all its possibilities. Also notable here is the fact that this design is one of the most highly developed of those with centralized plans and that the rooms, conveniently arranged, are placed around a two-story domed central hall, lighted by a cupola; passage on the second floor is both by corridors outside the hall and by balconies within it. The third story rises as a square "ring" around a central open court, at the bottom of which is the dome and cupola over the hall. It is all brilliantly direct.

Later Latrobe designed in Richmond another deep house with a cupola-lighted central hall, Clifton, built on Council Chamber Hill for Benjamin James Harris in 1808; the architect's beautiful perspective of it exists.[4] By this time he was living in Washington and his contacts with Virginia had been renewed. The front, like that of Mill Hill, has two semi-octagonal bays at the ends. Between them the broad wall is of compelling simplicity, with a single window in the center of the upper floor and a broad segmental-arched entrance motif below. Colonnades of three bays on each side lead to simple pedimented end pavilions; their small scale throws into exciting relief the commanding scale of the house itself. This central *corps de logis* is a deep structure; the ends show five full bays each, and to light the center there is a large domed cupola extending well above the roof.

Clifton reveals Latrobe's delight in houses with compact, squarish plans and top-lighted halls, so unlike the long narrow plans of the usual American house of his time. Even the Harvie-Gamble house and that for Dr. McClurg (discussed below) have greater depths in relation to their length than were common. The Pennock house was a perfect square of 43 feet. The Harvie-Gamble house, excluding the side porticoes, had a

4. See Scott, *Old Richmond Neighborhoods.*

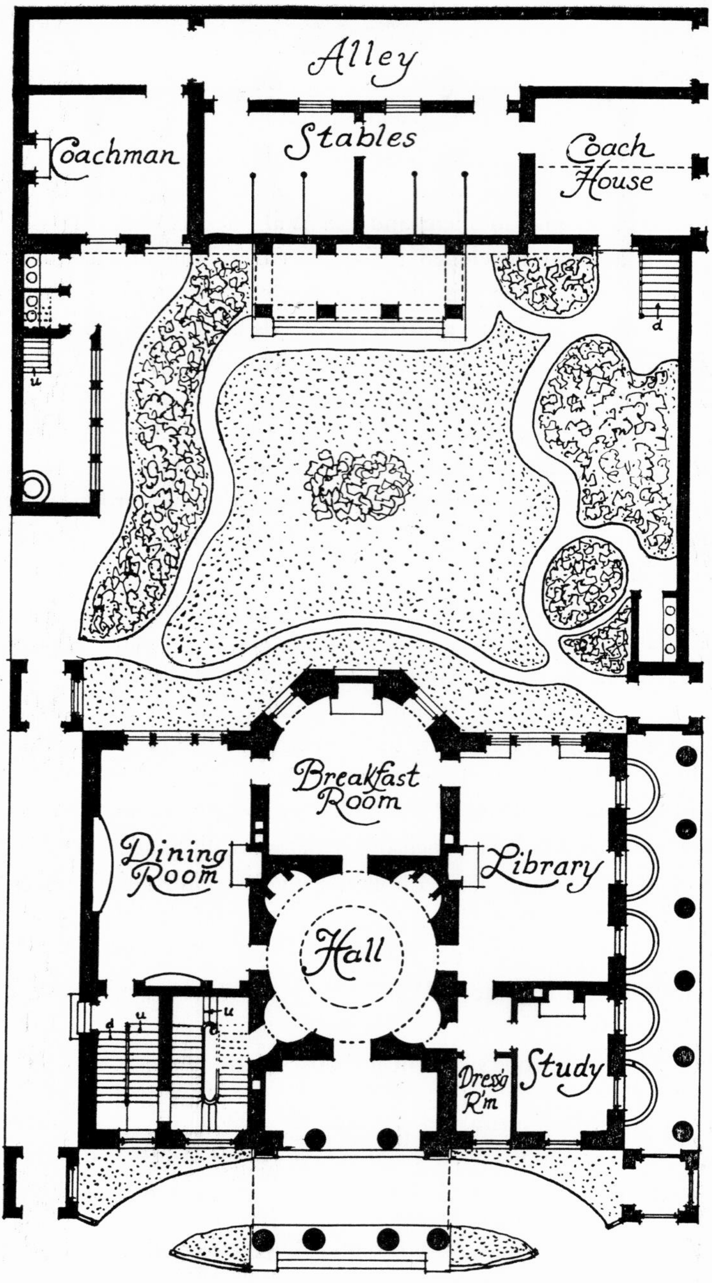
Alley
Coachman
Stables
Coach House
Breakfast Room
Dining Room
Library
Hall
Dress'g R'm
Study

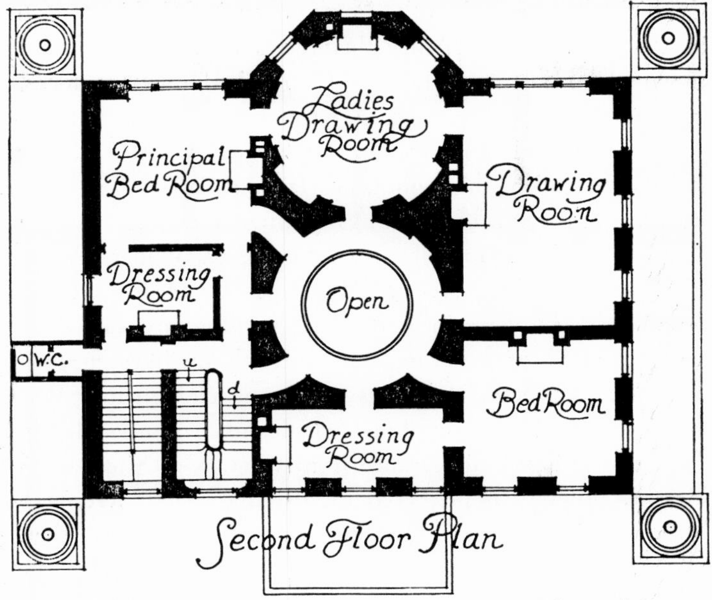

In Library of Congress

FIGURE 7. Proposed House for Mr. Tayloe, Washington. Plans. Redrawn from Latrobe's drawings.

depth of about 36 feet for a front of approximately 56 feet, and Clifton must have had a depth of nearly 50 feet. In large houses such depths bring in difficult problems of circulation and lighting, for both of which the central top-lighted rotunda is an obvious solution. Perhaps the desire for such a high interior may even have been a controlling aim in the development of the type.

The two finest examples of this are the house for Senator John Pope in Lexington, Kentucky,[5] and Brentwood in Washington. The plan for the Pope house, made as late as 1811, is included with the other Virginia house drawings in the Library of Congress collection. It is less grand than his Tayloe design but perhaps more delightful, and if the building had been erected according to the architect's design it would have been the most unusual house west of the Alleghenies. Latrobe had great hopes for it and he produced several sketches of different arrangements, each

5. See Clay Lancaster, "Latrobe and the John Pope House," *Gazette des Beaux Arts,* series 6, vol. 29 (1946), April, pp. 213-24.

one of which was a signal to the Popes—then in Washington—to make additional suggestions, until they themselves were so confused they did not know where to turn. All their friends had different ideas, which they freely expressed; Latrobe finally wrote his clients (January 18, 1811) that "the more friends you consult, the further you will be from your project." By the end of the month, however, a plan had been settled on and drawings and a bill of scantlings (timber sizes) sent to the senator. On March 1 Latrobe himself wrote to Pope's builder, Asa Wilgus: ". . . as I shall probably never see Mr. Pope's house, it is necessary that my house on paper & yours in solid work should go up exactly alike . . ."

But, alas, for all Latrobe's care, Asa Wilgus must have been at heart a conservative, and Senator Pope was not strong enough to withstand his suggestions. The executed building—which, much mutilated, still stands—was quite different in appearance from what its architect had so carefully drawn, although it preserved the original plan. Here, at last, Latrobe succeeded in introducing the English basement scheme that he had suggested unavailingly several times before. Entrance was in the center of the front, and a hall led into a central area from which the great stairs, well lighted by a large window in the side, ran up to the chief floor. On the other side of the central area was the service stair. The remaining space on the ground floor was used for an office in front at the left, a parlor at the right, and at the rear the ample service quarters—kitchen, wash and bake house, stores, and two rooms for servants.

Above, the stairs brought one to the central domed hall, cupola-lighted—a room of beautiful proportions with a great sense of space. Toward the front lay the drawing room (left) and the dining room (right), identical in shape and size, meeting in two large semicircular ends to give a little private "closet" at the front and a cleverly contrived niche in the circular hall. The dining room was served from the service stair through an ample, well-lighted butler's pantry; the service stair was continued up to the roof and was concealed by the mass of the large chimneys. The rear of the main floor contained three sizable bedrooms, two of them opening off a common vestibule. It was all most ingeniously contrived to give ample, beautifully shaped, and conveniently related rooms and to produce as well in the combination of large reception hall, drawing room, and dining room three volumes of a varied and almost monumental character—all in a nearly square house of relatively modest dimensions. It was one of the most tightly knit of all the Latrobe houses.

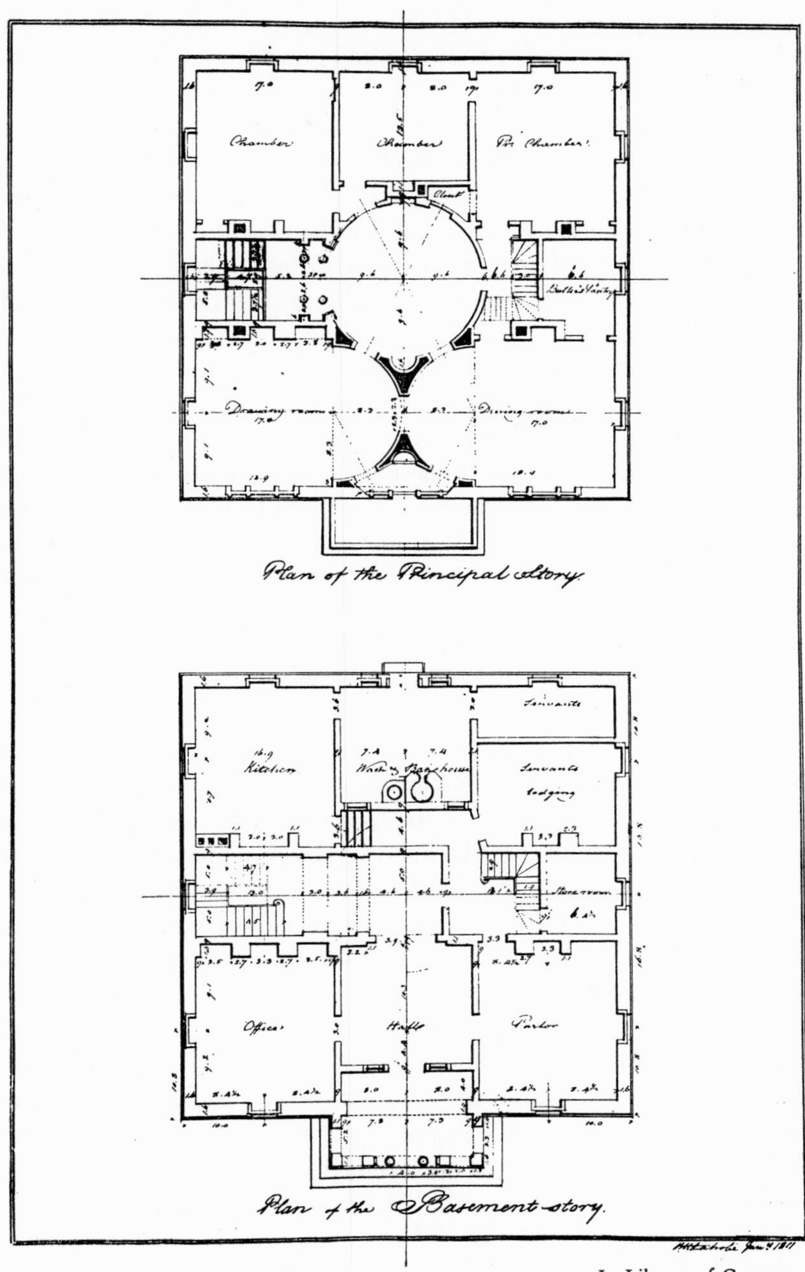

In Library of Congress

FIGURE 8. Senator Pope's House, Lexington, Ky. Latrobe's original plans.

The exterior, as the architect conceived it, was equally brilliant. He made two elevations, one of two stories and one of three; they are identical except for their height. In both the ground floor was kept low, with windows of relatively broad proportions; the second floor—the *piano nobile*—by contrast was high and had very tall windows running down to the floor. Above, in the three-story scheme, the windows were broader and less high. In both schemes Latrobe's characteristically simple eaves treatment and a hipped roof, with heavy chimneys at the sides and a cupola at the center, completed façades of unusual breadth, serenity, and charm.

For the entrance the architect had planned a broad low porch with solid brick end piers and two of his favorite primitive Greek Doric columns *in antis,* and over the windows he had indicated stone lintels supported at the ends on rosetted stone blocks. Neither this porch nor the lintels were included in the house as built, and even the proportions were destroyed by making all the windows the same in size. Thus, even without the subsequent mutilations that have resulted from the gradual transformation of a noble house to improvised modern apartments, the Pope house as built could never have been more than a sad caricature of what was intended.

The best of these rotunda-type houses was Brentwood, near Washington, built for Mayor Robert Brent in 1818 and destroyed only a few years ago. It stood on Seventh Street Northeast, not far from Capitol Hill, and its main axis was directed toward the Capitol dome. Fortunately it was well photographed and recorded.[6] Brentwood was more spread out than the houses just described, but its dominant element was still a large domed central salon, lighted by a cupola. Here this room no longer was a mere hall or distribution center but actually constituted the chief central reception or drawing room and formed an impressive setting for gay social gatherings. The front of the house was symmetrical, with a definite accent on centrality. It had a more formal composition than the other houses we have noted, for the walls carried cornices and an "attic" parapet which concealed the gutters; evidently Latrobe was seeking a strong horizontal stress as a contrast to the accented centrality. Only the central

6. See Harry Francis Cunningham, Joseph Arthur Younger, and J. Wilmer Smith, *Measured Drawings of Georgian Architecture in the District of Columbia* (New York: Architectural Book Publishing Co., 1914), and Joseph Arthur Younger, "Brentwood," in *Architecture,* vol. 37, no. 3 (March, 1918), pp. 55-6, plates 59, 60.

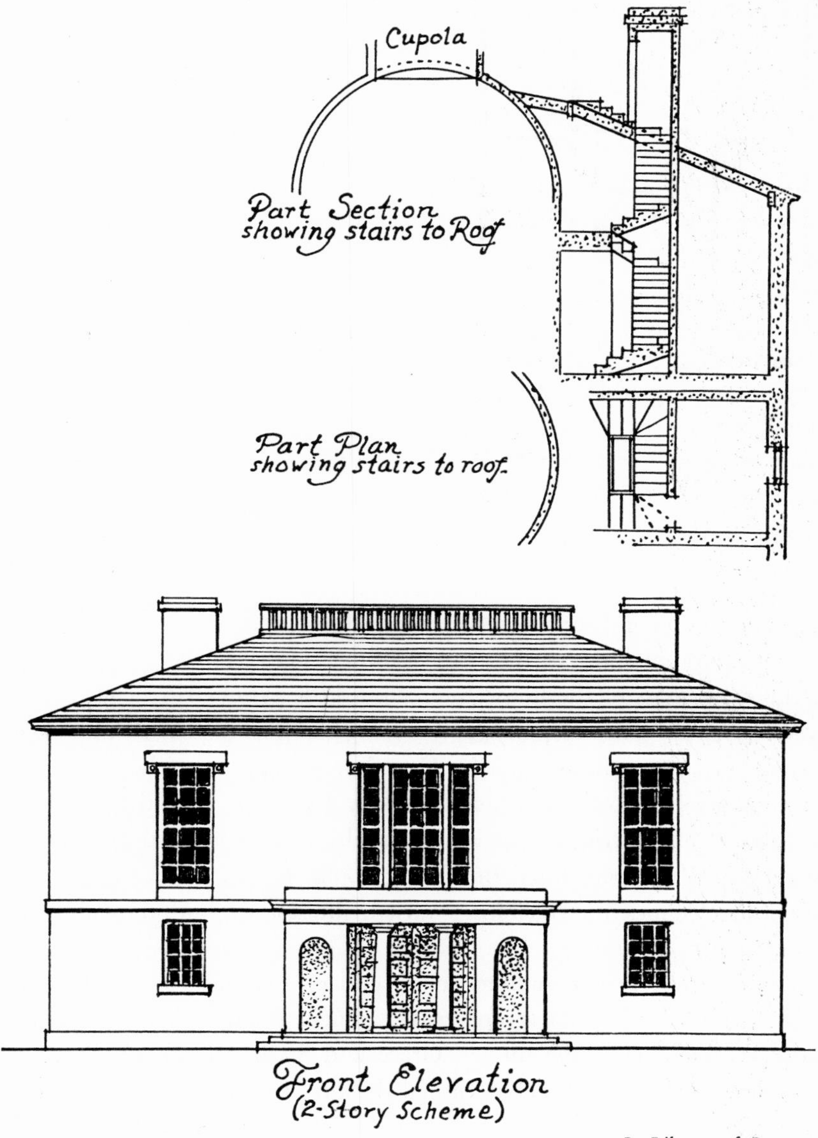

In Library of Congress

FIGURE 9. Senator Pope's House, Lexington, Ky. Elevation and Part Section. Redrawn from Latrobe's drawings.

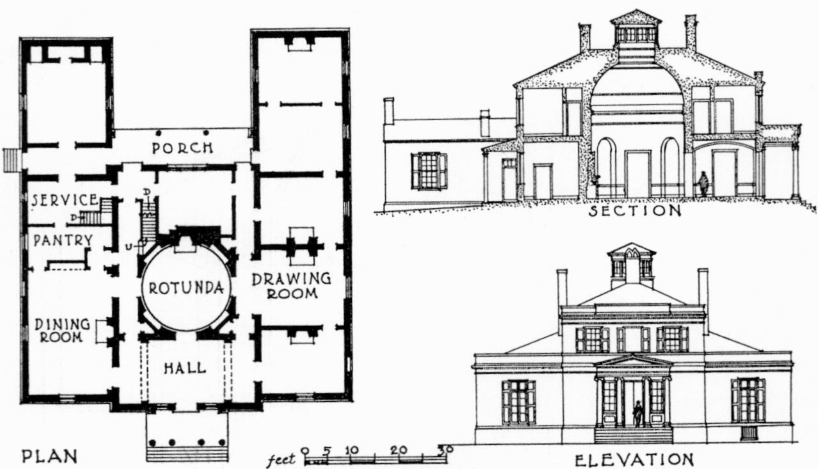

From Hamlin, *Greek Revival Architecture in America*

FIGURE 10. Brentwood, Washington. Plans, Elevation, Section.

portion of the house was two stories high, with two bedrooms in front and one behind the rotunda. The one-story wings contained, on the left, the dining room and service areas; on the right, a parlor, a drawing room, and an anteroom and two bedrooms *en suite*. These wings extended back of the main mass of the house to create a little symmetrical court, overlooked by a colonnaded porch and warmed by the eastern sun to make an ideal place for a flower garden. Corridors led back on either side from the entrance hall to the colonnade, and by means of wide doors the rotunda cross axis carried through into the drawing room at the right and on the other side penetrated the dining room. It was a superb composition, full of subtleties generating varied, interesting, and composed interior vistas.

After Latrobe left Richmond at the end of 1798 his connection with Richmond houses by no means ceased. There is, for instance, the fine house for Dr. James McClurg at Grace and Sixth streets. On April 16, 1804, Latrobe writes the distinguished doctor, "I thank you sincerely for the confidence you have placed in me," and goes on to request certain particulars of the lot; in the meanwhile, he says, he will study the problem as far as he can without them. The house was designed during the summer; obviously the information he needed had been forthcoming. No drawings of this house have thus far come to light and there is therefore no proof that the house Dr. McClurg erected in 1805 was built from Latrobe's design, although the beauty of the proportions suggests the possibility. Externally it was of a rather conventional five-bay type—but so was Mr. Pennock's house. Certainly the spirit of the delicate cornice and the hipped roof might well have been Latrobe's, though the flat arches over the windows, with their exquisitely detailed keyblocks, look more like the work of a skilled local craftsman than like the simple window penetrations or stone lintels preferred by the architect. If this house was built from Latrobe's plans it is unlikely that he superintended it, for he seems never to have returned to Richmond until the Burr trial in the summer of 1807. These arches, then, may have been additions which the builder considered necessary to complete the simple rectangular openings that were probably shown on the drawings.[7]

While he was working on the Pope house in 1811 Latrobe was also busy with another important residence in Virginia—Long Branch—for Robert Carter Burwell.[8] Burwell had considered building a house and apparently had been in contact with some unknown local builder-architect, but on meeting Latrobe he suddenly realized that a real architect's advice might be helpful. Latrobe wrote him (April 26, 1811): "Thank you for remembrance of our meeting at Mr. Page's. . . . If your foundations are not yet laid . . . I shall be happy to assist you." Two months later (July 6) he wrote again: "The plan you have enclosed is infinitely a better one than almost any other which I have seen adopted in Virginia, & the house would be a good one without any alteration." Yet here again we find him insisting on those qualities of privacy and of efficient service for which he always strove: "The great fault of your plan is want of private communication for your family . . . Your only staircase fronts the only external door. . . . Not a vessel, or nurse or servant can approach but through the hall . . . Another fault is that the dining room & cham-

---

7. A photograph of the house is shown in Scott, *Old Richmond Neighborhoods, supra.* In it we see Latrobe's favorite band-course story division, but this was also frequent in buildings by others. In addition it shows a Greek Ionic porch, which Miss Scott feels is an addition of the Greek Revival 1830's. Latrobe, however, had used the Greek Ionic in the Bank of Pennsylvania design as early as 1798, and there is at least a possibility that he used the same order for this house.

8. Latrobe had been in touch two years earlier with another Burwell, Congressman William Burwell, in connection with the design of a house; in a letter enclosing several letters of introduction to Philadelphia friends (June 30, 1809) he adds, "I will not forget your piazza."

ber are on the north side . . . How far are you advanced? . . . Is it possible to modify your plan . . . I will immediately . . . take it regularly in hand . . . and send you my ideas in a drawing . . . Is your house brick or stone?" Presumably Burwell's builder had already begun his work—had perhaps laid the foundations or even started carrying up the external walls. Latrobe sent on his final drawings in the middle of August, 1811; apparently they went astray, for on October 31 he wrote that he was sending copies of the drawings by letter mail so that there would be less danger of loss. With this evidence as to Latrobe's work, we can now turn to the house itself, which still stands with little alteration save the introduction of much trim of later periods.[9]

Long Branch has two-story pedimented porticoes at front and rear, and the porch behind the front colonnade is recessed to give greater protection and a greater sense of space. Obviously much of the plan may be due to Burwell's local builder-architect; almost four months went by from the time when Latrobe first heard of the project till the day when he first sent his drawings, and another two before copies of the drawings were forwarded and supposedly arrived. If construction was going on during this period, we may assume that at least the lower parts of all the exterior walls were well under way before Burwell received the architect's designs. Moreover, Latrobe states twice his general approval of the original scheme; his objections were largely confined to the lack of sufficient privacy and efficient circulation. The basic mass of the house, then—save perhaps its height—would conform to the original foundations; we should look to Latrobe only for details, perhaps for the handling of the roof and the colonnades and for any internal plan variations to give better communication.

The actual building bears this out. The house now has two exterior doors instead of the one Latrobe cites, yet the window widths and arrangements are almost completely "normal" and without any evidence of the broad concentrated wall surfaces and the tripled or otherwise unusual windows which the architect preferred. But the house has great distinction. It has the usual thin projecting eaves treatment that Latrobe always chose in preference to the conventional classic cornice; it has a hipped

9. I owe much of this information to Mr. Alexander Mackay-Smith, president of the Clarke County Historical Association, who generously sent me plans and photographs of the house.

roof with a central railed deck, something like his treatment of Adena in Chillicothe, Ohio, to be considered later; and it has a delicate glazed cupola, which originally may have been intended to light the upper part of the stairs.

Though now enclosed and much altered, there was a large open loggia facing the south at the end of the house proper and fronting the one-story flat-roofed wing. Its long south front at first consisted of four brick arches. There was a brick cornice above them, and the railing of the flat roof evidently was originally intended to have brick piers above the lower arcade piers, probably with simple panels of wood or iron railings between; as seen today, however, either because the builder misunderstood the intention or through later changes, intermediate railing piers have been introduced and the railing panels omitted to produce queerly awkward pseudo battlements. The first intention is clear from the treatment still existing on the other side of the wing.

The two great porticoes are a more serious problem in attribution, for they differ greatly in proportion and in spirit. The rear Doric portico is broad, with widely spaced columns; it reminds one slightly of the portico of Madison's Montpelier, near Charlottesville, the character of which is often credited to Jefferson's suggestions. The entrance portico, on the other hand, is much narrower and, with its recessed porch, in a sense more "architectural"; it uses Greek Ionic capitals. Actually, in relation to the plan, this difference between the two porticoes seems entirely natural, even inevitable, and it may well be that it resulted from the adjustment of certain work already done to the plans Latrobe was making; it results in a marked variation in atmosphere that is not unattractive and may express merely the normal differences between an entrance and a garden front.

In the plan the introduction of a second flight of service stairs, with the subdivisions dependent on it, is obviously Latrobe's. So, too, it would seem, is the planning of the entire central section—the recessed porch, the ample vestibule, the curve-ended stair hall—and on the second floor the remarkably monumental treatment of the upper floor hall. In its basic space arrangements the whole bears a certain resemblance to the plan of the Harvie-Gamble house, though here at Long Branch the stair is in a different place and the solution is simpler in details. But it is the spirit of the whole—the development of beautifully related volumes, the sense

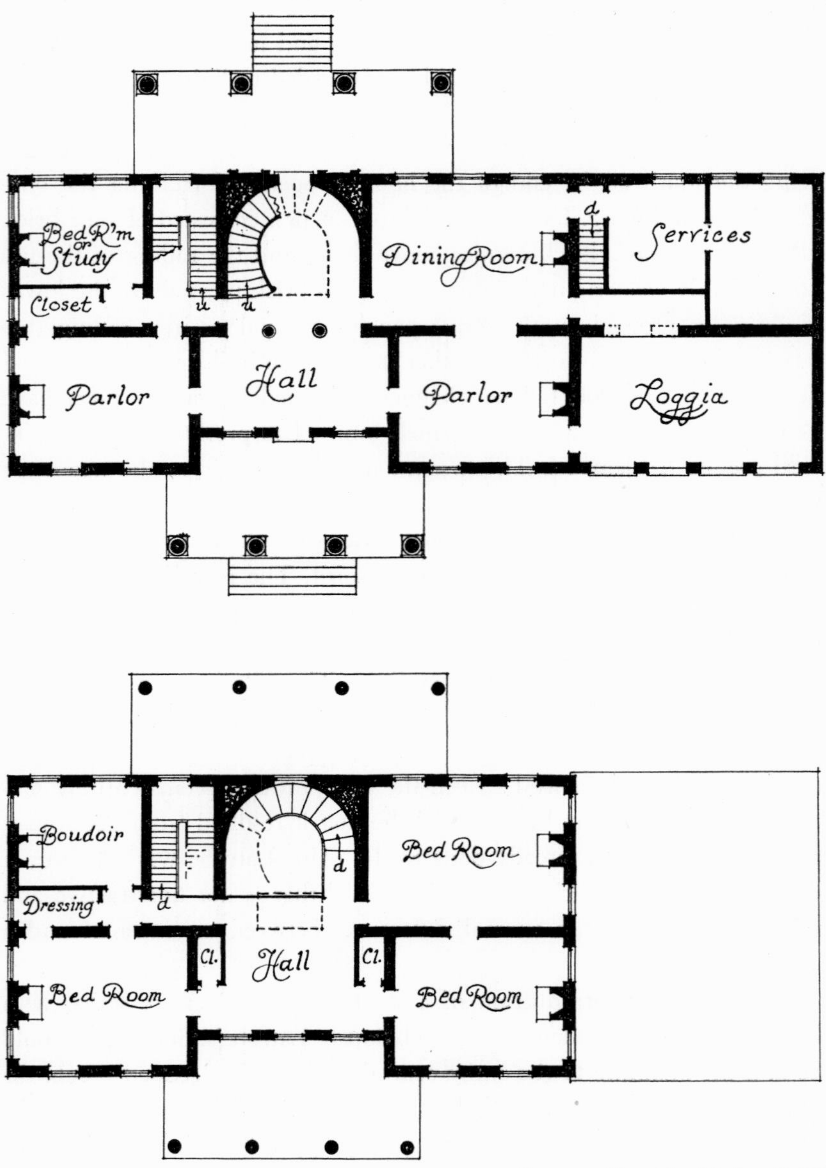

Courtesy Alexander Mackay-Smith

FIGURE 11. Burwell House, Long Branch, Clarke County, Va. From a measured drawing.

of great designed space—which in this case is particularly characteristic of Latrobe's architectural ideals.

About 1845 Long Branch was almost completely retrimmed, and other alterations were made. The piazza-loggia was enclosed, square-headed windows completely different in proportion and pane size from the earlier windows in the house replaced the open arches, and it may be that the quaint but incongruous "battlement" treatment dates from this time. Apparently the entire main stair was reconstructed also, and Corinthianesque Greek Revival columns of a common Lafever type supplanted the earlier supports. At present the effect is grand and harmonious in itself, but it is not the strong yet delicate effect Latrobe would undoubtedly have sought. New mantels and door trims, all characteristic of the often heavy taste of the provincial late Greek Revival, were installed at the same time. Fortunately, however, in the southeast corner bedroom one of the original mantels remains—the simplest kind of marble mantel, rather small in dimensions and of a type made in large numbers by the Traquair firm in Philadelphia. There is a low chair rail in the room, and all the walls above are covered by a superb French landscape paper which shows the elegance and the restrained lavishness that both Burwell and Latrobe envisaged. Long Branch, as one of the few existing houses Latrobe is known to have designed,[10] is an important monument in American architecture.

These houses are especially interesting as evidence of the way in which Latrobe's mind went about its creative task, through the repeated use of certain concepts—both general and particular—until their utmost possibilities had been exhausted. Thus we can see the earlier octagonal bays of the front of Mill Hill achieving an expression of complete and final perfection in Clifton a decade later; we find the concept of a central or rotunda plan appearing in an embryonic form in the complicated and confused plan of Mill Hill and evolving gradually through the untitled sketch into the monumentality and command of the Tayloe design, the ingenious perfection of the design for Senator Pope, and at last the great salon of Brentwood. Similarly the overweening end stairs of Mill Hill receive a chastened expression in the untitled sketch and yield finally to

---

10. Others are Adena, in Chillicothe; the Pope house in Lexington, today almost unrecognizable because of changes, mutilations, and additions; and the Decatur house in Washington.

the more functional and economic expressions of the later houses; just so, the apse-ended rooms of the Pope house are used in a much more refined and delicate manner in the drawing room and dining room of the design for the commandant's house at the Pittsburgh arsenal in 1814. And all of this impresses on one the extreme importance of the house for Captain William Pennock in Norfolk, Latrobe's first commission in the United States. It is a revolutionary work; in it so many of the qualities of his best later work already appear—the curve-ended rooms, the efficient handling of the service requirements, the architectural harmonies of volumes of differing but related shapes and sizes, the originality of the stair and stair hall, the love for compact arrangements. It was his first American building, but it was also a declaration of independence alike from English house standards and from the American colonial conventions; the house was a masterpiece of usefulness disciplined and shaped into beauty.

Also among the Library of Congress drawings are a plan and an elevation for an unknown church; there is no label or date. The church is long and narrow, with posts that seem to indicate a gallery. No stairs to the balcony are drawn, but apparently they were to have been placed in the towers that flank the porch, where there is space for them. The plan bears other evidences, too, of never having been completed. Since a central pulpit is shown, with an altar behind it, the church was probably Episcopalian.

If the plan is remarkable in the fact that it reveals a wide and open interior entirely unlike the usual Wren-Gibbs types that had been popular in America, the elevation is even more startling. It shows a relatively low, wide front, with a porch recessed between low towers; two widely spaced columns of Latrobe's favorite primitive Greek Doric type—here, however, made strangely slim—support a horizontal entablature. There is no pediment or visible roof; only a Latin inscription, *Deo Optimo Maximo,* decorates the sober entablature. The towers—square below and cylindrical above the entablature—in a way presage those he was to employ afterward in the Cathedral of Baltimore. They may owe something to his memory of St. Sulpice in Paris. The river seen at the right of the elevation suggests a Richmond site. It seems likely that this was a preliminary sketch for the rebuilding of Richmond's most famous Colonial church, St. John's, where Patrick Henry delivered his fiery "Give me liberty or give me death." The section of Richmond in which it was built was growing rapidly at the end of the eighteenth century, and there was considerable agitation in the parish for erecting a new and larger church.[11]

The second section of Latrobe's proposed publication of his works was evidently to contain his drawings for a theater, combined with assembly rooms and a hotel, for Richmond. This delightful design (already referred to) strangely enough was completed less than a month before the old theater burned down in 1798. But the building itself was obviously beyond the resources of Richmond at the time and was never erected.

Latrobe's design is remarkable for its time. The three parts are carefully differentiated on the exterior, the assembly rooms and the hotel section being expressed as pedimented end pavilions and the theater front projecting in a bold sweep between them. Entrance to the hotel and to the assembly rooms is arranged separately on the two sides of the building to permit the development of dignified entrance doors to each part without confusing the accent on the theater. The two sides, moreover, are treated differently to express the separate functions—the hotel façade unmistakable with the small rectangular windows of its bedrooms, the assembly-room section distinguished by the tall arched windows of its great rooms. The entrances differ, too: the hotel has a wide, low, inviting approach under a broad segmental arch; the assembly rooms are entered through a doorway of a more elegant and domestic character achieved by a simple semicircular arch with side- and fanlights. On both sides these approaches lead to the centrally located staircases, placed against the theater walls; it was probably Latrobe's intention to light the staircases from above with skylights.

On the hotel side—to the right of the theater—the ground floor is occupied chiefly by the great dining room and the public parlors, a coffee room, and sitting rooms; a coffee bar (on the coffee-room side of the entrance) and a liquor bar (on the dining-room side) are most ingeniously combined with the entrance vestibule; the kitchen and service areas are in the basement. No office as such is indicated, but the entrance is well controlled from the bars on either side. The whole is far in advance of the usual taverns and hotels of its time in the beauty of its rooms and the privacy of its chambers. Its greatest lack seems to be the omission of any service stair running through completely from the basement serv-

11. I am grateful to Miss Mary Wingfield Scott, of Richmond, for this information.

ice areas to all the floors, although this could easily have been furnished without appreciable changes in the plan.

The chief feature of the assembly room section is the superb ballroom, 52 by 26 feet, which occupies the left end of the principal floor. Charmingly proportioned cardrooms and supper rooms occupy the rest of this floor; beneath are the service rooms, more supper rooms, and three chambers; above are three more chambers. On this side a service stair gives completely private service to all floors.

In these drawings Latrobe included an exquisitely rendered perspective of the ballroom which reveals graphically the beauty of its proportions, its scale, and its detail. Had the building been erected this would have been the outstanding American interior of its day. It is covered with a segmental plaster barrel vault—with a semi-dome over the niche that ends the room—and is lighted by a range of arched windows with mirror panels across on the opposite side; above the mirror panels rise rich but simply detailed gilded reliefs like girandoles, patently of Adam inspiration. The walls have no cornices; instead there is a decorated band crowned by a single molding of rather flat profile, in excellent scale with the ribs of the arched ceiling. This drawing is particularly valuable, not only for its great beauty *qua* drawing but also because it is a rare expression of its maker's artistic ideals and of the influences that had played upon him. The Adam details are only such as had become the common vernacular of English architects of the 1790's, and the whole effect is different in atmosphere from the average Adam interior; there is a certain direct clarity in the whole which has other than Adam implications. In fact, it bears a distinct resemblance to the Grand Subscription Room in Brooks's Club in London by Holland, which was opened in 1788.[12] Latrobe had probably seen this room, for Brooks's was definitely a Whig or radical club and one to which Latrobe's political associations in London might well have brought him. Charles James Fox was a famous member and an intimate friend of Holland's and, as we have seen, an acquaintance and even a sort of patron of Latrobe a few years earlier. Memories of that clear, serene, yet lavish room in London were conceivably at the back of his mind when he laid out this exquisite drawing.

Yet the Richmond ballroom is not a copy; it is a new creation. Though

---

12. See Dorothy Stroud, *Henry Holland, 1745-1806* (London: Art and Technics, 1950), especially p. 19.

it owes something to what Latrobe had known in London, the recollections emerge re-created in accordance with Latrobe's own feeling for form and restraint and space. And the entire spirit of the exterior is as unlike Holland as can be imagined. Not a pilaster, not an excess molding clouds the simplicity of the brick, and the cornice is reduced to a narrow fascia on the projecting eaves. Aside from a discreet use of sunken horizontal panels, there is only the simple strength of the plain rectangular openings and the powerful recessed arches of the arcade which marches around the curved theater front.

It is the theater itself that is the climax of the design. The brilliant use of intersecting circular curves to give greater depth to the boxes and the gallery opposite the stage—and incidentally longer and roomier lobbies—would appear to be unique at the time. Equally remarkable is the interior, which like the plan is apparently without precedent. The ceiling over the auditorium proper is a shallow half dome. On either side, the fronts of the stage boxes are brought out toward the center sufficiently to create a narrow vertical plane, and this is carried across from side to side as a low, paneled, segmental arch, with a slightly conical coffered ceiling behind over the forestage and running back to the proscenium opening. This ceiling and the fronts of the side boxes form the only architectural "proscenium arch," for the opening of the stage runs clear from one side to the other and the lunette beneath the segmental ceiling is filled with drapery—probably intended to be a permanent valance—gathered up to a great American eagle in the center. An examination of plates of late-eighteenth-century theaters in England, France, Germany, and Italy reveals not a single scheme of this type; only a decade or more later do the nearest approaches to such a simplicity of ceiling design, so visually satisfactory, so definitely focused on the stage, appear in European examples.[13] Even Ledoux's famous theater for Arles has a colossal proscenium arch of heavily rusticated masonry.

Both the stairs and the exits may be criticized. There is a separate staircase to the gallery (an early example of an almost uniform American

13. Thus Smirke's Covent Garden in London dates from 1808-9, and Benjamin Wyatt's Drury Lane was built in 1811-12. The typical French and Italian theaters of the time usually strove for some sort of domical or circular treatment of the auditorium ceiling, or else—as in the theater at Versailles, by J. A. Gabriel—for a heavily architectural proscenium. The earlier Drury Lane by Robert Adam (1773) had straight sides, a polygonal plan opposite the stage, and a flat painted ceiling.

practice later), but the boxes can be approached only by stairs asymmetrically and rather casually placed and, according to modern standards, inadequate in size. The "pit" exit is also congested and bottlenecked; in a panic this theater would probably have been as lethal as the Richmond theater that *was* built (not by Latrobe) and destroyed by fire with such a tragic loss of life in December, 1811. Nevertheless, in form and elegant simplicity of treatment the entire composition is extraordinary and in advance of its time. Had it been built it would have given Richmond not only a ballroom the equal (except in size) of any in England but also a theater interior simpler, finer, and more distinguished as a unit than almost any standing anywhere in Europe in 1797.

The drawings Latrobe made for this project are delightful. On the title page there is a genre picture representing, he notes, nearly all the theatrical properties of the current Richmond company of players, and on an incompleted contents page there is a charming headpiece quaintly entitled "Tragedy begging, and Farce snatching the mask from Comedy." The sections of the theater itself are lively, not only because of the architecture they so graphically reveal but also because of the imaginative additions the architect made to give them scale—a painter, standing on a complicated scaffold plank, most peculiarly supported, painting the box-front panel; men apparently beginning to drape the box fronts for some special occasion; two men carrying a ladder. And the stage set depicted within the proscenium is impressive—the interior of a large primitive Greek Doric building looking out through columns to a distant landscape. The antae of the building are represented with huge, outcurving concave capitals, and the whole has a deeply evocative atmosphere—the romance of the ancient, the greatness of scale of the monumental. It would be a great play and great acting that would be worthy of that set.

The last great work of Latrobe's Virginia career, and in many ways the most important, was the Richmond penitentiary. Jefferson's deep interest in a more humane penology is well known, and it was fitting that just about the time of Latrobe's arrival in America the state of Virginia decided to build a new prison in which those ideals could be expressed. There was a competition for its design and on June 25, 1797 (as previously noted), he was informed by the governor that his plan had been awarded the premium and that he had been appointed to design and supervise the construction of the prison. Early in the construction Latrobe moved to Quarrier's Court, at the foot of Seventh Street, on the canal bank, to be nearer the work; there he had both his office and his dwelling. In March, 1798, he made his first visit to Philadelphia—mentioned in the letter to Scandella cited in the preceding chapter—chiefly, he writes the prison commissioner (March 5, 1798), to study the then famous Philadelphia vaulted prison;[14] from the summer of 1797 till his removal to Philadelphia the prison, slowly rising on a bluff overlooking the James, was his most compelling interest.

Though altered and added to many times and long since replaced, for nearly a century the Richmond penitentiary was a prominent landmark which shows strikingly in many of the existing early views of the city.[15] Furthermore, Latrobe's own drawings (perhaps those submitted in the original competition) still exist, and when M. Demetz and Abel Blouet were sent to the United States by the French government in 1835 to study the country's prisons, they carefully recorded the Richmond penitentiary as one of them; in their published report there is a rather sketchy perspective view and a carefully detailed plan.[16] Fortunately, therefore, we are able to gain a clear idea of Latrobe's complex building and to judge something of its fate in later years.

In general there is a striking similarity between the structure shown on the Latrobe drawings and what the French visitors recorded. The scheme consists of a large semicircular court, the cells—vaulted and in three stories—forming the outer circumference; thus every cell door is equally visible from one point in the center. (In the plan there is no suggestion of color segregation.) The straight side of the semicircle is closed by a wall, with the keeper's residence at its center—the point of maximum visibility. In front of this is a forecourt, closed at the sides with

---

14. This letter is in the Dreer Collection at the Historical Society of Pennsylvania. I am grateful to Mr. Charles Peterson, of the National Park Service, for bringing it to my attention.

For Jefferson's inspiration in his advanced prison design see Howard C. Rice, Jr., "A French Source of Jefferson's Plan for the Prison at Richmond," which reproduces the plan by P.-G. Bugniet for a solitary confinement prison in 1765, and also the other sections, "Early Prisons," "Latrobe Comes to Philadelphia, 1798," "Walnut Street Prison, 1774-75," and "Virginia Penitentiary, 1797," all in "American Notes," *Journal of the Society of Architectural Historians,* vol. 12, no. 4 (December, 1953).

15. The last remnant, by then surrounded with later shops and cell blocks, was not removed till 1927.

16. M. Demetz and Abel Blouet, *Rapports à Monsieur le Comte de Montalivet sur les penitenciers des États-Unis* (Paris: Imprimerie Royale, 1837), pp. 42ff.

blocks of building containing at the left an infirmary for men and at the right a woman's prison and infirmary; a wall encloses this court at the front and is pierced by a capacious guardhouse, which provides entrance to the prison through a wide, low, semicircular arch of great expressive power. The drawings show lower-floor walls of rough polygonal stone, with brick above. All the windows are arched, some are set back in arched recesses, and there is the usual thin eaves cornice which Latrobe loved. The guardhouse has a flat roof, but all the other roofs are low in slope and either gabled or hipped. Accented pavilions mark the corners of the main court and the entrance court, and there is a cupola over the keeper's house. The whole forms a visual composition that perfectly expresses the plan and, through its long ranges of arcades, its heavy rough-stone lower walls, and the rather sinister power of the great semicircular entrance, seems to have just the character of combined severity and humanity that Jefferson's penology envisaged.

Latrobe drew his plans for construction in two stages, the main court to be built first and the forecourt later. Apparently, however, the entire prison was erected at one and the same time according to the enlarged plan. The central building—the keeper's house—was burned in 1823, and after the fire the keeper's residence was rebuilt over the guardhouse. The building accounts, preserved in the State Library of Virginia, definitely indicate this change. At this time, too, the wall between the two courts was eliminated to give the prisoners more space and to simplify supervision.

By the 1830's, when Blouet drew his plan and view, many changes had been made. The state was then, Demetz reports, running the prison on a combination of the Pennsylvania solitary confinement system and the Auburn system of work in common. Also, the prison population had increased.[17] Large shops had been built behind the prison, and a new enclosure wall had been constructed around them.

Some of the details of the Latrobe design are of special interest. Ventilation of the entire scheme was assured by substituting for one cell on each floor, on the main axis, an open barred arcade and by creating open, barred, arcaded loggias on the lower floors of the infirmary and women's prison wings. The cells were entered from cantilevered balconies around

17. The prison was designed for a maximum of two hundred inmates. By 1820 the prison population had already exceeded that figure.

the semicircle; stairs evidently of stone were placed conveniently on each side, with turnkeys' rooms controlling them on each floor. A certain number of dark cells were provided for punishment purposes; instead of barred windows they had only crooked passages through the walls for ventilation. But, quite in line with the ideas of modern penology, Latrobe also furnished on each floor dormitories for three, five, or seven reformed prisoners to give them the advantage of some social converse.

In the building as Demetz and Blouet found it there were primitive individual water closets in each cell. Latrobe's drawings show not these but carefully grouped privies, though it is possible that the obvious difficulties in supervision of the prisoners on their frequent trips outside the cells may have suggested the inclusion of the individual water closets at the time of construction. Blouet's plan reveals, too, that because of the increasing prisoner population all the old carefully placed stairs Latrobe had shown had been removed to give more cell space and had been superseded by manifestly improvised wooden stairways in the court.

The French prison experts found much to criticize in the Richmond penitentiary. They noted that not only the dark cells but real underground dungeons, dank and wet, were used for punishment; of the latter there is no trace in the Latrobe designs, and they undoubtedly were added later when Jefferson's noble ideals had been at least partly forgotten. They reported that the cells were cold in winter—with only wooden doors to the outside court air—and that frozen hands and feet had occurred. No trace was found of Latrobe's dormitories; these had all been divided into cells. They objected to the fact that the cell windows overlooked the outside world and remarked that for this reason all the ground-floor cell windows had been blocked up except for a ventilation hole, so that these, too, were almost dark; and they criticized the close connection of the cells to the inner court. Objection was also taken to the character of the building, in that its exterior appearance lacked the "severity fitting to a prison." But here again Latrobe seems to have almost perfectly expressed the ideals which Jefferson had enunciated and which the state of Virginia in 1797 had sought to enshrine. For the cornerstone Latrobe himself composed the inscription, which is eloquent of those ideals: [18]

---

18. Manuscript journal, July 24, 1797.

The Legislature
of the Commonwealth of Virginia
having abolished the antient sanguinary criminal code
The first stone of an Edifice
The Monument of that Wisdom
which should reform while it punishes the Criminal
was laid on the 7th day of August
in the year 1797, and of American Independence the 22nd
by J^{n} Wood Esq. Governor
_______ Gr. Master of Masons

Council, Deputy, etc.
Lodges No. 10-19

As a building designed for such a purpose, the character of the Latrobe design seems almost perfect. There is a sense of enclosure; there is a single, solemn entrance; yet the ranked arcades and the scale of it all make one realize it is an enclosure for human beings. It is at the opposite extreme from the brutal rustication, the unbroken walls, the ironic false windows of George Dance's famous prison in London, which seems to groan, "Abandon hope all ye who enter here." Like Jefferson's concepts, Latrobe's building emphasized instead hope and reform.

As Latrobe designed it the building was a unique contribution to American architecture. It was the country's first large prison conceived architecturally. It embodied penological concepts that for their time were imaginative and advanced. And in its exterior of ranked arches, simple roofs, and stark entrance it can only be paralleled by some of the work of Claude Nicolas Ledoux. Memories of Ledoux's work in Paris might well have remained with him, to emerge—re-formed and re-expressed—in such of his designs as the Richmond theater and the penitentiary.[19]

Yet, despite the size of this important government commission, Latrobe's professional experience with it was not happy. He was embroiled in constant petty disputes. The superintendent in charge, Callis, questioned his estimates and his certificates and complained that the centering for the great entrance arch was unduly costly. Latrobe was even compelled, over his own bitter protests, to cut one of his certificates for pay-

19. For various early views of the prison see Alexander Wilbourne Weddell, *Richmond, Virginia, in Old Prints, 1737-1887,* published under the auspices of the Richmond Academy of Arts (Richmond [etc.]: Johnson, 1932).

ment to the head carpenter, Shortis, by eleven pounds. (It is interesting to note that the building accounts at this date are in both pounds and dollars—sometimes the one, sometimes the other—thus complicating the architect's work.) And for all this he was grudgingly paid, for the state authorities refused to honor the agreement with him which they had already made.[20] It was a dire portent—a prophecy of much that lay ahead of him in his efforts to establish in America a strong architectural profession, which alone could be depended on to give the young country a creative architecture worthy of its promise. He tells the story later in a long letter to his pupil, Robert Mills (July 12, 1806),[21] in which he has been advising Mills with regard to the professional attitude he should take in connection with the design and construction of a proposed prison for South Carolina. Latrobe has particularly insisted on the necessity of a clear written arrangement covering the fee to be received for the work, and he goes on:

> Some years ago I resided in Virginia. My object was not to live by my profession. The penitentiary law passed during that time. I was applied to for a design. No one there could have the same means of information as myself, for independently of my general professional character I had been surveyor of the police in the districts of London, & had not only erected the buildings belonging to that branch of the government of the metropolis but necessarily acquired a knowledge of all that others had done in the erection & improvement of prisons.—My design was adopted. I stated the terms on which I would execute it, 5 p. cent on the expenditure. The Executive Counsel [sic] made no objection. At the end of a year, when the work was considerably advanced, I requested a payment on account. I was directed to state my acct. I did so, but before I could present it, the individuals of the council with most of whom I was in habits of friendship, advised me not to adhere to my charge of 5 p. cent *for it would not be allowed*. After a great deal of most unpleasant wrangling, I was then offered *1000 dollars or nothing* for my services for 15 months in the actual direction of the work, & a salary for the future of 666.67$ p. annum. My

20. It is significant that in the prison accounts as preserved there is not a single item dealing with the architect's fee. In other respects they are so complete—even to vouchers for brick and timber and arch centerings—that this absence cannot be accidental. Perhaps the commissioners were ashamed of their actions. It is interesting to note that Colonel Harvie, for whom Latrobe designed the house mentioned earlier, supplied most of the brick (some of which came from England as ballast) and that Orris Paine, who later became a close friend of the architect, was the dealer from whom the lime was bought.

21. See Appendix.

actual expenses could not be defrayed by this sum,—but my reputation was engaged, & after much most degrading negotiation, I was persuaded by several of my friends not to ruin the work by quitting it, but at all events to carry it on so far as to leave a proof of my talents and knowledge of the subject to my successors. I therefore continued in the service of the state, to my infinite detriment, for another season, when I finally quitted it, disgusted & irritated at the treatment I received. The work was afterward continued by a very worthy man, a Millwright who has most materially injured the design by his alterations.—Had I not been able to live independently of my profession, I must have starved in conducting this work.

My subsequent experience of what is to be expected from public bodies has not differed from that which I gained in Virginia. . . .

Thus this, his first public building in America, became for him a bitter professional frustration. Though that was the way architectural genius was welcomed in Virginia, would he not find Philadelphia more understanding?

CHAPTER

7

Philadelphia at Last

LATROBE all through his pleasant but not particularly profitable residence in Virginia had been gradually gaining the realization that his professional future must be sought in Philadelphia. Of New England he had little direct knowledge; Boston in the 1790's was only on the threshold of its later economic and cultural growth. New York, too, which he was soon to know better, was but slowly climbing out of its wartime lethargy and was still repairing the damages from its occupation by the British and the great fire of 1776. But Philadelphia, the capital of the United States in more ways than governmental, was the largest and wealthiest city in the country and the undoubted cultural center of the young nation. It was here that Volney and Scandella resided; it was here that a considerable group of refugees from the French Revolution were gathered; and Philadelphia moreover was the seat of the American Philosophical Society.

After the warm but hardly intellectual hospitality of Virginia—its citizens almost entirely devoted to farming, to politics and the law, and to gaming and drinking—Latrobe must have craved a society more understanding of both his scientific and his aesthetic interests. He had given Richmond of his best, yet this had been received only fragmentarily and with an almost total lack of appreciation. To Philadelphia he was also drawn by family ties; for his uncle Frederick Antes, of Revolutionary fame, was still alive and several members of his mother's family were important people in Pennsylvania. We find him writing in February, 1798, the long, affectionate, and revealing letter to Dr. Scandella noted earlier. He sends with it designs he has made for a "hermitage" for Volney; he only wishes that he could be close to such inspiring company:

There is nothing I so much desire as to make one of the *garçons philosophes,* who live harmoniously together under one roof *et qui s'amusent à batir des châteaux d'Espagne. . . .*

We have at present here, a Mr. Palmer, with whom you dined at Caleb Lownes. He took it into his head that *your* name was Latrobe.—I am willing to agree with the change, provided you let me have your head & your heart into the bargain.—He is a plain sensible man, who has taken great pains to prepare his mind for cultivation by the eradication of prejudices. We are grown well acquainted without any introduction but the accidental discovery of his having seen you. Should he return to Philadelphia, I intend to accompany him.—He informs me that it is the intention of the Quakers to erect a very large school, in which not only the rudiments of literature, but also a great variety of mechanical trades are to be taught.—Such an institution would require a building large enough to encourage me to remove to Philadelphia were I *employed* and liberally paid,—that is,—were I paid *so much,* that I could employ all my personal income independent of my professional emoluments in my *own* way:—Books,—instruments, etc., etc. You would oblige me much by making an inquiry which you might feel yourself at liberty to do of Mr. Lownes. You see *self interest* will intrude itself into the intercourse of friendship,—but believe me my wish to be nearer to you is so intimately connected with a wish to go to Philadelphia, that I scarce know how to separate them.

Finally, in April, he left Richmond on his first visit to Philadelphia with the hope of becoming the architect of a new Quaker school there and also to study the prison. It proved a momentous step, for, although the plans for the school came to naught, the visit determined his future in many ways. He came to Philadelphia a man still almost unknown professionally, a widower lonely despite his Virginia friends, a man who notwithstanding his two years in the country still felt himself somehow an outsider, an observer—for he had laid down few roots. Two years later, through his work in Philadelphia, he had acquired a wide reputation as engineer and as architect, and he was on the verge of a happy marriage; no longer an outsider, he had become definitely a citizen of the United States, with a commitment entire and devoted. And he had begun to enter the business world, to put his capital to work, in ways that were to open out into strange fields.

The Philadelphia he found in the spring of 1798 was in some respects a shock to him. It was there that the Federalist-democratic schism was most passionate; there "society" was controllingly anti-French and anti-liberal, and John Adams was feeding the fires by his violent attacks not only on the entire French nation but even on liberals like the scientist Dr. Priestley—picking out Latrobe's friend Volney for a particularly virulent assault. Latrobe was acutely conscious of the tension. In his journal (April 19, 1798) after his return to Richmond he wrote:

> Political fanaticism was, during my residence at Philadelphia, at its acme. The communications from our envoys in Paris, the stories about XYZ and the lady, etc., were fresh upon the carpet. . . . To be civilly received by the fashionable people, and to be invited to the President's, it is necessary to visit the British ambassador. To be on terms [of friendship(?)] with Chevalier d'Yrujo, or General Kosciusko even, is to be a marked democrat, unfit for the company of the lovers of order and good government. This I saw. Many of my Virginia friends say I must be mistaken.

But he saw truly. War with France seemed imminent; the Alien and Sedition Laws, passed that very year, only put the final governmental approval on a popular hysteria that lumped together all Frenchmen as atheists and murderers. The group of French refugees and American intellectuals who gathered at Moreau de St. Méry's famous bookshop were increasingly fearful and uncertain; they were all suspect. The bitterness of the Philadelphia Federalist press knew no bounds; the frivolity and maliciousness of its attacks must be read to be believed. The prevailing atmosphere of fear, hate, and hostility to anything new or liberal has not been matched again in the United States until recent years. Gallatin and Jefferson were pictured as devils, as almost treasonable, as men inimical to what today would be called the "American way." William Cobbett's *Porcupine's Gazette* was but the most violent in its abuse—and Cobbett could write.

Latrobe, with his French name, was not spared, and even later when he had established himself in Philadelphia he was referred to—with the manifest aim of denigration—as a "French" engineer. Cobbett, of course, knew better than to assail him as French; but the fact that Latrobe had come from Richmond, where the democrats were strong, was enough to make him the target for a contemptuous note. On April 3, 1798, *Porcupine's Gazette* carried the following taunt:

> At Sans-culotte *Richmond,* the metropolis of *Negro-land, alias* the *Ancient Dominion, alias Virginia,* there was, some time ago, a *farce* acted for the benefit of a girl by the name of Willems, whose awkward gait and gawky voice formerly contributed to the ridicule of the people of Philadelphia.

> The farce was called the *Apology;* it was intended to satirize *me* and *Mr. Alexander Hamilton* (I am always put in good company), and some other friends of the federal Government. The thing is said to be the most detestably dull that ever was mouthed by strollers. The author is one *La Trobe,* the son of an old seditious dissenter; and I am informed that he is now employed in the erecting of a *Penitentiary House,* of which he is very likely to be the *first tenant.*
>
> In short, the farce was acted, and the very next night the playhouse was *burnt down!* I have not heard whether it was *by lightning* or not.

This was only the first of the Federalist attacks upon him which were to endanger his prospects for many years to come.

Yet in Philadelphia the foundations of his success were also laid. Among the letters of introduction he had brought with him was one to the president of the Bank of Pennsylvania, Samuel M. Fox. As they dined together, Fox told Latrobe of the bank's building prospects, and Latrobe made for him then and there a little sketch of what he thought would be suitable. Shortly after this, on April 17, he left Philadelphia and returned to Richmond, deeply disappointed, no doubt, at the failure of his Philadelphia hopes.

In the course of this initial Philadelphia trip he made his first acquaintance with the United States Capitol, with which he was later to be so intimately connected. On his way from Richmond he passed through Washington; there he was introduced to Dr. William Thornton by their mutual acquaintance William McClure, and Thornton escorted him over the building as it then stood. On his return he stopped again in Washington and wandered around the building by himself. Though he noted certain reservations, he was deeply impressed and jotted down in his journal (April 27, 1798): "The Capitol in the federal city, though . . . it is faulty in external detail, is one of the first designs of modern times. As I shall receive a plan of it from either Dr. Thornton or Mr. Volney, I mean to devote a particular discussion to it at my leisure." Unfortunately there is no record of this "particular discussion" in the existing papers.

At that time the external walls of the north (Senate) wing were complete, and much had been accomplished within. The area on the south was a maze of foundation walls, outlining the oval House of Representatives. In the central part the foundations were in an even more confused state, as a result of the controversies between Thornton and his assistant

Hallet about what the final plan was to be. Yet there was enough to make clear, to Latrobe's trained eye, the great size, the monumental plan, the daringly bold conception.[1]

The "faults" that Latrobe found in its exterior detail lay in the basically English Palladian treatment of its pilastered façade and the appearance of many touches of late Baroque detail, like the wreaths around the windows and the general pattern of the rustications and moldings. These were all in the Sir William Chambers vein—far indeed from the quiet surfaces, the restraint, and the power which Latrobe himself loved. Yet here was America making its boldest architectural statement, setting out in stone and mortar a striking expression of its faith; Latrobe admired the faith and the grandeur of the expression, though some of the terms seemed to him old-fashioned.

Architecturally alert in Philadelphia too, he comments on the white marble columns of the First Bank of the United States (by Samuel Blodgett) which gleamed in new brilliance on Second Street:

> Talk to an Englishman of white marble columns . . . thirty feet high, and he is astonished at the magnificence of such columns. In London indeed such columns would not only be magnificent, but really valuable. . . . As nine-tenths of our American, even our Virginian ideas and prejudices, are English, a very large proportion of the admiration . . . bestowed upon the said marble columns has been bestowed upon the material, white marble. Now it happens to be a fact that any other material besides white marble was not to be easily procured at Philadelphia. And so common is its use that the steps to the meanest house and cheeks to cellar doors are frequently made of it. . . .
>
> The white marble columns of the bank are full of bluish and yellowish veins, but they have, notwithstanding, a very beautiful appearance. Sufficient attention has not been paid to the successive heights of the blocks, nor are the joints level. The plain workmanship has been well executed. The sculpture is not good.[2]

One other building in Philadelphia impressed him with wonder more than admiration—the mad huge house L'Enfant had designed for Robert

1. See Wells Bennett and Fiske Kimball, "William Thornton and the Designs of the United States Capitol," *Art Studies*, vol. 1 (1923); Wells Bennett, "Stephen Hallet and His Designs for the United States Capitol, 1791-94," *Journal of the American Institute of Architects*, vol. 4 (1916), pp. 290-95, 324-30, 376-83, 411-18; Glenn Brown, *History of the United States Capitol* (Washington: Government Printing Office, 1900-1903).

2. *The Journal of Latrobe*, with an introduction by J. H. B. Latrobe (New York: Appleton, 1905), pp. 83f.

Morris, which stood unfinished as a result of its owner's bankruptcy. Fascinated, Latrobe writes:

I went several times to the spot and gazed upon it with astonishment before I could form any conception of its composition. It singularly made me wish to make a drawing of it, but the very bad weather prevented me. It is impossible to decide which of the two is the madder, the architect or his employer. Both of them have been ruined by it.

Either then or later, he made several sketches of its details and a general plan of its enormous exterior walls, nearly 120 by 60 feet; these, together with the existing engravings and the descriptions, explain his amazement. A few of Latrobe's own devastating comments give an interesting picture both of the building and of his own taste:

The windows . . . are cased in white marble with mouldings, architraves, and sculpture mixed up in the oddest and most inelegant manner imaginable; all the proportions are bad, all the horizontal and perpendicular lines broken to pieces, the whole mass giving the idea of the reign of Louis XIII in France or James I in England. . . . In the south front are two angle porches. The angle porches are irresistibly laughable things, and violently ugly. . . . There is a profusion of wretched sculpture. . . . The capitals of the columns are of the worst taste. They are a sort of composite and resemble those of ——— at Rome, the production of the worst times of the art.

Just as earlier he had been blind to the Early Renaissance of Silesia, so now he could feel nothing but astonishment and disgust at this almost surrealist unfinished pile which, had it been completed, would have been unique among American houses.

His Philadelphia trip, therefore, was grist to his mill. He returned to Richmond with new and wider visions of his adopted country, its building materials, its architectural hopes and achievements. And in Washington he had had his first glimpse of the city and the building that together were to engross him for so many years of his still undreamed future.

Seven months later, in November, he received a letter from Fox. Latrobe was informed that his design for the Bank of Pennsylvania had been approved, that he had been appointed architect, and that he should return to Philadelphia as soon as possible because construction would begin immediately. Here, at last, was his great chance—for the scheme he had sketched was revolutionary. Now Philadelphia would be able to judge what his capabilities really were; moreover, this opportunity came to him from solid citizens, highly placed both socially and financially. He hurriedly made his plans and said farewell to his Virginia friends, and December saw him at last ensconced in Philadelphia as the architect of the most important private building project of the day.

Personally, however, there were serious gaps in the Philadelphia to which he returned, for the two friends to whose conversation he had most eagerly looked forward were no longer there; Volney and Scandella were gone. Both had been frightened by the Alien and Sedition laws—Volney especially, for he had been in constant correspondence with the French government; Scandella because he realized that, if President Adams had bitterly attacked as innocent a person as the famous Dr. Priestley, his own freedom (libertarian and radical that he was) might be in jeopardy. Volney had fled to France in the autumn. Scandella had gone to New York to seek ocean passage, but as he traversed the Jersey marshes on his way from Philadelphia, where yellow fever had been rampant that summer, he felt the dread symptoms. He arrived in New York desperately ill, tried in vain to get a room at the Tontine Coffee House, and was mercifully taken in by a Philadelphia acquaintance, Elihu Hubbard Smith, at his apartment in 45 Pine Street. There, in a strange city, he died on September 17. Four days later his hospitable friend followed him, struck down himself by the same disease.[3]

Yet an earlier acquaintance with these two brilliant foreigners continued to be beneficial to Latrobe. It was to them that he had sent most of his observations on natural history and on geology, and it was probably through them that his scientific work came to the attention of the American Philosophical Society. In the winter of 1798 he sent to the Society the first of his formal papers, "Memoir on the Sand Hills of Cape Henry." Its receipt is acknowledged in the *Transactions* of December 21; on December 27 it was reported as worthy of publication, and Latrobe agreed to furnish an etched illustration. Seven months later (July 19, 1799) "Ben. Henry Latrobe, Engineer," was duly elected to full membership, and from then on, as long as he was in Philadelphia, he was a constant attendant at American Philosophical Society meetings. For two years, 1800 to 1802, he was on its council. He served on several impor-

3. Harry R. Warfel, *Charles Brockden Brown* . . . (Gainesville, Fla.: University of Florida Press, 1949), pp. 118-22.

tant committees and submitted a number of papers, notably one on the steam engine (May 20, 1803), his account of the descendants of Pocahontas (February 18, 1803) mentioned earlier, and a paper "On Building Stone made use of in Washington" (February 20, 1807). Among these aristocrats of American learning Latrobe found his rightful place, and over a long period of professional confusion and financial worry his membership in the Society must have been to him a continual source of satisfaction; here at least his talents were fully appreciated.

His first years in Philadelphia were busy and encouraging. His design of the Bank of Pennsylvania and the water system of Philadelphia established him as the most accomplished and imaginative of the architects and engineers in the United States. But this period after he moved to the city in 1798, a widower all but unknown save to the few to whom he had carried letters of introduction, brought him another advantage which in the long run may have been even more important. His personal charm, to which his life itself bears witness, won him rapidly the friendship and confidence of many of the most influential families in Philadelphia—especially those who constituted the financial and commercial rather than the political elite.

Meanwhile he was leading a professional life of frenzied activity. Suddenly he found himself not only the architect of an expensive, monumental building—the Bank of Pennsylvania—but also the engineer in charge of the Philadelphia water supply; and other clients came, too. He had to set up an office and to arrange for the purchase of the steam engines and pumps for the water supply, and both of these undertakings had eventful consequences. He employed in his office several persons who were to be important to him—some disastrously. Frederick Graff (1774-1847),[4] the engineer who became famous later on his own account, was at the beginning his clerk of the works on the bank and later the chief draftsman on the waterworks, receiving there a basic engineering training of the greatest value to him and to the country. A Frenchman, Breillat, is also mentioned as a draftsman at this time. But perhaps the most useful member of his staff was the draftsman Adam Traquair, the son of a well-known Philadelphia sculptor and marble worker, James Traquair, who sold busts of famous Americans on an almost mass-pro-

4. His grandfather, Jacob Graff, came to Philadelphia from Hildesheim in 1741 and ran a brickyard. Jacob Graff, Jr., Frederick's father, was a builder.

duction basis, employing several young sculptors in the process; the father also made marble mantels, as his son did after him, and from the Traquairs the architect later obtained many of the mantelpieces for the Capitol and the President's House. Latrobe retained a close friendship with this employee long after they had separated, and when Latrobe moved to Washington Traquair remained a faithful agent to watch over his interests in Philadelphia. Lastly, Latrobe employed as his clerk one John Barber, in whom he reposed an unwarranted confidence. In the summer of 1800, when the architect was away on his wedding trip, Barber absconded, taking with him a considerable sum of money and all the most valuable office and personal papers. He was never captured; he simply vanished. And this loss was a catastrophe. Exactly what the papers were it is impossible to say, but their removal involved Latrobe in untold anxiety, much threatened litigation, and actual money losses of several thousand dollars. It was a bitter blow.

Some of this trouble was probably connected with the confused problem of the waterworks financing. But if the waterworks job brought worry with it, it also brought valuable contacts. Latrobe's scheme was based on the use of two large steam-driven pumps. There was but one source for such pumps—Nicholas Roosevelt, the extraordinary New York inventor, promoter, and charming gentleman, who at that time was the only steam-engine builder of any consequence in the country. Latrobe therefore set out for New York to see him, in the bright October days of 1799; we can follow his course through sketches he made en route. He went through Scotch Plains and Springfield on October 16; two days later he was making sketches of the Falls of the Passaic, fascinated not only by the grandeur of the natural scenery—the vertical crags and the rushing water—but also by the evidences of L'Enfant's work there, for the French architect had built a powder magazine in a cave (which Latrobe sketched), had developed a grandiose scheme for diverting the stream and constructing a canal, and had also prepared a plan for the city. Latrobe tried to find the remaining fragments of the abandoned scheme. From there he went to Laurel Hill, Roosevelt's place near Newark, to Roosevelt's engine plant—the Soho Works, named after the Boulton & Watt factory in England—at Belleville, New Jersey, and then on to New York. Before he returned the two men had drawn up and signed a contract for the engines; but, still more important, Latrobe had gained a new friend—undoubtedly his most intimate associate in all the early American years.

Nicholas Roosevelt remains a baffling and fascinating personality. He was born in New York in 1767, the son of Jacobus, a prosperous goldsmith, and his early acquaintance with metals and the techniques of working them contributed not a little to his future career. But goldsmithing itself was too tame a career for him. He received an excellent general education and showed his delight in machinery even as a child; during the British occupation of New York, when the Roosevelts were living at Esopus, he claimed to have made a model boat operated by spring-driven paddle wheels.[5] Later he secured a patent on the use of paddle wheels for steamboats, but it was never tested in court. As a young man he had gone into the manufacture of steam engines in partnership with J. Smallman, an English-trained engineer for many years a foreman for Boulton & Watt, and by the time of Latrobe's visit he was acknowledged as the master engine builder in the country; only later was his supremacy to be challenged by Oliver Evans of Philadelphia and others.[6] Engine building, however, was but one of Roosevelt's interests. He became a speculator in land and in mineral resources; he had enormous paper assets and great actual debts. With a partner, Jacob Mark (or Marks), he tried in 1797 to obtain from Congress a monopoly in copper prospecting and mining in the United States, and in 1799 he was the proprietor of the famous Schuyler copper mine on the Passaic River in New Jersey—a mine that could be worked only because it was kept water-free by a steam pump which he had built.

Through his wide speculations and his reputation as an inventor, Roosevelt had become closely associated with Robert R. Livingston, "the Chancellor," and together, in 1797, they worked on the application of steam power to boats. Their first model, constructed in 1798, refused to run at a practical speed; it had an elaborate system of propulsion (devised by Livingston) consisting of a submerged box into which water

---

5. In an affidavit attached to his patent application, reprinted in John H. B. Latrobe's *A Lost Chapter in the History of the Steamboat,* Fund Publication 5 (Baltimore: Maryland Historical Society, 1871). The experiment was made near the house of Joseph Oosterhaudt, "four miles above Esopus."

6. Steam engines of a crude type had become fairly common in the United States by 1790, especially for pumping. The greater number were imported. See J. Leander Bishop, *A History of American Manufacture from 1608 to 1860* (Philadelphia: Young; London: Sampson Low & Co., 1864).

was to be received from ahead and ejected aft by means of steam-driven horizontal water wheels. Roosevelt tried to get Livingston to adopt his system of side paddle wheels, but Livingston, who was furnishing the money, refused. Finally, years later, Fulton came into the picture, and it is claimed that Livingston conveyed to him the idea of the Roosevelt side wheels; he used these to propel the *Clermont*.[7] Livingston, Roosevelt, Stevens, and Fulton were all "in" on these early steamboat efforts, sometimes in close co-operation, sometimes in open hostility.

Into this net of crisscrossing interests Latrobe, through his friendship with Roosevelt, was eventually drawn, just as, almost from the beginning, he was drawn into the tangle of Roosevelt's confused and optimistic financial concerns. One instance of this occurred when Philadelphia wanted some surety that Roosevelt would complete his contract for the waterworks engines. To use engines was revolutionary enough, but what if Roosevelt defaulted on his contract through accident, bankruptcy, or the plain visionary character of the scheme? When Roosevelt offered his lease on the Schuyler copper mine as his bond, the Councils—the two governing bodies that together ruled Philadelphia—were still hesitant, because the mine was not then being worked. Latrobe reported favorably on the mine and a year later enlarged his report into a pamphlet, *American Copper Mines* (1800), addressed to the Committee of Commerce and Manufactures of the United States Congress, in support of a petition by Roosevelt and his associates (probably Staudinger, an English-trained engineer, Smallman, and Jacob Mark) for an act of incorporation of a mine and metal company. Then, too, in 1797 Congress had authorized the building of a number of large warships—the "74's"—to be as heavily armed and well built as the best that England or France could construct. They were to have coppered bottoms, and Roosevelt had received the order for the sheet copper. Here also Latrobe later found himself disastrously involved, for he had freely signed notes for large amounts in connection with prepayments to Roosevelt.

Yet at the time of their first meeting all was glowing hope; the prospects of future demands for the services of both men seemed boundless. Steam was to conquer the world, American copper was to supersede

---

7. The fascinating story of the development of the steamboat is interestingly and colorfully told by James Thomas Flexner in *Steamboats Come True . . .* (New York: Viking, 1944). For Roosevelt's patent on paddle wheels, another extraordinary story, see the "lost chapter" on the steamboat by John H. B. Latrobe cited in footnote 6.

English copper, the prosperity of the new country was to be expressed in numberless beautiful buildings and great engineering schemes. The future was rosy.

And more than this common faith drew the two young men (Latrobe was thirty-four and Roosevelt thirty-one) together. Both were mercurial, emotional, optimistic. Both had a need for affection that their ordinary business associates could not satisfy. Both were brilliantly imaginative, and both had felt that crushing sense of frustration or despair which comes when the brightest visions, the greatest talents, and the widest generosities are received with misunderstanding, scorn, or open hostility. For years they remained the closest of friends, and Latrobe's letters—even when sharply critical of his friend's unwisdom or impracticality—usually end with the warmest, least conventional subscripts.[8]

The year 1798 brought to Latrobe another acquaintance who was to be of fateful importance to him—Justus Erich Bollmann (1769-1821), known in America as Eric Bollman, whose track we have already crossed. Bollman had been Mme de Staël's agent in helping to get her little band of refugees out of France and to safety in England in 1792. Then, two years later, after he had traveled widely around Germany and Austria, ostensibly on business but probably in the interests of French refugees, came his audacious, vain, but so nearly successful attempt (November 5, 1794) to liberate Lafayette from his Austrian prison at Olmütz. He and his colleague Francis Kinloch Huger of South Carolina, whom he had met in Vienna, were both arrested but set free in July, 1795. Most of the money for this extraordinary coup had come from Americans, through a Mr. and Mrs. Church in London. After the failure of the scheme it was natural for Bollman to think of coming to the United States, where his attempt to free the famous friend of America would, he thought, guarantee him a brilliant future. As a German compatriot said of him, on meeting him in London, he "is an amiable man, possessing imagination, and is very clever, but he is light-hearted and not accustomed to work continuously." Bollman sailed for America in October, 1795, and arrived in New York on New Year's Day, 1796. There he met Roosevelt, became interested in his steam engines, and then proceeded to Philadelphia. He

8. Two characteristic examples: "In the meantime, if there is anything certain under heaven, it is that you hold the first place in our esteem, good opinion, & friendship. Mrs. Latrobe joins in affectionate respect with yours, B. H. Latrobe" (December 17, 1804); "Heaven bless you my dear friend, Yours affectionately, B. H. Latrobe" (July 1, 1805).

had a letter to Alexander Hamilton, who sent him on to Mount Vernon; here he found young Lafayette solicitous that something more be done to aid his imprisoned father, and apparently Bollman pressed the matter. Washington himself was prophetically suspicious of him from the beginning and wrote Hamilton (May 8, 1796) that Bollman "will be found a troublesome guest among us." [9]

We do not know when Latrobe first met Bollman; it may even have been in London, in 1792, when Bollman was staying there with Talleyrand, or possibly it was in Virginia in 1796 or 1797. The first definite news we have of him in the existing Latrobe papers is in the summer of 1799, and it reveals them as already good friends. There was yellow fever in Philadelphia again that summer—not so devastating a scourge as the year before but violent enough to send many out of town. Among those who left were Bollman and Latrobe, who joined in taking a house (or part of a house) together in near-by Germantown. When they left it at the beginning of October, there was a dispute about the rent with the landlord, Creider; they refused to pay the total, and Creider kept Latrobe's horse as security. Bollman, who evidently felt in some way responsible, contrived somehow to get hold of the horse (he was always a believer in direct action) and returned it to Latrobe. Creider sued Latrobe for its value, and the suit dragged on for almost a decade. Nearly nine years later Latrobe wrote to Thomas Ross, his lawyer in Philadelphia (January 9, 1808): "I never dreamed that Creider's old affair was yet alive. It is now near 9 years ago, & all the witnesses are dead and absent, or worse than either. My servant is dead. Bollman is God knows where. Bollman is going to the Devil [this was after Bollman's involvement in the Burr conspiracy]. The constable who replevined [the horse] was dead drunk, and almost killed the horse in riding him home. . . . I can only beg you to accommodate the matter as much as possible for my interest." Bollman seemed to have a genius for involving his friends and associates in difficulties, yet so great was his charm that he succeeded in winning back the friendship of almost all those he had innocently or carelessly wronged.

In 1799 Bollman was still at the summit of his American career. With his brother Ludwig (or Lewis) he had opened a wide-spreading export-

9. Fritz Redlich, *Eric Bollmann and Studies in Banking,* in the series *Essays in American Economic History* (New York: Stechert [c1944]).

import house with notable correspondents abroad; in England, for example, it was the famous house of Baring which backed them, and in Germany they had friends of equal importance. Their business flourished, and they broadened it recklessly. This was during the English-French war, when American shipowners and businessmen were piling up fortunes as neutral traders. The Bollmans bought in Germany and sold in England or the United States; they bought in England and sold on the Continent or in America. This three-sided trade collected fat profits at each apex of the triangle, and to the adventurous Bollmans every profit gained was the signal for more extensive speculative plunges. While this neutral trade lasted the firm was opulent, but when the Peace of Amiens was signed in 1802 the bottom fell out and the firm crashed in a spectacular bankruptcy that involved even Latrobe, as we shall see.

One other acquaintance Latrobe made in these early years—with Charles Willson Peale—was significant, for the Peales painted the two best portraits of Latrobe that we possess.[10] Moreover, just as in the case of Roosevelt—though on a less emotional level—in Peale Latrobe found a man with many characteristics like his own. Both were artist-scientists; both were deeply curious about natural phenomena and at the same time devoted to the aesthetically creative. Both, like Jefferson, were excited by the new possibilities that invention offered for increasing efficiency, for making processes easier. From machines for taking silhouettes to devices for excavating and handling a mammoth's skeleton, and to arrangements for projecting changing lights on moving scenes, Peale's restless mind wandered, taking suggestions, improving upon them, and developing them into instruments of practical usefulness. Among the devices he developed, probably the most important was the polygraph. This was a highly organized kind of pantograph arranged so that copies—replicas—of letters and documents could be made at the same time that the original was being written. It had first been devised by an English inventor, Harrington, a visitor to Philadelphia, but it was refined, popularized, and sold by Peale. Over a period of years Peale was at work improving the first crude models and welcoming suggestions from its users. Latrobe was one of the first owners of the polygraph, obtaining it apparently in

10. The earlier, probably painted in Philadelphia between 1800 and 1805, and possibly a wedding portrait, was by Charles Willson Peale. The later, which shows a much more mature face—the face of one who has suffered much—and may date from 1816, has been attributed to Rembrandt Peale by the elder Peale's biographer, Charles Sellers.

September, 1803; it was through Latrobe that Jefferson obtained his own, and it is partly because of the polygraph that we now possess such full records of the correspondence of both men.

Thus the early Philadelphia years of Latrobe were immensely rewarding to him. By the end of this period he had close friends in the worlds of finance, of invention, and of art. He was a Fellow of the American Philosophical Society. His charm, his knowledge, the wide scope of his mind—these were all becoming ever more widely appreciated. And in Nicholas Roosevelt he had found his first really intimate American friend—a man who for years was to be closely associated with him and was to bring him much happiness and much pain in the time to come.

But a still more important relationship dates from this period—a relationship that made his hardships tolerable and his triumphs doubly worth while—for he found the perfect wife.

Among the important families he had met were the Hazlehursts. Isaac Hazlehurst and his brother Robert had a general mercantile business—export, import, and credit. The brothers had come from Manchester, England, where Isaac was born in 1742 and Robert in 1754. How Latrobe met them is unknown; it was very likely through Samuel Fox. Isaac had prospered in the import and export business he had set up in Philadelphia and had accumulated a sizable capital. When Latrobe became acquainted with him, he was less rich than he had been; for in the Revolution he had been a patriot, to his cost. As a close friend and associate of Robert Morris, he had thrown into the struggle the greater part of his funds and had been one of the signers of Colonial notes. Robert Morris had crashed in a disastrous bankruptcy, and his fall had brought hardship, failure, and poverty to his associates, Isaac Hazlehurst among them. But the Hazlehursts rose supreme over the troubles; their strong commercial connections with the other states—especially South Carolina, where Robert and his son had settled—as well as with European exporters saved them from bankruptcy. Isaac and his family could still live a life of gentlemanly comfort, and he maintained not only a large house in Philadelphia but also a more than comfortable estate, Clover Hill, across the Delaware at Mount Holly, New Jersey.[11] With all the Hazlehursts Latrobe was soon on terms of close intimacy.

---

11. On February 27, 1769, Isaac had married Joanna (or Juliana, as she was more frequently called) Purviance (1741-1804), of a fine Philadelphia family; their son Andrew

Mary Elizabeth Hazlehurst (1771-1841) was the daughter of Isaac Hazlehurst, and between her and the young architect a growing affection sprang up and ripened. During 1799, one gathers, much of his leisure was spent with the family, and Mary and he gradually grew more and more attached, while her father and Latrobe developed a mutual respect and affection that made their relationship much closer than the usual one between a son and father-in-law. Finally the couple were married on May 2, 1800, at the father's Philadelphia house, by the Right Reverend Dr. White, the Episcopal bishop. The marriage was obviously as warmly welcomed by all the Hazlehursts as by the bride and groom themselves.

It is impossible to stress too strongly the importance of this event and its consequences. The pair seem to have been ideally fitted for each other. Mary was the architect's constant helper, his constant inspiration; she understood him as few others did—knew his moods of elation and of depression, understood the strains behind his occasional outbreaks of tactless directness, and gave herself heartily and wholly to being his "helpmeet" in the fine old sense, his companion, and his love.

This was not the easiest of lifetime tasks for a woman to assume. The wife of any artist has a difficult time under the best of circumstances, and here was an artist of the greatest creative talent who was also professionally a revolutionary and was trying to establish architecture as a high and respected profession in a country which still thought of building largely in terms of the contractor-designer—a country widely permeated with a kind of basic anti-aestheticism. John Adams had well expressed this trend; he dreaded the time when Americans would become interested in the fine arts.[12] Yet only a few years after Adams's presidency we find La-

---

married his Baltimore cousin Frances Purviance, who was the daughter of Robert Purviance, Collector of the Port of Baltimore. The other children were Robert, Samuel, John, Richard, Isaac, and a daughter, Mary Elizabeth.

12. Adams's letters to his wife—see *Familiar Letters of John Adams and His Wife Abigail Adams . . .* (New York: Hurd and Houghton, 1876)—often give expression to this feeling. Examples include the following:

In 1778 (p. 334): "My dear countrymen! how shall I persuade you to avoid the plague of Europe! Luxury has as many and as bewitching charms on your side of the ocean as on this; and luxury, wherever she goes, effaces from human nature the image of the Divinity. If I had power I would forever banish and exclude from America all gold, silver, precious stones, alabaster, marble, silk, velvet, and lace."

In 1780 (p. 381), after a walk through the gardens of Versailles: "It is not indeed the fine arts which our country requires; the useful, the mechanic arts are those which we have occasion for in a young country as yet simple and not far advanced in luxury,

trobe pleading for and winning sculpture for the United States Capitol. Politically and socially Latrobe cherished firmly held ideas—often unpopular ones—and he was a man who had already been immersed in bitter controversy and was destined to be so enmeshed all his life. Here, too, was an artist and a scholar of the broadest capacity, a linguist, a man who was at least a theoretical musician and one who knew Hebrew, Greek, Latin, and most of the important western European languages. His was a cultural equipment that few in America could share, and this contributed to the feeling of isolation he had experienced. All of that feeling disappeared in the complete companionship that grew up between him and Mary Hazlehurst.

Physically, too, Latrobe needed the kind of home center and the kind of care that only marriage could offer. Tall and muscularly powerful though he was, he was never a robust person. He was subject to and periodically incapacitated by attacks of nervous indigestion and the various malarial fevers going around. A glutton for work, he was almost destroyed by overwork. At the death of his first wife he had had a serious nervous breakdown; later, when the Fulton-Livingston-Roosevelt-Latrobe steamship partnership collapsed in Pittsburgh in 1815, he had another almost like it—he became listless, could not concentrate, could not even read. It was Mary who rescued him then, with what sympathy and understanding only the imagination can picture. It was she who wrote to acquaintances in Washington, without her husband's knowledge; it was she who roused his friends to procure his second appointment as architect of the Capitol, and with this his spirits rose and he went on, again triumphant.

Nor was her value merely that of nurse and friend and lover. Socially as well she was an enormous asset. Brought up in the best Philadelphia society, she knew the ways of the great world of her time. She had an excellent singing voice, in talk she was warm and witty, and her conversation formed an admirable complement to his more exuberant and imaginative discourse. Later, in Washington, their house became one of

---

although perhaps much too far for her age and character. . . . My sons ought to study mathematics and philosophy, geography, natural history and naval architecture, navigation, commerce, and agriculture, in order to give their children a right to study painting, poetry, music, architecture, statuary, tapestry, and porcelain."

Adams's implied concept of the fine arts as unnecessary luxuries is characteristic. I owe this reference to Mr. Wayne Andrews of the New-York Historical Society.

the well-known *salons* of its time, largely through Mary's magnetic presence and her social skill.

On the eve of his marriage Latrobe had taken and furnished a house in Philadelphia, but Isaac Hazlehurst and his wife were loath to part with their daughter and for six months the young people lived with the Hazlehursts at Clover Hill. On their wedding trip they went to New York; altogether they were gone almost six weeks. On the way they visited Newark, where at the Roosevelt home, Laurel Hill, Latrobe introduced his bride to his closest friend. They went on to Paterson (May 28, 1800) and he showed her the thrilling sight of the Falls of the Passaic. We know they were in New York on the fourth of June, and from there they visited Gouverneur Morris at Morrisania. After another short stay with Nicholas Roosevelt at Laurel Hill, they returned to Philadelphia on June 14, for two weeks, and then rejoined the Hazlehursts at Clover Hill on the first of July. It was an exciting and rewarding trip for both bride and groom. She for the first time traveled away from her family and was warmly welcomed at Laurel Hill and elsewhere. He had the personal joy of being a tender and enthusiastic guide and the professional satisfaction of seeing Roosevelt's great engines for the Philadelphia waterworks well under way. Then the Latrobes had the pleasure of two weeks alone in Philadelphia (probably at the house he had taken for them), savoring their life together as he worked hard at the Bank of Pennsylvania drawings and the details of the waterworks.

His wife early appreciated that there was a lingering gap in the completeness of her husband's life. His two children, Lydia and Henry, were still in England and it had been more than four years since he had seen them. She insisted that they be brought over as soon as possible—in fact, she had made this a condition of their marriage. It was a daring and a generous impulse, and the necessary preliminary steps must have been taken at once, for mail to England was slow and passages back from England were long. Through the instrumentality of the ever helpful Christian Latrobe the matter was settled, and in October the children arrived, brought over in the charge of one of the Markoe family who luckily was returning to Philadelphia at the time. The two halves of Latrobe's life—in England and in America—were at last united.

The experiment was as successful as it was generous. Seventeen years later, after Henry's premature death in New Orleans, Latrobe wrote to

Henry's aunt, Miss Sellon, a long letter (November 15, 1817) full not only of his grief but of his love and admiration for his second wife:

> Of my wife I can only say that when I married her, her wit, her accomplishments, & her elegant person placed her at the head of the best society of her age in Philadelphia, but the kindness & benevolence of her heart gave her a much more exalted character, and when I took her from amidst the numerous poor neighbors around her father's estate in New Jersey, a scene occurred which I shall not easily forget, so much was her departure regretted. With such a step-mother, no apprehensions of neglect or severity could find room, and in fact, from the first hour of their meeting, little Henry [then seven] attached himself to her with peculiar fondness, while the approaches of Lydia were more cold and tardy. From that moment an affection grew up between Henry and his new mother, that had more of freedom and less of the constraint of duty, than might possibly have subsisted between a mother and a child. . . . To [her own children], acting without deliberation, she is as we all are, sometimes hasty, & always unceremonious, while to Lydia and Henry she mixed the truest affection, with much more consideration of their own wishes and feelings. . . . With him [Henry] she scolded, she wept, & she laughed & railed without restraint, and her correspondence with Henry in New Orleans, while it would do honor to the first pens of the age, was, in the course of our numerous vexations of the last four years, a never failing refuge to her in her most moody dispositions, & under her severest trials.

Latrobe's first visit to Philadelphia in the spring of 1798 and his final removal there in the early winter of the same year were therefore epochal for his career. In Pennsylvania, after all sorts of tentative beginnings in Virginia, he achieved a definite foundation for his life. Before unknown, now he had nation-wide fame. In Richmond a centerless wanderer, here he became a happily married man with a brilliant wife. All the foundations of his American future had now been laid and promised fair.

CHAPTER

8

Architect and Engineer in Philadelphia

Many of the difficulties Latrobe had faced in establishing his career were innate both in his own personality and in the conditions of the time; but his own too informal business methods and the political passions of the period were not the only barriers over which he had to climb in Philadelphia. Even more important was the fact that of all American cities this was the one in which the old system of builder design was most powerful. The Carpenters Company of Philadelphia was a strong, arrogant organization, assiduous in its attacks on everything that threatened its hold on the building industry. It had produced two great evils: first, a system that was by nature conservative in both taste and construction; second, the fallacious idea that *design costs nothing,* for the design costs were hidden in the total contract payments. Even good businessmen could not realize that the prevailing system opened the way to enormous abuses and was as uneconomic as it was deceptive.

This condition made Latrobe's practice difficult. The opposition of the Carpenters Company to his own ideal of complete architectural services was constant. People admired his work—and then, to avoid his fees, went to a member of the Carpenters Company for their own houses. When daring innovators commissioned him, they always protested his bills; what they paid seemed to them almost a gift rather than a payment for services, and again and again he was forced to accept a pittance or to endure endless delays in getting his final amounts.

The idea that full architectural services were an unnecessary luxury oftened bedeviled his later practice; it was but one of the hardships faced by a man ahead of his time who was giving his life to the task of molding the world more closely to his ideals and making it aware of the potentialities for better and more efficient living and working that it could possess by merely, so to speak, stretching out its hand. And Philadelphia brought these paradoxes particularly to the front; for, though without a doubt it was the cultural capital of the country, it was also a town permeated with a kind of traditional smugness. It was successful, and knew it; it was wealthy, and knew it; it had many of the finest buildings in the country, and knew that too. Why change the system under which these buildings had been erected?

And the system was strongly entrenched. The Carpenters Company of Philadelphia was a true guild. Its secrecy, its controlled prices, and its guild traditions of form and detail were all willingly subscribed to by the wealthiest and most powerful builder-designers in the city. Its *Price Book,*[1] published as late as 1784, contains typical details of dormers, windows, cornices, and mantels, all of which go back in style to the later Georgian Colonial; even the work of the Adam brothers had made but little dent on this impervious surface of traditional forms. And, five whole years after the completion of the Bank of Pennsylvania, Owen Biddle's *The Young Carpenter's Assistant,* published in 1805, which boasts on its title page that it was approved by the Carpenters Company (of which its author was a member), contains scarcely a hint—save perhaps for a slight attentuation of proportions in doors and door trims—of the changes in architectural style that were already under way.

This guild system naturally guaranteed a generally high level in building standards and a general over-all adequacy of design. The fragments of Philadelphia that remain to us from the last decade of the eighteenth and first fifteen years or so of the nineteenth century reveal that harmonious but backward character; repeatedly the forms used in some of these remaining buildings would lead the unwary scholar to date them twenty years earlier than their actual erection, so persistent and all-pervasive was the guild conservatism. And to this whole system the work of Latrobe was a ringing challenge.

Of course in the long run the architect system was bound to win out. It permitted experiment and novelty as the other system never could;

1. The secrecy of the guild is illustrated by the fact that in 1817, when Jefferson asked Latrobe to send him a copy of the Philadelphia price book (in connection with the building of the University of Virginia), he was unable to obtain it and was forced to send a Pittsburgh price book instead. In his letter to Jefferson (December 6, 1817) he notes that the Philadelphia price book is a secret document available only to the Carpenters Company and encloses a letter of Thackara, the plasterer, as proof.

it was flexible; it centralized the design and executive authority in one person; and it completely removed the architect from financial involvement in the work and enabled him to bring to bear on any question a mind completely free from economic pressure. But final victory was only to come after Latrobe's death, for the earlier system yielded ground slowly. It attempted to rejuvenate its products by wholesale copying of the style and the details developed by free architects. Undoubtedly it still had a definite function to fulfill; for the amount of building required in the rapidly growing cities of the early decades of the nineteenth century was far greater than could be handled by the relatively few trained architects, and it was a happy circumstance for Philadelphia that the Carpenters Company could keep the general level of building as high as it was and thus, by such copying, slowly popularize the new forms even when the copies were in themselves inept or unthinking.

Yet to Latrobe, eager to take advantage of his new fame by widening his practice, the opposition of the Carpenters Company was a hardship. Later he had more work of more kinds than he could take care of, but in 1800 to 1803—newly married, with a growing family and a high social position that entailed a relatively expensive standard of living—he was prepared, and eager, for more commissions than he could get. The problem in Philadelphia was continually troublesome. As late as January 23, 1812, in a letter to Joseph Delaplaine, the Philadelphia publisher, who had asked him to write a book on architecture for the firm to publish, he broke out in bitterness:

> . . . For my professional reputation I should have done enough had I only built the Bank of Pennsylvania and supplied the city with water. . . . As to the Carpenters Company, I do not thank that body, however much I respect individuals, for their praise. It is not their fault that I have maintained my professional character and standing. They have done me the honor to copy and to disgrace by their application almost all my designs from a moulding to a plan of a whole building. . . . I have changed the taste of a whole city. My very follies and faults and whims have been mimicked, and yet there is not a single instance in which I have been consulted in which some carpenter has not counteracted me. . . . If I write at all, it must be for men of sense, and of some science.

Latrobe was thoroughly aware of the historical basis for the system. For instance, in a letter to his brother Christian (November 4, 1804) he says:

You are probably right in the difference you imagine that there is between doing business here & in England in my profession. Had I in England, executed what I have here,—I should now be able to sit down quietly & enjoy *otium cum dignitate.* But in England the crowd of those whose talents are superior to mine is so great, that I should never perhaps have elbowed through them. Here I am the only successful Architect & Engineer. I have had to break the ice for my successors, & what was more difficult to destroy the prejudices the villainous Quacks in whose hands the public works have hitherto been, had raised against me. There, in fact lay my greatest difficulty.

Nearly two years later (July 12, 1806), in a long letter of advice to his pupil Robert Mills (who had gone to Charleston, South Carolina, in an abortive effort to establish himself in practice there), he writes:

The profession of architecture [which Latrobe had earlier in the letter termed "a liberal profession"] has been hitherto in the hands of two sets of men. The first,—of those who from travelling or from books have acquired some knowledge of the theory of the art,—but know nothing of its practice—the second—of those who know nothing but the practice,—and whose early life being spent in labor, & in the habits of a laborious life,—have no opportunity of acquiring the theory. The complaisance of these two sets of men to each other, renders it difficult for the Architect to get in between them, for the Building mechanic finds his account in the ignorance of the gentleman-architect;—as the latter does in the submissive deportment which interest dictates to the former. . . .

He goes on to criticize Mills adversely for tamely accepting clients' suggestions which jeopardize the integrity of his designs, and continues:

It will be answered, "If you are paid for your designs & directions, he that expends his money on the building has an undoubted right to build what he 'pleases.'" If you are paid!!—I ask in the first place, are you paid?—*No!* The custom of all Europe has decided that 5 p cent on the cost of a building, with all personal expenses incurred, shall be the pay of the Architect.—This is just as much as is charged by a Merchant for the transaction of business,—expedited often in a few minutes by the labor of a Clerk: while the Architect must watch the daily progress of the work perhaps for years, pay all his clerkhire, & repay to himself the expense of an education greatly more costly than that of a merchant.

Then he tells the sad tale of his experience in getting paid for the Richmond penitentiary referred to earlier.[2]

---

2. Additional excerpts from the letter are given in the Appendix.

There was one other difficulty that faced architects attempting to work in Philadelphia in harmony with the Carpenters Company—the matter of superintendence. Contractors would build from architects' plans, but only if the authority for the detailing and the supervision of construction was handed over to them. Latrobe tried this method once with disastrous result in Sedgeley, and he warns a subsequent client, Waln, against it in a letter (April 1, 1805) about his proposed house:

As to the superintendence of the building, I mean, merely, if I used that phrase, that which is a thing of course in Europe, namely the furnishing of drawings for the *whole detail* as the building progresses. Otherwise the architect becomes responsible in reputation for all the whims, the blunders, many of them perhaps expensive, of the various mechanics who execute. It is unfortunate for the profession that here the department of design & direction is not separate from that of execution, by which means, especially in the erection of Mr. Crammond's house on the Schuylkill I have been disgraced both by the deformity & expense of some parts of the building, because, after giving the first general design, I had no further concern with it.

And other later letters take up the same theme.

Nevertheless the architect found clients in Philadelphia besides the Bank of Pennsylvania—few at first, but in increasing numbers as time went on and the advantages of full architectural services gradually became evident. One of the first was Edward Shippen Burd, for whom Latrobe designed a large house on Chestnut at Ninth Street; it dates from 1801-2, according to a list of Latrobe's works which he sent to Robert Goodloe Harper (January 12, 1816). Old photographs show it as an almost arrogant challenge to the prevailing Philadelphia conservatism. Its motifs were familiar enough—arched windows under recessed brick arches, a Palladian window above a fanlight entrance door—but it is the way in which they are put together that shows the architect's hand. The central, three-bay, three-story body of the house is flanked by one-story wings, topped by a thin marble coping that aligns with the second-floor windows. The main cornice is thin—almost meager—as though to call no attention at all from the basic geometry of the whole and the power of its red brick walls. Power indeed is instinctive in every line, and the three-sided marble steps that sweep so boldly up to the door compose magnificently with the masses of the side wings. The Burd house is a strong chord of simple, clearly related notes struck with convincing authority. This is the most London-like of all Latrobe's American houses—nowhere else did he so severely restrict his window areas—and it bears a close relationship in form and details to the Admiralty Building in London which Cockerell planned while the young architect was one of his most important designers and on which Latrobe undoubtedly worked.

Another early house was Sedgeley, the William Crammond house (already mentioned), which stood just outside the town on the banks of the Schuylkill. Here again Latrobe was revolutionary, for the house was Gothic—the first American example of the Gothic Revival in house design. It was, in fact, Latrobe's first domestic commission in Philadelphia, and the controversy it aroused may have turned his mind back to quieter, more classic types for his future houses, though it could not entirely destroy the romantic appeal that Gothic held for him, as we shall see. The house is known to us today only through engravings, for it has long since disappeared. Like all the architect's work, it was basically geometric in scheme. The structure itself was a simple rectangle with a hipped roof, apparently a variation of the typical five-bay house; around this was a one-story porch, open and airy on the front and the flanks but at the corners emphasized by square masonry pavilions pierced with arched openings. Perhaps memories of the corner pavilions of many English Jacobean houses, such as Wollaton Hall, lay behind his use of these corner motifs. In classic guise they had already appeared in the designs for the Tayloe house mentioned earlier. The openings in these pavilions were topped with pointed arches. The porch posts were of a simplified Batty Langley Gothic type, and there were Tudor drip molds over the windows of the main house. The cornices were Gothic in profile as well; that is as far as the "Gothic" went. The house, though it aroused enthusiasm on the part of some Philadelphians, never pleased its designer. And rightly so; for at its best it was a piece of superficial design that was merely novel and at its worst an awkward attempt to marry incompatible elements. Of that triumphant integration of use, structure, and beauty which is so evident in Latrobe's best work there is hardly a trace.

Sedgeley was a bitter lesson to him. As we have seen, he claimed that in execution it was butchered and its details were caricatured, but it is doubtful whether it could have been a great success even if he had had the complete detailing and superintendence in his own hands; for Latrobe's Gothic, though sometimes picturesque, was never solidly based on a knowledge of the idiom and often showed itself awkward and crude. Yet Sedgeley is important in the history of Philadelphia, because it was the first of its type and because like the Bank of Pennsylvania and the waterworks it was unprecedented.

One of the earliest of Philadelphia's red-brick rows was also Latrobe's. Built between 1800 and 1802 for Joseph Sansom, the great real-estate magnate, it ran along Walnut Street between Sixth and Seventh Streets—fairly far out of town for its time. Latrobe mentions the row in a letter (February 10, 1814) to Richard Dale and William Wilmer of Philadelphia, who wanted him to design for them a building for Washington Hall. Warning his correspondents that they have seriously underestimated the costs, he writes: "In 1800, when Sansom's row in Walnut Street was built, I had the best means of ascertaining the actual cost—\$4.87½ p. superficial foot. . . . These houses were built in the most economical manner for sale. . . ." Though simple, the houses had doors of distinguished detail and excellent proportions, and they set a standard of general amenity for much future Philadelphia building; but they were not an important commission, and one hazards the guess that they brought in only a small fee.

Another project of this period, though it was never built—a house for the British minister, Liston—is eloquent of Latrobe's search for simple geometrical forms.[3] The sketches show a cross-shaped main-floor plan over a square basement, crowned by a cylindrical upper floor; obviously a dome was intended above this. The plans display a remarkable mastery not only in the development of exciting room shapes but also in the achieving of a workable and convenient arrangement of the whole. It is a tour de force; nevertheless it is a true building design and not merely a paper fantasy, and the structural thinking is sound.[4]

But it was the Bank of Pennsylvania, the building that had originally brought him to Philadelphia, which held the greatest import for his career and for the future of American architecture. Begun at the end of

3. This design is reproduced in Fiske Kimball, *Domestic Architecture of the American Colonies and of the Early Republic* (New York: Scribner's, 1922).

4. In the letter to Dr. Scandella mentioned earlier Latrobe notes his work on the *hermitage* for the *garçons philosophiques*—Volney and his friends. This, too, according to Volney's wishes, was to have been a circular house. Perhaps the idea had been bubbling away in Latrobe's mind ever since, until in this house for the British minister there came the perfect opportunity of expressing it in different terms.

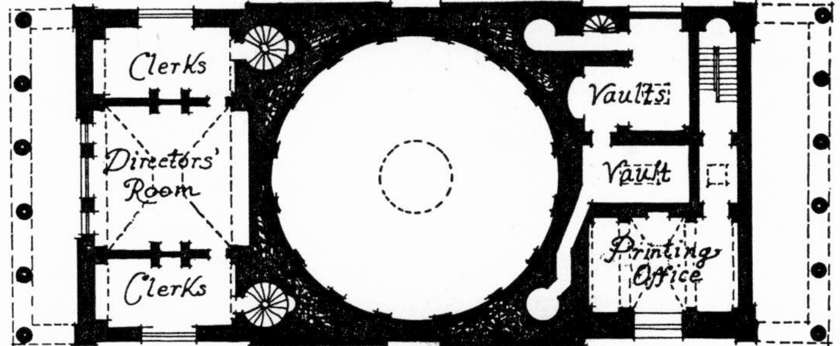

In Historical Society of Pennsylvania

FIGURE 12. Bank of Pennsylvania, Philadelphia. Plans. Redrawn from Latrobe's drawings.

1798 and complete by the summer of 1800, it was a landmark in the architecture of the United States. It was the country's first Greek Revival structure and also the first building in which masonry vaults were used integrally as a major means for achieving architectural effect.[5] And incontestably it was a beautiful structure, the destruction of which by the government in the 1860's is one of the tragedies of Philadelphia's long history of apathy toward its important monuments.

The building had a rare simplicity, of which the exterior was a direct statement. A central square block was lengthened by two rectangular

5. It was not the first large masonry-vaulted building in the country, however. That honor, so far as we know today, belongs to the old Philadelphia jail, built shortly before the Revolution as a fireproof and escape-proof structure.

wings, each with a portico at its end; above the central block rose the stepped stages of the shallow domed roof and a simply detailed cupola with large glass areas to light the space within. Four little stone lodges at the corners of the lot recalled the corner pavilions of the Tayloe design. It was all in all a composition of distinguished visual richness produced by a fundamentally simple geometry.

That form arose naturally from the plan. The nexus of the whole was the great central banking room, a circular space roofed with a brick dome and lighted by large windows on the cross axis and by the cupola crowning the whole. In one of the long ends was the entrance, through a barrel-vaulted vestibule, with offices on either side; above this was the money and security vault. On the other end was the stockholders' room, and above it the directors' room, both roofed with ingenious cross vaults, the upper room receiving its chief light from a skylight. For the needs of the time it was a simple and workable plan. One portico was the porch used by the public; the other, facing a little gardened area, served as the approach for the bank officials; in the center was the banking room where the public and the bank staff had their chief dealings.

Moreover, the spaces developed by this simple functional plan were beautiful both as units and in relation to one another. Their internal volumes, conditioned by the vaulted ceilings, were gracious and strong, and the almost stripped character of the detail only added to the total effect by emphasizing these shapes. Thus the vestibule had a strong directional sense, and the curved ends of the stockholders' and directors' rooms repeated in feeling the curves of the shallow groined vaults. Even in the climax, the banking room itself, there was the same reticence of detail. There were corner niches without impost moldings or archivolts; in shape and size they repeated the door recesses and the windows on the chief cross axes. Above these there was a frieze of delicately recessed panels with slightly raised frames; then, higher still, the impost for the dome, simplified into a raised band supporting a single projecting cap mold. The segmental dome had coffers sunk just far enough to create delicate lines of light and shade which made evident and emphasized the domical form.

Fortunately we know, from a long letter Latrobe wrote to Samuel Fox (July 8, 1805) when the plaster was sufficiently dry and the whole sufficiently settled for the final interior decoration to be applied, that the color scheme he planned for the interior had the same quality of restraint and precision. The banking-room walls were to be "pale but warm oker or straw," but a white bead was to outline the niches. The margins of the panels above were to be white, with the panels themselves a lighter straw color. He noted that "if the white is unmixed it will have a bluish cast." The frieze beneath the dome was to be white, slightly blued, bearing a painted Greek fret of a dark russet color. He advised that a sample should be tried in place, and added: "I have tried this Greek method of painting myself . . . and have always been struck with the beauty of the contrast and relief produced by it." The marble he wished left unpainted, and the dome itself was to have the ribs between the coffers pale blue, with the moldings and field of the coffers themselves like the wall panels beneath; the interior of the cupola above was to be either white or stone color. The entrance vestibule was to be a warm brown with a ceiling of white, pale blue, and red; and the directors' room and the president's room were both to have gray walls, with a pale-blue ceiling and the ornamented bands a light red, carrying ornaments of yellowish white.

How much of this scheme was adopted it is impossible to say, but Latrobe's recommendations reveal the clarity, the subtle harmonies, and the occasional accents he had in mind. For him the spirit of the forms had to be echoed in the spirit of the colors applied to them. These notes also show his fear that much that he advocated might seem strange to conservative Philadelphia. We trust that Samuel Fox took his advice and that the bank stood a monument to his color sense as well as his structural and creative genius.

It is interesting to speculate on the sources for the particular character of graceful and powerful austerity which Latrobe expressed with such skill in this building and which came to be the ruling characteristic of his best work. In 1792 Soane had completed the first of the great halls of the Bank of England—the bank-stock hall—and in it appeared many of the vaults with simplified detail which were the hallmarks of his later style.

In addition to Soane, there is another possible source of inspiration for the Bank of Pennsylvania—the work of Robert and James Adam. The unmolded niche is common alike in the work of the Adams and in that of Latrobe, as is the use of segmental arches and ceilings and of rectangular wall panels to contrast with curve-headed openings, but the way in which Latrobe used these motifs is quite different from that employed by the Adam brothers. Latrobe was fond of direct structural relationships and a simple continuity of major elements; the Adams, on the other hand, preferred a more complicated counterpoint of alternation and contrast. And, when one examines the moldings and the detail, the differences between Latrobe and the Adam brothers become much more striking, for in these matters Latrobe's own taste for simple and Greek-inspired forms was supreme.

The entire Bank of Pennsylvania, in detail as in plan and structure, was in fact a true creation bearing everywhere its designer's imprint. What he had seen in London before his departure, like what he had seen in Europe, undoubtedly remained with him, for his architectural memory was prodigious. Yet from that background, as from a rich and fertile soil, his own style grew as something entirely new. What Latrobe designed was his own; it was permeated with the geometricizing spirit of his time and was expressed with a power and a restraint then entirely unknown elsewhere in America.

The end porticoes are Greek Ionic. They are based on the simple type of Greek Ionic (as illustrated by Stuart and Revett) seen in the now-lost Temple on the Ilissus. How closely Latrobe's design followed the famous plate it is impossible to tell, but it is significant that even here he was detailing "out of his own head"; for most of his books, as has been noted, had been captured by the French and had never reached him in America, and later he boasted that he had designed the bank with no reference whatsoever to books.

In construction the bank was remarkable. Reversed arches below grade distributed the heavy pier loads to continuous foundations. The groined vaults over the smaller rooms helped to concentrate the loads and thrusts at points where heavy masonry masses could receive them. The major dome itself, 44′-6″ in diameter, was of brick 24″ thick in its lower portion and 1′-4″ thick above. It was received on a marble impost, and to enclose the oculus beneath the cupola another bold course of marble was used. The thrust was taken care of by two heavy iron bands around the marble impost; since the dome was segmental, this was the level of maximum thrust, and, to give still greater rigidity, the level was raised only slightly above that of the vault ridges of the rooms at either end. It was a project boldly conceived and boldly executed, and apparently it stood without movement or damage until it was taken down in the 1860's.[6]

6. On July 16, 1805, however, Latrobe wrote Fox, reminding him that the large marble slab forming the northwest corner of the covering of the dome was replaced in the spring

Thus the first monumental building by Latrobe can justly be called a masterpiece. In the new country it was the first building to be erected in which the structural concept, the plan conceived as a functional agent, and the effect both inside and out were completely integrated, completely harmonious. It was also a declaration of architectural independence, and it proved that design by a well-trained architect could go far beyond the ordinary usages of the time; its almost universal welcome proved, too, that the best popular taste of the period was ready and even eager for this kind of new vision. Latrobe always liked the building and felt that in it, through the co-operation of his sympathetic client, he had achieved a kind of success he was seldom permitted elsewhere. In his journal long years later he noted:

Walking up Second Street I observed two French officers standing opposite the building and looking at it without saying a word. I stepped into Black's shop and stood close to them. After some time one of them exclaimed several times, *"C'est si beau, et si simple!"* He said no more and stood for a few minutes longer before he walked away with his companion. I do not recollect anything that has happened that has given me so much particular satisfaction.[7]

Another major project that kept Latrobe busy at this time was the city waterworks. The evil taste and odor of Philadelphia water was notorious, the dangers to health were recognized by all, and nothing had been done to remedy the situation. Philadelphia, the metropolis of the nation, the home of culture and science, still depended on shallow wells. Latrobe had been acutely conscious of the condition during his spring visit. On April 29, 1798, Latrobe writes in his journal:

The soil consists of a Bed of Clay of different depth from 10 to 30 feet. It is excellent brick earth, being very smooth, & free, below the surface, from stone or gravel. Below this bed of clay is universally a stratum of sand. In sand runs a stratum of water . . . suppose that the waters of the two rivers unite through this sand stratum, which serves as a filtering bed. . . . The houses being much crowded, and the situation flat, without subterraneous sewers to carry off the filth, every house has its privy and its drains which lodge their sup-

---

of 1804. Apparently it had been cracked by frost. In the same letter he finds that damage to the interior plaster (about which Fox had evidently complained) was caused by the fact that after the dome was completed in June, 1800, frost set in before the marble covering was finally installed.

7. *The Journal of Latrobe,* with an introduction by J. H. B. Latrobe (New York: Appleton, 1905).

plies in one bog hole, sunk into the ground at different depths. Many of them are pierced to the sand, and as those which are sunk thus low, never fill up, there is a strong temptation to incur the expense of digging them so deep at first, to save the trouble and noisomeness of emptying them.

He also notes that the water is still good in pumps around large public buildings which have open squares around them, that "all the houses on the skirts of the town from 9th to 11th streets have admirable water, *as yet,*" and that the water in crowded places tastes as if it contained putrid matter. He concludes:

The great scheme of bringing the water of the Schuylkill to Philadelphia to supply the city now becomes an object of immense importance, though it is at present neglected from failure of the funds. The evil, however, which it is intended collaterally to correct is so serious and of such magnitude as to call loudly upon all who are inhabitants of Philadelphia for their utmost exertions to complete it.

The time of Latrobe's coming to Philadelphia was therefore propitious, for this engineering problem was in everyone's mind. An important group in town had long since planned to build a canal from the Schuylkill, above its falls north of the city, across to the Delaware. The company was incorporated in 1792 under the name of the Delaware and Schuylkill Canal Navigation. As a by-product the company proposed to build a gravity aqueduct some four miles long to bring the Schuylkill water into Philadelphia, where a reservoir could serve as a distributing center. The scheme sounded promising, but it had manifest difficulties. The length of the aqueduct required, the rolling terrain it would pass over, the achieving of a sufficient head once the water had arrived in town, and even the question of whether there was enough flow to permit the triple division of the system into canal, aqueduct, and the existing river bed were all problems to which the supporters of the scheme had no really convincing answers. It was to these that Latrobe now devoted his imagination and his engineering skill, and he soon arrived at his solution—one both revolutionary and efficient. Why not, he reasoned, take the water from the Schuylkill at the city itself? A settling basin could be built at the river bank; water could be taken from this through a tunnel to a well from which it would be pumped up, by steam power, to a second, higher aqueduct that would lead to Centre Square; there a second steam pump would raise it to a water tank high enough to guarantee a proper gravity flow wherever it was needed. This basically simple scheme he embodied in a report, *View of the Practicability and Means of Supplying the City of Philadelphia with Wholesome Water, in a letter to John Miller, Esq., from B. Henry Latrobe, engineer, December 29, 1798* (Philadelphia: Zachariah Poulson, Jr., 1799). The date shows the extreme rapidity with which Latrobe worked when he was smitten with an idea; for the letter, which describes a system almost precisely like the one executed, was sent less than two months after his arrival in the city, at a time when he must have been rushed with the drawings for the bank.

The whole matter was brought to a head when the citizens of Philadelphia, together with the managers of the Marine and City hospitals and also the Delaware and Schuylkill Canal Navigation company, petitioned the Pennsylvania legislature for help. A committee of the state senate approved granting some aid and proposed the mortgaging of the abandoned President's house in Philadelphia and the placing of a tax on auctions to purchase a thousand shares of the canal company stock at two hundred dollars each; this would permit the canal and aqueduct scheme to go ahead. But in the meantime the city itself was at last taking action, and eventually its energetic activity forestalled the scheme of building the canal and aqueduct with state help. As a result of Latrobe's letter, the committee set up by the Councils (the governing body of the town) appointed him engineer of the project to replace Mr. Huntley, who had been a supporter of the earlier canal scheme. This move was like shoving a stick into a hornet's nest; controversy raged and became bitterly personal. The canal company's supporters were many and important, and now their chance of completing their great scheme was being snatched from their hands.

Latrobe's plan was published by order of the "watering committee" of the Councils. Then followed at once *Remarks on a Second Publication of B. Henry Latrobe, engineer, Said to be Printed by Order of the Committee of the Councils; and Distributed among the Members of the Legislature* [Philadelphia], 1799. The author of the pamphlet is said to have been the Reverend Dr. William Smith, and he sails into his attack with all the weapons that satire and personal innuendo could furnish. He claims that Latrobe's publication misrepresented the canal company and maliciously set out to bring its efforts to naught. He takes special umbrage at the imaginative aspects of the Latrobe proposal, which, he claims, is "a confused and enormously expensive project of *'aerial Castles,'* and elevated *Reservoirs* of different stories [obviously a reference to the double-stage pumping of the Latrobe scheme], Fountains, Baths, etc." Of Latrobe's skill he writes that his *"professional abilities* [are] yet *unknown,* and *untried,* so far as the history of anything in his works in America has come to the public knowledge." Latrobe had claimed that the freezing of the canal might endanger the city's water supply; Smith merely states that water enough runs under the ice, and he objects to the fact that Latrobe quotes such foreign engineers as Bernoulli, Belidor, and Kaestner in support of his theories. Latrobe had found the estimate made by one Sambourne for the extra steam pumping that the canal scheme might necessitate in times of drought to be absurdly low; Smith ridicules Latrobe's criticism. The completion of the canal, Smith feels, "would give the death blow to all Mr. L's romantic and expensive projects, as well as to the emoluments and honours contemplated for him, from the projection and execution of a greater work than the *Canal."* Then he descends to the most vulgar personal remarks, intimates that Latrobe drinks too much and has too large a throat capacity, and ends with an extravagant climax: "If then he wishes to *save* his character and not become a *felo de se* (no matter whether the advice comes from a *merchant* or *divine,*) let him *write no more,* or strive to *write like a gentleman,* and a man of science and *consistency."* It is all typical not only of the literary quality of much controversial writing at the time but also of the prevailing spirit of many of the attacks upon Latrobe and his waterworks plans.

For months the discussion continued heatedly, even after construction according to the Latrobe plan had begun. As late as July 31, 1800, for instance, a letter to the Philadelphia *Gazette* calls the scheme a "ridiculous project" and expresses a hope "that the good people of my native city will no longer be duped by such chimaeras, but that they will turn out of Councils those men who have actively or, by suffering themselves to be duped by others, passively contributed to saddle the city with an unheard-of expense to accomplish that which, when finished, will be a public nuisance, and the probable cause of general calamity to our city, to wit: *a reliance upon steam-engines in the proper supply of water.* They are machines of all machinery the least to be relied on, subject to casualties and accidents of every kind."

Eventually the supporters of Latrobe and of city instead of state action won out. On February 9, 1799, the Councils authorized an address to the citizens asking for their assistance. Two days later they pledged all the estates of the Corporation except the High Street Bridge and Ferry to pay interest and amortization on a public loan of $150,000. Later still another $50,000 for expenses was raised by direct taxation. Work began almost at once; ground was broken on Chestnut Street on March 12, and contracts were let to John Huston for the approach canal and basin, to John Lewis for the lower tunnel, and to Timothy Caldwell for the vertical well at the lower pump house. The upper aqueduct was built by Thomas Vickers; on May 2 the first brick was laid on the three-arched portion that carried the water across a gully in Chestnut Street. The foundations of the central pump house were started on June 18, and the first pipes (of wood) were laid at the same time.

One is amazed at the speed with which the working drawings of this important work were made. Latrobe's chief draftsman on the waterworks project was Frederick Graff, later a famous engineer and the designer of the second Philadelphia waterworks some twenty years afterward. Latrobe chose well; existing drawings by Graff in the Historical Society of Pennsylvania and the Franklin Institute show a marked talent. In 1804 Latrobe, in writing to William Loughton Smith at Charleston, recommended Graff highly for the position of engineer in charge of the Catawba Canal in South Carolina and referred to him as "the first of my élèves." But the chief drawings were made, or at least finished, by Latrobe himself; they are examples of the exquisite engineering drafting that was developed in England—largely by Smeaton—in the eighteenth century. Yet they are more; there is in them the inevitable touch of Latrobe the artist, and in color, values, and the rendering of the rocks, the timber, and the water they are rare specimens of clarity and definiteness in working drawings—even the layman cannot fail to realize their import.

Despite such evidences of professional skill, however, the attacks on Latrobe continued all through the construction period. Here, in connection with this premier American enterprise, the first major engineering work he had had an opportunity to undertake, he found himself the unwilling center of a violent controversy—an experience, alas, that was often to be repeated. Around him swirled all the eddies of contradictory political and economic currents. To many Latrobe was "that damned

Frenchman"; to others he was a scatterbrained visionary. And at the heart of the contention was the continuing hostility of the Delaware and Schuylkill Canal Navigation stockholders, who saw the fruit of years of planning taken from their hands—who saw this stranger, this foreigner, employed to be chief engineer of a project they had initiated—who saw growing into actuality a water-supply system that had no need for their dreamed-of canal.[8] Even petty sabotage was indulged in. Only the fact that Latrobe's backers held firm—and the Councils refused to be budged—made possible the completion of the work.

And opposition appeared within the ranks of the watering committee itself. One of its most assiduous members was the well-known Quaker Thomas Cope, an enthusiastic Federalist and a very model of rectitude, with a whole-souled devotion to the interests of Philadelphia. He had been appointed a committee of one to take care of the detailed supervision of the project. At first he welcomed the Latrobe plan; but though he could grasp its daring he could understand neither the mind and the temperament that created it nor the difficulties that unforeseen conditions might produce. Latrobe, full of enthusiasm, was undoubtedly over-optimistic both about dates of completion and total costs; his estimates had already been exceeded when the system was far from complete. To Cope's factual mind the designer's optimism could only appear to be conscious dishonesty, artfully calculated to lead the city into terrific expenditures for the engineer's sole benefit.

Then in July, 1800, two months after Latrobe's visit to Roosevelt on his wedding trip, Cope in his official capacity also visited the Soho works to find out the actual state of the engines. Since Latrobe had told the eager committee these could be expected any day, Cope was shocked to discover that much still remained to be done on them. Roosevelt, with his customary charm, won Cope's confidence completely, asserting that Latrobe surely knew the exact state of affairs and thus leading Cope to the conclusion that the designer's statements to the committee had been consciously false. But Roosevelt went even further; he told Cope that La-

8. After the company's failure to obtain sufficient funds in 1798-9 and the replacement of its proposed aqueduct by the Latrobe scheme, it remained dormant for nearly thirty years. Eventually, however, in 1836, it used its charter to begin a canal from the Schuylkill to the Delaware in the southern suburbs of the city, not too far from the Navy Yard. The engineer was Samuel Kneass. The last recorded meeting of the company was January 18, 1842. (Minute books of the company in the Historical Society of Pennsylvania.)

trobe and he were partners in the independent use of the extra power of the lower engine. The whole scheme therefore appeared to Cope as a shrewd plan devised by a dishonest engineer to line his own pockets. And, furthering this view (though perhaps unconsciously), Roosevelt complained that his own costs were far exceeding the contract amounts.

Of course Cope could not know how Latrobe had become involved in Roosevelt's devious financial problems (a story that will be told in the following chapter); seeing the designer only as an accomplished villain, on his return to Philadelphia he became Latrobe's undying foe. Again and again he urged that the committee discharge its engineer, and to Poulson's *American Daily Advertiser* he sent several letters (signed "Machine") violently attacking Latrobe's competence and rectitude. But the watering committee continued firm in its support of the engineer, and the work went on.

But worse was to follow. Cope in his diary [9] (August 13, 1800) refers to Latrobe's two assistants Breillat and Barber as villains. With regard to the second he was undoubtedly correct, as the architect was soon to learn to his cost. And by March, 1801, Cope had discovered that for a period of three months the payrolls of John Grimes, one of the subcontractors, had been padded in favor of a former servant of Latrobe's, one Canin. Grimes said this had been done at the request of the architect. Cope's suspicious mind at once reconstructed the motive—a plan on the part of the engineer to discharge, at the city's expense, a debt to an old employee. Cope spoke to Latrobe on the subject, and Latrobe's agitation and apparent evasions were to him evidence enough of guilt. The circumstantial evidence *was* damning, but it depended solely on one man's word; Canin could equally well have been the villain, working hand in glove with someone in Latrobe's office—perhaps Breillat or Barber. If Canin had been discharged by Latrobe for cause (which may well have been the case), this arrangement could have been his revenge. But one thing seems certain—no money from the payroll padding got to Latrobe! Cope dutifully brought the matter before the full watering committee;

9. A transcript of the diary of Thomas P. Cope from 1800 to 1803, prepared by Mrs. George W. Emlen, was most generously put by her at my disposal. The whole is a fascinating document, for Cope has recorded vividly not only his side of this controversy but also interesting travels through Pennsylvania, New York, and parts of New England, in addition to thoughtful comments on ethics and metaphysics which reveal wide reading. It all gives a clear picture of Quaker life and of the thoughts and feelings of a confirmed Federalist and anti-Jacobin at a time of changing public opinion.

again it refused to believe his interpretation and, under the leadership of Samuel Fox and Thomas Parker (always Latrobe's good friends), continued its support of the engineer.

Cope twice offered strong minority reports recommending Latrobe's instant dismissal; the committee not only refused to accept these but voted that they be expunged from the committee records. Yet it also refused to accept Cope's resignation as its supervising committee of one! To the virtuous Quaker the whole affair was unexplainable except as another example of Latrobe's inexplicable and (in his view) reprehensible influence.

Toward the end of 1800 Cope had become disillusioned about Roosevelt, too. He was given to understand that both Roosevelt and Latrobe were in desperate financial difficulty, and to him—careful and successful financier that he was—this was but one more count in the indictment against them. Meanwhile the architect-engineer continued to puzzle and distress him. Latrobe, with the strange and naïve innocence in personal relationships that so often characterized his actions, made several friendly calls on Cope and wrote him a number of cordial letters, climaxing them finally by asking him for a loan. For the inflexible financier such behavior could not be what it seemed; it must be merely another "scheme," an infernally clever attempt to twine the meshes of ambition around another victim. But against the waterworks plan itself Cope had no complaints save its cost, and after a preliminary test of the lower engine had proved that the system was actually going to work he was as pleased as the designer himself.

The last act in this drama of complete personal misunderstanding was again characteristic of those involved. When the system was finally completed and in operation, Latrobe sent the committee a full report on what he considered the best form for the contract to be entered into with the subscribers to the water service. Cope was astounded; surely the committee required no such advice from the designer. What could have led him to give it? The answer, for Cope, could only be that it was an insidious move to make the city engage Latrobe as its permanent engineer, and another black mark was set down against the engineer; he little realized how time and again Latrobe offered suggestions, gratis, out of interest in his work and in his country's development. At last in September, 1801, Cope refused to continue any longer as a member of the Councils; he had given, he felt, too much time and effort, and though his services had been used gratefully his advice had been spurned. Yet as almost his final move he voiced his opinion in another letter to Poulson's paper (published on November 7) and wrote in his diary: "This will probably be the last of the controversy, as it must fix his [Latrobe's] character with every man of candour & common discernment." Latrobe by this time had already gone to the Susquehanna, and the attack remained unanswered.

Much of Cope's hostility to the engineer came from the mounting costs of the project. He did not realize that some of these could not have been foreseen and that the construction itself presented unexpected problems. The lower tunnel, for example, had to be driven through rock; the vertical well also entailed largely rock excavation. Then there were troubles with pipes. Like all the pipes of early American water-supply systems, these consisted of bored-out tree trunks or timber baulks. Perversely, too, many of them rotted even before the system was completed. Metal and terra-cotta pipes were proposed by hopeful inventors or manufacturers, but they were then economically impossible; wood pipes were inevitable in spite of their disadvantages, and the well-seasoned ones lasted once the water was let into them. Much later (November 8, 1812) Latrobe wrote to his son Henry, then in New Orleans superintending the building of the waterworks there: "If your suction pipe will lay one year without rotting, it is well . . . Our pipes in Philadelphia rotted in three months, being the time they were kept empty, & when the water was let in, it drove out a volume of carbonated hydrogen gas and poisoned a whole neighborhood . . ."

Nevertheless the work went on with surprising speed. The two pump houses rose in their simple grandeur, and by the beginning of 1801 the whole was substantially complete. On the night of January 26, Latrobe with a workman and three friends—Bollman and Roosevelt were probably two of them, and perhaps Fox was the third—went down to the new buildings and lighted the fires under the boilers. Latrobe had ordered the hydrants in the streets to be left open. Little by little the steam pressure rose; the pumps were started early the next morning, and when Philadelphia awoke water was flowing down the gutters in bright, clear streams. The system worked.[10]

---

10. The popular interest in the project is well shown by a letter (in the Historical Society of Pennsylvania) from Joseph Parker Norris to Charles Thomson at Norristown, dated January 7, 1801. A portion of it reads:

And the success of the enterprise was the signal for great civic rejoicing, for by this one dramatic morning event Latrobe's plan was completely vindicated and Philadelphia at last had pure water. Latrobe was hailed as a genius; his national reputation as an engineer was now secure, as the slightly later completion of the Bank of Pennsylvania assured his reputation as an architect.

Architecturally the buildings of the waterworks were significant. The lower engine house was of the utmost simplicity, but its proportions were beautiful and in its simple arched openings and undecorated walls there was a new note in American building—a strong, almost ascetic grace. The upper pump house on Centre Square (where the City Hall now uplifts its arrogant and awkward power) was quite different in character. The necessity for a raised storage tank to give sufficient head suggested a high circular drum; this was covered by a dome, and the smokestack was led up centrally from the boiler to end at an oculus in the dome, so that the smoke rose from the dome as from an altar. The machinery—half in a basement—was covered by a square structure that supported the drum and dome; this also enclosed the offices and was entered through a recessed portico of two Greek Doric columns. Thus a simple, strictly geometrical composition was created—hemisphere on cylinder on cube—again a striking innovation in the country at the time. Its basis was the function of the building; its flavor might be called distantly Byzantine, though any thought of any past style was probably entirely absent from its designer's mind. The moldings were simple and classic; only in the portico did a "style" as such definitely appear, and that style was Greek-inspired. Thus again Latrobe was treading a new path.

This little building was a famous landmark in the city until its destruction in 1827, some dozen years after the building of the enlarged waterworks system at Fairmount. The square in which it stood was prettily planted, and what is said to have been America's first decorative

---

"Dear Sir, It was with much pleasure I received yours of this date as it informed me of your continuing to recover your former health—a blessing which I sincerely hope may be long continued you—

"The lower engine of the Water Works is now compleated and has filled the tunnel about 5 or 6 feet—the Center One will not be ready in less than 2 or 3 weeks—but I presume it will be sometime before the Citizens will be reconciled to buying their Water—The engine which has been in operation is said to perform wonderfully well . . ."

fountain to be built with public funds was erected there in 1809. As its chief feature this had a wooden figure of a nymph, carved by William Rush;[11] she held a swan, and from its upturned head gushed the jet. A famous painting by Krimmel shows us the fountain and the pump house as the center of gaiety on the Fourth of July in 1812, so completely had this gracious structure built itself into the heart of Philadelphia.

---

11. Here was one result of Latrobe's much-criticized suggestion for fountains. For its carving, we learn from the reports of the watering committee, Rush received $200.

CHAPTER

9

The Unrelenting Web

DURING these years, professionally and personally so bright, another note begins to sound, a dull clang, resounding more and more menacingly, building up gradually to become almost the sound of doom itself. It is the noise of the want of money; it is the sound of creditors and of legal processes; it is the clangor of a sort of financial fate which dogged Latrobe, threatened his very freedom. It never ceased to toll through the rest of his life.

And it all grew up so innocently. Its roots were in generosity and friendship as much as in a lack of financial imagination or in financial ineptitude, and it began with his two closest friends, Nicholas Roosevelt and Eric Bollman. For them, too, it came as blamelessly as for Latrobe himself, though the main stupidities were theirs. They all had in common an incurable optimism coupled with a naïve belief in the innocence of mankind. But part of the cause of their joint disasters lay in plain bad fortune; for the times were still unstable, both within the country and outside, and there was not yet in the United States an integrated banking system to cushion financial blows.

To understand the web that ensnared Latrobe one must realize these precarious conditions. All of American business was floating on a sea of paper—mainly personal notes, endorsed by people of supposed property. One protested note might send a hundred others to the waste basket; endorsers became liable and were themselves perhaps drawn into bankruptcy. It was a house of cards on a slippery table, and any change of financial atmosphere or international policy might be the breath that sent the whole to ruin.

The weaving of the web began simply enough. President Adams was a big-navy man, and under his leadership Congress had authorized the construction of four great frigates—the "74's"—to be the equal of any in the navies of England or France. Roosevelt, because of his lease on the Schuyler copper mine, received the contract for the sheet copper for their bottoms. To produce this required more capital than Roosevelt possessed, and as part of the contract the Navy Department advanced him large sums against his notes; these Latrobe on his first visit to Roosevelt, in his enthusiastic discovery of a new and congenial friend, had blithely endorsed. Similarly, in the matter of supplying steam engines for Philadelphia Roosevelt lacked working capital. Not only was he forced to mortgage his engine works to the city in lieu of a bond for the completion of the contract [1]—a mortgage that was only finally discharged and returned to him in 1806—but the Corporation of the City of Philadelphia, like the Navy Department, advanced considerable sums to him on his notes, again endorsed by Latrobe. To back these endorsements, Latrobe's wealth lay chiefly in his Pennsylvania lands, together with other real estate he had bought on speculation since his arrival in the United States.

The solvency of this credit multiplication, of course, depended not merely on the completion of the two contracts but at least in part on the continued business and professional success of both Roosevelt and Latrobe. Of Roosevelt's career more will appear later; of Latrobe's enough has been said in the last chapter to show that the architectural conditions in Philadelphia militated strongly against his obtaining there the commissions his genius warranted. Actually, for a period after the completion of the Bank of Pennsylvania and the waterworks, he had not a thing to do—and he was newly married. Roosevelt, as well, was for the moment without work.

And worse things were to follow, for when Jefferson and the new Republican Congress came into power in March, 1801, work on the "74's" was abandoned and all the Navy contracts on them were canceled. Chancellor Livingston, Roosevelt's friend and collaborator in early steamboat experiments, was obviously worried. On June 13, 1801, he wrote to Secretary of State James Madison recommending Latrobe and Roosevelt

1. Even in the original engine works, called the Soho works, at what is now Belleville, N.J., near Newark, Roosevelt had been compelled to call in outside capital. The mortgage is made out in the names of Roosevelt, Jacob Mark and Rosetta his wife, and John Speyer and Catherine his wife. Jacob Mark was Roosevelt's partner in many enterprises, became a good friend of the Latrobes, and served as Latrobe's agent in many purchases made for his Washington buildings.

as competent engineers who had made great improvements in the Watt engine by using two air pumps instead of one.[2] He suggested that if the minting of money were done by steam power the coins produced would be more regular and less subject to counterfeiting. He hoped that Latrobe and Roosevelt would not leave the country, though since finishing the Philadelphia waterworks they had had nothing to do. Madison probably showed this letter to Jefferson, and it again may have brought Latrobe into his mind and helped toward the valuable future appointments that Jefferson bestowed on Latrobe.

Here, then, were these two men, jobless for the moment and indebted to the Navy Department (which had paid nothing on its contract for the undelivered copper) and to the City of Philadelphia (which, for various reasons, had delayed its payments) for large sums of money, backed on Roosevelt's side by nothing and on Latrobe's by his entire personal land holdings. Who suffered the more may well be anticipated.

The Navy copper affair dragged on for years. It was a source of terrific worry to Latrobe until Roosevelt, sometime between 1806 and 1810, assumed the entire debt and Latrobe was cleared of responsibility. Not till February, 1813, did Roosevelt finally clear himself by pledging land holdings worth $50,000.[3] But with the Philadelphia waterworks it was otherwise, for there Latrobe was involved professionally and, contrary to his best judgment, financially as well. The story is peculiar, and at the heart of it is the city's strange contract with Roosevelt. To allow for the growth of Philadelphia, the power of the pumping plant had to be designed far in excess of immediate needs. This excess power was concentrated in the lower of the two engines. Here Roosevelt, with characteristic optimism, saw an opportunity for great individual profits, and the contract specified that this excess power, together with land adjacent to the pumping station, should be leased to Roosevelt for forty-two years. Roosevelt agreed to supply the city with 1,000,000 gallons a day for $3,000 a year for each engine and to supply any larger amounts up to 3,000,000 gallons at half that figure. In return Roosevelt was to pay a sliding scale of rent for the leased extra power and the land—for each of the first seven years, $500; for each of the second seven, $800; for each of the third seven, $1,000; and for each of the remaining twenty-one years,

2. In the Livingston papers in the New-York Historical Society.

3. See page 375.

$1,800. On the leased land Roosevelt built a metal rolling and slitting mill, run by the lower engine's surplus power. At first Latrobe had nothing to do with all of this, save as a regular professional adviser; but by midsummer, 1800, Roosevelt, in gratitude to the architect for his advice and the endorsement of his own notes, considered Latrobe his informal partner.

Trouble arose almost immediately. The costs for the waterworks far exceeded the original estimate of $127,000; by 1806 the total costs levied against the project were $349,016.50. Of this Latrobe's fee represented $6,358, plus an extra $1,050 voted to him by the Councils on February 20, 1805, making a total of $7,408. John Davis, the clerk of the works selected by Latrobe, up through 1803 had received $4,191. The wooden boiler for the lower engine leaked and was insufficient to maintain pressure; two men had been suffocated in repairing it. A second boiler was installed and later replaced by the city with a cast-iron boiler made by Large & Smallman. The pump power was found to be erratic; sometimes there was a plethora of water, sometimes a drought. In 1805 the city refused to pay its agreed fee for the water on the ground of non-compliance with the contract, and the rolling and slitting mill was not yet making the profits Roosevelt had expected. Meanwhile, sometime in 1801, Roosevelt, cashless as always and needing more capital to carry on the works, turned to Eric Bollman, whom he had known ever since Bollman's arrival in the United States.[4] Bollman at this time was at the height of his meteoric financial career, and in attaching him to the enterprise Roosevelt thought he had guaranteed its success. Since Bollman agreed with Roosevelt that the anticipated success of the metal-rolling plant would be largely due to Latrobe—primarily because of his skill and imagination but also because he had endorsed Roosevelt's notes—they decided to make him a full partner with a one-third interest, although he had put up no capital. Of course from the strictly professional point of view Latrobe should have refused the offer, but here were two intimate friends importunately urging him to share with them. Reluctantly he accepted. Another strand of the web was encircling him.

And that strand was tough. Latrobe had received $7,000 as his total professional fee for the design of the waterworks. Against this stood the Roosevelt notes, for much more than that, which he had endorsed. Roose-

---

4. See page 138.

velt and the city were at loggerheads, and Roosevelt was too busy devising more mercurial schemes to spend the necessary time in Philadelphia to straighten things out. Matters went from bad to worse. The watering committee, reporting for 1803, stated: "Although considerable efforts were made towards a settlement of the accounts and concerns existing between Nicholas J. Roosevelt and the corporation [of the city], and for the establishment of the relation, which is hereafter to exist between them, upon simple and equitable terms, yet they have not been able at this time to arrive at any conclusion in this part of the business." A year later they repeated: "Your committee have not yet been able to make a settlement of the accounts and concerns with Nicholas J. Roosevelt." Meanwhile the Peace of Amiens, in 1802, had suddenly stopped the enormous profits of the neutral trade which had been the mainstay of Bollman & Company, and the firm had crashed in a spectacular failure. Bollman's interest in the rolling mill was taken over by William Crammond, Latrobe's old client of Sedgeley; later Roosevelt's former partner Smallman and Samuel Mifflin, the industrialist son of Thomas Mifflin (one-time Governor of Pennsylvania), were also brought in, the agent Mifflin taking actual charge of operating the lower engine and running the iron mill. Crammond had discounted the Roosevelt notes to the corporation of the city and later had sold them to the New York financiers Corps & Casey, who in turn, hopeless of obtaining a single cent from Roosevelt, brought pressure on the architect for payment. Even Latrobe himself did not know how much was involved, and he wrote repeatedly to Roosevelt in vain, asking for the details; it was only from Corps himself that he finally learned he was their debtor—if Roosevelt could not come through—to the extent of $20,700! And Roosevelt could not be counted on; in March, 1805, he had written the Councils that he had lost $47,000 by his contract to build the engines.[5]

On December 1, 1803, Latrobe had written Corps & Casey for details of their claims; nearly two weeks later (December 13) he writes Roosevelt about the matter:

I need not assure you that my attachment to you, whatever may be the difference of our opinion, remains unaltered, through all the disappointments, suf-

5. John T. Scharf and Thompson Westcott, *History of Philadelphia* (Philadelphia: Everts, 1884), p. 519.

ferings and apprehensions for the future that have attended our connexion, and to which I see no end.

A passage follows deprecating and regretting his own connection with Bollman and Roosevelt in the workings of the rolling mill and stating that any new partners, now that Bollman is out, must be bound by the same conditions as the old. He goes on, with regard to Corps & Casey:

I have declined in the letter I have written to them giving any answer until I shall have copies of all the papers under which I may be liable to them. . . . And here the bills retained by them will come into question & all the evils which I formerly predicted, and of which you made so light will come into view.—What they may amount to, and how they will influence a man like myself, whose infant family is likely to become numerous,—you,—where so alive to your own situation, will no doubt be well able to anticipate.

The most distressing circumstance in anything that can be said or written to you on this subject is, that you appear to consider it,—(as it certainly has been between *you* and *me,* as friends,)—as a matter not of business, of figures, & of calculation but of *sentiment,* when treating with others, who never felt, or pretended to feel friendship for you. The disinterested and *lumping* settlements of mutual confidence and generosity, have always been expected by you from men, whom you must have known well enough, to have looked for nothing from them but mercantile exactness,—and whom you could not possibly believe to have any reasonable motive to depart from the usual method of settling money concerns. Among these I reckon Bollman.—Believe me with sincere affection yours truly. B. Henry Latrobe.

In another ten days he writes Roosevelt again asking him what he has done under the power of attorney; he himself has had no answer from Corps & Casey. Again he ends on a personal note: "Mrs. Latrobe unites with me in sincere affection for you and Mrs. Marks [sic]." It was February 6, 1804, before Latrobe learned the amount of his obligations to Corps & Casey. Mr. Corps was then in Washington, and Latrobe was to see him that evening. Evidently the whole business continued to drag on, as did the negotiations with the city for a new lease and a settlement of its controversy with Roosevelt, for nothing important concerning it is mentioned until November 2, 1804, when in another letter to Roosevelt possible drastic action is indirectly suggested by Latrobe:

I assure you that I know as little about the negotiations with the corporation as you do. I have seen Mr. Mifflin [Roosevelt's agent] only twice in these three months. He then told me that Stephen Girard, who carried on the negotiations on the part of the Corporation, carefully avoided committing himself on any proposal. My opinion is that nothing short of withholding the water will bring the matter to an issue. . . . The supreme court will inevitably have to decide them all [the points of controversy] on an action for withholding the water. . . .

In respect to Corps & Casey, the matter is so simple, that your mode of treating it always surprises me.—I became your security for bills of a large amount. I had no interest but that of my reputation & friendship in the completion of your contract with the corporation. The bills were protested. By an arrangement with the Navy Department the security was changed as to the persons who held it & ruin was postponed.—That ruin must one day or other fall upon the drawer & acceptor. The only indemnification I hold is the share in the works. We shall see what it is worth when our partners state their accounts. I am in their power. I cannot even *give away* my share because it is mortgaged.—There was some comfort while the Bankrupt law existed. That is repealed. It is a fearful abyss to look into. But a bachelor need not care about it.—

A few weeks later a new note appears in the correspondence. Roosevelt had written Mrs. Latrobe that he had fallen in love with Lydia. Of that, more later. But Latrobe ends his current letter: "In the meantime, if there is anything certain under heaven, it is that you hold the first place in our esteem, good opinion & friendship."

In January, 1805, the negotiations with the corporation remaining fruitless, Latrobe writes Roosevelt: "If you were to manage the business yourself with the corporation I should not doubt of a successful event. But I have not the same confidence in our Lawyers . . ." Why was Roosevelt so reluctant to undertake these things himself? On July 1, concerning the matter, Latrobe writes that he cannot come to Philadelphia, "so that you and Mifflin must do as you can. I fear you will at best make a bad hand of it.—You should in the mean time keep possession, & speak a high toned language threatening the worst if a speedy decision be not obtained."

In July, Roosevelt with his customary optimism writes proposing the sale of the lease to the corporation for $35,000. Latrobe questions the possibility of such a transaction but asks if he should send Mifflin his power of attorney. On August 21, Latrobe writes again discussing with Roosevelt the real value of the lease:

By our lease, the corporation are at its expiration to pay for all *permanent* improvements *at a valuation*. Therefore if we now sell,—we ought to receive in addition to this value of permanent improvements the value of the extra power for 40 years about. I suppose the permanent improvements to be worth at least $10,000. What then is the value of the other item? . . . As to Mifflin, I dread writing to him, plagued as he is with Crammond.—I have heard once or twice from Bollman lately on business. This man distresses me exceedingly. I have a long, & most eloquent defense of his conduct moral & mercantile. His talents are astonishing. I wish his heart were to be trusted.

Later, writing to Bollman, Latrobe says of Crammond, who with Smallman and Mifflin had taken over Bollman's share of the waterworks when Bollman & Company failed: "As to Crammond,—his opinions, liberally laid before me, have had no weight. . . . I believe insolvency may be outdone in criminality by actions that receive applause among us.—Crammond can furnish examples." Perhaps his sale of Roosevelt's notes with Latrobe's endorsements to Corps & Casey was one such instance.

But matters were coming rapidly to a climax; in true tragic fashion violence stepped in. Roosevelt had taken Latrobe's suggestions literally and had turned off the water for three hours. About the same time there was a serious fire in Philadelphia. Latrobe wrote Roosevelt almost in panic, on September 24, 1805: "I hear . . . that the spread of the fire was owing to the withholding of the water. I hope this representation is not true. . . ." Roosevelt hastened to reassure him on this point, but Latrobe's answer of September 26 seems to indicate that Roosevelt had threatened to blow up the engines unless his asking price for the lease, $35,000, was accepted. Evidently he had made such a threat, for the Councils had immediately secured a writ against him. Roosevelt foolishly locked the gates against the sheriff. The city was enraged; a mob, led by the sheriff himself, charged the waterworks, broke open the locks, threw out Roosevelt and the men working under him, turned the whole works over to municipal operation, and replaced Davis and Mifflin with Graff as manager. It was an ugly business from every point of view, and it redounded to the credit of neither party, but that the watering committee's ire was not directed against the designer of the system is shown by its appointment of the new manager—a man who had been Latrobe's chief assistant on the project and was still his close friend.

Yet it is also true that the watering committee had as little legal right to possession as Roosevelt had had in his highhanded defiance of the writ. Some accommodation finally had to be made, if only to guarantee the continued operation of the system. The city had been put in a position where to be assured of its water supply it had to buy Roosevelt's lease. Roosevelt, on the other hand, was now powerless to do anything but sell. By his ill-timed, impulsive actions he had lost whatever respect and influence he had enjoyed before, and he had no capital to fight the matter further; the price his syndicate received—$15,000, with a few additional sums—reflects these two facts. The total, less than half what he had asked, was actually, according to the report of the watering committee (which tactfully makes no reference to the riot), $15,886.[6]

Where did this leave Latrobe? Theoretically he stood to gain a third of the value of the sale to counterbalance the $20,700 debt to Corps & Casey. In reality things worked out differently. The syndicate still had many outstanding debts to pay, and Mifflin was supposed to take care of them. Crammond and Mifflin were entitled to Bollman's third between them; the other third was Roosevelt's. From Crammond Latrobe could expect no consideration; in fact, Bollman had entered on the account of Bollman & Company a claim on Latrobe for several hundred dollars that Latrobe's absconding clerk, John Barber, had stolen, and Latrobe had had difficulties in removing this absurd claim. Naturally the New York

6. The *Annual Reports of the Watering Committee* (at the Historical Society of Pennsylvania) are fascinating documents. They should put to rest at once the still popularly believed canard started by Mencken, who has spent many years trying to kill it, that bathing was considered immoral in the early United States and that bathrooms were nonexistent till the 1840's. The *Report* lists the numbers of subscribers to the water system for each year and, since private baths for a period paid a special rental, gives these separately. Thus the first year 63 houses, 4 businesses, and one sugar refinery paid water rents, whereas in 1805 there were 685 houses on the system and the next year 848. At some later date the special rate for baths was introduced; these climbed rapidly in number. In 1815, when 2,883 dwellings paid rentals, 228 (nearly 10 per cent) had bathrooms, and in 1819 the number of baths had climbed to 380, twelve of them located in houses beyond the city limits. The 1819 receipts for water rents amounted to $24,884. When the Fairmount works, which supplemented and later replaced the original Latrobe-designed plant, were changed from steam power to water power in 1819, the city was forced to buy the entire water rights at this point. These were held by the Schuylkill Navigation Company, chartered in 1812 to improve the river channels and to build canals where necessary. With the development of the use of anthracite coal, the company's earnings grew to unexpected levels, for the Schuylkill and its canals offered the most economical route from the coal fields to the city. Ironically the price the company received for the water rights purchased in 1819 was $150,000, nearly ten times what the city had paid Roosevelt and his associates. Latrobe and Roosevelt only achieved, from all their actual contributions, near ruin.

group headed by Roosevelt hastened to realize as much as it could while it could.

The final sales contract was closed early in January, 1806, and on February 20 Latrobe wrote to Roosevelt begging for some share in the liquidation. He summarizes his debts and says that he has consulted a lawyer as to the advisability of declaring himself insolvent and that he is even threatened with arrest for Philadelphia debts of $950. First of all, he wants two-thirds of the Corps & Casey claim removed—as we have seen, this was solely the result of his backing of Roosevelt. The Chesapeake and Delaware Canal notes with which his salary on that development was paid were no longer accepted anywhere. To prevent his arrest, he says,

> it occurred to me that if of the money due from the corporation I could have obtained 1300 dollars, I could discharge all my personal debts, & be free from *detention* here. For you must understand that my stay in Philadelphia is not voluntary, & that an attempt to leave would be fatal to me. . . .
>
> As security that this sum together with 700 Dollars already advanced by you should be applied to the object of liquidating my debts as your security, I proposed to give my personal bond conditioned as the case requires—and as security real estate in Delaware, in the city of Richmond Virginia & in Pennsylvania to the amount which I believe I could do by regular Mortgage or by a Judgment. . . . [What an expression both of Latrobe's dire need and of his business naïveté—as though such a bond would be required of him either by right or by law, when the payments it suggests are actually due him legally! The result would have been that his remaining assets would have been heavily mortgaged to the very man for whose benefit the debts had been unwarily assumed.]
>
> I have however learned that Mr. Mark [ever the prompt businessman] took with him to New York 3000 $ cash [of the city settlement]. . . . In common course it ought to be applied to the reduction of our debt but such are my necessities, that I cannot help think that it would be equally just to relieve with part of it my present necessities in the manner I hope.

Then the same day he writes another letter to Roosevelt, complaining that Roosevelt's answer to an earlier letter was full of insults and practically insane! And on March 8 he writes Jacob Mark urging him to explain to Roosevelt the facts of the entire case. In the meantime, Roosevelt had associated Latrobe with him in a speculative purchase of New Jersey salt-meadow land. This had been done without investment by

Latrobe as an expression of gratitude; on April 8, 1806, Latrobe writes him that any profits from the deal should be applied to reducing the Navy debt; he, Latrobe, had invested nothing and desires nothing.

But all was of no avail; the debts, the lack of income, the threatened arrests and judgments remained. Philadelphia had proved itself far from grateful; the architect's early heady prospects there had been fool's gold. Latrobe had had enough of it; now he wanted to move to Washington, to which his professional position as Surveyor of the Public Buildings called him. Isaac Hazlehurst, his father-in-law, evidently objected to the move; to explain the necessity of going, Latrobe wrote him on July 19, 1806, about his present position:

> But it is well known that two months after my marriage, Barber's conduct involved me in such a manner that I have paid the last of the burthens he threw upon me only this spring. His delinquency exceeded 6000 $.—The *necessary* interest which devolved to me in the rolling works,—the failure of Bollman,—the transfer of all personal concerns with me, as an individual, both as debtor and creditor,—to me as a partner in the concern, has cost me $7000. . . . I have made good all deficiencies excepting to you partly by the observance of the most rigid oeconomy in my domestic & personal expenses, partly by the *private sale*—I might say, the sacrifice of my patrimony of lands in this state. All this is now past. . . . But from the end of 1802 to the middle of 1804, I, in fact, was little better off than the dogs who relied upon what fell from the rich man's table. I had nothing but scraps and leavings, & have often spent my last dollar in the market, when I did not know where to get another. . . .

And in another letter to Hazlehurst two days later:

> And when the Canal [the Chesapeake and Delaware Canal, of which more will be said later] was finally suspended, I came to Philadelphia "to begin life anew." . . . [But the prospects are bad.] As to private business,—*I shall get none.* There are now building in this city two capital houses by the Fishers, who call themselves my friends. Do they employ me?—John Dorsey has now no less than 15 plans now in progress of execution, because he charges nothing for them. The public affront put upon me as a professional man, in the erection of the Academy of Art from the design of John Dorsey,—by a vote of all the men who pretend to patronize the arts in this city,—would have driven any Artist from it,—but one held by the strongest family ties and affections. . . .
>
> I cannot in any emergency, *lay down & die quietly* . . .

Latrobe was bitter, and justifiably so. As an architect Philadelphia regarded him not; in his role as engineer, fate had seen to it that the waterworks project had cost him $7,000 more than he had received as a fee.

He had, it is true, temporarily cleared himself by the sacrifice of most of what he owned, most of the capital that before had been his mainstay; but even then the web was not broken, the outstanding debts against the old syndicate and the rolling mill continued to vex. A controversy arose between Latrobe and Mifflin (the titular agent of the works) as to who should meet these debts. Mifflin claimed he had no authority to pay anything after the date of the sale to the city; the creditors leaped upon Latrobe as a man of substance—though of how little they did not dream.

At last, in despair, he writes to Richard Peters of Philadelphia (February 14, 1807), asking him to arbitrate all the matters relative to the syndicate and Mifflin. In his letter he summarizes the story and adds another detail:

> I had in fact ceased to be a partner in the first six months [of the rolling-mill company] . . . having given Mr. Roosevelt a power of attorney under which he conveyed my share, as well as his own, to Messers Corps & Casey [obviously as additional security on the old notes]. . . . As this was for very good reasons not published [I was being held to account]. . . . The dispute of the partnership having risen to great heights about the time of Bollman's failure both parties agreed to leave them [the matters at issue] to my decision. They were satisfied with the award I made. . . . Under this award Crammond & Mifflin became partners. . . . In the latter end of 1805, the corporation having withheld all compensation for the supply of water . . . we determined to get rid of the concern. . . . At last a price was agreed to be received . . . and it was agreed that Mr. Mifflin should receive [all amounts due] and pay all debts outstanding. . . . I have no business to enquire why the outstanding debts were not paid . . .

Some months later Mifflin finally paid, and the disastrous incident was closed. On February 14, Latrobe also wrote to President Jefferson in connection with a possible increase in his government salary. He states that his professional life has cost him, thus far, $15,000 of his patrimony. If he were to move to Washington he must be promised real security.

That, then, is how the waterworks were built. Six years and more from the time when the clear water first flowed sparkling down the

Philadelphia gutters, Latrobe was at last rid of the whole affair. It had brought both Roosevelt and himself to the brink of ruin and disgrace, and Latrobe had broken free of the web only by the sacrifice of most of his capital. From that time on, he was no longer a comparatively well-to-do man who could (as he had written to Scandella in 1798) spend his professional income on books and instruments. After 1807 he was a professional man in all seriousness, dependent on his professional income for the nourishing of his growing family and for supporting the style of living expected of one in his station in life. Such was his reward for his brilliantly conceived and swiftly executed design for the waterworks, such the price paid for his professional skill. It is a depressing picture but one not entirely unparalleled either then or later. The city of Philadelphia was the gainer, of course; it had the waterworks—and for a fraction of their cost!

CHAPTER

10

Professional Struggles: 1802-1807

THE first eight years of Latrobe's second marriage were strangely compounded of professional success and financial failure. Of the happiness that his marriage brought it is impossible to speak too strongly; Mary Elizabeth afforded him a kind of companionship and emotional security he had never known before. In addition to her gentleness and generosity she had the talent of the creative homemaker. As Latrobe wrote to his brother Christian (May 16, 1805): "She is besides one of those women who without expense have the art of making everything that belongs to them wear the appearance of exquisite taste. Cleanliness & order reign from my Garret to the cellar, & I am myself surprised at the unseen Art by which all is produced."

Their first child, a daughter named Juliana after Mrs. Latrobe's mother, was born June 9, 1801, and died of "summer complaint" on August 7 of the same year at Clover Hill, the Hazlehurst estate at Mount Holly, New Jersey. The monument Latrobe designed for her still stands, exquisite in its simplicity. Yet in those days of heavy infant mortality the Latrobes were unusually fortunate. Their second child, christened John Hazlehurst after a recently dead maternal uncle and Boneval for his father's ancestor, was born on May 4, 1803, and lived till 1891. A daughter, named Juliana like her dead sister but generally known as Julia, followed on July 17, 1804, and then on December 19, 1806, there came another son (who died in 1878) named Benjamin Henry for his father. (A third daughter, Mary Agnes, born November 5, 1805, had died in infancy.) John H. B. Latrobe, a bright, talented youth, was for a time his father's able draftsman; later, after the architect's death, he switched to the law, became one of Baltimore's most respected lawyers and financiers, and was deeply interested in the colonization of Negroes. During most of his life he was general counsel of the Baltimore & Ohio Railroad, and he went to Russia to represent the Winans railroad interests in the new Russian railroads. But he remained part architect and artist all his life and in his hundreds of accurate water colors he handed down something of the technique and the vision he had learned from his father.[1] Ben was also interested in railroads; scarcely more than a child at the time of his father's death, he followed his elder brother into the law but later took up engineering and became one of the notable railroad engineers of the country, known especially for his magnificent viaducts for the Baltimore & Ohio Railroad between Baltimore and Washington and also for his layout of its western lines from Cumberland to Wheeling. The two sons were a remarkable pair, and it is interesting to see how they carried on many of the talents of their father—imagination, skill in delineation, engineering ability, and interest in technical progress. There were also, of course, Lydia and Henry, who in the earlier days of the marriage were the children in the home, as contrasted with the infants. Later, as the new family grew, they were sent to boarding schools, at least for part of the time.

The Latrobes, ensconced in their new Philadelphia home with a cook, a chambermaid, and a manservant (as Mary later described the household) [2] and with the Bank of Pennsylvania and the waterworks approaching completion, looked forward to a bright future. Happily, too, in Clover Hill at Mount Holly they had almost a second home and were often there on visits, sometimes extended ones; the proud Hazlehurst grandparents indeed were always ready to receive a child or two if the parents wished or were compelled to be away.

With the summer of 1801, however, when the bank and the waterworks were completed, no further work was in sight. It was a worrisome period, for Latrobe had a position to preserve if he wished to make his way in purse-conscious Philadelphia; but by fall a providential engineering job saved them. This was a survey of navigation on the Susque-

---

1. See John E. Semmes, *John H. B. Latrobe and His Times, 1803-1891* (Baltimore: Remington [c1917]). This is an extremely interesting account, though marred by occasional minor inaccuracies. A large collection of John H. B.'s water colors is in the Maryland Historical Society.

2. Her memoir of her husband was transcribed by John H. B. Latrobe and is preserved in a large manuscript notebook (also containing much other material dealing with the Latrobes) now in the possession of the family.

hanna. In September, Governor McKean appointed Latrobe one of the commissioners of the survey and also the engineer of the project. The architect's uncle, Colonel Frederick Antes, had been made the agent two months earlier, and it was probably he who selected Latrobe as his chief assistant.

The Latrobes therefore set out together in the soft early autumn days, leaving Henry and Lydia at Clover Hill. The survey party, under the architect's direction, was to start at Columbia, some miles down the river from Harrisburg, and work gradually to the Maryland line. It was to make an accurate survey of the banks, reefs, rapids, and existing channels and wherever possible to remove boulders and even blast off projections and dredge shallows in order to make the channel safer. Maryland was to do the same thing south of the boundary; the result was to provide barge navigation, even in periods of low water, from Columbia to Chesapeake Bay.

In early October, soon after the work began, Colonel Antes died of kidney trouble, at the age of sixty-seven, and his nephew fell heir to his responsibilities. The work was arduous but pleasant; the country proved picturesque, and Latrobe's workbook (now in the Maryland Historical Society) is full of rapid pen sketches of the rocky valley, done *con amore*.

As the survey progressed (with Christian R. Hauducour as assistant engineer and surveyor) contracts were let for digging and for the removal of rocks, and on November 18, the work being substantially complete, Latrobe wrote Governor McKean a report of what had been accomplished. But in addition he had to make adjustments of a myriad of accounts and untangle carefully all the unfinished business left by Colonel Antes. The final accounts were not presented till mid-March, 1802; for the entire job Latrobe received $1,000.

The whole project was embodied in a single long annotated map, graphically rendered in color, which was sent from Pennsylvania to Washington in connection with Gallatin's proposed Federal support of internal improvements. The map disappeared when the British looted and fired the Capitol in 1814. Later (in 1817), when Latrobe was living in Baltimore, he made a replica of it from his notes and from memory and presented it to the Library Company of Baltimore; it is now in the Maryland Historical Society. The map's indications of rocks, rapids, reefs, and promontories are so compelling that it is as legible to a layman as to an engineer.

ceiling
Wall

In Maryland Historical Society

FIGURE 13. Sketches on the Susquehanna. Top, Culley's Falls. Second, Bear Island. Third, A Cave. Above, Fulton's Ferry House. From the Latrobe workbook of the Susquehanna survey.

Latrobe was back in Philadelphia by mid-November; Mary had returned earlier. An affectionate letter to her from Buckhalter's Tavern (November 10, 1801) while she was living at the Hazlehursts' at 117 North Second Street reads in part:

If I could bring myself to write to anyone but you, I could furnish a letter entertaining enough. . . . The very reception we have met with has been so various that I could fill a letter with descriptions of character & manners, that would often make you laugh. . . . But after writing the first words of my letter, after calling you, my dearest Mary, my beloved wife, the whole world vanishes from my imagination, and I see none but you. I seem to stretch my arms from the rocky walls of the Susquehannah in vain towards you, all my spirits, and strength exhaust themselves in the exertion, and I scarcely am capable of guiding my pen, just to give a bare dry narrative of our daily labors. . . .

When I think of you, my dearest love, my heart melts with tenderness, such as I never before knew; but it soon rests itself firmly on that superiority of mind, that soundness of reasoning, and that command of your feelings that I know you to possess, and then I take my level on my shoulders and march forth as strong as a lion to push forward to the end of my labor, when your arms and your kisses, if I dare to think of them shall reward all my fatigues. Oh my love! What virtue can deserve such a woman as you are! Were I but half worthy of you, how superior to all should I be, and how just would be my pride. . . .

I pray God you may have been well. Love to the children and to our father and mother, and to the boys [the Hazlehursts],

Your most tenderly affectionate husband.

During the winter he had to make several trips to Lancaster in connection with the final accounts. In a letter from there on one of these trips (March 18, 1802), addressed to his wife at 186 Arch Street, their own house, he gives his impressions of the local political scene:

. . . I have attended the house [of representatives] this morning, and regretted that I durst not use my pencil as freely as I wished. Some of the figures there exhibited, are fit only for the pencil of Hogarth. I counted only twelve combed heads and two woolen nightcaps. . . . There is neither favor nor comeliness among them that we should desire them. Some of the countenances unite coarseness & brutality with stupidity in a superior degree. And yet I was much disappointed in hearing sound sense proceed from many of the least promising in appearance, though dressed in very uncouth language. . . . After the House broke up, I had occasion to go to the Governor. He had just received a petition from Meadeville on Lake Erie praying for the removal of a Mr. Kennedy, a prothonotary whom he had appointed, and who is said to be a very worthy man. [In the petition] he was stated to be an aristocrat, a tyrant and a Tory. The petition was signed by more than 500 names, written on papers of various sizes pasted together so as to form a roll of about 7 feet long. On looking over the roll it appeared, that the signatures consisted of old Muster Rolls, of the signatures to other petitions the heads of which had been cut off, and so clumsily pieced, that . . . on separating two pieces the head showed the names to be a list of taxable inhabitants of Erie County. So abominable a forgery excited not a little of his Excellency's choler, and the fellows who brought it sneaked away in the utmost confusion. . . .

A great disappointment in these early years was Latrobe's failure to win the competition for the New York City Hall in 1802. He had two good friends in New York, Aaron Burr and Nicholas Roosevelt; both hoped eventually to make him a permanent New Yorker. It was at Burr's solicitation that Latrobe entered the competition, and (according to Latrobe's memorandum to Gallatin on December 15, 1806, shortly before Burr's trial for treason) through Burr's influence all the commissioners save one voted for the Latrobe design. Burr's report on the voting may have been one of his bits of accomplished deceit; in any case, the final vote was for the design of Mangin & McComb.[3]

Latrobe's design for the City Hall was in its way superb. His competition drawings are now in the Library of Congress, and a comparison of these with the Mangin & McComb scheme is revealing. The building Latrobe designed is smaller and more tightly organized than the other. Its plan is beautifully studied, excellent from the functional point of view; compared to it, the Mangin & McComb plan seems loose. On the other hand, the Latrobe scheme has no such superb central rotunda stairs as the winning design, nor does it include so fine a public suite of state reception rooms, and the very looseness of the chosen design has proved to be much more susceptible of all those changes that historical development has necessitated.

Creative as Latrobe's plan is, the exterior nevertheless is far from perfect. The height relation between the ground floor and the *piano nobile* above is weak; the great entrance steps are too high, and the Corinthian portico to which they lead becomes too small by contrast. As the crowning motif of the exterior Latrobe uses his favorite low Pantheon-type dome, and the distribution of the openings and all the detail have the perfection of relationship and of detail to be expected from him; but these virtues do not make up for the fundamental errors in judgment.

The Latrobe design, moreover, was perhaps too conscious a search for economy to appeal to the committee, who were thinking in a remarkably large way; looking forward to a great future for New York, they were seeking a building of equal grandeur. The Mangin & McComb scheme, with its great length, its projecting wings, and its ample entrance vestibule, had much more of this quality than did Latrobe's simple rectangular block. No one can study the two designs candidly without realizing that in spite of the economy, the organization, and the reticent distinction of the Latrobe design the committee members made the correct choice. The admiration and affection in which the New York City Hall has been held for a century and a half sufficiently prove their wisdom.

Latrobe bitterly regretted his failure to win the competition; he felt

---

3. This competition was finally judged on October 4, 1802. John McComb was appointed the architect to carry out the work. The result was the present building.

he had produced by far the better design of the two. Some time later (November 4, 1804) he wrote his brother Christian:

> Three years ago, I presented a design for the new city Hall at New York. It was I think my best design. It was rejected, & a vile heterogeneous composition in the style of Charles X of France, or Queen Elizabeth of England was adopted,—the invention of a New York bricklayer & a St. Domingo Frenchman in partnership. . . .[4] Now, this very city of New York, have appointed a Committee to solicit my undertaking their business *on my own terms* & I have been obliged *twice* to refuse them, on account of my present engagements.

The "business" referred to here was the design of a system to drain the Collect Pond as well as the construction of suitable docks. For this, J. F. Mangin had submitted a scheme that was deemed impractical by the authorities. The committee consisted of Wynant Van Zandt, Jr., Jacob Morton, and Clarkson Crolins. Their invitation to Latrobe had come, he believed, through the influence of Burr.[5] Latrobe wrote them (June 17, 1804) regretting that he could not accept their invitation "to be useful to their city" and going on to discuss the problem of drainage and the construction of docks along the North and East rivers. The unexpected fullness of his letter and its valuable suggestions led the members of the committee to think that his refusal was far from final—they little understood how his ebullient imagination seethed and ran over when any problem was presented to it, pay or no pay—and they wrote again urging him to come. Latrobe firmly declined the job on August 5; he could not leave the canal or be so far removed from the United States Capitol, on which he was already at work. This nevertheless was not the only effort to bring Latrobe to New York, as we shall see.

One particularly exciting project for which the architect made preliminary estimates was a bridge from New York to Long Island across Blackwell's Island. Communication between Manhattan and Long Island was becoming more and more of a problem; the small ferries of those pre-steamboat days were manifestly insufficient. Roosevelt was the instigator this time, in the fall of 1804. John Stevens[6] had suggested a tunnel

---

4. This is an important new piece of evidence on the life and origins of Joseph François Mangin, the brilliant co-author with McComb (the "New York bricklayer") of the winning design.

5. See the "Memorandum" referred to earlier and given on page 222f.

6. John Stevens (1749-1848), a brother-in-law of Chancellor Livingston, had been as-

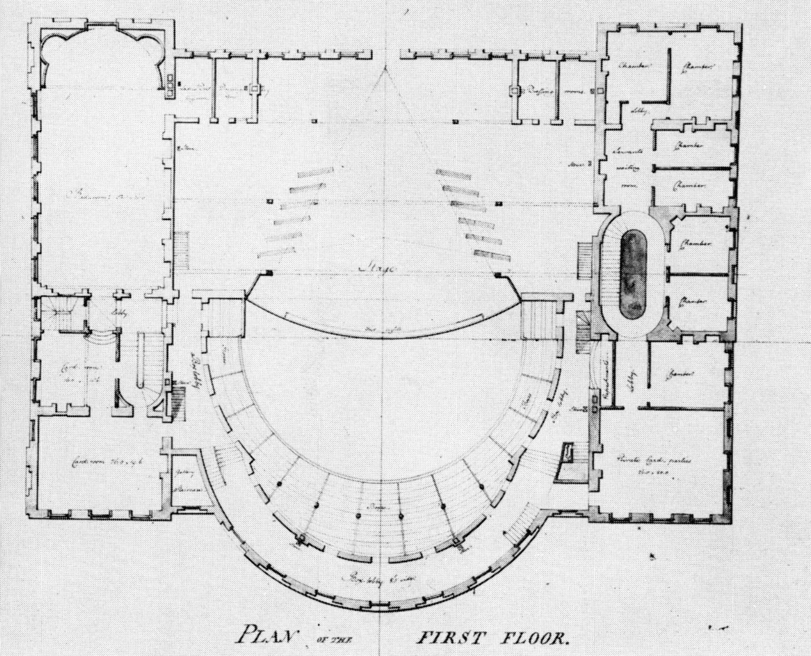

be's main-floor plan. Library of Congress

Proposed Theater, Hotel, and Assembly Building, Richmond. PLATE 9

be's section of the theater. Library of Congress

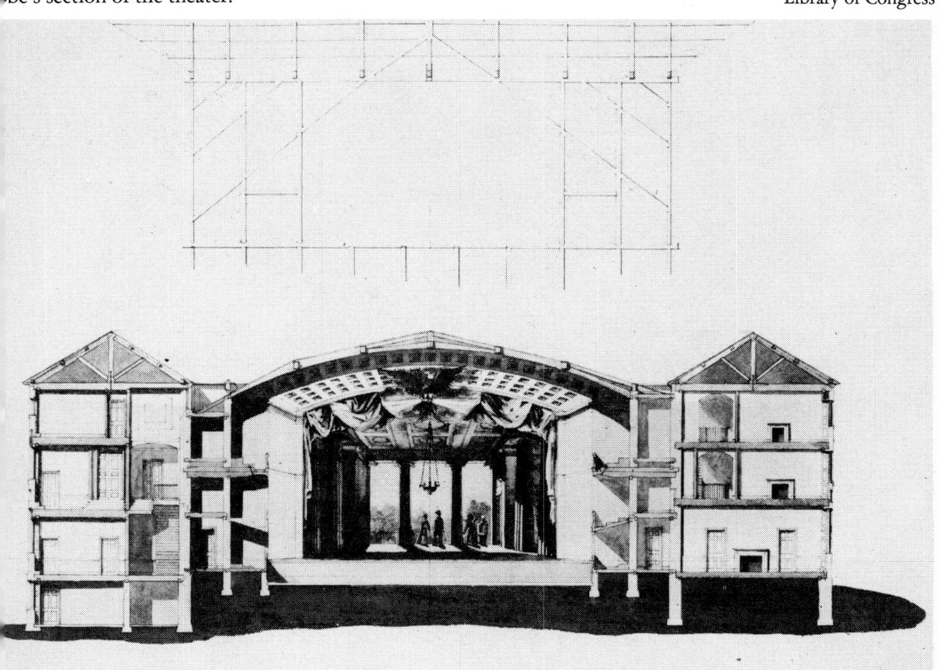

Library of Cong

Proposed Theater, Hotel, and Assembly Building, Richmond. Latrobe's perspective of the assembly roo

PLATE 10

The Penitentiary, Richmond. Latrobe's main-floor plan. State Library of Vir

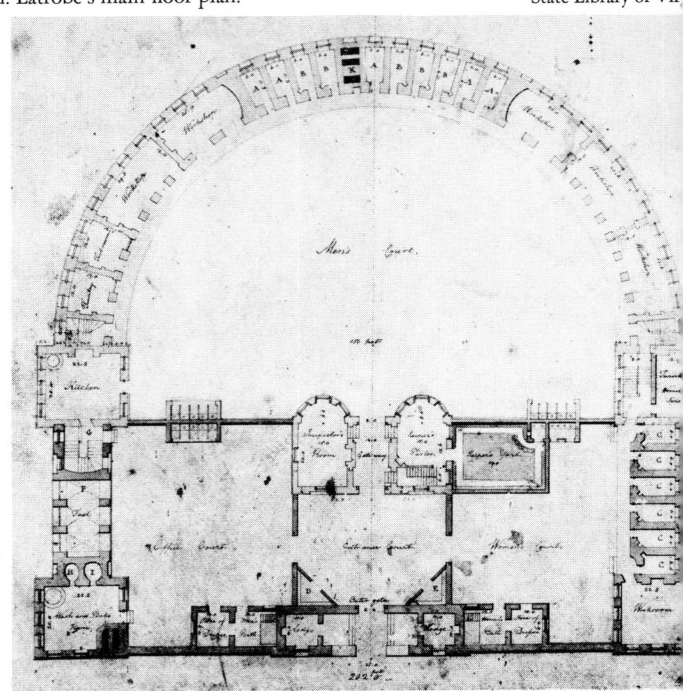

A, Dark cells.
B, Solitary cells for men.
C, Solitary cells for women.
D, Receiving room for men.
E, Receiving room for women.
F, Open arcade for ventilation.
G, Stair to infirmary.

State Library of Virginia

Penitentiary, Richmond. Latrobe's perspective of the entrance.

Old photograph, courtesy Valentine Museum, Richmond

PLATE 11

Penitentiary, Richmond. Cell block (with added top story).

g Branch, the Burwell House, Virginia. B. H. Latrobe, architect. Entrance front.

Photograph Rohden, courtesy Alexander Mackay-Smith

Library of Con[g

Competition for the New York City Hall. Latrobe's perspective.

PLATE 12

Bank of Pennsylvania, Philadelphia. Latrobe's preliminary perspective. Slightly modified in execution.

Maryland Historical Soci[e

Historical Society of Pennsylvania

k of Pennsylvania, Philadelphia. B. H. Latrobe, architect. Engraving of a drawing by George Strickland.

PLATE 13

k of Pennsylvania, Philadelphia. Latrobe's section.

Historical Society of Pennsylvania

Philadelphia Academy of

Philadelphia Waterworks. B. H. Latrobe, architect and engineer. Centre Square Pump House on the Fourth of July. A painting by Krimmel.

PLATE 14

Philadelphia Waterworks. Settling basin on the Schuylkill. Latrobe's drawing.

Historical Society of Pennsylva

Historical Society of Pennsylvania

Chestnut Street Theater, Philadelphia, as altered by Latrobe. Engraving by Birch.

Historical Society of Pennsylvania

lgeley, the Crammond House, Philadel-
ia. B. H. Latrobe, architect.

PLATE 15

ıe Burd House, Philadelphia.
Old photograph, courtesy Historical Society of Pennsylvania

Historical Society of Pennsylv

University of Pennsylvania, Philadelphia. Medical School. B. H. Latrobe, architect. Drawing by William Strickland.

PLATE 16

South front. Photograph W. Boone, courtesy Dickinson Col

"Old West," Dickinson College, Carlisle, Pennsylvania. B. H. Latrobe, architect.

North front. Courtesy Dickinson College

of brick, or even one made of continuous sheets of heavy waterproof leather. Latrobe thought these suggestions impractical and remarked that Stevens was always the dupe of his fantastic ideas; then he made an elaborate estimate for the bridge that would be required. Roosevelt may have been thinking in terms of a wooden-pile bridge, but Latrobe was convinced that the difference in cost between that and a stone bridge would soon be offset by the heavy maintenance required on the wooden structure;[7] accordingly his estimate was founded on stone arches and the costs were calculated on the basis of work actually done in Philadelphia; the final total amounted to $950,000.[8] This at the time was a sum beyond the capacities of either the city or any private company, and the matter passed into limbo. Manifestly Latrobe was not destined to be a New Yorker.

Meanwhile architectural jobs in Philadelphia remained coy. One of those on which he worked intermittently for several years was the radical alteration of the Chestnut Street Theater. Latrobe apparently made his designs for this sometime in 1801, but construction was only completed early in 1806. The building, supposedly a copy of the theater in Bath, England, had been erected in 1791 by Thomas Wignall and Hugh Reinagle—the latter an architect, scene painter, and master mason all in one. By 1801 it had become insufficient for the growing town, its lobbies and entrances were inconvenient, and its rich gabled brick exterior was considered old-fashioned. Latrobe changed the spirit of the whole front by adding an entirely new entrance complex on the ground floor. At each end were projecting marble-faced wings; these were ornamented with sculptured panels and connected by a colonnade. The supper rooms and withdrawing rooms were above, on either side; evidently they were not finished or used for some time after the theater opening. The auditorium interior was not Latrobe's but, as often happened, was designed by the theater's scene-painting department. The new front had a classic quality unwonted in Philadelphia. The sculptured panels of the new end

sociated with Livingston and Roosevelt in their 1798 steamboat experiments. An inventor with a restless imagination, he was in later life chiefly instrumental in railroad development.

7. In 1812, Robert Mills and the engineer Lewis Wernwag completed the timber Upper Ferry bridge over the Schuylkill. It was an arched bridge of low rise, the sides concave for lateral stability. It stood till 1818, when it burned. At the time it was built it had the longest single span (344 feet) of any bridge in the world.

8. See Appendix for the complete text.

pavilions harmonized with the figures of Comedy and Tragedy, carved by Rush, in the niches of the older front which showed above and behind the new work. Over the colonnade the architect had hoped to use an "emblem" (of English Coade stone) with the arms of the state in the center, but existing engravings show that this was not included. The colonnade was Corinthian—apparently the simple Greek Corinthian of the Tower of the Winds—but, alas, as a matter of economy and against Latrobe's wish, it was of wood and the leaves of the capitals were of papier-mâché, made by the decorator Holland.[9]

The work, like many alteration jobs, was a taxing one; yet payment for his services was almost indefinitely postponed. We find him writing again and again about his bill all through 1804. In 1805 he says, "I have waited four years for any payment," and he states (February 6) that he is putting the matter into the hands of his attorney; on April 1 he writes Richard North in Philadelphia that there is $800 due him from the theater. Whether he ever received it, or any part of it, is problematical; apparently an architect's fee for making the theater usable had the last call on the treasurer's till.[10]

Another job phizzed into smoke entirely—the Philadelphia Exchange, planned for the Philadelphia Chamber of Commerce through a certain J. P. Broome. This was a most ambitious project, to occupy a lot on Second and Dock streets directly opposite the Bank of Pennsylvania. The design had originally been made as early as 1800, but subscriptions lagged. As late as 1805 the idea was still considered "alive," and Latrobe wrote David Cox on February 4 to refresh his mind about the lot size (106 by 209 feet) and the contemplated method of building in three stages corresponding to the three units of which it consisted. In front there was to be an open colonnaded court—a summer exchange—with four large rooms around it; next, a winter exchange room eighty feet square, bordered by small offices; then, at the rear, rooms for auctions and a customs house. More than a year later (May 27, 1806) Latrobe wrote J. P. Broome, then in New York, that he felt that subscriptions

9. Letter to the agents of the new theater, July 4, 1806. In this letter Latrobe also pleads for the final completion and decoration of the retiring rooms for subscribers.

10. It was probably this failure of the theater to pay that he refers to in a letter to Roosevelt (March 26, 1805): ". . . a most serious disappointment to the amount of 850 dollars, on which I counted with the fullest reliance has thrown me into the utmost difficulty . . ."

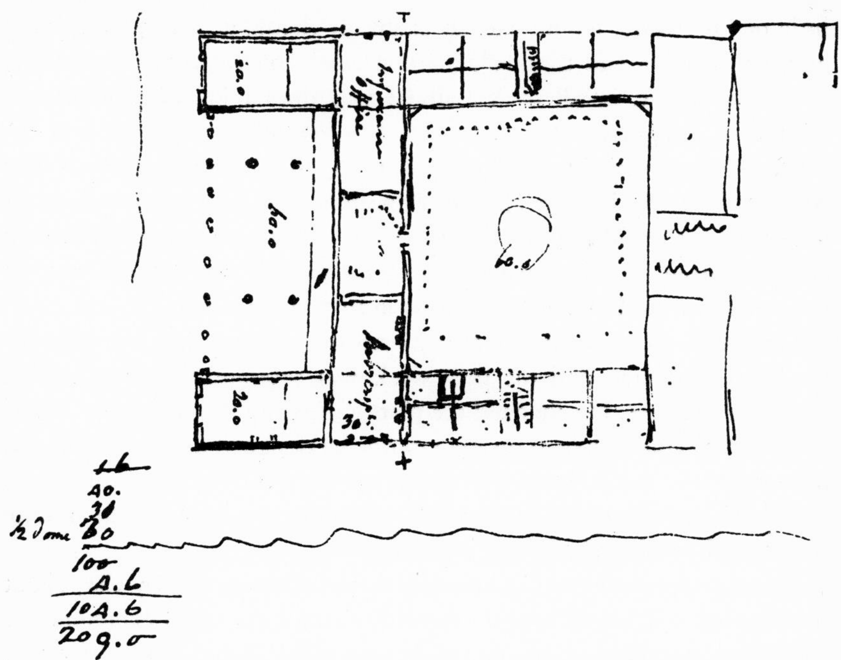

From the Latrobe letter books

FIGURE 14. Proposed Philadelphia Exchange. Rough Sketch Plan. From Latrobe's letter to Daniel Cox, February 4, 1805.

would eventually be forthcoming. But the matter had become snarled in real estate speculation, for Broome had seen an opportunity to unload a piece of property he owned, and Latrobe told him, probably with secret pleasure, there was no possibility of the Exchange's moving to Broome's lot; the definite action of the Chamber of Commerce had specified the Second Street site. Latrobe still counted on the job, and the gradual fading out of the grand scheme must have been a severe blow.[11]

There was still another taunting will-o'-the-wisp: the alteration of Bingham's great mansion into a "Tontine" coffee house—a luxurious cooperative club for Philadelphia businessmen, like the Tontine Coffee House which McComb had designed in New York. Latrobe was the natural choice for architect. But here again subscriptions failed to materialize, and eventually the aim was changed; the Bingham house became the Mansion House Hotel. The hotel job, too, brought Latrobe

11. On May 6, 1806, he wrote his father-in-law: "The Chamber of Commerce has no fund out of which to pay me."

little or no money, for he had no claim on Renshaw, the lessor; it also brought vexation and trouble. Financial confusion reigned, much litigation ensued, and in all of it Latrobe was drawn in, willy-nilly, as a witness.

But other commissions did materialize in that difficult period. There was, for instance, Nassau Hall at Princeton. This had been completely gutted by fire on March 6, 1802; the roofs, floors, and partitions had all been destroyed, but the greater part of the exterior walls (of stone) remained. It was to Latrobe that Princeton turned for the design and carrying out of the restoration. He contributed his services, charging only for the actual expenses, and the new work was substantially completed in the following year. He changed the plan somewhat, laying out the rooms on a more regular scheme; on the exterior he designed a new, wider, and taller cupola of great elegance of detail, and over the old simple entrances he added pediments to make them more consonant with the monumental scale of the whole long building.[12]

The architect was proud of his work there and wrote Henry Clay about it (May 15, 1812) apropos of Transylvania College in Lexington, for which he had made a design (to be considered later): "In Princeton, they lodge three or two [students] in a room of 16 or 12 by about 15 [feet] . . . divided into 2 or 3 cells for study thus . . ." (adding a sketch). Further on he continued: "The renovation of Princeton, the College of Carlisle, the Medical Schools of Philadelphia are among the most gratifying exertions of my art . . ." Although he had contributed his services, Princeton's gratitude was grudging. He had used iron for the roof—and the roof leaked. The Princeton authorities were much disturbed and wrote to Elias Boudinot in Philadelphia suggesting angrily that Latrobe "be held strictly to account." Latrobe wrote to Samuel Mifflin, manager of the rolling mill at the waterworks, about this iron, but there is no further reference to it in the correspondence.[13]

Dickinson College at Carlisle, Pennsylvania, was a more satisfactory engagement, though here again his services were donated. In 1803 he was approached with regard to this commission by Hugh Brackenridge, the famous judge and satiric author, who had made a special hurried

12. Latrobe's reconstructions produced in large measure the Nassau Hall of today, save for the arched entrance, the modifications in the cupola, and the interesting end stair towers of stone that were added by Notman some half century later.

13. See "Mr. Duffield's Letters," *Princeton Alumni Weekly,* Friday, August 10, 1934, p. 5.

trip to Philadelphia to catch Latrobe before he left on one of his visits to Washington. The two men seem to have developed an instant understanding and mutual liking, and Latrobe attacked the design with pleasure. Before long (on May 18, 1803) the designs were sent to James Hamilton in Carlisle by Brackenridge, together with a long explanatory letter by Latrobe:

. . . I will beg leave to state to you the principles which have governed me in the distribution, & arrangement of the apartments.—

The two aspects, the most unpleasant in our climate are the North East & the North West. The extreme cold of the North West winds in winter, & their dryness, which causes a rapid evaporation so thoroughly chills the walls of every house, exposed to them, that when the wind, as is almost always the case, changes afterwards to the West & S.W. & becomes warmer & moister,—the water is precipitated upon the Walls from the air, by their coldness,—as upon the outside of a Glass of cold Water in warm weather,—and they soon stream with humidity.—The North East winds bring along rain & sleet,—& their violence drives the moisture into every wall of which the material will permit it.—The unpleasantness of the winds is aggravated by the suddenness with which the Northwest commonly succeeds the North East.—I have stated these things, which are indeed known to every body, in order to explain a *law,* which is thereby imposed upon the Architecture of our Country: It is,—to reserve the Southern aspects of every building in the erection of which the choice is free, for the inhabited apartments, and to occupy the Northern aspects by communications, as Stairs, Lobbies, Halls, Vestibules, etc.

This Law governs the designs herewith presented to you.

On the North are the Vestibule & Lobbies, or passages. They protect the Southern rooms from the effect of the Northern winds. On this Aspect I have also placed the dining room, a room only occasionally occupied for a short time,—& the School rooms above it,—which by means of Stoves, & the concourse of Students are easily kept warm. There are indeed two Chambers in the N.E. wing on each story.—If these Chambers be inhabited by Preceptors, the one as a study, the other as a Bedchamber, the disadvantages of the Aspect must be overcome by such means, of Curtains & Carpets, as a Student does not so easily acquire. The South Front affords on each story 6 rooms for Students. The angle rooms will accommodate 3, and each of the other, 2 Students; in all 14 on each floor.[14]

14. See William W. Edel, "Hugh Brackenridge's Ride: How We Got 'Old West,'" in *Bulwark of Liberty,* vol. 1 of The Boyd Lee Spahr Lectures in Americana, Dickinson Col-

Brackenridge reported to Hamilton in his letter that Latrobe much preferred stone to brick as the building material.

Two of Latrobe's original preliminary drawings—the basement plan and the north elevation—exist in Dickinson College. They indicate the basic scheme as built, although the proportions of the details of the elevation differ somewhat from the executed work and the sketch shows no cupola. Since the changes between drawing and building were clearly intended to produce a more coherent whole, and since the details (especially the cupola) are in a spirit that is obviously Latrobe's, it seems likely that they were the result of further study by the architect and that the lost working drawings which he made incorporated them. The building is a U-shaped structure with projecting wings on the north side to shelter the main entrance (originally on the north also, though now closed); there is an off-center corridor, with only small rooms to the north and deeper ones to the south; and on the sunny southern side are the "hall," below, and above it a large room at first intended as the library. The exterior—except for the closing of the north door—remains substantially as Latrobe planned it and has all of his love for simple, strong forms. It is built of stone, as he suggested, with brick for arches here and there. Its proportions are eminently satisfactory, and its deft handling of scale is obvious. Almost the only purely decorative features are the inscription panel on the north front and the exquisite cupola with its quaint iron weather vane—now called the Mermaid but probably intended as Aeolus pointing into the wind. Perhaps someday the old north entrance will again be opened and the original sheltered forecourt on that side brought back to its pristine charm. Yet even changed as it is it remains one of the most distinguished, and certainly the most subtly designed, of all early American college structures, for its distinction is founded not on ornament but on solid qualities of functional planning, good proportion, and excellent materials beautifully used.

The third of Latrobe's educational projects was the Medical School of the University of Pennsylvania. With the removal of the national govern-

---

lege, Carlisle, Pa. (New York: Revell [c1950]), pp. 115-45. Latrobe's remarks on orientation are particularly interesting. In the "Observations" before Chapter 10, of part II, vol. II, book 3, in Hugh Henry Brackenridge's satiric potpourri, *Modern Chivalry,* first published in 1805 but later reprinted (New York, Cincinnati, etc.: American Book Co. [c1937]), there is a passage on house design very similar. He may well have expanded it from Latrobe's ideas.

ment to Washington, the great house that had been built for the President on Walnut Street in Philadelphia was purchased by the University of Pennsylvania as its chief building. As early as 1800 Latrobe had been consulted about the necessary alterations and on December 29 of that year had submitted plans (now lost); a detailed report exists in the University archives.[15] Latrobe furnished all the accommodations that had been demanded—including quarters for the "charity schools" for boys and for girls—except residences for four professors; for these, he found, "the arrangement of the house is extremely unfavorable." He did, however, provide accommodations for the master of the charity schools and for one other professor; he says, "I have endeavored so to arrange his apartments, that their convenience and number may entice the principal Professor or Provost to solicit the use of them." He wished to remove the old double stairs in the circular hall, replacing them with new stairs and using the old north service stairs as the main stair of the new arrangement; then the large circular hall could be made into a handsome combined chapel and exhibition room two stories high.

Exactly how much, if any, of Latrobe's plan was carried out at this time is unclear, but four and a half years later he obtained from the University a more important commission. The institution itself had been formed by the merging of the College of Philadelphia and the Medical School, and in 1805 a large wing designed by Latrobe for the Medical School was added at the rear. The architect was introduced to this commission through his always helpful friend Samuel Fox, who wrote him on May 9 with regard to the needs of the University. Latrobe answered (May 11) pessimistically in respect to the likelihood of his design's being accepted: "I well know that the probability of its adoption will be in inverse ratio to the excellence of the design. But it will be an ample reward to me have complied with a wish of yours . . ." Then on May 25 he sent on the completed sketch, with a letter in which he noted that he had had in mind the "famous anatomical hall in Paris" in his design of the chemical lecture room and that the best way of heating such a large room was "by steam pipes of tin."

The trustees did accept the design, and construction went forward at once under Latrobe's direction. No views or plans of the interior have

15. "Report of the Committee to Provide for the Payment of the President's House, &c.," pamphlet XIII of University Papers in the University of Pennsylvania archives (n.p., n.d., printed by Z. Poulson, Jr.). I owe this reference to Mr. Charles E. Peterson.

as yet come to light, but there is a charming little drawing by Strickland (in the Historical Society of Pennsylvania) which shows the exterior. It is a characteristic Latrobe design, of great elegance, and one in which simplicity adds markedly to its geometric grace. A low Roman dome over the anatomical hall crowns the composition, and a cupola and large semicircular windows give light. Below, the mass of the building, apparently T- or cross-shaped and two stories high, is interesting in proportion and has the triple rectangular windows of which the architect was fond. The whole is distinguished and serene, set though it is behind a high masonry wall. A severe gateway with a segmentally headed door—probably also by him—gives access from the street.[16]

Latrobe also handled numerous alterations within the mansion itself, perhaps carrying out the suggestions contained in his report five years earlier, changing partitions and modifying and adding to the stairs to make circulation easy for the various departments of the University. All in all it was a large commission and one of which he was proud, yet he gained from it little save reputation. He complains to Isaac Hazlehurst (July 21, 1806): "With the Trustees of the University, my bargain was disgraceful—$250 in lieu of $500 . . ." Even learned and professional Philadelphia could not see its way to pay an architect his due! Nor did he have better fortune with his own Masonic brothers, for whom in 1807 he designed a Masonic Hall, to contain also a dancing and assembly hall; in 1811 he was still trying (May 30) to collect from them the $150 which he felt they owed him for his work.

He could not even get paid for some domestic work actually completed from his designs. In 1804 S. Goodwin wanted to build a house, *vaulted throughout,* at Ninth and Market streets. The client had agreed to pay Latrobe $100 for the design, and the house was built from his drawings and under his supervision. He was never paid; seven years later (May 30, 1811) he wrote from Washington to a Philadelphia attorney, S. Ewing, asking him to sue for the amount owed him. If, as it appears, this was

---

16. In 1817 William Strickland was engaged to design a new Medical Hall and in the following year he made various alterations and repairs to the older existing one. These chiefly consisted of repairs of the flooring of the first and second stories and certain additional sinks and drains, the total amount involved being some $600. See Agnes Addison Gilchrist, *William Strickland, Architect and Engineer, 1788-1854* (Philadelphia: University of Pennsylvania Press, 1950). A few years later, in 1829-30, the old house built for the President of the United States was demolished, along with the Medical School, and two new buildings were constructed from Strickland's design.

the country's first masonry-vaulted fireproof house, it is doubly unfortunate that no other record of it than Latrobe's letters seems to exist.

But 1805 brought him another job that was more rewarding—his first large Philadelphia house since the ill-fated Sedgeley. This was the Waln house, on the southeast corner of Chestnut and Seventh streets. Among Mary Elizabeth's closest girlhood friends had been Mary Wilcocks, who at this time was engaged to William Waln, the successful and wealthy China merchant. On March 12 Latrobe answers a letter from her brother, J. S. Wilcocks, who had written him (March 5) about a house that Waln was thinking of building for his bride:

> I have also received a letter, on the same subject, from another gentleman [Fox, perhaps] in Philadelphia who in naming the proprietor of the lot has given me a motive for the exertion of my best talents & industry by leading me to believe that the house I may design, will be inhabited by a Lady, more loved and esteemed by Mrs. Latrobe than any of her friends . . .

By March 21 he had developed a preliminary sketch and sent on a book of the designs. Then (March 26) he wrote Waln a long explanatory letter in which he incorporated the basic theories of his house designs. Every good building, he says, is adapted to both climate and to manners, and though American manners are English the American climate is entirely different from the English climate; hence copies of English houses in the United States are faulty. French houses, on the other hand, have many elements more suited to the American climate than do the English; yet, since our manners are still basically English, to copy French houses would be equally silly. "All we require," he writes, "is the greatest possible compactness, & convenience for the family, expressed in the very comprehensive word *comfort,* and moderate means of entertaining company."

He describes the typical French house, divided so that its functions do not overlap and recommends the French system of having "two distinct apartments on the principal floor,—l'appartement de Madame & l'appartement de Monsieur." He calls for a bathroom and a water closet, as well as a private service stair. Conversely, in the English house of four rooms to a floor and a central hall and staircase, this hall becomes "a kind of turnpike road through the house over which everyone, whether visitor or member of the family, male or female, sick or well must pass, paying toll to curiosity." In the Waln design, he continues, he has striven to combine the advantages of both the English and the French types and to avoid "back buildings" (rear extensions) in order to keep the rear of the lot free for gardens and stables. This he has achieved by putting the kitchen, service stair, and services on the rear of the low-studded ground floor, with only a small entrance hall and stairs at the front, and by placing all the main rooms above on the main floor—the scheme generally known as the English basement house.

The house Latrobe envisaged had many similarities in plan to the Tayloe house design made seven years earlier in Virginia—again an example of how he liked to work all the possible variations on an architectural idea that appealed to him. As in that scheme, the stairs here were centrally placed and lighted by a "lanthorn," with the rooms ranged around to get the greatest benefit from the external windows. Fearing that this design would seem too radical, he sent at the same time another set of plans, which he also describes; but these, too, called for a central main staircase and a separate service stair. Neither design, however, seems to have completely pleased the Walns, for on May 6, 1805, he sent a third set—perhaps combining elements from the first two—and on June 25 a fourth design, probably the final one, for with it he encloses his first bill for one hundred dollars.

Latrobe laid great stress on this commission and wanted to make sure that it got started in the right way. He dreaded a possible repetition of the Sedgeley experience and insisted on keeping the detailing and the supervision in his own hands. The vehement letter to Waln already quoted [17] reveals his deep anxiety on this point. The house was slow in construction and was only completed in 1808. Robert Mills acted as superintendent on the job. As a residence it seems to have been the success Latrobe had hoped, and he not only designed all the furniture but also advised on the planting of the grounds. Its richness is indicated by the drawing-room frieze representing scenes from the Iliad and the Odyssey based on Flaxman and painted in "Etruscan colors." [18] The painter was George Bridport (the brother of the architect Hugh Bridport), who later painted the ceiling of the House of Representatives in Washington. Latrobe was very proud of the Waln frieze and recommended the painter to all his friends.

---

17. See page 150.
18. Letter of Latrobe to Joseph Norris, June 6, 1809.

Unfortunately no plans and no photographs of the Waln house have been preserved; the only graphic record of its beauty is a charming little water color now in the Ridgeway Branch of the Free Library of Philadelphia.[19] The house was placed well back on the lot, and the ground rose somewhat from the street level. It was rectangular in plan, with a hipped roof, and there were square one-story pavilions at the front corners (like those in the Tayloe design) which created a sort of forecourt. The openings were few and large, and the detail was extremely reticent. Like the Burd home, the house was large in scale and a striking addition to the Chestnut Street ensemble.

Two other houses of this period warrant notice: one (already referred to) for Latrobe's old Virginia friend Dr. McClurg, in Richmond; and Adena, the mansion that Colonel Thomas Worthington commissioned in Chillicothe, Ohio. Latrobe had met Thomas Worthington in Washington, where he was serving as a member of the House of Representatives, and had started work on the designs sometime in the late summer of 1805; on September 2 he wrote Worthington that the sketches were ready and that he was sending them to him by one of the draftsmen, Louis de Mun; by the end of March, 1806, working drawings were well under way.

Adena still stands and has been restored to its original state. It is an impressive residence, all of cut stone, with a large central block, hip-roofed, and two one-story wings; between these there is a terrace, and a colonnaded porch across the central block connects the wings on the north, or entrance, side. The details are of the simplest; the emphasis, as in so many of Latrobe's houses, is on geometrical power and the distinction that comes from restraint. Since the architect could not superintend the construction in far-off Ohio, alterations may have been made in his design when the house was built. But according to local tradition Worthington brought two skilled workmen from the East with him to do the actual building and Latrobe's drawings were carefully followed.

Certainly the plan bears every evidence of being Latrobe's. The orientation, with the entrance to the north between sheltering wings and

---

19. A tiny photograph of this water color is included in Casper Souder, Jr., *The History of Chestnut Street, Philadelphia* . . . (Philadelphia: King & Baird, 1860).

William Waln found himself in financial difficulties only a few years after the house was completed. He therefore sold it to Dr. Swain, who had made a fortune with a popular panacea. Later still, Swain changed the house into a public bath called Swain's Baths.

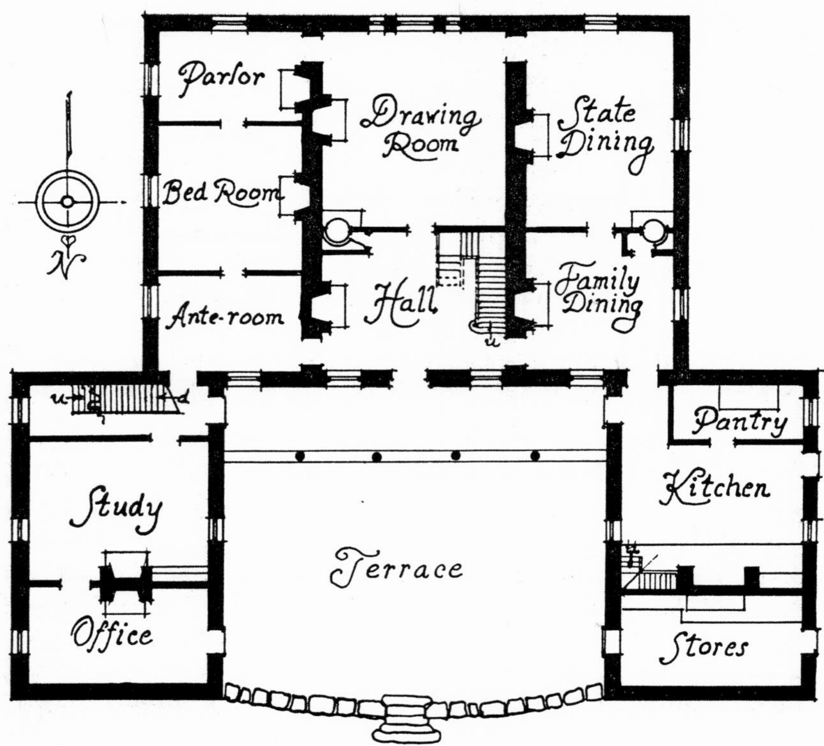

with the chief rooms to the south, follows the scheme of the Dickinson College building. Heavy stone cross walls, containing the fireplaces, divide the main block into unequal thirds. The eastern third, together with the east wing, forms just such a private suite—with its own exterior door—as Latrobe describes in his Waln house plan, and the circulation is ingeniously designed to give ease of passage and yet to preserve perfect privacy for the bedrooms. Similarly, the western portion, containing the kitchen, the private dining room, and the state dining room, is carefully arranged for ease of service. Upstairs, too, there is the same kind of *en suite* planning. The two heavy cross walls continue up through the second floor; the eastern section is obviously intended for the family and is connected by a separate private stair to the owner's suite below. There is also direct connection to a large storage or work space—possibly a spinning and weaving room—in the attic of the one-story eastern wing.

At Adena there is one other evidence of Latrobe's original thinking: the ingenious cylindrical rotating servers leading to the state dining room

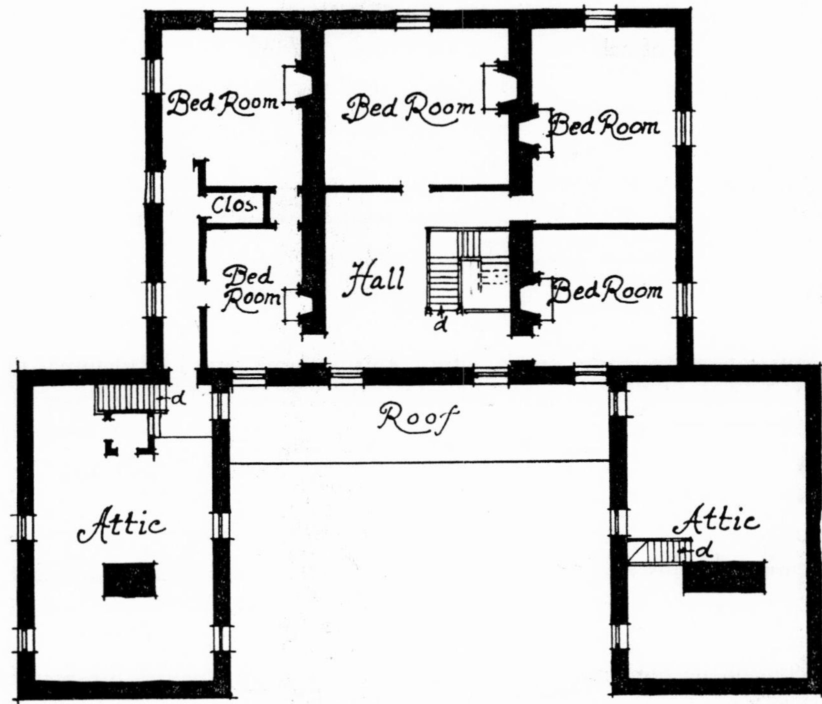

Courtesy James H. Rodenbaugh

FIGURE 15. Worthington House, Adena, Chillicothe, Ohio. Plans. From measured drawings.

and the drawing room. In his report to Waln, cited above, he had objected to the lack of privacy in the ordinary course of domestic service as provided for in the conventional plan. Here, although service to the drawing room is through the hall, the designer made it possible for food and drinks to be served in the important rooms without having the servants enter the rooms at all, and he arranged it all so that when important state dinners are given the family dining room becomes itself a commodious serving room. These rotating servers would be used again when Latrobe designed the Van Ness house in Washington ten years later; they are typical examples of Latrobe's ingenuity.

Latrobe's largest private architectural commission of these early years was the Roman Catholic Cathedral of Baltimore, so important that it warrants a later chapter of its own. This occupied him off and on for years, beginning with the spring of 1804. To the architect its design was a ringing challenge, as well as a magnificent opportunity, to prove himself as capable of achieving true monumentality in a large building as in the much smaller Bank of Pennsylvania; he rose magnificently to the occasion.

Other little jobs we hear of in these years—the designing of a seal for the Bank of Philadelphia (later he was to design its new building), and of a pedestal for the metal statue of William Penn in the Philadelphia Hospital, for which he billed the committee in charge $25.00; that is nearly the complete list.

This, then, is almost the total of Latrobe's non-governmental architectural work in those crucial years; this was all that Philadelphia, in a time of rapid growth, could offer him. And the record, as we examine it from the financial side, becomes even sparser. Among his commissions, only the Bank of Pennsylvania and the Waln house were complete enterprises, carried through from beginning to end and bringing fees compatible with the effort involved. The McClurg and Worthington houses required designs and drawings only, and the bills for them must have been correspondingly meager. The theater job, which should have paid him liberally, brought nothing or nearly nothing. For Princeton and Dickinson he donated his services, charging merely expenses. From the University of Pennsylvania he received only a pittance; it was the Richmond penitentiary experience all over again. No man with a growing family and with Latrobe's social position could hope to live on that basis!

Moreover, this was during the years when the financial web of his association with Bollman and Roosevelt had ensnared him in unforeseen and burdensome debts—the years during which, to save his credit and his reputation, he had been forced to sacrifice all his current permanent assets. Had the Latrobes depended entirely on architecture, they would have faced actual destitution; indeed, they skated several times along its perilous and terrifying edge.

Two things came to their rescue: Latrobe's reputation as an engineer and important appointments from the national government. Both, however, turned his interests away from Philadelphia—where he and Mary so ardently wished to live—and finally forced them to leave it. From 1803 on, the family home was successively in many places, their longest single stay in Washington. It is one of the great achievements of Mary Elizabeth Latrobe that she had the courage and the adaptability to welcome cheerfully each new abode and make it a delightful home for her husband and children. That quality shines out everywhere—in Latrobe's letters to his English relatives, in the accounts of her son John H. B. Latrobe, in various social notes on Washington—and it gleams between the lines through a hundred of Latrobe's business letters.

Their wanderings began as a result of his connection with the long-contemplated Chesapeake and Delaware Canal, which had been projected before the Revolution. Benjamin Franklin had supported the idea, Thomas Gilpin had been an enthusiastic advocate, and preliminary surveys had been made, though no actual work had been carried out. But at the turn of the nineteenth century many canals and turnpike roads were being built; increasing commerce and industrial development combined to make closer communication between the cities and their hinterlands, as well as between the cities themselves, more and more essential. If a canal could be cut between these two great estuaries, water-borne traffic between Philadelphia and Washington, Annapolis, or Baltimore could save the long and frequently dangerous voyage down Delaware Bay, around Cape Henlopen and Cape Charles, and up the Chesapeake. Accordingly some of the most important men of Philadelphia—under the stimulus of Thomas Gilpin and his son Joshua—formed the Chesapeake and Delaware Canal Company. This was organized under the aegis of the state of Pennsylvania, which contributed some of the capital and retained a certain supervisory power exercised through commissioners appointed by the governor. Early in 1803 Governor McKean appointed Latrobe as one of these; it was an almost inevitable appointment in view of his efficient and economical handling of the Susquehanna River survey. And the canal company, in order to cement its bonds with the state as well as because of his reputation, commissioned him to make a careful survey of the canal route.

Such a survey, of course, required residence close to the area, and in the summer of 1803 the family moved to Newcastle, Delaware—the first stop in their wanderings. It was close enough to Philadelphia to allow easy visiting there for a day or a week and, at the same time, close enough to the general area to be surveyed so that Latrobe could be home at least for week ends. "Having a pleasant carriage and excellent horses," Mary Elizabeth Latrobe says of this period in her memoir of her husband, she would drive over on Friday evening to get him, usually at Elk Forge—he was generally away from Monday to Friday. Their little boy John, his nurse, and Lydia would accompany her; Henry was at Drake's boarding school in Philadelphia. Mary's father wished them to return to Philadelphia; but on October 11 Latrobe wrote his father-in-law that living there would be impossible, and he started looking around for a residence near Elkton, Maryland, where the most time-consuming work was centered. In the autumn Lydia also was sent to school in Philadelphia—Jaudon's Academy—and in December the Latrobes were already planning their first extensive trip to Washington and writing their friend Samuel Harrison Smith, the famous Washington editor, about lodgings. The Latrobes remained in Washington for roughly two months, from January 8 to the end of February, 1804, Latrobe making a short trip back to Newcastle in the meantime.

It was during this visit to Washington that Latrobe learned of his promotion in the canal company; he had been appointed engineer in charge, with complete control of all design and construction. The salary, for the time, was excellent—$3,500—and this, with the fees from his Washington work (of which more later), seemed to assure him the security for which he had vainly been seeking. But he was in a quandary about where he should live—Philadelphia? near the canal? Washington? There were objections to any of the alternatives; all meant working at a distance from important commissions or prospects. But immediate pressure from the canal company determined his decision, and during his journey from Washington to the canal at the end of January he purchased a farm on the top of Iron Hill (near Elkton) for nine dollars an acre, from one "Mrs. McDonald (late Miss Polly McDaniel)." The farm consisted of between fifty and sixty acres, as he wrote his father-in-law (February 4, 1804), and he intended it chiefly for a summer residence. His wife was pregnant at the time and apparently none too well. Two days later he withdrew Lydia from the Jaudon Academy, informing Mr. Jaudon that she was needed at home. At the same time he withdrew Henry from Mr. Drake's school, although much pleased with his progress there, in order to enter him in Father Dubourg's college or seminary in Baltimore—not from any religious motive but because he liked the continental atmosphere there and the Latin type of education that was offered.[20]

---

20. Father William Dubourg was a French Sulpician monk, a refugee from the French Revolution, who in 1800 had established an academy in connection with the Sulpician monastery in Baltimore. Most of his faculty, like himself, had come direct from the Acad-

To understand the choice of Iron Hill, one must know something of the progress on the canal. When Latrobe was engaged as engineer, its route was still unsettled, save that it should start somewhere in the Elk River neighborhood on the Chesapeake and debouch into the Delaware either through Christiana Creek and the Christiana River, flowing by Wilmington, or else close to Newcastle and directly on the Bay. John Tatnall was president of the company; in Latrobe's letters to him, as well as to his own particular friend among the directors, Joshua Gilpin, one can follow the discussion. On October 10, 1803, Latrobe sent Gilpin a sketch map showing the various possibilities, and he wrote him again on October 18; disgusted with quarrels among the board of directors—each wanting the canal to be run according to his prejudices or property holdings—he was almost willing to throw up the whole job.

Seven months later the matter was still undecided. Latrobe wrote Isaac Hazlehurst (May 14, 1804) that everything pointed to Newcastle as the best eastern terminus but that the majority of the stock subscriptions pointed the other way. Even Latrobe's advice could not overbalance that economic pressure! But his advice did have one effect—the change of the western end from Frenchtown, up the shallow Elk River, to Welch Point, the promontory where Back Creek joins the Elk. A series of locks here would, in one flight, lift the canal from relatively deep water in the Chesapeake to almost the highest point it would need to reach, and from there on the route would be comparatively level; enormous economies over the original other route would result, and the canal mouth would be much easier to approach from the bay.

He made numerous surveying trips to this area in those early days, apparently enjoying them thoroughly; the rough living and the spice of danger in making wild passages in small boats were welcome anodynes for his almost constant financial worries. And he appreciated to the full

---

emy of St. Sulpice in Paris. This academy, later called Saint Mary's College, offered a classic education—largely in the manner of a French lycée—from the secondary-school through the college level; the closely related St. Mary's Roman Catholic Seminary (founded in 1791) offered the more advanced theological training. The educational standards of the college were high, and for a period it enjoyed a great popularity even among non-Catholics. Latrobe wrote Dubourg (January 14, 1805) urging that the academy-college be officially chartered, and later that year it was legally incorporated as a "university." In 1805 Maximilian Godefroy, the architect, came to Baltimore to be professor of civil and military architecture and of the fine arts at the new university and a few years later designed for the seminary a remarkable Gothic chapel, which still stands.

the beauty of these headwaters of the Chesapeake—the woods, the sand bluffs, the little towns—and as late as August, 1806, on a final tour of the canal work, he stopped long enough to make a series of charming water colors of various spots in the area—scenes that appear not too different today.

The route the canal was to take was at last determined in June, 1804—Welch Point to Christiana Creek—and construction could actually begin. Already large orders had gone to Philadelphia for shovels, spades, and wheelbarrows, and on May 10, 1804, John Strickland, carpenter, builder, and father of William Strickland the architect, was engaged as construction foreman and was set up temporarily in the existing log cabin on Latrobe's farm at Iron Hill, where his first job was to build barracks for the expected workers; Latrobe sent him (May 3) a sketch of what he wanted. One foreboding note was sounded on the same day: Latrobe wrote Gilpin that the canal construction was feeling a shortage of funds.

The first work planned for the project itself was the construction of a feeder line to bring water from the Elk River, above its falls, to the proposed canal, since water was necessary for the canal itself as well as to facilitate its construction. This feeder left the Elk near Elk Forge and passed beneath Iron Hill, not far away; hence the purchase of land at Iron Hill both by the company and by Latrobe himself. Early in 1804, too, Latrobe was searching for a quarry of good building stone for the locks. He had written Traquair in a preliminary way about stone blocks for the lock construction almost a year earlier, for Latrobe considered the wooden locks used on many early canals to be wasteful makeshifts. The feeder went forward rapidly. It was to be twenty-one feet wide, with a water depth of three and one-half feet, and could itself serve as a branch canal for light-draft scows and barges. Yet as it progressed the crucial need for money became ever more harassing—on July 6 the work needed two thousand dollars immediately and on August 26 there was a "desperate need of money"—for the subscribers to the canal stock were laggard in paying up their subscriptions, and Latrobe was beginning to have difficulty in collecting his salary.[21]

---

21. In a letter of October 29, 1804, to a stockholder of the canal company (John Helmsley, of Centerville, Maryland) Latrobe gives some estimated costs of the canal, as follows: Total amount of subscriptions expected, $350,000. Cost of the water of the Elk, $66,000. Cost of the feeder, $40,000. Distance of the feeder from Welch Point, 8½ miles at an average of $15,800 per mile. (This makes the total cost of the western half of the canal $335,300.)

And the canal had its share of labor troubles. Suddenly to place a hundred or more common laborers in barracks in a quiet rural community which had few facilities for recreation created a critical situation, which finally erupted early in October, 1804, in a riot that developed from arguments surrounding a horse race at Elkton. It was a serious riot—one man was killed and thirty were wounded—but the fault, Latrobe thought, lay not on the side of the laborers. He wrote to Joshua Gilpin about it (October 7): "I have a body of evidence on that subject, which must some day come forward and which will redound to the honor of our people, as to the disgrace of the *gentlemen* jockies and gamblers of the neighborhood . . ."

In other ways, too, this was a bad period for the Latrobes. The financial difficulties surrounding the Philadelphia waterworks and the rolling mill were mounting steadily. Even the mill itself seemed to be producing less well than was expected, and Latrobe was forced to write constantly to Samuel Mifflin, the manager, urging him to hasten deliveries of sheet iron needed for this, that, or the other job—especially for the public buildings in Washington and for President Jefferson's Monticello. And more personal troubles intervened. At the end of May, 1804, Mary's brother Robert Hazlehurst died, and on July 11 their mother, Mrs. Isaac Hazlehurst, passed away. Mrs. Latrobe was not told of her mother's death immediately, for on July 17 a daughter, Juliana Elizabeth (Julia), was born to the Latrobes in Philadelphia; a little later they moved there to stay with the bereaved Hazlehursts till September.[22]

---

22. On March 22, 1805, Latrobe sent Samuel Hazlehurst suggestions for the inscriptions to be carved on the tombstones of Mrs. Hazlehurst and Robert at Mount Holly, as follows:

In Memory
of Robert Hazlehurst, son of Isaac Hazlehurst
born ———
died ———
With talents to serve
Virtue to adorn,
Wit to delight
Affections to enjoy
this world
He departed in the bloom of his youth
Leaving to his afflicted friends
The consolation of immortal bliss
The admiration of his worth
The instruction of his example

When the family returned to Delaware, it was to a different residence. This was a house in Wilmington, owned and lent to them by Isaac Hazlehurst. It required major repairs and complete redecoration, for which Mr. Hazlehurst paid; the total costs were over six hundred dollars, a sizable amount at that time. This place was their home until the next summer (when again they moved to Iron Hill) and also from October through December of 1805; from then on till they finally settled in Washington in the spring of 1807 they lived chiefly in Philadelphia, though Latrobe himself was absent in Washington almost half the time. Of all their homes, Iron Hill was probably their favorite. High on the summit of the hill, the house commanded a superb view embracing both the headwaters of the Chesapeake and the gleam of Delaware Bay, thus overlooking the entire terrain the canal must traverse. In addition it was restful and far removed from the bustle of traffic or the hurry of towns; it was a wonderful refuge from the day's business, a palliative to worries and fears. When the Latrobes bought the farm it had a two-

---

22 (cont'd).

To the Memory of
Juliana, wife of Isaac Hazlehurst, Esq.
and daughter of Sam[l] Purviance late of
Salem County in this state
She was born March 18, 1740, and
died July 11, 1804, at Cloverhill
in the 65th year of her age
To her
Tender, prudent, pious, intelligent
one daughter and six sons
owe
their being and their virtue
To her
The solitary mourner who erects this tomb
The pride and the consolation
That for 33 years, her love and her counsel
Blessed their union
To her
In the search—now vain—for happiness
in this world
The cheering certainty that he shall share
Her immortality

At the present writing (1954) there is no trace in the Mount Holly churchyard of the stone for Robert Hazlehurst and no record of his burial there, but Mrs. Isaac Hazlehurst's stone is intact and shows that a slightly shortened version of Latrobe's text was used for the inscription.

story log house on it, and it was here that John Strickland was first installed; later it became the nexus of the larger house into which it grew as Latrobe added to it to meet the needs of his growing family. Yet, though they liked it so much, they were fated to live in it only one full summer and part of another.[23]

In all this period Latrobe was busy—frantically, almost maniacally so. Jobs in Philadelphia, the Cathedral at Baltimore, the endless details of the canal, the growing work for the national government—these would have filled any two other men's time, yet in actual income how unprofitable! He made one ill-fated attempt to obtain something of real value for his work in the "American" way, by speculation. Judge Kinsey Johns of Newcastle suggested it to him in the spring of 1805; it was the plan that they should be partners in purchasing, at its current low value (nine dollars an acre), a sizable tract of land where the canal and the feeder met. Of the ethics of such a speculation—by which the engineer and a stockholder would benefit from the construction of the canal—it is perhaps better not to judge; Latrobe's dire need of money may have blinded him to the actual issues involved. In any case he was well punished. "The speculation is a great one," he wrote to Roosevelt on March 28, "but a most serious disappointment to the amount of $850, on which I counted with the fullest reliance has thrown me into the utmost difficulty. I have given bond to pay on the 10th of April 750$ [elsewhere he mentions notes to Johns of $675], being the amount of my half, and have not a dollar towards it, nor know where to borrow it . . ." But by June 14 he had somehow scraped together enough to pay Johns $425

23. On June 5, 1805, he wrote to Eric Bollman from Wilmington before his move to Iron Hill, about the inconveniences of living far from his work:

"The board [the canal directors] broke up only yesterday, & left me vexed & fatigued, & I am now in an hour again going to the works 17 miles from hence where I spend all my working days of the week, seeing my family only on Sunday & part of Saturday & Monday morning. This is one of the features of that enviable profession you sometimes speak of & write about, a profession the outside of which appears calculated to gratify every species of laudable & elegant ambition, but of which the practice is fit only for a servile & cold mind inhabiting an iron body. As a wheel in the great machine of the world, I however believe, it right that extreme irritability & restless activity should be given as a spring to force forward the movement of public works to those who are to perform the part of engineers, and that the painful reaction of the pressure of ignorance, meanness, selfishness & egotism of public boards is a mere regulating contrivance, like the lump of lead on a pendulum."

on account. On July 2 he wrote him again, attempting to straighten out the accounts between them; then the matter dropped out of the correspondence. Latrobe saved himself from arrest on his bond in some way and retained title to his half, using it later as security to cover certain Washington debts. But he never received a cent from the sale of the property; the speculation which was to have been "a great one" actually cost him $425 which he badly needed—perhaps a small price to pay for the lesson he learned.

His Philadelphia work, as we have seen, brought little income, and the Baltimore Cathedral paid for actual expenses only, providing nothing toward the family living. Even the Washington work in these early years cost him almost as much to carry out as it brought in. The canal company, because of his necessary absences on trips to Washington and elsewhere, voted to dock his salary pro rata for the time he was absent. In a letter to President Jefferson asking for an adjustment in salary (April 28, 1806), he showed that against the $1,700.00 he received in 1805 for work on the Capitol and the White House he had been forced to write off actual costs of $1,639.46—$940.80 deductions from his canal salary because of time spent in Washington, $215.66 as excess costs of living in Washington, travel expenses of $108.00, and half of a draftsman's time, $375.00. This left him for all this work a personal gain of exactly $60.54! He told Jefferson that he was in an impossible situation; he could not go on like this. In 1805 he had received $450.00 from the Navy Department, and he expected $200.00 on the fireproof vault he had designed for the Treasury Department. He suggested that in the future he should be paid annually $1,700.00 for the Capitol work, $1,300.00 for Navy Department work (he was in complete charge of the building of the Washington Navy Yard and advised the Department on other matters), and $500.00 from other government departments for miscellaneous services. This would be equivalent to the $3,500.00 he had been given by the Chesapeake and Delaware Canal Company and would justify his moving to Washington permanently.

The letter reveals Latrobe's acute anxiety about the future. As the canal work creaked to its close—its treasury drained dry, its subscriptions everywhere in default—the company paid Latrobe his salary in checks or notes, not in cash; as rumors of the company's plight circulated, these checks and notes were everywhere refused. To all intents and purposes, for the last five or six months of his employment he was working for literally nothing. On August 5, 1805, he complained to Joseph Tatnall, the president, that the company was settling its accounts with notes; he needed and wanted cash. Five days later he wrote Samuel Hazlehurst that he was starting to settle up and close the canal affairs, and by the middle of November the company had voted (November 19) to discharge all the employees except the officers on December 1.[24] Latrobe, as an officer, was not discharged, and for another several months he devoted much time and effort to the final winding up of its affairs. Creditors of the company were besieging him; on May 29, 1806, he was forced to write John Partridge of Elkton that he was not responsible, and could not be held responsible, for the debts assumed by the company. The whole ambitious project was in a coma.[25] The failure of the canal company to collect or increase its subscriptions was the result of world conditions, as Latrobe wrote his brother Christian (June 2, 1806) from Philadelphia:

> My business here is to meet the Directors of the Ches. & Del. Canal, which is . . . now at a stand[still]. . . . The true reason, however of the suspen-

---

24. Letter to Isaac Hazlehurst (November 25, 1805); letter to Lenthall (November 19, 1805), in which he writes: "The canal is aground, and all that are embarked with them must go overboard, except the officers, & they may stay by the wreck & starve if they chuse . . ." Eventually, however, Latrobe's widow recovered $600 from the company when it was resurrected and the canal built after 1823.

25. The canal company remained dimly alive, however. There was a flurry of reawakened interest in 1807-9, when Gallatin's imaginative proposal for extensive internal improvements was being prepared and put before Congress. He and Latrobe had corresponded busily on the whole scheme, and Latrobe had been his chief adviser in connection with roads and canals. The completion of the Chesapeake and Delaware Canal was high on the Gallatin list. Nothing came of these proposals, nevertheless, and another period of dormancy intervened. Then, in 1821, the company employed William Strickland to make a completely new study of the problem. This was published in 1823 as a *Communication from the Chesapeake and Delaware Canal Company; and a Report and Estimate of William Strickland to the President and Directors* (Philadelphia: J. R. A. Skerrett, 1823). The report changed the route so as to terminate the canal at Back Creek on the Chesapeake and north of Reedy Point on the Delaware—substantially the present route. This time the United States government invested $300,000, Pennsylvania $100,000, Maryland $50,000, and Delaware $25,000. Work was recommenced immediately, and the canal was finally opened to traffic in 1830 at a total cost of $2,250,000, or about $165,000 per mile. It was bought by the national government in 1919 and was widened, deepened, and eventually changed into a sea-level canal, without locks and deep enough for medium-sized ocean freighters. See Alvin F. Harlow, *Old Towpaths, the Story of the American Canal Era* (New York & London: Appleton, 1926); also [George Amroyd,] *A Connected View of the Whole Internal Navigation of the United States* . . . by a Citizen of the United States, corrected and improved from the edition of 1826 (Philadelphia: the author, 1830).

sion of the internal improvements of the country, is the absorption of all our active capital by the Neutral trade. The turnpike roads which have been opened near Philadelphia, as well as the Ch. & Del. Canal were children of the peace of Amiens. They sickened, & our canal indeed has died in consequence of the abstraction of pecuniary support by the foreign trade, which revived with the new War—a War which, by the accounts which have arrived here seems scarcely beyond its commencement. In the present volcanic state of Europe, we cannot help congratulating ourselves on the peaceful state of our shores . . .

With the canal scheme now dead, Latrobe wrote (July 19) from Philadelphia to his father-in-law about his plan to move to Washington. But it was not to be Washington yet; instead the family leased the Iron Hill place and moved back from Wilmington to Philadelphia. They tried to rent a house on Arch Street from Elias Boudinot, but the scheme fell through. Eventually they rented a house at 132 North Second Street; this was their residence during the rest of their stay in Philadelphia.

The canal work led indirectly to two other planning commissions. The first was a survey of the town of Newcastle, undertaken largely at the suggestion of Latrobe's friend Judge Kinsey Johns. This was much more than a survey, since it included plans for the future growth of the town. The actual surveying work was done by Strickland and an assistant, both working under the supervision of Robert Mills; but the plans for further development were of course Latrobe's. The survey and the accompanying report are still extant.[26] The plans include little elevations of all the existing buildings on the most important streets, and among these is the front gable of a brick house as purely Dutch in concept, shape, and detail as any seventeenth-century house in New Amsterdam or Albany—a lovely relic of the early Dutch settlements on the Delaware. Like all the drawings from the Latrobe office, the sketches are extremely legible. The report containing Latrobe's criticisms and suggestions is another evidence of its author's interest in the hygiene of cities and the enormous importance of correct orientation in street and house design.[27]

Larger in scope, the other commission was the design of an entire new city on the banks of the Susquehanna, an enlargement of the village called Nescopek. Samuel Mifflin, the manager of the Roosevelt-

26. See Appendix for the report.

27. In the Historical Society of Delaware, Wilmington.

Bollman-Latrobe rolling mill in Philadelphia, owned a tract of land ripe for development and, naturally enough, he turned to Latrobe for the design of his proposed town. Unfortunately the plan cannot be found, but the long descriptive report (dated March 30, 1805) which accompanied it is preserved.[28] Latrobe found the opportunity an exciting and congenial one, and into this town plan he poured all he knew of American needs and all he dreamed of for the American town of the future. He planned ample promenades along the river bank and a large town square, around which he would group the important public buildings. The streets were oriented so as to take the best advantage of the sun and of prevailing winds. Vistas were considered; most of the major streets, he says, have either public buildings or the water as climaxes. And, asking the owner—or the trustees—to retain an ample area for public uses, such as the support of an academy, he remarks that such a scheme is so cheap in America and its results so beneficial to a town that even selfish interests rather than public spirit should endorse it. All this, alas, passed over Mifflin's head; he was no city builder but merely an all-too-common type of real-estate speculator. What he wrote Latrobe is not known, but Latrobe's next letter to him (April 12) tells the story only too clearly:

> It cannot have been my intention by sending you the plan of the town of Nescopek to interfere with your views of immediate profit. . . . I had understood that you were proprietor of the shore of the Susquehannah for near a mile above the fall. Had I known that your property was so very limited. . . . I certainly should not have proposed the sacrifice of even so small a gratuity as 300 feet for public use. [One wonders if Mifflin caught the irony.]

He goes on to say that he has one request to make of Mifflin—that he never, never use Latrobe's name in connection with his subdivision and never suggest that Latrobe had a thing to do with its design. So, again, American speculation defeated a forward-looking vision; "immediate profit" prevented true creation. And here, as usual, the architect received not a penny for his pains.

---

28. In the Latrobe letter books. Its wording largely repeats that of the report on Newcastle.

CHAPTER

II

Colleagues and Quandaries

DURING these busy years Latrobe's office force had changed. His early draftsmen Graff and Traquair had left him, Barber had absconded, Breillat was dead, and an entirely new group of brilliant young men collected around him. The most important were Louis de Mun, Robert Mills, and William Strickland, and it was their hands that prepared many of the drawings that flooded out from the office—all to be revised by Latrobe himself. In the case of the more important jobs the draftsmen merely laid in the basic control lines and Latrobe added the details and the ornament.

There were three De Mun brothers, and all became the architect's good friends. They were royalist French army officers who had fled from France to Santo Domingo and, at the uprising there under Toussaint L'Ouverture, had fled in turn to America. Latrobe was drawn to them by their background, their broad culture, and their charm. Louis de Mun became in effect his chief draftsman, working especially on the Cathedral and the Capitol and often acting as the architect's confidential agent. But perhaps, despite his brilliance and conscientiousness, he was not the "born architect." Latrobe sent him to Washington to act as his agent in the Navy Yard work; then when apparently this did not work out—De Mun's aristocratic manners may hardly have suited the ways of the United States Navy, and Latrobe himself complained of De Mun's delay in sending on necessary information [1]—he moved him to the office

1. The letter containing the complaint (November 12, 1805) is characteristic in its expression of Latrobe's affection for De Mun. He apologizes for the brusqueness of his reproof. "But I also wrote in great haste & ill-humor . . . wishing to compleat all the drawings of the details before Mills goes to Charleston . . . William Strickland has entirely left me . . . Mills goes to Charleston to visit his churches & with a chance of remaining there. If you could then become a member of our little circle again it would be highly

of John Lenthall, clerk of the works at the Capitol. This, too, proved unsatisfactory, for neither Lenthall nor De Mun had an easy personality, and De Mun returned to Philadelphia. Latrobe did not forget him, however; in the spring of 1806 he recommended him to Gallatin as a suitable person to survey the site of the lighthouse proposed for the mouth of the Mississippi. De Mun was appointed, and Latrobe saw that he was furnished with the proper instruments and tools and that he took a refresher course in surveying under the mathematics professor at the University of Pennsylvania, Robert Patterson; he even saw to the making of a special boring machine designed to take core borings on the site of the lighthouse foundations.

De Mun's appointment came through on April 29, 1806, but he did not sail till August; Latrobe wrote him a final letter (August 2), adding: "Of all things, give me a picture of Dr. B. [Bollman had gone to New Orleans ostensibly to practice his profession.] I have served that man most zealously wherever I could. . . . He is, however, the only human being that ever taught me to hate, for which I do not thank him . . ."[2] De Mun returned about the beginning of May, 1807, his mission satisfactorily completed but himself having somehow become involved in the Burr conspiracy, as noted in a letter marked "private" from Latrobe to Gallatin (May 4): "De Mun arrived here 4 or 5 days ago . . . He found on his return to N. Orleans, that not the slightest notice had been taken of his letters . . . but was informed that Col. Wilkinson had given orders for his arrest." Both De Mun and his friend Colonel de Peyster, with whom he had gone to stay in Burlington, New Jersey, after his return from the South, were suspect for a while but later cleared. We shall return to the conspiracy shortly. Afterward De Mun joined his brothers in Havana and dropped out of the picture.

---

pleasant to me & Mrs. Latrobe . . ." Earlier (April 8) he had written Louis's brother Augustus de Mun at Baltimore: "Your brother, who is with me, is become absolutely necessary to my business, as well as to my domestic circle. In this money getting country, a friend who does not consider it the object of human existence to scrape dollars together, & who has a heart as well as a pocket, is an invaluable companion to me, whose nature, education, & habits have also taught me a different doctrine. Such a one is your brother Lewis [sic], and such a one I am sure I shall find Amadée. The sooner I gain this addition to my circle, the better . . ." But apparently Amadée did not come or, if he did, stayed but a short while; there is no evidence of his work. On December 12, though, Latrobe wrote to him that he would speak to Robert Smith, Secretary of the Navy, on his behalf.

2. Later, however, Latrobe relented and restored Bollman to his good graces, even his affection.

Of the other draftsmen, William Strickland (the son of the canal foreman, John Strickland) was the youngest and the most brilliant, the one for whom Latrobe had the greatest admiration, but he was also the most ebullient and the most intractable, so that finally he had to be discharged. Strickland worked chiefly on the United States Capitol during the nearly four years he was in Latrobe's office, which he had first entered in Philadelphia in August, 1801. Two years later (July 1, 1803) Latrobe had moved him to the Newcastle office. But as Strickland grew older he became more self-willed and rebellious. On March 10, 1804, Latrobe writes John Strickland: "Your son, has bethought himself that he has both a father and a mother alive, and is seized with such a violent inclination to see both, that I have given him a furlough for a few days." But the next letter to the father (August 18) has a different tone: "Although I am still of the opinion that your son William has the best talents and disposition I have almost ever seen in a boy of his age [he was at that time in his sixteenth year]—his conduct has been such as to render it necessary to use him with great severity. For the last fortnight he has been with me in Philadelphia." William had been sent on ahead to air the Latrobe house, but he had forgotten or neglected his commission and the family arrived to find the house damp and a "mass of mildew." The young man was sent home as a punishment; later he was taken back and continued to work with Latrobe until the middle of the summer of 1805. Then he was finally discharged, after he had neither appeared at the office for two days nor given any notice whatsoever. The father was deeply distressed and begged the architect to take William back, but Latrobe could not be moved. Perhaps he realized that he had given the boy all the training he could and had obtained from him all the service that William, with the personality he had, could offer. Yet for many years Latrobe retained his admiration for William Strickland's talents and took pleasure later in recommending him in the highest possible terms [3]—until 1818, when controversy about the Second Bank of the United States in Philadelphia again estranged them.[4]

---

3. For example, to the Secretary of War (June 10, 1812): "Mr. William Strickland, the bearer, is desirous of obtaining a commission in the Corps of Engineers. . . . He is an excellent draughtsman, perhaps the best of those I have educated. . . . I should consider the talents, the spirit, & the acquirements of Mr. Strickland to be an acquisition to the Corps . . ."

4. See pages 500-503.

The wheelhorse of the office was the ever dependable, the conscientious, the hard-working Robert Mills. Mills wanted to be an architect, knew he could learn more with Latrobe than with anyone else, and came to him in 1802 on the recommendation of President Jefferson—a good friend of both—after having worked with Hoban and spent more than a year at Monticello learning what Jefferson could teach him. He was a superb draftsman and made beautiful if somewhat cold renderings. Yet, though Mills was of inestimable value at the office, Latrobe never warmed to him as he did to De Mun and Strickland, and his attitude toward him after Mills had left was often ambivalent; he admired Mills's abilities while at the same time he distrusted, and even actively disliked, his sense of design. He was fond of him; but there was something in Mills's constant energy, in his continual forging along no matter what the obstacles, that seems to have disturbed and perhaps frightened Latrobe. Mills had a kind of unshakable purpose, combined with a narrow though serious rectitude, that was essentialy alien to Latrobe's more mercurial temperament. Latrobe apparently wanted to like him more than he actually could.

Perhaps there was a little unconscious envy in Latrobe's feeling. Mills was a much younger man but possessed an equal enthusiasm for architecture; though he had none of Latrobe's advantages of wide European travel and lacked his breadth of education, he was already in 1805-6 obtaining commissions with an ease that astonished Latrobe. Obviously he was going to be a success professionally in a way that Latrobe could never be, but in a way, too, that would have been impossible had not Latrobe broken the ground. This was bound to lead to a certain restraint in Latrobe's admiration of his pupil—even at times to a certain suspicion. Yet he tried unceasingly to be helpful. In 1805 Mills had already designed two churches for Charleston and, as we have seen, had left Latrobe's office to superintend them, with the possibility of remaining in Charleston. Latrobe was deeply concerned with Mills's professional future; he wanted to make doubly sure that the younger man preserved his professional attitude unsullied, hence the full letter (July 12, 1806) on the architectural profession in America, which was quoted in part in Chapter 8.[5]

When the prospects in Charleston evaporated, Mills returned to Phil-

5. See also in Appendix.

adelphia and to Latrobe's employ, remaining with him as his invaluable assistant, superintendent, clerk of the works, and agent all through 1807, 1808, and into 1809. He acted thus for Latrobe on the Waln house, the Markoe house, and the difficult and unusual Gothic Bank of Philadelphia. If Mills got from this an education of the greatest importance to his future, Latrobe in turn received from him unquestioning loyalty, devoted hard work, and the greatest possible skill in interpreting his own wishes with sympathy.

And Latrobe helped and advised Mills on commissions received while he was still in Latrobe's employ. In addition, he helped him when Mills was asked to design a jail for Burlington County, New Jersey, in Mount Holly—a particularly generous gesture when one realizes the Hazlehursts' close association with Mount Holly. Mills had written Latrobe asking his basic philosophy of prison design and had sent specific questions about the relative advisability of a city or a country site, and so on; Latrobe answered the questions at length (November 17, 1807). But there was still something missing in their relationship.

The whole situation was pointed up years later, in 1812, in connection with the proposed monument to the seventy-two persons (including the governor of the state) who perished in the dreadful fire of the Richmond theater on December 26, 1811. Latrobe had written to the mayor offering his services, and at about the same time John Wickham had written directly to Latrobe asking for his suggestions; Latrobe replied (January 21, 1812) with a long letter. He had learned that it was planned to build both an Episcopal church and a commemorative monument on the old theater lot. But he disapproved of the idea; the money collected for the church could only build "a plain brick building such as we see everywhere." Instead, Latrobe proposed that only the monument should be erected; this should consist of a block 32 feet square, on which a pyramid 48 feet high should rise, and within there should be a chamber 20 or 24 feet square. On the inner walls should be carved the names of the victims and the appropriate inscriptions; in the center there would be a memorial statue, "a kneeling figure, representing the city . . . mourning over an urn." A sketch embodying the idea still exists. Then suddenly, two months later, he learned that Mills had received the commission. He wrote in astonishment to Dr. John Brockenborough of the building committee (March 22). Latrobe had understood he had authority to proceed; he had already received preliminary estimates from a Mr. Douglas for the construction and had procured from Franzoni a model of the figure the sculptor was to carve. He was at a loss to know what to say to these men, for, he added:

Mills has furnished you with designs, one of which you approve . . . You wish for a design for a church from me also. . . . I feel reluctant to enter the lists against my own professional child . . . especially when the principle on which Mr. Mills has made his design is my own idea, communicated to him, though much modified. . . . Of Mr. Mills, I cannot . . . speak but in terms of respect . . . [He is] of the strictest integrity. . . . He is of a religious turn of mind . . . Whatever design you adopt, it would be infinitely to your interest . . . to engage him to direct its execution. . . . In the design of private houses, he is uncommonly excellent, in . . . public works, he wants experience, as yet, to a sufficient extent. . . . As you have explained Mr. Mills' design . . . it is a monument . . . in front of a church, so as to serve as its vestibule. . . . The church itself has no trace of monumental character, and as its roof . . . [is] of boards . . . covered with shingles . . . it has every property in a superior degree to that of permanence. A Monumental Church ought to be such a monument as that in extent & arrangement it could serve as a church . . . [In connection with] Mr. Mills' circular vestibule . . . with columns of permanent materials and of impressive size, his estimate of $35,000 would fall infinitely short. If you will favor me with the ideas of the committee and are at all desirous of my further assistance, I will prepare a design in which they shall be embodied . . .

Latrobe was deeply hurt at what seemed like Mills's attempt to wrest a commission from him. He wrote Mills (May 26) enclosing some drawings of Mills's that he had found in Lenthall's office:

I regret that after knowing that I had been consulted on the Monument once proposed to be erected at Richmond . . . you should have transmitted to them a number of ideas & drawings, which rendering decision difficult has I believe defeated the object. . . . I am far from supposing you intended [it] . . . yet you have already not only injured but disgraced me, because I had already made a conditional contract with respectable men, whom I had to disappoint with an explanation not very creditable to myself, namely that your plan was preferred. . . . I am very far from being jealous of the preference of such judges . . . but I am most sensibly hurt, that you should not have become aware of the indelicasy. . . . It is also singular that you should propose setting marble panels into freestone margins, exactly in the same manner in which I had proposed, without being informed of my intention. It is however impossible to suppose you had been informed, because you would hardly have waged war against me in my own armor. Had you had the special information . . . the committee furnished to me you would have given a different design . . .

But the whole matter was a misunderstanding, the result of the clients' thoughtless ineptitude in handling professional matters. Mills and Latrobe had been consulted independently, and neither had been informed that the other had been approached; Mills hastened to put Latrobe straight on the facts, and Latrobe was mollified. He wrote Mills (July 22):

> I can only say that if you did not know that I was consulted by the Richmond Committee, & had given them a design & was wholly unapprized of my intentions as to the mode of recording the names, although your father in law told me that he should write to you on the subject, before you sent in your different plans, then all ground of offense is certainly removed, & nothing remains but astonishment that in so novel a mode of setting marble in freestone we should both have invented the same thing at the same moment. But such extraordinary coincidences do actually happen sometimes. . . . I shall always endeavor to serve you, & although my period of ability is passed for the present, it may again arrive . . .

The Monumental Church (as it is known) that Mills designed and built, though the final structure was much altered from his original sketch, stands today as one of its architect's most original and successful achievements.

Latrobe's influence on his draftsmen and superintendents was incalculable. It is certainly no accident that two of the greatest American architects of the generation coming up should have been with him for years; perhaps his training of these younger men in aesthetic design, in fine and permanent construction, in meticulous detailing, and in professional idealism was one of Latrobe's greatest contributions to the architecture of America that lay ahead.

This is no place for an account of the alleged Burr conspiracy to create a new country in the American Southwest, with Burr himself as king, president, or leader; yet that tragic, ambitious, embittered character, who by a hair had failed to become President of the United States, hypnotized and misled a remarkable group of people, including Latrobe. He had an uncanny sense of those who were brilliant, adventurous, and unappreciated, of those who found themselves in positions of personal hardship or had become bitter because of unjust fortune, and of those whose talents could be useful to him. Before a chosen few of these he dangled baits cleverly chosen to appeal to them most, the chief one being the dazzling opportunities of gain offered by the gradually opening West.

Such a man was Bollman, now since his failure struggling with visionary but often prophetic scientific schemes. Such a man was Latrobe in the years from 1804 to 1806, with judgments hanging over him, debts everywhere, and the Chesapeake and Delaware Canal about to fold up in ignominious failure. The enticing bait hooked Bollman, who became one of Burr's most important agents; it almost caught Latrobe. How deeply Burr confided in Bollman we shall probably never know; in Latrobe he confided a little, for he wanted Latrobe's engineering and architectural skill, which he appreciated even if Philadelphia did not. The canal project did collapse, and Burr seized the opportunity to make a definite offer, as Latrobe wrote his father-in-law (July 21, 1806):

> When the Canal company's operations were evidently on the point of failure, I received, through Colonel Burr, proposals respecting the Canal to pass the falls of the Ohio, a project in which the whole western interests of the Union are at present engaged, which I fear the misfortunes of our country in the separation of the Western from the Eastern states will in a few years develop. I stated my terms . . . they were acceded to . . . I did not go Westward, as I otherwise, on my own judgment should have done . . . I came to Philadelphia instead . . . [A narrow escape!]

Meanwhile Bollman had gone on to New Orleans as Burr's chief emissary to the ineffable play-both-sides-against-the-middle General Wilkinson, and in the summer, through pure coincidence, Latrobe's former employee Louis de Mun sailed to survey the mouth of the Mississippi. Latrobe was shocked and astounded when, toward the end of the year, rumors of Burr's duplicity and his real purpose began to circulate. Early in January, 1807, Wilkinson proclaimed martial law and shortly afterward summarily arrested Bollman, Col. Samuel Swartwout, Peter V. Ogden, and General Adair, without warrants. Bollman and Swartwout as the most dangerous were put on board a vessel bound for the East coast; Ogden and Adair were released by the courts in New Orleans and their arrest was declared illegal. Wilkinson had suspected De Mun, too, and as we have seen had ordered his arrest, but De Mun escaped before his arrest was accomplished. Communication from the New Orleans area was slow, however, and Latrobe at first knew nothing but these rumors. Then Gallatin writes him asking what he knows of Burr, and Latrobe answers (November 15) with a long account headed "Memorandum":

My first acquaintance with Col. Burr was in the year 1797 or 8. He introduced himself to me . . . Since that time I have received from him nothing but civilities, and he has taken pains to render me essential services. For instance,—when the City Hall at New York was projected, his interest procured me all the votes of the corporation, *save one,* as his persuasion had at first induced me to become a competitor for the design & decoration of that building. I was afterwards, thro' his means, applied to by the corporation to undertake the general superintendence of the city & Island, but declined . . . and whenever we were in the same place we have seen much of each other . . . but he seemed always a little embarrassed even in talking to me of *State affairs,* as he knew my individual feelings to be in favor of Mr. Jefferson's election in 1800, at the very time of his election; for I had very innocently & indiscretely opened myself to him. At least I thus account for his reserve to me in matters of politics, while on other subjects he was as open as possible.—About the year 1803 I had a long conversation with him on the *Western navigation,* then, as I told you this evening, the New York periauger [6] was discussed between us, as the best boat, probably, for shallow & rapid rivers, as well as deep water,—as being capable of navigating both;—the latter by the help of the [lee] boards.—I promised to obtain him a *building* draft of one, & succeeded. I finished the project of the boat at once,—he requested me about the 15th of July last that I would procure him half a dozen copies to be made. I did so, in my own office, Mr. Mills & Mr. De Mun each hav[g] each made 3.—The dimensions of the boat I do not recollect, but I know well that I advised him to [use] boats 80 feet & not more in length, & not more than 18 feet beam. . . . I understood him to want these in order to distribute them more diffusely among his friends on the Western Waters.

In 1805, about June, [I received the offer of the canal job at Louisville. I answered and heard no more] till one evening in June last he walked into my house. The subject of the Canal was then renewed. I saw him almost every day as he lodged near me, & I was very ill. We talked of almost every subject. Miranda's expedition for instance, the rise & origin of which he was well acquainted with, & which he said he had from the beginning considered a most precipitate & ill considered scheme. And on this subject he told me many things which astonished me, both as to the names he introduced, and

6. A type of shallow-draft lighter.

as to light thrown upon many characters & much conduct, which the public appear to have viewed "through a glass darkly."

[In August I showed him articles in the *Aurora* on the] old & new Western conspiracy, mentioning Burr. He considered them personal attacks due to Marshall, & said they would cause "great uneasiness to the Westward." [I spent the last days of July in fitting out De Mun.] De Mun's Brother in law, Depestre came to town to wish him farewell.—On this occasion I had much conversation with Depestre on his affairs. He had sold part of his Jersey farm & intended to part with the remainder provided he could get *more* land of good quality for his money, even if it lay further back.—Having had much conversation here, on the land in Ohio with Col. Worthington, I advised him to look about him in that state, & promised him letters, which I afterwards wrote & sent to Burlington after him when De Mun was gone.

[Burr also asked me about sounding out my Irish friends to see if they would go out & dig.] I accordingly treated with three of my contractors, Sands, Stuart, & Grimes, who were all inclined to take land & provisions & some money for their Labor; & I went so far as to arrange for having 500 men . . .

Latrobe states that, since the separation of the eastern and western states had been openly voiced in Congress, he asked Burr what he thought of it; Burr considered it imprudent at the time, but he thought there was already a majority of two to one for the separation. Then Latrobe goes on to report a long conversation with Depestre on "Saturday last" (after Latrobe had had dinner with the President), on the eve of Depestre's leaving for Havana, evidently low spirited and greatly disappointed in his western tour:

The effect of what he said on Col. B's offer to me, was that of an advice not to accept of it.—In fact the more I consider it,—the more I think, that my presence is the only thing desired. The rest is sham. I forgot to mention that I am in a bad scrape with my Irishmen, for Col. B. has never once noticed the subject of the Canal since I made conditional arrangements with them. . . .

On December 15 Latrobe sends to the Secretary of the Navy, Paul Hamilton, a copy of the "draught of a boat, made in my office for Col. Burr, when in Philadelphia June last. . . . I will also . . . mention . . . that, at the instigation of Col. Burr, I did also make arrangements to engage and send to the Western country, 500 Irish laborers, to be employed in cutting a canal at the falls of the Ohio . . ." He mentions De Mun's employment, and he also writes Roosevelt (January 22, 1807): "Bollman as you will see by the papers is arrested and at Charleston. . . . Burr is not taken . . ." Later rumor had it that Burr had disappeared and that $2,000 was offered as a reward for his apprehension.

Innocent though he was in his connection with Burr, Latrobe was worried. On April 3 he wrote his brother Christian a short account of Burr's "curious conspiracy" and told him that he had heard President Jefferson say that Burr's treasonable intent could be proved if there were time enough to collect witnesses. Bollman and Colonel Swartwout, as is well known, were released almost immediately upon their arrival in the East; the Federal courts held that their arrest without warrant was unlawful and that there was no evidence of treason. Exactly what their complicity was in the scheme has never been ascertained. But Bollman's hopes of a successful future in the United States were dashed—who would trust him now? Burr was arrested and indicted for treason; his trial is one of the great monuments of American jurisprudence, and he was at last acquitted of the charge. Having been held up to the scorn and hatred of all good Americans, however, he fled to Europe to avoid the universal detestation with which he was regarded.

Latrobe was subpoenaed as a government witness against Burr and was held under bail in Washington for several months. When the trial began he was summoned to Richmond and made an official report on the security of the room in which Burr was detained, but he was never called to the stand. Again, when Colonel Wilkinson was brought to trial in connection with his most circuitous behavior in the supposed plot, Latrobe was subpoenaed as a witness but was never actually called; Wilkinson, too, was acquitted. Little by little, then, the matter faded into the background. It is largely a mystery still, and historians have yet to reach unanimity on what actually happened, on what Burr's and Wilkinson's dealings with each other and with the Spanish meant, and on which of the two was the stranger and the more crooked character. Burr was gradually reinstated in Latrobe's friendship, for who could withstand his charm? And five years later, Latrobe writes Bollman in Philadelphia (August 14, 1812) his final summing up of the affair:

> Aaron Burr . . . is another guess sort of person. . . . I love him still, tho' I would not trust him with the conduct of an intrigue to elect a common councilman. . . . Wilkinson may be rotten, as you say, & whatever Burr's

plans were, God knows neither side have ever explained them to me. . . . But the rottenness of Wilkinson was not nearly so cankerous to their success as the lawyer like management of Burr himself. . . . To me, Mr. Burr revealed a project of cutting a Canal round the falls of the Ohio. . . . I committed myself accordingly . . . $10,000 would have commanded 500 Irishmen. . . . I am told he could not command the money . . . he ought to have known in July what he could do in September. . . . He combines within his own, two most opposite characters—the most sanguine and the most suspicious, while he is careless of his interest, and even of public opinion, he is cautious to a degree of folly.

Besides professional work and financial worries, as well as the Burr matter, there was another factor in the Latrobe family life between 1804 and 1808 which brought them much anxiety, many misgivings, but finally a deep satisfaction. It concerned Roosevelt and, like everything surrounding that extraordinary personality, it was strange, at times ambivalent, and unexpected. Roosevelt, scarcely four years younger than Latrobe, had fallen in love with Latrobe's daughter Lydia! The news broke upon the family like a thunderbolt in a letter from Roosevelt to Mrs. Latrobe. Latrobe himself could hardly believe it. At the end of a business letter to his friend he wrote: "On the subject on which you have written Mrs. L., we had better *talk* than *write*. Perhaps it will be still better *to laugh. 13 years & 6 months*" (Lydia's age). Of Lydia at that time, Latrobe wrote his older brother (February 6, 1805): "I must tell you that Lydia though only 14 on the 23 of March next is a fine sensible young woman, inheriting the faults of her mother's character as to unevenness of temper, but abounding also in excellent qualities of solid value," and he asked Christian to send on to him evidence of the registry in London of her birth and Henry's.

The attraction between Lydia and Roosevelt was deep, but it created a dilemma in the minds of her parents. Not only was he old enough to be her father; he was also financially unstable and unduly optimistic, and at this very time his actions were threatening Latrobe's entire future. Everything on the worldly plane was against such a connection. On the other hand, Roosevelt was Latrobe's most sympathetic friend, and Mrs. Latrobe was equally fond of him. At last, when Roosevelt proved persistent—as evidently did Lydia—her parents gave in and accepted him as a serious suitor for their daughter's hand. On March 28, 1805, Latrobe wrote Roosevelt, at the end of one of his worried business letters:

Now for the other subject.—

We on the 22nd of March celebrated the entrance of our Daughter into her 16th year.[7] How does that look as to our consent and even wishes?—But I declare I would rather be responsible for your whole fortune than for your happiness. Come & see us when you can.—Mrs. Latrobe will no doubt write you fully on this head.

Early in April, therefore, Roosevelt visited them at Wilmington and became the accepted if unannounced fiancé of the young woman, scarcely out of childhood. Latrobe wrote him again on April 13: "We are all well, excepting Lydia, who, since you left this place, has been seized with a dreadful fit of affectation, and can scarce speak so as to be heard. Yours very affectionately . . ." But, still troubled as to the prospects of such an April-December match, he wrote three days later to Isaac Hazlehurst for his advice—

[On a matter] so situated, as you will see, that not even my own or Mary's judgment was left to decide.—R[oosevelt] already proposed a settlement of about $20,000 value in landed property which he has designated:—but I have declined entering into any discussion as premature. L[ydia] is, since this grand event, silent, & as affected as a Cat. I don't know what to do with her . . .

And on May 16 he wrote to his brother Christian:

As to Lydia, we have lost her.—Mr. Roosevelt of New York, a man who in every respect but age is exactly what I could wish, has contrived to persuade her that she will live more happily with him than with us.—I regret most sincerely that a man past 30 [he was actually 36] should have made the proposition to her who is only in her 15th year. But before I dreamed that anything serious was meant things were so far settled between them as to put it out of my power to prevent their union but by an exertion of authority to which I hardly conceive I have a right. A year's probation is put upon them, & I sincerely hope that in the year something to break off the connexion will occur. If not, I must depend upon his good conduct to prevent that unhappiness which seems inevitably to belong to so very unequal a union.—Mr. Roosevelt is a man of exceptionally good moral character,—and of one of the oldest families in the State of New York,—has a very handsome fortune [did Latrobe actually still believe this?], and inhabits one of the most enchanting country seats in Jersey, on the river Passaic. He calls himself 33,

7. A typical example of Latrobe's occasional carelessness about dates. The "22nd" should be "23rd" and the "16th" should be "15th."

but is suspected to be a year or two beyond that . . . [Did not Latrobe know his real age?]

Anxiety still shows through the words, in spite of attempts to brighten the picture. But Roosevelt was impatient. The year's delay seemed irksome, and he tried direct action. On May 18 Latrobe wrote him again about a letter Lydia had given her parents in which Roosevelt had pressed her for an immediate union:

> On this subject I must most seriously repeat to you what before I said,—that my duty to my child, my anxiety for her happiness & for her education, and above all my *well considered principles* of propriety, will never permit me to consent to her marriage before next year. . . . I beg you will therefore desist from persuasion *to her*. Her consent you can no doubt obtain by pressing solicitation. Mine is better worth having . . .

And on June 4, still fearful of the impetuosity of the lovers, he admonished him further:

> Early next week I shall go to Washington with Mrs. L. & leave Lydia in charge of the house & little folks. You will I am sure understand the delicacy of her situation in this scandalous town, & I need say no more . . .

Roosevelt nevertheless visited Wilmington and Lydia, and Latrobe was forced to write once more (July 1):

> On referring to my letter on the subject of your visit to Wilmington during my absence, you will find that I could not usefully intend to prohibit your visit. I only cautioned you as to the time and duration of it. You have acted as you ought, but I am sorry if I have caused your inconvenience by it. . . . You will know how much I have regretted your *infatuation* from my first knowledge of it. . . . All I can do now is to prepare for your happiness as well as I can. . . . As a daughter there can not be one more dutiful, & *convenient* in every respect. She is an excellent housekeeper & nurse both for the children & the sick. Her behavior must necessarily win our warmest affection. —But a daughter is not a wife, nor are the qualities which are required of *an inmate* exactly those which the *head* of a house should possess. In a few years more she might do us and you honour. We ask only a few months, and you think it too much.—I am not in very high spirits in this affair. . . . Now I look round in vain for a subject of congratulation.—A little more instruction may make me change my opinion and cannot possibly be against your interests.—Be assured that every part of my conduct which displeases you is dictated by my affection for *you* rather than for L.—She cannot help but be

happy with a man of your kind heart, and perfect principle. . . . The delay we ask is but a short one, tho' I know a week seems an eternity to lovers. Heaven bless you, my dear friend. Yours most affectionately.

From this strange and confused letter of a confused parent are we to understand that Latrobe was becoming conscious of a certain lack of full frankness on Roosevelt's part, just as he was increasingly struck by Lydia's immaturity? His financial difficulties with Roosevelt were in part the result of a lack of frankness; here too were growing the seeds of misunderstanding. And Latrobe needed so much the continuing friendship of his prospective son-in-law. Yet apparently he bowed to the inevitable; on November 3 he wrote his brother, whom he had urged to try to get some of the money due from the Sellon estate:

> Lydia is now going to be married. Must I describe her English relations to Mr. Roosevelt as a panel of speculators on her property [which of course they were] or must I save their character at the expense of truth & of my own. . . . As to my own fireside, I have no idea of anything on this side the grave more calculated to attach the mind to sublunary happiness. And yet the longer I live the less does human existence appear to me of importance. The laborious uphill climb to my present *hour* in which I have always engaged has given me a restlessness which all my activity of employ scarce satiates.—What should I do without the *sedative,* of the kindness & example of my beloved Mary?

At last 1806 came round—but there was no marriage and a new note arose. Perhaps Latrobe's hopes that a delay would cause a break in the connection were to be realized. In a letter to Roosevelt on January 5 he intimated that he had learned that Lydia had refused to answer Roosevelt's last letter! But worse was to come. The Latrobes, shocked, discovered that over all the past months, when supposedly Roosevelt had not approached Lydia directly, Lydia and he had been carrying on a secret correspondence weekly; neither of them had been frank and open with the parents. Their distress was great—a beloved daughter and a beloved friend both seeming underhanded and insincere. This was something Latrobe could not stomach, and to increase his distress there was the additional sorrow that the correspondence had in some way backfired and brought unhappiness to Lydia through the end of a romance which Latrobe, though questioning it, in his heart had welcomed. He wrote to Roosevelt in protest; Roosevelt replied in a letter that Latrobe called "insulting and insane." In a letter (March 8) to Jacob Mark, Roosevelt's partner, Latrobe asserted that all Roosevelt's troubles were based on his deep bitterness at the breakup with Lydia.

The basis of Latrobe's feeling for Roosevelt had now changed completely; ". . . you have taught my child deceit," he wrote on March 21, and for months he signed his letters (which were rigidly impersonal and dealt only with business) "Yrs etc." But time softened Latrobe's anger, and there may have been personal explanations and apologies; for eventually, and with great relief, the two old friends resumed their former relationship and the infatuation appeared to be a thing of the past. Yet actually it had not died in the hearts of either Roosevelt or Lydia. They went on with their ordinary lives, Roosevelt increasingly busy on a thousand nebulous projects, Lydia gradually growing into a fascinating and much sought-after young lady both in Philadelphia and in the delightful and exciting society of Washington.

In September, 1808, Roosevelt visited the Latrobes. Mrs. Latrobe was upstairs, ill, recovering from a miscarriage a few days earlier. Latrobe was called out on business, and Roosevelt and Lydia were left alone together for an hour and a half. That was enough; he proposed again, and she, with a year and a half more of experience behind her, accepted. On September 8, after Roosevelt had returned to New Jersey, Latrobe wrote him that Mrs. Latrobe and he were in perfect agreement about the marriage and welcomed it—but what about Roosevelt's financial state? Roosevelt, Latrobe knew, had debts of almost $75,000 and assets of only about $36,000; how was Roosevelt going to pay the $30,000 to the United States Navy, which he should do at once, in order to clear his credit? Latrobe knew the facts only too well—the Corps and Casey notes, the Navy copper affair—all things that had dragged him into the picture, whether he would or no. But apparently Roosevelt satisfied him on this score, for Latrobe wrote his father-in-law the story of the resumption of Roosevelt's suit and Lydia's acceptance. He went on to say that the example of President and Mrs. Madison had convinced him that a difference in ages was no bar to happiness. The fact that the failure of the Sellons had taken with it all of Lydia's own inheritance was referred to, and he said that Roosevelt on a final summing up of his assets and liabilities had between forty and fifty thousand dollars. And he related that Lydia had had several proposals and had refused them all:

One of them, from Captain Porter [the famous officer] of the Navy, now married, was of such a nature that I could not well have objected to it, either on grounds of prudence or character. I therefore left her to her own feelings, but she rejected him so firmly that the matter dropped at once; and on this occasion she said to her mother, that he was not to be compared with Mr. Roosevelt. This circumstance among others persuade[s] me that she is as seriously attached to him as her calm disposition admits; and he is certainly sufficiently devoted to her.

So at last they were married, and Latrobe wrote to his father-in-law:

Yesterday evening [November 15] our daughter Lydia was married by the Revd. Mr. McCormick to Mr. Roosevelt, who arrived here in his own carriage. He picked up Henry at Baltimore, & brought him hither. No one was present at the ceremony but our own family, Mrs. Madison, Miss Brent, Lydia's particular friend, Captn. Tingey [of the Navy Yard] & James Eakin. Mr. Madison promised to come, but he was so ill as to be confined to his room . . .

The marriage proved a happy one—much happier than the preliminaries might have presaged. After several exciting, worrisome, adventurous years the couple finally retired in modest affluence to Skaneateles, New York, where they were honored citizens till the days of their deaths.

Even more important to the future of the Latrobe family, of course, was the removal to Washington, as an inevitable result of Latrobe's growing governmental work. This will be discussed in later chapters, but in order to get a true perspective on the life the family lived in this troubled period some consideration of it is necessary here.

Latrobe had met Jefferson in 1798, at Fredericksburg, and had written him about possible canal work in the Charlottesville area in the same year. Evidently reports of Latrobe's growing reputation in his early Philadelphia years had reached Jefferson and impressed him. When, in 1802, Jefferson had the idea that the best way to preserve naval vessels out of commission would be in huge covered dry docks, he turned naturally to Latrobe as the man best fitted to design the necessary structures. Long letters were exchanged between them, and finally Latrobe was summoned to Washington to develop the designs in co-operation with the Navy Department. He was invited to dinner at the President's House on November 29, 1802, and much of the next day he spent writing his wife a full account of it.[8] The dinner was small—only three besides himself—

8. See Appendix.

and the conversation was largely scientific and professional: "on the best construction of arches,—on the properties of different species of limestone,—on cements generally,—on the difference between the French and English habits of living as far as they affect the arrangement of their houses,—on several new experiments upon the properties of light,—on Dr. Priestley,—on the subject of immigration,—on the culture of the vine . . . on the domestic manners of Paris, & the orthography of the English & French Languages . . ." Then to lighten the atmosphere the President told amusing anecdotes of life in Paris, and especially one, slightly ribald, about the Quaker Dorcas at Benjamin Franklin's.

Latrobe's design for the docks so impressed Jefferson that three months later he appointed him Surveyor of the Public Buildings of the United States; in addition the architect received much work for the Navy Department and eventually was made Engineer of the United States Navy.

With all this Federal government work, eventual residence in Washington became inevitable, though the Latrobes were long in making the final move. They first considered it seriously in 1806, when the cessation of work on the Chesapeake and Delaware Canal was imminent. They had made extended visits in 1804 and 1805. Later, after all bright hopes in Philadelphia had collapsed, they were again uncertain. Latrobe wrote his father-in-law (July 19, 1806) that he could not make up his mind whether to move to Washington or not; every visit there had cost him more than he received. Two days later he wrote again, explaining his indecision, citing the lack of Philadelphia commissions, but adding: "Even my dependence on the Government . . . must be precarious while a single vote of Congress, to abandon the crazy project of forcing a national metropolis by paltry appropriations of 50-60000 Dollars a year, must draw the foundation on which I depend from under me."

By November, nevertheless, he seemed convinced of the necessity of the move, and he wrote Jefferson (November 8) that he planned to bring his family to Washington on the first of June and had leased his Philadelphia house. He said that he had tried to rent a house in Washington from a Mr. Wheaton, but the lease fell through and he had had to come on alone; that he had been called home by illness and since then the serious illness of himself and various members of the family had deferred the move.[9] He added: "I confess candidly that the addition

9. This illness, which Latrobe calls dysentery, may have been cholera. The architect was called home at the beginning of September by the serious illness of his son John H. B.,

[to the salary] proposed would be very convenient for me . . . I have engaged a house here [he was writing from Washington] to which I shall move in the spring, should I still be engaged in the service of the Government."

But when 1807 came round his uncertainty came again to the fore. He wrote the President (February 18) that it would be useless to move to Washington unless Congress passed the appropriation for the north wing and Latrobe was assured of full pay. Friends and relatives, he added, "consider it madness in me to leave a populous & wealthy city where I am known & where I may obtain much business, less honorable indeed, but more lucrative, for a situation so precarious & depending on appropriations."

Yet the logic of events inevitably overcame his doubts. As early as February 9, even before the letter to Jefferson, he had apparently made the decision, for on that day he wrote to Dr. Bullers, who had offered to rent him his own Washington home, that he could not take it; he had made other arrangements. The house he took, between the Navy Yard and the Capitol, was owned by Robert Alexander, a builder then absent in New Orleans as contractor for the customs house there which Latrobe had designed. The lease ran from May 1, and on May 20 Latrobe wrote Robert Smith, Secretary of the Navy, that the next day he was "putting the whole family on board the packet for Washington." Actually the move seems not to have been made for another two months; all his letters till July were written from Philadelphia. Beginning with July 1, 1807, Latrobe was a Washington resident for six consecutive years.

Philadelphia again had failed him; the Waln house and the Bank of Philadelphia (the commission for which he had just received) could not justify his further residence there. The Philadelphia home which he held on a long lease he sublet to an art dealer, Delormeric; unhappily, and characteristically enough, Delormeric's rent was not forthcoming. This seemed a final example of Philadelphia's ingratitude. Perhaps Washington would be more kind.

---

whose life was for several days despaired of. He himself caught the infection in an attack of almost equal violence, and his recovery from the immediate attack left him completely prostrated; between August 27 and October 6 not a letter of his left the house, and for two weeks or so longer all the letter copies are in the hand of either Robert Mills or Mrs. Latrobe. He was not well enough to return to Washington until the end of October.

CHAPTER

12

The Baltimore Cathedral

FROM the spring of 1804 on throughout Latrobe's years in the East he worked spasmodically on the Roman Catholic Cathedral of Baltimore. In his search for good building stone for the United States Capitol he had become well acquainted with the city, and later when his son Henry was put in St. Mary's College, the Sulpician academy, his connections with Baltimore became even closer. The Diocese, under the farsighted Bishop Carroll, had for some time seen the advantages of having an impressive cathedral, and someone had prepared a sketch. This sketch was given to Louis de Mun by one Fitzsimmons, and De Mun passed it on to Latrobe for his comments and criticism, perhaps at the Bishop's suggestion.[1]

The result was a letter from Latrobe to Bishop Carroll (April 10, 1804), in which he attacked the proposed design on two counts, both practical. In the first place, there was no adequate support for the dome shown at the crossing or for the indicated tower. Then there was the cost; the proposed design included 54 Corinthian columns 30 feet high, and these alone would cost at least $54,000, or approximately the total proposed cost of the entire building. He concluded by offering his services free. Apparently the Bishop thought well of the offer, for a month later Latrobe was hard at work on his design. Here was a magnificent opportunity for all the best he had to offer.

---

1. See Fiske Kimball, "Latrobe's Designs for the Cathedral of Baltimore," *Architectural Record,* vol. 42, no. 6 (December, 1917), and vol. 43, no. 1 (January, 1918); and Walter Knight Sturges, "A Bishop and His Architect: The Story of the Building of Baltimore Cathedral," *Liturgical Arts,* vol. 17, no. 2 (February, 1949). See also J. M. Riordan, *Cathedral Records from the Beginning of Catholicity in Baltimore to the Present Time . . .* (Baltimore: Catholic Mirror Publishing Co., 1906).

In 1804 Latrobe was still the rebel, still under the influence of the Romantics in the England he had left. What could be more fitting, he thought, than that America's first major cathedral should be Gothic? But what sources could he use, what documents for details? At this period he was engaged in work on the Chesapeake and Delaware Canal, living in quiet Newcastle and later at Iron Hill and Wilmington. Joshua Gilpin was important in the direction of the canal, and Gilpin was his good friend and a man of cultivation. Latrobe had lent him his own copy of "Gothic Hints" and in the middle of May wrote to see if he could get it back and at the same time borrow a few volumes of "Picturesque Scenery," which Gilpin owned.[2] The books came a few days later, and Latrobe set to work in earnest.

But the designs proceeded slowly. Latrobe was almost unbelievably rushed. Daily oversight of the canal operations, thronging questions about the Capitol requiring many drawings and numberless long letters to Lenthall, and visits to Washington and Philadelphia left little time for the Cathedral save occasional evenings and Sundays and odd hours when De Mun or Mills could be put to making drawings. It was not till the following February (1805) that the designs were nearing completion. On February 6 he wrote his brother Christian (in a letter already quoted in part on page 225):

> Your account of your rambles carries me to the spots I have visited among those you describe.—I forget the year I went to Bath, Bristol, Wells, & Salisbury with Mr. Lloyd. I think you were in Germany on the Gnadenfrey business. . . . I am obliged as to the Baltimore Cathedral to design from memory. I cannot procure here a single technical account or representation of a Gothic Building of any superior merit; but the style, & even the detail is so impressed on my imagination that I hope to succeed, in escaping the censure you so justly bestow upon Wyatt, whom among architects, I have always put in the same rank that Shenstone & Phillips hold among poets.—

---

2. These books are difficult to identify, since the titles Latrobe gives do not agree with any recorded book titles. The "Gothic Hints" might possibly refer to Batty and Thomas Langley's *Gothic Architecture, Improved by Rules and Proportions* (London: Taylor [1742]) or, more probably, one of the works of John Carter or of John Britton. The earlier volumes of Carter's *Ancient Architecture of England* (London: n.p., 1795-1807) had already appeared. Britton's *Architectural Antiquities* had also begun publication and included King's College Chapel in Cambridge and the Henry VII Chapel at Westminster Abbey. The "Picturesque Scenery" perhaps refers to William Gilpin's *Remarks on Forest Scenery . . .*

I have, as I believe I have told you, made a good campaign at my great Canal. I shall send you such another book of this work & of the buildings at Washington as soon as I can get it drawn as your last,[3]—& will add to it my Cathedral, & any other work I have not yet sent to you . . .

Another two months passed before the Cathedral design was finally ready. Along with the Gothic scheme Latrobe included one he called Roman; obviously he wished to give the Cathedral authorities the opportunity of such an important choice. With the designs went a long letter of explanation (April 27, 1805) addressed to the Right Reverend Bishop Carroll and the building committee; it is entitled "Remarks on the proposed erection and on the designs submitted." This communication is remarkable not only as a treatise on church design but also because it shows so clearly that for Latrobe, as for any really creative architect, the making of a suitable program and the development of a plan to fulfill its demands must be the basis of any good building. He starts out:

A Cathedral of the Latin Church, has a prescribed form, from which that propriety, which ought to be uniform in the practise, to produce the respect which is always given to consistency—does not permit the architect to deviate. This form is that of a cross, the *style* of which is *longer* than the head, and either of the arms.—The head of the cross is also necessarily the Choir, the arms the Transepts, & the style the nave of the *Church*. . . . The Choir, being that part of the church which is devoted to divine service, must be of a size to admit of the commodious arrangements, & movements of the Clergy engaged in its performance.—If it be ascertained, what is the smallest space, in which the ceremonial of high festivals of the Church can be *decently,* that is commodiously exhibited—(for embarrassment arising from a crowd, destroys solemnity) the smallest possible size of the Choir of a Cathedral would be determined. The Choir governs the dimensions of the remaining parts of the Church.

But generalities are not enough; basing his estimates on a nave width of 25 feet, he assumes a depth of 50 feet for the choir, and from this di-

---

(London: Blamire, 1791). It is barely possible that this William Gilpin was a relative of the Philadelphia Gilpins.

3. "Your last" refers evidently to Latrobe's volume of drawings, now in the Historical Society of Pennsylvania, which contains the designs of the Bank of Pennsylvania and the waterworks of Philadelphia. Its title page informs us that it was made for Christian Latrobe. The book this letter promises has never been found.

mension in turn he arrives at a total length of 177 feet for the entire church. These dimensions are for the Gothic scheme, which he refers to as the "first design," and he comments that such a length is "a small dimension, compared to the length of any European Cathedral with which I am acquainted." With regard to the second, the Roman design, he writes:

In the second design, I have very considerably contracted the length of the Nave, the style of the building admitting it better than that of No. 1.

The length of the choir in this design from the back wall to the Screen is 37′-6″. The center is covered by a dome 40 feet in diameter, and the nave is 58 feet long, making, with the width of the arches on which the dome rests (6 feet), 141 ft. 6 in., or 36′-6″ less than the 1st design.

Only after presenting a complete table of dimensions for the two designs does he bring up the subject of style:

The Veneration which the Gothic cathedrals generally excite, by their peculiar style,—by the associations belonging peculiarly to that style, and by the real grandeur, & beauty which it possesses, has induced me to propose the Gothic style of building in the first design submitted to you. The Gothic style of Cathedrals, is impracticable to the uses of common life, while the Greek & Roman architecture has descended from the most magnificent temples to the decoration of our meanest furniture.—On this account, I claim that the former has a peculiar claim to preference, especially as the expense is not greater in proportion to the effect.—The second design which is Roman, has, as far as I can judge of my own works, equal merit with the first in point of plan, and structure, and I therefore submit the choice to you, entirely, having myself an equal desire to see the first, or the second executed,—my *habits* rather inclining to the latter, while my reasonings prefer the first.

He refuses to make an accurate estimate for either plan:

. . . if the building is to be erected at all events, and the least possible size be determined,—everything else follows of course: for an estimate made with the best care & judgement cannot bind the expense.—All that is to be done then is to execute the smallest work with the greatest economy which is consistent with solidity, for no extravagance is so profligate & ruinous as that of bad workmanship.

The letter ends with practical advice on the materials and on choosing a competent clerk of the works. For the clerk of the works he suggests

William Steuart, son of Robert Steuart the stonecutter, from whom Latrobe had purchased stone for the Capitol. He concludes:

> In offering you my professional services I have to request that you will do me the honor to accept them in their fullest extent. In this you will do no more than to gratify the jealous desire I feel to be as useful to you, as if my love of fame & of independence were as much interested,—as are the feelings of my heart in serving you.—When you are ready to lay out your building, I will do myself the honor to wait upon you & to perform that duty . . .

A day later, in a letter sent personally to the Bishop, Latrobe elaborates upon his offer, explaining that donating his services does not mean donating the services of his employees, and continues:

> But as neither my private or professional income,—nor the measure of what a single individual ought to offer to a numerous society, or that society to accept, extend to actual expenditures in your service,—I mean very candidly and unceremoniously to deliver to you an account of all, & every [one] of the trifles, which affect my purse.

Still more important, he includes here his first tentative estimates: either design, he believes, can be built for $55,000 or $60,000. Even for that period, however, these figures seem (and proved) low for a building of the size and elaborateness planned.

Hastening to accept this generous offer, the Diocese chose the second—the Roman—design for execution. But the building committee, finding even this smaller scheme too long and too wide for the selected site, wanted the plan reduced, and Latrobe sent on (July 9, 1805) a revised design which also included a change from the square east end to a semicircular apse, as the Bishop desired. Continual minor changes were made, and it was not until the end of the year (December 26, 1805) that Latrobe wrote that the construction drawings were at last ready.

The ensuing four months were crucial. On February 15, 1806, he pleaded with the Bishop for an additional twenty feet, fifteen feet, even ten feet; ten days later he wrote again that he was now satisfied with the fifteen feet more he had been allowed and asked (apparently in vain) if he might design the rectory. By then it had been decided to omit the transept porticoes, and Latrobe inquired whether the transept doors were necessary. Finally, on March 6, the first of the actual working drawings, the foundation plan, was sent; two days later Latrobe wrote the Bishop saying he could not see any way to reduce the length further. Apparently the whole would impinge on an existing earlier building, and Latrobe suggested that the erection of the apse be postponed until the old building could be taken down.

With this first working drawing trouble began. The builder had read the sections upside down, had mistaken the crypt vault for reversed foundation arches, and had complained to the Bishop that they were absurd. On March 26, 1806, Latrobe wrote the Bishop reassuring him on this point and explaining the builder's error. Toward the middle of April Latrobe submitted his first bill for expenses [4] and made his first visit of inspection. He was appalled at what he found. A certain John Hillen, one of the Cathedral trustees, had been appointed the builder, and a Mr. Rohrback clerk of the works. Not only was Hillen incompetent enough to misread Latrobe's plans, but he was continually running to the building committee and the Bishop with objections to the plans. The Bishop, architecturally innocent, brought up all these complaints with Latrobe. From Washington, on April 18, Latrobe wrote the faithful Louis de Mun, who had been the principal draftsman on the project: "I had a terrible battle at Baltimore, with Hillen whom I found at the bottom of all the Bishop's objections. Another such battle will drive me from the field."

Early in August, 1806, Latrobe made another visit to Baltimore and hastened to write the Bishop in high dudgeon:

> Near three months have now elapsed since I have seen or heard anything of the Cathedral, excepting a few words . . . that it was progressing. On my arrival here this morning, I find that alterations which appear to me very material have been made, & that others are projected. I might complain on this occasion in strong terms. But I content myself with requesting that you will please to return to me all the drawings of the church . . . & designate the person to whom I may return my actual expense . . .

And a little later, from Washington, he wrote his good friend Maximilian Godefroy (August 18) telling him of his trouble.[5]

---

4. The total bill was $247.00: Louis de Mun, 66 days, at $2.50 a day; Robert Mills, 26 days, at $2.00.

5. Maximilian Godefroy was a French ex-officer and a thoroughly trained architect and designer of no little skill. A refugee from the trouble in France, he had come to the United States in 1805, to be professor of fine arts at St. Mary's College in Baltimore. Nine years later he completed the layout of the Virginia state capitol grounds in Richmond. This was a formal garden with two axial apse-ended compositions of walks and hedges,

During all the rest of 1806 the Hillen matter rankled. Bishop Carroll did his best to smooth matters over, but Latrobe's professional pride was involved. The disastrous occurrences at Sedgeley had been lesson enough to him; they should not happen here! Reluctantly the Bishop returned the drawings, and finally, on December 12, Latrobe wrote the building committee a virtual ultimatum:

> It is now time that all the drawings necessary for the erection of the Cathedral . . . should be made. . . . Before any steps of this kind can be taken a very perfect understanding ought to exist, as to the plan you mean to execute. . . . All the drawings are now in my possession. Alterations have been made in them and in the work by Mr. John Hillen, in direct violation of the stipulations under which I have given my services to you. . . . I shall, I am sure, not be thought unreasonable in making a further proposal . . . that either I, or Mr. John Hillen, be wholly discharged from all share in the design & construction of the Cathedral.

The next day he sent an explanatory letter to the Bishop suggesting the firing of Rohrback as clerk of the works and the hiring of Robert Mills instead; he added what amounted to a threat:

> I sincerely hope that hence forward everything will go on agreeably to all parties. . . . If it is such . . . I will proceed actively and zealously, if I decline I shall publish the whole correspondence, and thus prevent my name being ever connected with the building that will be erected . . . under the auspices of Hillen & Rohrback . . .

---

one on each side of the capitol; the capitol hill itself was terraced high between these in three rectangular terraces with an axial walk and steps. The present informal grading and planting superseded the old formal layout about 1830. Godefroy married Eliza Crawford, the daughter of a well-known physician and herself something of a blue stocking. She was the editor and publisher of a periodical called *The Companion* (published between November 3, 1804, and October 25, 1806) and its successor, *The Observer* (November 29, 1806, to December 26, 1807), to which Latrobe contributed several pieces of architectural interest. Godefroy himself became famous as the architect of the chapel of St. Mary's College (for Father Dubourg)—a design of great verve in a sort of strange picture-book Gothic—and later of the superb domical Unitarian Church in Baltimore. Still later, he entered into a somewhat unfortunate collaboration with Latrobe on the Baltimore Exchange, as we shall see. Embittered by this experience, the Godefroys sailed for England in August, 1819, and, equally unsuccessful there, in 1827 they went to France where he became the official architect for La Mayenne. Here he designed the Prefecture of Laval. Mrs. Godefroy died there in 1839, and he apparently left Laval in 1842. No date for his death has thus far been ascertained. See Carolina V. Davison, "Maximilian Godefroy," in *Maryland Historical Magazine,* vol. 29, no. 1 (March, 1934), and William D. Hoyt, Jr., "Eliza Godefroy: Destiny's Football," in *Maryland Historical Magazine,* vol. 36, no. 1 (March, 1941).

And to show his good faith he wrote to Bishop Carroll some three weeks later (January 6, 1807) that he was still working on the Cathedral drawings and waiting for word of his re-engagement.

The Bishop's position was not enviable. Between the pressures from Hillen (a trustee) and Rohrback on the one hand and Latrobe's professional attitude on the other, and with a building committee largely ignorant of the real points involved and eager to get on with the job, all his skill and diplomacy were needed. He urged Latrobe to continue; Latrobe answered that he would do so on receipt of an official letter, and on January 26, 1807, he again wrote Bishop Carroll a new, extended account of the whole controversy, marked "private." Then, on the first of February, Latrobe sketched a letter he would like to send the trustees, but he had the wisdom to send it to the Bishop first. The Bishop at once seized the opportunity to make a final attempt to clarify the problem and to mollify the architect in a direct appeal to him dated February 9:

When I received four days ago your favor of the first inst. inclosing the draft of one intended for the trustees, it gave me too much concern to comply with your request by writing an immediate answer. My concern did not arise merely from the foresight of the fatal consequence which would result to our undertaking by the withdrawal of your direction in its present state, but likewise because it appeared to us that the loss of your talents and knowledge would be chargeable in some degree to my imprudence, not indeed for having exhibited to the trustees your private letter of December 13 (which I was careful not to do), but for having verbally informed them of your repugnance to act with Mr. Hillen, (one of the trustees) or to have the building superintended by Mr. Rhorback [sic]—repeating this part of your letter from memory, I may have used unintentionally expressions from which they inferred that they were to be restrained from employing agents best approved by them, for the immediate superintendence of the building, and therefore they required that their answer should assert their authority. But as they expressly added that these agents should have no authority to make alteration in the design or construction without your knowledge or approbation, is it yet forbidden to hope that more attention will be paid hereafter to this, and that you will reconsider and suspend at least, if not change your resolution? . . . It does not escape me that this is a selfish and interested request; it is soliciting you to sacrifice your own feelings to those who have rashly undertaken to rejudge your work and modify without knowledge a design formed on the principles of science and directed by experience. Conscious of my inability to give any opinion on the combinations required for the various detailed parts of a great piece of architecture, I have constantly refrained from every interference, but seeing now the mischief into which we shall be plunged without your aid, I am determined to interpose my voice more decidedly, and I shall insist peremptorily on a strict compliance with your directions . . .

Having offered these observations, and despairing almost of their having the effect of producing a change in your determination, I send you back the copy of your intended letter. If, however, you can think more compassionately for our ignorance and presumption its daughter, you will find it advisable to soften some expressions (a few marginal notes on your copy will direct you to the passages) which have appeared most likely to me to give displeasure—perhaps you will note the others. . . .[6]

This letter succeeded in its aim. On March 26, at last, all seemed settled and Latrobe wrote gratefully to the Bishop: "I thank you sincerely for your kind interference in the work of peace, & will do all I can to give success to your wishes . . ." A new agent was appointed—the Reverend Francis Beeston—to whom Latrobe could send his technical directions and his drawings, and a chastened George Rohrback continued as clerk of the works. Latrobe had won his main point—no changes whatsoever were to be made in the design without his express approval or his direct and specific orders. Already nearly three years had passed since the architect's first letter, but many details of the final design had not yet been decided on and only the excavation and some foundations had been carried out. The three years had brought to Latrobe hope, disappointment, and trouble and to the Bishop difficult problems of human relations; both of them must have felt a great relief to have the controversies settled. Now the work could proceed!

All through 1807 the drawings were piling up and being sent on to the Reverend Francis Beeston—sections of the foundation walls and details of the transept, the gallery and gallery stairs, the vestry windows, and the bases for pilasters and columns. Latrobe had planned to visit Baltimore in the last week in July, but the weather was unfavorable and later his subpoena as a witness in the Burr trial held him in Washington. He was in Philadelphia from the end of November, 1807, until mid-January, 1808, when he returned to Washington; during that period he probably visited Baltimore, for another important change occurred about this time. The Bishop and the trustees wanted the four central piers that had been planned removed, so that the crossing dome, instead

6. Sturges, *op. cit.*

of being only as wide as the nave, could be the total width of nave and aisles. On February 5, 1808, Latrobe wrote that the desired drawings were being delayed by this change—"wholly altering & I think spoiling the design." He recapitulated the matter in another letter to Bishop Carroll (February 11):

> All the difficulties of the piers arise, like all our other difficulties, out of the alterations made by desire of the Trustees. Side aisles in every Cathedral of the world are passages, or walks. I made them 7′-6″ wide. But the Trustees would add 10 feet to them. I added the 10 feet, & then they became of consequence to the room of the church, and the piers were then too big. Thus a seventh design becomes necessary, & I am making it . . .

This "seventh" design was completed in March. In its preparation Latrobe had to consider not only the final effect he desired—the great open central space—and such alterations in other parts of the original interior design as were necessary to make them consistent with the new vision, but also the existing foundations. He had to plan in such a way as to utilize as much of the old and necessitate as little new foundation work as possible. This problem he solved brilliantly; only small diagonal wings were necessary, added to the inner side of the eight central piers, and to even the bearing on the foundations he used four diagonal reversed arches to tie each of the four diagonal corners together. The existing work shows no trace of unequal settlement, although the weight of the central dome was transferred from the four central piers to the eight that were adjacent. On March 4, 1808, the final section drawing went forward to Bishop Carroll, and in transmitting it Latrobe wrote that "the Church as it now is proposed must necessarily be vaulted . . ."

At last the Cathedral design had taken its final form, and construction now went ahead slowly but surely. The finished drawings were made largely by George Bridport and were billed for on October 10. It was this seventh design that produced the Cathedral substantially as it stands today, except for the additional domed bay used to lengthen the choir in 1890, when Latrobe's pleas for greater length were found to have been warranted; the space which he had wanted in front of the altar and had shown in his earliest designs ultimately had to be provided.

All through 1809, 1810, and 1811 the building progressed gradually and without friction; apparently the trustees had learned their lesson. The exterior walls had risen to the level of the panels above the side windows

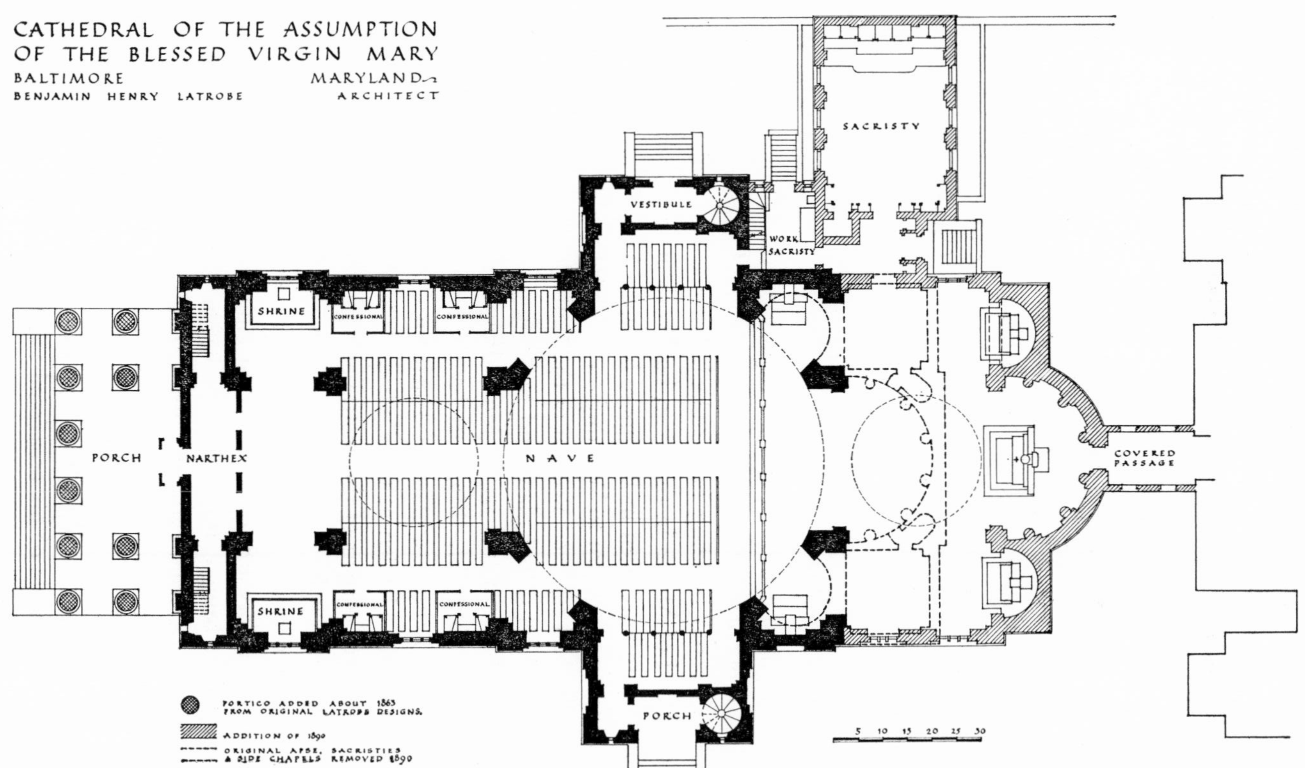

FIGURE 16. Baltimore Cathedral. Measured Plan, showing additions.

Courtesy Avery Library and Walter Knight Sturges

by the autumn of 1809; in November there was correspondence about the special cut stone for these panels, obtained from "Mr. Robertson, the quarrier." In the following July (1810) the interior was almost ready for the Ionic column capitals for the galleries and the apse, and Latrobe wrote the Bishop that he would have them carved in Washington by Andrei, one of the Italian sculptors who had been imported for the Capitol work, and by his assistant Somerville; in February he wrote again saying they would cost $200 each for the sanctuary capitals and $120 each for the smaller capitals beneath the galleries, plus $200 more for the stone. On July 4 and July 12, 1811, he wrote two letters pleading for payments to the carvers. Latrobe visited the Cathedral twice that year—sometime between July 23 and July 30, and again on September 20. Apparently he found everything in order. All bade fair for continuing progress and the completion of the Cathedral at not too distant a date.

But these hopes were vain; the War of 1812 intervened and, with the consequent financial confusion and the depression that accompanied and followed it, brought a total cessation of the work for almost five years. Only in 1817 could building be resumed. Latrobe was called to Baltimore at the end of March in that year, but work at the Capitol delayed him; he seems to have been in Baltimore between April 12 and April 25, however, and on his return to Washington he wrote the Reverend Enoch Fenwick (who had replaced Beeston as the Cathedral's executive agent), sending some dimensioned plans and requesting him to check their dimensions against the actual work. More drawings of the central dome followed, and on May 21, 1817, Latrobe wrote asking Fenwick to call for them at the Baltimore office of Hazlehurst Brothers. Two months later he wrote Mr. Hayden at the Cathedral: "The heads of the niches [in the two eastern corners of the central area] must have caissons, otherwise they will be as bald as a monk, & cost more in painting them . . ." And by August 1 he stated that "the great dome is under way." Details of the dome went forward to Baltimore on August 6. Meanwhile the interior details were being completed; but what had become of the column capitals ordered six years earlier? Latrobe wrote Fenwick (August 21, 1817): "I had an indistinct recollection that I had formerly all the capitals of your internal columns carved here by Andrei. This morning I . . . found them . . . in a log shed, where they have remained these ten years [a typical example of his occasional vagueness in dates]. They are among the most beautiful things . . . Andrei will engage to carve over and repair all those that require it." Andrei's assistants in the work were Henderson, Somerville, and McIntosh. The capitals were finally shipped on October 22; the cost of the carving, we learn, was $142.50 each.

At the end of that year Latrobe resigned his position as architect of the Capitol under distressing circumstances, as we shall see, and went to Baltimore to live, primarily to be close to the Exchange then under construction. But this removal also brought him in immediate touch with the Cathedral and he had the satisfaction of seeing it enclosed during 1818, its vaults and its roof complete and most of its interior finished. Only the exterior portico and the towers remained to be built.[7] The great church was ready for use. It was dedicated in 1821, its noble interior a mute witness to its architect's skill.

Thus the first major Roman Catholic cathedral in the United States gradually came into being. It is now a fitting time to consider its design and its construction, for both offer convincing testimony to the architect's vision.

Latrobe's first design was Gothic. In this, as he wrote to his brother, he had "to design from memory." What was this memory and how accurate was it? He had traveled extensively in Europe; undoubtedly he had seen at least the chief Gothic cathedrals of France and certainly some of those in Germany and England. Of his acquaintance with English Gothic monuments we can place him definitely in Bath, Wells, and Salisbury, and he must have known the Gothic churches of London. We also know that as a lad in Fulneck he had sketched Kirkstall Abbey in near-by Leeds. His general acquaintance, therefore, with important Gothic monuments was large. Yet we must remember, too, that in those early years Latrobe's chief architectural interest was in the new, rationalist, classic revival buildings which were rising all over Europe; to him the Gothic monuments were merely historic and picturesque backgrounds.

As an ardent young architect in London, however, he was necessarily under the Romantic influence, which must have been nearly as strong for

---

7. Latrobe's drawings show simple domical tops to the belfry towers; the present onion-shaped outline, dating from 1832, is not his work. The portico was not completed until 1863, and John H. B. Latrobe served as the architect to carry it out and thus complete his father's creation. The choir was lengthened in 1890, as we have seen, and the whole was carefully examined, repaired where necessary, and redecorated in 1945. The lengthening in 1890 followed the original details meticulously, but the more recent decoration seems to follow the fashions of its time more than the spirit its original architect would have preferred.

him as the classic rationality that underlay his thinking and his design. In his painting he was a romantic of the romantics, disciplined by his sense of reality rather than by any classic rules. He was a water-colorist of the school of Girtin, with occasional atmospheric touches not too unlike the early Turner; not infrequently one sees in the work flashes of Fuseli if not of Blake. To one formed in such an environment, at a time before any profound analysis—either historic or structural—of Gothic monuments had been made, "Gothic" was pre-eminently an atmosphere rather than any strict category of definite forms. It connoted an emotion about buildings rather than any specific way of building them. Moreover, this Gothic was still not a revival, in the strict sense of the word. For Wyatt, in Fonthill Abbey, as for Wren in his Gothic work a century earlier, the architect's freedom in design remained untrammeled by notions of historical consistency. Nostalgia rather than archaeology reigned. And in Latrobe's Gothic work—Sedgeley, the Baltimore Cathedral design, Christ Church in Washington, the Bank of Philadelphia—the same holds true.

Apparently, nevertheless, in this design for the Cathedral, one precedent predominates—Kirkstall Abbey, the ruin that had enthralled the architect as a boy. In the treatise on landscape which he prepared for Miss Susanna Spotswood, there is a romantic picture of it, painted either from memory or more probably from early sketches which he still preserved. In general mass its effect is strikingly like that of the Baltimore Cathedral project. In both a relatively low central tower covers the crossing; in both there is the same rather high-shouldered appearance, derived from high side aisles and a low clerestory. Latrobe's painting in the Spotswood sketchbook includes, too, a revelatory little detail vignette of the end of the nave or choir. It shows an enormous single window running the entire height of the structure and flanked by large corner pinnacles. Significantly, the sketch depicts the wall beneath the window sill as almost completely destroyed, giving the effect of one colossal door or porch. Here then, rather than in the quite different Peterborough, is the source of the tall recessed porch that dominates the front of the Cathedral design.

It is futile to seek direct precedents elsewhere. Latrobe was designing within an atmosphere, not aiming to re-create the past. The tall lancet windows of the side aisles and the equilateral arches of the clerestory are his own. Possibly these clerestory windows recall the low arches of the Salisbury cloister; perhaps they are merely the result of the effort to obtain large scale in conjunction with modest height.

In the interior, however, the spirit is more that of German than of French or English Gothic. The nave vault is essentially a barrel vault with penetrations, rather than a true groined vault, and like some late Gothic German church vaults it is covered with a lace of surface tracery. Everything is done, too, to exaggerate the slim verticality of the nave; there is little here of the long horizontals so frequent in England. It is characteristic of the atmospheric quality of the entire design that this vault is apparently intended to be of lath and plaster, for the supports (only three feet thick) and the thin strip buttresses are manifestly insufficient to support or to buttress the thrusts of a vault of masonry. In plaster the non-structural, reticulated vault ribbing is as consistent as any other form could be; in masonry the pattern would be absurd. Similarly the primitive and sometimes awkward window tracery seems designed for wood rather than for stone. Here the architect's emotional feeling for Gothic led him far indeed from the structural logic that so largely controlled his classic buildings.

But Latrobe's chief difficulty in this design was in the matter of scale. As he wrote the Bishop, the length of the church was "a small dimension compared to . . . any European Cathedral," and the nave width (only twenty-five feet) was from ten to fifteen feet narrower than the average in European Gothic cathedrals. The whole scheme was of necessity a miniature, and—since that very fact made the copying of typical Gothic monuments absurd to a thinking designer—Latrobe went to great lengths to avoid in it any sense of the toy. Hence the use of stretches of plain wall, the single lancets of the side aisles, and possibly the use of what is virtually a barrel vault. Yet even in this relatively short cathedral the designer's search for the emotion of mystery led him to use a complete choir screen (with an organ) across the west end of the choir. Here, of course, it was the memory of the broken perspectives of English abbeys that controlled.

The total result was interesting but not convincing, vivid but somehow unreal. And Latrobe's memory of Gothic detail, despite the accuracy he boasted of in his letter to Christian, played him false in many places, so that his moldings are too thin, his tracery wiry and without conviction. The design displays a compromise between emotion and structure, between memory and imagination. One hazards the opinion that Latrobe himself, despite a certain disappointment, felt a deep relief when the Cathedral authorities chose the "Roman" design. Later Latrobe's own view of the desirability of Gothic changed. On May 30, 1813, he wrote from Washington to David Hare, of Philadelphia, about a proposed Washington Hall there. Hare had mentioned the possibility of making it Gothic, and Latrobe protested:

> You even speak of a Gothic arch. The Bank of Philadelphia [which Latrobe had designed in Gothic] has done more mischief than that of Pennsylvania has produced good. The Free Masons' Hall [designed by William Strickland], which is anything but Gothic, has made me repent a thousand times that I ventured to exhibit a specimen of that architecture. My mouldings & window heads appear in horrid disguise from New York to Richmond.

In his other design for the Cathedral the effect is entirely different. Latrobe himself commented on the fact that with the Roman inspiration he could make a satisfactory design considerably shorter than in the case of the Gothic. The fewer and more definite architectural details allowed a much truer sense of scale throughout. In the earliest classic sketches the aisles are narrow, and the dome over the crossing—some forty feet in diameter—occupies the total width of the nave and aisles. By using semicircular windows above as a sort of clerestory lighting, the side-aisle scale has been cut down; the exterior rusticated walls beneath are unpierced. The highly developed transepts are fronted by six-column Corinthian porticoes, and above them the treatment (recalling distantly some of Soane's eccentricities) is somewhat inept in tying the transept pediments to the paneled octagonal dome base.

The plan in essence is a Greek cross, with an added short bay in the nave to transform it into a Latin cross, the plan Latrobe was seeking. Noteworthy is the large choir with its square end, and some kind of screen is indicated to separate it from the crossing and the nave. Four low saucer domes on pendentives cover the bays of transept, nave, and choir and lead up to the larger and higher central dome.

Thus the plan of this first classic scheme is logical and consistent, but the total design is still far from the simple grandeur eventually achieved. The scale is still in certain places too small, and particularly on the exterior the planes are too broken up; for instance, the use of horizontally rusticated stone up to the sills of the "clerestory" windows, though not without ample precedent, makes for confusion. From this project the final design was arrived at, but only by means of drastic simplifications.

The first major change—the increase in aisle width to seventeen feet, made at the behest of the trustees—was accompanied by another: the marked shortening of the choir and the substitution of an apse for the domed square. Both caused major changes in the interior. Once the aisles were widened, they became essential parts of the entire interior volume; to express this, large arched windows, one in each bay, were inserted to replace the earlier semicircles. Immediately the interior was clarified and the sense of openness increased. At the same time the nave saucer dome was replaced by a square cross vault, and sections of barrel vaults were used over the transepts and the choir. Only the central dome over the crossing remained. This was to have been vaulted in masonry, but its outer drum walls were placed, most unfortunately, over the middle of the side-aisle bays, and the section appears almost unbuildable. Yet this second version of the design is in general still a confused compromise. The simple clarity of conception of the first—four saucer domes surrounding a larger central one—has been irrevocably lost, despite the gain in volume. And the central dome, now reduced to the nave width, has lost its commanding scale. No wonder Latrobe was irked.

But salvation of the scheme came with another suggestion from the client—the omission of the four inner piers at the crossing. Latrobe again regarded the interference as a difficulty, but he made no serious attempt to change the client's mind; evidently he, too, felt the narrower dome a blemish and to the challenge of the new problem he rose magnificently in what was the final design. He approached the entire problem anew, bound only by the position of the exterior walls and the major pier positions and sizes; the lower parts of these were already built. For the first time he realized what the changes already made had created—the opportunity of orchestrating the entire interior volume as a single, richly rhythmical whole. In line with this new thinking the upper clerestory windows disappear; the walls now count as single areas, with emphasis on their height from floor to vault. The earlier saucer dome over the nave goes back into the design again as a preparation for the central dome over the crossing, and this central dome now has its proper commanding dignity and a diameter of more than sixty feet. All the difficulties of its structural relation to the rest of the building have vanished; again everything is integrated. It is unconventional—a copy of no known building—but it is a whole in which use, construction, and effect have been united at last with true Vitruvian power.

Structurally the Baltimore Cathedral is a masterpiece. When in the spring of 1808 Latrobe submitted his "seventh" design to Bishop Carroll, as we have seen, he had decided that the entire church was to be vaulted. This at the time was a daring decision; except for a few Spanish mission churches in Texas, no other American church of that day was completely vaulted in masonry. And here it was a question not of mere barrel or groined vaults but of coffered domes and pendentives and of a major crossing vault some 65 feet across (more than 20 feet wider than the architect's earlier dome over the Bank of Pennsylvania). The nave dome is two feet thick to the bottom of the coffers; apparently these coffers were built in the solid vault brickwork. In the nave and transepts the width of the aisles and the weight of the exterior stone walls take care of the thrusts; longitudinally the extension of the nave and the belfries make spread improbable if not impossible. The crypt is divided by cross walls, pierced with several low segmental arches; these in turn carry segmental transverse barrel vaults that support the nave floor. It was these barrel vaults, shown in section, that Hillen had read upside down and taken for reversed arches in the foundations. No important thrust considerations occurred here.

In the central dome the case is different. This is a double dome, the outer one of timber, metal covered, and the inner of brick, 2′-8″ thick to the bottom of the coffers and 3′-6″ thick over all. Built into its spring there is probably a continuous iron band similar to that used in the Bank of Pennsylvania, though Latrobe did not depend upon this alone to withstand the thrusts. The dome is low, and the heavy barrel vaults over the transepts and the first bays of nave and choir would do much to prevent the dome drum from deforming; but in addition he weighted the haunches of the inner dome heavily with a mass of solid masonry (4 feet thick at the base and 2 feet thick at the upper rim) which forms the external visible drum and the lower steps of the visible outer dome. This masonry domes inward slightly and receives the ends of the radiating laminated timbers of the outer dome, thus carrying their weight down on the outer haunches of the inner dome and then to the cross arches and the piers. It is a brilliantly conceived scheme, and its success is proved by the stability that has held all without apparent cracking or movement for a century and a third. And it is something of this stability that seems expressed, perhaps unconsciously, in the quiet directness of the architecture, both inside and out.

When it was first built, the shortness of the choir, which brought the apse so close to the crossing, must have made the climax seem unduly sudden; yet from the first the Cathedral of Baltimore won an almost universal admiration, alike from the untutored public and from the sophisticated. Mrs. Trollope found it, like the Capitol, remarkable. She writes:

> . . . Its interior, however, has an air of neatness that amounts to elegance. The form is a Greek cross, and a dome in the center; but the proportions are ill-preserved; the dome is too low, and arches which support it are flattened and too wide for their height.[8]

Yet today, as one enters the great west door, the beautiful openness of the space envelops one, and the way in which part leads to part and the little to the big—all so simply detailed, with just the right amount of ornament in the dome coffers and on the Greek Ionic capitals of the columns around the apse and under the galleries—makes for one of America's truly distinguished interiors, which even the present inept "decorations" and boudoir colors cannot destroy.

Mrs. Trollope notes one criticism—the fact that the use of segmental arches throughout makes the interior too low. Two reasons evidently determined the architect's use of this form: the fear of exceeding a limited appropriation by building to an undue height, and the fact that such segmental arches were a commonplace in the English architecture of the late eighteenth century.[9] Latrobe liked and used them elsewhere. Perhaps here the arches are too segmental, with too little rise for their span, but somehow the relation of heights to widths seems fundamentally right.

There is another peculiarity of the design less easy to justify—the treatment of the central dome without pendentives, together with the odd soffits that result in the four chief arches at the crossing. Perhaps Latrobe was afraid that pendentives so large would be difficult if not impossible for the local masons to construct. Perhaps he felt that the necessary scaf-

---

8. Mrs. [Frances Milton] Trollope, *Domestic Manners of the Americans* (London: Whittaker, Trecher & Co., 1832; New York: reprinted "for the booksellers," 1832).

9. As, for instance, in the Old Park Church of St. Mary, Paddington, London, built between 1788 and 1791, from the designs of J. Plaw.

folding and centering would entail too great an expense. Or perhaps he remembered the design difficulties in which Wren had found himself through his desire to have eight equal pendentives at the crossing of St. Paul's in London and the awkward means he had been forced to adopt to produce them. Latrobe's taste was always for the straightforward, the untroubled, the continuous plane. And by the omission of pendentives he certainly achieved at the crossing in Baltimore a simple and direct power of effect, for which he felt the unequal soffits of his arches—curved in plan on the crossing side though straight on the other—were but a small price to pay. To have added further segmental arches over the corner faces of the crossing, as the use of pendentives would require, would have destroyed this lucidity.

On the exterior the design is equally compelling. Except for the onion tops of the belfries, the Cathedral stands much as Latrobe designed it. The simplicity of the masses is superb, the handling of the wall planes direct and unforced. The large arched recesses in which the windows are placed define on the exterior the scale of the interior and suggest the vaulting within, just as the cut-stone panels express the membering of the plan. The shortness of the nave allows the dome, low though it is, to dominate as it should, and the 1890 addition to the choir length enhances the uniformity of the rhythms. It is an exterior worthy of the interior it surrounds, and that is high praise indeed.

PART III: The Climax Period

CHAPTER

13

Work for the United States Government: 1798-1812

Within two years of Latrobe's arrival in the United States he found himself working for the Federal government, and from 1802 to the end of his life there were only four years (1813-15 and 1818-20) during which he had no Federal commission. Thus government work was a continuing thread running through his life; for long periods it was his chief interest. Personally, too, this connection was important to him. It brought him into close contact with the most influential men in the United States; it won him wide professional esteem as well as savage criticism; and for years the salary he received from it was, if not his chief, at least his most secure source of income.

His first Federal employment arose out of the French war scare of 1798. The fortifications at Norfolk, largely destroyed in the English bombardment during the Revolution, had never been rebuilt. Latrobe therefore was asked to survey the ruins of the old forts and make recommendations about what should be done to make the city secure, and he spent weeks in the summer of 1798 on this work. His findings were embodied in two vividly graphic plans, still extant.[1] In addition he made two designs, one small and one large, for a powder magazine—a circular, masonry-vaulted building with a conical roof.[2]

These plans contained the best that European practice had to offer, and Latrobe had even been informed that it was the intention of the military authorities to appoint him their architect. But the commission

1. In Records of the United States Army, National Archives.

2. A similar structure was built from his designs on Judiciary Square in Washington during the War of 1812.

never came—he belonged to the wrong party. Since political passions were high in those frightened years, any governmental appointment at all seemed an impossibility for him; not only was his French name almost a sufficient barrier in itself, but he was also known to be in the closest sympathy with all the Virginia democrats. He had also hoped to become the designer of a new arsenal to be built at Harpers Ferry, but he soon learned how fantastic his expectation of either job had been.[3]

With the election of Jefferson in 1800 the pattern changed. Latrobe was now in Philadelphia and enjoyed an acknowledged position as architect and engineer. Was it with this political change in mind that in January of that year he made a design for a military academy?[4] The drawings show a building on three sides of a deep court, with an entrance gate on the axis in front, connected to the ends of the wings by ditches. Opposite the gate the building is both heightened and widened to produce a striking central motif. This is dome crowned and at the rear accented with a semicircular projection containing a large lecture room on each floor; in front of the lecture rooms are a dining hall (below) and a library (above), so that the whole forms the functional center of the structure. Dwelling rooms and minor rooms occupy the wings. It is not an entirely successful plan; the entrances are awkward, some connections are forced, and the whole seems to need more study as well as a more closely reasoned program. The simple exterior, like the Richmond penitentiary, owes its effect to the rhythmical repetition of the arches. Yet it has coherence and is marked by an appropriately bleak military character. Latrobe felt acutely the need of some such academy and kept coming back to the idea again and again, but in vain. As late as 1808 construction of the military academy was still under discussion, and in a letter to Colonel Williams in New York (December 28, 1807) Latrobe remarks that a possible Washington site—"Camp Hill"—had been selected and that the plans were in the hands of General Dearborn.

His next government venture was on a totally different plane. In 1802 Jefferson, then President, found himself in a political dilemma between his pacific ideals and a desire for government economy on the one hand and the preservation of national security on the other. The order for the

3. As disclosed in his letter of November 29, 1798, to Joseph Perkins in Philadelphia.

4. The drawings are in the Library of Congress. The United States Military Academy at West Point was not established until 1802.

74's—the great frigates—which had been issued by the Adams administration had since been canceled. Jefferson wished to keep the navy small, yet he realized that under such a policy the preservation of existing ships became all the more important. Ships when afloat require maintenance crews; could they not be more economically stored and better preserved in drydock and under cover? The President decided to find out whether such covered drydocks could be built and if so what their cost would be. There was but one person in America, he felt, who was fitted to handle so large a project, and this was B. H. Latrobe. On November 2, 1802, therefore, he wrote the architect proposing his scheme for a covered drydock 175 feet wide and 200 feet long, with a roof "like that of the Halle aux Blés in Paris." He asked Latrobe's help and told him that the job would require a visit to Washington and that only four weeks remained till the opening of Congress.

Latrobe accepted the assignment on November 8, on condition that satisfactory arrangements for payment could be made. On November 12 the Secretary of the Navy, Robert Smith, set the architect's mind at rest on that score, and Jefferson confirmed this a day later, suggesting that the first payment be an advance of $100. Latrobe then hastened to Washington, examined the conditions, and in the short time available produced an extraordinary design. The roof, as in the Halle aux Blés, is supported on tremendous laminated-wood arched girders, built up of planks in a manner first suggested by the French Renaissance architect Philibert de l'Orme; [5] these are received on and against heavy masonry buttress-like piers which, with the arches between them, establish a powerful and expressive rhythm. On the center of each side a monumental Greek Doric portico forms an imposing entrance; at the landward end a low pediment hides the curved roof, and three great arches provide light and ventilation. This covered drydock, 165 feet wide and 800 feet long,

---

5. This roofing system is based on the use of curved girders made of two layers of timber bolted together in relatively short pieces and given strength by horizontal purlins that are keyed through the joints. Latrobe knew this system best through the publications of the Prussian architect David Gilly (1748-1808), father of the brilliant architect Friedrich Gilly. David Gilly, a man of wide curiosities, was the editor of Prussia's first architectural magazine, *Sammlung nützlicher Aufsätze und Nachrichten, die Baukunst betreffend,* in 1799-1800. He was the author of *Ueber Einfindung, Construction und Vortheile der Bohlen-Dächer* (Berlin: Vieveg der Aelter, 1797), which is entirely devoted to the de l'Orme roof and its possible modern uses. It was probably through this book, which Latrobe knew well, that he was introduced to this type of roof.

was to be approached through two large masonry locks, designed with equal care, and the whole vast scheme proved to Jefferson at once Latrobe's ability not only to handle a project of large scale but also to integrate its demands and its construction into a building of power and beauty. Jefferson had an extensive correspondence with Secretary Robert Smith about this covered drydock and was deeply disappointed when Congress refused to appropriate the large sum of money—$417,276—it would cost.

While Latrobe was in Washington, Jefferson invited him to dinner. The party, a small and intimate one, has already been referred to (pages 230-31); but its real purpose, besides the pleasure Jefferson always found in stimulating company, was probably to give the President an opportunity of observing the architect more closely and of finding out if he could become a congenial collaborator. For Jefferson had another pressing architectural problem on his hands—the completion of the United States Capitol.

Work on the Capitol had reached a virtual impasse; the realization of Thornton's great plan was becoming more and more difficult.[6] The north wing had been in use since 1800, but already the roof leaked, the plaster was cracking, and fundamental repairs were necessary. Since only the south-wing foundations were in, the House of Representatives was using a temporary building (known in local slang as the "Bake-oven" because of its shape and its lack of ventilation) which Hoban had built on the foundations of Thornton's oval House chamber. The central portion was a maze of foundations that were based on at least two entirely different plans.

Three superintendents or assistants had worked on the Capitol, trying to overcome Thornton's technical ignorance: Étienne Hallet, who had been awarded second prize in the original competition; George Hadfield (the brother of Jefferson's friend and correspondent Maria Cosway), who had been brought over specifically for the job at the suggestion of Colonel Trumbull; and James Hoban, the Irish-born architect who had designed

6. As early as March 26, 1793, Jefferson had sent Washington a new plan of the Capitol made by Hallet, with a description in which fundamental faults of the Thornton plan were noted—especially poor lighting and bad circulation. Washington had answered from Mount Vernon (June 30, 1793), somewhat testily, "It is unlucky this investigation of Dr. Thornton's plan . . . had not preceded the adoption of it," and suggested a meeting between Thornton, Hallet, and Hoban to straighten out the confusion.

the President's House. Thornton had rendered the position of each of them unbearable, and one by one they had resigned. Hoban, the last, had been given a special title, Surveyor of Public Buildings, but even this move had been unavailing. All of the work had been carried out under the direct financial direction of the three commissioners of the capital, who were responsible for street layout and construction as well as land sales. This board (of which Dr. Thornton was a member) had also proved ineffectual. As a result, responsibility for the financial administration of the development of Washington and for the construction of the government buildings had been centralized in one commissioner, Thomas Munroe, who proved a faithful and efficient public servant. But the vacuum in the architectural administration of the construction of the Capitol and the President's House still remained.[7]

On March 3, 1803, Congress appropriated $50,000 to start the south wing of the Capitol, and the President had to choose a new surveyor—preferably a man with the necessary artistic and technical skills and one who had not been embroiled in the former controversies. From every point of view Latrobe seemed an ideal choice; accordingly Jefferson in a letter on March 6 offered him the position of Surveyor of the Public Buildings of the United States, and the architect accepted. Thus only five years after his arrival from England Latrobe found himself in the most

7. There is an extensive literature that deals with the building of the United States Capitol. Glenn Brown's *History of the United States Capitol,* 2 vols. (Washington: Government Printing Office, 1900, 1903) is a terse narrative valuable for its excellent illustrations, including many reproductions of existing drawings; but its handling of Latrobe's work is marred by an unjustified pro-Thornton bias. The *Documentary History of the Construction and Development of the United States Capitol Building and Grounds,* Report 646 of the 2nd Session of the 58th Congress (Washington: Government Printing Office, 1904), prints many (but not all) of the pertinent documents *in extenso.* Charles E. Fairman's *Art and Artists of the United States Capital,* Senate Document 95 (Washington: Government Printing Office, 1927), contains many interesting details. *Thomas Jefferson and the National Capital, 1783-1818,* edited by Saul K. Padover, with a preface by Harold L. Ickes, U.S. Department of the Interior, Source Book Series no. 4 (Washington: Government Printing Office, 1946), makes available in convenient form an enormous amount of valuable correspondence. Elinor Davidson Berman's *Thomas Jefferson Among the Arts, an Essay in Early American Esthetics* (New York: Philosophical Library [c1947]) also contains much valuable material. Paul Norton's *Latrobe and the United States Capitol,* a dissertation for Princeton University, 1950 (available at the Princeton University Library), is an almost day-by-day account of the construction of the Capitol and contains reproductions of a large number of previously unpublished drawings; the same author has in preparation a revised and more complete account of all Latrobe's governmental architecture. I have used all these sources in this chapter.

important architectural position in the country. It was a great triumph, but it was an even greater challenge.

After a visit to the capital city in March and April, 1803, Latrobe set seriously to work. Since at that time he did not contemplate moving to Washington—for in the letter of appointment Jefferson had expressed some uncertainty about the permanence of the job—the first requisite was the selection of a clerk of the works in whom he could put absolute trust. John Lenthall was his choice, and in many ways a perfect one; Latrobe appointed him on April 7. Lenthall was English born, two years older than the architect, with wide experience in building and in architecture both in England and in Washington. Furthermore, his wife was the daughter of Robert King, the city surveyor, and a sister of Nicholas King, who followed his father in that job. Lenthall therefore had an intimate knowledge of Washington conditions and personalities. The earliest letter we have from Latrobe to Lenthall—in which he requests him to ride over to the Capitol and informs him that he is being given a house near the Capitol to live in—is written with a kind of playful intimacy that suggests a previous acquaintance and sets the personal tone that was to distinguish all their future relationship.

This fundamental sympathy was of great importance. Lenthall was highly emotional—and tender-skinned almost to the point of abnormality. He was easily offended, could at times be rude, and was often silent when speech was called for. Occasionally he was at odds with Munroe and sometimes with Jefferson; for a period in 1807, thinking himself slighted by Latrobe, he sulked like Achilles in his tent for several weeks. Yet basically he worshiped his employer and was absolutely devoted to the great work—the completion of the Capitol. Latrobe on his side was fond of Lenthall, finding him so congenial that again and again in letters to him he unburdened his mind as he did to no one else. He encouraged, he twitted, by turns he was playful and somber; but always the letters were affectionate, always written as if the two of them alone knew the magnificence of their common opportunity. Continually Latrobe urged on Jefferson the justice of Lenthall's demands for more salary; he explained away Lenthall's testiness and lack of tact. Each was a true friend, a loyal supporter, of the other. Yet invariably Latrobe remained the designer and decider of questions, welcoming Lenthall's suggestions but accepting or rejecting them impersonally, and ever ready, as we shall see,

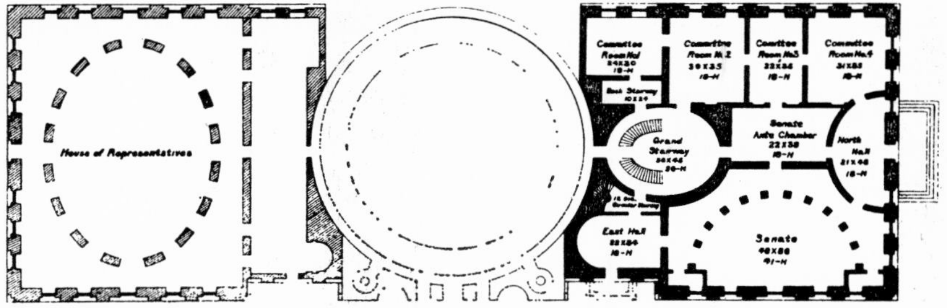

From Brown, *A History of the United States Capitol*

FIGURE 17. The Capitol, Washington. Ground-floor Plan as proposed by Thornton.

to acknowledge responsibility for his own decisions in the most wholehearted manner.

Obviously Latrobe had to begin by examining Thornton's plan for the south wing; and here the troubles began. Latrobe had received five different plans of the Capitol, and they were not in agreement.[8] The completed north-wing walls indicated the lines the exterior of the new wing must follow, but as for what was intended inside—beyond the mere room shapes—there was no evidence. The commissioners had complained earlier that they could get no sections from Thornton, and still none were forthcoming. The entire interior design would have to be created anew.

After his first month of work Latrobe wrote a long report (April 4, 1803) to Jefferson; in it he described the conditions as he had found them and set forth the futility of a visit he had made to Thornton at Jefferson's suggestion. The construction that had been completed was of what seemed to him a shockingly low standard and would require extensive demolition in the interests of safety; and the more he studied the plans he had received (none of which were in exact accordance with the executed foundations), the more practical difficulties he found in them. There were large areas of waste space and equally large areas that could not be well lighted; there were almost no committee rooms and similar auxiliary spaces. Latrobe's mandate had been to construct the building

8. One plan was given to him by Volney, one he received in 1801 from James Greenleaf (Robert Morris's partner in early Washington land speculation), one from George Blagden (the stone contractor), one from Thornton, and one from Jefferson. All were small-scale plans of the main floor.

in accordance with the competition plan that Washington had approved. But could he justifiably go ahead and build an expensive structure when he knew it would lack essential usefulness? To Latrobe as an architect there could be but one possible answer—it was his professional duty to call the attention of the President to these inadequacies before he proceeded.

Hope of any co-operation from Thornton was fruitless. He had already taken his stand—that Latrobe was an intruder and that any changes Latrobe might suggest would constitute not only affronts to himself but also direct violations of Latrobe's orders, which were to build according to the plan approved by Washington. Latrobe requested drawings; Thornton either had made none or they had been lost—he stated that they were no longer in his hands. Thornton did, however, describe the colonnade that would surround the oval House of Representatives, but he brusquely declined any further responsibility.

In this first report Latrobe also found fault with the Thornton layout for aesthetic as well as economic reasons. The oval shape, he felt, was bad acoustically; there was no relation between the exterior and the interior, and the plan would produce a badly lighted room. Moreover, the construction would be extremely expensive, for each stone of the pedestal wall would have to be cut to a special pattern and not to a single radius; he suggested that the oval be replaced by a semicircle or by two semicircles connected by a rectangle. Then he stated his impressions of the completed north wing: everywhere he found evidence of badly designed construction; rot was already appearing in many of the wood beams; a new roof that did not leak was imperative; and some way of heating the Senate chamber had to be found—Latrobe suggested steam.

Latrobe's immediate tasks were to get as much stone cut as possible, to strengthen and complete the foundation walls, and to carry up the exterior (in which there could be no changes) as high as possible. Jefferson was especially anxious to get this exterior up; he was politician enough to realize the excellent effect on Congress of such a showy evidence of progress. Quarries had to be examined, especially the one the government owned at Acquia, in Virginia. Additional sources for stone had to be found, for unless a sufficient quantity was delivered to the job at once the masons could not be used to their full efficiency during the coming months. Thus the summer of 1803 was devoted to preparing the necessary foundation drawings, taking down and replacing that part of the existing work which was so badly constructed as to be unsafe, and letting contracts for stone.

During Latrobe's absence on Chesapeake and Delaware Canal work after the middle of April, the Capitol building continued under Lenthall's efficient direction. Letter after letter passed between the architect and his clerk of the works, and Latrobe was able to settle many questions by means of careful drawings or little sketches in the letters. In the middle of June, after one of his many bouts with sickness, caused in this case perhaps by the conflict of interest between his two chief jobs, he was back in Washington for a short time to see that everything was going well. By the end of the building season the cellar vaults of the south wing had been completed and the cellars under the north wing cleaned out and ventilated to prevent further rotting of the wood floor beams. Yet difficulties in this method of handling the work were arising. Between July and September there was not a letter to Lenthall, and Thomas Munroe, the commissioner, was forced to write Jefferson of Lenthall's consequent embarrassment. Latrobe himself, however, returned at last for a week in mid-September.

Criticism in Washington had already become vocal on the slow progress being made, and Mrs. Latrobe records in her memoir that she felt her husband's absence from Washington was the basis for it. The President, in his eagerness to speed up the construction, even suggested the use of wooden columns for the House of Representatives; but Latrobe, writing to Lenthall (November 27, 1803), stated firmly: "The wooden column idea is one with which I never will have anything to do. On that you may rely. I will give up my office sooner than build a temple of disgrace to myself and Mr. Jefferson." Later, when Jefferson suggested brick columns stuccoed, the architect had to convince him that these, too, would be unworthy of the capitol of a nation; for Latrobe from the beginning had the concept that the United States Capitol, as far as he could make it, should be a solid structure, masonry built and of only the finest materials.

As 1803 wore on, another problem which was to dog the architect throughout his service in Washington raised its head. This was the difficulty of obtaining labor and materials. Washington itself was still but a village; skilled labor had to be brought in from outside and, since the work was seasonal only, labor recruitment was annually a bothersome and discouraging task.[9] Stone was a problem, too. Daniel Brent had a near monopoly on good freestone in Washington, and he forced up the prices unmercifully. The government quarry had proved expensive to operate; it was closed, then reopened, then closed again. Finally Latrobe found a quarrier in Baltimore, William Steuart, to whom he let a large contract. Brent then saw the light and reduced his exorbitant demands, and from that time on the cut stone was purchased from both sources. The architect's task was proving much more than one of designing, detailing, and, through Lenthall, superintending the work; it was one that required a broad knowledge of the sources of supply and much business negotiation, as well as all the tact Latrobe could command. How could an impatient Congress be aware of these endless but inevitable troubles?

When Latrobe visited Washington again at the beginning of 1804, remaining from January to March, the final plan of the House of Representatives was still undecided except that it should be raised one floor from the ground level, leaving the space beneath for required service and committee rooms.[10] Thornton was asked to supply a plan showing how he had contemplated providing committee rooms, and he complied with a plan showing a ring of them around the outside of the oval foundation wall of the House. Latrobe at once countered with the observation that this still left the entire central area an unusable dark hole. Some other solution had to be found. At Jefferson's suggestion, the architect went to call on Thornton again in late February to attempt to get his consent to the changes Latrobe felt necessary, and again the call was unavailing. Meanwhile he had several talks with Blagden and Hadfield in order to assemble the actual facts of their respective connections with the Capitol earlier; armed with this information, he made a report (February 22, 1804) to the Congressional committee in charge of the public buildings explaining to them the "absurdities" he found in the Thornton designs and the absolute necessity of changes. Then, that same evening, he went to Jefferson and carefully described to him all that he

9. In 1806, for instance, when skilled stonecutters were urgently needed, the New York City Hall and the State Capitol at Albany were both attracting so many that Latrobe was forced to send Mills to Albany to recruit possible employees there.

10. Thornton claimed that he had originally wanted the House and the Senate to be placed on the upper floor but that Jefferson himself had been responsible for moving them to the ground floor, and the north wing had been planned and built according to this decision.

felt was wrong and what he proposed. The President appeared convinced and asked him "to transmit to him drawings of a practical and eligible design retaining as much as possible the features of that adopted by General Washington."[11]

Under this Presidential command, therefore, during the first days of March (immediately after his return to Newcastle from Washington) he labored at the plan, embodying the necessary changes, and eventually found his answer. He wrote Lenthall of it at once (March 10, 1804):

> Instead of the ellipsis I am going to propose two semi-circles abutting against a parallelogram in the center. Of this I can make a *very good thing of the sort.* As old Mr. Izzard, who hates the New Englanders, said of Mr. Coit from Connecticut . . . [when asked if he were not a good sort of man] . . . "N, N, Neneno!" said Mr. Izzard, who stuttered violently, "He, he, he's a googood man of a G, G, God damn'd bad sort." This I say of my plan and no more.

The plans were all in Jefferson's hands by the first of May, the President approved, and the work went ahead; but Thornton was by now the architect's implacable enemy, and in October the Washington *Federalist* published the first of its many attacks on Latrobe.

Congress meanwhile, becoming restive over what it considered the slowness of the work and its cost, threatened to stop further appropriations. Latrobe wrote Lenthall of his discouragement at the delay: "As for our business, I give it up for lost at once. We must now continue to make what money remains cover the President's house, and when that is finished, knock off altogether . . ." But only the day before, March 27, Congress at last, despite hot and acrimonious debate, had actually made the appropriation for another year—again $50,000—and now the work could go on. In his report to Jefferson at the end of the year (December 6, 1804) Latrobe recounted the year's accomplishments and a little later (December 30) estimated that it would require $134,300 to complete the south wing.

---

11. From a memorandum dated February 27, 1804, in the Latrobe papers in the possession of the family. Two months later (April 28) he wrote Hadfield: ". . . I am now at open war with Dr. Thornton. He has written me a letter in which he asserts that my report to the Commissioners on the Public Buildings to be *false,* in terms which according to fashion ought to produce a rencontre with a brace of pistols . . . In the meantime, if you could go over your drawing, and as nearly as possible ascertain what is his, and what stolen property in the plan now *said* to be the original plan I should be infinitely obliged to you."

On January 25, 1805, Congress appropriated $110,000—a special victory for the architect, for Thornton on New Year's Day had had a printed letter issued to all the members of Congress virulently attacking Latrobe, refuting in a somewhat casuistic way Latrobe's statement to the committee that none of Thornton's drawings could be found, and violently supporting his own plan for the south wing. This had all been fodder for Federalist criticism in general, but it had failed to affect the action of Congress.

The same winter, however, brought Latrobe a disappointment. Justice Chase of the Supreme Court was to be impeached, and because of the importance of the case—the first impeachment of a high-placed government official—Vice-President Burr wished the surroundings of the trial to be as dignified as possible and asked Latrobe for a plan. Having left Washington on December 13 after a short stay, the architect immediately set to work to design the fitments and rearrangements of the Senate chamber the trial would require. He sent off his drawings to Burr on the seventeenth—surely not an excessive time for the job. But mail was slow and Burr impatient; before receiving the Latrobe drawings he awarded the commission to Samuel Blodgett (the Massachusetts architect of the First Bank of the United States in Philadelphia), and all Latrobe's work went for nothing. Blodgett's design, Latrobe felt, was both more expensive and less convenient than his own.[12]

Meanwhile he had taken time to search for proper stoves for the Capitol and for Monticello, to look for possible American sources for window glass, and to study new ways of making the roof of the President's House tight—since it, like the roof of the north wing of the Capitol, had become a veritable sieve. Latrobe wrote the President (January 26, 1805): "I am almost in despair about parapet roofs in this country . . ." And on the same day he wrote Lenthall that one of the difficulties was the fact that the roof drained directly into the water-closet cistern in the attic: "Those who can afford to perform the *stircatory* functions by machinery, can always afford a forcing pump & the labor of a man to work it. I mean to propose to the President *once more* the drainage of the roof by external pipes, & the filling of the . . . cistern by a forcing pump." [13]

Again in Washington during the first week of March, 1805, the archi-

12. See the letter to Lenthall on page 275.

13. This is interesting evidence that a water closet existed in the White House apparently from the beginning. Two years later the installation was still giving trouble, as we

tect found a much more congenial task confronting him. The south wing had now progressed to the point where it was time to plan for the decorative carving. Still more important, Latrobe with Jefferson's backing had proposed for the House of Representatives the decorative sculpture that he deemed essential, and where could good sculptors be found in America? Rush, the country's best sculptor, was a woodcarver only. Who in the United States could be trusted to carve even the rich Corinthian capitals—based on those of the Choragic Monument of Lysicrates in Athens—which Jefferson was insisting on? Latrobe had already written the President (November 17, 1804) that he could not understand "how economy and anything like an exact imitation can be united—for it's a most complicated piece of sculpture." But Jefferson had been stubborn; he felt that only the richest effect would do. The sculptors, then, must be imported—naturally, from Italy. The architect therefore wrote (March 6, 1805) to his acquaintance (and Jefferson's) Philip Mazzei [14] in Italy, asking him to find and send over two sculptors as well as to inquire what Canova would charge for a large figure of Liberty. Mazzei's answer, long delayed, brought such a fantastic estimate for the proposed Canova statue that the idea of employing this famous artist was abandoned; but the following year Mazzei did find and send over two young sculptors, Giuseppe Franzoni (1786-1816) and Giovanni Andrei (1770-1824), who brought a new standard of skill and taste to America.

The two Italians arrived in the United States toward the end of February, 1806.[15] One wishes that they had left us some account of their adventures. What could they, fresh from Leghorn and Carrara, make of the young country? In a letter to Lenthall from Philadelphia (March 3, 1806) Latrobe mentions that he is going to write them in Italian to cheer them up; perhaps they had been appalled at the raw newness of Washington, the swamps, the muddy roads. He also informs his clerk of the works that Franzoni (according to Mazzei) "is a most excellent sculptor, & capable of cutting our figure of Liberty, & that Andrei excells more in decoration." [16]

---

know from a letter to the President on August 7, 1807, in which Latrobe suggested a revision of the cistern arrangement.

14. Philip Mazzei was an Italian scientist and scientific farmer who at one time had visited Jefferson in Monticello and become a close friend and frequent correspondent.

15. See Charles E. Fairman, *op. cit.*

16. The two sculptors were paid $85 a month each and were furnished with living quarters for themselves and their families, as well as their traveling expenses to Washing-

Franzoni came of an excellent family—an uncle of his was a Cardinal—and he proved to be a sculptor of more than ordinary ability and a swift and enthusiastic workman. He was acutely aware of his professional standing and took an early opportunity of calling on President Jefferson and leaving at the door, when he found the President out, a group of little marbles he had carved, intending them as presents. What must have been his astonishment at their strange American reception when they were returned with a gracious note from Jefferson explaining that it was his irrevocable policy never to receive gifts of this kind while he held an official government office. But a friendship sprang up between them, and Jefferson later gave the Franzoni family a silver sugar bowl. Latrobe soon realized the sculptor's skill and the dignity of his character; it may even have been Franzoni's own presence in Washington that suggested a richer sculptural decoration of the House of Representatives than had been contemplated. There was to be a great eagle, fourteen feet from wing tip to wing tip, in the frieze over the Speaker's desk; near the entrance there were to be four over-life-size relief figures representing Agriculture, Art, Science, and Commerce; and behind the Speaker's chair was to rise a colossal figure of Liberty nine feet high—plenty of work to keep a sculptor busy for two years and more.

Andrei, on the other hand, was chiefly a modeler and carver of architectural decorations. He was "not only a good sculptor, but a man of rare personal virtue, united to first-rate talents, and firmness of character," as Latrobe wrote to Senator Nathaniel Macon later (January 9, 1816); he was observant and adaptable too, for in the same letter the architect added, "He has also a perfect knowledge of the temper of our country." But Andrei was slow—a careful, plodding workman who refused to be hurried. Three years after he arrived on the job Latrobe wrote to Thomas Munroe, the commissioner (September 14, 1809): "[Andrei] is the slowest hand ever I saw, especially in modelling, and in fact our clay models of his work have cost more than the same thing in marble . . ."

The architect kept a sympathetic but critical eye on all this decorative work. Franzoni's first task was the great eagle, and as the model pro-

---

ton; in addition the government contracted to pay for their return to Italy when their work was completed. The house taken for them was near the Capitol; it provided each family with two rooms, besides a common kitchen and a servant's room. Franzoni objected to the crowding and later bought a house for himself at 121 Pennsylvania Avenue, S.E.

gressed Latrobe found the result too conventional, too Roman; he wanted an eagle that would be definitely American. Latrobe accordingly called on Charles Willson Peale for aid, writing him (April 18, 1806): "May I therefore beg the favor of you, to request one of your very obliging and skilful sons to send me a drawing of the head and claws of the bald eagle, of his general proportions . . ." Peale at once sent on not only the drawing but also an actual head and claw from the stores of his museum, and the eagle when completed won universal acclaim. About the Liberty Latrobe also had his reservations and when he received Franzoni's sketch[17] wrote, somewhat facetiously, to Lenthall (December 31, 1806): "It may be correct symbology or emblematology to give Dame Liberty a club or shelelah, but we have no business to exhibit it so very publicly . . . I must have one arm close to her side, resting on her lap. The other may be raised, & rest on a wig block, or capped stick . . ." He also reduced the height from nine to seven feet. This figure was never carved in marble, but a finished plaster cast was erected in place of it in the completed room. The architect was delighted with the four allegorical figures near the entrance. Plaster casts of them all were sent to C. W. Peale in Philadelphia for exhibition at the Academy of Arts, for Latrobe wished Franzoni's talent to be widely known and appreciated.[18]

Thus the completed House of Representatives had a rich panoply of expressive sculpture: Liberty, above and behind the Speaker, a constant reminder presiding over the meetings of the House; crowning all, the daringly colossal eagle, the incarnation of the country; and at the entrance, as though handmaidens to Liberty and to the nation, Art, Science, Agriculture, and Commerce. It was a noble iconography which the architect had conceived and with the President's support had so boldly carried out. Any such use of sculpture was undreamed of before in the country, and it is a tragedy that we know it only from descriptions and from Latrobe's few indications on his drawings, for all of it was destroyed when the British burned the Capitol in 1814. And, as if to under-

---

17. The carefully rendered pencil sketch preserved among the Capitol drawings in the Library of Congress probably represents the Athena designed for the Supreme Court. Contrary to the common attribution, this drawing does not seem to be in Latrobe's manner and is more probably by Franzoni.

18. When work on the Capitol slowed up in 1808, the two sculptors were "loaned" to Godefroy, in Baltimore, to help him with the statues and decorative detail required for St. Mary's Chapel.

line its loss, Giuseppe Franzoni died two years later in Washington, when the rebuilding of the Capitol had scarcely begun.

The work of the plodding Andrei was more fortunate. Probably from his models and his chisel came not only many of the decorative details of the Capitol as rebuilt after the fire but also the beautiful corn capitals (in the Senate stair vestibule) which he modeled and carved from Latrobe's detail.[19] The architect was immensely proud of these and on August 28, 1809, had a model shipped to Monticello as a gift; Jefferson, equally pleased, used it to support a sundial in his garden. With pardonable pride Latrobe says in his letter to Jefferson: "This capital, during the summer session obtained me more applause from the members of Congress than all the works of magnitude . . . They called it the Corn Cob Capital, whether for the sake of the alliteration I cannot tell, but certainly not very appropriately" (for the capital uses the full ears, not the cob).[20]

Other newly originated capitals, based on the tobacco plant, crown the columns of the oval lobby on the upper floor; these date from the rebuilding after the fire and were modeled and carved by another Italian, Francisco Iardella. One of these also was sent to Jefferson (October 28, 1817); the architect in his letter at the time admitted that it was not so effective as the corn capital had been and suggested that the leaves be stained pale umber to bring out the flowers just as was to be done in the lobby.

Latrobe designed (1809) one more capital based on the country's native flora—a cotton capital. It was intended for an upper range of miniature columns forming a sort of cupola over the Senate lobby. These columns were cylindrical and without entasis; with their broadly spreading naturalistic capitals they had an effect almost Romanesque. From the existing evidence it is impossible to say whether or not they were actually used, for all that part of the north wing was rebuilt after the fire. What

---

19. Mrs. Trollope was much impressed by the novelty of the corn capitals. In *Domestic Manners of the Americans,* describing her visit to the recently completed Capitol, for which she expressed an astonished and enthusiastic admiration, she writes: "In a hall leading to some of these rooms the ceiling is supported by pillars, the capitals of which struck me as peculiarly beautiful. They are composed of the ears and leaves of Indian corn, beautifully arranged and forming as graceful an outline as the acanthus itself. . . . A sense of fitness always enhances the effect of beauty . . ."

20. The Senate stair vestibule was completed in the spring of 1809 and was so little damaged by the fire of 1814 that much of its present detail goes back to that early period.

is significant is the fact that in the Capitol the architect sought for novel decorative forms expressive of the country itself.

Still another artist participated in the Capitol decoration—George Bridport, the decorative painter. We have already come across his work in connection with Latrobe's Philadelphia houses; he was evidently a thoroughly competent craftsman, with imagination and an excellent decorative sense. Obviously in the House of Representatives the wide, curved ceiling could not be left in naked plaster, and, pierced as it was with wedge-shaped rows of dazzling skylights (considered in greater detail below), it required more than a mere protective coating to give it coherence and scale. At first Latrobe thought of employing for the work the Philadelphia scene painter Holland, for whom he had a great admiration, but Holland's price was exorbitant. The architect's next choice —and probably, as things turned out, the best he could have made—was Bridport, who accepted the contract for $3,500. One can surmize from various indications that the scheme was probably a matter of simple lines and panels of color with discreet classical ornaments. As to its final effect, however, there is no question. To those who saw the work it seemed a perfect treatment, completely in harmony with the architecture and with the sculpture beneath it. It was the final touch which, together with the handsome hangings at the windows and around the Speaker's chair and the red curtains between the columns, made the whole room as distinguished in hue as it was in form.

This rich panoply of color and of sculptured decoration, carried out in a city that was still a raw village, and in a country where any such conception had previously been unknown, would have been impossible without the hearty support of the President. Rightly Latrobe wrote him (August 13, 1807): "It is not flattering to say that you have planted the arts in your country. The works already created are the monuments of your judgment and your zeal and of your taste. The first sculpture that adorns an American public building perpetuates your love and your protection of the fine arts." Latrobe and Jefferson were both familiar with many of the greatest buildings in Europe, and for both of them the ideal of what the United States Capitol should be was far higher than any that could readily be accepted by the majority of Congressmen; this was one of the difficulties under which they labored. To men like the peppery John Randolph of Roanoke the Capitol was merely a matter of shelter and of dollars; to the architect and the President, on the other hand, it was an opportunity for achieving a building that should not merely equal but even surpass the great government buildings of Europe, one that should stand out as a superb visible expression of the ideals of a country dedicated to liberty. It is a mark of their greatness that they succeeded, for the House of Representatives when it was completed in 1811 was undoubtedly the most beautiful legislative chamber in the Western world.

In a work of this magnitude it is not strange that labor troubles should have arisen. During the summer of 1805 the masons and the bricklayers presented a petition requesting "that the hours of work may begin only at six o'clock in the morning and end at six in the evening"—a system that had been in use earlier in the building of the north wing. Latrobe instead had followed the usage current elsewhere of working the masons till dark; they had an hour and a half off for dinner in the middle of the day. "At the Navy Yard," the architect wrote in his answer to the petition, "the same hours are observed which are kept at the Capitol, & though two hours are allowed at dinner time, no rest is permitted in the course of the morning or afternoon as with us . . . Allowing, however, the justice of your statement as to the inconvenience & heat of the place . . . two hours will be granted at dinner time, from this day (June 18) to Sept. 1 next, and one hour and a half from the 1st of Sept. to the 21st, after which the old regulation will again prevail. The usual times of refreshment in the morning & afternoon will also be continued." Apparently this compromise satisfied them and there was no more trouble then.

By the fall of 1805 the details of the great domed roof were being considered, and now the most serious of all Latrobe's controversies with Jefferson began.[21] The President, having been overwhelmed in Paris by the effect of the Halle aux Blés, wanted the new House of Representatives lighted in the same way—by wedge-shaped skylights radiating out and down from the center. The architect saw endless objections to this scheme. The light from such skylights would be dazzling in Washington summers, condensation impossible to avoid, and waterproofing difficult. He made a graphic sketch to show how the light would fall; Jefferson answered that Venetian blinds could be used to control the light,

21. See Paul Norton, "Latrobe's Ceiling for the Hall of Representatives," in *Journal of the Society of Architectural Historians,* vol. x, no. 2, pp. 5-10.

and Latrobe obediently worked out a mechanism for operating them. The President minimized the practical difficulties and implied that to solve them was part of the architect's task. Latrobe stubbornly continued objecting to the scheme; he wanted to use a lantern with vertical glass that would diffuse the light and would be easy to make waterproof. In London he had known at least one of Soane's great halls in the Bank of England and been delighted with the dramatic effect of light pouring in from sources almost concealed; and he himself had used such a scheme in the Bank of Pennsylvania.

All during the summer letters on the subject went back and forth between Latrobe in Washington and Jefferson at Monticello; neither would yield, until at last in September Jefferson threw the onus for the decision entirely upon the architect. Latrobe hastened to answer (September 13, 1805): "I cannot possibly decide the point of the Halle aux Blés lights of myself . . ." and on the same day he wrote to Lenthall that the President's decision placed him "in a most unpleasant situation," and continued: "I shall therefore let [the skylights] lie over till it is absolutely necessary to decide, & then my conscience & my common sense I fear will reject them in spite of my desire to do as he wishes . . ."

In the summer of 1806 as the roof approached completion the matter cropped up again, and Latrobe had Lenthall frame the great roof in such a way that either the panel lights Jefferson wished or his own lantern could be used; he even had the lantern framed up, perhaps hoping that the sight of it would convince Jefferson. Instead, it had the reverse effect. Jefferson, arriving in Washington in October—an illness had kept him at Monticello—saw the lantern and was enraged; apparently he expressed himself in no uncertain terms to Munroe. Latrobe wrote him an apology (October 29, 1806)—"I have heard with the deepest mortification that I have had the misfortune to displease you"—and explained that since for the want of glass the lights could not be opened that year he had taken the liberty of building the roof so that either scheme could be adopted. Yet he stuck to his guns: "I am convinced by the evidence of my senses in innumerable cases, by all my professional experience for near 20 years, and by all my reasonings, that the panel lights must inevitably be destroyed after being made . . ." It was impossible to put the thing more strongly.

Some two and a half weeks later, perhaps wishing to emphasize the impersonal character of this difference of opinion, he sent Jefferson a colored perspective of the Capitol with a letter: "In presenting to you the drawing of the Capitol, which I herewith leave at the President's House, I have no object but to gratify my desire, as an individual citizen, to give you a testimony of the truest respect and attachment . . ." Even as late as the spring of 1807, when the roof was already almost complete, Latrobe still hoped he could persuade the President to give up his panel lights. One of Jefferson's objections to the proposed lantern was that he could find no ancient classic precedent for such a form. Latrobe answered (May 21): "What shall I do when the condensed vapor showers down upon the heads of the members from 100 skylights . . . ?" And then he adds the famous statement of his artistic credo:

> My principles of good taste are rigid in Grecian architecture. I am a bigoted Greek in the condemnation of the Roman architecture of Baalbec, Palmyra, and Spalatro. . . . Wherever, therefore the Grecian style can be copied without impropriety I love to be a mere, I would say a slavish copyist, but the forms & the distribution of the Roman & Greek buildings which remain, are in general, inapplicable to the objects & uses of our public buildings. Our religion requires a church wholly different from the temples, our legislative assemblies and our courts of justice, buildings of entirely different principles from their basilicas; and our amusements could not possibly be performed in their theatres & amphitheatres . . .

Nevertheless the President finally prevailed, but on a compromise basis; instead of the long wedge-shaped skylights he had originally suggested, a series of relatively small square lights between the great structural ribs was adopted in the final building. But Latrobe's prophecies proved only too true. The lights caused endless trouble, because of leaks, until the adoption by the architect of a new detail using single sheets of glass that projected beyond the sides of the openings. Condensation did drip on the bald heads of the Congressmen below, a condition later mitigated when some of the lowest lights were arranged to open to allow ventilation of the upper air of the room. And eyes were so dazzled by the glare that all the western lights had to be permanently covered. The huge ribs of the domed roof, it is interesting to note, were built of New England white pine, for yellow pine from Virginia and the Eastern Shore (called by Latrobe the best of American woods) could not conveniently be obtained in sufficiently large pieces.

The campaign to bring the Capitol to completion was carried on in spite of a long series of vexations that had little to do with the actual construction. For instance, there was the problem of keeping Lenthall happy and co-operative. As early as the summer of 1804, for example, an antagonism for Thomas Munroe had begun to grow in Lenthall's mind. Why should this person, who he felt was an outsider so far as Latrobe and himself were concerned, have so much to do with the conduct of the work? Why should Latrobe consult him? Lenthall's jealousy of Munroe even became apparent to others, and Latrobe was forced to write him a letter (August 22) putting him clear on the subject, for nothing more fatal to the carrying on of the work could be imagined than an open break between the architect's clerk of the works and the commissioner who served as the direct agent of Congress—the man through whom all payments came. And in the letter Latrobe assured Lenthall of his continued regard and affection.[22]

Later that same year, in September, it was George Blagden, the master mason, who came under Lenthall's disapproval. The fact that Blagden was doing the stonework for the Navy Yard gate concurrently seemed to Lenthall's exaggerated devotion to the Capitol a dereliction of duty. Again Latrobe had to intervene to straighten matters out; but Blagden was still suspect in the eyes of the clerk of the works, and, when a difference of opinion arose between Lenthall and Blagden about whether to use iron or lead cramps in the stonework, Latrobe's upholding of Blagden almost broke the ties of friendship between Lenthall and the architect and all of Latrobe's tact was necessary to repair the damage.

As the job progressed, Lenthall grew abnormally sensitive and increasingly rude to those he disliked. At last Latrobe wrote his employee (September 5, 1807) reproving him for his uncivil actions and his constant complaints and asking him if he wished to resign; at the same time he was compelled to write the President, apologizing for Lenthall's be-

22. The playful confidence between the two men is well shown in another letter Latrobe wrote Lenthall when he learned that Blodgett had been chosen to design the arrangements in the Senate for the impeachment of Chase (January 7, 1805): "You and I are both blockheads. Presidents and Vice Presidents are the only architects and poets for ought I know, in the United States. Therefore let us fall down and worship them! As for the Ladies behind the piers [at the trial] and the respondents at the long table, they shall ogle the Vice President, the Vice President may ogle them, as much as they please"—and he goes on to conjure up a picture of "Little Hamilton and Little Burr, standing in the temple of Lingam (the Hindo Priapus) like the columns of Jakin and Boas in the Temple of Solomon . . . for their sins."

havior but acknowledging the "spirit of mutiny" it had caused among the Capitol laborers. Then, thinking better of his curt letter to Lenthall, he later on the same day wrote him another long letter of explanation and appeal:

> When you were first appointed it was against the wishes of the President, who was prejudiced against you by false reports. . . . I adhered to my nomination with the same pertinacity that I have exhibited in respect to the skylights, & he acquiesced. [Latrobe goes on to remind Lenthall that he had procured him and his family a healthy dwelling near the Capitol at public cost though Lenthall had insisted on moving to an unhealthy place where they had all been sick; to this illness Latrobe attributes all Lenthall's ill humor. He continues by recalling how he had tried to find him an assistant,] but if such an assistant had been found, he would have been useless to you had anybody but you chosen & appointed him. I have tried De Mun & Mills . . . Strickland, Courtenay, & Carpenter [and none of them could work with the clerk of the works;] whether you remain or not depends not on me. If you remain till I desire you to go, you will go only to sleep with your fathers. I can easily put up with all your humors.

Lenthall was moved, and he answered, "I mean not to employ you to dress my wounds any more—you make them worse . . ." Yet the trouble continued. To improve the morale on the job, Latrobe on October 7, 1807, gave a dinner to all the Capitol workmen. It was a festive occasion to celebrate the near completion of the House of Representatives, and apparently it served its purpose. Only one thing marred the harmony that reigned—Lenthall's absence, for he obstinately refused to come, and Latrobe wrote him a sharp rebuke the next day.[23] For a while thereafter Latrobe's letters to Lenthall were strictly on a business basis; then, little by little, the old friendship triumphed, Lenthall forgot his trials, and the playful, intimate co-operation was renewed.

All the more tragic, then, was the death of Lenthall, crushed as the vault of the Supreme Court fell when the centerings were taken down on September 21, 1808. The original conception had contemplated a ribbed semi-dome; the ribs were to have had conical vaults built over

---

23. Latrobe in vain tried to have himself repaid for the expenses involved in this dinner. He wrote Jefferson about it in 1811; Jefferson answered that he had no memory of it and could not help. Latrobe gave another dinner to the Capitol workmen in 1809, when the centering of the rebuilt Supreme Court vault was struck. In this case, too, the expense had to come out of his own pocket.

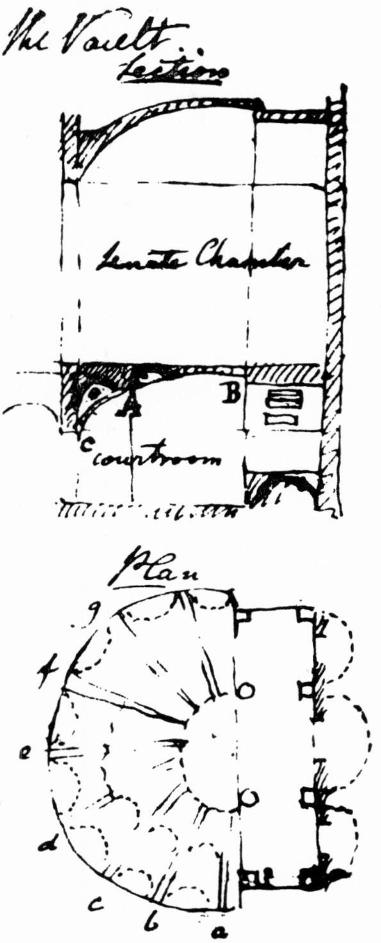

and between them to support the Senate chamber floor above. While Latrobe was away from Washington, Lenthall suggested another scheme which would save a great deal in centering and labor: instead of the conical vaults radiating from the center, annular barrel vaults would be run over the lower semi-dome circumferentially. Latrobe accepted the advice but with some reservations. As he wrote Jefferson two days after the tragedy, he had placed too great a dependence on Lenthall's skill and experience. The Lenthall system had brought heavy concentrated loads on the dome at places ill-adjusted to receive them, and when the supports were removed the whole collapsed. All in the room escaped except Lenthall.

There was intense local excitement over the disaster. The Capitol workmen, out of respect and affection for both Latrobe and the clerk of the works, voted to donate a week's labor toward repairing the damage. There was even talk of sabotage—for the continued Federalist attacks on the entire project enraged many besides Latrobe—and the mayor of Washington offered a reward for the apprehension of any who were found guilty. But Latrobe in a letter to the *National Intelligencer* (September 23, 1808) assumed the responsibility, for he was not one to lay public guilt on the shoulders of the dead. And, as a final tribute to his late friend, he

From the Jefferson Papers, in Library of Congress

FIGURE 18. Sketch Explaining the Fall of the Supreme Court Vault in the Capitol. From Latrobe's letter to Jefferson, September 23, 1808.

Instead of the radiating lobes originally planned, Lenthall substituted annular vaults. These brought concentrated loads (as at A) on the ribs (a, b, c . . . g), which were insufficient to carry them.

sent the *Intelligencer* a long letter that contains the only trustworthy biography of Lenthall we possess; in the course of it he says:

The full utility of so many and such extraordinary qualifications of mind and body, seldom united in the same man, was somewhat abated by a reserved exterior and a rigid adherence to his own principles and opinions which nothing could bend . . . In the execution of the public duty, and especially in the control of expenditure he was so inflexibly just, as to be often thought harsh; but when acting in his individual character, the benevolence of his heart could not be mistaken, and he was by all those who had known him long as much loved as respected. . . . Since the year 1803 he had been clerk or immediate superintendent of the public works, and had in that situation acquired a reputation for talents and virtues, unanimously conceded to few. His loss to the public will not be easy to repair.[24]

It speaks well for the true esteem in which Latrobe was held by Congress and the Administration that, despite the fall of the vault, the Federalist attacks, the Thornton letter, the Thornton libel suit (of which more later), and the continual charges of extravagance, appropriations for the Capitol continued to be made and for another three years the architect continued in his position.

It has always been a piece of popular American mythology that architects are high-priced luxuries. And, as Congress and the rest of the little Washington world scanned the high and to them expensive standards both of appearance and of construction in the Capitol that was rising before them, accusations burst forth. Every year the annual appropriation bills were passed only after violent debate; frequently they were severely cut before final passage. What finally brought the antagonists of Latrobe

24. Lenthall was born in Chelmsford, Derbyshire, in 1762. In England he had had wide experience in all phases of mining, as well as of cotton manufacturing, and had picked up an extensive knowledge in many other phases of engineering and building; he was also an accomplished draftsman. He was married to Jane King, the daughter of Robert King, City Surveyor, "about 1800 or 1801." Lenthall built two houses, apparently on speculation, at 612 and 614 Nineteenth Street, N.W., which stood until comparatively recent times. See Maud Burr Morris, "The Lenthall Houses and Their Owners," in *Columbia Historical Society Records,* vols. 31-2 (1930), pp. 1-35.

Lenthall's position was not filled immediately; since Latrobe was then at the Capitol almost daily, there was less need for a permanent clerk of the works. Slightly later, however, Latrobe obtained the President's permission to take on his own son Henry, fresh from college in Baltimore, as his assistant, and Henry served in this position until his departure on his first visit to New Orleans.

to the very brink of victory was another most unfortunate happening—the overspending of the 1807 appropriation by more than $50,000.

The reasons behind this seeming extravagance were many. In the first place, since all the building accounts were kept by Thomas Munroe, the architect had to plan his work on the basis of whatever summaries of the actual state of affairs he could get from the commissioner's office, and apparently Munroe had given no hint that a deficit was about to occur. A second and to Latrobe even more important factor was the President's continued insistence on getting the House of Representatives finished and the President's House and grounds into more acceptable shape. Toward this end Jefferson asked Latrobe to take on more hands and exert the greatest possible pressure to see that Congress at its next session would be able to use the new hall, and at the same time he kept writing anxiously to ascertain how the work at the President's House was progressing; under this double pressure money was spent hurriedly. And a third reason was that always in carrying on a complex building operation, particularly where many structural elements are concerned, it is literally impossible to draw a sharp line in the work and the expenditures at any given moment and say "Stop." Both safety and efficiency demand a certain planned continuity.

In any case, when the year's accounts were finally made up they showed an expenditure for the year of approximately $118,500 instead of the $67,000 that had been appropriated. A little over $3,000 of this was not chargeable to the Capitol but was spent on the State, War, and Navy buildings and would be repaid by those departments; but even with that deduction the deficit was enormous. Fortunately, the House was at last meeting in its new home; fortunately, too, the vast amount of work that had been accomplished on the north wing was obvious. Otherwise the results might have been much more serious than the floods of oratory and newspaper criticism that did pour forth.

Jefferson himself was deeply shocked—all the more, perhaps, because of a realization that his own overeagerness had helped produce the discrepancy. He wrote Latrobe at this time the most severe letters that ever passed between them—one on April 25:

You see, my Dear Sir, that the object of this cautious proceeding is to prevent the possibility of a deficit of a single dollar this year. The lesson of last year has been a serious one, it has done you great injury, & has been much felt by myself—it was so contrary to the principles of our Government, which made the representatives of the people the sole arbiters of public expense, and do not permit any work to be forced on them on a larger scale than their judgment deems adapted to the circumstances of the Nation. . . .

and six weeks afterward, on June 2:

When I was obliged to state it [the deficit] to Congress, I never was more embarrassed than to select expressions, which, while they should not charge it on myself, should commit you as little as possible. As short as that message was, it was the subject of repeated consultations [with department heads] to help us find expressions which should neither hurt your feelings or do you any injury.

Later in the year, whenever Jefferson wrote Latrobe about the Capitol or the work on the President's House, he added a cautionary note, a warning—"if there is money enough."

Among the ringleaders in the Congressional attacks on Latrobe's supposed extravagance was John Randolph, that strangely warped genius who was one of the foremost orators of his time. To him, therefore, in order to vindicate himself in the eyes of so eloquent a man in such a strategic position, Latrobe wrote a spirited defense (April 23, 1808). In it he begins by apologizing for taking notice of what had been said in Congressional debate, "but you have been too long known to me, and to the public, to permit me to doubt your receiving this proof of my confidence in your candor otherwise than it is meant." Then, acknowledging gratefully Randolph's recognition of his competence as an artist, he states that the point of importance now is his competence as a businessman; it is this that he wishes to vindicate. He goes on:

Nothing has so much injured my utility to the public & to my family, as the very prevailing opinion that men who unfortunately for themselves are called men of genius are incapable of the management of money. . . . It is a mark upon me,—the effect of which I feel daily, and which keeps me from acquiring that independence which a dull usurer, or a dealer in dry goods easily and *honorably* attains . . .

Now it happens also very unluckily that the professions of architecture and painting are supposed to be of the same grade, & to require the same sort of head & habits;—and that as Stuart, the greatest painter we have ever seen, was a profligate, the only architect we know, may possibly be just such another.—But I am sure the professions, & I hope the men, are widely different. . . . When the castle in the air [the architect's original conception] has been made to descend into the office, and such instructions in writing and drawing are to be manufactured as to guide the hard hand & the iron tool of the mechanics, imagination is busy only to disturb.—To execute such a building as the Capitol without relaying a brick or altering the shape of a single piece of stone, a competent knowledge of 18 mechanical arts is necessary . . . and above all a correct mastery of accounts. . . .

If I could lay before you the accounts of all the buildings in which I have been engaged, I am very certain that you would never again pay a compliment to my imagination at the expense of my common understanding . . . wherever I have committed myself upon an estimate I have never exceeded it, unless gross alterations of the design have been made to induce greater expense. For instance:

	Estimate	Expense
Portico of the Bank of Pennsylvania	58,500	57,650
Great tunnel of the waterworks	23,500	23,350
Philadelphia Bank	30,000 (not finished but contracted for)	28,500
Plaisterers' work, South Wg of the Capitol, Washington	12,500	12,240

and many others which I could quote. . . .

He goes on to explain the details of the way in which the south wing of the Capitol was erected and the careful measurements he made before authorizing payments; he says the measurements of the "plaisterers' work alone occupy 128 columns in my measuring book." Continuing, he writes:

But the truth is that previous estimates have never but once, in 1804, been required of me, & the responsibility of an estimate for such a work as the Capitol will never be courted by me for a salary of 1700 $ p. annum, which for several years did not pay the expenditures of my office, but left me the honor of presenting my labors to the public.—In the course of the debate, I am informed, I was by some gentleman supposed to be a contractor to build the Capitol for a certain sum, & that if it exceeded that sum, I ought to lose it. I wish I had been such a contractor at the cost of the north wing. I should have put 60,000 dollars into my pocket instead of being poorer than when I undertook the work.

I might pass this over with the very proud but little satisfactory consolement of *Virtute mea me involvero*. But this will do for myself, not for my wife & children. That which robs me of reputation, robs them of bread.—

The freedom with which I have written this is the best evidence of my respect for you. I will therefore say no more but to assure you of its sincerity.

The Capitol appropriation was finally passed, carrying $36,500 for 1808, plus the deficit of $51,500, and Randolph voted aye.

But the greatest vexation of all was Dr. Thornton's undying enmity.[25] In 1804, as we have seen, Thornton had distributed to the members of Congress a printed letter defending his own design and accusing his successor of making false statements in his report to Congress. Latrobe took no active steps to refute it at the time; but in the spring of 1806, as Thornton's attacks and those which he had inspired in the Federalist papers continued, Latrobe also, feeling himself compelled to follow Thornton's technique, had a long justificatory letter printed and distributed to the members of Congress. In it he told the story of his own association with the Capitol and of the difficulties involved in the work, and he included a long and devastating criticism of Thornton's original plan in order to bring out the reasons why he was forced to depart from the scheme Washington had approved. He also contrasted the vaulted, solid construction he himself was attempting to use with the old wooden framing (already rotting) and the bad stone- and brickwork he had found in the structure when he was appointed.

Latrobe's letter was a complete answer to all the attacks Thornton had made on him, but its forthright manner was perhaps not the most effective way of mollifying an enemy—its very forcefulness could only rankle. Thornton, seeing that his whole crusade against his successor's Capitol designs had failed, determined on a new approach—an assault on the architect as a man; perhaps if Latrobe could be made odious enough on general grounds his resignation could be forced. He launched

25. When Latrobe came to Washington in April, 1806, at his first visit to the Capitol a brick fell from the scaffolding, hit him on the head, and stunned him. He was senseless for a while, and for nearly a week afterward, as he wrote President Jefferson (April 21), he was so troubled with giddiness that he could not see to write. Eventually, of course, he recovered completely. Such accidents—bricks falling from scaffolds—are always suspect. No suggestion is intended that Thornton was directly involved, of course; but the uncertainties which resulted from his campaign against Latrobe may have helped to produce in some unbalanced workman an unreasoning dislike of Latrobe. I have no wish to overdramatize this incident, and the fall of the brick may well have been pure accident; but the other possibility does exist.

his offensive in a signed letter to the editor of the Washington *Federalist,* dated April 20 and published on April 26, 1808. The letter, a column and a half long, not only assails Latrobe's architectural competence but also accuses him of habitual falsehood.

Thornton begins by justifying the choice of a doctor (himself) as architect of the Capitol by citing the case of Claude Perrault (also a doctor), who was chosen over Bernini as architect of the Louvre. Then he states that Latrobe might present a similar justification on his own behalf, for Latrobe (like Perrault) was not trained as an architect; he had come to the United States as a Moravian missionary, and in London he had been only a carver of chimney pieces. He mentions Latrobe's alleged antipathy to General Washington (thus subtly bringing in the Federalist-democratic rivalry) and hints at a reason for it by saying, "for that great man was asked by a very respectable man now living why he did not employ Mr. Latrobe. 'Because I can place no confidence in him whatever,' was the answer." Proceeding to a detailed criticism of the changes his successor had made in his own plan for the House of Representatives, he inserts the claim that Latrobe was so prone to alterations that he even changed his name from Latrobe Boneval to simply Latrobe; he implies, too, that Latrobe was not, as he professed, a native of England. He attacks the acoustics of the House of Representatives, claiming his own ellipse would have been better than Latrobe's plan; and he ridicules the sculpture, saying that the great eagle is more like a goose and that most people take the figure of Liberty to be meant for Leda and the Swan. Then he cites the lantern that Latrobe had wished to use for lighting the House chamber and remarks, "I wonder how the idea of that lantern ever entered the head of this architect; for if Diogenes had now lived he would never have blown out his candle on meeting Mr. Latrobe." As for the architect's extravagance, Thornton cites an occurrence in Philadelphia: "So much are his calculations depended on that in Philadelphia it was published in the newspapers that proposals would be received for one of the public buildings from any persons except Latrobe." [26] Closing with a blistering attack on the architect's taste, he ridicules the Navy Yard gate and also the entrance arch which Latrobe—forced to work with a pittance—has made in the wall around the President's House:

---

26. So far as I know, the source of Thornton's statement—if any—has never been identified. He gives no supporting evidence in the answer he later filed in Latrobe's suit for libel.

. . . for such an arch as the interior one [in the Navy Yard gate, the rear arch of which was a large semicircle] was never made to a Gateway before, and till the extinction of taste will never be made again. The eagle, which crowns it, is so disproportionate to the Anchor, that we are reminded of the Rook in the Arabian Nights Entertainments; but on reviewing it the Eagle looks only like a good fat Goose, and the Anchor fitter for a cock-boat than even a gunboat.—If the American hope rested on such an anchor she would soon breathe her exit in a sigh of despair! The next object of taste is the wall around the president's square!—Every ten steps we are reminded of point-no-point! To emphasize the whole he has put up a Gateway, that instead of being adapted to the termination of a grand Avenue, and leading to the Gardens of a palace, is scarcely fit for the entrance of a Stable Yard. Though in humble imitation of a triumphal Arch, it looks so naked, and disproportioned, that it is more like a monument than a Gateway: but no man now or hereafter will ever mistake it for a *monument of taste.*

This letter was so outrageous—and many of its claims were so malicious and untrue—that Latrobe felt he had but one course to take, and he entered suit against Thornton for libel. On April 30 he wrote Walter Jones at Alexandria, asking him to serve as his attorney and asserting that "the two paragraphs in Dr. Thornton's letter . . . aim so directly, the first at the destruction of my respectability in society, the second at the means of supporting my family, that I cannot help conceiving it to be my sacred duty . . . to appeal to the laws of the land . . ." Later he sent the Thornton letter to John Law with a similar appeal; it was Law who actually acted as his attorney, and the complaint was dated May 28, 1808. Thornton chose as his lawyer Francis Scott Key, later to become famous as the author of "The Star-Spangled Banner."

Both Latrobe and Thornton left voluminous memoranda with regard to the case.[27] They are characteristic of the two men. Latrobe's are simple factual statements of his meetings with Thornton, the history of the Capitol, his vain attempts to win the doctor's co-operation, the efforts of friends to reconcile the two in the summer of 1807, and his surprise at the attack. He tries to get in touch with Ferdinando Fairfax, the man who, he had learned, had reported Washington's disapproval of him. He tells his attorney of his only meeting with Washington, on his visit to

27. Latrobe's are scattered through the letter books in the possession of the Latrobe family; Thornton's are among the Thornton papers in the Library of Congress. The official records of the case are preserved in the National Archives.

Old photograph, courtesy Historical and Archaeological Society of Ohio

Adena, the Worthington House, Chillicothe, Ohio. B. H. Latrobe, architect. View from the garden.

PLATE 17

Adena. The rotating server.

Courtesy James H. Rodebaugh

The Waln House, Philadelphia. B. H. Latrobe, architect. Old water color by J. Kern.

Ridgeway Branch, Free Library of Philadelphia

Courtesy Diocese of Baltimore and Walter Knight Sturges

Latrobe's Gothic side elevation.

PLATE 18

Roman Catholic Cathedral, Baltimore

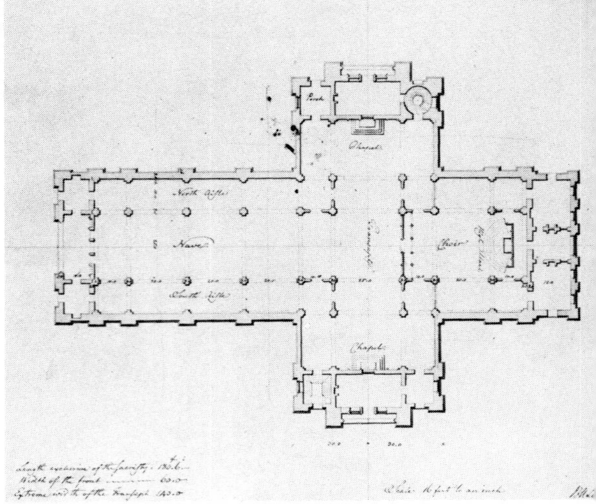

Courtesy Diocese of Baltimore and Walter Knight Stu

Latrobe's Gothic plan.

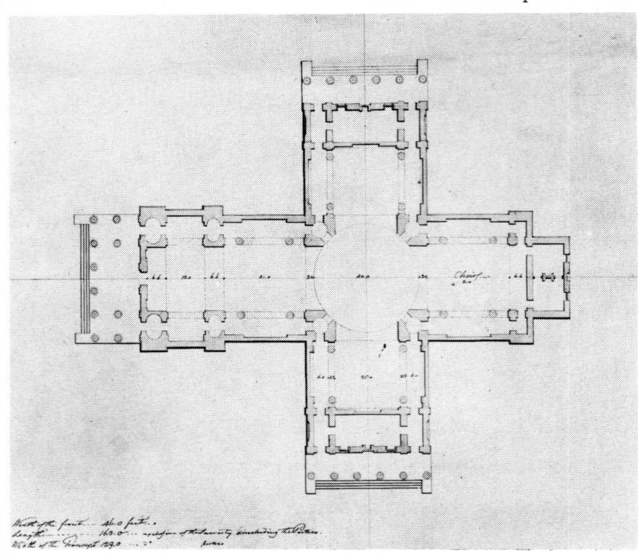

Latrobe's first "Roman" plan.

Courtesy Diocese of Baltimor
Walter Knight Sturges

Courtesy Diocese of Baltimore and Walter Knight Sturges

an Catholic Cathedral, Baltimore. Latrobe's section of the "seventh" design.

PLATE 19

an Catholic Cathedral, Baltimore. B. H. Latrobe, architect. Part measured section showing actual dome truction.

Courtesy Diocese of Baltimore and Walter Knight Sturges

Exterior. Photograph J. H. Schaefer anc

PLATE 20. Roman Catholic Cathedral, Baltimore

Interior. Photograph J. H. Schaefer and

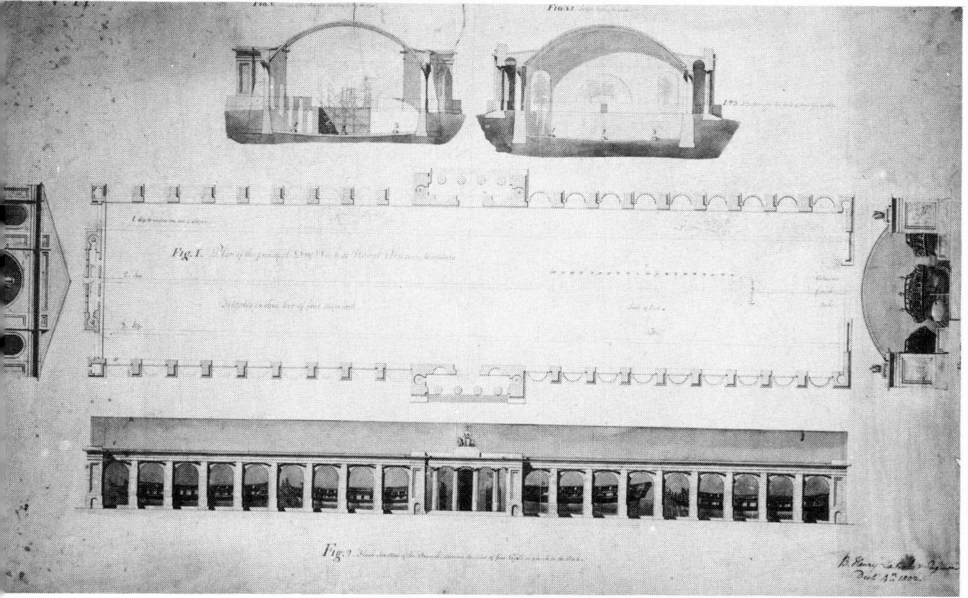

Library of Congress

ɔosed Storage Drydock for the United States Navy, Washington. Latrobe's preliminary design.

Library of Congress

ı of the United States Sloop of War *Hornet*. Latrobe's sketch for the rebuilding.

PLATE 21

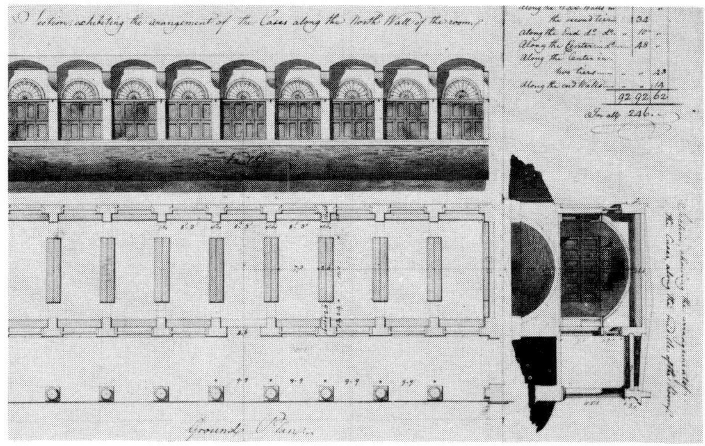

ɜury Fireproof, Wash-
ɔn. Latrobe's plan and
ɔn.

ɾy of Congress

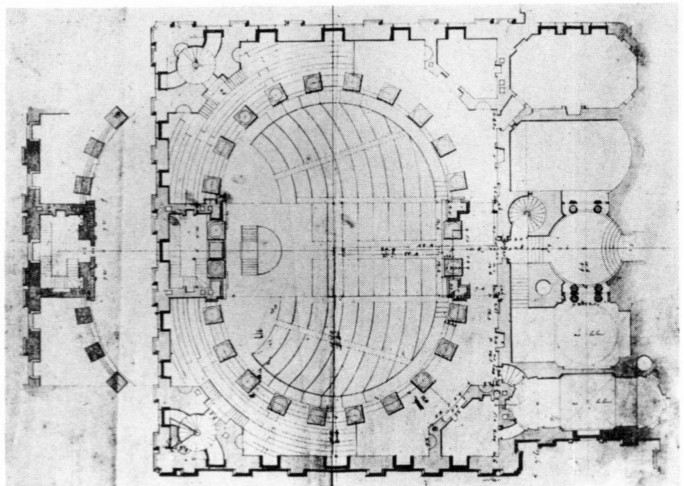

Latrobe's plan for the S
Wing.
Library of Congress

Latrobe's preliminary section through the House of Representatives, showing the penetration of light through the skylights.
Library of Congress

PLATE 22. United States Capitol, Washington, before the War of 1812

Latrobe's section showing arches and vault of the Supreme Court, 1808.

Library of Congr

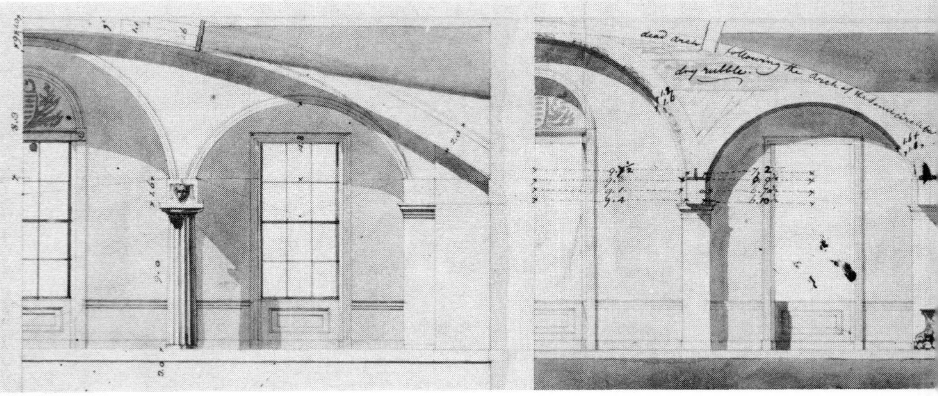

G. Brown, *History of the United States Capitol*

Senate vestibule with Latrobe's corn capitals.

Photograph I. T. Frary

ate rotunda with Latrobe's tobacco capitals.

PLATE 23
United States Capitol, Washington

robe's section through Senate and Supreme Court, 1808.

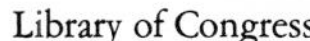

Library of Congress

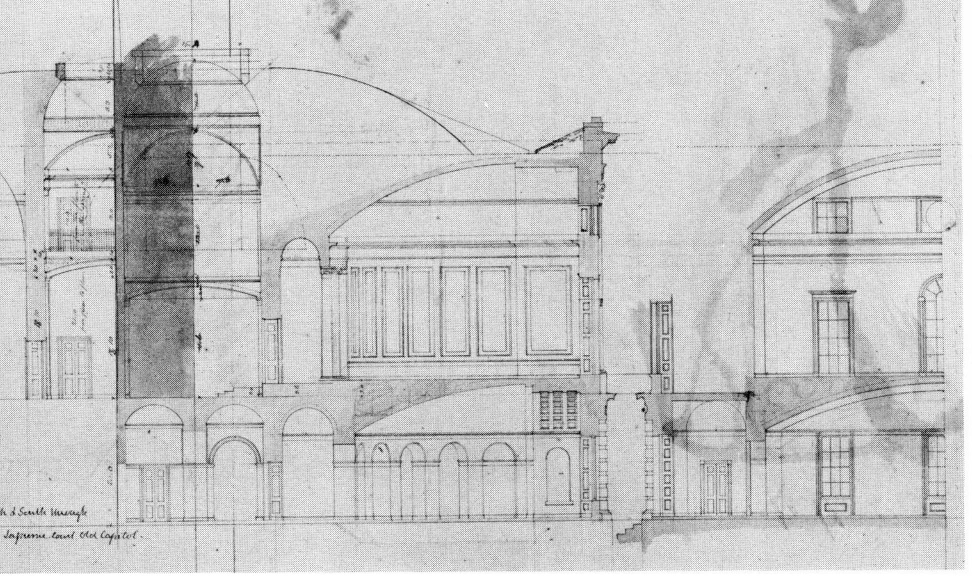

Library of Cong

Latrobe's south elevation with proposed propylaea.

PLATE 24. United States Capitol, Washington, before the War of 1812

Latrobe's west elevation with proposed propylaea.

Library of Cong

Mount Vernon in 1796. It seems that the basis of Washington's supposed remark lay in the fact that Latrobe had promised to send him a Rotherham plow; Latrobe had given Washington's request to the man who had previously offered it and then forgot all about it; evidently the plow man never fulfilled the request. He explains his occasional use of the name Boneval Latrobe or Latrobe Boneval instead of the simpler Latrobe, and obtains certificates of his children's baptism to prove his right to the more complex form.

Thornton's memoranda are an extraordinary hodgepodge of fact and fancy, of prose and bad verse. They contain no real evidence but they reveal plenty of his almost indecent spleen. He rakes up all the gossip of the last years to find anything that might involve Latrobe. He mentions a Mrs. Turner, a notorious and disreputable woman of the town, whom he claims Latrobe had ruined—no dates, no facts, only a verse:

Epitaph

The monument of poor Moll Turner,
Whose clay's so soaked that Hell can't burn her.
How died poor Moll? Moll died of spleen
Because she found L—— too keen;
In other words, he broke poor Moll's heart.
What! Outmatched Moll? Yes, rough or civil
He can out-jaw, out-lie the devil.
Hell dries the clay of poor Moll Turner
And waits L—— as fuel to burn her.

Other examples of the doctor's poetic genius may be cited from the same collection:

This Dutchman in taste, this monument builder,
    This planner of grand steps and walls,
This falling-arch maker, this blunder-roof gilder,
    Himself still an architect calls.

Benny's hatred to Washington never can end
    He hates both the name and the place—
For he knew that this good man could ne'er be his friend,
    Having fully pronounced his Disgrace.

Out of such nonsense Thornton's lawyer had to build his case.

Year after year the case was called, and Key reported that he was not ready because witnesses he needed were unavailable. At last, in the June term of 1813, the judge, disgusted with the defendant's continual postponements, called the case to trial. On June 27 Latrobe wrote to his son Henry in New Orleans: "On Thursday last, the old cause of Thornton came on to be tried. My counsel did not press damages, however. I got a verdict with costs. This plague is therefore off the list." Although the award was only one cent with costs, it was nevertheless a moral victory for Latrobe, and the filing of the suit had actually put a stop to Thornton's public attacks. The certificate of satisfaction is dated September 1, 1813.

The impact of all these troubles—the deficit of $50,000, the explanations to Congress, the reproofs of Jefferson, and finally the attack by Dr. Thornton—proved too much for Latrobe and early in June, 1808, he suffered one of his typical nervous and physical prostrations; for the rest of the month he lay sick at home.

From 1808 to the War of 1812, progress on the Capitol continued steadily and with a minimum of troubles. Early in 1809 Congress requested a complete and detailed estimate of what would be necessary to complete the two wings. In order to make such an estimate Latrobe needed more assistance, and he had the satisfaction of hiring George Hadfield, whom he had always liked and had often tried to help. Hadfield worked for him till his pay amounted to $300 (roughly three or four months); for this the commissioner had allowed Latrobe $150, but the architect paid the other half out of his own pocket.[28] On the basis of the appropriation that followed, the completion of the redesigned north wing was seriously undertaken.

That drastic repairs and replacements were necessary here had been obvious to Latrobe from the moment he became Surveyor of the Public

---

28. Later, in 1812, the final settlement of accounts between Latrobe and Commissioner Munroe brought into his hands a gold medal that Hadfield had given Munroe as security for an unpaid loan of fifty dollars. Latrobe hastened to return it to Hadfield. It was the prized gold medal awarded him by the Royal Academy in 1784—the highest architectural honor that England could offer to aspiring young architects. Latrobe wrote him (August 19): "It gives me much pleasure to return it to you, as I should feel abhorence at the idea of possessing it. In losing the prospect of an independence arising from your professional talents, it would be too much were you also to part with the honor you have so deservedly obtained . . ." In his published *Journal* Latrobe notes of him further: "He loiters here, ruined in fortune, temper, and reputation, nor will his irritable pride and neglected study ever permit him to take the station in art which his elegant taste and excellent talent ought to have obtained."

Buildings, and in his reports to the President and to Congressional committees he had pointed to the dangerous condition of the wing. Yet it had been impossible, with the limited labor and material at his command and the pressing necessity of concentrating on the House of Representatives prior to 1807, to carry out more than the most urgently needed repairs.

And there were profound faults. Much unventilated wood had been built into the masonry, and all of it was rotting; some was no better than powder, and the brickwork above was threatening complete collapse. The Senate columns themselves consisted merely of plaster over a wood framing; this had started to warp and to rot, and the plaster was bowing out and cracking. Latrobe's letters to Jefferson between 1803 and 1807 are full of accounts of this dangerous condition, becoming progressively worse every year. It was all a sad commentary on the lack of knowledge or care in supervising on the part of the original builders; for the wing had been completed and put into use only in 1800.

Even more radical changes than mere repair were necessary too. The original Senate chamber was still on the ground floor. After the House of Representatives had been brought up to the main floor to permit the inclusion of committee, clerk, and storage rooms below, it seemed imperative to raise the Senate to the same level, and in 1806 Latrobe sent the President complete plans showing the new arrangement. Here for the first time the Supreme Court was assigned an adequate and dignified home in the room beneath the new Senate chamber. In addition, by changing the uneven shape of Thornton's old Senate into a semicircle, several committee rooms and a more convenient circulation were achieved. All of the new construction involved was to be carried up in "solid work" —as the President and Congress had directed—and Latrobe interpreted this to mean solid masonry construction vaulted in brick.

Congress in March, 1807, seeing that the House was rapidly approaching completion, appropriated $25,000 for the new work on the north wing; in 1808, a similar sum; and in 1809, $16,650. At the end of that year the Senate voted to occupy its new chamber at the beginning of 1810. It was in 1807-8 that the distressing deficit was discovered, and on July 6, 1808, Jefferson wrote Latrobe suggesting that the Senate floor be installed at the new level and the chamber opened to the roof, but that the old cracked wood-and-plaster columns should remain until there was absolute proof that there would be money enough to replace them with stone. It is an interesting letter because it shows so clearly Jefferson's limitations as an architect. Apparently he still had little realization of the profound difference between the basic ideals of building expressed in Latrobe's scheme and those revealed in the work being supplanted; nor had he any real understanding of the complete integration of construction, use, and appearance that was always dominant in Latrobe's designs. To save money, therefore, Latrobe concentrated on the changes in the eastern half of the wing, which was to be completely rebuilt. The western half, containing the Congressional library and various smaller rooms, was left for future attention and now only repaired. He had, of course, made plans for its rebuilding, including a superb Egyptian design for a new and larger Congressional library; but the growing war clouds prevented Congress from making any sizable appropriations, and this section remained much as it had been built originally.

Latrobe began by entirely rebuilding the roof, thus enabling construction to go on continuously beneath it, unhampered by the weather. The semicircular walls around the Supreme Court and Senate were carried up and vaulted in brick, a brick dome was built over the oval staircase hall, stone steps with iron railings were substituted for the old wooden stairs, and a new vaulted entrance vestibule (with Latrobe's corn capitals) replaced the inconvenient earlier entrance. The vaulting was a tour de force. The Supreme Court vault that had fallen was replaced by a new ribbed semi-dome carrying the radiating conoidal vaults which the architect had originally intended, but in the rebuilt vault these radiating forms were exposed beneath, so that the whole had a sort of umbrella shape. Above, the Senate chamber was covered by a continuous brick half dome sixty feet in diameter, supported at its circumference on a semicircle of closely spaced Greek Doric columns. Latrobe notes that when the first Supreme Court vault collapsed the Senate dome stood undamaged. Even after the terrific conflagration of 1814, which utterly destroyed the western or library half of the north wing, all this masonry-vaulted area, together with the vaulted lobbies of the House and the vault over the House galleries, came through virtually intact—a striking vindication of the soundness of the architect's construction.

Between 1803 and 1812 the Capitol, under Latrobe, was carried to a point that assured safe and beautiful accommodations for the House of Representatives, the Senate, and the Supreme Court, together with all the necessary minor rooms. Except for the House roof and the old library section, the greater part of it was solidly built (masonry vaulted) of the finest materials the architect could command. The decorative detail was of cut stone or marble and the floors were chiefly of marble slabs, though Jefferson would have preferred hexagonal French tile, then completely unavailable because of the English blockade. And pre-eminently there was the continuous interest of designed space—successions of lobbies, stairs, and great rooms, all harmonious with one another and with the whole.

Criticism naturally did arise. The acoustics of the House, for example, were bad. Latrobe had warned Jefferson from the beginning that any oval shape would be unsatisfactory, and even his modification of the oval was little better. When Congress first used the chamber (October 18, 1807) and it became obvious at once that echoes rendered even the best speakers unintelligible, a committee was appointed to consult with the architect. His solution, reached on December 14, was to hang heavy red baize curtains between the columns (he wrote Lenthall on that day showing how it was to be done) and to paint the ceiling with flock colors (this Bridport did). He had always intended curtains, but Congress in cutting the appropriation from $21,000 to $17,000 had rendered it impossible to install them; now at last even Congress saw the necessity, and they were ordered. John Rea, the Philadelphia upholsterer, made them; they finally arrived on February 25, 1808. Three stripes of red velvet and a wide fringe in red, yellow, and black, all designed by Latrobe, decorated their lower edges. Not only did the curtains solve the problem, but their rich color added greatly to the beauty of the room; again the architect had made a practical requirement into an opportunity for creating effect. As he described the earlier condition and its cure in a letter to his Philadelphia friend Colonel Duane (February 29, 1808):

. . . the noisy echoes; who having no respect of persons, repeated with equal impartiality the speeches of the eloquent, the reveries of the stupid, and the negotiations carried on upon the Washington Exchange, alias the lobby of the house. To hang [the curtains] tastefully & usefully has been . . . my almost sole employment. They have produced the fullest effect, & even Mr. Rhea of Ten. is distinctly heard, & almost understood in every part of the house. . . . But besides this effect on voice & ears, the eye is now extremely gratified by the appearance & proportions of the room to the full extent I expected and intended, for the curtains were part of my design . . . Hitherto

I have been distressed by the praises bestowed upon the room, knowing what a bad effect the angular forms peeping thro' the circular colonnade necessarily produced on the eye of taste; now one single & simple image presents itself to the mind in a splendid colonnade backed by the folds of well hung drapery.

There were dignified hangings in the Senate too. In this smaller area, the color was more subdued than the crimson and gold-yellow of the House; here buff, straw-yellow, and blue predominated. In both rooms the furniture was of mahogany; the throne-like desks and chairs of the Speaker and the Vice-President were restrained in design, with spots of rich ornament, and there were handsome draperies behind them. It is important to remember these colorful fitments, all designed by Latrobe, for as we look back on the Capitol of that distant time we are prone to evoke a vision of cold whiteness instead of the color harmonies, the subtle richnesses, and the human touches of ornament and sculpture and furniture which as an integral part of the architect's original scheme made it the building it was.

Latrobe now took the occasion to make a careful new study of the entire building, including the central section. By this time it was apparent that the Senate needed the entire north wing. Latrobe therefore added a bold projection on the west, containing a magnificent library room extending its whole length and fronted by a long Corinthian colonnade to give an imposing elevation from the Mall below. In addition he planned at the foot of the hill a monumental Greek Doric propylaea, with an impressive flight of stairs within to lead up to the west entrance of the Capitol. The flanking buildings of the propylaea were for guard rooms, fuel storage, and the like. It was a superb conception which made full use of the slope and effectively tied the Capitol to the long axis of the Mall that stretched out on the lower ground toward the west. It is unfortunate that this brilliant scheme was not carried out in the rebuilding of the Capitol after the fire.

By 1811 the working parts of the Capitol were virtually complete. Now, with the difficulties in trade which the European blockades produced, the falling revenues, and the growing military expenditures, Congress could only see its way to closing down all the work, especially since accusations of extravagance were still being flung at Latrobe. In vain did he point out that the north wing as originally built in wood and plaster, with cheap, slipshod construction, had cost nearly $100,000 *more* than the south wing (of which he had had charge) with its vaulting, its solid masonry, its sculpture, and its furniture. To the Congressmen accounts were merely figures on paper, meaning little, whereas any fool could see the costliness of brick vaults, of color and carving! To them *it was beauty itself that was the extravagance*—no cost comparisons could contradict that! What could any architect do in the face of such an attitude?

The final appropriation made by Congress in April, 1812, allowed only for the payment of outstanding debts and the cost of returning Franzoni and Andrei to Italy. Latrobe was referred to as "the late Surveyor of the Public Buildings," and no money was appropriated to pay the salary due him. This shocking oversight he took at once to the President (then Madison), but it was not till July that Congress relented and passed a revised appropriation based on reality and not on emotion. It did allow for the completion of the carving of the House capitals and did provide for the arrears in salary, though it paid Latrobe only up "to July 1, 1811, when his duties in that capacity ceased." This, of course, was the least they could honestly do. There was not a word of gratitude anywhere for the architect's accomplishment.

Jefferson was more appreciative. He understood Latrobe, realized the struggles he had had, and was gratified at all he had achieved. After Latrobe had written him (April 5, 1811) out of deep discouragement, even doubting that Jefferson had retained his old cordiality toward him (so universal seemed the disesteem with which he was regarded), Jefferson answered (April 14):

> Besides constant commendations of your taste in architecture, and science in execution, I declared on many and all occasions that I considered you the only person in the United States who could have executed the Representative Chamber, or who could execute the middle building on any of the plans proposed. . . . Of the value I set on your society, our intercourse before as well as during my office, can have left no doubt with you; and I should be happy in giving further proofs to you personally at Monticello.

And fifteen months later, when Latrobe had written him of the cessation of the Capitol work, Jefferson said in another letter (July 12, 1812):

> With respect to yourself, the little disquietudes from individuals not chosen for their taste in art, will be sunk into oblivion, while the Representative

Chamber will remain a durable monument of your taste as an architect. I can say nothing of the Senate room, because I have never seen it. I shall live in hope that the day will come when an opportunity will be given you of finishing the middle building in a style worthy of the two wings, and worthy of the first temple dedicated to the sovereignty of the people, embellishing with Athenian taste the course of a nation looking far beyond the range of Athenian destinies.

But perhaps the most forceful comment on Latrobe's success in the Capitol was made later by his son John H. B. Latrobe:

> I can still recall, among the shadowy impressions of my earliest boyhood, the effect, approaching awe, produced upon me by the old Hall of Representatives. I fancy I can see the heavy crimson drapery that hung in massive folds between the tall fluted Corinthian columns to within a short distance of their base, and I remember, or I think I remember, the low, gilded iron railing that ran from base to base, and over which the spectators in the gallery looked down upon the members on the floor. I seem to see, even now, the speaker's chair, with its rich surroundings, and the great stone eagle which, with outspread wings, projected from the frieze, as though it were hovering over and protecting those who deliberated below. Of course, after so many years, it is not impossible that form and color have been given to the memories of a boy, nine years old at the time, by what he had seen in the portfolios which were almost the picture-books of his childhood. Be this as it may, however, there can be no question that the old Hall of Representatives was a noble room. Even the British officer, who was ordered to destroy it, is reported to have said, as he stood at the entrance, "that it was a pity to burn anything so beautiful." [29]

Meanwhile Latrobe had been busy with other Federal work. Work to be done for the Navy had increased and won him the position of engineer for the Navy Department, with a welcome addition to his stipend. Then, in the early summer of 1807, as we have seen, he had moved his family to Washington. But two years before that two other important government commissions came his way, chiefly through his contacts with Albert Gallatin, the Swiss-born genius who was Secretary of the Treasury under Jefferson. Both jobs came at almost the same moment. One was a lighthouse for the mouth of the Mississippi; the other, a fireproof archive room for the Treasury Department, to be included in one

---

29. John E. Semmes, *John H. B. Latrobe and His Times, 1803-1891* (Baltimore: Norman, Remington [c1917]).

of the long one-story colonnaded wings which Jefferson wished to add to the President's House and for which he had made the first drawings himself.

Latrobe devoted much time to the design of the lighthouse, and there was a busy correspondence about it between the architect and Gallatin. Of the details of the design there is now no existing record, but from the correspondence we learn that it was in essence a conical masonry tower with a spiral marble stair inside. We may perhaps gather some hints of it from the design which Henry developed in 1816, for the plans of this exist and we know from the correspondence that B. H. Latrobe gave his son all the help he could by sending him (December 19, 1816) his own calculations of cost and probably sketches as well. The soil was soft and fluid, so that the base had to spread wide; in the final design by Henry Latrobe advantage of this was taken by surrounding the cone with a colonnade and connecting the complicated ring-shaped foundations by reversed brick vaults, in the hope of wedding the parts into one almost monolithic whole. Gallatin wished to make an over-all lump-sum contract for the construction of the lighthouse, and although the architect could—and did—assemble accurate bids for its masonry (largely of stone to be cut in Philadelphia) he could find no one to undertake the risk of construction on that distant and lonely site. The project was therefore abandoned. Some ten years later, when Henry Latrobe was established as an architect-builder in New Orleans, the proposal was revived and Henry was finally awarded the contract. But the foundation design was faulty; the masses of masonry in the building were too heavy for its piles; the building settled unevenly and collapsed just before its completion. It was rebuilt, without the colonnade, in 1823.[30]

The Treasury "fireproof" also caused Latrobe much trouble during 1805 and 1806. Jefferson had planned colonnaded one-story wings stretching east and west from the main block of the President's House, to contain a stable and executive offices and to connect with the departmental buildings that flanked the President's dwelling—the Treasury Department to the east and the War and Navy Departments to the west. The Treasury fireproof was to be in the eastern wing. For this wing Jefferson had

30. See Benjamin Henry Boneval Latrobe, *Impressions Respecting New Orleans,* edited with an introduction and notes by Samuel Wilson, Jr. (New York: Columbia University Press, 1951), pp. 124n., 169-73.

made elaborate drawings, which nevertheless left many practical points unsolved, and it was within the limits set by these drawings that Latrobe had to work. He disliked the wings fundamentally; again and again he refers to the President's Palladian taste as old-fashioned. In a letter to Lenthall (May 3, 1805) he unburdened himself on the subject:

> . . . a post or two will bring you the President's colonnade, etc. I am sorry that I am cramped in this design by his prejudices in favor of the old French books, out of which he fishes everything—but it is a small sacrifice to my personal attachment to him to humour him, and the less so, because the style of the colonnade he proposes is exactly consistent with Hoban's pile—a litter of pigs worthy of the great sow it surrounds, & of the wild Irish boar, the father of her . . . [So much for Hoban.]

There was difficulty in adjusting the levels of the new work to the old, and the planning was an exacting task. In a letter to Gallatin, Latrobe calls it "damned hard work"—but, he adds (May 4, 1805): "I have made something of it which does not altogether displease me, & of which your fireproof is infinitely the best morceau, for with that, I am entirely satisfied . . ."

As designed (the architect's beautiful drawing is dated April 27, 1805), the archive room took up nine bays of the colonnade, with an entrance in the center bay. Light came in from semicircular windows, which were on both sides between the piers, and the piers were connected across the long room by built-in timber tie rods. Segmental arches crossed from pier to pier above the ties, and these in turn carried shallow segmental vaults. In this way the over-thin walls and piers were enabled to bear the weight of the fireproof covering. Large cases in which the papers were to be preserved lined the walls, and additional double-faced cabinets were placed transversely at each bay. The floor was carried on another long segmental vault over the cellar. It was a light and daring solution of a difficult problem, and it demanded the most meticulous construction.

In the original design an open vaulted loggia extended over the road that bordered the ground to the east of the mansion in order to give undercover approach to the colonnade from the Treasury building. This loggia was double-arched, with a narrow arch over the sidewalk and a wider carriage arch. In December the vaults were complete and the mortar was sufficiently set for the temporary centering to be removed. The removal was disastrous; either because of badly designed centering or through carelessness in removing the posts that supported it, the westernmost of the supports over the carriageway was shoved out of plumb and the entire vault collapsed. Latrobe in Philadelphia heard of the accident at the end of the month and wrote Lenthall (December 31, 1806): "I am very sorry the arches have fallen, both on account of the expense & the disgrace of the thing. But I have had such accidents before, and on a larger scale, & must therefore grin & bear it"—and he continued with an elaborate explanation of what must have been the cause. But the vaults were reconstructed successfully as originally designed, and the Treasury fireproof eventually went into use.

Another commission from Gallatin came just afterward—a customs house for New Orleans. This was given to Latrobe in March, 1807, and on the fifteenth he wrote his acquaintance Daniel Clarke, who was living there, asking for permission to send him the plans in order that they might receive criticism from someone thoroughly acquainted with the local conditions. The completed designs were sent to Gallatin on April 28, along with a cost estimate of $19,193.26 and the interesting news that Robert Alexander, who had been one of the contractors for Latrobe's Navy Yard work, was planning to move to New Orleans to open a building business and would take the contract for $19,000.

The job was rushed. All the joinery was done in Philadelphia, and it was practically complete by August 1. The contractor had purchased a brig there and was loading her with bricks to ship around to New Orleans; on the way she was to go to Alexandria to pick up all the ironwork and other manufactured parts that had been made in the Washington area. On August 20, Alexander obtained permission to use all the materials he could salvage from the old wooden customs house in New Orleans which was being replaced, and soon afterward the brig sailed. Alexander himself arrived in New Orleans in May, 1808, and the building was completed in 1809.

This was an ambitious project to be undertaken at such a small cost. The lower floor, for stored goods, was covered with fireproof brick vaults. Above it rose walls faced with Philadelphia brick, the main front had a recessed loggia with two Greek Doric stone columns *in antis,* and there was a wood-shingled hipped roof. In refusing to follow the New Orleans custom of building all walls on horizontal logs laid in the foundation trenches, however, Latrobe made a serious error; for his masonry footings did not give the perfect continuity the logs would have provided, and the ground was so soft as to make that continuity necessary. Moreover, Alexander skimped his walls; instead of building them throughout of good Philadelphia brick he used that material for facing only, and the backing was of local soft brick inadequate for the loads. Unequal settling and serious cracks were the result, but when expensive repairs became necessary in 1813 the war prevented any appropriation for them. Four years later the building was an unusable ruin, and a new customs house by the local architect Benjamin Buisson was erected to replace it. The whole vain attempt was a disappointment to its architect—and to New Orleans.[31]

Two other important projects in Washington had long occupied Latrobe's busy hours—the Navy Yard and the necessary repairs and completion of the President's House. The architect's design for the covered drydock had naturally brought him to the attention of the Secretary of the Navy; when, therefore, the Navy Yard organization was rearranged in 1804 and Captain Tingey was officially made commandant (he had served in that capacity earlier, from 1799 to 1801), a large building program was decided on and it was to Latrobe that the Navy looked for assistance.[32]

The Navy Yard in 1803 was an incoherent group of sheds and slipways on the northern shore of the Eastern Branch, extending from Seventh to Ninth Streets Southeast. It had one long wharf running out to the channel, and in 1801 a house had been built for the commandant (at that time Captain Cassin) near the northern boundary. Latrobe's first task, then, was to regularize what existed as far as he could and then lay out the area so that the new buildings would form an efficiently related group. For his plan we are forced to depend on the description of it which he sent to Secretary Robert Smith in the winter of 1804-5; for, as Latrobe himself wrote later, no plan could then be found in the Navy Department of either the Washington Navy Yard or that at New York, and no Latrobe plans can be found today.[33]

Secretary Smith approved Latrobe's ambitious scheme, and work on

31. See Latrobe, *op. cit.* pp. xiii, xiv.

32. See Henry A. Hibben, *Navy Yard, Washington; History from Organization, 1799, to Present Date,* 51st Congress, 1st Session, Executive Document 22 (Washington: Government Printing Office, 1890).

33. Mr. Nelson Blake, of the Navy Records department in the National Archives, has been kind enough to make a thorough search for such plans—but in vain.

it began at once. Robert Alexander was the chief contractor for the buildings. The plan called for building first a new permanent stone-faced wharf adjacent to the existing one of timber, second a similar section to replace the old, and then annually 150-foot sections until the entire channel frontage was complete. Westward of this wharf section were the slipways, which were to remain in their original locations but were to be rebuilt in a more permanent manner. Meanwhile, as the wharf sections were erected the shallows were to be filled in to meet them, thus adding nearly 30 per cent to the yard's area. Still farther west, a canal was to be dredged that would pass back of the ends of the slipways and allow barges or rafts to be floated deep into the yard; along this canal, on both sides, were to be placed rows of important storage and shop buildings. The timber shed, the mast shed, and other storage units for bulky and heavy articles opened also on the open space around the shipbuilding slips. The main gate was placed on the axis of Eighth Street Southeast and fronted on Georgia Avenue; from it a street called Gate Street led to an open area on which were located the residences of the "master artificers," and the rear doors of these gave approach to the central open yard and thence to the shipbuilding slips and the major shops. Along the eastern boundary were placed the slaughter house and the salting house (for producing the salt pork and salt beef that formed the basis of navy rations); these, being "nuisances," as Latrobe calls them, were situated as far from the other parts of the yard as possible. The old commandant's house was close to the north boundary and east of the entrance; a second good house, also built before Latrobe's appointment, existed not far away on the eastern lot line. To these the architect planned to add another and better home for the commandant west of the entrance, but this was not built until 1807.

The whole plan was a study in providing the most efficient relationships for a large group of essentially industrial buildings. The structures themselves were of the simplest types. Architectural display was limited to the main gate. This was a most interesting composition consisting of a double gateway, with guard rooms between the inner and outer gates. The entrance toward the street was a miniature triumphal arch; that toward the yard was the wide, low, semicircular opening that so enraged Dr. Thornton; the passage between the two was bordered by two Doric columns on each side, with the guard rooms behind them;

and the whole was crowned by a great eagle and anchor carved by Franzoni.

Of all of this large composition little is left today. At the time the British entered Washington (August 24, 1814) Captain Tingey ordered the yard to be burned before evacuating it, and a thorough job—completed by the British—was made of the fire. The two old houses still stand, much altered, but neither of them was designed by Latrobe though he may have carried out some decorative work in them. His main gate, however, still exists, almost hidden by an amorphous mass of later additions, and the eagle and anchor vanished when the inharmonious upper floor was built.

An addition made to the Washington Navy Yard by Latrobe in 1810—one he was even prouder of than he was of the gate—was a large steam engine (bought from Smallman of Philadelphia) which was specially designed to provide power for both the bellows and a trip hammer in the yard forge. Later it was attached to a sawmill, and it could be used for a blockmill as well (to make the hundreds of pulley blocks required). The architect wrote with justifiable pride to Secretary Paul Hamilton (June 29, 1811) that the engine could operate the forge, the bellows, and the sawmill at the same time—or the blockmill, the bellows, and the forge—and to Jefferson (July 2, 1812) that it saved the Navy at least $16,000 a year besides the saving in time. As in all those early engine installations, there were troubles of one kind or another. Smallman was supposed to erect the engine, and a controversy arose whether he or the Navy Department should pay the wages of his employees in this work; a compromise settlement was arrived at. There were times when the engine would not run; Latrobe discovered that the well driven through the clay to furnish condensing water was subject to tidal action, and that when an unusually low tide occurred there was no water in the well. Most of the time, however, the engine performed satisfactorily, to the immense advantage of the yard.

The following year brought another Navy job—the design of a new stern for the brig *Hornet,* which, much rotted, was largely rebuilt in the spring and early summer of 1811. Latrobe's preliminary sketch for this, still preserved, is our only evidence of actual ship detailing by him, though he may have done more.

An interesting special problem that Latrobe solved was the erection of the famous Tripoli Monument in Gate Street, on the axis of the

Navy Yard gate. This had been carved in Italy to memorialize the officers who lost their lives in the Tripoli war. It had been shipped over in cases, and the architect found that the building of a heavy core was necessary to support the thin marble slabs; Franzoni and Andrei were put in charge of repairing and setting the statues. Later, after the war, during which it had been knocked down, Latrobe was responsible for its reconstruction. Washington hoodlums had looted the yard after the fire, and a discussion arose whether the monument had been destroyed by them or by the British. Tingey thought it was the Washingtonian looters, but the discovery of a fragment of one of the statues in the possession of a British officer who had been captured at New Orleans was evidence enough that the British were the guilty parties; a new inscription stating the fact was therefore installed at the Navy's request.[34]

Two other commissions for the Navy Department deserve notice. The first was the replanning of the Brooklyn Navy Yard. Latrobe was sent to New York in mid-August, 1808, to examine conditions there and to suggest improvements. He enjoyed this visit, for it enabled him to see the Roosevelts and to renew his acquaintance with friends there—the Marks, Robert Fulton, Dr. Hosack (with whom Latrobe dined after having been shown his botanical garden, and for whom the plans for a house were apparently under discussion), and Colonel Williams. On his return to Washington his observations of the Brooklyn yard resulted in a complete new plan for it; nothing, however, was done at that time to carry out his recommendations, and four years later in a report to the Secretary of the Navy he noted that his plan had long since disappeared.

Much more important, though it also resulted in no construction, was his scheme for a naval hospital to be placed on New Jersey Avenue, close

---

34. From Latrobe's letters of July 31 and October 5 and 19, 1815, to Commodore Porter. The Tripoli Monument, now in the grounds of the Naval Academy in Annapolis, is an ambitious if awkward example of the classic revival Italian sculpture of the turn of the nineteenth century. In my opinion Latrobe, Franzoni, and Andrei made a serious error in the arrangement of the statues. There are unexplainably but three figures placed on three of the four corners of the square base, leaving the other corner empty and naked. It would seem probable that the Victory (or Fame), instead of crowning the whole and conflicting with the monument's outline, was probably intended as the fourth corner figure, with her outstretched arm pointing toward the inscription that refers to fame. This arrangement, with a slight change in the placing of the other three figures, would then agree perfectly with the inscriptions on the four faces of the pedestal. Since the present arrangement, however, appears on the earliest prints we possess, which show the monument as it was first erected in the Navy Yard, the error (if it is one) must have occurred then.

to the Navy Yard gate. This occupied him from time to time for four years, from 1808 to 1812, and, as the war grew more and more imminent, interest in the project increased. In 1812, accordingly, at the request of Secretary Hamilton, he prepared an elaborate set of plans. At one time it seemed as though the building would surely go ahead; but the final breaking out of the war prevented it, and Latrobe's modest bill was never paid. His design shows a large U-shaped structure, with residences for doctors and the commanding officer at the corners and the wing ends. The court is arcaded on the ground floor, and a large formal garden occupies the center. It was the architect's intention that half of the long western wing would be built first to take care of immediate and emergency needs—the rest to be added as conditions warranted. The plan is carefully studied throughout for ventilation and convenience, the quiet exterior well composed. It would have produced a building both useful and beautiful and together with Hadfield's marine barracks and the Navy Yard gate near by would have created a handsome naval center.

The work on the President's House extended over the entire period from 1804 to 1812. Jefferson had found the building incomplete—the great east room unfinished, for example—and moreover the roof leaked and the plaster was falling. The entire construction indeed had been as slipshod as that of the north wing of the Capitol. And the grounds had not been touched; the house rose starkly above a wilderness. The wooden sewer that carried the wastes from the water closet and the kitchen discharged at the surface, over a temporary roadway of approach—on a hot summer day not a pleasant prologue to a visit to the President! To Jefferson, himself an architect of fastidious taste, the whole was a challenge and drastic improvements were an urgent necessity. The President needed office space as well as stables; he needed privacy, too, and surroundings that had some modicum of decency. For service elements, Jefferson designed the one-story colonnaded wings already described, in which Latrobe (as we have seen) incorporated a fireproof section in the eastern wing for the Treasury Department in 1805-6 and one in the western wing for the Post Office in 1810, during Madison's administration. Vaulting troubles occurred in this later wing too, but in this case they were caused by imperfections in the old walls.

In 1806 and 1807 the surroundings were studied by Latrobe and received the close attention of the President. A stone wall was built around the immediate private grounds, with an arched gate on the north, and a road was constructed around the whole to produce not only an essential connection between the various avenues that focused on the President's House but also a convenient approach to the executive office buildings which flanked it on the east and west. The sewer, in addition to being an unhygienic nuisance, was threatening to destroy the road by erosion and had to be reconstructed and covered. Within the wall extensive grading was undertaken, to open the view from the house over the Potomac toward the south; the earth removed was used to form little hills on either side to give privacy to the wings and to a private garden. It was a brilliantly conceived landscape plan of the popular English informal type. Since appropriations were scant, every means was sought to keep down the cost of the wall and the road. Still the expenditures mounted, and still Jefferson's pressure to finish the work continued. It was this pressure, Latrobe claimed, together with the fact that he could not get actual figures from Commissioner Munroe, which caused the $50,000 deficit in the season of 1807-8.

Latrobe never liked the President's House. Hoban's design for it was purely in the eighteenth-century English manner; to Latrobe, trained in the more efficient planning of the classic revival, the great entrance hall was absurd ("all stomach" he called the plan) and the lack of convenient service a disgrace. He found the central oval projection on the south ill-proportioned and the central entrance pavilion on the north undistinguished. As a result, during 1807 he prepared a new plan for the entire building. This showed not only an almost complete change in the plan of the central section but also a semicircular portico on the south and a boldly projecting entrance portico—incorporating a dignified porte-cochère—on the north. The interior alteration was never undertaken, but Jefferson saw at once the tremendous value of the two porticoes, and work on them was begun; the entire stone foundation, platform, and steps were completed before Jefferson left office. The main-entrance stonework was large in size and costly; to those who could not visualize the grandeur of the portico that would one day rise upon it, it was but one more example of Latrobe's extravagance. Actually, of course, these foundations determined the porticoes that were constructed later, and it is to Latrobe's designs—incorporated in a series of superb drawings—

that we owe these salient features of the White House exterior today.[35]

Thus except for the north and south porticoes, the President's House was almost complete when the Madisons took possession in March, 1809. From that time on till the beginning of the war Latrobe was busy acting as interior decorator and purchasing agent for them in their ambitious scheme of making the interior as beautiful and as distinguished as its purpose dictated. Since Mrs. Madison was an old and intimate friend of Mary Latrobe's and since the President—much older, often ill, and rather aloof—left all such matters largely in the hands of his wife, it was on an unusual basis of personal understanding that these missions were carried out.

First it was necessary to procure new and suitable carriages, but this proved almost fatal to the continuation of the work. They were ordered by Latrobe from the Philadelphia coachmaker Peter Harvie, who had made various carriages for the architect's friends and had won their admiration for his work. On this of all jobs, however, everything went wrong and when the carriages were delivered one of them was found completely unacceptable in both workmanship and finish; it had to be returned and the contract for it was canceled. This was not an auspicious start, but the Madisons' faith in their architect was unshaken.

The Madisons had in mind no less than the complete refurnishing of all the most important rooms in order to make them for the first time worthy to be parts of the executive mansion of an important nation. This included everything—carpets, furniture, new marble mantels,[36] stoves, plate, china, lighting fixtures, great mirrors, and hangings. Not only did Latrobe have to select, but much had to be designed. The furniture he designed was manufactured in Washington and Baltimore; the hangings were made locally by Mrs. Sweeny, the fashionable upholsterer of the city; the carpets, plate, china, and lighting fixtures were purchased in Philadelphia; the mirror and table linen were bought from Jacob Mark in New York. Because of the embargo, the later Non-Intercourse

---

35. The restoration of the President's House after the fire of 1814 was put into the hands of Hoban, and it was under Hoban's direction that the porticoes following the Latrobe drawings were built in 1824.

36. It was probably for the President's House that Latrobe ordered a marble mantel from Adam Traquair on October 17, 1810. He wrote: "Forward hither as soon as possible the best marble mantel piece you have . . . You know my taste. I want no spindle shanked columns, nor elliptical pilasters. A plain good thing, of well chosen marble will please me best."

Act, and the English blockade of the Continent, many European materials were in short supply. It was therefore a tragedy that the largest mirror, ordered from Mark for $1,500, was broken in transit; it could not be replaced, and two smaller mirrors (at $1,060 for the pair) had to be substituted. Since German stoves were also unavailable, Latrobe used instead an ordinary iron-plate stove in the hall, surrounding it with a handsome hollow pedestal crowned with an urn of masonry.

From Bradford & Inskeep, of Philadelphia, Latrobe bought the lamps, as he did some of the plate. They were of the new spiral-burner type with glass chimneys—a great improvement over the more common candles—and the architect used them in parts of the Capitol as well. There were twelve double lights in the great East Drawing Room alone. Latrobe wrote the firm (November 21, 1809) that he would prefer bronze to brass or glass, for cut-glass lamps ornamented with drops and festoons "would soon be demolished by the clumsy & careless servants of this part of the world." When the lamps came the architect wrote them again (December 23) that the fixtures gave the greatest satisfaction to President and Mrs. Madison, "and, permit me to add at a proper distance, to myself, altho' I cannot say that I admire the mixture of Egyptian, Greek, & Birmingham taste which characterizes them." As early as May 29, 1809, the bills for furnishings amounted to more than $5,000; for his own extra work Latrobe charged only 2 per cent.[37]

The final achievement was worth all it had cost and all the labor and imagination which the Madisons and Latrobe had put into it. Contemporary accounts vouch for the elegance and beauty of the drawing room. The colors of its hangings and upholstery were red, light blue, and yellow, and the carpet harmonized with them. Over its mantel hung the largest of the mirrors; the great Stuart portrait of Washington dominated the dining room.[38] But all this elegance was ruthlessly destroyed when the British burned the President's House on that dread day (August 25, 1814) so painfully recalled by Mrs. Madison in a letter to Mary Latrobe (December 3, 1814):

---

37. See Katherine Anthony, *Dolly Madison: Her Life and Times* (Garden City, N.Y.: Doubleday & Co. [c1949]), and Allen C. Clark, *Life and Letters of Dolly Madison* (Washington: W. F. Roberts, 1914).

38. Mrs. Madison had wished to hang the general's picture in the drawing room but had yielded to Latrobe's advice.

Two hours before the enemy entered the city, I left the house where Mr. Latrobe's elegant taste had been justly admired, and where you and I had so often wandered together; and on that *very day* I sent out the silver (nearly all) and velvet curtains and General Washington's picture, the Cabinet Papers, a few books, and the small clock—left everything else belonging to the public, our own valuable stores of every description, a part of my clothes, and all my servants' clothes, etc., etc. In short, it would fatigue you to read the list of *my* losses, or an account of the general *dismay* or particular distresses of your acquaintance. . . .

So came to a close Latrobe's work on the President's House, for when he was recalled to Washington in 1815 to rebuild the Capitol the reconstruction of the President's House was put in other hands. Here again, as in the Capitol, all that he had created—the product of a decade of toil and genius—literally went up in smoke.

CHAPTER

14

Washington Years: 1807-1813

It must have been with a deep feeling of relief that Mary Latrobe finally settled her family in Washington in July, 1807. At last they had a home that promised to be permanent, or at least as permanent as could be expected of any busy professional man's menage. The Capitol would be several years in the building, and Latrobe's position seemed for the moment secure. Of course she would be days away from her beloved Hazlehursts, but that too was not an unmixed hardship; now she and her husband could establish a center that was theirs alone, to be formed and managed as they saw fit. Disappointed in their hopes for a home in Philadelphia, they must have seen Washington as a new foothold in pleasant contrast to their temporary abodes in Newcastle and Wilmington. Iron Hill, at least, had been all theirs and much loved by them both, but it was a summer home only.

And their removal to Washington was the inevitable end of a long process. Latrobe had collected a large circle of friends and acquaintances there, and to Mary it was hardly a strange city; she had been there with her husband in 1803-4 and again in 1805. Then, too, many important Philadelphia acquaintances were often in Washington, and some made it their chief home. Mrs. Madison had been a close friend of Mary's when they were both young girls in the Quaker City, and what more perfect introduction to Washington society could be wished?

Their house, disclosed as a large one by its use as a landmark in an advertisement of a furniture dealer in the *National Intelligencer* and further identified as being "half-way between the Capitol and the Navy Yard," belonged to Robert Alexander, who had gone to New Orleans as the contractor to build the customs house there from Latrobe's designs. It was a pleasant and commodious home, and in an addition which he had designed, Latrobe set up his office. He roofed it with a cement invented or marketed by a Russian officer who called himself Baron de Niroth, whom Latrobe had befriended as he had so many other European travelers and refugees. The cement was worthless, the roof leaked while Latrobe was away, and many of his precious drawings were defaced or destroyed. This was not the only trouble he was to have with this strange individual, however, and a brief account here may throw interesting sidelights on the Latrobes and their times.

Five years after the Latrobe family settled in Washington, "Baron" de Niroth, encumbered by debts in the city and with no more prospective victims to fleece, decided to leave town. Unfortunately his plan became known and he was arrested and jailed for debt in Alexandria, leaving his daughter Charlotte (apparently in her late teens or early twenties) penniless at the inn there. Dr. Dick, of Alexandria, was kind enough to take her in for a time, and either he or De Niroth called on Latrobe for aid. Evidently the Latrobes had met Charlotte, liked her, and felt some responsibility for her, for the architect wrote Dr. Dick (October 29, 1812) thanking him for rescuing the girl, who later joined the Latrobes in Washington as their guest. Meanwhile, he added, a "fellow debtor's" generosity to the "old Baron" had accomplished his release and he was then at McCleod's Tavern, and the letter goes on to describe the situation:

> He is an accomplished brute; accomplished only so far as he possesses various knowledge, and a command of various languages, but a brute in morals, and in habits. . . . but [I] foresee it will be impossible to do what humanity points out—as the most effectual mode of preserving her innocence and happiness (if she ever can be happy)—to separate her from her father.

Writing the same day to the Baron that he must take care of his daughter, Latrobe says he cannot accept the responsibility for keeping her. De Niroth had suggested she be committed to Bishop Neale; Latrobe thinks the suggestion excellent and agrees to be responsible for her board. There things rested for a week—Charlotte staying with the Latrobes and anxious not to join her father, the Baron evidently planning ways and means, Latrobe all puzzled and considerate. Charlotte wished to return to the Dicks in Alexandria, and Latrobe wrote her (November 10): "We worked 2 hours on your father last night, & he at last agreed to allow you $200 a year through a merchant in Philadelphia who is at present anonymous." Suspicious, Latrobe wrote the Baron (November 15) asking who the merchant was, and it is not altogether surprising that his identity never appears. For, earlier, when the Baron had suddenly displayed a recommendation from Latrobe's own brother, apparently signed by him as president of the Imperial College of Medicine, near St. Petersburg, Latrobe had indignantly written to Dr. Dick: "I have a brother, a physician,[1] in Russia but I did not know before, and I doubt now of his being, President of the Imp. Col. of Med.!" De Niroth had been overplaying his hand; this was a patent hoax.

Now the Baron takes the attitude of a wronged nobleman. He wants his daughter back—what right have they to interfere in the affairs of a Russian noble? Latrobe, increasingly skeptical, at once institutes an inquiry through the Russian embassy, with which he is on terms of special intimacy. The result, which Latrobe hastens to convey to De Niroth (November 18), is that the embassy denies any knowledge of De Niroth personally, or of any Russian nobility of that name. The Baron is now caught fairly out. He has lived off Washington for at least five years; his pretended waterproof cement has been widely used and later widely deplored; he has displayed a genius for borrowing money and for running up bills. Obviously he has personal charm; but even that is no longer good coin in Washington, and finally Latrobe in disgust writes Dick (November 23) suggesting that the Baron be locked up. Charlotte, it appears, is at last settled with the Dicks as a sort of governess, and the Baron disappears from the pages of history. But the whole episode is expressive of Latrobe's deeply considerate kindness as well as of his naïve trust in others.

The new Latrobe residence was situated in what was then one of the most rapidly growing areas of the city. Washington in 1807 was less a city than a grotesque expression of faith and hope. The L'Enfant plan was still chiefly on paper; only a small number of its streets had actually been laid out and even fewer of them paved. It was a city of summer dust and winter mud—a city where occasional short rows of brick houses, entirely urban in type, rose incoherently out of vacant land (thicket-grown) or dotted the ubiquitous market gardens. Here and there an elegant mansion, like Colonel Tayloe's "octagon house," proudly faced the confusion, haughty and disdainful of the unkempt and often un-

1. His younger brother Frederick, who had married a Livonian countess and lived at Dorpat.

drained land it overlooked; here and there older mansions of the original Maryland patrician landowners were gradually giving way to the new city pattern. Yet this was the city that boasted one of the country's greatest houses—Hoban's home for the President, then without its north and south colonnades—and by far the country's noblest building project —the daringly conceived United States Capitol, crowning the city's most imposing hill. When the Latrobes came to Washington, the exterior walls of the two wings of the Capitol were practically complete, but nothing had been done aboveground on the central section; the building was as magnificent in conception, and still as incoherent in appearance, as the entire city for which it was the sole *raison d'être*. Only on the far side of Rock Creek, along the Potomac and the canal around its falls, was there any considerable district of cohesive development, for Georgetown had existed even before the Revolution and its quiet brick houses and occasional mansions were the result of its favorable situation.

Foreign diplomats laughed at Washington and at what seemed to them its extraordinary pretensions; they disliked its climate and hated its dust and its mud. Tom Moore displayed his anti-Republican prejudices in reviling it. Congressmen from New York or Virginia, from New Hampshire or the Carolinas, were appalled at its rawness and the crowded inconvenience of its boarding houses; their wives were struck by the primitiveness of the city, by the difficulties of keeping house, and by the fact that a horse or a carriage was absolutely necessary, since their friends might be far away in Georgetown or miles up the hill near the Capitol. As it had been christened by the witty Portuguese Abbé Correa, it was the city of magnificent distances, and those distances usually had to be traversed over unpaved and undrained roads. It is perhaps no wonder that there arose in Congress frequent agitation to move the government away—back to New York or Philadelphia, even to Baltimore or the West—so hopeless seemed the struggle to create a real city. But these movements were often mere expressions of pique or disappointment; there was no force behind them when it actually came to collecting votes. Latrobe called them "intrigues."[2] The men of vision prevailed, and the capital little by little came into being.

Latrobe himself was acutely conscious of this strange, unfinished char-

2. In a letter of February 13, 1808, to George Clymer, president of the Bank of Philadelphia.

acter of the city, but he was conscious too—as were hundreds of others—of the opportunity for gain its growth might bring. On an earlier visit he had leased a lot at Sixth and C Streets Northwest and, instead of holding it for investment, as most men did, had tried to make it income-producing by building on it a "painting room" or studio for Gilbert Stuart. When Stuart left, Latrobe held on to the lot and later added to the original building to make a little factory for steam engines—an equally profitless venture, as it turned out. Typical of the replies he made to acquaintances who had invested in Washington real estate and were continually writing him for information about their holdings is that to James Martin, Jamaica, Long Island (July 21, 1810):

Your lots all lie in that district of the city which may be called Terra Incognita Borealis—to the north of Massachusetts Avenue, a part of the town which is admirably calculated for the pasturing of lean cattle . . . for some years to come. . . . Between the President's House and the Capitol & in the neighborhood of the Navy Yard, lots are now selling at a price above their value, namely from 10 to 25 cents p. superficial foot, but in every other part they are a mere drug . . .

During the last years of the decade, however, the growth of the city accelerated, and building for speculation became the ruling passion. Latrobe tells of this new development graphically in a letter (July 17, 1810) to his friend Thomas Law, who had gone away from the town for an extended stay:

Between the Capitol & President's house, there is a great bustle of building. Huddleston, the stone cutter fills up with good brick houses the space between Lindsay's & Charles Jones, so that square will be complete. They are also building on the other side . . . & in a variety of other straggling situations. The Bank of Washington are also going to build next door to your house occupied by Poydras. . . . Carol [sic] [3] complains of ill treatment. He has now almost all his houses on the hill on his hands. . . .

---

3. The Carol referred to was Daniel Carroll of Duddington. Julien Poydras was elected Orleans Territorial delegate to Congress in 1809. Thomas Law, to whom this letter was written, may well be considered one of the founders of the city of Washington. He had come there, in 1794, with a large fortune made in India, where he had had an important government position. This fortune was invested in Washington real estate through the ill-fated firm of Morris, Nicholson & Greenleaf (part of Robert Morris's overextended real-estate ventures), and Law had built numbers of the earliest brick mansions in the city. He had married Eliza Parke Custis, a granddaughter of Martha Washington, but they were divorced

Yet in this unkempt, uncomfortable town there was a gay, often luxurious and vivid social life—a life of free association with some of the most influential personalities of the time. The very smallness of the population made for intimate acquaintanceship; the inconvenience of the great distances usually transformed even a routine call into a stay of some hours or the sharing of a meal. Essentially this was a quadrapartite society: the President and his official family (the Cabinet members and their staffs), a fairly permanent group for at least the life of a single administration; the ministers of foreign countries and their entourages; the members of Congress (especially the senators, who came for longer terms than the representatives); and a group of important professional people, especially lawyers, ministers, and army and navy officers. Unlike New York or even Philadelphia, Washington was a world in which it was men of official position who dominated, not businessmen; though money had its place, money alone counted for little. It is significant, for instance, that the Thorntons, though their comparative poverty was notorious, held a high position in Washington society.

During the Latrobes' earlier years in the capital, Jefferson was President and his idealistic and intellectualized democracy was in control. Some of the more stuffy Federalists might complain of the letdown of social barriers, yet the tradition Jefferson had set was evident long after he had been replaced. And the Madisons, though Mrs. Madison was a thoroughly sophisticated and socially trained hostess, never forgot their Jeffersonian principles. The new First Lady might be the most fashionably dressed American in the town, but the Presidential levees were as democratic as any that Jefferson had held and, except for the comparative absence of Westerners, as any that Jackson would hold later. Latrobe

---

in 1810. He was probably at his Vermont farm near Westminster, where he often spent his summers, when this letter was written. All his life he was an enthusiastic believer in the future of Washington and a worker for its betterment, and he was instrumental in obtaining the early passage of the Act authorizing the rebuilding of the government buildings after they were burned by the British in 1814. His brother Edward was chief counsel for the defense in the famous trial of Warren Hastings and was later created Lord Ellenborough. Two sons born of an earlier marriage in India were also famous in Washington history: John Law as an attorney, and Edward as a financier. Thomas Law was one of the organizers of the Columbia Institute in 1816, and Latrobe was a member of its first executive committee. See Allen C. Clark, *Greenleaf and Law in the Federal City* (Washington: Roberts, 1901).

himself was surprised; even after twelve years in the country he could hardly imagine such wholesale hospitality. He wrote George Harrison, in Philadelphia (June 30, 1809): "Mrs. Madison gives drawing rooms every Wednesday. The first one was very numerously attended by none but respectable people. The second, La, la. The last by a perfect rabble in beards and boots . . ."

Mrs. Samuel Harrison Smith has left such a vivid picture of the day-by-day activities of a Washington hostess at that time [4] that little more need be added. In reading her graphic pages, however, it is well to remember that although she was the wife of one of Jefferson's most enthusiastic supporters—and herself fell a victim to his natural and honest charm—she had been brought up a Pennsylvania Federalist, with just that little touch of primness and innate feeling of superiority which so often distinguished the genus. To her, genuine democracy always seemed a little shocking. That is one of the reasons that lay behind the feud which developed later between the Latrobes and the Smiths and thus perhaps kept the Latrobe name from ever appearing in Mrs. Smith's fascinating pages.

This family feud was particularly unfortunate not only because of Mr. Smith's eminent position as a publicist and his wife's as a social arbiter but also because earlier the two families had been on such intimate terms that the Smiths had invited the Latrobes to stay with them on their first visit to Washington; they had been, as well, close friends of the Hazlehursts in Philadelphia. The bad feeling was the result of an unavailing letter Latrobe had written to Governor Snyder of Pennsylvania (who had married one of Latrobe's Antes cousins) recommending that Mrs. Smith's brother, Andrew Bayard, a Federalist, be continued as state auctioneer despite his party. Latrobe had no reason to love Andrew, for it was Andrew, he claimed, who had prevented the passage by the Select Council of Philadelphia of a resolution of thanks to Latrobe on the completion of the waterworks. Solely out of friendship for the Hazlehursts and the Smiths, however, he wrote the letter (November 20, 1808) and later pressed the matter personally when he happened to be in Lancaster that winter. But the governor was obdurate; his election vote, he claimed, had been so overwhelming that he could keep

4. *The First Forty Years of Washington Society,* edited by Gaillard Hunt (New York: Scribner's, 1906).

no Federalist in office. Latrobe reported this to Samuel Hazlehurst and said that the only effective pressure would be for the Smiths to obtain a letter to Snyder from some highly placed officer in the Federal government, and he added that he doubted whether in their position they would descend to such tactics. Andrew Bayard apparently took umbrage both at his sister and at Hazlehurst, and Mrs. Smith in turn seized on this as an opportunity to break off all relations with the family. From the long letter of explanation which Latrobe wrote his friend Smith (September 22, 1809), it would almost seem that Mrs. Smith had used the Bayard episode as a convenient hook on which to hang some long-felt resentment—probably a combination of politics, spleen, and even some envy. She was instinctively distrustful of those more daring and more imaginative than herself.

An instance in point—trivial perhaps, but interesting for the light it throws on that early Washington society—is furnished by Mme Jerome Bonaparte, née Elizabeth Patterson of Baltimore. She was very beautiful, and knew it; she was at the peak of fashion, and knew that too; and she combined awareness of both in her actions and her dress. Empire fashions were the reverse of concealing, and she outdid even the beauties of the imperial court in Paris in the low cut of her gowns, the sheerness of the materials, the small amount of what she wore beneath. Washington was scandalized—and loved it. Latrobe was diverted; as he wrote Joshua Gilpin in Philadelphia from Washington (February 20, 1804):

> Jerome and Madame Bonaparte have amused us considerably for the last fortnight. She is certainly pretty, her youth and singular fortune excuse her if she be not very wise; of her it might be said, "I see thee beautiful; I believe thee wise" [a translation of Latrobe's Italian]. She has much scandalized the lovers of drapery, and disgusted the admirers even of the naked figure . . .

Later, in 1817-18, as recorded by Latrobe's son John, Mme Bonaparte became an intimate of the Latrobe household. But to Mrs. Smith and her particular friends Elizabeth Patterson Bonaparte was not a source of amusement; she was an outrage, a threat to the sacredness of the American home. Mrs. Smith therefore took the lead in organizing a group of Washington women who agreed to attend no parties at which Mme Bonaparte was to be present, unless she put on more clothes—a boycott in the cause of convention. The difference between the two attitudes is basic.

There is one more element in the break, and this is perhaps the most fundamental, though neither side ever mentioned it. Mrs. Smith's most intimate Washington friend was Mrs. Thornton. Each was continually trotting to the other's house for petty aid, for advice, or for gossip. But Mrs. Thornton, though she never descended to the level of her husband in her prosecution of his controversies, was definitely his worshiper and his partisan. She was a passable draftsman and helped him with his drawings. In a way, when Jefferson had appointed Latrobe Surveyor of the Public Buildings and Latrobe for good and sufficient reasons had radically altered the Thornton design, could she help feeling involved herself? Was it not an affront to her as well as to her husband?

The Thornton-Latrobe antagonism was indeed inevitable, since Thornton was a rabid Federalist, proud as a peacock and combative as a robin. Friends of both families tried to patch things up between the two; possibly even the Smiths had been among these peacemakers. But by 1808 the breach had become complete, and Latrobe had been forced to sue Thornton for libel. In the almost daily chats between Mrs. Smith and Mrs. Thornton could this have been overlooked? Mrs. Smith was under Mrs. Thornton's influence in many ways; perhaps in breaking with the Latrobes, as in the Patterson matter, she was "taking a stand" and supporting her friend Mrs. Thornton rather than merely showing umbrage at the Andrew Bayard imbroglio. No wonder the Latrobes, in some things strangely innocent, were perplexed.

Yet even this break could not deeply affect the Latrobes' Washington life. Those with whom they most loved to associate were above such petty schisms. For friends like the Madisons, the families of the two successive Secretaries of the Navy Robert Smith and Paul Hamilton, the Russian minister Dashkoff and his American wife, Robert Goodloe Harper (the Senator from Maryland, who though a Federalist was a staunch and lifelong friend and customarily had Sunday dinners at the Latrobe home whenever he was in Washington), and the Joel Barlows (he a diplomat, poet, and radical—a fellow spirit), the Smith break could have been merely a subject for smiles. And among Latrobe's old Virginia friends were the Bushrod Washingtons, now the owners and residents of Mount Vernon. One of the British embassy secretaries, Foster, later the British Ambassador, had married an English cousin of Latrobe's, and the English embassy was always open to him and his family. The French embassy also sought them out, and with Sérurier Latrobe had close social relations. His linguistic ability and his wide European background created common interests with the foreign colony. It is obvious, too, that Latrobe was one of the Administration's inner circle. His position as Surveyor of the Public Buildings necessarily involved frequent contacts with the President, but the bonds were stronger than that. Again and again he refers in letters to dinners with the President, sometimes tête-à-tête.

Outside the political world there were also many close contacts. The Hunters, the family of a well-known Presbyterian minister, were near neighbors of the "Navy Yard House." The famous Commodore David Porter, then a Captain, was an assiduous visitor at the Latrobes' in 1807 and early 1808, as well as a suitor for Lydia's hand. There were the Robert Brents, among the wealthiest of Washingtonians; their daughter was Lydia's closest Washington friend, and Brent was at one time mayor of the city and later owner of the magnificent house Brentwood which Latrobe designed for him. Then, too, a continual string of visitors to Washington called on or dined with the family. The diminutive Miss Juliana Miller, a maiden lady from Philadelphia, witty and kind—a favorite companion of Mrs. Latrobe's—made them extended visits, bringing with her the latest gossip from Philadelphia and thus uniting, for Mary, the past and the present. She was a continual and special delight to the children, John, Julia, and Ben—almost the ideal "maiden aunt." And behind the scenes, to keep the household running easily and quietly, was the ever faithful and efficient if sometimes crotchety Kitty (Catherine McCausland), who for years until her death was the family factotum—nurse at first, then housekeeper and friend.

The Latrobes, in fact, had what was virtually a salon in Washington—another indication that in that milieu money had not the all-powerful importance it later achieved. Robert Fulton, introduced to them by their friend Joel Barlow (who had been Fulton's patron in Paris), was often in and out and before long became an intimate associate and friend—a fact that rendered the later developments in Pittsburgh all the more distressing. Washington Irving, visiting Washington in 1811 for a week, dined with the Latrobes and records the fact.[5] Paul Svenin, or Svinin, the hawk-eyed, inquisitive, and understanding secretary of the Russian

5. In a letter to Henry Brevoort, in *Life and Letters of Washington Irving,* edited by Pierre Monroe Irving (New York: Putnam's, 1862-4), vol. 1, p. 268.

legation—an artist, too, like Latrobe—was a frequent visitor. Mr. and Mrs. Henry Clay were often guests, and Latrobe helped them professionally in the design of their house Ashland in Lexington, Kentucky.

One is struck by the varied character of those represented as well as by the fact that all had some similarities. A broad foreign background, wide intellectual interests, a brilliant and forceful type of imagination, an excellent education, artistic skill of some kind—these seem the hallmarks of the frequenters of the Latrobe drawing room. Even the famous Salem merchant and financier Derby was included because of his musical skill. Latrobe himself was a trained musician. Mary had a lovely singing voice—"cultivated," wrote her son John, "under the instructions of the best masters of Philadelphia of the day." [6] Some of their parties were musical, with Mary or Miss Brent at the piano and occasionally singing, and Latrobe perhaps playing the clarinet. But it was more than pleasure in music that was the attraction there, more even than Mary's wit and warm-heartedness or her husband's imaginative and forthright conversation; it was doubtless the feeling that here was a home where innocence and affection reigned and where in addition there was learning coupled with imagination—a center that welcomed all who dreamed or worked for human betterment and freedom—a place, however gay, of essential idealism, free from the boring chatter of the marketplace and from the rankling bitterness of political controversy. Here poets and scientists, artists and writers, men of the world and men of ideas could meet without restraint.

Himself at least half artist, Latrobe had an especial fondness for artists and a deep interest in their success. The story of the Gilbert Stuart painting room is indicative. Learning in 1803 that Stuart was moving to Washington and wished a studio there, Latrobe erected expressly for his use a small building on the lot he himself had leased. This Stuart was to rent from him, to help Latrobe carry the lot as well as to benefit the artist. On learning that Stuart had finally started for Washington in December of that year, Latrobe wrote John Lenthall on December 13:

> I have understood that Mr. Stuart has departed for Washington. If so, you will see one of the greatest, if not the most pleasant, originals in the United States. His presence, and probably his conduct, leaves me nothing certain to

---

6. John E. Semmes, *John H. B. Latrobe and His Times, 1800-1891* (Baltimore: Remington [c1917]).

say respecting his painting room, but . . . I shall come prepared to make good all deficiencies on my arrival . . .

Stuart came, took possession of his atelier, and remained there for over a year, but the uncertain condition of his health and his erratic habits made it basically an unproductive period for him. Latrobe, in Washington in the spring of 1805, was shocked at what he found and on March 12 he wrote to John Vaughn, a friend of them both in Philadelphia, that Stuart was in a bad way:

All last summer he had a violent ague & fever. It is now returned upon him, and he cannot paint at present. I fear indeed that he will lay his bones in Washington, and it seems of the highest importance that some of his family should attend him. He is miserably off, though his life & his residence . . . are of his own choice. He has one man servant, who does exactly what he pleases, & is seldom with him. He has shut himself up in a little building never intended for a habitation but only for a painting room; where he boards himself, *after a fashion,* with the assistance of his man servant when he can get him to the place, and where he sleeps. The house is remarkably comfortable & warm, but in the present state of the drainage of the city the situation must be unhealthy in warm weather.—I could do nothing with him, not even get him to paint my own portrait,—which, if he ever paints it, will cost me 1000 dollars, & more. He had resolved when I last saw him, to finish the pictures he had in hand, which he thought he could do in six weeks,—begin no new ones,—and move off to the northward. But should he continue sick there will be an end to all his exertions, & I think he runs the risk of dying for want of good nursing where he is.—I shall write to him,—but he is a man who answers no letters. Thank heaven—at least my family ought to thank heaven,—that I have no genius,—if this is the orbit in which genius must move.—And indeed it generally is so . . .

Latrobe did write Stuart the very next day (March 13). He begins by attempting to arouse his interest by sending him a print as an example of the kind of engravings that could be made of some of his portraits. There is a suggestion, too, of another portrait in Stuart's hands—perhaps one of Jefferson—that apparently was finished and ready for engraving (John Vaughn seems to have been connected with this in some way). He goes on:

Let me in the meantime intreat you to leave that sink of your health, your Genius, & your interests, Washington. I often am angry with you for having staid so long. Get into the packet at Georgetown if you cannot bear a carriage,—get away any where, but get away.

As to myself, I was very sick for four or five days previously to my departure, and had I staid longer, it would not have been so easy to have moved me. My illness prevented me calling upon you.—

God bless you & give you resolution to start off to a climate more healthy & less tainted with fraud, speculation, marsh miasmas, & the insolence of clerkships.

But Stuart lingered on until July, when he left the city. He never paid Latrobe a cent of rent; nor, so far as we can tell, did Latrobe ever dun him for the debt—such was the consideration he felt was due to artists. Later the building was "rented" to a Mr. Boyle, another painter, who maintained a kind of museum there; he was connected in some way to one of the Hazlehurst cousins, and evidently he paid no rent either.

Latrobe had good reason to doubt the ability of artists or art dealers to discharge their debts. When he left for Washington in 1807 (as has already been noted) he sublet his Second Street house in Philadelphia to a certain Delormeric, who had a valuable collection of paintings for sale but no buyers, and Delormeric remained there till the expiration of Latrobe's lease without paying him a cent. Four years later when Delormeric wrote for further help, Latrobe's answer was a firm negative (October 3, 1811):

You inform me you were the loser by occupying my rooms in Second Street, at an expense to me of $125. If you made a bad speculation at my expense, I cannot help it . . . I have a house in this city. Mr. Stuart, the painter took it of me, occupied it for two years, & went to Boston without paying me a cent . . . Mr. Boyle, of Baltimore, then succeeded. He painted also & had a museum. He also remained two years, filled the house with negroes, & decamped $125 in my debt. Having thus paid for the encouragement of painting & Museums above $500 in cash without any advantage whatever to myself, except the acknowledgment which you are willing to make me, I must decline during the rest of my life having anything whatever to do with paintings, museums, or their proprietors . . .

Yet Latrobe's enthusiasm for art and his vision of its importance to the new country continued. He fought for sculpture in the United States Capitol and was instrumental in bringing over Andrei and Franzoni from Italy. An ardent supporter of decorative painting, he employed George Bridport whenever he could and gave him letters of introduction to all his influential friends. Similarly, he tried to help a French painter and miniaturist, E. Boudet, with introductions to the Claiborne family, Bishop Carroll, and others. And he took care to see that "his Italians" Andrei and Franzoni got other work when their Washington labors lagged and that models of their figures for the Capitol were exhibited at the Academy in Philadelphia.

Deeply, too, Latrobe felt the need for artists' associations. He knew what the American Philosophical Society had done for American thinkers, naturalists, and other scientists and how it had raised American ideals at home at the same time that it had enhanced American prestige abroad. Thus he became an early member of the Academy of Arts in Philadelphia, in 1805, and a frequent exhibitor in its exhibitions.[7] When later several artists, thinking that the Academy had become too much dominated by its wealthy lay patrons, formed the Society of Artists of the United States, he joined that as well and had the honor and the pleasure of conveying to President Madison (January 16, 1811) the Society's invitation to become its chief patron; Madison graciously accepted, and he did more—he offered a present. As Latrobe wrote George Murray, one of the founders (January 31):

> I enclose the answer of the President U.S. . . . He gave it to me in the form in which I sent it, himself, & asked . . . whether having accepted the office, he ought not to promote our views in some way or other . . . I told him, that I doubted not but it would be agreeable to his feelings, so it would be highly flattering & acceptable to the Society to receive from him any work of excellence in the arts . . . to place in their exhibition room . . . He begged me then to look out for some suitable object to present. . . . Will you suggest something of the kind. We have nothing here. I think perhaps he had best send to Paris for something . . .

Latrobe's efforts on behalf of the Society were crowned by what he always considered one of the pleasantest and most flattering offers he ever received: he was invited to give the Society's annual oration in May. The

7. According to the catalogues of the Pennsylvania Academy of Fine Arts, the 1811 exhibition included, by Latrobe, a landscape on the Schuylkill River, a view of the Richmond penitentiary, and five large drawings of the Capitol at Washington—two plans, two elevations, and a perspective. In 1812 he exhibited a view of the seat of Myers Fisberg, Esq., and another Schuylkill River landscape, and in 1818 a perspective of the Baltimore Cathedral. His wife also painted; Mary Latrobe is credited with two views from nature in the 1812 exhibition. I owe this information to the kindness of Miss Anna W. Rutledge.

address was given and printed and is an important document in the early art annals of the country.[8]

The notes of the architect bring us also a vivid picture of Washington life in another field—the purlieus of "enthusiastic religion." In a notebook labeled III, containing comments on life, philosophy, and literature made between 1806 and 1809, there is a full description of a camp meeting (August 6, 1809), beginning with an interesting sidelight on his wife:

> I have always endeavored to prevent my wife from being led by her curiosity to attend the meetings of the Methodists.—With the most rational, but very pious & sincere religious sentiments,—she joins a warmth of imagination, which might receive a shock, if not an impression from the *incantations* which form the business of their assemblies. A camp meeting however is a thing so outrageous in its form & in its practices, that I resolved to go to one held a few miles from Georgetown in Virginia, under the auspices of some very good citizens,—principally Mr. Henry Foxall the great Iron-founder.—

The meeting was held about seven or eight miles out on the Leesburg road, and as the Latrobes got within a mile of it the crowd increased, with

> parties of well dressed blacks of both sexes returning on foot towards the city, & of ill dressed white boys hurrying forward . . . [further on] we could distinguish among the trees, half concealed by the underwood, houses, chaises, light waggons, hacks, & a crowd of men & women, in the midst of whom we presently arrived . . . Crowds of negreos & mullatoes tastily dressed stood

8. *Anniversary Oration Pronounced Before the Society of Artists of the United States on the eighth of May, 1811,* by B. Henry Latrobe, Fellow of the American Philosophical Society, of the Academy of Arts, and one of the Vice-Presidents of the Society of Artists of the United States [New York, 1811]. This address starts with a refutation of the notion that the fine arts have no place in a republic; Latrobe cites Greece and Rome as examples and emphasizes the value of monuments to great citizens. Similarly he attacks the notion that the times are not ripe for art; all times are ripe for it. Art is a hardy plant, the author states, which will spring up everywhere, and he mentions the figureheads carved by Rush, which he says "seem rather to draw the ship after them than to be impelled by the vessel." He would like to see engravings made of them and broadcast. But art needs support; artists need sympathetic patronage. As an example of such an understanding patron, Latrobe names Samuel H. Fox, recently dead, and praises him as the real force behind the building of the Bank of Pennsylvania; to him, rather than to the architect, should go the gratitude of Philadelphia—"to the mild but powerful influence and discriminating taste of this one man." The artists are here; with patronage like that of Fox, the arts in America will prosper. Incidentally, Latrobe states that he considers Philadelphia his real home.

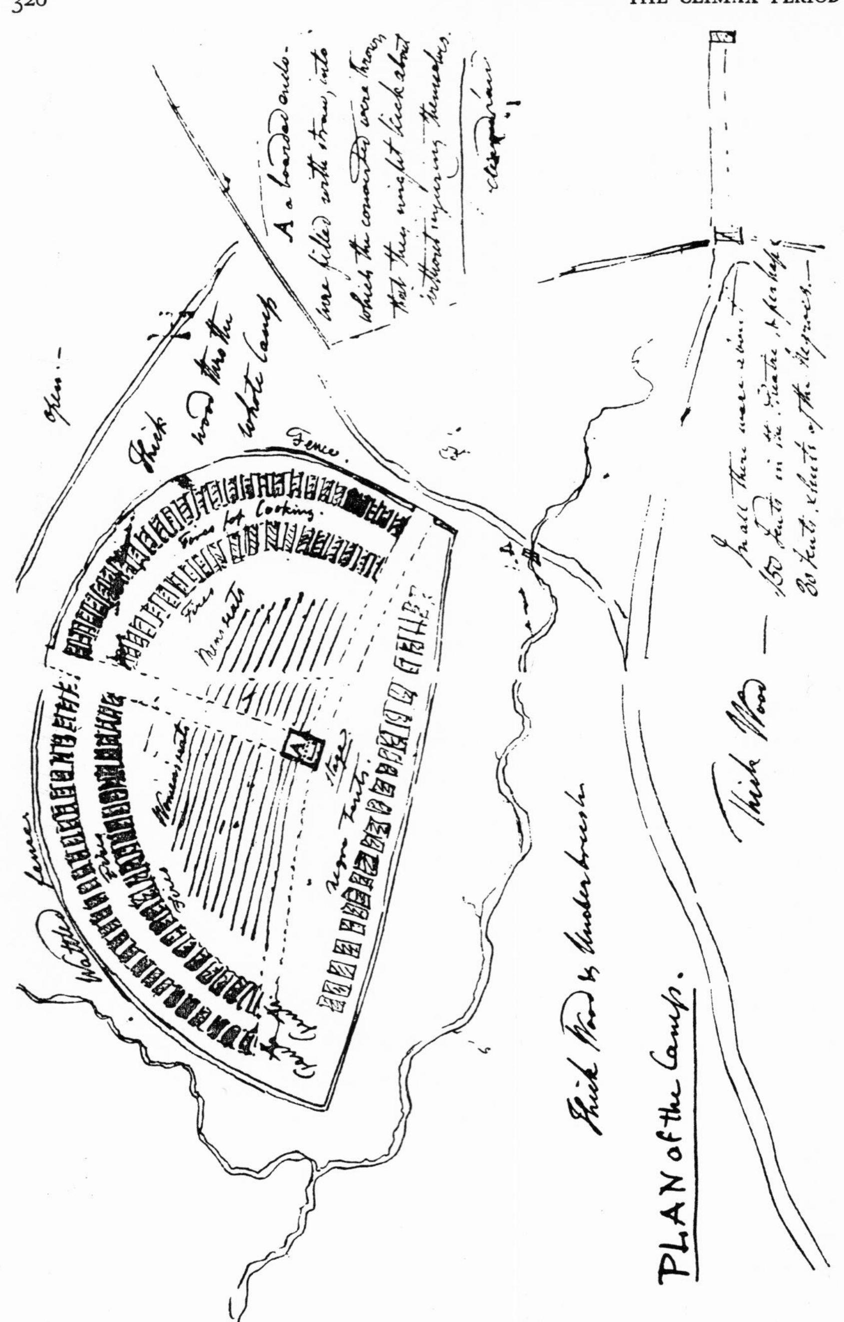

PLAN of the Camp.
Thick Wood
Fence.
Fires for Cooking.
Fires
Mens seats
Womens seats
Stage
Negro Tents

From the Latrobe journals

FIGURE 19. Camp Meeting near Washington. Plan and Sections.

among the trees, & the groups looked as if any motives but religious ones had assembled them. . . . We at length reached the camp . . . It was placed on the descent of a narrow ridge, at the foot of which ran a small stream . . .

The camp itself, of which Latrobe gives a plan and section, consisted of two concentric semicircular arcs of tents, separated by a street for cooking fires, surrounding a roughly semicircular swale in which were the benches—for women on one side and men on the other—focused on the stage or pulpit. Behind the stage was a row of tents for Negroes, and directly in front of it "a boarded enclosure filled with straw, into which the converted were thrown that they might kick about without injuring themselves." When the Latrobes learned that men and women could not sit together they took their places, standing, at the head of the center aisle,

from whence everything could be seen & heard. There I staid for about an hour during which Mr. Bunn, a blacksmith of G. Town, one of the most eminent Preachers of the Methodists spoke [with] immense rapidity & exertion to the following effect. . . . It appeared that his subject was the preaching of St. Paul before Felix & Festus. He was in the midst of his discourse when I heard him exclaim:—"Temperance, Temperance, Temperance.—I say & so says St. Paul *temperance,*—not self denial, no he asks no favors of you, no, only temperance.—And what is temperance,—Paul had no communication with women, none at all. Peter carried about with him a sister named Lucilla, I suppose she was his wife, else he had no business with her, this I call temperance,—one woman was enough for Peter. . . ." Then he spoke of the judgement to come—"That's the point, the judgement to come,—when the burning billows of hell wash up against the soul of the glutton & the miser,—what good do all his victuals & his wine, & his bags of gold;—do they allay the fiery torment, the thirst that burns him, the parching that sears his lips, do they frighten away old Satan who is ready to devour him, think of that: this is the judgement to come, when hell gapes, & the fire roars,—Oh pour [sic] sinful souls, will ye be damned, will ye, will ye, will ye be damned,—no, no, no, no, don't be damned, now ye pray & groan & strive with the spirit." (A general groaning & shrieking was now heard from all quarters which the artful preacher immediately suppressed by returning to his text)—"and so it was with Festus, he trembled, he trembled, he trembled, (—during these words the Preacher threw out both his arms sideways at full length, & shook himself violently, so as to make his arms quiver with astonishing velocity . . .)—he trembled every bone shook, he strove with the spirit, & he was almost overcome, but he conquered, he was afraid of the Jews, saving grace was not for him, etc.—"

[A little later] I found him further advanced in his business. A general groaning was going on,—in several parts of the Camp, women were shrieking, & just under the stage there was an uncommon bustle & cry, which I understood arose from some persons who were under conversion.—

He was proceeding thus: "There, there, stands an unconverted coxcomb; dressed in his God & his delight,—will it help him then, when he must face the fiery gulph, when he cries mercy, mercy, mercy, & there is no mercy,—when hell burns & roars, what then is his smartness & his buckishness, of no use, none, not any, any use to allay hellfire, which calls for him to devour him;—but there I see another,—a woman. Oh, how grace strives & the spirit works, oh for power, power, power,—see how her bosom heaves & throbs, how her whole form is agitated, how the tears start from her eyes, how they burst forth, oh, my brethren pray for her, pray for her, see how she trembles, how she trembles, how she trembles."

(Here he repeated his trembling) "how she trembles,—and now comes the stroke of grace, the stroke," (at every time he pronounced the word he struck his right hand into his left palm so as to produce an astonishingly loud clap)—"the stroke again, and another stroke (repeated about 20 times) and now it works, it works, it works, Oh God for Power, power, power, power,

power, power, power, power, power (roaring like a bull),—there it is, now she has it, glory, glory, glory, etc." *By this time the noise of the congregation was equal to that of the preacher, & he took the opportunity to receive a drink of a glass of water, of which he seemed in very great need, for he was quite exhausted.*

[And so on and on, till B. H. and Mary left.] Henry our son, who remained at the Camp till midnight reported that the conversions were numerous, & in the same hysterical style in all the tents, & that the negroes after the Camp was illuminated sang & danced the methodist turnabout in the most indefatigable & entertaining manner.

Enthusiasm has its charms, & as this is the only public diversion in which the scattered inhabitants can indulge, it would be a pity to suppress it, even by the ridicule to which it is so open.—The night scene of the illumination of the woods, the novelty of a camp especially to the women and children, the dancing & singing, & the pleasure of a crowd, so tempting to the most fashionable,—are in fact enjoyments which human nature everywhere provides for herself, in her most savage as well as most polished state.—Let the congregation rejoice & wellcome. But as to the Preacher, who lives by such dishonest means,—"to his own Master he standeth or falleth."

Thus Latrobe, with his customary understanding, closes his account of one of the country's most characteristic early customs.

Latrobe himself, though keeping as aloof from political battles as his position permitted, was anything but a political agnostic. He was part of his age, a convinced democrat, an ardent patriot. Soon after the tragic Burr-Hamilton duel, he wrote George Read in Newcastle (July 22, 1804): "I have not been able to work myself up into the fashionable pitch of grief for the death of Mr. Hamilton. Other folks besides myself are also refractory . . ." He despised chicanery and deplored the compromises to which politicians descended (his letters are often eloquent on that), but he bore his own part staunchly. He tried to preserve a native dignity and gentle manners even when enemies (chiefly Federalist) were yapping at his heels. The Washington *Federalist* contained attack after attack on him, on his competency, on his work at the Capitol. He was accused of extravagance, of feathering his own nest, and—by innuendo—of dishonesty. It hurt him profoundly but until Thornton's final outrageous letter forced him to act he bore it patiently, secure in his own rectitude. He was bitterly opposed to dueling at a time when dueling was achieving a new status in American life—to the endless harm and disgrace of the country—and his distaste increased as he grew older and more aware of the fantastic lengths to which gossip could go in many Washington circles. Thus in a letter of protest to Thornton as early as April 28, 1804, he speaks of the insults—planned and carefully arranged—that Thornton has offered him and that according to custom would lead to a challenge, but at the same time he acknowledges the hospitality he had received at his hands:

> For a considerable time I have been convinced that an open rupture would be more honorable to me than even that show of good understanding which has prevailed between us; and which was kept up last winter by the respect of my wife for the ladies of your family: a respect which led me to accept an invitation to a Ball at your house. For the civility of this invitation . . . I feel myself indebted and particularly for the transmission of your essay on Negro Emancipation; a mark of respect, as unintelligible on any principle of consistency, as it would have been flattering had it been possible for it to be sincere. . . .

He goes on to recapitulate the entire controversy and to remind Thornton of his own constant efforts to preserve peace and pleasant relations between them and continues:

> My last call upon you is the strongest proof of how far I was willing to go. The insulting treatment I received closed all further prospect of amicable arrangement, which I might have expected from your politeness or your understanding.
>
> I now stand on the ground from which you drove Hallet, and Hadfield to ruin. You may prove victorious over me also; but the contest will not be without spectators. . . . I shall not court public discussion. It is in my power, *however,* more than in my inclination, to show you in a more ridiculous light, even, than were I, as is the fashion after such a correspondence, to call you to the field . . .

Seven years later the matter of dueling came up again. Under date of August 15, 1811, there is a "Memorandum of what passed between Captn Jones, Commander of the U.S. sloop Wasp and B.H.L. in the Navy Yard on Monday evening, Aug. 12," which reads:

> About six o'clock on Monday evening, prior to my leaving the yard, I went as my custom is to the Bell Post, where Captain Cassin, Commandant, . . . in the absence of Captn Tingey, sat in conversation with Mr. Geo. Beale . . . I took my seat also, and in a few minutes Captain Jones came up . . . I asked Captain Jones, when he was likely to sail from Alexandria,

where his ship lay. He told me, ironically, that for aught he knew he might lay there all winter. . . . Which led to his opinion of the yard, answered by Cassin. His opinion of the waste of money in architecture and machinery, answered by B.H.L., & finally his opinion of the Secretary, answered by all. Just before he left, he told me that I should hear from him next day. I answered, that if by that he meant that he would send me a challenge, he would be disappointed if he expected me to meet him. That I should certainly not prove my courage by risking the life of a man of my age, family & standing in society against the common calumniator of all those with whom I acted . . . He was very near me the next day on the Common, but he kept his distance . . .

And the next day (August 16) Latrobe reported the matter in general to the Secretary of the Navy but did not send his "Memorandum." It is shocking to realize on what frivolous grounds challenges were sent and duels, sometimes fatal, were fought.

Latrobe had frequent opportunities for the exercise of patience under attack. Not only did he become the target for Thornton's disappointment, anger, and envy; but also as an important appointee of Jefferson, in a position where his every move was open to scrutiny and where he had control (or part control) of the spending of large sums of public money, he was a logical target for all the Federalist writers. Long before, in 1798, he had had his taste of their bile, in Cobbett's sneering paragraph about his play, *The Apology.* Six years later the Washington *Federalist* was in full cry, and from Wilmington Latrobe wrote Lenthall in Washington (November 2, 1804):

I find by the [Philadelphia] *Aurora* that the *Federalist* has commenced an attack upon me. Pray get me the papers collected in which the filth is thrown, that I may have the pleasure to see how I look when dragged through the Kennel. . . . The attack will help our Democratic Congress to appropriate in opposition. Anything to cure the headache in the pocket . . .[9]

On December 1, 1806, Latrobe took cognizance of a further attack by Thornton and of more yapping by the *Federalist;* he wrote Thornton:

The pamphlet you caused to be laid on the desks of Members of Congress attacked me by name, and in a manner which, in my opinion, nothing

9. The *Aurora* article stressed both the low quality and the high cost of the work that had been accomplished on the United States Capitol before Latrobe's appointment, suggested that corruption had been rampant, and complimented Latrobe on bringing order out of chaos.

could have provoked. I did not notice it at that time, nor yet the very scurrilous abuse of me in the Washington *Federalist,* some of which public report attributed to you . . .

But Thornton could not be placated; the attacks continued and culminated at last in the letter of April 20, 1808, which Thornton had printed in the *Federalist* and which led to Latrobe's suit against him for libel.

Another of Latrobe's long-term enemies was Oliver Evans, the great American engineer—inventor of the mechanized flour mill and popularizer of the high-pressure steam engine. Evans thought Latrobe had done his engine less than justice in a report to the American Philosophical Society [10] and he, too, saw an opportunity to join the pack, perhaps egged on by Thornton himself. He sent a letter to the *Federalist* supporting Thornton's attack but changing some of its charges. Latrobe, thoroughly aroused, wrote Jonathan Findlay, editor of the Washington *Federalist* (May 20, 1808):

I understand that Evans has sent a piece to the press contradicting Dr. Thornton's statement as to my having been a carver of chimney pieces, & reducing his assertion to the keeping of a statuary yard . . . It is a most humiliating task . . . to vindicate my professional character against the rage of a Thornton & the stupidity & officiousness of an Evans . . .

Even then, however, the *Federalist* kept the matter alive. Hoban, the original architect of the President's House, joined the fray and Latrobe, after discovering his attacker's identity, wrote the *Federalist* editor (October 17, 1808):

I thank you for your letter . . . in which you communicate to me that the author of the piece published in your paper of the 8th inst. signed "a plain man" is James Hoban. . . . As to Mr. Hoban, his personal attack is the more extraordinary, as I certainly could not positively swear to his person . . . I once saw him in 1797, when I del'd to him a letter from one of the Commissioners requesting him to show me the public buildings; and as he did not accompany me . . . his person was soon forgotten.

With this was enclosed another letter to the editor for publication:

---

10. "First Report in Answer to the Enquiry Whether Any and What Improvements Have Been Made in the Construction of Steam Engines in America," read on May 20, 1803, and printed in the *Transactions,* vol. 6 (1809).

> Having discovered the author of the piece . . . I have to answer to the personal abuse . . . that the work which it has been my duty to condemn & tear down was erected while he was superintendent of the public buildings. . . . This notice may serve as a general answer to all he may choose to publish against me . . .

Even the clergy was not free of Federalist fanatics; such a firebrand was the Reverend Mr. Wilmer, to whom Latrobe felt himself forced to write (May 24, 1809):

> A paragraph in the *Monitor* of Thursday last, signed Moses, is generally ascribed to you. The respectability of your professional as well as . . . of your personal character . . . forbids me to believe you capable of that kind of scurrility, which without pretension to wit or even truth disgraces our American press. . . . The scurrilous allusion to me would be undeserving my notice [except that I feel it my duty] to apprize you . . . that . . . the next attack on the part of Moses will not be privately noticed.

The letter apparently was efficacious; no libel suit was necessary.

Most of the anonymous letters sent or handed to him he disregarded, but one contained rumors that could have been dangerous and had to be scotched. When Lenthall was killed (September 23, 1808) by the fall of the Supreme Court vault in the Capitol, his affairs were placed in the hands of his brother-in-law Nicholas King, one of the city surveyors and a friend of Latrobe's. To him Latrobe wrote (August 28, 1809): "Ten days ago I received an anonymous letter, in which is the following passage . . . 'Mr. Lenthall has left . . . a long list of charges against you . . . Mr. King . . . is going to bring them out.'" Of course the whole rumor proved baseless. The anonymous letter, over which Latrobe had pondered and worried for more than a week before writing King, had merely been a malicious attempt to wound. The year before, in 1807, there had been a similarly dangerous anonymous letter, attributed to J. P. Van Ness, which started rumors that circulated widely in Congress. This letter stated that Jefferson had once said that Latrobe had arranged the whole north wing of the Capitol, particularly the courtroom, without the President's knowledge and against his wishes. These rumors were becoming such a threat to the entire project that Latrobe, thoroughly discouraged, felt forced to write directly to Jefferson (April 5, 1811): "I beg that you will have the goodness to communicate to me your own conviction on this head. I do not expect the public buildings to be finished under my direction. As far as I have conducted them, they will not disgrace your presidency . . ." Jefferson, his true friend as always, sent him a full vindication,[11] and Latrobe acknowledged it gratefully in a letter to Jefferson at Monticello (August 1): "For the very full & honorable testimony which you have been so good as to bear to the zeal and integrity with which I conducted the public works during your presidency, I cannot express the satisfaction & gratitude I feel . . ." One canard, at least, had been effectively stopped.

The letters, nevertheless, were gradually wearing down Latrobe's confidence, disturbing his sense of values. Occasionally he came even to doubt himself and his friends. Several anonymous letters, for instance, stated that Mrs. Sweeny, the seamstress-upholsterer who was working on the furnishings for the President's House,[12] was telling everyone that Mrs. Madison herself was talking of Latrobe's extravagance, of his absences from Washington and his inattention to the government business. Latrobe, worried, wrote Mrs. Madison at once. Her answer (September 12, 1809)[13] is a little masterpiece—gentle, strong, tactful, dignified, understanding. It alone would explain the worship she received from so many of her contemporaries. She begins:

> Incredulous indeed must be the ear that receives without belief the "varnished tale," but most happy would it be if you could listen without emotion, to the variety of falsehoods framed but to play on your sensibility . . .
>
> [Then a gentle reproof for his lack of trust.] The letter I have this moment rec[d] from you, gives me uneasiness; because I find my conduct, which always contradicted any opinion, or expression against you, has been insufficient to assure your judgment that I would at least—be consistent.—In the first place my affection for Mrs. Latrobe would in itself prevent my doing injustice to her husband—and in the next I always knew that *I* had no right to animadvert on his journeys, or conduct as a public officer, as it is one of my sources of happiness, never to desire a knowledge of other people's business. Thirdly, I never for a moment doubted your taste or honour in the direction of public buildings, or even in the building of our *little* carriage

11. Dated April 14, 1811. This letter is quoted on page 291.

12. Mrs. Sweeny was the proprietress of Washington's best upholstery store—she was almost what would be called today an interior decorator. She advertised continually in the *National Intelligencer* and evidently had a large and wealthy clientele.

13. This letter is reproduced in Allen C. Clark, *Dolly Madison, Her Life and Letters* (Washington: W. F. Roberts, 1914). The writing is as precise as the style is clear and direct.

. . . [This was the coachee, ordered from Peter Harvie of Philadelphia, which had been unsatisfactory.]

Mrs. Sweeny is a woman of many words—I have never talked with her, or before her, but of her work. In your absence she would release to the Household *terrible* tales of dis-affection from the Capitol—which I lamented for your sake. I can account for Mrs. Sweeny's mis-information to you, only by supposing her offended at my leaving her but little to do, in the house. . . .

I shall be strict in my examination of the servants, when I return, as I wish to know those who have taken the liberty to misrepresent me. I will say little of the anonymous letters but that you excite my surprise at suffering *them* to have the slightest effect upon your spirits. . . . Allow me again to thank you, with all my heart, for the trouble you have taken, in many instances, to oblige and accommodate me—and tho' our enemies may strive to throw around me ungrateful appearances, I shall take a pleasure in contradicting their designs. [The "our enemies" is masterly.]

So again anonymous letters had been proved baseless; yet these continual harassments, public and private, coupled with the uncertain state of public affairs, made him susceptible to offers of other employment, as will appear.

Nevertheless Latrobe was much more than a mere democratic scapegoat for Federalist barbs. All through his Washington residence—temporarily till 1807 and permanently from 1807 to 1813—he was in the closest touch with the most salient figures in governmental administration, who, at least till the War of 1812, backed him and gave him encouragement. And his contacts with these men were not limited to the multitude of questions brought up in connection with the Navy Yard, the President's House, and the Capitol. His letters are full of graphic comments on these important men and of accounts of what they thought and believed. In the days of bitter controversy with England which filled the four years preceding the war he kept his Hazlehurst relatives and his Philadelphia friends well informed on the turns that events were taking.

Another political matter occupied him occasionally during this period—the aftermath of the Burr conspiracy. We have seen how he was subpoenaed as a witness at the Burr trial, though never called to the stand; yet as a potential witness he was in a way a marked man, and when General Wilkinson was tried by a court of inquiry he named Latrobe as one of his witnesses. In a letter to Robert Goodloe Harper (April 15, 1808) Latrobe says of this:

I attended the Court of Inquiry . . . of Genl. Wilkinson . . . He was asked . . . as to the nature of the evidence expected from me . . . He answered, that he believed that I could prove a connexion between Burr and Clarke [which would] strengthen his other proofs, that the foundation of the persecution he suffered was a sympathy in the designs of Burr. . . . I immediately rose & stated that I was unacquainted with the nature of the connexion, but that I would very willingly give testimony . . . as far as my knowledge . . . went . . . I said that my motive . . . was the very contemptuous light in which I was held . . . in Genl. Wilkinson's testimony before the Court in Richmond . . . I repeated all that related to Daniel Clarke [which] amounted to his having given me letters of recommendation to De Mun [evidently when De Mun went south to the Gulf of Mexico on his surveying trip].

A few weeks later Latrobe, apparently feeling that a talk with Wilkinson (who had asked him for a memorandum of his evidence) was necessary in order to clarify his own position, wrote Wilkinson (June 4) to suggest a meeting. But the conference never took place.

The effect of Wilkinson's attitude, however, continued to plague Latrobe. Burr was unforgettable, and all those he had been close to were still under a cloud. Almost three years later Latrobe was still disturbed and wrote Dr. Thomas Ewell in Washington two letters (March 22 and March 25, 1811) telling him at length of the entire matter—exactly what Burr had offered him (the job of building the canal around the Falls of the Ohio), his association with Burr five and six years before, his complete ignorance of Burr's plans, and finally the damage done to him unjustly by General Wilkinson's words at the Wilkinson trial. "It is unfortunate for me," he says in the second letter, "that Gen. Wilkinson did not permit the interview to take place, which I asked . . . I rely on the exertion of your friendship to put an end to this business in the way that may point out . . ."

Burr had helped to wreck Bollman's life; was it to be the same with Latrobe? The architect wrote Bollman, who despite everything still admired Burr (August 23, 1812): "I have found myself sometimes in company with half a dozen of Mr. Burr's friends, all cursing him for having duped them, & all duped in different manner . . . always adapted to their peculiar characters." Nevertheless, three years later, when Latrobe feared suits would be entered against him in New York in connection with the Fulton steamboat debacle (which will be dealt with in due course), it was Burr, then returned to New York, whom he called in to be his attorney.

Latrobe's opinion of Wilkinson altered, too. Could some new personal interest have had its part in the change? Or was it merely that the existence of such an interest made him examine the evidence more closely? For Wilkinson's father-in-law, Charles Trudeau, was acting as mayor of New Orleans, and his support was essential at a time when the New Orleans waterworks—Latrobe's most important enterprise at the moment—were at a crucial point revolving around the site of the pump and the engine house. In any event, Latrobe wrote Wilkinson on Christmas Day, 1811: "I have lately become much indebted to your father-in-law, Mr. Trudeau, who has acted as Mayor . . ."; and on May 17, 1812, he wrote to his son Henry in New Orleans his final judgment: "I have taken great pains to study the evidence for & against the General, & am convinced that he has been most infamously used by men who ought to have protected him at all hazards, but who have sacrificed him to popular clamor, & to the hatred of fellows who in talent, in military knowledge, in virtue even, are not worthy to be named in the same day with him . . ."

The *Chesapeake-Leopard* affair in the early summer of 1807 was a shock to Latrobe. At first he could not believe that a British war vessel would fire on an American frigate when the latter rightly refused the request of the *Leopard's* officers to search the American vessel for deserters. He wrote Henry (July 3, 1807) that he felt there must be some mistake in the reports; then, when he was convinced of their accuracy, his Americanism roused him to righteous wrath and on July 4 he offered his services to Jefferson as a military engineer. There was no doubt where his loyalty lay. And in the letter he avowed his American ancestry—"descended in the fourth generation from American ancestors." Two days later (July 6) he wrote his father-in-law:

> I may, however, venture to say, that it is not their [the Administration's] opinion that we shall have actual war with England, but that we shall go as near to it as possible, so as at last to avoid it.

And on August 2:

> I have had lately many very confidential conversations with Mr. Gallatin, Mr. [Robert] Smith, & the President. . . . The terms proposed to England . . . are the giving up of seamen "proved to be American," an apology for the conduct of Berkeley, and a reprimand . . . if he acted without orders.

. . . I asked the President [Jefferson] if he thought we should have war: he answered—From the interests and professions of England we may expect everything, but from their pride, nothing. . . . Gallatin, Smith & the President believe in war, Madison and Dearborne in peace . . .

Then on August 15, 1807, to Isaac Hazlehurst again:

These rumors of war are equally fatal to your and to my repose . . . Suppose the money now expended in public works should go to buy blue cloth & pork for our army—where am I? Not here at all events—I must go to New York, or to Norfolk [or return to Philadelphia]. There I have . . . retained my house in Philadelphia [sublet to Delormeric, the picture dealer] for another six months, during which time & not sooner we shall probably know all about it.

In the ensuing winter the crisis remained imminent. Latrobe wrote Joshua Gilpin (February 25, 1808):

On the subject of public affairs . . . my conversations with men in office are numerous & frequent . . . The tone of Mr. Erskine's opinions [Erskine was the British minister] with whom I have the pleasure of particular acquaintance . . . points out the tendency of his ideas. In discoursing on the probable election of Mr. Madison to the presidency, I evidently found him decidedly against it . . . He would rather see a man . . . whose knowledge of the connexion between the nations . . . obtained on the spot, would correct his theoretical opinions . . . A decisive proof to my mind that affairs are not in good train . . .

Then follows a note on the proposed embargo. Later that year, in mid-March, Latrobe's English connection Augustus Foster, the secretary of the British legation, returned to England, and through him Latrobe took the opportunity to send some drawings to the Athenian Society in London. But the threat of war continued to grow; by November Jefferson's embargo was in full force, and Latrobe wrote Samuel Hazlehurst (November 20, 1808):

[The present administration plan is to make the] embargo more strict, the naval little armament fitted out to watch the coast; perhaps a non-intercourse bill, this is doubtful but not improbable; the militia called out, & then wait till news arrives from England . . . By what Mr. Erskine, who is an indiscreet man, says, the British calculations have been on the certainty of a President being elected who would arrange matters with England . . . That France in resentment would declare war, & of course, we be enlisted by the side of England . . . To use his own words 4 months ago, "the Eastern states who live by the carrying trade would sooner quit the Union & return to a colonial state than see the destruction of their commerce! . . . The election of Mr. Madison gives us a chance for peace." I think the calculation a wrong one. We shall obtain no terms from England. . . . Were I a merchant I would calculate all my plans for a twelve month's embargo & get hold of English goods, especially hardware. . . . I'm only giving you the cream of my conversations at the President's, Madison's [not yet inaugurated], Pickering's, & Quincy's, taking in both sides . . .

A few days later (December 4) Latrobe wrote his brother Christian, telling him of the Lenthall accident, and added:

Mr. Madison is President. I have for many years been on an intimate footing with him. Mary has known his very excellent and amiable wife from a child. . . . I do not approve entirely the rigid adherence to theoretic principles of policy which mark the conduct of our administration . . .

To Isaac Hazlehurst, too, he offered his opinion of Jefferson and Madison (January 16, 1809):

. . . As to embargo or war . . . to judge the possibility of the latter by the efficiency of the armament that is going on—on paper, I should suppose it will not take place very soon . . . Mr. Madison is not, I think, half so obnoxious a man to the Federalists as the present President. Mr. Jefferson is a man out of a book. Mr. Madison more a man of the world. With equal honesty, I think the latter will adapt his measures more to the actual state of the world & of opinions, while the former seems to have in many cases attempted to force the state of things into the mould of his theories . . .

Then political matters in so far as they affected Latrobe quieted down, the embargo was repealed, and all through 1809 there are but slight references to them in his papers.

Erskine returned to England, leaving things in their still unsatisfactory status. As a sign of British displeasure at the bold line taken by the upstart new country, he was replaced by mere chargés d'affaires—first by Jackson, whose rude stupidities alienated American opinion still further and eventually caused his recall; then by John Morier, who brought with him revived hopes of peace, soon to be disappointed. Meanwhile, of course, the two countries were still technically friendly, and Latrobe's social relations with the British legation continued. One encouraging note was the evident desire of the British to have at Washington a convenient and impressive legation building. Morier consulted Latrobe about the possibility, and Latrobe in a long letter expressing his own views (October 27) notes, first, the original scheme (which he credits to Washington) of setting aside the lots on either side of the Mall—"one of the most beautiful sites in the city," as he calls it—for the accommodation of the foreign ministers. "Letters were sent to the several ministers," he continues, and "not one accepted but the Portuguese Minister. Tho' the deed was actually made to him . . . his successors have neglected to have it recorded . . . Another difficulty arose afterwards [which] rendered this disposition entirely nugatory . . ." Latrobe then discusses various possible sites and the probable cost of the building—at least $25,000 to $30,000. The house in Georgetown which had been rented by the last three British ministers was now in the hands of the Russian ambassador, Count Pahlen. And Latrobe believes that the rent for any suitable building would be at least $1500 to $1700. But Morier, Latrobe felt, had little real knowledge of American opinion; he was almost entirely under Federalist tutelage, fundamentally hostile to the democratic point of view, and almost blind to its strength. Madison's strong Message to Congress on the situation (December 5, 1810) brought matters to a head, and Latrobe wrote Joshua Gilpin in Philadelphia (December 5, 1810) of its effect:

> Morier spoke to me very freely . . . on the President's speech—"They may wait long enough . . . for anything more than a chargé d'affaires if this is the spirit in which they chuse to treat John Bull!" . . . He considers the country to be still under the influence of Jefferson, & believes even that Mr. Barlow is not without considerable weight in biasing the opinions of the President. This latter opinion I believe to be unfounded, tho' I doubt not but that the former is to a certain extent correct. . . . There is a wretched kind of policy which I think both parties are pursuing . . . I am to dine with Morier . . . The Federalists will cling to him . . .

And to his brother Christian two days later:

> [The President's message is] ill humored as respects Great Britain [but] Mr. Morier . . . is I think more than necessary out of temper with it. . . . As a sort of war, perfectly bloodless indeed, we have taken possession of the whole of West Florida . . . The President has recommended the erection here of a National University & of a Military Academy . . . Both, if adopted, will give me ample employment. . . . It is probable that the non-intercourse act will be renewed with England prior to Feb. 2 as I do not suppose the obnoxious Orders in Council will be repealed . . .

Thus the two countries blundered on in their stubborn course toward war. By January, 1811, the lines were growing tighter, and Morier showed himself more obstinate and misled. Latrobe kept Joshua Gilpin apprised of developments and wrote him (January 3, 1811):

. . . Morier has been sick for a fortnight or three weeks . . . He is miserably off here for society. A few members of Congress associate—I am told—much with him. They are of the high Federal caste, of course they will do him no good . . . With our heads of departments, I do not find that he has any associates [sic] at all. Mr. Jo. Tayloe is his principal acquaintance. When I dined with him last, Tayloe & Law were present. Tayloe maintained [that] the Democratic party were ready to receive a prince of the house of Bonaparte, & to find him a throne, that Jefferson governed the country now, & was sold to France . . . that the eastern states alone saved us by their threats of separation of the Union . . . Law made an admirable defence of the administration to a certain extent . . . But Morier, I found, listened with more pleasure to the very inferior speech of Tayloe . . .

Nor did Latrobe hide his sentiments from his English acquaintances; in fact, he made sure that they reached the one most highly placed of them all—Lord Gambier, whom he had met twenty-five years earlier at the house of the famous Mrs. Bouverie. To him he sent by the British navy ship *Gleaner,* in a packet through the courtesy of the British embassy, a long letter (October 23, 1811) praising Captain Rogers, commander of the *President,* whom the British had said they would have hung at the yardarm had they been able. Latrobe also attacked the behavior of the British officers in the *President–Little Belt* informal battle, as well as those of some of the British privateers that cruised off the American coast. He characterizes the "gross ignorance of the English ministers who come hither, in every point of importance relative to the country," as "astonishing." He tells of the tremendous development of American manufactures as a result of the embargo and the English wars. He denies that Mr. Madison is partial to France; "there is no such thing as a French party." The letter is a powerful indictment of British policy and a strong declaration of American strength. It is tragic that Britain paid no attention whatsoever to all the warnings it received, of which Latrobe's was but one. It had not yet learned to think of the Americans as other than rather uppish colonials. It would have to learn the truth the hard way—hard for both countries.

It is strange, perhaps, but typical of Latrobe's strong support of the basic aims of the Administration that there is hardly a word in his letters about the French blockade of Europe and the French seizure of American ships. Evidently he still retained his fundamental love of France; he seemed to feel, like William Hazlitt in England, that foreign powers—and especially England—were responsible for forcing the French to take such extreme measures. The Latrobes were intimate friends of the Francophile Barlows, and when Barlow was sent on his ill-omened mission to arrange things with Napoleon the Latrobes accompanied his family to Annapolis to bid him farewell as he sailed.[14] And Latrobe wrote Barlow several long letters of gossip, both personal and political. Thus on November 15, 1811:

> The meeting of Congress last week has probably produced matter for letters of all your correspondents. The insolence of Foster, the steady & cautious candor of Monroe & the ultimate amende honorable of the Br. Minister . . . also the sandy [?] opposition furnished to the Federalists by the late settlement of the affair of the *Chesapeake* . . . In the house . . . there will be 38 to 40 sturdy 39 article men, including Randolph from whom I borrowed the designation . . . on the side of our country we shall count 100. Clay, the Speaker, is as firm as a rock . . . Macon had a few votes, being expected to be a Randolphian before the close of the session . . . On the Senate, the administration cannot place the same dependence. Pope will desert them, I think . . . Bradley is doubtful, & Leib not very firm. . . . Yesterday Mr. Monroe's appointment [as Secretary of State] . . . was before the Senate . . . I hear it was debated . . . today it was referred to a committee . . . It will no doubt pass. . . . Giles is also doubtful . . . Varnum fills clumsily the chair of Pickering . . . Randolph begins to . . . lash away as formerly at the City, "We are again met in the Capital & the Capitol, and we also find ourselves in the same desert!"

---

14. The vilification of Joel Barlow as an atheist, a traitor, and a subversive character at the time of this appointment lends an ironic coloration to similar attacks on distinguished governmental servants in the mid-twentieth century. But Barlow was so obviously the only person qualified for the job that his appointment, despite the violence of the attacks, was finally accepted by the Senate. Barlow, pursuing Napoleon in vain, died in Zarnowiec, near Cracow, on December 18, 1812. See Charles Burr Todd, *Life and Letters of Joel Barlow* (New York: Putnam's, 1886), and Milton Kantor, *Joel Barlow* (in preparation).

After Joel Barlow's departure, and until the end of the war, the Barlows rented Kalorama to the French Ambassador, Sérurier.

This is a typical commentary. Such glimpses must—if Barlow ever actually received them—have awakened in him thoughts of home particularly pleasant in his icy trek north and east, following Napoleon's march to Moscow.

These years of approaching war brought changes to the Latrobes as well. In the autumn of 1811 Robert Alexander, their landlord, died in New Orleans, and the Latrobes were forced to move. Their second house, to which they moved on March 1, 1812, belonged to Thomas Ridgeway; the rent was $350 a year. It was larger, a little grander, and much nearer the center of things than their first. On Pennsylvania Avenue, in the neighborhood of the Washington Theater, it was almost directly across the avenue from the residence of Latrobe's good friend Paul Hamilton, the Secretary of the Navy. Here the family continued to lead a busy social life, remembered later with great pleasure by their growing son John. It was from this house that they joined President Madison on his second inaugural parade; even John rode in the procession up the hill to the Capitol. Another social note at the time of the war places Mr. and Mrs. Latrobe at the naval ball held in Washington on December 8, 1812. As the architect, writing to Henry in New Orleans (December 9), describes it:

Captns. Hull & Morris being here, it was decided to give them a Naval Ball, as it was called, at Tomlinsons, Lon's formerly. About two hours before . . . handbills arrived from New York, announcing the *U.S.* frigate, Com. Decatur, had captured the *Macedonian* . . . It was immediately resolved to illuminate the city, & the Pennsylvania Avenue & the scattered houses on the hills, cut, I assure you, a most singular & splendid dash of scattered fires. The company assembled, all the secretaries & wives. . . . Doubt was then thrown on the truth . . . People were ashamed to have wasted their candles . . . The dancing, however, went on, & the illumination was placed to [the] account of the *Guerrière*. About 9 o'clock, young A. Hamilton arrived at the door with the colors of the *Macedonian* . . . the applauses were absolutely boisterous . . . At last he arrived in the midst of the room, where in an open circle stood his mother & sisters, Mrs. Hamilton leaning on your mother . . . Her son was soon in her arms . . . The colors were taken up and spread over the heads of Captns. Hull, Morris, Stewart, & other Naval men, including the Secretary, & marched like a canopy round the room, & at last spread at the feet of Mr. Madison . . . Nothing could be more affecting, at the same time dramatic, as the scene . . .

Thus the last month of 1812 brought with it this sudden upsurge of enthusiasm and brilliance to lighten momentarily the gathering darkness. At the naval ball, with Mary the chosen companion of Mrs. Hamilton (wife of the Secretary of the Navy) Latrobe must have felt proud indeed—this was a sign of achievement of high place; this was a kind of vindication. But in every other respect he knew his prospects were growing constantly dimmer. Congress in its session of 1811 had passed no appropriation for his salary or for further major work on the Capitol; Latrobe's income from this source was at an end. The Navy work continued, but on a more and more uncertain basis. For his main support, and for cash to fight suits or to settle various outstanding debts—chiefly those resulting from his endorsements of the notes of others—he was reduced to depending on his non-governmental work and on the business ventures into which, with such frequent misfortune, he entered. Mrs. Latrobe, in her unpublished memoir of her husband, portrays their situation vividly:

> His salary was $3000 a year, the promised addition being made from the Navy Department. With this salary we might have laid up something, as I was a rigid economist, having been educated never to go in debt. My dear husband's generous character was soon discovered and in consequence he became a prey to the worthless and improvident, being repeatedly applied to to become security for men who had no claim upon him, thus involving himself in the debts of others and drawing upon his salary every year to meet their notes. He never could bring himself to use the important monosyllable—No—when asked for his signature. At this time I possess a schedule of his property in which list is $10,000 of money lent to unprincipled men.[15]

Thus encumbered, Latrobe's further residence in Washington—particularly on the wide social scale to which the family was accustomed—was becoming more and more problematical.

---

15. This memoir, transcribed by her son John H. B. Latrobe in a large notebook of family memorabilia, is in the possession of the family.

CHAPTER

15

Private Professional Practice: 1807-1813

LATROBE's work on the Capitol, the Navy Yard, and the President's House by no means occupied his entire time during his Washington residence. Although he himself made by far the greater number of the drawings required and spent many hours in personal inspection, there was still ample opportunity to carry on private practice at the same time. Economically this was a necessity, for his government salary was insufficient to support his family, furnish the capital necessary for his speculative ventures, and at the same time take care of the raveled financial ends of his Philadelphia debts.

A major portion of these private architectural jobs naturally were in Philadelphia, some of them brought with him to Washington in 1807 and some newly commissioned. Work on the Baltimore Cathedral continued all through this period. The Waln house, already discussed, was under construction, and just before he left his old center he was asked to design two more houses, those for Captain John Meany and for John Markoe, which we shall come to presently. Soon after this he was appointed architect for the new Bank of Philadelphia, and there were even a few slight attentions required by the Bank of Pennsylvania, now six years old.

At the same time there were minor commissions for Washington and Philadelphia acquaintances. We hear, without particulars, of a house for a Mr. Craig. Apparently a stable and outbuildings, possibly in Gothic, were designed for his Philadelphia friend George Harrison, to whom he writes (July 25, 1807): "Don't be frightened. The enclosed is a sketch of what I have designed for you . . . About 100 dollars more than the expense of a common front will give you your abbey glimmering through the foliage." And a month later in a letter to Robert Mills (August 20) he mentions the job. On the Eastern Shore in Maryland, he seems to have helped Charles Goldsborough with the alteration or rebuilding of a house Goldsborough had just bought; he writes him (March 18, 1807), expressing his regret at not being able to complete the "proposed arrangement" with him personally, and continues: "I hope still to render you every possible service in your proposed re-edification of the house you have bought . . ." He recommends a certain Mr. Grimes of Elkton as the best carpenter for the job, and concludes: ". . . if you will forward me an exact plan of your walls, ground plan & elevation, I can send you as clear & useful advice as if I were on the spot." The house referred to was probably Myrtle Bank, near the Wye River in Talbot County.

Among the other, more important commissions was the house for Captain John Meany. About this Latrobe never grew enthusiastic as he did over the Waln house; he made the designs, to be sure, and Mills acted as occasional superintendent for him. But evidently Meany's taste and the architect's were often at odds, and Latrobe felt his client had made undesirable changes or used inept details. Why the black water table, the architect asks Meany, and to Mills he writes of his disgust at the exterior brick panels (mere collectors of dust, he calls them) which Meany wanted. On August 5, 1807, he wrote to Mills objecting to the design for the front door: ". . . this is congruous . . . with the taste and wishes of the Captain, for nothing could better remind him of the decoration of a binnacle, excepting . . . a chimney piece. I should think those imitations [in stone] of cabinetwork incongruous with good taste . . . I am a little sick of Captain Meany. I shall never get the least credit by his house . . ." Latrobe billed Meany only $100 for the design (December 23, 1807); it would seem that Mills detailed the job as he saw fit, working directly with the owner.

Robert Mills superintended all Latrobe's work in Philadelphia at this time, and his careful, meticulous handling of it took a load of worry off the designer's shoulders. But in taste and temperament the two men differed markedly. Mills, brought up in a purely native American architectural tradition, was still in matters of detail strongly under the influence of the Federal and Late Colonial manners; he loved tiny moldings and richness of surface modulation, and he never quite came to grasp—until much later in his life—the values of the strong quiet planes and the muted accents of Latrobe's classical taste. Latrobe's opinion of him was equivocal, a mixture of admiration and disapproval. Thus to

John Markoe, in Philadelphia, Latrobe writes (August 10, 1810): "Notwithstanding my believing the pious Robert Mills is not absolutely the most minute inspector into the proceedings of your workmen . . . yet his answer[s] to my string of queries are so detailed that it would have been more trouble to have invented the statement of things than to have copied them from observation . . ." And, after Mills had left his employ, Latrobe answers a question of John Wickham concerning his house (now the Valentine Museum) in Richmond (March 16, 1811): "[Brackenridge] requested me to give you my opinion upon a stucco for your house, which it appears your man of taste, who has designed it, says is absolutely necessary to render the work complete."[1] He goes on to refer Wickham to his report on stucco in India, published in Volume 6 (1809) of the *Transactions* of the American Philosophical Society. In a later letter (April 26, 1811) Latrobe states his own dislike of certain features of the house as he had heard them described—particularly the front hall and staircase, which seemed to him to be in the worst taste of Charles IX of France! Nevertheless Mills, in addition to superintending the houses for Waln and Meany, was also in 1808 overseeing Latrobe's two other Philadelphia jobs—the house for John Markoe and the Bank of Philadelphia.

The Markoe house, on Chestnut Street, was brilliantly original in concept. It made the most efficient use of its narrow lot by having its service stair placed near the middle of the garden side of the house and the main staircase near the front, in a hall approached through an octagonal porch and a square vestibule. The rooms, lighted at front and back, spread to meet between the stairways and could therefore be excellently approached or served; at the same time the greater part of the floor area could be utilized to the best advantage. Closets and beautifully proportioned recesses filled every inch, yet the effect was open and welcoming. The outside was elegantly simple. On each floor large triple windows on both sides flooded the interior with light, and the entrance door, restrained in detail, gave just the right note of elegance.

Naturally the house, for so wealthy and distinguished a client, embodied all the "latest improvements." It had a bathroom complete with

1. Although the "man of taste" is not named, it seems probable that Mills, to whom the house is usually attributed, is meant. The spirit of these letters and the references to the Wickham house designer are precisely similar to other passages referring to Robert Mills. This parallelism can hardly be accidental.

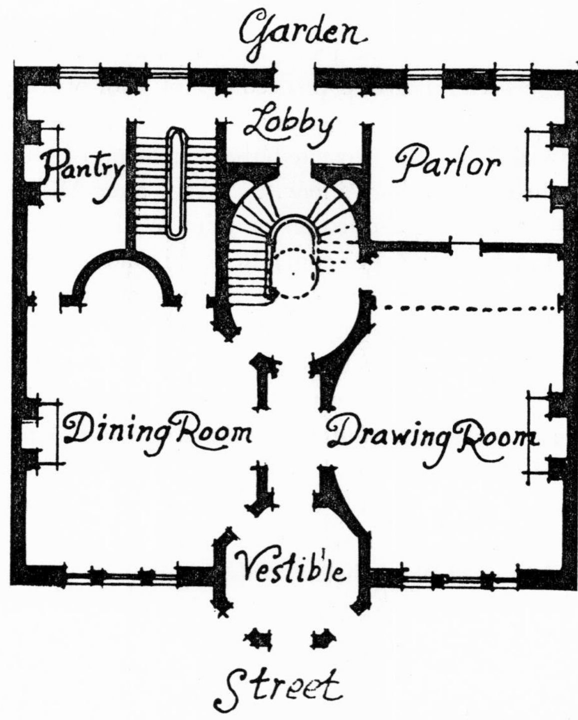

Redrawn from the Latrobe sketchbooks

FIGURE 20. Markoe House, Philadelphia. First-floor Plan.

water closet and bath. A letter to Mills (January 23, 1810) suggested a slight rearrangement so that the furnace that heated the water might be more conveniently vented to an adjoining bedroom chimney. The rough sketch that accompanied the letter is perhaps the earliest existing American drawing of a complete bathroom.

Latrobe had evidently begun the Markoe designs in February, 1808; by December the contract was ready to let; a year later the interior details were under way and there were questions to settle about the very unusual stairs. And it was at this moment that Mills had to be absent for several weeks, called to his father-in-law's house in Georgetown by the tragic death of his wife's brother in a duel. Latrobe wrote Markoe, reassuring him and explaining the superintendent's absence, and himself went to Philadelphia to see that all was well. The railing of the marble entrance steps and platform was of iron; for this Latrobe followed a pattern he had designed for the Capitol stairs, having the parts cast in

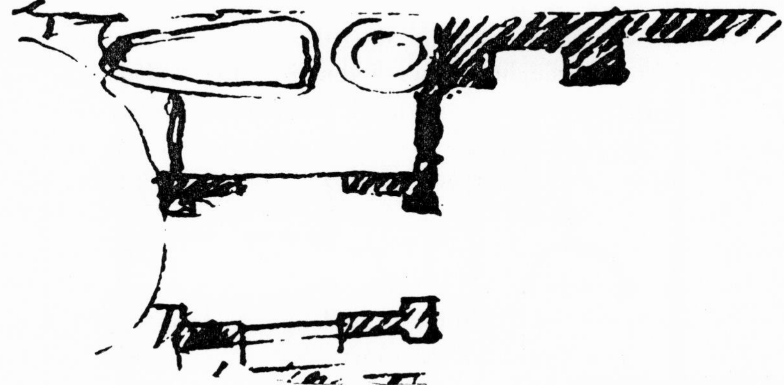

From the Latrobe letter books

FIGURE 21. Markoe House, Philadelphia. Sketch for Rearranging Bathroom. From Latrobe's letter to Mills, January 23, 1810.

Washington from the Capitol original. He visited Philadelphia to oversee his jobs in March, 1810, and again in June; of the latter visit he wrote Mills (June 10): "My sole object is Mr. Markoe's house. I shall stay as long as I want . . ." The house by then was rapidly approaching completion, and on August 10 Latrobe promised Markoe that he would certainly be able to move in in October. Yet in November the house was still "almost finished" except for the delayed entrance-step railing, and as late as the end of January Latrobe was still writing his superintendent about the installation of the iron. The Markoe house, according to the architect, cost $8.00 per superficial foot, and he remarks that it was the cheapest house "of the first class" in Philadelphia.[2]

The Markoes were delighted with their new home; their reception of it was a heartening thing indeed in a time of discouragement. In early December, 1810, just before they moved in, they showed Joshua Gilpin around it and expressed their admiration of the architect; Gilpin passed on the good news to Latrobe, who answered his letter on December 5: "Your good opinion of Mr. Markoe's house flatters me very agreeably. As to the exterior, it is created by the interior, & was with me a secondary thing altogether. It has certainly no merit . . ." But in this he did him-

2. The square-foot cost of the Markoe house reveals that building in Philadelphia was expensive even then. In 1953 the cost per square foot of a house "of the first class" would be likely to run to $30, or over three times the Markoe figure. But the general buying value of the dollar has in the meantime risen to from five to seven times its value in 1810.

self an injustice, for the exterior, by its frank expression of the unusual plan, had a power and a directness altogether winning; the house, with its triple windows, brought a new rhythm into the Philadelphia landscape. When the Markoes moved in at last, in mid-winter, they were even more elated, and Mrs. Markoe hastened to write Latrobe of their pleasure. He answered (February 19, 1811): "Delightful as my profession is in most of its circumstances, it would be infinitely more so, did every architect receive as flattering a reward from his employers, as you have bestowed upon me . . ."

But the family did not live in the house long. Chestnut Street was rapidly changing, and Philadelphia's growth had no regard for personal convenience. Business was creeping up the street inevitably, and what a few short years before had been the finest of the city's residential districts became instead a confused region of shops and taverns, public baths and circuses. Two of Latrobe's most beautiful houses fell early victims to this march of "progress"—the Waln house, sold to Dr. Swain, became a public bath; the Markoe house was converted into a hotel. Eventually two more stories were added to the original three of the latter, smothering its proportions and concealing its original elegance; for decades it stood, a caricature of its former self, succumbing again to economic pressure and finally being replaced by a characterless commercial structure. *Sic transit* . . .[3]

Another notable Pennsylvania commission of these early Washington years was the Bank of Philadelphia. This institution, of which George Clymer was president, was one of the large number of local banks founded in the first decade of the nineteenth century to take care of the enormous increase in business activity and to fill the void caused by the demise of the First Bank of the United States. Latrobe's selection as architect was almost inevitable, for his Bank of Pennsylvania was universally admired not only as a beautiful incident in Philadelphia's streets but also as a functionally satisfactory building. The site of the new structure

3. The relative rapidity of change in the United States and England can be well illustrated by the history of Latrobe's own work. All his major houses in England are still extant, the house his family lived in near the center of London stood till the bombings of the Second World War, and the house he and his wife inhabited still stands. Of the American city houses which he designed, only the Decatur house is preserved; his own various homes in Philadelphia and Washington disappeared long ago, and of his other Philadelphia work—the two banks and the theater—not a trace remains.

was close to that of the earlier bank; this makes all the odder the fact that Latrobe in designing it chose to make it Gothic. A rather blocky composition of brick with stone trim, its doors and windows had pointed arches and projecting hood moldings; it had battlements of a sort, and stone pinnacles; the profiles of the moldings were what Latrobe considered Gothic, and on the interior the plaster vaults were webbed with tracery. Nevertheless, as one sees it in old engravings—for it had but a short life—it is far from the conventional Gothic building, for its firm, symmetrical composition, strong horizontals, and broad wall surfaces are still, as could be expected, more classic than Gothic in feeling.

This commission was received in the spring of 1807; by December construction was well along. Latrobe wrote his brother Christian (December 1, 1807): "Your fondness for Gothic architecture has induced me to erect a little Gothic building in this city, the Philadelphia Bank. Externally, it will not be ugly, but internally, I mean it to be a little cabinet. The boardroom is a Gothic octagon Chapter House with one pillar in the center . . ." Robert Mills superintended the work and made many of the details from the sketches (often quite rough) that Latrobe sent on from Washington. It is interesting to notice in all of this correspondence the architect's care in handling the purely practical necessities —the rebates on the iron bank shutters, for instance, "to prevent fastenings from being sawn through"; the iron angles or corner beads set in the plaster at the corners of piers and reveals, to prevent damage to the plaster; the ventilation of the book and money vault; and so on. In the course of the work he took occasion to further Mills's architectural education by giving him (February 13, 1808) the first two parts of "Britton's Gothic Architecture,"[4] realizing also that Mills's increased knowledge would be of great service to the building. By March the contract for the plastering was awarded—to Latrobe's favorite plasterer, William Thackara, whom he had trained in the skills his own designs required. This contract was of special importance, for much of the effect of the interior would result from the perfection of the intricate tracery to be formed in the plaster ceilings. Sketches in letters to Mills give fascinating glimpses of the rich plasterwork. Evidently the banking room had an

4. Probably John Britton's *The Architectural Antiquities of Great Britain* (London: Longmans, Reed & Orme, 1807-26), which was issued in parts from 1805 on. The first volume was completed in 1807, the second in 1809.

elaborate fan vault; the radiating ribs had cusped panels between them, cast in advance, and there were elaborate modeled bosses at the intersections. In the center was a large pendant. Latrobe had this manufactured in Washington, under his own eyes; it was framed in iron, like "a birdcage" (as he wrote Mills). This was to be fastened securely to the ceiling framing, and the radiating ribs were to be brought down and adjusted to it. The whole must have been a fantasy in Gothic ribbing not too unlike certain English ceilings of a decade earlier. The vault was completely non-structural, but in those pre-Pugin and pre-Viollet-le-Duc days Gothic was less a structural system than a dream of richly decorated curving surfaces to puzzle or please the eye. In the Philadelphia of 1808, the vault must have been a source of wonder; at least it was unique.

Late in November of that year the bank moved into its new premises, just as the contracts for the Markoe house were signed. Latrobe had designed all the bank furniture, and in a full letter to President Clymer (June 18, 1808) he described its location. He felt the matter especially important because some of the directors, he understood, wished all to be left in abeyance till the bank moved in; they did not realize the advantage of careful planning ahead of time. With his intimate knowledge of the bank's functioning and with the advantage of his experience in the Bank of Pennsylvania, he knew better than they how the various portions interlocked and had consequently designed the whole as a unit. The arrangement he proposed, he told Clymer, was even more efficient than that of his earlier bank. The entrance to the banking room was on the east. On the left (south side) he had placed the first teller, convenient to the vaults and the cashier's office. Across the west side stretched the desks of the bookkeepers, conveniently accessible to the first teller and the currency scales. On the north side was the second teller, equally convenient to the bookkeepers. The note clerk was in the northeast corner, close to the entrance to be easily available to the public and yet also next to the second teller, "to whom the money for payment of notes is paid." In the southeast corner, across the entrance passage from the note clerk and equally near the entrance, the discount clerk was to reign. Latrobe noted that the range of bookkeepers' desks along the west side might not be required at once, but as the bank grew they could be added as necessary. As for the furniture for the cashier's and president's offices, that, he added, could wait until his next visit to Philadelphia.

The bank did expand and rapidly outgrew its first building. Less than two decades later Latrobe's Gothic structure on which he had lavished so much care was destroyed, to be replaced by a much larger classic building designed by Strickland. It was the all-too-usual history of Latrobe's work.

The year in which the bank was finished (1808) saw the completion of another Gothic building by Latrobe: Christ Church in Washington, on G Street near Sixth Street Southeast, not far from the Navy Yard.[5] The church still stands—surprisingly little altered, though somewhat changed in appearance by a particularly knobby white stucco applied in the early twentieth century—and offers an opportunity today of judging Latrobe's entire Gothic achievement. A relatively small structure, the church is a simple rectangle with a square tower over the entrance; the chancel arch was not constructed until after Latrobe's death. The composition of the tower itself is excellent, and its connection with the gable-roofed nave is handled with simple and satisfactory directness. Though the church is in brick, it has a stone hood molding around the entrance arch, and little stone key blocks on the smaller arches reveal the classic foundation of their author's taste. Yet these are not intrusive; the feeling of the whole is right. The doors and windows are pleasantly proportioned. When first built it was a sort of village church, and seen from a distance its tower rising over the scattered houses must really have given to this part of Washington much the effect of an English country village. Even today the tower carries its dominant message above the little two- and three-story row houses that line the near-by streets, and the placing of the church well back from the street line—so that it is approached over a green churchyard—adds immeasurably to its effect.

Inside, the building is not without charm. Between the nave and aisles the roof is supported by two rows of slender, slightly tapered, cast-iron columns; the nave ceiling is elliptically vaulted in plaster; the side-aisle ceilings are flat. The proportions are high, the windows narrow but tall; pointed arches lead into the chancel and the tower gallery; and, for the small dimensions, there is a surprising sense of airiness and space. Of course, as in the Bank of Philadelphia and the Gothic design for the Cathedral of Baltimore, the interior is in no sense historically Gothic; yet

---

5. Latrobe, as architect, signed the final brickwork and plastering accounts on March 9, 1808.

the pointed windows, the slim columns, and the high-seeming space give a genuinely churchly effect, faintly reminiscent of antiquity—an effect of Gothic as seen through a child's eyes or imagined from the reading of a fairy story. Its merits, naturally, are those that result from the fact that its creator was an artist; for its ineptness as an interpretation of Gothic cannot entirely conceal his genius. Later, as has already been noted, Latrobe's own feeling for Gothic changed, but it is a boon to have still standing, still serving its original function, this quaintly attractive church to show another facet of its designer's mind.

There were other private Washington commissions, several of them still problematical—like the Bank of Columbia in Georgetown and the Bank of Washington. For the first Latrobe had installed an iron roof as early as 1805 and perhaps had done more; old photographs show a simple exterior with a large and commanding central arch that might well have been his, though it is clothed in the prevailing manner of the time and either Thornton or Hadfield might have arrived at a similar solution. In any case a dispute arose between the bank officials and the contractors, litigation ensued in 1810, and Latrobe was the chief witness in the affair.[6]

The work for the Bank of Washington is even more puzzling. On September 9, 1809, Latrobe wrote Daniel Carroll of Duddington about it: "If I expected either to make my fortune or to increase my reputation by directing the execution of the design of the Washington Bank, it might be well enough to persuade you . . . that I have nothing but your interests in view in what I advise or direct . . ." And he goes on to tell of the mortification caused him by Carroll's countermanding of his orders. "You have rendered my drawings useless . . . You would not use either your attorney or your physician in this manner, and why should you suppose your architect to have less skill or honesty or blunter feelings?" Obviously he did serve as the architect; obviously, too, things did not go as he wished. His feelings about the work were mixed, and in all his existing correspondence he never once referred to it again. Yet the structure as built (if we can trust old views) was, on the exterior at least, a worthy work of which he need not have felt ashamed.

He had pleasanter experiences on a much smaller commission carried

6. Letter to Robert Mills, January 23, 1810: "I am detained by being subpoenaed as the principal witness for the Columbia Bank . . . ."

out during 1810—alterations and improvements to Kalorama, the estate on the hills of northwest Washington belonging to his dear friends the Joel Barlows. The work was small; apparently it dealt largely with a gate and gatehouse but included some new marble mantels (probably for the main house) bought from Traquair in Philadelphia. Here Latrobe had the pleasure of working for a family he and his wife both admired and loved; fortunately the job went well, with none of those unforeseen imbroglios that so often cloud professional dealings with personal friends.

Another fascinating project arose in 1812, but nothing came of it. Thomas Law, the farsighted, felt that one of the difficulties in Washington was the great distance between the residences of the Cabinet members. Could not efficiency in the government be improved if they were nearer the President, the Capitol, and one another? He wrote Latrobe asking his advice about the best location, and the architect, at once enthusiastic, answered (March 20) suggesting a site north of Pennsylvania Avenue near Seventh Street Northwest, where the ground sloped steeply down to the avenue and the Mall beyond. Not only was this just halfway from the Capitol to the President's House, but it was also high enough to possess a broad prospect over the Mall to the Potomac. "It is perhaps the handsomest situation in the whole city, excepting the President's house," he wrote. He would place the houses on the north side of the lot, they should be 27′-6″ wide, "and the slope of the hill to the south would furnish a handsome garden . . . as far as the line of the Avenue. I have made a design and estimate for such a block of houses . . ." Complete with a stable, each would cost $12,000. But in June the war broke out, and another forward-looking dream of Law's and of Latrobe's fell a victim to it.

For Governor Claiborne of Louisiana Latrobe designed two New Orleans monuments: the first, in 1810, for a Mr. Lewis who had perished in a duel; the second, and the more important, in the following year, for Mrs. Claiborne, who had died in childbirth. For this the architect had Franzoni carve a relief; as he wrote the governor (September 17, 1811): "Franzoni had bestowed upon it his best talents, and the group of figures in *basso relievo* are exquisitely sculptured in marble." The monument still stands, and although the relief has been much eroded it bears witness to its designer's delicate taste and expressive conception.

During the early months of 1812 Latrobe was also busy on a design for a dormitory at Transylvania College in Lexington, Kentucky, made for Henry Clay, to whom the architect wrote (May 15) enclosing a long list of questions and explaining the different methods used in existing colleges for housing students. In the final plan sent to Clay at Lexington (June 24), Latrobe adopted the Princeton dormitory scheme, in which each student has an 8-foot-square sleeping cubicle, arranged with one or two others to form a room 16 or 24 feet long. Unfortunately the plan was not preserved and the first building of Transylvania College has long since perished. From existing old views it does not seem to have resembled Latrobe's work; if Latrobe's design was used at all, it was probably in matters of plan only. At about this time the architect also began to work with Clay on the design of Clay's own house, Ashland, which engaged them both for over a year.

As an engineer, too, Latrobe was in demand. He was consulted about the silting up of the Hog Island bar in the Delaware, with which he was familiar through his residence in Newcastle and Wilmington. Recommendations were made by him and on November 19, 1807, he submitted his bill of $150 to Thomas Fitzsimmons of Philadelphia. Three years later he was asked for advice about the Potomac bridge at Washington: how could the channel through it to Georgetown, which insisted on silting up, be kept open? Mr. Thomas More of Brookville, Maryland, had suggested wing walls or dykes to narrow the opening in the hope that the increased current would scour out the channel between. Latrobe had been retained by the Washington Bridge Company as consultant, and, although the wing dams were an integral part of the scheme, he wrote General Mason at Georgetown (January 8, 1811) that this would not affect his giving an unbiased judgment. The matter had come up before a Senate committee, for the channel was essential, and the committee through Mr. Carroll had referred the question to Latrobe, who found against the proposal; his experience both in England and in the United States had made him skeptical of such "scouring works," for though they deepen a certain point they are responsible for building up other shoals which may be even more dangerous. Here he feared that the result would completely close navigation in the Eastern Branch up to the Navy Yard. On January 20, 1811, he wrote More explaining his objections and appended a long disquisition on America's innate suspicion of trained professional men and on his own consequent difficulties.

Just how much Latrobe had to do with the actual design of the Potomac bridge is difficult to judge; from the existing correspondence it would seem that he was more consultant than designer. But he designed other bridges. As early as 1797 he had made a design for a Schuylkill River bridge in Philadelphia. As we have seen, he had made a complete report on a bridge to connect New York and Long Island via Blackwells (now Welfare) Island. And in 1806 he had taken out a patent on a stone arch-ribbed bridge, which will be considered later. During his Washington years he designed a bridge, probably over Acquia Creek, for Daniel Brent, the quarry owner, and with his customary honesty he told Brent that no bridge in the location could possibly be built for $1,000, the sum Brent had named, especially if it had to be furnished with a draw.

But his largest private engineering work of these years was the Washington Canal. Toward the end of 1809 he was asked to make a report on the project, and this he did; he received $300 for it. As a result he was pestered with questions about both the canal and the bridge. The directors of the proposed canal company were Elias B. Caldwell (the president), Dr. May, Daniel Carroll, Robert Brent, George Blagden, and Edward Law. To them Latrobe wrote (January 17, 1810), somewhat testily, asking where he stood in the scheme and refusing to give any further opinions gratuitously. The letter was effectual; the directors at once appointed him engineer, and on January 19 he wrote Elias Caldwell accepting the appointment and agreeing to do all the work for $2,000 if the work cost $48,000 or over, or at 5 per cent of the cost if it fell below that figure—payment in either case to be in canal company shares. A little later (January 23) he wrote Caldwell again agreeing to consider the $300 already received as part of the over-all figure.

The Washington Canal was designed to connect the Anacostia River and the Eastern Branch with the main channel of the Potomac, thus cutting across the peninsula that occupied the central part of the city. Thomas Law had long been an enthusiastic supporter of its construction and had even spent two years in Holland trying to raise capital for it. But no work resulted, and the American corporation that finally built the canal was not chartered until 1808. The canal had been shown in the L'Enfant plan. It had two entrances to the Eastern Branch, and for much of its length it paralleled and regularized the little Tiber Creek. The necessity for the canal seems questionable today; but in the early nineteenth century, with few improved roads and with many of the Washington streets still impassable, there was great dependence on barge and scow transportation to bring food and building materials into the city. Some supplies, from the east, came down the Anacostia; from the western hinterland materials arrived by the upper Potomac and the Georgetown Canal. The proposed waterway, therefore, would not only allow easy interchange between these two routes but also offer transportation by either of them to the heart of the city. Law, moreover, hoped to establish a series of packet boats on the canal, to run from the canal entrance on the Potomac to the Navy Yard and thus furnish a sort of primitive rapid transit which would be both more economical and more comfortable than that furnished by the usual hackney coaches. The Tiber River already poured its waters down from the northwestern hills, affording an ample supply to feed the proposed canal.

In the plan the canal led from the Eastern Branch, crossed the axis of the Mall a little to the west of the Capitol at the foot of Capitol Hill, and then turned west, following Pennsylvania Avenue and the north edge of the Mall to the Potomac. There were to be tidal locks, a harbor basin, and docks at both ends; two intermediate locks of small lift; and, to connect the whole definitely with the Washington plan and the Capitol, a formal settling basin on the Capitol axis. Here, according to one of Latrobe's plans, was to be erected the Tripoli Monument, as the chief element in a compact, integrated monumental center just beneath Capitol Hill. If this had been carried out and the Greek Doric propylaea which Latrobe designed for the Capitol had been built, together they would have formed one of America's first serious attempts at site composition in the grand manner. The propylaea was never erected, and the Tripoli Monument (now in Annapolis) was placed instead in the Washington Navy Yard; but the basin was built and formed a most effective recall of the Capitol axis in the undeveloped Mall. This part of the canal was twice changed. The government wanted to sell some of the land along Pennsylvania Avenue, and Latrobe in 1815 made a plan to permit this. In it he shows the Tiber flowing into a great circular basin on the Capitol axis, with an axial feeder connecting it to a semi-octagonal "mud lock" at the canal. But even this did not suffice, and in 1818 the entire eastern part of that run of the canal was shifted to the Capitol axis; a plan by Frederic C. DeKrafft [7] shows this. The circular basin has gone,

7. Frederic C. DeKrafft was a draftsman and surveyor, apparently well trained. Some of the Capitol drawings of 1818 bear his name.

but the semi-octagonal mud lock remains. As actually built, apparently this last refinement had vanished, and the canal turned a stark right angle onto the Capitol axis at the bottom of Capitol Hill.

The Washington Canal was completed in about two years, but it was far from being the monument Latrobe had contemplated. He had hoped its locks would be of stone and its construction as permanent as possible; but evidently only one of the directors, Dr. Frederick May (who became a close friend), agreed with him. In the search for cheapness the canal was lined with timber, its locks were built of wood, the docks and basins were skimped, and eventually—as Latrobe had foreseen—trouble developed. Thus in a heavy storm in the summer of 1811 one of the locks was completely destroyed, as the architect wrote Robert Fulton (July 31), and by 1816 the linings and locks had both tumbled down or washed away to such an extent that Latrobe considered them beyond repair. These were the results of cheapness, of the failure to accept the architect's advice.

For the excavation and grading the contractor was James Cochran of Baltimore, who had been one of the contractors on the Philadelphia waterworks a decade earlier. He had an excellent record and reputation and had worked on the National Road as well, where he had earned the admiration of Gallatin. At the very beginning of the canal work a difficulty arose: there was no official survey of the city. The only approved legal plan was the first printed one, and many private owners had already altered this. Nicholas King, the city surveyor, helped as best he could, furnishing the levels of streets at various canal crossings, but in large measure Latrobe had to make a new survey. For this he employed a German immigrant, Eugene Leitensdorfer, who was a scientific agriculturist as well as an accomplished surveyor. (Later Latrobe tried to help him to some position more worthy of his talents.)

The canal contracts apparently covered only the canal itself, leaving the docks and basins for future consideration. Latrobe wrote the directors (July 20, 1812) a full report on what remained to be done. Cochran would need a small payment to complete his digging in order to provide a depth of fully three feet and to secure the canal from erosion. The locks already required considerable maintenance; wharfs must be built, and Latrobe recommended one at Twelfth Street and another "opposite the Rope Walk." He also insisted that dredging at the canal entrances under existing conditions would be futile and the cost of permanent improvement too great for the company's treasury; but he did suggest a tide dam, lock, and "tumbling bay" at the Potomac end, to cost about $3,000.

Eventually the canal proved more useful for drainage purposes than commercially. To Latrobe the project was another financial blow. The war came, then the long depression. He had accepted his fee in canal company shares (and in addition he had purchased other shares); then in a time of dire need he could find no one who would discount the canal notes or purchase them. For him his service was, in actuality, merely one more contribution to material improvement; it was the Chesapeake and Delaware Canal experience all over again.

Yet another engineering project took form at this time. It was to be his own undertaking; he alone would design, organize, and arrange the financing for it. This was the furnishing of city water to New Orleans. His designing of the New Orleans customs house and the Mississippi lighthouse had given him some familiarity with the conditions there, and letters to and from Robert Alexander (his Washington landlord as well as the contractor who had built the customs house) had provided further insight. He had met and become friendly with Governor Claiborne, and through him his own interest deepened; he knew that New Orleans was the growing Mecca of restless Americans and restless American dollars and that its prospects for the future were brighter than those of any other American city. Yet its water was atrocious and its health record terrifying. Would not a plentiful water supply improve both? At a time when dirt was often blamed for yellow fever, would not good water abolish that scourge? And, with yellow fever gone, to what heights might not New Orleans rise?

Perhaps, too, the fact that Roosevelt and Lydia had gone to New Orleans to prepare for the opening of steam navigation on the Mississippi may have turned Latrobe's thoughts in that direction and reminded him of a suggestion given him years before by Jefferson. At any rate, we first hear of the scheme in a letter to Samuel Hazlehurst (December 7, 1809): "I have . . . digested two schemes, which, as Tibbs says, are 'as yet a secret' . . . One is to supply the city of New Orleans with water, on which object I have a communication from the Governor of the territory, the other a canal around the falls of Niagara, on which I am consulted by the Government [8] . . . The exclusive right of the supply of

8. See pages 361-3.

New Orleans to me & my associates is proposed if I effect it. I have associated with me a Mr. Alexander . . ." And ten days later he wrote his father-in-law that he had already petitioned the legislature for the requisite franchise and that "Mr. Poydras, the representative from N.O., an old French miser, worth $75,000 p. annum, says that we shall assuredly succeed . . ."

But there was an infinity of delays, and at times the political difficulties seemed almost insuperable. The city asserted its rights, and a certain Monsieur Blanqué led the opposition. Latrobe also, he wrote Alexander (April 29, 1810), feared Wilkinson's objections. To handle the affair more expeditiously as well as to gain a more personal view of affairs, Latrobe decided to send down his son Henry, who at eighteen, besides his excellent academic education and all the knowledge his father had been able to give him, had had experience as surveyor with the National Turnpike Commission. Henry left in December, with letters of introduction furnished chiefly by Poydras.

Meanwhile Alexander had had no success whatsoever in getting the charter passed, and Latrobe now used Henry as his direct intermediary, thereby, he believed, ending any claims Alexander might have in the project. Naturally Alexander protested, through his Washington attorney Joseph Cassin. Latrobe was enraged at his tone, for, so far as he could see, Alexander had contributed nothing at all to the scheme—neither engineering skill, original ideas, nor effective political or financial activity. What possible claim was left? [9] In a long letter to Alexander (July 27, 1811), Latrobe tells the story as he saw it:

> The idea of supplying the city of New Orleans [with water] was first suggested to me by a French gentleman from thence to whom I was exhibiting my works in Philadelphia . . . But I dismissed the subject from my mind until it was renewed by a conversation with Mr. Jefferson while you were in N.O. building the custom house. On your return we seriously entered into a partnership for accomplishing the work. The duties of each of us were determinate & equal . . . You engaged to procure the charter on terms drawn up by me . . . You failed in your application . . . Gleize of New York applied immediately afterwards and obtained a grant . . . of this you did not inform me . . . When Governor Claiborne arrived . . . I received the first

9. Latrobe was particularly disturbed because both Cassin and he had endorsed a note for Alexander, who had never paid it and owed him, Latrobe claimed, $378 (letter to Alexander, July 27, 1811).

clear account of the matter. [He goes on to state the reasons he considers responsible for Alexander's failure—his ignorance of the French language and French manners, and the existence of a French majority in the City Council.] All of these reasons . . . made me resolve to send . . . Henry . . . depending on his . . . knowledge of French . . . the French manners [received] from a French college . . . & his French name . . . 2 days before he left . . . several gentlemen from N.O. . . . entered warmly into the scheme . . . & suggested a project . . . on the condition you be left out. . . . I resisted . . . Henry departed. . . . The success of my son . . . was almost miraculous. . . . Now put the question . . . whether there exists any partnership . . . in these proceedings . . . after you had failed . . . If there is & you will state it . . . I will sacrifice every advantage . . . to justify you . . .

Apparently Alexander accepted Latrobe's explanation, but less than six months later he died, a victim of yellow fever, which was afterward to claim the two Latrobes—first Henry, and then his father. The waterworks seemed indeed ill-fated.

Even with the charter finally granted, however, political difficulties continued. A site for the pump house had been determined on; supposedly it was on city property. But the city discovered it held no valid title to the lot, over which the Federal government claimed jurisdiction. The matter caused endless confusion to the plans, and mountains of correspondence; eventually that site, however advantageous, was discarded and farther down the river another to which no legal objections could be raised was adopted.

The financing, too, was difficult. All sorts of business associates of Latrobe tried either to insinuate themselves into the scheme or to destroy his general leadership in it. Eric Bollman, poor and almost forgotten, saw in this project opportunities for spectacular profits; he besieged Latrobe with suggestions, wanted a partnership in the concern, and boasted of all the money he could bring in—he even intimated that the original idea was his. Latrobe was forced to write him (August 11, 1811): "I am very sensible I am under obligations to you of the most important kind, but certainly not for the idea of these waterworks . . ." Later Bollman declared to Latrobe that everyone with whom the architect dealt was "a ruined man"—a harsh accusation indeed—but sent a list of people he thought he could interest. Latrobe wanted none of them but later he relented enough to offer Bollman the privilege of selling the stock, when and if he could, on a definite percentage commission.

Actually the financing was largely done through the always helpful and solid Jacob and Louis Mark, who handled the New York end, and through Godfrey Haga of Philadelphia and Frederick C. Graff of Baltimore.[10] Money came in easily at first, then more and more slowly as the shadow of the oncoming war grew darker, and finally in a trickle only. Latrobe began by selling one half of his privilege to Jacob Mark, for $40,000, and pledged his other half to his agents Haga and Graff as security that the work would be completed; it was of course Mark's cash, supplemented by Latrobe's, that enabled the work to go ahead.

As soon as the basic layout was completed, the next and most expensive requirement was the steam engine—and here began a long and complicated story that was not to end until several years later.

Latrobe's favorite engine builder, after Roosevelt had embarked in other pursuits, was James Smallman, of Philadelphia, who had built the engine for the Navy Yard. But Smallman's prices were mounting, and just at this moment (in 1811) he was engaged in a long business controversy with the Philadelphia iron founder Large, who was evidently becoming a feared rival. The controversy ended with Smallman's purchase—forced on Large by want of cash—of all of the Large interests. Except for Oliver Evans, Smallman now had a monopoly, at least in Philadelphia, and he was fully aware of the advantage he had gained.

The result was that eventually Latrobe, disgusted with Smallman's antics, decided to build the engine himself, buying the castings from Foxall—who was a great Methodist zealot as well as an excellent foundryman—in Washington. The plan seemed to offer many advantages. Latrobe's position at the Capitol had become ever more precarious as the war grew closer; in 1811 no appropriation for his salary was made. With commerce to England closed, American manufactures seemed to have a flourishing future ahead, and the demand for steam engines was increasing. What better means could there be of assuring himself an income? So now Stuart's old painting room found another use; to it Latrobe added a few necessary sheds and there he set up his factory. Its first job was the engine for New Orleans. He wrote Jacob Mark (August 24, 1811): "I have now a shop & men waiting." For the project he wanted Samuel Hughes of Havre de Grace to cast the iron pipe as well as the engine cylinder; he bought boiler iron from Bishop & Malin at Bishop's

10. Letter of May 18, 1809, to Louis Mark.

Mills, near old Chester in Pennsylvania; and he ordered other castings from Foxall. Everything seemed ready for rapid progress. But Hughes could not cast the cylinders, and the order went to Foxall. There was a flurry of correspondence throughout August and September about the project, and many letters were sent to prospective investors. Haga dropped out of the scheme; others had to be interested. And then, as if to cap the climax, the Latrobe children fell sick, and the architect was obliged to take them out of the city for three weeks. On his return from this necessary but worried rest, uncertainty arose about the house the family was living in, now since Alexander's death the property of his estate. Then, in December, Graff withdrew as Haga had done—was it because they foresaw the delays and difficulties the war would bring? To compensate for these setbacks, however, the city of New Orleans itself, in May, 1812, bought twelve shares, and later in the same year Latrobe persuaded Graff to reconsider and re-won his support.

Meanwhile Henry had returned from New Orleans and was helping his father as his emissary in New York and Philadelphia; but now, what with the engine under way and the controversies about the site still going on—for Congress had refused to validate the title—it seemed best to have him in New Orleans again. In January of that year he sailed, never to return.

The certainty of war in June, 1812, brought a sudden end to this optimistic planning. Latrobe already had thirty-three cases of machinery ready to ship—and few ships were sailing. Could such a valuable cargo be risked? He wrote Henry (June 7, 1812): ". . . of course my 33 boxes and all my castings will remain at Baltimore till I can send them by land to Pittsburgh. At Pittsburgh, also, I shall have to build my boiler . . ." It was just at this juncture that Latrobe received from Henry an order for another steam engine for New Orleans—not for the waterworks but for the sugar mill of one Chevalier de la Croix—and with it came a welcome draft for $1,500 to cover the preliminary expenses. At once he rushed to enlarge his plant, bought more land adjacent to the "painting-room lot," ordered fire bricks and crucibles for brass founding, and built a new shed to house the new machinery. But, alas, suddenly came news that De la Croix had failed, and the draft became uncollectible.[11]

11. The De la Croix engine was apparently the one that was later completed and sold to Mr. Hartshorne of Baltimore for a grist mill. When Hartshorne gave up the mill idea, Latrobe

Everything Latrobe touched that year seemed to have a curse upon it.

It was during this troubled time that B. H. Latrobe almost became a New Yorker. New York had fascinated him ever since his early visits in 1799 and 1800; he had close ties there with the Marks, and both Aaron Burr and—for a time at least—Robert Fulton seemed anxious for him to move to the rapidly growing city. He had been disappointed in the outcome of the competition for the City Hall (1802) and he had refused the job of regulating the Collect Pond and the city drainage. But that had been in 1804, when professional opportunities in both Philadelphia and Washington seemed glowing. By 1808, however, his Philadelphia prospects had almost vanished, his Washington future was already fogged with doubts, and he felt increasingly distressed at being so constantly the Federalists' target and the democrats' scapegoat.

Accordingly offers of jobs outside of Washington became ever more attractive as time wore on, and the growing tensions between Great Britain and the United States only increased Latrobe's desire to get away. At one time—as early as his visit to New York in August, 1808—he was consulted by his New York friend Colonel Jonathan Williams, a co-founder and the president of the Military Philosophical Society,[12] about

---

tried to sell the engine to various other individuals to benefit both Hartshorne and himself, for the payments on it had not yet been completed.

12. See Sidney Forman, *West Point, a History of the United States Military Academy* (New York: Columbia University Press, 1940), pp. 20-35. The Society was formed by the engineer officers of the United States Army at the suggestion of Col. Jonathan Williams, the first superintendent of West Point, on November 12, 1802. Its purpose was to stimulate the study of all the sciences and arts which had any bearing on military or naval problems; thus included were astronomy, navigation, geography, and all the forms of engineering. The Society sponsored the publication of several important scientific pamphlets and was directly responsible for the fact that the United States Military Academy in the years after the War of 1812 furnished the best technical, scientific, and engineering education to be found in the country. Membership in the Society meanwhile had widened to include men like Madison, Monroe, Marshall, DeWitt Clinton, Bushrod Washington, Joel Barlow, and Latrobe. The Society was dissolved at a meeting in New York City on November 1, 1813, because of confusion resulting from the War of 1812 and the fact that many Army men were hostile to it and its influence. Latrobe's good friend Colonel Williams was himself an extraordinary individual, a grand-nephew of Franklin. Born in Boston in 1750, he was in France during most of the American Revolution. Thomas Jefferson thought that he resembled his famous grand-uncle in the breadth of his scientific interests. It is noteworthy, too, that Joseph G. Swift, one of the first cadets to graduate from West Point as an army engineer, also became a good friend of the architect in his later Washington years.

Latrobe was in New York in August, 1808, having been sent by the Navy Department to

a house John McComb was designing there for one of Williams's friends. Williams sent the drawings to Latrobe, who returned them with sketches showing the alterations he would suggest. In the covering letter Latrobe concludes: "I hope Mr. McCombe [sic] will not be offended at the alterations. If I come to New York . . . I shall certainly have the inclination to help him . . ." Did he hope to become McComb's partner?

The same year he designed a "hydraulic temple" for the famous Dr. Hosack, whom he had met during former visits to the city. And, when in November Lydia married Roosevelt and went to live with the Marks at 62 Greenwich Street, there was still another thread pulling him northward. The flurry of fortification that followed the *Chesapeake-Leopard* battle—if such an unjustified attack on an unprepared ship can be called a battle—offered another opportunity. Latrobe wrote General Morton, in New York, asking to be considered as a "practical engineer" to carry out the works his friend Colonel Williams had suggested, and saying frankly (February 2, 1809): "My wish for some years has been to reside in New York, and as my daughter has lately chosen her residence in that city, I have an additional inducement . . . Any certain engagement producing not less than $3,000 per annum would be a sufficient inducement . . ." Significantly enough, he wrote on the same day to Orris Paine in Richmond: "It is my opinion, from my own experience, . . . that the worst situation a man with a family can be in is to be a salaried officer under U. States Government . . ." And he had still another vain dream of going to New York, for, as he wrote to Thomas Carpenter of Philadelphia (April 9, 1807), he was being considered as the architect to redecorate and complete the Park Theater there; he writes of it as a probability—disappointment again.

But of far greater appeal to him was the most important engineering job in the United States in those years—the design and construction of the New York Western Navigation—the Erie Canal. Latrobe's prospective connection with this came from two sources—the first, and most significant, his part in Gallatin's controversial road and canal bill; the second, but more immediate, his friendship with Robert Fulton. When Gallatin had his daring vision of enormous public improvements to be financed by government surplus funds, roads and canals occurred first to

---

report on the condition of the navy yard in Brooklyn. His letter to Colonel Williams was written shortly after his return to Washington.

him as the most necessary objectives, and he asked both B. H. Latrobe and Robert Fulton to make reports.[13] Latrobe's was a complete analysis of the communication needs of the eastern part of the country, and in it he emphasized canals; he laid out a comprehensive system which largely anticipated actual improvements that have since been made and which called for a Cape Cod Canal, a Raritan-Delaware Canal, the resumption of work on the Chesapeake and Delaware Canal, the improvement and enlargement of the Dismal Swamp Canal, and various minor connections between rivers farther south. To this system the West would feed its products and its trade by two means: first, the connection of the Great Lakes and the Hudson River (already projected and in part begun by the state of New York); and, second, a canal from the Potomac River or Chesapeake Bay to the Ohio River. Fulton's report dealt largely with railroads for horse-drawn traffic.

During late 1809 and early 1810 Gallatin's bill was the subject of wide interest and controversy. Latrobe wrote letter after letter to his friends and associates about it; according to him this was the time, if ever, when such a bill could pass. The chief problem was whether Congress could constitutionally take such action. Finally presented by Senator Pope on January 5, 1810, the bill received its third reading in the Senate on January 10—and then quietly went to sleep. But Latrobe's activities in connection with the project did not go unperceived. He was in large measure its initiator; as he wrote Richard Rush in Philadelphia (December 31, 1809): "A plan which I conceived some time ago, for the general improvement of the internal navigation . . . which appeared to be so Utopian, & if not beyond the means, yet so far beyond the temper of our national government, I never even produced it till about a month ago. . . . In a few days you will see the features of the gigantic infant in the newspapers." One of the indefatigable workers for this ambitious scheme was Colonel H. P. Porter, member of Congress for New York, and with him Latrobe worked in close association. It was but natural, then, for the architect's name to come to the fore when the state decided to complete the New York Western Navigation and appointed a commission. He himself sent a copy of the bill to Gouverneur Morris, one of the commissioners, on April 10, 1810; in his letter he says: "I have been

13. The two reports were published in the *National Intelligencer,* Latrobe's on September 23, 26, and 30, 1808, and Fulton's on October 3 in the same year.

asked in a preliminary manner whether if the offer were regularly made to me, I would attend them [the commissioners] as their engineer. There would not be a moment's hesitation on my part . . . were I not the head of a large & expensive family." He goes on to enumerate the losses that would accrue if he left Washington and his private practice, including the expense of a deputy to carry on his Capitol work. "But," he writes, "if . . . I may look forward [to it] as the employment of the rest of my life . . . it would then be my interest . . . to attend." He adds a personal note: "Should I come to New York few circumstances would give me more pleasure than to see at the head of your family a lady [once Nancy Randolph] whom I had known in Virginia . . . who may recollect my visit to Bizarre . . . in 1797."[14] The informal inquiries he refers to came from Governor Clinton; Latrobe wrote Roosevelt asking him to give the Governor his sincere thanks.

Yet the matter was far from dead. The commissioners were evidently anxious to obtain Latrobe's services and took the matter up with him a second time a year later (in May, 1811). And again Latrobe wrote a noncommittal answer. "My intention and wish," he said, "is to accept of your proposition," but he added that circumstances would prevent his immediate decision. Commissioners Robert Fulton and Thomas Eddy had proposed that he visit New York for a conference; they wanted at least a consultation with him. He replied that he could be with them in August, provided his terms were acceptable—his traveling expenses from the time he left Washington till his return and twelve dollars a day in addition. As a precedent he cited the fact that Weston, the famous English engineer, had received $1,000 and expenses for a two-week trip to Richmond. Then at last, on August 1, in a letter to Commissioners Eddy and Fulton, Latrobe accepted the offer to survey the New York Western

14. Actually in 1796. Mr. Howard Swiggett, in *The Extraordinary Mr. Morris* (New York: Doubleday, 1952), suggests that this letter is a veiled threat to compel the offering to him of a permanent position or he will reveal, or reawaken, the scandal surrounding Richard Randolph's death. In the light of Latrobe's character, principles, and generosity, this seems absurd. As an acquaintance of several members of the Randolph family, he must have known of the gossip; but the reference here would seem to mean just what it says—it is a message of greeting, a statement that can be understood to mean, "Whatever I may have heard, I am still her friend and would be glad to meet her again." Morris evidently answered that the position was far from a permanent one, and Latrobe's acknowledgment (April 29) is a letter the patent sincerity of which should be ample proof that there was no sinister threat in the reference he had made.

Navigation. All seemed settled, and on August 20 he wrote Fulton that he was preparing to leave for New York.

But again circumstances prevented. The commissioners refused to advance funds for the trip and complained that his arrival would be too late for their purposes. Indubitably the trip depended on their advancing him the cost, for Latrobe was at this point desperately poor—a man with many projects of the greatest importance before him, architect of the country's greatest building yet one whom Congress had cut off without a salary, a man harassed by duns and debts and almost literally without a cent.[15] Except with the commissioners' aid, the trip to New York was an actual impossibility, though he could hardly tell them this. The trip therefore fell through, and regretfully Latrobe refused the commission. He was not to be a New Yorker after all.

Meanwhile, in Washington, the architect-engineer was constantly busy in all kinds of attempts to raise the cash he so drastically needed. Several of these were connected with the wide enterprises of the Marks in New York, some with his mercurial son-in-law, Nicholas Roosevelt. The Marks were agents for many German interests, including various manufacturers of arms. Now, with the air full of rumors of war, what better time could there be for selling these in America? And what better person than Latrobe to act as the firm's Washington salesman? He had bought from the Marks much equipment for the President's House; here was a chance for them to reciprocate by throwing what seemed like sure business his way. There were swords and cutlasses, for example, excellent in quality and cheap in price; Latrobe devoted letter after letter to these in correspondence with Jacob Mark, Louis Mark, and the Secretary of War. The Federal government turned down the offers; it wished to support American manufacturers and had found a man in Connecticut (probably the famous Collins) who could turn out such equipment in large amounts at a price only slightly higher than that of

15. A letter to Father Dubourg (November 12, 1809) is eloquent in its account of the situation in which Latrobe found himself in those harassed years. Dubourg was trying to collect from him a sum he claimed was still due on Henry Latrobe's tuition, and the architect writes explaining why he cannot pay; moreover the bill is a surprise to him, because he had for one year placed Henry in the University of Pennsylvania (in order to avoid the cost of St. Mary's) and had returned him to the Baltimore college only because St. Mary's had granted Henry what Latrobe took to be a full scholarship. This was in 1809; now, in 1811, with the imminent cessation of the Capitol salary, the architect's condition was still further straitened.

the Germans. Latrobe tried the states; first Pennsylvania, then Maryland, was on the verge of ordering the cutlasses for the militia, but no state apparently went over the verge. All his time, his letters, his contacts seemed futile; no orders came in.

Then, too, there were knapsacks made by one L'Herbette. Over these Latrobe also labored in vain; nobody seemed to want them, excellent though they were. Finally, in desperation, he advertised them in the *National Intelligencer.* Week after week in 1809 the advertisement, with a crude engraving, appeared, with "Apply to Mr. Latrobe" as an address. This shows how low his sense of professional dignity had sunk in his frenzied efforts somehow to make ends meet, somehow to cover his notes and those he had so generously and so rashly endorsed for friends. It is tragic to think of the time and energy wasted by the brilliant architect, the careful engineer, in this struggle to make money in "the American way"—time and energy that, had the United States appreciated what he had to give, might have been so creatively applied.

Another will-o'-the-wisp was a projected railroad to run from the Virginia coal mines to the waterside at Amthill. The use of coal as a fuel was increasing; in the East one barrier to its use was the long and expensive trucking necessary to bring it to Richmond or Washington. A railroad—horse or mule powered, of course—would vitally expedite shipments; again the potential profits were fascinating. The scheme was first evolved in connection with an owner of coal lands, one Harry Heth of Manchester, Virginia. Latrobe wrote Eric Bollman of the plan in the late spring of 1809 (May 21); here, he thought, was a chance to bring Bollman into a profitable speculation. A week later he wrote him again, listing men he thought would be most likely to invest. But capital was elusive; nothing was done, and another opportunity to raise himself from the morass of debts vanished into oblivion. Latrobe was becoming desperate and bitter; as he wrote at last to his colleague and friend Godefroy in Baltimore (May 20, 1812): "I . . . am every day becoming more a Goth. I shall at last make cloth, steam engines, or turn tailor for money, for money is honor."

Among the outstanding notes that worried him, the most emotionally wearing were those connected with Eric Bollman. When Nixon—the wealthy father of Bollman's late wife—died, he left a certain amount of money to Bollman's children, and Mary Elizabeth Latrobe had been named their legal guardian to watch over their interests. Bollman himself, well-nigh penniless, was eking out a miserable existence in all sorts of strange enterprises—running a factory for artificial flowers, experimenting with dyes, developing chemical means of producing verdigris, discovering new methods of refining platinum. Some of his discoveries were potentially of the greatest importance, yet in the America of those years they went without appreciation and yielded him nothing. His former connections with Burr alienated possible investors, as his indiscreet affair with his children's nurse had alienated his rich father-in-law. Yet he retained his high notions of what the world owed him, and he determined that his children must have the best education possible.

Bollman and Latrobe were sufficiently similar in their devotion to science on the one hand and architecture on the other, and sufficiently alike in their present ill-success, for a close bond to exist between them. Latrobe, though he often disapproved of Bollman's actions, could not help liking him and admiring the keenness of his mind. He owed him a deep debt of gratitude for helping him freely when Barber had absconded in 1800, taking with him all the office assets and the office papers. Bollman had then been top dog, partner in a spectacularly successful firm. Now it was Latrobe's turn to help; poor as he was, he had a substantial government position and contacts with the most influential men in Washington. To them he took every opportunity of pleading Bollman's cause, and now when Bollman needed money for the education of his children—titularly under the guardianship of Latrobe's own wife—what could he do but sign Bollman's notes? Bollman borrowed the money from his cousin Hoppe, and, when Bollman could not pay, Hoppe turned on Latrobe. What had begun as a friendly accommodation became the opening for Hoppe to bring continuous and unpleasant pressure on the architect.

Meanwhile Bollman had produced the two essays on banking that were to make him famous.[16] Latrobe welcomed these enthusiastically. He saw to it that they were widely distributed among the powers in Washington. At last, he thought, Bollman's brilliance had given birth to something that must win him popular favor and eventually some financial position worthy of his talents. But the essays, though generally admired and actually of great value in the fiscal development of the country, brought

16. See Fritz Redlich, *Eric Bollmann and Studies in Banking,* in the series *Essays in American Economic History* (New York: Stechert [c1944]).

Bollman no cash and no job; he remained as poor as ever. And his cousin, Hoppe, continued to harass Latrobe with threats of suit. Bollman, he knew, had nothing and probably never would have anything; but Latrobe had a position to protect. Thus the architect was put in a situation where payment became imperative. Hoppe at last got the thousand dollars Bollman had borrowed—got it from Latrobe, already deep in a morass of debt. Now it had become almost entirely a matter of Latrobe's borrowing on a new note to pay an old one, and the total of uncleared debts was little by little mounting.

Then Latrobe became embroiled with one Henry Hiort, a manufacturer of hydraulic cement in Richmond. The details of the affair are vague. Hiort advertised his product in the *National Intelligencer* at various times in 1809, and in the advertisement he quoted Latrobe's praise of the product. Latrobe admired the cement sincerely and apparently did everything to back it, lending money to Hiort and most recklessly endorsing his notes. But Hiort was evidently not so reliable as his cement, and he disappeared sometime in 1811 or 1812. All his creditors of course turned for redress to Latrobe as Hiort's endorser; five separate suits descended on the architect's head. He had no defense, for Hiort could not be found, and every single one of the claimants had to be satisfied. The writs of attachment were dated between 1809 and 1812; each year a few hundred hard-earned dollars vanished in the settlements. Hiort, Latrobe claimed later, joined the British in the War of 1812 and left the country with them, leaving Latrobe to settle his bail.[17]

The final worry was the old matter of Roosevelt's Navy copper debt of $30,000 to the United States government. Roosevelt was at times, Latrobe felt (as he wrote his son Henry in New Orleans), the *sinister cornix* of his fortune. Yet for him he performed endless services. The government was beginning to feel restive about this long-unpaid debt. Roosevelt was seeking delay after delay and apparently thought that Latrobe, through his contacts with the great and the powerful in Washington, could work wonders. Throughout four years—1808 to 1812—the situation rankled. Again and again Latrobe was forced to write Roosevelt that the matter was not a personal one, that he could do no more than

17. Records of trials in the Washington Courts, now in the National Archives, contain many particulars. I am deeply grateful to Professor Louise Hall, of Duke University, for a microfilm of all the Latrobe court records.

he had done, that even his friend Gallatin had come to feel that Roosevelt's nonpayment of the debt was outrageous, and that this was no longer a Navy concern but one in the hands of the United States Treasury, which had received directions to collect all moneys due it at once.

What would be the effect if the government actually entered suit against Roosevelt? Latrobe knew his son-in-law's nebulous financial position well enough to realize that a sudden suit might be disastrous. And how would it affect the life of his beloved Lydia? Financially, to be sure, Latrobe was no longer involved in the affair, but emotionally it was all deeply troubling, and he wrote repeatedly to Roosevelt to force him to take the initiative in arranging a settlement. But Roosevelt still procrastinated, hoping as usual for miracles. It was all a continuing threat to Latrobe's peace of mind.

Nor were these the only disturbing problems. With all sorts of financial entanglements, with his salary for the Capitol work at an end, with a drastic need for money to carry on the New Orleans waterworks—both for eastern materials and for construction at New Orleans—Latrobe whirled around like a squirrel in a cage, continually evolving new schemes that were to make the family fortunes. For instance, he entered into a partnership with Louis Mark in a steam-powered plant to make furniture ornaments, buttons, and other articles of stamped metal; the agreement is dated January 8, 1811. Nothing came of the scheme, for capital could not be found. As financial matters grew worse, Latrobe's correspondence mounted, letter after letter not only to carry on his ordinary professional work but to get cash for New Orleans, to extend notes —anything to keep his head above water.

The button factory may have been the most grotesque of the enterprises Latrobe considered, but the most heartbreaking was the plan for weaving cottons on a power loom. Here, surely, with English manufactures barred from the country, would be a bonanza. Sometime in the summer of 1810 the architect had been introduced by a Massachusetts congressman to a certain Samuel Blydensburg, then in Washington to interest the government, obtain a patent, and collect capital for a new model power loom he had invented.[18] In Latrobe he found his ideal in-

18. About Samuel Blydensburg little can be found. He was actually granted a patent for a power loom in 1815, but it is unclear if it was ever widely adopted. He evidently continued his interest in textiles, for in the 1840's he appears as the editor of the periodical *The*

strument, and the architect's imagination fired at once. Always excited by the problem of the simplification of manufacturing by the use of power, Latrobe was prophetically aware of both the immense social benefits and the massive profits that would accrue from the industrialization of the United States. He had come from a country where at the very time of his departure industrialization was proceeding by leaps and bounds, and he realized full well that America's dependence on England for all kinds of manufactured goods—and especially for cheap cloth—was not only dangerous but also, granted the proper support of American enterprise, unnecessary. The new country's quarrel with England made the opportunity particularly favorable. Blydensburg undoubtedly had a loom that worked; Latrobe had himself seen it produce "50 yards of excellent plain cloth a day" by the mere turning of a crank.[19] The machine was as yet crude, but with some development would it not soon be immensely useful?

Latrobe entered into the scheme with immense enthusiasm. In 1810 his position at the Capitol still seemed secure, and he poured into the loom project his capital, his enthusiasm, his time. Yet he appears to have been almost totally unaware of the details of the other vast developments in the New England cotton industry, or of the fact that Blydensburg was far from the only creator of power looms. He at once sought a mill site—for water power this time—and found one on the canal at Georgetown, where he could rent all the power he needed at $450 a year, and where a good water wheel already existed. On August 14 he wrote Blydensburg of his determination to back him; on August 26 he was already writing to his wealthy Baltimore friend William Lorman, telling of his discovery of the mill site and his plan to build there a factory (20 by 30 feet) to hold forty looms, and explaining the terms under which Lorman could share in the scheme. Lorman accepted; then caution reasserted itself and he withdrew. So sanguine was Latrobe of success that he wrote Blydensburg that he welcomed Lorman's withdrawal—it would mean more for them!

But others were prospecting the field, apparently to Latrobe's surprise. The Washington Manufacturing Company had advertised a plan to in-

---

Silk Worm, and his *Manual of the Silk Culture* was appended to I. Richard Barbour's *The Silk Culture in the United States* (New York: Greeley & McElreth, 1844).

19. Letter of September 1, 1810, to Isaac Hazlehurst. But Latrobe adds that Blydensburg's loom is "loose and badly constructed."

stall power looms designed by another inventor, and Latrobe warned the company that he was likely to enter suit against it for patent violation. Then he heard of a third loom, and a fourth—all seeking patents—and wrote Blydensburg, again back in Massachusetts, of his perplexity. But evidently Blydensburg, a tardy and un-co-operative correspondent and an even more slippery partner, was sometimes in Massachusetts, then again in Rhode Island. Continually seeking more money to improve and refine his loom, he promised to send looms to Latrobe's waiting factory "soon." And Latrobe, refusing to lose faith, sent on what money he could; his hope, he wrote Blydensburg (January 18, 1811), was eventually to build a steam-powered weaving factory in the city itself, "the present water-powered plant being merely a preliminary experiment . . ." And (June 20, 1811): "In the meantime I have been patient, because I have been very poor, & in fact I have been poor because I have been patient. Let me know what you are about . . ."

So it continued for nearly two futile years. "Send on the Looms," wrote Latrobe again and again. At last thoroughly aroused, he wrote Blydensburg (February 2, 1812): "One year & 3 months have elapsed since you were to furnish me with ten looms. I have paid you $1600 . . . 400 for a mill site rent & 600 for a building . . . Can you inform me how I am to get back to the point from which I started?" Nothing happened; four months later Latrobe besought him to send looms and to return the little polygraph the architect had lent him. A month later: ". . . at least send 2 looms . . . I *must* do something to support my family . . . If I had *10* looms here I know I could work them most advantageously." Again in August he pleaded for his two looms, but in vain. That was his last despairing note. So far as Latrobe knew, Blydensburg had vanished into thin air, taking his backer's two thousand and more dollars along with him. And this was no longer 1810, when Latrobe as Surveyor of the Public Buildings and Engineer of the Navy had the security of a government salary; it was now 1812, with the Capitol work stopped and even the Navy job problematical—a time when every cent was precious indeed. There remained but one hope—Robert Fulton, friend and close associate, wealthy and ambitious, full of schemes for making continually more money by widening his steamboat empire. Could the future lie here?

CHAPTER

16

Prelude to Pittsburgh: Steamboats and War

NICHOLAS ROOSEVELT was both indirectly and directly the cause of Latrobe's becoming a steamboat constructor and of his choosing Pittsburgh as the place where at last he might rebuild his fortune and find the security he had lost when work on the United States Capitol ceased. And again, as in the case of the Philadelphia waterworks, Roosevelt became in part the agent of the architect's financial ruin. Yet still the two remained friends; Latrobe in his new position as Roosevelt's father-in-law now found himself the protector of his daughter's interests as well as of his own.

In the winter of 1798-9, it will be remembered, Latrobe had gone to New York to contract with Roosevelt for the Philadelphia steam pumps. It was in this year that Chancellor Livingston, John Stevens, and Nicholas Roosevelt were up to their ears in steamboat experiments; the future possibilities and the design of steamboats, the power plants they required, and especially the matter of how power should be applied had become their chief interest, their chief subject of conversation and of speculative thinking. During his visit to Roosevelt Latrobe met both the other men; naturally, too, he visited the steamboat they had built, for it lay in front of Roosevelt's place on the Passaic, Laurel Hill. He was told that the vessel had made a bona fide run from New Jersey to New York but that its speed was only three miles an hour in still water;[1] this was not sufficient to secure the hoped-for monopoly of steamboat service on the Hudson. Two years later Livingston was appointed Ambassador to France. When he sailed from Philadelphia, Latrobe saw him there on

1. See letter of October 1, 1798, from Roosevelt to Livingston reprinted in John H. B. Latrobe, *A Lost Chapter in the History of the Steamboat,* Fund Publication 5 (Baltimore: Maryland Historical Society, 1871).

the eve of his departure and Livingston urged him to do anything he could to help Roosevelt and Stevens carry the steamboat project to a successful conclusion. Then Livingston apparently forgot them, for in France he met Robert Fulton at Joel Barlow's—and the rest is history. In due time the *Clermont* appeared; Fulton and the Chancellor received the New York monopoly, but it was granted to them alone; Stevens and Roosevelt had been dropped by the wayside.

A sequel was to follow. Roosevelt had suggested the use of side paddle wheels to Livingston, and Livingston had refused to adopt them. Yet he never forgot the suggestion, and when he met Fulton in Paris and they discussed steamboats—a passion with both of them—he passed on (so Roosevelt and Latrobe both believed) Roosevelt's side-wheel suggestion; Fulton at once adopted it as the basis of his future work.[2]

Roosevelt had not yet patented his notion; his later patent is dated December 1, 1814. The success of the *Clermont,* nevertheless, put Roosevelt in a dilemma. Should he sue Fulton and Livingston at once for the share he felt was his due and thus antagonize the two men who were most able to make his own invention useful and association with whom would be warrant of immediate prosperity? Or, instead, should he try to make with them some kind of new arrangement that would express their recognition of his part in the creation of steamboats? He chose the latter course and, knowing the intimacy between Latrobe and Fulton in Washington, brought in the architect as his emissary. At the beginning of 1809 Roosevelt was in dire need of both money and a job; only recently married, he was without any single project or commission, and prompt action was imperative. His father-in-law was the obvious person to help him.

Accordingly Latrobe wrote Fulton (February 7) suggesting that there should be a new "union of all three interests and abilities"—Fulton's, Livingston's, and Roosevelt's—to further the good cause of steamboat monopolies in an equitable manner profitable for them all. Whether

---

2. See John H. B. Latrobe, *op. cit.,* for significant Livingston-Roosevelt correspondence in 1798. A letter of 1802 from Barlow in Paris to Fulton in Brest, given in Charles Burt Todd, *Life and Letters of Joel Barlow* (New York: Putnam's, 1886), is also revealing. Barlow is telling of a conversation he had just had with Chancellor Livingston. In the course of it Livingston stated that Fulton's "wheels over the side" were not patentable, since they had been suggested earlier "by someone else." Evidently Fulton later overcame Livingston's scruples!

Fulton was afraid of Roosevelt's prospective patent or not, he was favorable to the suggestion—claiming he acquiesced out of pure friendship for Latrobe—and as a result, when the Mississippi Steamboat Navigation Company was organized, Roosevelt appeared as one of the founders and was appointed the company agent to build the first boat at Pittsburgh and to collect company subscriptions there. This was in the spring of 1809, and when Lydia wrote her father asking his advice about the whole matter he answered (May 11):

> As to Fulton's scheme of sending your husband to the Ohio I highly approve of it so far. It will give you a charming jaunt, & will effect a separate housekeeping, an object of the first importance to your happiness. . . .[3]
>
> My great objection to the Western water scheme (independently of your distance from us) is the unhealthiness of that country, and the sacrifice of Mr. Roosevelt's commercial pursuits, which he understands better than the steamboat business, & which he can always live by.—But on the footing on which you have now put it I think it a very good scheme. . . .

He went on to suggest that Louis and Jacob Mark be brought into the scheme, and continued:

> Fulton I respect & love & believe him to be honest, tho' devoted to his interest. Of the Chancellor I have no good opinion. I hope your husband will treat safely with them, & not be in a hurry to conclude.

Lydia, it may be noted in passing, had inherited from her father a strong sense of adventure and love of new experiences; for, when it became Roosevelt's first duty to explore thoroughly the possibilities of direct navigation between Pittsburgh and New Orleans, his wife, then pregnant, accompanied him on the long voyage—now tedious, now perilous—down the Ohio and the Mississippi on a flatboat borne by the swelling current.

Actually, things did not work out as Latrobe had hoped; in Roosevelt's case they scarcely ever did. The Marks did not come in, and Roosevelt sold far fewer shares in Pittsburgh than the company had planned. But he did build the boat—the *New Orleans*—and in the fall of 1811, with Lydia along and again pregnant, made the passage down the Ohio

3. The reference to "separate housekeeping" is interesting. Roosevelt made his New York home with Jacob Mark, at 62 Greenwich Street, and it was there that Lydia and he lived whenever they were in the city. Mark, as we have seen, was one of Roosevelt's partners, and for his wife at least the Latrobes had a warm affection. Yet they resented a little their daughter's transfer so wholly into another household.

and Mississippi from Pittsburgh to New Orleans in this—the first steam vessel to make the run. It was an exciting and at times a terrifying trip, with earthquakes, floods, and washouts so serious as to change the shores of the Mississippi. That autumn of 1811 was a famous time of strange natural phenomena in the West; yet through it all the little boat puffed her way down, day after day, somehow escaping snags and new shoals, finding new channels, and at last arriving at her goal. In every civilized town or settlement along the banks she was received with enthusiasm, acclaim, or dire predictions of future disaster. Nevertheless she succeeded, and the trip ever after was a treasured memory to Lydia and, through her, to later generations of Roosevelts and Latrobes.[4] In New Orleans the vessel was placed in the Natchez–New Orleans trade and was run under the supervision of Edward Livingston, the Chancellor's much younger brother. Enormous profits were made on every trip, and all looked fair for the Roosevelts.

But Fulton and Roosevelt could never work happily together. Fulton cast disapproving eyes on Roosevelt's fame as well as on his accounts. All the local papers along the river route were full of tales of Roosevelt's accomplishments and of his heroism in making the dangerous trip on a vessel people feared would blow up at any moment. Fulton and Livingston were not mentioned; that rankled. And the boat cost far more than Fulton had dreamed it would. At once the company arranged matters (for Roosevelt's one-third interest could always be outvoted) so that not only did Roosevelt receive none of the profits that should have been his when the boat started actually to work but he was also confronted with threats of a suit to recover much of the company funds he

4. See John H. B. Latrobe, *The First Steamboat Voyage on the Western Waters,* Fund Publication 6 (Baltimore: Maryland Historical Society, 1871). The *New Orleans* was delayed by low water at Louisville, where she arrived on October 4, 1811. She took the occasion to make a return trip to Cincinnati, thus proving that she had speed enough to go upstream as well as down. She remained at Louisville for some time; it was there that Lydia's second child was born. Shortly afterward the river started rising and reached a level to permit the boat to pass the "Falls of the Ohio," where the river poured over an almost continuous ledge of rock. They passed in safety, and almost immediately the earthquakes began. John H. B. Latrobe's account, based on the memories of his sister Lydia, is vivid and valuable.

The *New Orleans,* 371 tons, was 148.5 feet long, 32.5 feet beam, with a molded depth of 12 feet. She was wrecked and sank in July, 1814, but her engines were recovered and re-used in the second *New Orleans,* a slightly smaller vessel of 324 tons. See Louis C. Hunter and Beatrice Jones Hunter, *Steamboats on the Western Rivers . . .* in Studies in Economic History (Cambridge: Harvard University Press, 1949).

had expended in Pittsburgh. Furthermore, Fulton refused to have anything more to do with him. Unfortunately Fulton's action was not entirely without justification, for Roosevelt was as careless in his accounting as he was dilatory in writing letters—and the letters he had written en route and mailed along the way were all lost in transit.

Disagreements flared. Early in 1812 Fulton refused to pay Roosevelt amounts actually due, and Latrobe was again called in by Roosevelt as a sort of ambassador. The architect saw Fulton in New York, they talked over the matter at length, and Fulton—again, as he claimed, solely because of his friendship for Latrobe—agreed not only to cancel the unjust claims but also to pay Roosevelt something on account of the profits, this amount to be made over to Lydia and her heirs in view of keeping it safe against any action the Federal government might undertake to recover the old Navy copper debt. But Fulton sought to delay his payments by substituting a six-month note for cash, and Latrobe was forced to write him a letter (February 1, 1813), in which he also objected to the terms Fulton had used in a letter to him about the affair:

> There is in the remarks, some reason,—& I think as you are on the high ground it would be *kind* in you to let the thing go as they wish it. . . . I, as you know am only the *Gobetween,* & give no opinion.—In fact, *believing as I do, that Roosevelt is an honest man,* altho' one of the most wrong headed in the world,—I want the thing *done with* because while it remains afloat, my poor daughter will know no peace,—& God knows, her afflictions of mind & body since her marriage have exceeded those of any woman I have known, & will most assuredly, in their *permanent* consequence, make an old woman of her before her time. For instance in her first trip down the river [in the flatboat], her husband being sick, & every hand on board laid up,—she for three weeks cooked & baked for the whole crew, at a time when she was within 2 months of her own confinement,—nursed all the sick, scoured & washed what was absolutely necessary, & one night at Natchez, the crew being ashore, & Roosevelt & her maid sick, the boat got aground on the mast of a sunk vessel ahead, & the water falling fast, the stern of the boat, badly caulked, leaked so much, that they would have gone to the bottom had she not baled her with all her might from *Nine* in the evening till *One* in the morning when the crew returned.—In the steamboat, when her boy was a fortnight old, the Earthquakes began, & continued without intermission until their arrival at Natchez. Their effects, as described by her, were indeed tremendous.—All this & a thousand times more,—together with the pecuniary

difficulties of her husband, while they have matured her understanding & given her the air of a much older woman, have . . . depressed her courage, & very materially injured her constitution.—I am hardly able sometimes to contain my silent anger against her husband for exposing her to such hardships, and yet she makes his defense with much affectionate zeal, & attributes it all so entirely to her own determination to share every fatigue with him,—and in fact is so entirely attached to him, that nothing can be said upon the subject. He indeed appears attached to her, for which I do not thank him;—for no man of sense or feeling would be insensible of so much merit & loveliness as belong to her,—united with possible talent.

All this I have written perhaps very imperfectly but with that confidence which always inspires me when I write to you. . . .

The handwriting shows that this letter, which apparently was efficacious, was written at terrific speed and under deep emotional stress. Latrobe's paternal love obviously blinded him to the fact that what to his more mature hindsight seemed terrific hardship may have been for Lydia and Roosevelt high adventure as well as evidence of a new kind of complete, almost modern, partnership between them.

The same letter, however, concludes with a bit of welcome news: the virtual end of the Navy copper affair, which for years had been a millstone around the necks of both Roosevelt and Latrobe. As we have seen, Roosevelt had contrived to clear up the architect's personal financial involvement. But emotionally Latrobe was still deeply enmeshed; he could not see the matter otherwise than as a threat both to the future and to the good name of his daughter's husband if not to Lydia herself. Roosevelt for years had sought some way of clearing off the obligation without sacrificing any of his capital; but, though he felt the whole situation a deep injustice to himself, his income was so precarious and his cash position always so uncertain that no solution had offered. At last he made up his mind to the inevitable, as the final paragraph of Latrobe's letter to Fulton suggests:

Mr. Roosevelt is gone to Philadelphia finally to conclude his business with the U. States. He has about $50,000 worth to offer them as security which sets him completely free for 7 years, & as most of this security is land, valued in his inventory at $2 p. acre, there is every reason to believe that it will 7 years hence be much more valuable.—He will return in 10 days. Lydia in the meantime remains with us, & is daily increasing our regret that we cannot always be together.—

Mrs. Latrobe joins me in sincere respects to Mrs. Fulton & yourself, & children.

The triumph of the Mississippi boat, which was astonishing the world and piling up profits in its regular trips between Natchez and New Orleans, proved conclusively that steamboats on the western rivers could be hugely profitable. A second boat, the *Vesuvius,* was being built in Pittsburgh; John Livingston, Mrs. Fulton's brother,[5] was Fulton's agent in this project, and Staudinger, one of Roosevelt's early associates, was foreman. But even more profitable would be steamboat commerce on the Ohio and its tributaries. If Fulton wished to corner that rapidly growing market he would have to hurry. In these years he was in a state of chronic anxiety: his monopoly was being attacked on every side, his basic patent itself was threatened, and rival boat builders were already contemplating work at Pittsburgh. If the monopoly legislation was to be held illegal and his monopoly on steam commerce should therefore fail, at least he must be the first in the field; he knew well the prestige his name held and the confidence it engendered.

Accordingly he and his New York collaborators set up a new company, the Ohio Steamboat Navigation Company. A trusted agent was required to build the boats; who better than Latrobe? Fulton knew that Latrobe, in 1812, was out of a job and harassed by debts and that his architectural prospects were dim. He knew that because the British blockade had disrupted coastwise commerce the engines for the New Orleans waterworks, which by now were desperately needed, would have to be completed inland and floated down the Ohio and Mississippi, and that Latrobe was already considering a move to Pittsburgh to build

---

5. The Livingston clan was deeply enmeshed in Fulton's steamboat affairs. After the Chancellor's death, his younger brother Edward acted for his heirs and handled the Mississippi business from his home in New Orleans. Mrs. Fulton was a Livingston; Latrobe refers to her as the Chancellor's niece—and in a letter to Captain Tingey (June 22, 1808) calls her "a very learned lady, somewhat stricken . . . rich, elegant, spirited & able to manage any man"—but actually she was the daughter of Walter Livingston, the Chancellor's second cousin.

The profits earned by the early steamboats were fabulous. Thus in 1814 the *New Orleans* cleared a net $20,000 on a capitalization of $40,000, and in 1818 the *Vesuvius* in one trip up the river received freight charges of $47,000, of which over half was clear profit. See Hunter, *op. cit.* p. 20.

them.[6] Was it friendship or a shrewd sizing up of affairs and a clever seizing upon another's hardships as a means of furthering his own ends that prompted Fulton? His character was so volatile, his actions were occasionally so erratic, and his record of turning against former associates was so chronic that today, as in his own time, it is impossible to make any final judgment. Latrobe believed implicitly in Fulton's good will and acknowledged his gratitude to him for settling the Roosevelt affair. And Fulton in those years had become more than a business friend; he was a welcome visitor at the Latrobe home.[7]

Evidently they discussed the move to Pittsburgh during the visit Latrobe made to New York in the autumn of 1812 (September 27 to October 9), as well as steamboat projects for the Washington area. When he departed he traveled by steamboat to New Brunswick and on his way spent two days at Clover Hill, where he had left his wife. It was on this visit that he finally made up his mind, and from then on he devoted his keen attention to the whole steamboat situation. On October 15 he wrote Fulton from Philadelphia about Daniel French's steamboat at Cooper's Ferry—French was one of Fulton's most serious rivals—and he wrote Cooper his opinion of the French boat. The same day he wrote to Roosevelt to find the "actual rate of going" of the Mississippi boat; then a day later he wrote Fulton again about business conditions in the West, the possible competitors on the Ohio, and the lowering of river freight rates which the mere threat of steamboats had already forced; much of this information he had obtained from a Mr. Gratz, "who does by far the greatest quantity of western business in this city." Again from Washington he wrote Fulton more about competitors (October 28):

6. Latrobe had written Roosevelt as early as July 1, 1812: "I am very well convinced that I must go to Pittsburgh & organize affairs there. I have a serious intention of being there as soon as I can get money to bear my expenses." And the next day in a letter to Jefferson he said: "I intend as soon as possible to employ myself in some manufacturing occupation, & to quit, if I can, the public service in which my mind has suffered a very disadvantageous change."

7. Much of the material dealing with the relation of Roosevelt and Latrobe to the development of steamboats comes from a long letter Latrobe wrote to a Pittsburgh attorney, Henry Baldwin, Mrs. Barlow's brother, on October 10, 1814. This is so important a source that it is given complete in the Appendix. See also James Thomas Flexner, *Steamboats Come True* . . . (New York: Viking, 1944). There is a small amount of interesting material dealing with the Mississippi and Ohio companies in the Gilbert Montague Collection of Robert

[Roosevelt] has promised to look up Baker for me. [Baker, who had been the engineer of the *New Orleans,* was desired as a mechanic for Pittsburgh.] . . . He found him in your service, & ascertained his terms . . . the same offered him by Oliver Evans, who is going to build boats on the Ohio. . . . I fear this opposition of Oliver Evans will knock us up as to filling our subscriptions [note the "our"]. . . . As French uses wheels [on his boat] in the Delaware without opposition, from you or Stevens, I fear Oliver will be emboldened to adopt the same plan. . . . The races & the incessant rain have prevented a meeting of the gentlemen who wish to put forward the Georgetown-Alexandria boat. E. Riggs of this place heads the subscription list with $1000. . . . The Potomac Creek boat is not likely to take so well. I cannot get Forrest to move in it. . . .

By January, 1813, he had definitely decided on moving to Pittsburgh and wrote the news to his brother Christian in London (January 13):

It is a long time since I have heard from you. But this unfortunate war accounts for everything that is abominable. I expect it will end either in a few months or last for many years, in which case your Congreve Rockits [sic] may be tried on our towns & our Torpedoes under the bottoms of your ships. Hitherto in the Naval engagements which have occurred the Yankees have had the better, twice with small odds in the point of weight of metal & once (in the case of the Frolic) against superior force. But against your ships our few Frigates can't long have an existence so we'll say no more about it. . . .

This war has among many other changes, totally changed my plan. It is my intention to resign my public situation & go & live at Pittsburgh in Pennsylvania. My reasons are these. The new demands on the Treasury for the expenses of the War, have occasioned a suspension of all work on the Legislative building in this city, which I have so far completed as to accommodate the houses of Congress, & the Supreme Courts of the U. States now admirably. What remains to be done is not immediately necessary & may be postponed. The Navy Yard in this place which is entirely of my creation is also pretty well compleated. I have done enough for my reputation here. I have therefore engaged with Mr. Fulton in the establishment of steamboats to the Westward, and next year I shall build at least three at Pittsburgh of 3 to 400 tons each. I have already compleated a line of boats from hence to Potomac Creek where the land carriage to Richmond necessarily commences, & from hence to Norfolk steamboats of 400 tons will compleat the line to Norfolk. I gave

---

Fulton Manuscripts in the New York Public Library; there are also many letters dealing with the subject among the Livingston Papers in the New-York Historical Society.

you in my last a full account of this new mode of navigation. If I live to finish what I have undertaken & which will occupy three or four years, I shall very probably be able to sit down at my leisure [the ever hopeful Latrobe!] for the rest of my life & deliver the Bar at which I have pulled devotedly so long to my son Henry now at N. Orleans, where he is as industrious & active as I could possibly wish him to be. A second edition of the same boy is growing up in John, now 9 years old. Our next Juliana is 8, and our youngest Benj. Henry a great rogue of 6. I wish I had your half dozen boys here.—We have business for them all, and I am afraid, in spite of the victories of Lord Wellington the same embarrassment exists in England respecting the provisions for children which existed 20 years ago. . . .

. . . We expect in a few days Lydia & her husband here, with her *two* children, a boy & a girl. Thus I am a generation ahead of you.—This goes by a Cartel which takes over Mr. Baker late Secretary of Legation to Mr. Foster. He is a very well informed & I believe well disposed man, but can do no good between the two nations. . . .

Two weeks later (February 1), through George Poe, he rented a house in Pittsburgh belonging to James O'Hara; when his delay in Washington prevented his using it, he wrote O'Hara in April asking that it be turned over to John Livingston for the time being. But nine full months were to elapse before he could finally leave Washington—probably, as he thought, for good—and it was already July before he went to New York again to make the final agreements with Fulton.

Many things caused the delay. The Potomac Steamboat Company, which had elected Latrobe its secretary, required much work. The state of North Carolina had granted the exclusive privilege of steam navigation within its waters to Stevens, not to Fulton, and to counter this action Fulton's agent DeLacy [8] was working with North Carolina congressmen. Latrobe arranged for DeLacy to get an opinion on the validity of the Fulton-Livingston patent from Robert Goodloe Harper, who re-

8. John Devereux DeLacy, or Delacy, was a charming, improvident, optimistic, ambitious Irish-born gentleman who for some time acted as one of Fulton's traveling agents. In 1815, in a letter to Henry Latrobe on February 23, the architect gives his final summing up of the ebullient Irishman: "But he has proved himself a very honest man lately, and he certainly is a man of most excellent understanding, & of a true good Irish heart. He however overwhelms his excellent qualities by manners the most extraordinary. He left Ireland at 14 and has lived in America ever since, and yet it is not easy to find a more intolerable brogue than he has. . . . He is a handsome man of about 40, with an iron constitution, and a countenance of unblushing but good natured candor. Such a man is the Knight errant that has arisen in defense of our family . . ."

ported: "The powers of the central government expressly given by the Constitution extend over the whole U. States, and are paramount to the powers of the states; among these is the securing to the inventor the fruits of their [sic] ingenuity." But the legislature of Virginia, on the other hand, as Latrobe wrote Fulton (March 3), had granted "us" a charter on both the James and the Potomac for fifteen years; Latrobe also was seeking a similar grant from the legislature of Illinois to cover steamboats on the upper Mississippi, the Wabash, and the Illinois.

Another controversy arose over the question of towboats. Fulton had heard of certain proposals to use steam tugboats, and he hurried to assert his rights by applying for a patent on the idea. Latrobe sent to Secretary of State Monroe (June 10, 1813) a formal application for the patent signed "B. H. Latrobe, attorney for and on behalf of Robert Fulton." But Fulton's claim was contested by a certain New Englander named Sullivan who claimed priority in the scheme. The Secretary of State, as was usual at that time, referred the matter to a three-man commission, each claimant appointing one member and the third being appointed by the Secretary. At Fulton's suggestion Latrobe named Eli Whitney, the famous Connecticut inventor, to represent the Fulton interests (as he wrote Fulton September 3). There the matter rested so far as the architect was concerned, swallowed up in the larger interest of the war.

During this last Washington summer, Roosevelt and Lydia on their way home to New York from New Orleans visited the Latrobes briefly, and the architect took the occasion to discuss with his son-in-law the state of steamboat affairs in Pittsburgh, including the size and equipment of the building yard (then at work on the two additional Mississippi boats, the *Vesuvius* and the *Etna*), so that he might be thoroughly prepared. He learned too of Roosevelt's investments in Pittsburgh, for the incorrigible plunger while he was a resident in that city had bought a whisky distillery and a snuffbox factory.

In addition to all these steamboat affairs, other engineering matters required the architect's attention. There was, for instance, Roosevelt's scheme for an engine to be driven by gunpowder—a scheme into which Roosevelt was pouring his immense energy, trying vainly to interest New York financiers in his invention.[9] And there was the matter of

9. Latrobe was not sanguine of its success. On March 22 he wrote Roosevelt: ". . . I have also a letter from Mr. Graf, which very much embarrasses me. He puts me on my honor

Latrobe's own steam-engine factory. This, though busy, was an expense instead of a profit maker, for the war rendered deliveries from Washington difficult if not impossible and the purchasers paid only on delivery. Something had to be done with the enterprise. Latrobe felt he had sunk so much capital in it that to liquidate at once would endanger whatever credit he possessed. Finally he succeeded in making an arrangement with his associate in the business, John Wark, an Alexandria (Virginia) millwright, who assumed the direction and the ownership of the works without loss—or gain, for that matter—to Latrobe. He was thus well rid of a concern that in those precarious years of war and inflation was bound to become a grievous burden; but with its passage from his hands went another vain hope of financial security. It was a bitter blow, yet the pain of it was buried under his new great hope—a fortune from steamships!

And there was still some architectural work to be finished before he could move from Washington—the Marine Hospital, for instance. This great scheme, which had occupied him intermittently from 1808 on, was alive again under the stimulus of wartime needs, and Latrobe was busy making a complete set of final drawings; his bill for $300 for consultation and drawings went to the Secretary of the Navy on March 27, 1813. Then, too, he was still in charge of some work at the Navy Yard and had to make a final report on it, and the steam engine he had installed there required constant supervision.

He also had many other architectural and engineering interests to hold him. There was a mill for George Brent, in Washington. There were odds and ends in connection with the Washington Canal, for, as Latrobe had foreseen, maintenance of the wooden locks was a constant problem. There was some work on the Marlborough courthouse[10] and some for the courthouse at Allentown, Pennsylvania. There was a portico for Charles Carroll of Bellevue. And Henry Clay's residence, Ashland, in Lexington, Kentucky, then under construction, required many draw-

---

as to my opinion on your machine, which I find you after all proposed to him. I told him I had had the same sanguine spirit which animated me 25 years ago . . . but that I was considerably cooled by disappointment . . ."

10. July 7, to William Beanes, Marlborough, Maryland: "It will be utterly impossible to put up the bars at the court house on the 13th. My part is done, but the castings [being made by Henry Foxall] will delay the business."

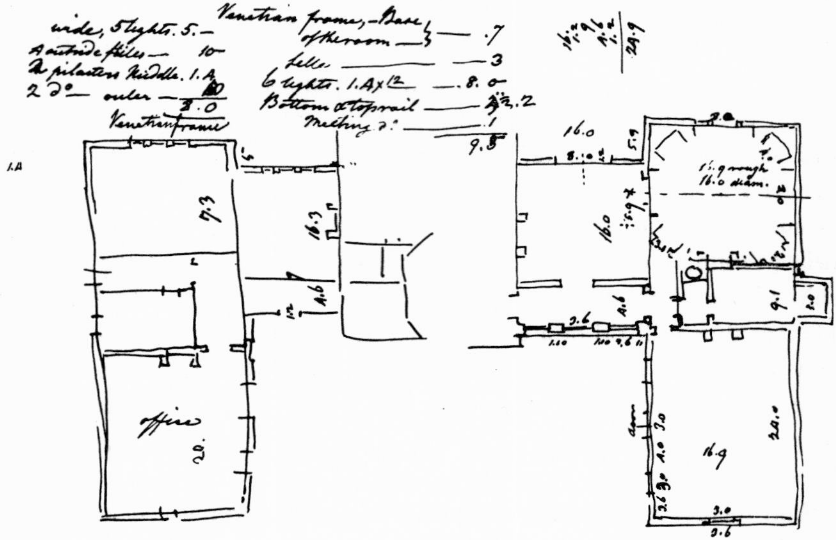

Courtesy Clay Lancaster

FIGURE 22. Henry Clay House, Ashland, Lexington, Ky. From Latrobe's sketch in a letter to Clay.

ings.[11] There were the drawings for Transylvania College, also in Lexington, for the same client—an ambitious scheme that failed to materialize at that time. There was a house for J. C. Williams of Baltimore. This was evidently a project of considerable size, and Latrobe gave it his best efforts. But its construction was postponed, probably because of the war, and Latrobe, anxious to collect as many of his bills as he could before he left for Pittsburgh, billed the client for the work to date. Williams refused to pay, in a letter (written in November, 1813) that only reached Latrobe in Pittsburgh several months later—a missive so galling to Latrobe's notions of professional standing that it drew from him a full and angry letter expressive of the difficulties under which he labored:

11. August 15, to Henry Clay: "As to your house, I think you said that you had reversed the use of the wings. . . . I also understood that you are at present engaged in building the wing containing the chambers & nursery. . . . In the meantime I shall make my design without regard to the corner houses . . . and shall send you the drawings." He sent an additional plan on September 5.

Pittsburgh, April 3, 1814

Sir

Your letter of Nov. . . . 1813 arrived here while I was confined to my bed by a dangerous illness, and withheld from me by the kindness of my wife, for a long time.—I have delayed to answer it chiefly by my astonishment at its contents. It is *in point of fact* the greatest insult I ever received in my life, & yet I am so well persuaded that every man acts with as much propriety as he is capable of, that I am readily conscious that you did not mean to insult me.—You have besides a further excuse,—you acted upon false information.—I will now put the case in a form which will be intelligible to you.—

Supposing you were to offer a cargo to Mr. Gilmore, & demand a certain price for it and Mr. Gilmore, taking the matter into consideration were to offer you one third of the price you ask, & were moreover to tell you that you were either so ignorant of the practice of your profession, or so inclined to impose upon your customers, that you had exceeded by 200 per cent the demands of the very first merchants for the article, & that he had this information from persons, whom he did not name. If on receiving this answer you had knocked him down, I for one would have given you great credit for doing so.—

I asked you 150$ for a design which detained me two days in Baltimore, out of which had you executed it, all the conveniences & elegance of the best house in Baltimore would have arisen,—& you offer me 50$ & tell me into the bargain that 10 Guineas is the common charge for a design by the first architects in Europe!

Whoever gave you the information knew nothing of the matter. That in Europe there are men of talents who are starving is certain, & that many young artists feed their profligacy & dissipation by selling their productions at an under value is also certain, just as merchants sell an article with which the merchant is overstocked at a loss, if they cannot afford to keep it on hand. But that any architect of character & eminence in England or France ever made a design for such a house as yours for 10 Guineas is a ridiculous error, not to say a falsehood. I have been in no inconsiderable business in England myself; and . . . Shaffer, Harris, Wyatt, Soane, Grave, Harrison, Cockerell etc. would not make a design unless to be executed under their direction. For their direction & the design they charged,—for fair drawings,—a set is 50 Guineas, for each consultation half a Guinea, from 5 Guineas to 20 Guineas per day for going into the country to view the grounds & personally to direct the work, & 5 per cent commission on all monies expended. Having been 3 years in Mr. Cockerell's office & made many of his designs,

I must know this in detail, & my intimacy with other architects proved to me that these charges are uniform. Being very young I charged at first 3 Guineas per day in attending Mr. Fuller's & Sperling's houses in Sussex,[12] but 5 Guineas in attending parliament on the Marsden Canal business; I received 100 Guineas as gratuity on the success of my evidence. *The English Courts* have decided that for a *perfect design, which is ordered but not executed 2½ per cent on the estimated cost is a fair charge.* And with us even the Carpenters receive 3 per cent only for measuring & valuing the work, without any design. You must therefore in England have paid me 500$, & had you built your house you must have paid 600 for measuring it.—And I have charged you only 150$.

In order to close the business however, I am willing to receive 50$, you paying the same to Mr. Hazlehurst who will give you a receipt in full and returning him the drawings. If this is agreeable to you there will be an end of this very unpleasant business, which if further correspondence is necessary, I shall beg leave to transfer to Mr. Harper [Latrobe's attorney].

Respectfully Yrs.
B. H. Latrobe

More and more, however, as the year 1813 passed, it was the war that filled the architect's mind and his days. Latrobe was intensely patriotic and deeply distressed as events seemed to be turning more and more against the United States. Chesapeake Bay was now to all intents and purposes British territory. British fleets navigated it at will; they lay off Norfolk, and, a hundred strong, British warships barricaded the entrances to Baltimore and Annapolis. All coastwise commerce was at an end, and land transport was jammed on the roads.

In connection with this blockade there is a curious note—so characteristic of the unreal character of that peculiar war, strangely compounded of chivalry and wanton destruction—concerning the steamboat (then being built in New York) which the newly organized Potomac Steamboat Company wished to buy from Fulton. The boat had been ordered before the British blockade was complete; but now, with the British in command of Chesapeake Bay, how was it to be delivered? Christened the *Washington,* it was eventually delivered, after the war, in May, 1815. But by that time Latrobe's company had dissolved and a new one (in which he had no interest) managed her operation. Latrobe in a letter

---

12. Hammerwood Lodge and Ashdown House. See pages 44-6.

to Fulton (May 8, 1813) on the general condition of affairs remarks that he supposes the danger "which surrounds us will assuredly prevent the steamboat being brought around." Yet in the middle of August the Potomac Steamboat Company was still expecting its delivery from New York, and Latrobe was forced to write twice to Fulton about the impatience of the company. No passport difficulty was expected, for the scheme had august backing, it appeared: "The President & Mr. Monroe [Secretary of State], it seems, have both interested themselves exceedingly about the boat, and have given assurances that an arrangement for getting her round would be made . . ." Conceivably the President and his Secretary of State could have somehow—perhaps through a friendly legation—put before the British admiral their desire that the steamboat be permitted to pass the British blockade; but what an extraordinary request that would have been! And the company's confidence that such a request would be granted is even more remarkable. Whether or not some preliminary inquiries had already been made we do not know, but the entire episode reveals a kind of give-and-take between hostile forces that is almost unprecedented. Three weeks later the company was still waiting, and Latrobe pled with Fulton (September 5) to do something to quiet the impatient purchasers: "They are outrageous. They accuse me. It seems they had a license to bring her round to Annapolis in a cartel, which is expired or expiring." A week later the architect left Washington, and the matter is not referred to again.

The defenses of Washington seemed to Latrobe inconceivably chaotic, the entire Washington administration shot through with incompetence and confusion, the army authorities arrogant, over-confident, and planless. These impressions come out in letter after letter, as in this to Adjutant General Duane at Philadelphia (March 13, 1813):

I shall remove to Pittsburgh this summer. I offered my services once to General Dearborn. He told me *engineers* were of not much use in our Army;—anybody could *dig* a fosse and that they ranked with Brigade [infantry?] at the commencement of the present war. I waited on Dr. Eustis & pressed him exceedingly to do something for the Corps of Engineers, & offered him the services of 5 or 6 French officers, among the rest of Godefroi (Count La Mard),—men hating the English, & royalists whose French attachments were worn out, who were married here, etc., etc. "I know it, I know it,"—says he, "but we do not want them till we are at the walls of Quebec."—Our honest, patriotic, *firm,*—but influenced President tells me plainly,—that he dare not employ me, because I am *unpopular.*[13] So I am going to be a blacksmith at Pittsburgh: & there the feathers which I have for many years pulled from my pen, to keep her down to the level of my dependent state will again sprout . . .

and in one to Mr. S. Gordon of Philadelphia (January 14, 1813), about another French engineer seeking service:

There is, you know, a violent prejudice among the Federalists against everything French. . . . It arises partly from the inveterate habit of the nation before the Revolution, which is not yet worn out. . . . With the exception of Colonel de La Croix, whose position has arisen from very peculiar patronage, not a single Frenchman has, since the Revolution, been entrusted with public duties, and those who were in the army, Rivardi, Rochefontaine, Vermanet, Toussard & many others have been, by degrees, got rid of. . . . The Republican party entertain a violent jealousy against all foreigners, Frenchmen particularly. I have been laboring these six years to get employment for Mr. Godefroi (Count La Mard). . . . General Dearborn told me, they had no occasion for engineers, that he never would consent to employ foreigners, especially not Frenchmen . . .

To his son Henry he unburdens his soul with respect to the Washington scene:

[January 14:] . . . Mr. Madison, whom your mother, in her way, compared to a little shrivelled spider, in the midst of a large flabby cobweb shaking in the wind, will be nobody at all. Mr. Gallatin has in fact been president for some time. . . . [January 24:] There has been miserable work under Granny Dearborn to the Northward. But your apprehensions about the Indians have not the least foundation. Tecumseh is prisoner, & they have already broken up. Pittsburgh, at all events, is safe, let things go as they will. . . . [February 21, with good news of the capture of the British frigate *Java* by Commodore Bainbridge in the *Constitution:*] She was so crippled, he was obliged to blow

---

13. On April 24, 1813, Latrobe sent Secretatry Jones of the Navy a long letter which is an apologia for his way of life: "My time has been fully employed. I have had no assistance in the most laborious parts of my operations.—My family has been my greatest, and almost my only scene of short relaxations & of enjoyment—I could only have devoted my evenings to the members of Congress, scattered thro' an extent of 4 miles in length, had I had the talent or inclination to visit & to entertain them. But, in truth, I neither felt the wish nor the propriety of *appearing* to consult anyone on my designs, or the mode of my operation, while I felt myself competent to perform my duty without assistance. . . .

"My unpopularity therefore has arisen [from my character and my ideals of public service], not from extravagance."

her up. Br. 60 killed, 170 wounded. Am. 9 killed, 29 wounded. This uniform disparity is astonishing and inexplicable.

A month later, in a letter to Fulton (March 13), he is bitter:

There is now a most formidable force at Norfolk, at which the Federalists here rejoice, saying that it will bring Madison to his senses. I have by this time convinced myself that we have no national honor to defend, & therefore had as well make up the quarrel as well as we can, & go to making children, tobacco & flour as hard as possible, giving up Detroit & what else we have lost, appointing a committee of merchants to govern the country, & offering our trade to European nations at auction under the hammer of Mr. L. Davis . . .

The next day he writes to Henry Baldwin in Pittsburgh:

General Wilkinson is to have command of the Northern Army, an express having been dispatched for him 10 days ago. Norfolk is in a state of siege, a formidable British force being in Hampton Roads. But they are not afraid, having 30 gunboats, the *Constellation* & a narrow channel, with two tolerable forts & 3000 men in arms. Oh, the folly of this War . . .

As matters worsened and spring wore into summer, he wrote General Duane at Philadelphia (May 2):

There are now in the Bay, perhaps 100 British ships of war. . . . At the Navy Yard are 3 or 400 guns . . . [they] lie in rows on rotten logs like sea lions snoring on the ice. Not a carriage on which to mount them. To be sure we have some very fine soldiers. 100 marines at the barracks. Major General Van Ness, Lt. Col. Tayloe, lately appointed over the heads of all the majors . . . Capt. Thornton's troop of horse, himself, a trumpeter & 1 trooper, Capt. E. B. Caldwell's troops, 40 strong, a good corps, *quo ad* horse, men & courage, Capts. Cassin, Lenox & Davidson, 60 strong . . . 2 rifle corps, I believe in all perhaps 400 men, as many in Georgetown, & as many or more in Alexandria, good stuff, rather more like soldiers than mahogany logs are like dining tables. And yet the constant cry, "Oh, they won't come" . . . There is no more preparation at Alexandria than at Cape May. Fort Washington, Dearborn's design, the magazine the most conspicuous spot on the top of the hill . . .

Latrobe could not even get his regular work at the Navy Yard performed properly and was forced to write William Jones, the Secretary of the Navy (May 7):

> I have, by direction of Com. Tingey . . . given such directions for the driving of the piles in the new slip as appeared to be necessary. . . . I acknowledge the support of the principal commanding officer . . . but from the counteraction of others my efforts are useless, & the public interest suffers. I therefore solicit either to be relieved from all responsibility in respect to the slip, or to receive such authority as shall ensure obedience to my instructions . . .

The British had burned Havre de Grace and Frederick; these attacks Latrobe referred to as "Cockburn's fires," for that redoubtable admiral was rapidly accumulating the burden of hatred for his ruthlessness that has pursued him ever since. On May 8 the architect wrote Fulton of the danger to Washington:

> An express arrived this morning stating that the British were preparing to burn Annapolis. . . . The postboy who is since come in, says that no bombardment however has taken place. . . . Madison and [General] Armstrong declare that there is not any danger. A town meeting, however, this evening has appointed a committee of vigilance, & will, I hope, rouse the sleeping administration a little. . . .

And the same day, in a letter to Samuel Hazlehurst in Philadelphia, he made a prophecy that turned out to be all too true: "I have little doubt of this city faring exactly as did Havre de Grace."

Latrobe wished desperately to have some part in the defense. Largely in vain, he busied himself trying to get commissions for various engineer and architect friends. For several harmless English acquaintances he obtained exceptions from the military order that Englishmen had to leave the eastern coastal regions, though he complained that one of them, a certain Mr. Greatrakes, talked too much against the government. Another of those he helped to remain was William James, who had briefly been his pupil and draftsman in London and of whom he wrote to General Mason (May 31): "While I was in England I knew his family intimately. His father put him into my office, but his tendencies led him more to the turf than to the fine arts & I advised him to change his profession."

But this vicarious activity could not satisfy his desire to be of use. He offered suggestions to Brigadier General Young at Alexandria (May 15) —that the authorities use fire rafts, moor the frigate *New York* as a floating battery, mount the ample supply of guns, commandeer the stage horses for cavalry, form a company of riverboatmen and merchant seamen for shore defense, cut abatis in the woods—and he sent a sketch to make sure the general understood the last of these recommendations. But above all, Latrobe says, the government must wake up and do something.

He had tried, too, to sell various useful arms or supplies to the government for the Marks: hemp for rope, sauerkraut, and, most important, a large ship described in a letter (March 12) to William Jones, Secretary of the Navy, as "the *American Eagle,* 1000 tons, cost $125,000, pierced for 28 guns on gun deck, 16 guns on upper deck, fully found . . ." But this was also in vain; the hemp, the sauerkraut, and the *American Eagle* had all been refused, as Latrobe wrote Louis Mark (March 16):

> The Secretary told me that the law would not permit the purchase [of the vessel]; that an appropriation was made . . . to purchase vessels of a certain description, namely sloops of war carrying their guns on one deck, vessels light & not expensive, such as could be built & equipped for $60,000. That your ship was in fact a 28 gun frigate, too large to be employed as a sloop of war, too small to lay alongside any of the enemy's ships on our coast. . . . The Secretary informed me that the Government had resolved to build all their vessels themselves, on one particular mould and of a particular size & timber . . . [and] that the purchase of merchant vessels in the year 1798 had proved ruinous . . .

Nevertheless, he did at last find his niche—and, in its way, a not unimportant one. It arose out of his close connection with Fulton on the one hand and with Secretary Jones on the other. Fulton had for years been interested in submarine vessels and submarine torpedoes; here was the ideal situation in which to test them. Here were great groups of hostile warships, arrogantly holding complete control of the waters but for that very reason over-confident and careless. Latrobe, keenly aware of the possibilities, wrote to Fulton (March 21): "If I were unmarried, & under 25, I would borrow a few pairs of torpedoes, & if I am not much mistaken, they should succeed in some stormy night at Norfolk, with the aid of two canoes . . . or, rather whaleboats. The more dreadful the wind is, the darker, the better . . ." Both he and DeLacy had lobbied for the passage of Senator Bradley's bill to grant a bounty of half the value of every enemy ship destroyed by citizens not commissioned by the United States, and he had written Fulton (March 12) about a certain

Mr. Perkins [14] of Boston, a man of great practical acumen, who was proposing a range of torpedoes across the Narrows in New York harbor "to be set on fire by an electric wire."

By the middle of March the prospects of using the Fulton torpedoes had brightened. Latrobe had succeeded in interesting the Secretary of the Navy, and orders for the necessary materials were being prepared. "We shall hear more of this, I think," he wrote Fulton (March 29). The result was that Latrobe himself became the secret agent through whom the whole enterprise funneled, and he in turn worked through his friend General Duane in Philadelphia. Several of Fulton's torpedoes were in Washington; they had been sent over from France years before, along with Fulton's model submarine, by Joel Barlow, who had been Fulton's patron. On March 27, Latrobe devoted hours to searching for them.

> I found them [he writes Fulton], with some difficulty in an upper story thrown into a heap, some in a barrel, others lying about. . . . I spoke to the storekeeper, Mr. Buller Cocke, a Norfolk man, & told him you had delivered these things to Mr. Barlow [and] you wished me to inquire where they were. . . . I requested him to say nothing. . . . He became very anxious that they should be used in Norfolk and said ". . . 12 desparate fellows . . . could easily be found to hang a pair of them across a hauser."

The torpedoes were dismantled. How to get them into use secretly? It was here that General Duane came in. Latrobe had implicit faith in him, and he in Latrobe. Since he was in the army rather than in the navy, his was the ideal address to which the torpedoes could be sent without giving any notion to the rank and file of what they were or what their ultimate destination was; they were consequently packed and shipped to him. The Secretary of the Navy told Latrobe that no Navy money could be expended on the project itself but that gunpowder, boats, and men—volunteers—would be at Fulton's command. Three weeks later the commander of the expedition was chosen: Elijah Mix. Latrobe writes Fulton (April 13) about the torpedo volunteers; he has engaged a Captain Lawton, and had been considering a Commodore Kennedy, who was in charge of a flotilla of gunboats, for the command,

> but [he continues] today the Secretary has sent me a man born for the service . . . Captain Elijah Mix . . . He is here to claim & receive half the value of

14. Jacob Perkins, inventor and industrialist, chiefly remembered for his invention of a widely used machine for making nails.

the *Emolus,* supposed to be lost by accident, but, in fact, run ashore by Mix, then a prisoner on her. He, at the same time, took & brought back her dispatches, & he has since contrived to procure the treasonable Bostonian correspondence, which will come out next meeting of Congress. . . . I shall be the means of getting him the necessary boats & hands, confidentially from the department.[15]

On April 24 Latrobe informs Fulton that he is sending Mix to see him and that the mouth of Chesapeake Bay should be the first scene of action, for Mix has a friend at Old Point Comfort, "a creek at the door, a solitary house," and "a few leagues from the house, often only a few miles, the ships lie at anchor. . . . God bless you, my dear Fellow, & prosper your torpedoes, as he has done your steamboats for the benefit of humanity."

By May 7 the expedition has largely crystallized, and Latrobe writes Edward Johnson, the mayor of Baltimore, enclosing a letter of instructions for Captain Mix. "If the enterprise miscarries, it will be in consequence of its becoming the subject of conversation," he warns; "if Capt. Mix succeeds, your city, indeed all the cities of our seaboard are safe." And to make secrecy doubly sure, the enclosed letter to Mix merely asks him to call on Captain Gordon, commander of the flotilla at Baltimore, for further orders. At the same time, Latrobe is busy forwarding the torpedo parts to General Duane at Philadelphia; they are sent carefully boxed in several crates marked "Mathematical Instruments." The torpedoes are soon assembled, and Mix and his crew are already on their way, so that on May 15 Latrobe can write Fulton: "Mix should be at Old Point Comfort. The English Fleet is collected in Lynnhaven Bay." Yet secrecy in the navy is hard to preserve. Captain Stewart of the *Constellation* is in Washington on June 5, and Latrobe is distressed to hear him talk about the proposed attack on the frigates before Captain Tingey and others who are unsympathetic to the bold scheme.

Then comes the first attempt—a total failure, but a near success. Latrobe has had a letter from Mix, he tells Fulton (June 10). Mix, in the dark, had hooked the hauser of a "74" instead of its rudder, and had been forced to flee, leaving the torpedo behind him; but the next night

15. The *Emolus* that Latrobe refers to was probably the British Navy cruiser brig *Emulous,* lost early in the war. Elijah Mix was commissioned a Sailing Master on January 12, 1813, and in the winter and spring of 1812-13 served on Lake Ontatrio as commander of the *Growler.*

he had boldly gone out and retrieved the torpedo safely. The Secretary of the Navy is afraid Mix's unsuccessful attempt may have given warning to the enemy, and through Latrobe he sends Mix more directions for another attempt. The moon is waning, and they are to wait till the dark of the moon. Latrobe writes Mix on June 17: "I watch the decline of the moon with more anxiety than I ever watched her increase." But on June 24 Mix with his men is back in Washington, swearing that he will eventually succeed, and that the British fleet is bombarding Norfolk. Mix needs more money; Latrobe writes Secretary Jones that he is lending him what he needs, hoping for an advance on the fire engine Latrobe has designed for the United States Navy frigates.[16] Mix tries again in the moonless period of July; four successive nights see him seeking the *Plantagenet,* chosen for destruction, and each time he is forced to return because of untoward accidents or near discovery by the enemy. Then he makes a fifth and final attempt; it is almost successful, but actually a failure. Latrobe writes Mix in Norfolk (August 15):

> I wrote to you while in New York [where Latrobe had gone to settle final points about the Pittsburgh scheme], and have since then seen in the newspapers the account of your attempt on the *Plantagenet,* which had so nearly proved successful, that had you been 20 feet nearer her, she must no doubt have been destroyed.[17]

---

16. Apparently neither Mix nor the Navy ever reimbursed Latrobe. Four years later (June 15, 1816) Latrobe wrote Jacob Mark in New York: "Enquire for me . . . after Elijah Mix, who, I understand keeps an auction store in New York. He owes me some hundred dollars."

17. According to T. H. Palmer, editor, *The Historical Register of the United States* (Washington: the editor, 1814), Part II, vol. II, Mix made his attempted torpedo attacks on the nights of July 18, 19, 20, 22, and 24; Palmer does not mention the attack in June. It was the last attempt, so nearly successful, to which Latrobe refers. Palmer's account is vivid. He tells us that Mix dropped his torpedo 100 yards from the *Plantagenet,* and goes on: "It was swept along by the tide, and would have completely effected its errand but for a cause not proper to be named here, but which may easily be guarded against in future experiments: it exploded too soon. The scene was awfully sublime . . . [The tremendous column of water thrown up] fell in torrents on the deck of the ship, which rolled into the yawning chasm below and almost upset . . . [The red glare of the explosion revealed] that the fore-channel of the ship was blown off, and a boat which lay alongside with several men in her, was thrown up by the dreadful convulsion of the waters . . . and they are certain that nearly the whole ship's crew hastily betook themselves to the boats."

According to a letter of Captain Mix in the Navy archives, the Secretary had issued him a sharp reprimand for not continuing his attempts to sink the *Plantagenet.*

He goes on to tell Mix of Fulton's latest scheme: cannon that fire under water. One of these has sent a 100-pound ball through twelve feet of water and three feet of oak, and Fulton has designed a boat for them—a sort of bombproof craft with sides of pine seven feet thick, designed to carry four of his heavy underwater cannon. Thus ends Latrobe's active connection with the war, resulting only in another disappointment.

Meanwhile the question of a possible peace was being discussed everywhere. As early as January 10, 1813, the architect had reported to Charles Gwynn at Baltimore that peace "is the talk of the day . . . but it takes two nations to make peace, while only one can provoke war, & declare it." Latrobe was bitter at the English behavior and wrote Thomas Johnson at Frederick (January 4):

> I am of your opinion as to English art. I love it as much as I detest the morality of the English Government, by far the most unprincipled & cruel of modern times in its conduct to foreign nations, & the most unjustifiably so, as she pretends to uncommon humanity, justice & religion . . .

The burning of Havre de Grace—like the later burning of Washington—seemed to him inexcusable in its wanton brutality. He wrote to Godefroy (May 6): "Fools, not to suppose that this is the only possible method of uniting the nation, & rousing us from the sleep of ignorance & folly in which we are sunk." Yet despite the prevailing American wrath it was obvious that little could be done by the Americans save to prolong a stalemate. Peace was inevitable, and it was equally desired by the American and the British governments—by the American in order to save its own seaboard and resurrect its sea-borne commerce, by the English to rebuild its economy shattered by the French war. To his father-in-law, Isaac Hazlehurst, Latrobe wrote on May 23: ". . . Peace in the autumn, Mr. Madison says so without reserve . . ."

In June came rumors that the Russians were offering their services. The Latrobes were socially intimate with several Russian diplomats, whose charm and unfailing courtesy had made them much loved and everywhere trusted in Washington. Latrobe himself knew especially well Paul Svenin, the Russian consul at Philadelphia and a fellow artist,[18] as

---

18. Svenin, Svinin, or Svennin, as Latrobe spells the name, was an amateur artist who left a sketchbook (now in the Metropolitan Museum in New York) containing superbly accurate water-color impressions of many facets of American life. A selection of those has been published in Avrahm Yarmolinsky's *Picturesque United States of America, 1811, 1812,*

well as the legation counsel Swertchkoff. When in early June it became known that the Russians were unexpectedly leaving the country, Latrobe wrote Svenin (June 5) that he had hoped to send him a finished set of the plans of the Capitol; he had been too rushed to complete them, but in their place he was sending mere outlines which his Russian artist friend could complete at his leisure. Incidentally, he took the occasion of the Russians' departure to help Mrs. Madison with her servant problem, for one of the legation employees had a valet who would be left jobless. Perhaps this man, Latrobe wrote Schwertchkoff, would be willing to serve as the Madisons' major domo; "if so, for the bien etre of our Queen, you will add to the obligations we owe you . . ."[19]

Reporting Washington gossip to General Duane in Philadelphia (June 27), Latrobe wrote:

Gallatin, it seems, said, or procured it to be said, thro' Richard Brent, in the Senate, that the Russian minister had expressly asked that he [Gallatin] should be of the mission [the peace commissions]. On the other hand, it is stated that he had also arranged with the President that he should retain the Secretaryship . . . The senate say that Armstrong complains bitterly. It is asserted that as to the issues of money G. has left positive orders that they shall not exceed 1½ million a month, so that though absent his ghost still governs us . . .

As the summer wore gradually away, the Russians departed and so did the American negotiators.[20] But the war was to drag on for many more

1813; Being a Memoir on Paul [Pavel Pavlovitch] *Svinin, Russian Diplomatic Officer, Artist, and Author* (New York: Rudge, 1930).

19. On September 4 Latrobe wrote to Mr. Douhar, this prospective steward, that Mrs. Madison could not use him till November 1. He then enumerates his duties: "Your duty will be to undertake the business of confectionery & cooking with a woman & a young man, pretty good cooks, under you; to market, to set out the table, & superintend the waiting upon the guests, & the arrangement during the dinner in the dining room, to keep correct accounts. . . . Your wages are to be thirty dollars a month." To Mrs. Madison, the same day, he described Douhar as a little man wearing spectacles and "very decent in his exterior."

20. Albert Gallatin and James Bayard. But the Senate refused to approve Gallatin's appointment unless he resigned from the Treasury Department, and at the same time the British refused to negotiate through the Russian good offices. Gallatin did resign as Secretary of the Treasury, and the British agreed to negotiate directly; Latrobe later said that Eric Bollman, then in England, did much to persuade the British government to undertake negotiations. The peace commissions met finally in Ghent; the third American member was John Quincy Adams, then minister to Russia. (The Peace Treaty—as inconclusive as the war itself—was signed on Christmas Eve, 1814.)

bloody months. Washington would be burned and Latrobe's decade of work in the Capitol largely destroyed. Andrew Jackson would win the battle of New Orleans after peace had already been signed in far-off Europe.

Meanwhile Latrobe's financial position became steadily worse; suit after suit, chiefly for amounts that were small but frightening in their sum, descended upon him. Writs against him multiplied as the year wore on and he could not collect his bills. Finally he found himself compelled to part with a pair of horses, valued at $200, to satisfy a long-due claim —a claim that had started originally with an unpaid bill of less than $15 and by 1813 had climbed, with damages and interest, to over $100. He was in despair, and anxious—how anxious—to leave the doomed city, to flee the process servers, but chiefly to get to Pittsburgh where he could get on with creative work again. Fulton, too, was eager to start the new boats and finally lent Latrobe $1,500 to clear the Washington debts and provide cash for the trip. Latrobe sent Fulton's note to Roosevelt in New York, for money was scarce in the capital, and wrote frankly of his position (September 12). He could not even collect the $600 the government owed him for his work on the Marine Hospital and the furnishing of the President's House; he owed Graff for material he had bought for the New Orleans waterworks; he owed Barker, of Philadelphia, for a cylinder Barker had cast for him. Going on, he writes:

I have got thro' all my heavy affairs but Graf. I cannot raise a dollar on my shares as yet [the stock he had received in payment for his services on the Washington canal]. But I have some hopes left. If I can only get $500 I will take the whole, or even 400$, & send it to Graf. I do not write to him for fear of a quarrel. I shall set all to right if I can only raise 500$. . . . My best love to Lydia. I fear we cannot see her. I shall stay only one day in Philadelphia & two at Cloverhill—I am heartily sorry for it but tho' one of the dearest wishes of my heart is to have her with me as often as possible I must forego it as I do so many others.

And to Fulton on the same day:

May you never have 10 years engagement with the public to wind up,—neither you nor your children after you.—Several times I had nearly thrown myself into the Potomac.—I cannot receive 600 [$] on *two* appropriations (the President's furniture & Marine hospital).

But by mid-September, thanks to Fulton's loan, Latrobe was free to leave the chaotic city and, by way of Baltimore and Philadelphia, to travel west to a problematical haven in Pittsburgh. Bitter and depressed, he penned a final farewell to Washington in a letter to Nathaniel Ingram at Charleston:

> . . . bidding an eternal adieu to the malice, backbiting, and slander, trickery, fraud, & hypocrisy, lofty pretensions & scanty means, boasts of patriotism & bargaining of conscience, pretense of religion & breach of her laws, starving doctors, thriving attorneys, whitewashing jail oaths, upstart haughtiness, & depressed merit, & five thousand other nuisances that constitute the very essence of this community . . . the more you stir it, the more it stinketh. . . . So you really think that my good word would be of promise to you with the President. Wonderfully sagacious . . . what pray, does Mr. Madison care for you or for me? Every dog has his day, & ours is past. And, in general, honest & right intentioned as is our cold-blooded President, you might as well stroke an armadillo with a feather by way of making the animal feel, as try to move him by words from any of his opinions or purposes . . .

It was September 17 or 18, 1813, when at last he departed and set out with his family to make his fortune in a new and strange environment. Disdained, disregarded, almost forgotten, Latrobe, by far the country's greatest, most creative, most idealistic architect, was now forced to make his living by building boats.

CHAPTER

17

Pittsburgh Debacle

FINALLY, in the latter half of September, 1813, the Latrobe family set out on their long trip to the West. On the way they stopped at Baltimore and stayed for some time in Philadelphia and at Clover Hill; it was in mid-October that they at last said farewell to the East. Most of their Washington furniture had been sold—another way of collecting cash—and the rest had been sent on ahead by wagon; the faithful Kitty had preceded them by stage to oversee the opening of their new home. They traveled in their family coach, drawn by their own horses; the weather was rainy much of the time, the autumn proved cold in the mountains, and the inns along the way were primitive and uncomfortable. Their great comfort was their own vehicle, one that Latrobe himself had designed—a characteristic example of his ingenuity. It was a large olive-green carriage with seats for four face to face in the center, as in the usual coach; but in this one the driver sat inside, not out in the weather. On either side of him was a "nest" for the children, John, Julia, and Benjamin Henry, Jr.; there they had their own little spaces and were not constantly in their parents' way, though completely under their supervision. Furthermore, in what was usually waste space at the bottom of the high-slung coach body, a water-tight box had been inserted for especially valued luggage; this could be opened from the coach interior. There were leather side curtains; but these, instead of being merely buttoned in place and flapping awkwardly when loosened, were tightly stretched and slid up into the curved coach top by the pulling of cords. The door was at the back so that there would be no danger of the children's falling under the wheels should the catch be faulty.

There is no record of the exact route they traveled except in the reminiscences of their son John H. B., in which he recalled only Montgomery Courthouse and Boonsboro' (near Hagerstown), both in Maryland, and the log house of General Arthur St. Clair in a clearing in the wilderness; they followed generally, he thought, the National Road, then still new.[1] It seems probable that they turned aside from the course to visit Carlisle and see Latrobe's building at Dickinson College, for in one of the architect's sketchbooks there is an undated sketch which shows it. Then, too, one of Latrobe's most assiduous correspondents was the Dickinson professor of natural philosophy, Thomas Cooper, and in the letters to Cooper there is a tone of friendly intimacy which suggests more than an epistolary acquaintance.

The trip was slow and it was not till October 31 that at long last they approached their goal. Several gentlemen, forewarned and riding out on horseback to meet them, escorted them to their new home, "a handsome new three-story brick house" on the southeast corner of Grant and Second streets—the property of Colonel James O'Hara—which Latrobe had rented some months before.[2] The house was not far from the site where the new vessels were to be built. Soon the family was comfortably settled, and Latrobe plunged into work.

Pittsburgh in 1813 was already past its infancy; it had gained the awkward and arrogant swagger of the adolescent, full of confidence in its future. Hilly, with badly paved or unpaved streets, it flanked its embosoming rivers with a raw clutter of buildings where new brick structures scraped elbows with slatternly cabins, occasional handsome mansions told of rapidly growing wealth, and improvised sheds for factories bordered the shores. Planless confusion reigned, and over it all—as travelers tell us—there already hung a heavy pall of soft-coal smoke. David Thomas, a year later, says of the city: "Pittsburgh was hidden from our view, until we descended through the hills within half a mile of the Allegany River. Dark dense smoke was rising from many parts, and a hovering cloud of this vapour, obscuring the prospect, rendered it

1. The details of Latrobe's coach and the trip, together with much personal material concerning the Pittsburgh story, I owe to John E. Semmes, *John H. B. Latrobe and His Times, 1803-1891* (Baltimore: Norman, Remington [c1917]).

2. The welcoming party probably included O'Hara, John Livingston (Mrs. Robert Fulton's brother, who was in charge of building the Mississippi steamboats *Vesuvius* and *Etna*), and Staudinger (Livingston's foreman and an old acquaintance of Latrobe's). The house was on the outskirts of the built-up part of town and is mentioned in Colonel O'Hara's will, where it is left in trust to his daughter Elizabeth. See Charles Shetter, "James O'Hara's Landholdings in Allegheny County," *Eastern Pennsylvania Historical Magazine,* vol. 34, pp. [23]-33.

singularly gloomy."[3] Coal and iron joined to produce not only their characteristic nineteenth-century progeny—dirt, squalor, and ugliness—but also, for the lucky few, undreamed-of profits. As the architect himself wrote DeLacy the next spring (March 17): "Mud & smoke are the great evils of the town. Whoever can make up his mind to breathe dirt, & eat dirt, & be up to his knees in dirt, may live very happily & comfortably here . . ."

There are times in some men's lives in which numberless strands of both character and events weave together in an inexorable pattern; in which fortuities seem to be not merely accidental; in which the setting of the drama—the place, the landscape, even the weather itself—contrives to cast over the whole production a mood of somber doom. So it was now with Latrobe, as, after what he terms "a terrible trip," the coach rolled into Pittsburgh accompanied by escorts who like heralds in an Elizabethan tragedy seemed to establish a false pomp around them.

John H. B. Latrobe, then ten, retained vivid pictures of contemporary events and atmospheres, and he describes their home as a pleasant one, kept in order by the zealous Kitty. To John, Julia, and young Ben the excitement of the new place was endlessly fascinating; there were steep hills to climb, a strange town to wander in, the boat traffic of three rivers to watch, and all sorts of strange factories (including soon their father's own works)—banging and puffing and whirring and screeching as they hammered, sawed, rolled, bored, or ground—to gaze into or explore. There were new schools and new friends; later, too, after the Battle of Lake Champlain, several British prisoners, paroled, were quartered in Pittsburgh to add their own spice of novelty. John was sent to the Reverend Mr. Stockton's only a block or so away in Cherry Alley (the best school in Pittsburgh), where he began Latin. One of the paroled British officers, a sergeant of marines, taught him the English manual of arms, which later in West Point he was forced painfully to unlearn. There was the children's first circus (Pepin and Brechard's) and the excitement of seeing the three Latrobe horses, borrowed for the occasion—Peacock and Turkey, who had pulled them across the mountains, and

---

3. *Thomas's Travels through the Western Country in the Summer of 1816* . . . (Auburn, N.Y.: Rumsey, 1819), quoted in *Pittsburgh in 1816*, compiled by the Carnegie Library of Pittsburgh on the One Hundredth Anniversary of the Granting of the City Charter (Pittsburgh: Carnegie Library, 1916).

Codger, the new acquisition—come prancing by as part of the Grand Entrée.

But to the parents the town, though it was a challenge, was scarcely a delight. They were cut off, as they had never been before, from the stimulating society of Washington, from the Hazlehurst connections in Philadelphia, even from the sometimes devious fascination of their son-in-law Roosevelt and their beloved Lydia. Pittsburgh society had little to offer of intellectual or artistic inspiration, and the available evidence seems to be that they entered into it scarcely at all.[4]

And Latrobe immediately discovered the first snag in the steamboat scheme—the fact that the yard where the *New Orleans* had been built and where the *Etna* and the *Vesuvius* were now being constructed (under John Livingston, David Cooke, and Staudinger) was cramped even with the two boats then on the stocks; it was impossible to build other new boats there, and a fresh site had to be selected. Latrobe solved the problem with a bold stroke. At first, as we see from a letter to Fulton (March 15, 1814), he had tried to rent shops; one of these had proved impossible, and from another he had been ejected because the owner had received a new contract for work and wanted it himself. Purchase thus became necessary, and he bought from Colonel O'Hara a large area on the Monongahela river bank, to be paid for on a monthly basis. On this he erected the ways for the boats and an efficient forge and machine shop. He informed Fulton of this at once (November 11, 1813), and Fulton gave his approval.[5]

The shop was simple, cheap, and efficient; frankly a temporary structure, it was built lightly of boards and consisted of four 40-foot squares in the form of a T. At the intersection of the two arms of the T was the power plant, a great horizontal wheel to the underside of which four yokes for horses were attached. The wheel was cogged and meshed with

4. See the letter to their son Henry quoted on page 416.

5. The land bought by Latrobe was just on the outskirts of the town. It stretched from the inshore side of Water Street to the river bank and from Ross Street 375 feet to the boundary of the property on which the Beelen foundry stood; a creek—Sukes Run, later canalized and later still covered over—curved down to the Monongahela through its easternmost portion. The town reserved a 60-foot right of way through it for a cross street that had not yet been constructed as well as for the extension of Water Street. It is well shown on a sketch map included in a letter to Robert Fulton on November 11, 1813. This map also shows the position of the house in which the Latrobes lived. At the present time the Baltimore & Ohio freight station and yards occupy part of the site.

From the Latrobe letter books

FIGURE 23. Part Plan of Pittsburgh, showing land purchased from Colonel O'Hara and, at upper left, the house in which the Latrobes lived. From Latrobe's letter to Fulton, November 11, 1813.

gear wheels on the power shafts, which extended into the three arms of the T. On the west was the machine shop, well equipped with lathes; on the east was the boiler shop and foundry; and in the stem of the T was the blacksmith's shop and forge. This arrangement gave great flexibility in the use of the power and at the same time minimized both the building size and the length of the power shafts required. Yet, cheap and efficient as it was, it was later destined to become a great source of worry to its builder.

Latrobe was almost fanatically busy. He sent men into the mountains to get out timber. He bought materials for the boats as he could. He assembled the large castings for the engine that had been ordered earlier from the Pittsburgh foundry of Anthony Beelen. But anxiety was growing. Prices for everything were proving higher than the estimates. The impossibility of using the yard where the Mississippi boats were being built was a bitter blow. And the ever-present question of money was wearing; actually he had come to Pittsburgh on money borrowed from Fulton. These worries, and perhaps the odious climate—so damp and dreary as the winter approached—along with the smoke and grime and commercialism of the city, proved too much for him; just at the mo-

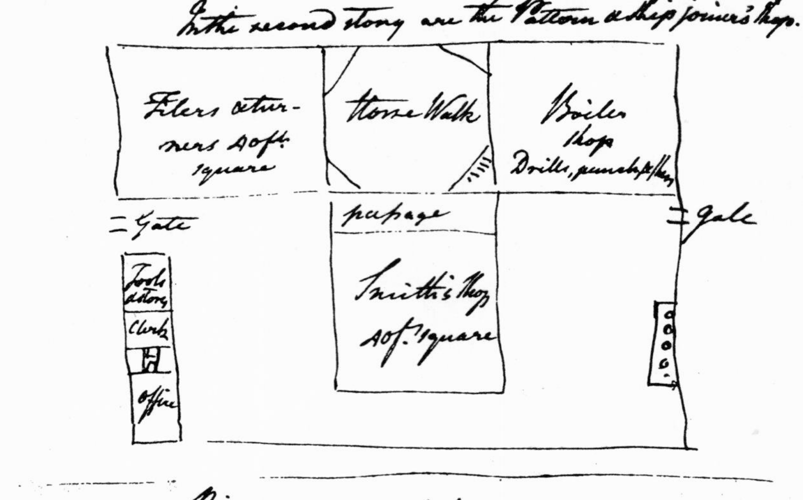

From the Latrobe letter books

FIGURE 24. Latrobe's Shipbuilding Shops, Pittsburgh. Sketch Plan. From Latrobe's letter to William Stackpole, May 24, 1814.

ment when the clearest mind and the strongest will were necessary, he fell desperately ill. The attack was called a bilious fever, and later a nervous fever; actually it was close to a nervous collapse, and for six weeks he was in bed, all his mail kept from him and his business almost at a standstill. Luckily he had sent his chief shipwright, Hurley, on to Pittsburgh ahead of him, and before his sickness Latrobe had ordered most of the timber necessary; but during his illness no letters went to Fulton and no schemes could be started to help get in the money he so urgently needed to settle old debts and to make the monthly payments to O'Hara for the purchase of the land.

But the first worry, already mentioned, was the question of prices. When Latrobe was with Fulton in New York in 1813, they had together estimated the cost of the proposed boat as between $21,000 and $25,000 (using figures obtained by Roosevelt when he was building the *New*

Orleans). The Ohio Steamboat Navigation Company—financed largely by New York money—was set up on this basis. But since the launching of the *New Orleans* the War of 1812 had begun and was playing hob with prices. When, after his six-week collapse, Latrobe got seriously into the construction of the ship, he was appalled. Prices everywhere and for everything were skyrocketing. He wrote at once to Fulton (January 20, 1814): ". . . What are we agents to do in the abominable rise in price of iron & every article necessary to build the boat?"

Apparently Fulton never answered this question in detail. What went on at the company meetings in New York may never be known, or Fulton's part in them. Latrobe was aware that the *New Orleans* and the two other boats Livingston was building for the Mississippi Steamboat Navigation Company had all cost far more than the projected sum and that there had been no protest. He knew that the *New Orleans* had paid for itself in an unbelievably short time. His own accounts had been sent regularly, and of course he believed that his job was to build his boats not only as cheaply but also as rapidly as possible, in order to take advantage of the enormous profits the growth of the Ohio River trade promised as well as to anticipate the efforts of Fulton's rivals, Evans and French.

Then suddenly, early in March, Fulton writes Latrobe that any future notes he may make against the company in New York will be protested and not paid. On March 15 Latrobe writes to Fulton in bewilderment:

In this dilemma I called on Mr. Livingston, for I found myself placed in the situation of a Contractor engaged to build the boat for 23,000$ *compleat* (deducting 2,000$, my salary for one year). As no steamboat of this size has ever been built for that money I did not believe, altho' the company's capital of which a dividend is to be made is only 25,000, that that was to be the limit of the cost of the boat to be built by me. I took it always for granted that the object was to be accomplished *at all events*. If on examination of my accounts it should be found that I had incurred improper expense, had wasted the Companies money, or that, upon the whole, by neglect or bad management, I had occasioned their boat to cost an unreasonable Sum, I knew that my account might be disallowed, that in that respect I was under an effectual check, & responsible for my stewardship, but I had not any idea that I had engaged to build the boat & the freight boat for a limited sum.—As therefore Mr. Livingston was exactly in my situation, & there was no secret made of his having very largely exceeded the capital stated to be that on which the dividend was to be made (30,000$ for each boat) and as his name was mentioned in your letter on the same footing as my own,—I asked his advice as to what I should do,—and also requested him to state what were his actual expenditures on the boat.—I learned in consequence, that by the time his boat could be finished he would have expended from 45 to 50,000$ on one boat, & that the two would probably cost from 80 to 90$ say 45,000 for each boat, leaving an excess of 12 to 15,000 on each boat beyond the *dividend* Capital stated in the article of incorporation.

He continues with a careful comparison between the Mississippi boats and the ones he is building and, because of the greater simplicity of his, figures that the price of his boats should probably be about $10,000 less than Livingston's. But in addition to the direct cost of the boats there is the further cost of yards, shops, tools, and the like—all assets that can be sold after the boats are complete. About these he goes on:

When we were together at New York, it seemed to be our impression that the Shops & tools of the Mississippi company would be of infinite service to me in my proceedings as to economy. We supposed that by the time I should begin they would have finished.—But on my arrival . . . the first sight of the works convinced me that the very idea of using any part of them, for the present, was vain. . . . Then I began & put up shops on my own ground,—as I have already told you—& so energetic & rapid were my proceedings, that in one month during which I occupied Mr. Copeland's shops after notice, I was compleatly under way on the company's own premises. I shall send you a plan explaining fully the construction of these shops, which are of rough timber & boards.

I also had to build a wharf 40 feet front (as formerly stated) which cost about 500$ (Staudinger told me their ways cost 1500$).—My smith's shop is 40 feet square, boiler shop 40 feet square & the filer's shop the same dimensions, the ship joiner's & carpenter's shops over the whole. The Boat shed & saw pit 80 feet long. All this cost less than 5,000$. But you will see the exact amount to a Cent when my accounts are made up to the present time, which will be in order this week.

He appends a complete report on the state of the works to date—showing amazing progress for the time involved—and sends a valuation of the shops, tools, and materials on hand, amounting to $9,000. The final valuation, he suggests, will make the company property "independently of the boat about 10,000$. At this sum at least Mr. Livingston values the property of the Mississippi company which will remain after the boats are finished." After asking Fulton to check the values against New York prices, he concludes his letter:

I have now to ask, whether taking all this into consideration, I am obliged to finish the boat for 23,000$. The size of the Engine, the whole mode of constructing it, the quantity of brass, so enormously expensive, has not been a matter of my own choice. All this is prescribed to me. The enormous price of iron, of steel, of tools, of anvils, vises, etc., I cannot regulate. The Mississippi boats with the same Engines have cost 45,000$. How is it possible that I can build the same engine & two boats, but little less expensive for 25,000$,—and yet, if I expend 35,000, your books, I believe will show that your boat will not stand in more than 25 to 28,000, for if you will give me time I will buy your shops, tools, etc., for the value, & you shall have security in *Land* & *Wharf,* & *Warehouse,* productive of infinitely greater value.—And *moreover* I if I am not obliged to stop short as your letter implies, discharge all hands, & shut up shop,—your company will in freight pay their excess in *three trips.*

I have fatigued myself & you by this long letter. I must close by saying, that altho' it is highly unjust that you should advance the money, I *must* draw on the 17th a bill at 60 days date, for no other paper is worth a Cent, or discharge all my hands. By next post I will write again.

Yours very truly & gratefully,
B. H. Latrobe

As yet he has no realization that catastrophe threatens; he is puzzled by Fulton's conduct yet still writes to him with trust, as to a friend. It would almost seem that Fulton, in view of the success of the New Orleans–Natchez boat, had begun to regret the generous contract he had made with Latrobe—a one-third interest in the company and a salary of $2,000 a year—and that he and the Livingstons had decided to squeeze out the architect, using the excess cost of the boat Latrobe was building as a lever, now that the boat and its engine were well along and the shops and yard well organized.[6] Having already obtained from him the

6. The Fulton and Livingston boat companies were set up on an extraordinary basis. Fulton and Livingston reserved to themselves and their agents 90 per cent of all profits; the investors in the companies were to receive and distribute as dividends only 10 per cent. The arrangements with Roosevelt in the Mississippi company and with Latrobe in the Ohio company granted them one-third of the 90 per cent received. One wonders how investors were obtained at all! Fulton's own consuming greed appeared when Chancellor Livingston died; he then wrote Livingston's heirs that he would demand not only his half of the 90 per cent but half of their shares too, as recompense for his "activity." See note dated November 27,

services they needed, they could now do without them. Edward Livingston meanwhile had written Latrobe from New Orleans asking him to build a boat for the Natchez line on a fixed-price contract. Was this just another bait thrown out to lead him to ruin? Fortunately he did not rise; instead he wrote Fulton (March 21) that a careful estimate showed that "no possibility exists at Pittsburgh of erecting the Engine & Machinery, *wholly independently of the Boat & its ironwork & inboard work for less than 24,000$* . . ." Then, returning to the boats he is building, he goes on:

You will please, my good friend, to consider that I was not to build a boat which should cost only 25,000$ Engine & all,—but that the *size* of the boat & engine were the data prescribed, & the expense was the consequence necessarily resulting. Now please compare prices here with prices at New York. Staudinger says there are about 40 ton on board in the engine & beneath 20 in the boat. Say in all:

60 tons	Cast *here*	140 Per ton
	Wrought	200
	Rolled	400
		3)740
		243$
In New York	Cast	150
	Rolled	250
	Wrought	120
		3)520
		173$

In this important article alone then there is a difference of 70 in 173 or 40 per cent against us. The only things in which we have an advantage are fuel, & timber, but then everything else is against us.—However, *do not* now leave me in the lurch, unless you find me guilty of extravagance or neglect, or inadequacy. . . .

If you [could hold off] a little longer (for I shall not intrude upon you for anything but time) I shall do admirably well here. . . .

Still Latrobe cannot believe that Fulton has determined to ditch him. All through April he continues to plead for money from the company

1813, in the Gilbert Montague Collection of Robert Fulton Manuscripts in the New York Public Library.

to complete the boat, and at the same time he pours in what cash of his own he can raise to keep the work going. He sends Fulton a power of attorney to make possible the mortgaging in New York of Latrobe's own share in order to raise cash. On April 22 he tells him of the final completion of the *Vesuvius*[7] and its departure, and the next day he writes a glowing description to be inserted in the *National Intelligencer:*

This morning the Steamboat *Vesuvius,* intended as a regular trader between New Orleans and the falls of Ohio, left Pittsburgh. A considerable fresh in the river renders it probable that notwithstanding the great size & draft of the vessel she will pass the falls without difficulty, after which she will meet with no obstruction in the rest of her passage. There is now on the stocks here, just ready to be launched, a boat adapted to the navigation of the Ohio above the falls, which will be finished in time to meet the *Vesuvius* on her return from New Orleans at the falls. The boats are built by Mr. Fulton under the agency of Messrs. Livingston & Latrobe, for companies who have vested very large capitals in the establishments.—The departure of *Vesuvius* is a very important event not only for this place but for the whole western part of the Union, & its influence will be felt over the whole of the U. States. In describing it, it is not necessary to use the inflated language, which unfortunately for the credit of our own taste, too often renders real facts incredible or at least lowers their importance by the manner in which they are suffered into notice. It does not require the ornament of metaphor to impress upon the public mind the incalculable advantage of an intercourse by water, effected in large Vessels which move with certainty & rapidity through an extent of internal navigation embracing a space almost as large as the whole continent of Europe, and comprising in it the productions of almost every climate. This intercourse, tho' now only in its infancy, must in a few years become of immense magnitude.—About 3 years ago a steamboat of about 400 tons burthen was built here, and now navigates the Mississippi, between N. Orleans & Natchez. The *Vesuvius,* which, with another boat of the same size & construction now building, is intended to form the 2nd link in this chain

7. The *Vesuvius,* like all the first Mississippi boats, was built as a mere modification of the coastwise or ocean-going ship but with increased beam and decreased draft. In the larger *Washington,* built by Daniel French and Henry M. Shreve in 1816, all the cabin accommodations were within the hull and occupied an entire deck. See Louis C. Hunter and Beatrice Jones Hunter, *Steamboats on the Western Waters . . .* in Studies in Economic History (Cambridge, Mass.: Harvard University Press, 1949). Édouard de Montulé in *Voyage en Amérique* (cited in Hunter, *op. cit.*) gives an account of the *Vesuvius.* The *Etna* (or *Aetna,* as it was sometimes spelled), the freight boat built at the same time as the *Vesuvius,* was used successfully in the New Orleans–Louisville trade in 1814-15 and then became a towboat for sailing vessels coming up the Mississippi from the Gulf to New Orleans.

of navigation, is of 480 tons burthen, Carpenter's measurement. She has 160 feet keel, 28′-6″ beam, & will when loaded draw from 5 to 6 feet of water. The whole of her hold below deck, excepting a neat cabin for ladies & the space occupied by her machinery, is appropriated to the cargo. On her deck is built what in a ship would be called a Round House, extending nearly half her length, elegantly fitted up as a cabin, having 24 double berths each side. Previously to her departure she had been several times tried in going up & down the Monongahela & Ohio for four or five miles, & performed very satisfactorily. This morning (Saturday, April 23rd) everything being in perfect order, she passed at 10 o'clock up the Monongahela in front of the town to its Eastern limits & returning down the opposite shore went down the Ohio, firing a Salute. Most of the citizens were assembled on the bank as she passed. In order to witness & ascertain her speed, I crossed the Allegheny, & mounting a very capital horse, I endeavored to keep pace with her along the road which skirts the river. But she moved so rapidly that after riding 3½ miles in 19 minutes I gave up the attempt. In one hour & 30 seconds, she was at Middletown 12 miles below Pittsburgh, where several Gentlemen who had proceeded in her so far came ashore. If therefore the current in the Ohio be rated at 4 miles an hour in the present fresh, she has gone at the rate of 8 miles an hour in still water. In coming up the rapids of the Ohio below this town on Monday last, she passed the shore at the rate of 4 miles an hour, a speed which would exactly agree with her descent this morning.

. . . Situated as I am at present, on the spot where the advantages which the public will reap from the introduction of steam navigation, with a very sensible effect, it is difficult to repress the expression of feelings which arise towards the person to whom we owe it, that this mode of navigation so often before attempted and laid aside in despair, has become *practical,* and its principles reduced to mathematical certainty. But it is unnecessary to give them vent. The obligation which the nation, I had almost said the world, owes to him, will be freely & fully acknowledged by history, when the envy & cupidity of his detractors will be remembered only with disgust & reprobation, etc., etc. . . .

When the late Chancellor Livingston applied for his grant for the exclusive navigation by Steam on the North river, to the legislature of New York, for 30 years on condition that he should actually accomplish it,—a very sensible member of the legislature told me that he could have easily had a grant of any further extent, as the navigation by steam was thought to be much on footing as to practicability as the navigation by the Reindeer in the Chancellor's park. The case is altered since then, for many people have found out that it's an old invention, open to everybody who can read Mr. Fulton's specifications or look at his boats.

The last sentence of this quotation is significant, especially after the glowing tribute to Fulton which has preceded it. On the surface, it is an attempt to make the prospects of the company independent of Fulton's patent, for Latrobe knew that Fulton had not prosecuted either French or Evans for infringement. But in addition may we not suspect that it is also an almost unconscious declaration of independence on the part of Latrobe himself? Was Fulton supposed to read into it more than a statement of fact? [8] In any case, the New York company backed down from its stand, and Fulton advanced another $3,500; the immediate crisis was over, but the climax had only been postponed.

Two weeks later Latrobe's boat, the *Buffalo,* its hull complete, was launched. The launching narrowly escaped being disastrous. The ways, designed for the expected spring water level, had necessitated the deep excavation of a portion of the bank. But the river was low that year, the beautiful dry spring days had not yielded the usual rainfall, and no complete weather or river-depth reports from upstream were then available. The launching was postponed several days as the river slowly rose —painfully slowly. On May 13 it reached its apparent summit—several feet beneath the expected level—and when it started slowly to fall Latrobe gave the word, the wedges were hammered out, and the boat slid down the ways. At the end it hesitated, almost stopped, and hung there, its whole after half unsupported. Then with agonizing slowness it moved again, pivoting on the end of the ways, and its stern finally crashed down into the river; a moment later it was afloat, and Latrobe was enormously relieved to note that it floated level, with no sign of hogging and little damage from its hazardous launching. Afloat at last—on Friday the thirteenth. Seemingly the fates had hung undecided but at the end been kind.

This was one of the few triumphant experiences of that calamitous period. In New York, however, Fulton and the company remained

8. Objections to the Fulton-Livingston monopolies, on the ground that they were hostile to the public and national interest, were widespread. Thus in David Thomas's *Travels through the Western Country in the Summer of 1816,* already cited, the author while discussing the steamboat building of Pittsburgh remarks with considerable asperity that, though the support and encouragement of inventors is desirable, the method chosen in the case of Fulton—monopoly of navigation—is severely penalizing the development of steamboats and hampering trade on a necessary national trade route. The first hard blow to the Fulton monopoly occurred in 1817, when the Louisiana courts in a suit entered by the Mississippi Steamboat Navigation Company declared they had no jurisdiction in the case.

adamant, unmoved alike by the success of the *Vesuvius* and the launching of the *Buffalo*. Fulton answered none of Latrobe's letters. Then, on May 17, John Livingston, who reigned inscrutably over the Mississippi company's boats at Pittsburgh, refused to honor a draft Fulton himself had sent and informed Latrobe he could accept no more notes. Mrs. Latrobe, writing much later in her memoir of her husband, accused John Livingston of being Latrobe's chief enemy, acting as a spy for Fulton and concealing behind his apparently friendly exterior a treacherous hostility. And Latrobe himself, little by little, was waking up to Fulton's true purposes. The company's refusal to honor drafts was soon common knowledge in Pittsburgh. On May 21 Beelen himself, who had invariably been cordial and co-operative and whose foundry had made all the large castings for both the Mississippi and the Ohio boats, declined to endorse any drafts of Fulton or of the Ohio company, and no Pittsburgh bank would accept them. Latrobe, now in deep distress, wrote Fulton (May 17) that it was not pleasant to see ruin staring him in the face.

Meanwhile in New York the ever busy John DeLacy, always the architect's friend, was trying to patch matters up. He wrote Latrobe that he ought to come to New York, and Latrobe answered (May 22), in a letter so incoherent as to reveal his harassed state: "I cannot possibly come to New York. The devil is sure to be at work there against me, but he has shown his cloven foot only by protesting a draft of John Livingston on Mr. Fulton was to leave me high & dry with 60 workmen on hand and not a dollar to pay them with." Only the day before, he had written a long letter to Fulton begging the company if necessary to mortgage the *Buffalo* in order to raise money to finish its engine and to bring the freight boat to completion. Still no answer.

So events march inevitably toward catastrophe. On June 3 the not unexpected happens: the Pittsburgh creditors of the company attach the boat, and two days later Latrobe writes Henry that they are also putting an attachment on the Pittsburgh work for the New Orleans waterworks. Then, on June 8, Latrobe tries to use a New York emissary, the Reverend Mr. Benjamin Mortimer, pastor of the First Moravian Church in New York, who had been his schoolmate in those faraway days at Fulneck. Mortimer is close to Fulton and the New York company (as well as apparently an investor), and Latrobe begs him on the basis of their own boyhood friendship to go to Fulton and assure him that Latrobe is "honest and no fool." By June 16 Fulton refuses to pay a draft to Graff for materials used in the boat. In July the rift between Fulton and Latrobe becomes complete—at Fulton's instigation—and Fulton orders Latrobe to write to McNeven, the secretary of the company, and not to himself. Nevertheless, in an attempt to preserve relations between them, Latrobe does write Fulton again (August 9) describing Evans's boat and finally (September 24) sends a moving appeal: he and the company and the future of the boats are hanging over an abyss of ruin for want of $6,000 to $7,000.

It was all in vain. Latrobe mortgaged his shops for money to continue. On September 1 he had had a notice printed and distributed in Pittsburgh:

OHIO STEAM BOAT COMPANY'S OFFICE,

Pittsburgh, September 1st, 1814

SIR,

THE capital originally assumed to be sufficient to complete the Ohio Steam Boat and the freight boat, was 25,000 dollars. The experience not only of our Company, but that of the Mississippi, has proved that this assumption was exceedingly erroneous.

There has been received by me on account of the original subscription, ... $24,250

The subscribers in New York have become personally responsible to the Banks for $12,000, which has been remitted to me, or paid on my drafts on account of the boat, } $12,000

750 dollars are due on account of the original subscription.

On the first of August I had expended of my own private funds on behalf of the company, as per account furnished the Secretary at New York, August 28th, } $ 5,073.68

And during the month of August, my personal advances have been upwards of . . . . $ 2,000.—

Mr. Fulton at New York, has advanced out of his private funds also, ... $ 2,000.—

This total includes the expense of the shops, office, tools and materials now on the ground. After much correspondence with Mr. Fulton and the secretary of the company, I was required to propose to the Stockholders residing *here,* to raise the sum necessary to complete the boat, on their personal responsibility, pledging the first receipts of the boat as security for the repayment of the loans. It is now my duty to make this proposal in *form*. In order to remove the objections which may occur to this measure, finding my interests as well as my reputation irretrievably involved in the undertaking, and having the fullest confidence in its success, I am ready to come forward personally and to propose the following security to the subscribers.

I have given the company credit in account, for the value of the shops and office, which are now my own property,	$ 4,002.—	
Prior to this transfer to myself, and while they were the property of the company, I received, and possess, a power of attorney to sell or pledge them and the tools, for the purpose of raising the necessary funds to complete the boat.		
The tools are worth at least	$ 2,000	
I am proprietor, by a deed, of ⅓ of the Patent Right on these waters, that is, of ⅙ of the revenue of the boat above 10 per cent. per annum on $25,000, worth, say	$10,000	16002.

Independently of the pledge of the first revenues of the boat to the repayment of the whole sum borrowed here and in New York, I will convey to a trustee the above property to secure payment of the sum of 7,500 dollars to be borrowed (if practicable) here, and which will enable me to get the boat underway by the rise of the water this fall.

The state of my funds are now such that I must stop our operations immediately, without further assistance, and I therefore respectfully and earnestly solicit your attendance at Morrow's tavern on Tuesday evening the 6th inst. to consider this subject, where all the accounts shall be laid before you.

Respectfully yours,
B. H. Latrobe, Agent

Thus, at last, under the combined influences of wartime inflation and the attitude of Fulton, Latrobe publicly announced his inability to go on unless more funds could be borrowed locally, the security to be his own pledge of almost his entire assets and prospects. Perhaps it was fortunate for him that the appeal failed.

But impending failure of the steamboat enterprise was not Latrobe's only worry. There still remained all his old uncollectible bills against the government for the Marine Hospital and the furnishings of the President's House. And there were Roosevelt's Pittsburgh affairs to straighten out—a distillery and a speculation in snuffboxes. A fire wiped out all the snuffboxes, but the distillery apparently was a going and profit-making concern. And Roosevelt had left debts—especially a large claim from one James Tustin (who had furnished material for the *New Orleans*) for which the Mississippi company claimed Roosevelt alone was responsible. Tustin threatened suit and later obtained an attachment on all Roosevelt's Pittsburgh properties. Again and again Latrobe wrote his son-in-

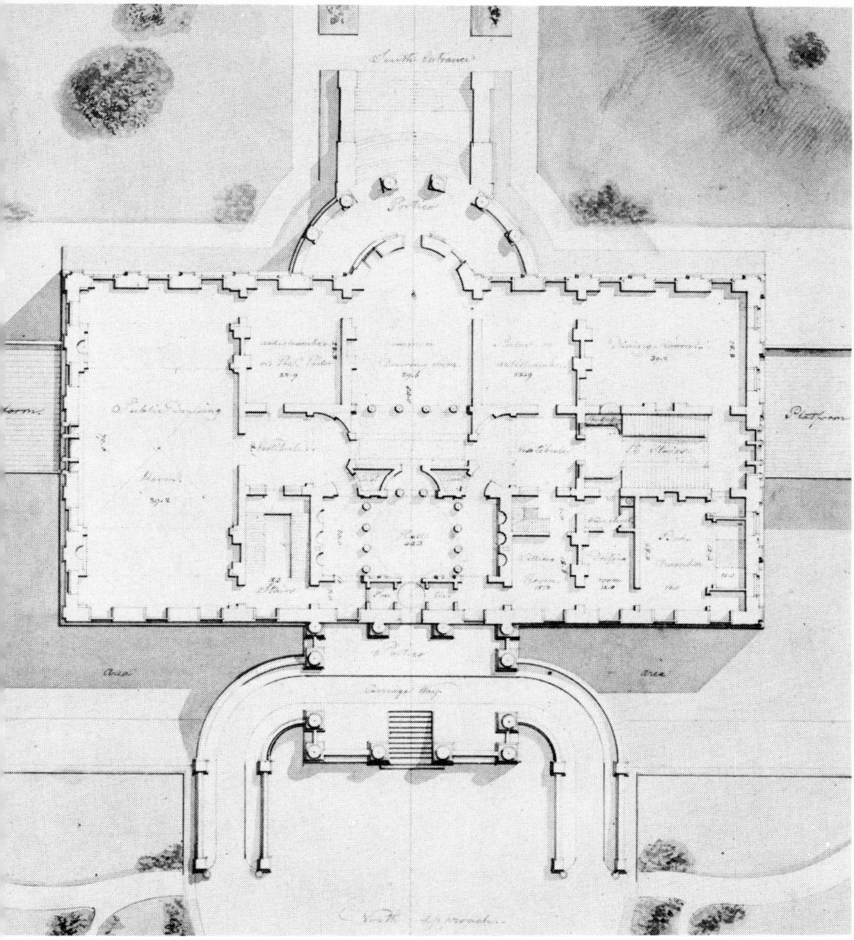

Library of Congress

President's House, Washington. Latrobe's plan of first floor showing proposed alterations.

PLATE 25

be's "Egyptian" design for the Library of Congress, 1808.

Library of Congress

Photograph author

Photograph author

Exterior. Christ Church, Washington. Interior.

PLATE 26
Gothic Buildings
by B. H. Latrobe

St. Paul's Church, Alexandria, Virginia.
Exterior.

Drawing by Bontz, courtesy John O. Br

Bank of Philadelphia.

Old engraving, courtesy Historic
ciety of Pennsylvania

Early Mississippi Steamer *Paragon*.

F. B. Read, *Upward to Fame and Fortune*

Library of Congress

Proposed Central Building, Pittsburgh Arsenal. Latrobe's elevation.

PLATE 27

Library of Congress

roposed Commandant's House, Pitts-
urgh Arsenal. Latrobe's east elevation.

r. Herron's Church, Pittsburgh, after
dditions by B. H. Latrobe.

Old view, courtesy Fine Arts Department, University of Pittsburgh

PLATE 28

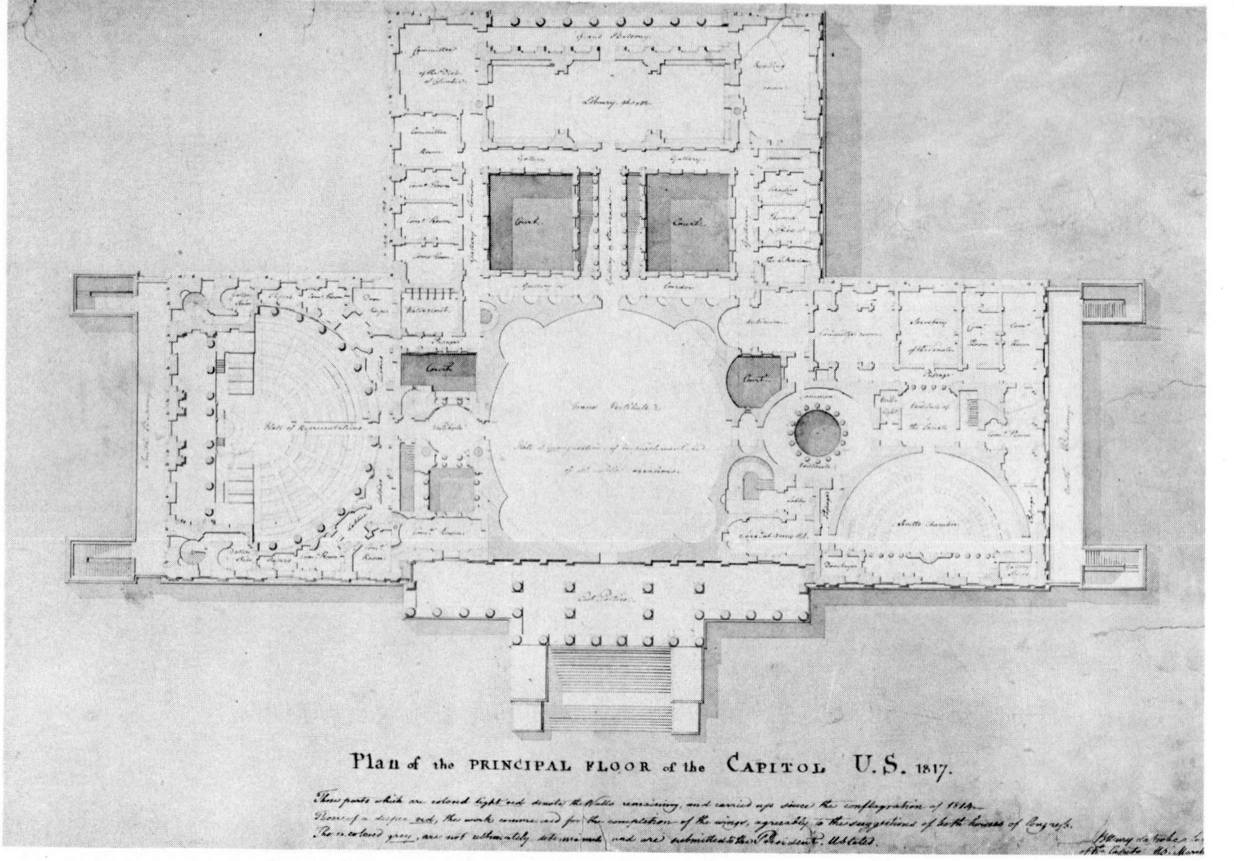

United States Capitol, Washington. Latrobe's plan for rebuilding after the War of 1812.

Library of Congress

Corcoran Gallery

House of Representatives at lamplighting time. Painting by S. F. B. Morse.

PLATE 29

United States Capitol, Washington, as rebuilt after the War of 1812

G. Brown, *History of the United States Capitol*

Old Supreme Court.

The Old Senate Chamber.

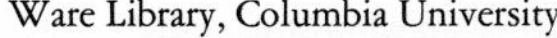

Ware Library, Columbia University

Courtesy Mrs. Truxtun Beale

The Decatur House, Washington.
Latrobe's details of the parlor doors.

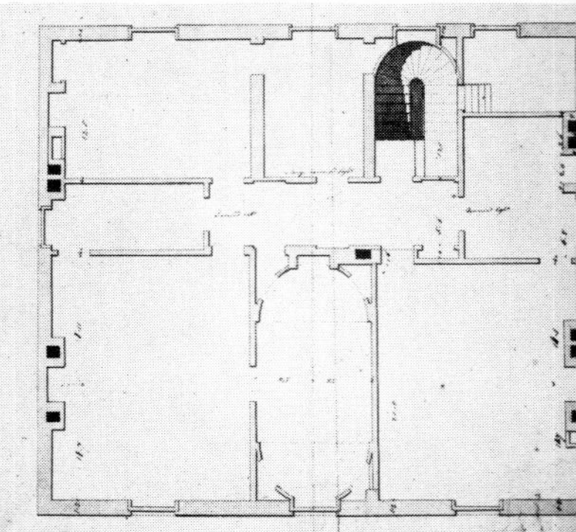

Courtesy Mrs. Truxtun

The Decatur House, Washington.
Latrobe's second-floor plan.

PLATE 30

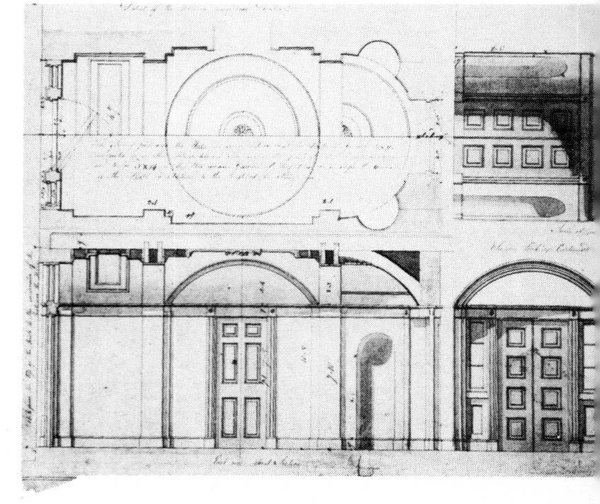

The Decatur House, Washington.
Latrobe's details of the vestibule.

Courtesy Mrs. Truxtun Beale

St. John's Church, Washington. Latrobe's sketch perspective showing the burned-out President's Hous the background.

Courtesy St. John's C

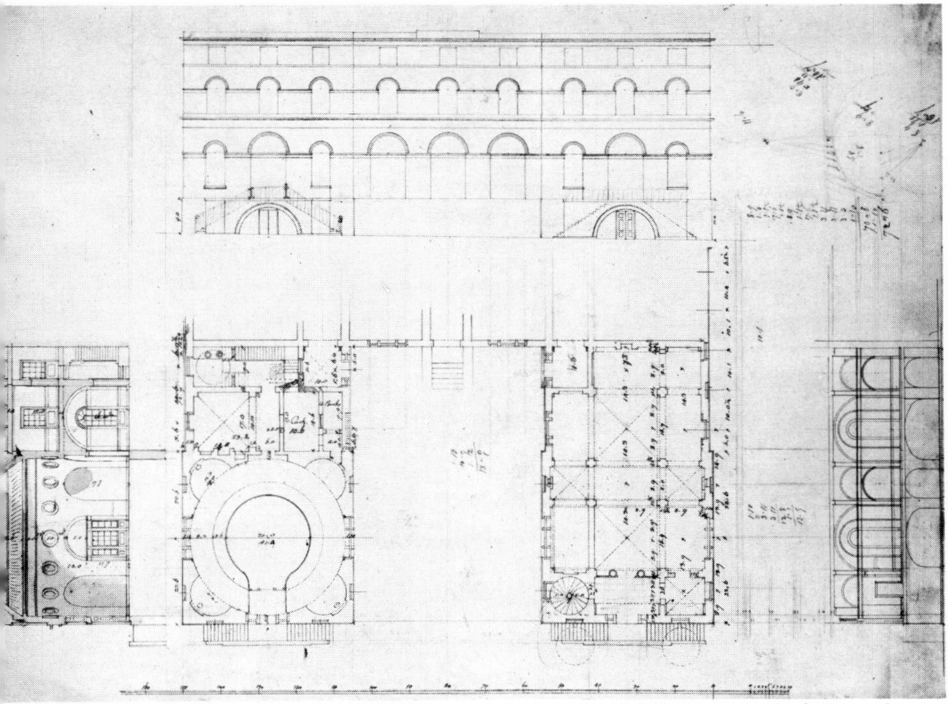

obe's study plan for Post Office and Customs House.

Maryland Historical Society

The Exchange, Baltimore. Godefroy and Latrobe, architects. PLATE 31

obe's perspective of the Gay Street front.

Maryland Historical Society

Old photograph, courtesy Richard Borneman

The Exchange, Baltimore. Godefroy and Latrobe, architects. Exterior.

PLATE 32

The Exchange, Baltimore. Interior of the dome, looking up.

Old photograph, courtesy Richard Born

Proposed Library, Baltimore. Latrobe's original design.

Maryland Historical S

law to settle the matter and warned him that if it ever came to trial the courts, since Tustin was locally much loved and admired, would undoubtedly award Tustin all he claimed. When Beelen wished to buy the distillery, Latrobe urged Roosevelt to sell at the advantageous price offered; but still his son-in-law procrastinated, as he had in the Navy copper affair, apparently hoping for some sudden gift from heaven that would clear up his obligations. As soon as the property was attached, of course no sale was possible, and Latrobe was forced to put up bail to remove the attachment (May 8, 1814). The matter was still hanging fire before referees when the architect left Pittsburgh.

Then there was the problem of competing steamboats and the threat to his own steam-engine business from the new high-pressure engines that Oliver Evans had developed. French was running a small sternwheeler [9] between Redstone and Cincinnati; George Evans (Oliver's son), with the backing of some Philadelphia Quaker capitalists, was using a still smaller boat, driven by an Evans engine, in local trade. As John H. B. Latrobe later recalled, in the Pittsburgh of that time steamboats were a dominant interest; evidently Fulton and the Ohio Steamboat Navigation Company would enjoy no monopoly, and Fulton's patent was too shaky to risk infringement suits.

To Latrobe's natural worries about the rivalry an Evans boat might offer was added his old distrust of the Evans engine. He had spoken slightingly of it in his report for the American Philosophical Society, "First Report in Answer to the Enquiry Whether Any and What Improvements Have Been Made in the Construction of Steam Engines in America." [10] But Evans claimed that Latrobe's first language had been much more violent in expressing his disapproval and was the result of prejudice pure and simple, and that the committee had had to edit the report in deference to the facts. Evans broadcast this charge and Latrobe was forced to a written denial. Then in 1814 when Evans applied for an extension of his patent, which was about to lapse, Latrobe thought him-

---

9. The tug *Charlotte Dundas,* built by William Symington, had a stern wheel in 1802, with a B & W engine, and was operated briefly on the Forth and Clyde Canal.

10. *Transactions,* vol. VI (1809), pp. 89-99. It is significant that even the low-pressure engines employed in western steamboats were using continually higher pressures, sometimes averaging between 20 and 40 pounds per square inch. Low-pressure engines, however, were generally preferred for steamboats until 1860 or thereabouts, because of their relative safety from boiler explosions and their fuel economy. See Hunter, *op. cit.*

self called upon to write to the Secretary of State protesting against any extension on the ground that Evans's patent was meaningless since it claimed to cover any engine working at more than atmospheric pressure —which of course would have included all Boulton & Watt engines also. And now in Pittsburgh Latrobe thought he had actual evidence of the shortcomings of the Oliver Evans engine, for Evans had built a large flour mill there and powered it with one of his own engines. It was making tremendous profits, but Latrobe did not credit its success to its engine; investigating, he found support for his doubts. In a letter to Roosevelt (January 20) full of Pittsburgh news he says of the engines:

> Oliver Evans's Engines are going to the devil here as fast as possible. His own mill drives badly two pairs of stones, & consumes 70 bushels of coal a day.—To drive two pairs of stones, a Bolton & Watt Engine of 20″ cylinder is competent & power to spare. Such an engine consumes 1¼ cords [of wood daily] at $2—the price here is 2.50 cents; 70 bushels of coal at 7 cents—the price now—$4.90. The prime cost is the same of the two engines. I need not say more.

Of the enormous possibilities for economy in the use of high-pressure steam, Latrobe had apparently no conception. The engines that he had built and was building, those his son-in-law Roosevelt had built, and the ones that had powered Fulton's *Clermont* and its immediate successors were all low-pressure Boulton & Watt engines. They worked; they had revolutionized both steamboat travel and mill design. Why look for more? Thus Latrobe, usually so farsighted, was brought by his own somewhat limited experience not only to denigrate the high-pressure steam engine but to dislike and distrust the greatest American inventor of his time.

These were all little matters, to be sure, but they were genuine annoyances, additional pinpricks of worry, of antagonism, of frustration; on top of the great anxiety about the steamboats and his own future and reputation, they were too much. Again his harassed body and mind rebelled and in the middle of August he had another warning sickness—what he calls in a letter to Henry "my old Hemicrania"—but at least his illness brought him two weeks or so of rest, enough to nerve him for the drama's final scene.

How was it that, for so many months after the first ominous rumblings, construction on the two steamboats—the large *Buffalo* and the smaller freight boat (later named the *Harriet* after Fulton's wife)—continued? How were the materials secured, the men paid? The printed notice of the Ohio Steamboat Navigation Company gives part of the answer: Latrobe had contributed some $5,000 out of his own pocket. Yet we have seen that he arrived from Washington in November, 1813, almost penniless and burdened with debts. Where did the $5,000 come from? For the solution of the mystery we must turn to another, brighter side of Latrobe's Pittsburgh career.

We know, for instance, that he came there partly to build an engine for the New Orleans waterworks, and at least some work was accomplished on this project. But there were other orders for steam engines; the West was greedy for them. Pittsburgh was pioneering in their use; its new factories, unhampered by the conservative traditions of the East, were more and more powered by steam.[11] Latrobe was a pioneer in this field. He wrote to Henry, asking him to get engine orders in New Orleans, and he had several orders from the Pittsburgh region itself. One of his last Pittsburgh activities, just before his return to Washington, was a visit to Steubenville, down the Ohio, to make final adjustments on a large textile mill there which he had apparently designed and for which he furnished the engine. This steam-engine business undoubtedly brought in some cash; but, because at that time engines took months to build, all except the Steubenville engine—even that for the New Orleans waterworks—remained unfinished and were handed over to creditors when the Latrobes left Pittsburgh in the spring of 1815.

The bulk of the money, then, came from another source—a flourishing building business. Latrobe's fame as an architect had preceded him. An enormous amount of construction was going on; even the war itself, by turning capitalists' eyes from the blockaded East, was aiding in Pittsburgh's extraordinary growth. There was an insistent demand for the architect's talents. But in Pittsburgh, he discovered, to handle design on a strictly professional basis was impossible. To try to do so would have been to undertake the old futile Philadelphia struggle all over again, this time in a town still culturally primitive, with little understanding of the arts or the professions, and geared only to the rapid accumulation of

---

11. In 1816 six of Pittsburgh's factories were steam-powered. By 1818 the city's own steam-engine factories were producing $300,000 worth of engines. See Erasmus Wilson, *Standard History of Pittsburgh, Pennsylvania* (Chicago: Cornell, 1898), pp. 214-15.

money. The good Pittsburghers were prepared to pay well for tangible things; design, however, they would have regarded as a luxury and the alleged economies of professional service as at best a pig in a poke. Latrobe desperately needed the architectural work; very well, if the Pittsburghers wanted design merely as a part of actual construction, so be it. He would put his pride in his pocket and become an architect-contractor. And, since in the spring of 1814 funds for the completion of the steamboats were being held up by Fulton and the New York members of the company, money was an ever more compelling need. In a letter to Henry in New Orleans (May 29), he enumerates the buildings he is putting up and gives an interesting picture of the O'Haras and a glimpse of the Latrobe household:

. . . I have now nothing particular to say, but that I am crawling slowly along with our N.O. works. . . . I should indeed be now entirely stopped had I not a most wonderful run of architectural business for which I get ready money, & thus keep on. The Mechanics here are such slow dogs, that the speed with which I proceed occasions perfect astonishment. I have formed a building connexion with a Mr. [Henry] Holdship whom I knew 16 years ago in Philadelphia, who is the most active & industrious carpenter I have ever employed. We have built a circus in a fortnight & made 500$, Barracks for the British prisoners & made about 300$, a range of stores 160 feet long for Beelen in three weeks which were no great catch, a warehouse for Col. O'Hara, a profitable business just finished. I am tomorrow going to begin a farmhouse for him & today I finally concluded a contract with Mr. Beltzhoover for a country seat which will come in all with Stables, etc., to 10,000. Thus I am getting on very well, having got over my squeamishness about being interested in the execution of works. Two years' struggle however will be necessary to set me free, & to send you to Europe.

You may easily imagine how my time is taken up. Of course I visit little. There are few families here in fact worth visiting. Our principal friend is Col. O'Hara. As far as the immensity & valuable situation of his landed property goes, he must certainly be one of the richest men in America. He is in all matters of business close & demands his own. But out of dealings he is as liberal a rich man as it is easy to find anywhere.

His wife is a woman of uncommonly fine understanding, well cultivated by a long and extensive intercourse with the world, but very little polished by education. They have had three sons. One after going thro' the usual course of education at Princeton, came home & promised to be one of the most prominent characters in this part of the world. He had learning, manners, uncommon personal beauty, and a correct moral character. He married a niece of his Mother's, a very fine woman. But there his rise ended, for a fortnight after his marriage he died suddenly of a violent cholic.—The second son, James, succeeded with prospects not less flattering. But by degrees he became addicted to the vice of the place, married a very charming woman, & died of intemperance a few months ago. The third is an idiot just able to go about without injury to himself or others, but also addicted to drink, he spends much time & drinks among my workmen. There are two daughters, one about 18 or 19, a most admirably sensible but not handsome girl, the other about 10, a spoiled child but of uncommon talents. If you come hither, you may with my leave set yourself in battle array against Betsey O'Hara, because with her immense fortune she is said to have heart & certainly has understanding. But that is your affair not mine.

Thus you see I have filled a side or two on a subject not connected with business. We are all well in the family. Kitty must go. Her fury is intolerable.[12] It is impossible to live longer in the house with her. Your brothers & sister surpass all our wishes as to their talents & dispositions. Julia is daily improving and is the comfort of our lives. I foresee that you will love her most warmly when you again see her. Lydia & her husband are well. Your Mother joins in affection to you with

Yr. father

B. H. Latrobe

There were other, later jobs in Pittsburgh, too, some evidently of considerable size. For Christian Cowan he designed a large house, which apparently was built and for the design of which he billed Cowan $150 on January 16, 1815; he also designed houses for William Robinson and William Foster.[13] And other construction jobs fell his way. When he

---

12. Catherine McCausland, the Latrobes' invaluable servant, had been with them eleven years and had served successively as nurse, maid, and housekeeper. As she aged she became increasingly erratic and tyrannical, and Latrobe was forced to write to her brother Alexander in Philadelphia, uring him to take her home. She had developed a complete disregard of clothes; though she was being paid thrice what she had received earlier, she still was not decently dressed. She gave the children to understand that the McCauslands had been people of affluence in Scotland, developed illusions of persecution, was arbitrarily autocratic, etc. Alexander wrote back urging the Latrobes to try to put up with her, and she remained with them till her tragic death by fire some two years later.

13. Letter of April 5, 1815, to William Robinson: "I hold myself bound to furnish you such plans as are necessary to execute the house I have designed for you"; and letter of July 18, 1815, from Washington, to Henry Holdship: "Of Robinson's house I had only loose memoranda. But my memory has supplied the rest . . . [The details] the present sheet contains will enable you to go on for some time." In connection with the Foster

bought the O'Hara land, for example, he found on it a large barge, partly built, which the drunken builder was long overdue in delivering. Latrobe, partly out of kindness, took over the completion and made a considerable profit both for himself and for the original contractor. In addition, there were houses—if we can trust the correspondence—for a Mr. Ripley and a Mr. Anderson in Bedford, though these may have been merely design commissions; and there are references to other Pittsburgh work. Then there was a certain continuation of his earlier architectural practice. The correspondence with Dale and Wilmer in Philadelphia about a project for Washington Hall in that city was resumed; Latrobe warned them (February 10, 1814) that their wants exceeded their appropriation, yet evidently he made a set of drawings:

> You state that your building is proposed to be about 115′ long by 65′ wide. Such a building will cover 7,475 s.ft.—You will therefore assuredly exceed your estimated expenditure of 40,000$.
>
> [After discussing building costs in Philadelphia as he had found them, he continues:] Suppose your Hall to be only rated at 6 dollars, its amount will be 44,850$. I state this for your consideration. If the design which I shall send you appears too expensive at first sight—do not reject it merely on that account. I shall have a copy of it and can then furnish you with data on which to proceed with certainty as to the expense.—I presume of course that you want a permanent building, not a magnificent piece of Scenery, which for a moderate sum will make a great show. Such a one I could give you, but I should consider it as an insult to your taste and understanding.

Actually, Washington Hall was finally built from a design by Robert Mills. And there was additional work for Henry Clay. Clay was building Ashland slowly, bit by bit, and Latrobe was also planning for him a row of tenements—apparently shops and houses for rent—in Lexington, Kentucky. He wrote Clay of the difficulties of arranging so many dwellings on such a small lot; each of the houses or shops, it appears, was only fourteen feet wide. Through much of this period, too, he seems to have been working spasmodically on the designs of the Van Ness house in Washington, which will be discussed in a later chapter. Van

---

house, Latrobe wrote his client on January 16, 1815: "I beg Mrs. Foster's acceptance of the landscape herewith sent, representing such a house as she seemed to approve. . . . In the background I have imagined the appearance of your village of Lawrenceville, with the Arsenal. . . . Should you resolve to build under my direction . . . working drawings will be required. . . . If not, I will thank you to return me the plan and section."

Ness had given him the commission shortly before Latrobe left Washington and was pressing him for sketches.

Finally, there was the great United States arsenal in Pittsburgh. Latrobe had done his best to obtain this job for Thomas Pope, a bridge engineer, poor and without work, then in Pittsburgh.[14] Latrobe wrote Captain Wooley of the United States Army (June 9, 1814) on his behalf:

> Mr. Pope, who is well known for his knowledge of the subject of bridges, has with a large & expensive family shared the fate of others in our seaport towns and is now out of business. He is now in Pittsburgh in hopes of finding employment here & the means of supporting himself. He is not only perfect master of the practice of building & surveying, having been brought up in that line, but he is a good draughtsman. He is besides a most respectable man in his private character, and will never disgrace his employers by bad conduct.
>
> I therefore take the liberty to recommend him to you as likely to be very useful to you in the great public undertaking of which you have the direction. His expectations will be moderate, & he will trust to his own conduct & abilities to deserve encouragement, & to receive it.—
>
> In giving to Mr. Pope a situation in which he can be useful to the public, to you, & to himself, you will not only be rewarded by the benefit derived from his services,—but by the satisfaction you will enjoy in having given support to a highly meritorious & amiable family.—To me you will grant a favor also which will not be forgotten.

Yet Latrobe did make certain elaborate drawings (dated October, 1814) —now in the Library of Congress—and the construction did go ahead. The arsenal still stands, in part; a comparison of the actual buildings and the Latrobe drawings, however, reveals more differences than similarities, although the general over-all shapes of some of the buildings agree. The preliminary drawings which he made are among the most brilliant of the architect's designs; they are original, admirably fitted for their purpose, with clear, simple, and distinguished details. In these drawings more than anywhere else is embodied the most perfect expression of his later style, which so wonderfully combines austerity with

14. Pope was the inventor of an ingenious if impractical method of building cantilever bridges of great span; with this method he was sure even the Hudson River could be bridged in a single span. He illustrated his proposed Hudson bridge and explained the method in *A Treatise on Bridge Architecture . . .* (New York: printed for the author by A. Niven, 1811).

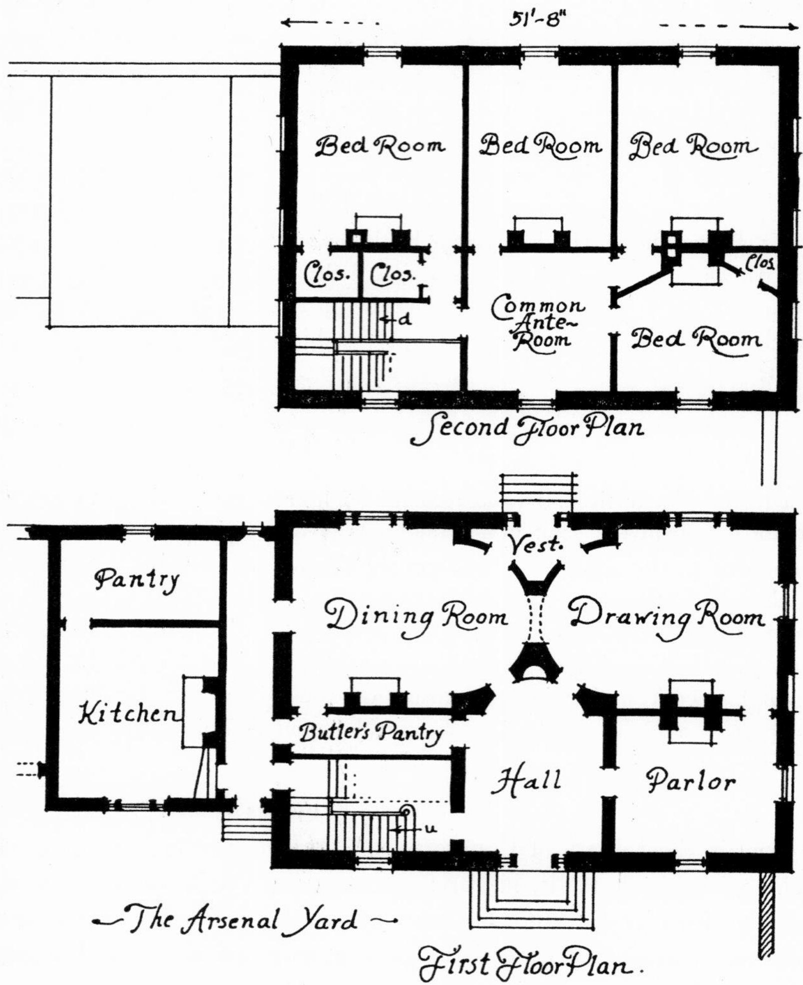

In Library of Congress

FIGURE 25. Proposed Commandant's House, Arsenal, Pittsburgh. Plans. Redrawn from Latrobe's drawings.

grace and in spite of its simplicity avoids the mean or the merely stark. Of all this the executed work offers but little evidence. In the commandant's house, doubled projecting brackets, widely spaced, support and decorate the snubbed roof-eaves cornice; these are almost the only recognizable Latrobe motifs. And the central building—the arsenal proper—is but a caricature of the magnificent vaulted structure the architect had designed. His exterior was a perfect expression of what went on within; the executed design has small rectangular openings only and at some period acquired awkward and ugly battlements that hide completely whatever resemblance it may once have had to the clear and serene Latrobe design.

Latrobe's plan of the commandant's house is distinguished. All the living rooms are placed on the outer side, away from the working area; the yard or inner side is reserved for the entry, stairs, halls, and minor rooms. The drawing room and dining room meet in curved walls that create a useful closet on the hall side and an entrance vestibule on the other; the kitchen and service areas are grouped in a wing with a separate service entrance to the outside and a service stair. On the second floor the planning of the bedrooms is convenient, the circulation is minimized, and there are a number of closets. The entire plan, economical and carefully studied for orientation and function, has a surprisingly modern appearance. As it exists today, the house has been drastically altered with the addition of a later and inharmonious wing, so that it is difficult to determine whether Latrobe's arrangement was preserved in the original construction.

Among the rest of the buildings that remain, the storage warehouse and the powder magazine are the two that reveal the most of what seems the true Latrobe character. The beautiful masonry and the clarity of conception seen in both are remarkable, and the stepped cornice of the warehouse—in two projecting courses of squared stone blocks—is effective and expressive, just as the great gable coping stones (keyed up at the outside edge) of the powder magazine and its simple arched entrance have a character of exciting power. The gate posts in the surrounding wall of the arsenal, excellent in proportion and with strong, well-studied moldings and a successful handling of the rustication, may also have come direct from the architect's drawing board. The non-commissioned officers' quarters, with their low, inviting arches and the triple windows above, although without any recognizable details definitely attributable to Latrobe, seem somehow to have something of the directness and the common sense associated with the architect. No drawings for them are known to exist, but these features might well be based on simplifications of his designs, as is the general geometric composition of the whole layout.

The building of the arsenal, which was not completed till 1820, extended over a period of five years and more, and for only part of one of those years was Latrobe in Pittsburgh. And after he left the city in the spring of 1815 he never returned, kept away not only by the press of other interests but also by fear of local judgments against him in connection with the steamboat debacle. And Thomas Pope *was* employed on the project, for on October 3, 1814, Latrobe wrote Captain Wooley to arrange a conference with him on the matter of Pope's bill for professional services; two days later he wrote Wooley again a formal opinion and sent a copy to Pope. Thus it seems probable that Latrobe acted informally as consulting architect only and that Pope served as the draftsman for the first buildings as actually erected. This is rendered all the more likely by another letter from Latrobe to Wooley (October 21, 1814) after the captain had written to ask his advice about the roof of the warehouse:

> . . . Shingles, therefore, are inadmissible; lead, I have found . . . in the Middle states, to be impossible . . . as the great range of temperature [from winter to summer] expands & contracts it so much as to tear it to pieces in a few years. . . . The leakage of the public buildings in Washington had their [sic] cause in the leaden roof. . . . Tin is not to be procured. . . . Tiles & slate are not to be had here. . . . All these considerations induced me fourteen or 15 years ago [actually, twelve] to cover Princeton College, after it had been burnt down, with sheet iron, and since then I have covered all the public buildings of the U. States [with it]. I have not heard or observed a single objection to it, & the roof of Princeton College, as far as I have information, is as good as the day when it was put on . . .

This sounds much more like the advice of a consulting architect than a letter to an active client. But apparently Pope did not remain long on the job, for in a final letter to Wooley from Washington (October 10, 1815) Latrobe wrote: "I feel most exceedingly sorry for Pope. . . . He is besides crazy about his patent lever bridge. My shyness about the Arsenal has been useless to him. On his account I declined, much as I wished to . . . engage in that work . . ."

Of the work in western Pennsylvania outside Pittsburgh, the Anderson house still stands.[15] It is a large brick structure, seven bays wide; a central hallway divides the main block between Dr. Anderson's quarters

15. It is illustrated in Charles M. Stotz, *The Early Architecture of Western Pennsylvania* . . . (New York: W. Helburn, for the Buhl Foundation, Pittsburgh, 1936).

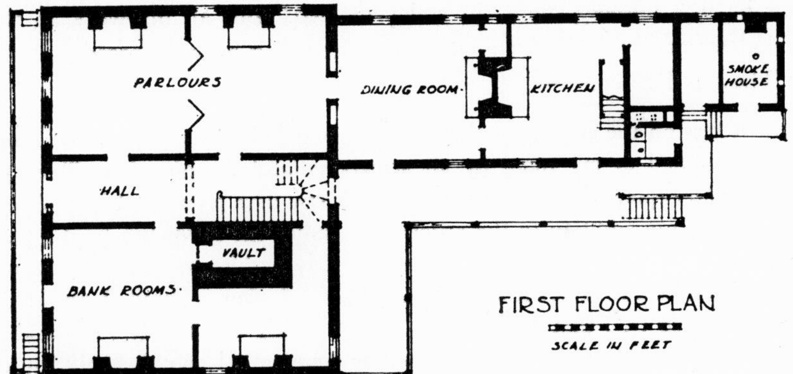

From Stotz, *Early Architecture of Western Pennsylvania*

FIGURE 26. Anderson House, Bedford, Pa. Plan.

and the rooms assigned to the local branch of the Bank of Pennsylvania, which shares the building. The present rich iron porch is an addition of a much later period than that of the house itself (1815), and a vertical joint at the front corner suggests that the front itself may have been reconstructed or refaced. Since Latrobe evidently did not superintend the building, it is difficult to say how closely the structure follows his original drawings, but one may surmise that at least its over-all dimensions and its general spirit are due to him; of the interior detail it is impossible to speak with certainty. The excellent relation of the roof slope to the whole, the basic austerity of detail, the stone lintels with molded paterae in their square end panels, the excellence of the plan and the existence in it of separate service stairs—these all point to an architect's careful study and resemble closely many elements we have come to recognize as typical of Latrobe's work. In Pittsburgh itself, except for the arsenal, everything of Latrobe's has perished.

During his troubled years in Pittsburgh the architect found time to do some writing. For the Philadelphia publishers Parker & Delaplaine's proposed encyclopedia he had been asked to write the article "Acoustics," and he had complied. Now they wished him to undertake the entire revision of the article "Civil Architecture" which they were printing from the Edinburgh Encyclopaedia, together with the addition of whatever he felt necessary to bring it up to date and to incorporate American achievements. They sent him the proof sheets in April, 1814, and by August 4 his revisions and new material were ready; he wrote them that he was mailing these "in a day or two." But all his work in this period seemed to be under a curse; on October 7 he was forced to write to Thomas Parker:

Your letters on the subject of the article on Civil Architecture arrived while I was confined to my room by an acutely painful disorder [the illness of August and September referred to earlier]. A few days previous, I had labored to compleat my addition to the article . . . under the following heads: Convenience of arrangement of private houses; City architecture; Rural architecture; Arrangement of town & cities as to general plan & detail. I found the work grew so . . . that I could not satisfy myself entirely, & [was taken] ill before I compleated it. . . . Your letters were entirely withheld till my recovery. But what was my surprise to find that the papers in my private drawer in my desk were not as I left them, but that they had been shifted, & that the article . . . was nowhere to found. . . . My mortification cannot be expressed in words. . . . What can I say or do to repair the mischief? Any terms you can prescribe, I accede to. But I cannot create again the lost sheets . . .

Therefore when the first American edition of the Encyclopaedia finally appeared (published by Joseph and Edward Parker, in 1832), although it carried his "Acoustics," the "Civil Architecture" was the old British article unchanged and we have been deprived of what might have been by far his most important architectural essay.

In addition, there was his correspondence with Professor Cooper of Dickinson College in Carlisle already alluded to. Cooper was then producing an interesting magazine, the *Emporium,* and urging Latrobe to contribute; but their letters cover much more than that. They make learned puns in Latin and Greek; they discuss the potentialities of lighting by gas and the proper apparatus necessary for it; they even discuss cooking, for Cooper boasted of his imaginative culinary skill. On January 8, 1814, for example, Latrobe writes:

There is not a gourmand in the United States who could have written the Epicurean pieces but yourself, so that I give you the credit of being *unus e grege Epicuroporcus,* for the pieces are unique. But as to Say of Tomatos [a sort of tomato ketchup] you are mistaken. We have made it (I will send you a bottle next season) for 14 years . . . [Going on to the subject of Eric Bollman, who had been writing Cooper about his chemical and metallurgical experiments:] Bollman I fear will never forget you. What is to be done with him? Right or wrong, the Laws of Society are firmly established for his lifetime. He complains bitterly that he is an outlaw, defends his mode of life & connexion—& yet he expects to be admitted to all the advantages to which every married fool, rogue, wise & virtuous man is admitted, on terms contrary to all law. [Evidently Bollman had told Cooper of his ostracism on account of his liaison with his children's nurse as well as because of his association with Burr.] No one indeed has anything to do with the manner of his life, further than as he invites censure by his complaints,—& I should not now mention it, if it did not bring him with every disadvantage on his side into the field of Science. Poor fellow! excluded as he is from free intercourse with all who could assist his researches, it is pitiable to see the efforts & shifts he makes to do as much as he has done. Pray then use him gently, & above all don't laugh at him, and never hint that King George was a button maker . . .

Let me hear from you, & give mine & Mrs. Latrobe's love to Mrs. Cooper & the charming girls that hover about your retorts.

Latrobe had sent Cooper his "Report on Turnpikes" (submitted to Secretary Gallatin) to be inserted in the *Emporium* and now writes (February 8) that he is trying to get a piece of marble smooth enough to allow him to engrave on it the necessary illustrations. A week later (February 14) he sends Cooper the story of Newcomen's discovery of the steam engine as he had heard it from his father; he thinks the *Emporium* might use the story in the form of a letter to the editor:

The following anecdote was told by my father in the presence of Mr. Boulton of Soho about the year 1786, and is so probable, that altho' it rests on tradition only, it is worthy of being preserved. My father gave it on the authority of a Gentleman of Exeter, whose name I do not remember.

"Mr. Newcomen having been out late & having drunk freely one evening, felt himself feverish & unable to eat his breakfast the next morning. He called for a glass of cold water, and having drunk part of it, his attention was caught by the Tea Kettle which was boiling violently upon the fire. The lid, which happened to be well fitted, was thrown up by the steam, & alternately fell, so as to keep up a rattling noise;—a circumstance not at all infrequent. Having the remains of the Water in the glass in his hand, he capriciously dashed it upon the kettle. A Vacuum was instantly created by the condensation of the steam, & the weight of the Atmosphere forced the lid into the kettle. This was the hint that produced Newcomen's Engine, & from which has originated the present perfect mode of using the agency of Steam."

On May 5, 1814, Latrobe writes Cooper about the retorts for his potassium experiments, says that Bakewell (who ran a famous Pittsburgh foundry) had Cooper's order partly completed, and wonders if it is possible to weld cast iron: "I honestly confess that I never knew that it could be done, tho' I do not see why not . . ." A month later he writes: "Bakewell told me your order is ready . . . I shall send you a paper on that monster the Harmony Society."[16] The famous Abbé Correa[17] had meanwhile been visiting Carlisle and had come on to Pittsburgh. Latrobe reports on his visit (July 10): "The Abbé Correa stayed here only 3 days, & was Smolletting the whole time, venting his dislike of all around him. . . . He seems a man of the world, & a politician, as well as of letters." All this correspondence is personal and informal. Evidently the two men, in their broad curiosities and their speculative and imaginative pursuits, were deeply congenial. Thus it was with double regret that Latrobe (October 11) acknowledges the report from Cooper that the *Emporium* is to cease, the victim of wartime depression. In the same letter he adds his own bit of distressing news: "Bollman has gone to Europe owing me $1000 for the education of his children."

There are letters to other friends in the East, for Latrobe's mind turned back increasingly to more serene days as the troubles in Pittsburgh mounted. He writes friends and associates in Washington. He sends a running account of the steamboat imbroglio to Roosevelt. For William Stackpole (a famous nail manufacturer in Boston) he arranges the purchase of Cowan's works in Pittsburgh for conversion to a nail factory, and he hopes for a commission on the sale. He has various debts still plaguing him in Washington and as security to cover one of them he offers his title to part of the Delaware farm he has held jointly with Judge Kinsey Johns.

An even deeper pleasure to Latrobe was his correspondence with his

---

16. The Harmony Society—the Rappites—after settling first in Economy, Pennsylvania, and then in New Harmony, Indiana, had acquired considerable wealth. The Society was based on religious communism and demanded the absolute continence of its members. Latrobe's paper never appeared, for the last number of the *Emporium* was that of October, 1814, and evidently Latrobe in the press of his confused affairs had not had time to prepare it by then. The discussions about steam engines appeared in the numbers of December, 1813, and February, 1814 (vol. II, nos. 1 and 2); Latrobe's turnpike report was published in August, 1814 (vol. III, no. 2). I owe this information to Professor Milton Flower of Dickinson College.

17. José Francisco Correa da Serra, 1750-1823, Portuguese minister to the United States, 1816-20.

son Henry in New Orleans, where the young man in addition to keeping the waterworks project alive was rapidly making a name for himself as an architect and builder. Toward the end of December, 1813, for example, Latrobe (according to the record in his letter book) sends Henry a box of drawing materials, paper, Chinese ink, "a book of architectural scraps, —and the drawing made by [Henry] of the Temple of Theseus, etc.—& a letter & some books from his mother." [18] A month later (January 30, 1814) he writes Henry a characteristically intimate and playful letter:

> . . . Yesterday I received yours of the 21st of Dec. 1813 [more than a month in transit]. I am very sorry that you have had so serious a cut, by dint of gesticulation. Gesticulation if properly managed (& yet it cannot be governed by any rules) has assuredly great effect in producing that effect on an audience, which the orator feels himself. It governs the mind thro' the eyes, as the voice does thro' the ears. It is said that some of Burke's most celebrated & exciting speeches, were made while his hands were groping in his breeches pocket. But vehemence of manner always produces effect, & it is almost always accompanied by gesticulation. Fox gesticulated violently & most ungracefully, *pawing the air,* & yet the vehemence of manner & the good earnest which his gestures inspired contributed much to the effect of his speeches.—An extraordinary instance of gesticulation, if it may be so called . . . I have frequently heard mentioned and altho' it appears almost ludicrous its effect, I am assured was outstanding. The celebrated Patrick Henry, in his famous speeches against the adoption of the present federal constitution in the Virginia Convention used this expression: I dread this constitution in its tendencies,—*it has an awful squinting at Monarchy;* at the same time he turned up his head obliquely to the speaker, & squinted most horribly during some seconds.—It is peculiar to the English . . . to condemn gesticulation, all other nations use it. In our family it is a sort of disease, our children come gesticulating into the world, I think. Henry, & John, & Ben all gesticulate, & so do I your father. I hope your thumb is convalescent, & I offer it the condolence of the family. It is of less importance to you, who do not operate by *rule of thumb,* than it would be to others . . .

---

18. Henry left at his death a surprisingly extensive library, including not only many large and valuable architectural and engineering volumes but also an excellent general collection of English and French literature. Much of the architectural collection consists of French rather than English books and these were probably purchased by Henry in New Orleans. Undoubtedly some of the English literature came to him from his parents and included the books referred to here. I owe this information to the kindness of Mr. Samuel Wilson, Jr., of New Orleans.

He keeps Henry informed of his own progress and of the state of the New Orleans waterworks engine: (January 8, 1814) "I am now making patterns for our engine"; (February 14) "I am head over heels in great things. The steamboats, & two barges on the stocks, 4 gangs of bricklayers at work, smiths, pattern-makers, filers & turners, ship-joiners, & boiler makers, are all as busy as possible." In a letter about sugar kettles and engines for sugar mills (March 4), he remarks that "it is evident that planters are bad pay . . ." and again (April 2): "Beelen cannot fill the orders [for sugar kettles] he has. Pittsburgh has arisen to its present flourishing state in a very few years . . . Three years ago, Beelen's Foundry was the only one"; in 1814 there were three others—the McClurg, the George Evans, and the Stackhouse & Rogers. Later in the month (April 23) he sends Henry a letter of introduction for Captain Francis Ogden of the *Vesuvius*. On May 23 he sends the letter (already quoted on page 416) describing his building and architectural business, and on July 17 he writes that the New Orleans engine is under construction.

Then there is a long break of two months; apparently the failure of the steamboat scheme and the frantic attempts to patch it up were occupying Latrobe so completely that there was little time left for any other correspondence. As he wrote Henry (September 24):

I am this evening writing for the first time after a very severe attack of my old Hemicrania. It has hitherto generally lasted for three weeks, but I have got over it after 10 days' severe suffering. Dr. Barton's remedy, Magnesia, appears the best I have yet discovered. Every other from Blisters to Bleeding & starving, to wine of Laudanum had been tried in vain for many years. . . .

The state of things to the Eastward, the taking & burning of Washington, the danger of Baltimore & of all our seaport towns, the active & successful efforts of the federalists in defeating the loan & withdrawing the specie from the Southward & sending it to Canada, the brutal ignorance & gross mismanagement of our affairs by the democrats, all this affects the current credit & facility in doing business of every individual, & is most sensibly felt everywhere. . . . But as to your apprehension of a change of Government for New Orleans, altho' I do not deny the possibility of a temporary occupation of the place by the English or Spaniards of which I am no judge, yet I think a permanent possession of the mouth of the river against all the Western states, is not to be counted upon. But I am glad of your apprehensions if they induce you to learn Spanish, & I beg you will make a point of learning to speak it well, let what will happen. For nothing is so practically true as the observation of the Emperor Charles V, that a man's powers & existence is multiplied in proportion to the number of languages he speaks . . .

This is his first reference to the burning of Washington, which had taken place almost a month earlier. With what relief, then, the loving parents learned early in February, 1815, of the successful defense of New Orleans on January 8 and the safety of their son in that threatened city! A month later, when General Jackson's official report came to hand, deep pride was theirs, for Andrew Jackson had picked out Henry Latrobe for special commendation as one of the engineers. Latrobe wrote Isaac Hazlehurst (March 5): "We have been highly flattered and delighted by General Jackson's handsome mention of our Henry." Truly a son to be proud of.[19]

Meanwhile the steamboat picture grew ever blacker. As the enterprise marched along inevitably to failure, it was as if a sudden whirlwind had developed among the glowering and threatening clouds; no longer was it a simple Fulton-Latrobe controversy, but so confused became the cross purposes that it is almost impossible to find a pattern in the outburst of charges and countercharges. Not only the Ohio boats but the Mississippi boats as well were involved, for there was a tangle of debts left dangling when the builder of these, John R. Livingston, sailed gaily off down the river on the *Vesuvius*.

On September 30, 1814, Fulton suddenly and without warning, in an insulting letter, declared Latrobe no longer his agent. Latrobe wrote at once to Dr. McNeven, the secretary of the New York company:

Considering myself no longer either the agent of the . . . Company . . . or for Mr. Fulton, and finding that a few days ago two attachments had been issued for a small amount against the Company's property, which were invalid . . . as a common creditor I have issued an attachment against the whole property here. . . . I shall take care that it receive no damage, & charge the Company with the expense.

---

19. Later, after a more careful study of the report, Latrobe declared himself a little put out that Henry was mentioned as "Mr. Latrobe" instead of "Captain Latrobe." On September 3, 1815, he wrote to Major General Jackson himself of the mortification felt by his son and quoted from the report: "The services of the chief engineer Col. Latour have been useful, as well as of his assistants *Captain* Lewis Livingston & *Mr.* Latrobe" (titles underscored by Latrobe). He added that Henry Latrobe "believes that his commission on the staff was of prior date to Captn. Lewis Livingston, & that he had the rank of Captain . . ."

He also sent a copy of part of this letter to David Cooke, in Pittsburgh, who at Fulton's order had claimed possession. Fulton and the company were threatening suit, and Latrobe wrote to the Reverend Mr. Mortimer again (October 1):

> You, who have known me from a child . . . You will excuse the warmth of an old schoolfellow. . . . But I cannot be expected to be so made, as after such conduct to me to step down from the ground on which I now stand, unless ample justice is done me. . . . Our object is to get the boat a-going, not to succeed in a law suit . . . [Nevertheless in January, 1815, he asked Aaron Burr, in a letter, to act as his attorney in any New York suits that might eventuate.]

It was on October 11, 1814, that Latrobe wrote to Henry Baldwin, the attorney, the long letter (referred to on page 377) in which he relates the complete history of his association with Fulton and Roosevelt in steamboat building.[20] Fulton had wished Baldwin to take his own case against Latrobe, but the attorney, believing Latrobe to be innocent, had refused. Now Fulton, too, was beginning to worry; he wrote David Cooke (October 24)[21] that Latrobe had been penniless when he left Washington and had been enabled to travel to Pittsburgh only by virtue of a loan from him that now amounted to $1,703.22; how then had he been able to advance the company large sums of money? What other business had he been conducting?

Later he wrote Latrobe direct, and from then on it was open war. Fulton continued to bombard Latrobe with minatory and accusing letters; Latrobe wrote back dignified answers. Thus on November 6 Latrobe lists the accusations Fulton had made, one by one: First, that Latrobe had speculated with the company's money; this, the architect says, is absurd and the vouchers prove it absurd; Fulton moreover had approved Latrobe's land purchase from O'Hara. Second, that Latrobe was carrying on a private building business; the architect acknowledges that he has and that *all the profits have gone back into the boats.* Third, that Latrobe had used company money to build the shops in which he carried on other business; the architect counters that he had been informed that Fulton had had a correspondent in Pittsburgh to spy on him, a fact he

20. See Appendix.

21. Incomplete draft in the Gilbert Montague Collection of Robert Fulton Manuscripts, New York Public Library.

could not at first but now begins to believe. This third accusation, Latrobe says, is completely false; he had built an engine on the Ogden plan, but all its parts had been made elsewhere. Fourth, to use his own words:

I now come to the only charge which has a shadow of foundation, the failure to pay my note endorsed by you for my accommodation. Had the banks continued to discount this note (you being willing to continue to endorse) or had I been able to apply the monies received by disposal of property R[oosevelt] gained to that use, this failure would not have occurred. . . . In the meantime all my profits of business which would have taken it up, went into the boat.—I acknowledge the obligation I am under on this account, & regret the course it has taken. I could have avoided it had I done as Livingston did, & kept my own money to pay my debts instead of advancing all I could earn & borrow to the Company.

Then, suddenly, the New York directors of the Ohio Steamboat Navigation Company rebelled against Fulton also, as they had earlier against Latrobe. They wrote Latrobe that they had a contract with Fulton to supply the boats at a fixed price and that they were prepared to force Fulton to make good, and the Mississippi Steamboat Navigation Company threatened similar action.[22] Fulton's greed had finally overreached itself. "Fulton, the First, cannot sleep on a bed of roses," wrote Latrobe to Roosevelt (November 15).

One could wish for the drama's sake that all these stresses had united in some great catastrophic event. But reality often destroys the dramas it has suggested, and so it did here. Instead of one great crash there was a sort of raveling out of the threads into a tangled confusion. Yet some settlement of the conflict had to be made, and eventually it was decided that the boats and engines should be handed over to the Cooke-Staudinger combination and that the shops should remain temporarily in Latrobe's hands.

By the end of November Latrobe at last realized that any further attempts at reconciliation were impossible. DeLacy, disgusted with the treatment he had received from Fulton, was attempting to become an ally of Latrobe and Roosevelt; the battle of the patents was on. Latrobe had refused to believe DeLacy's rumors about the invalidity of the Fulton

22. Yet later accounts suggest that the Mississippi Steamboat Navigation Company at least agreed to the actual rather than the stipulated price, and for the *Vesuvius* a capital of $40,000 is mentioned. See Hunter, *op. cit.*

patent because of irregularities in the application; he had refused even to support Roosevelt's claim to priority in the invention of the side paddle wheel. As late as November 13 he wrote Fulton warning him of DeLacy's "powerful opposition," and his letter of December 13 to DeLacy shows that he still distrusted the wily and eloquent Irishman: "You have given us so dashing an account of your crusade against Fulton, with such a variety of incident, perjury, conspiracy, & the state prison in perspective, that I absolutely am ignorant of the real state of the case, as if I never heard of the thing."

But Roosevelt is now applying for his patent, and Fulton goes to Washington to fight it; he blames his old enemy Thornton for the attack on his own patent. Latrobe has fresh dreams of new Western steamboat companies organized by DeLacy, Roosevelt, and himself; he writes Fulton that he, Latrobe, had been present when Roosevelt suggested side wheels to Livingston, and he offers DeLacy an affidavit to that effect (January 25, 1815). On February 13 he writes a formal letter to Thornton, the Commissioner of Patents, giving the Roosevelt specifications and asking protection till the patent is granted. To cap the campaign he sends letters to Dr. McNeven in New York (February 20) and to Edward Livingston in New Orleans (February 22) stating that all future inquiries about steamboat affairs must be addressed to Roosevelt, the rightful owner of the only valid steamboat patent, since Fulton's was invalid.

Again his efforts were vain—the chimerical hopes of a man without capital, without credit, to pursue dreams created out of his own distress. The whole country was on the verge of a financial panic. Great debts in Pittsburgh hung over Latrobe, since many suppliers of materials for the boats were still unpaid; the company refused responsibility, and Fulton was an enemy. Then, to bring on ultimate chaos, at the beginning of March, 1815, Latrobe heard of Robert Fulton's death from pneumonia, caught on a visit of inspection to a new boat being built for the Hudson River trade. So far as Pittsburgh and steamboats were concerned, Latrobe was doomed and knew it; his frenzied correspondence all through January had been only the struggle of a prisoner against his shackles.

Of the burning of Washington Latrobe had heard the previous September; his friend Dr. Frederick May had written him of the condition of the Capitol, and Latrobe had answered (September 24, 1814):

> I thank you for your remarks so flattering to me on the Capitol. But I fear that it cannot be repaired. The frost will come on & destroy much. . . . I

know exactly what it would be best to do, but I cannot intrude my advice & Mr. Madison will never employ me again, I am told. All I can do is to lie by & wait. If called upon, I will give all my talents & industry to restore, or to build something new & better & cheaper & more beautiful in place of the former room. Perhaps Congress will call on me . . .

Two months later, as the Pittsburgh prospects grew ever darker, his mind turned back again to the possibility of more work in Washington, and he wrote tentatively to Secretary of the Treasury Dallas: "Should the restoration of the Capitol call for the activity of a professional man, you will lend me the assistance of your old friendship." But for a time, in the confusion of all his Pittsburgh affairs, the matter seems to have been forgotten; evidently his cautious inquiries had brought no result.

Meanwhile the incessant worries, the constant frustrations, the never-ending harassments of the steamboat debacle and Roosevelt's Tustin affair, the growing doubts and fears about the future of the New Orleans waterworks, the terrifying debts, and the increasing sense that every road to the future was being closed all began to take their toll as the gloomy Pittsburgh winter dragged on. Suddenly, at the beginning of February, Latrobe's nerves snapped, in a collapse like the one he had had twenty-two years earlier at the death of his first wife, and he slipped into a state of listless, will-less, silent melancholy, unable even to read or to write except at the tactful insistence of Mary Elizabeth, who strove mightily to raise his spirits and arouse his interest. All the letter copies of this period are in her hand. At her suggestion he did write on February 17 to Thomas Munroe, asking his support in obtaining the commission for rebuilding the Capitol and acknowledging that he was unpopular with the President and had little hope; for Madison's thoughtless words eighteen months earlier (referred to on page 386) had cut him deeply and now in his despair returned to plague him. He closed his letter: "I have not forgotten tho' with shame, that I am your debtor; but all my means have since my arrival here been in Mr. Fulton's hands, who has used me very ill."

Then, in spite of his lethargy, Mrs. Latrobe urged her husband to write direct to President Madison. Finally he did so (February 25), as he informed Munroe in a letter on the same day:

. . . I have however, observed that a Law is passed authorizing a loan for [the reconstruction of the Capitol and the White House.]—[I have] been prevailed upon by Mrs. Latrobe to write the letter to the President of which a copy is on the other [side]. She is anxious to live near her father & brothers, & our children begin to require more education than they can obtain here. I confess however that I have no hope or expectation from this application however desirable its success may be to me. I beg you therefore not to mention that I have applied, altho' it is due your situation and our former relations, as well as to my respect for you that it should be known to you.

Latrobe's copy of the letter to the President is only a draft. It is crossed out and revised and shows a mind bewildered and unsure. The final wording runs:

Sir,

I beg leave respectfully to offer you my services in the restoration of the public buildings in the city of Washington. I have devoted the best years of my life to the public. I need not trespass upon your time in stating the professional qualifications which I should bring to the office. That I have shared the charge of extravagance with every architect to whom the expenditure of money has been committed in every nation, and from the most ancient times, I am very sensible.

I am conscious that I do not deserve it—still more so, that if I do, my error has produced no advantage to myself, for independently of that excusable ambition which prompts me to wish that I may restore the works which I erected & avoid the implied censure of another appointment, consideration for my family would render the situation I solicit highly desirable to me.

B. H. Latrobe

Of Latrobe's own depression his letters tell little. To Thomas Munroe he writes (March 1) that he has been afflicted with hemicrania and that a long convalescence is necessary; to DeLacy (March 5): "I have many letters hinting at a recall to Washington, which I shall accept if offered. Here I am done up completely, & am sometimes ready to lay down in despair. We are otherwise well & with appetites & teeth strong enough to have eaten up part of our furniture"; and finally to Roosevelt (on March 5): "I go tomorrow for a week to Steubenville & expect afterwards to decamp & vegetate somewhere till I can get salt to my porridge perhaps at Clover Hill. There is some talk of my return to Washington. I must do something otherwise . . ."

But Mrs. Latrobe had not confined her efforts to encouraging her husband and selling part of their furniture. She had written fully to all her closest Washington friends, and especially to the Madisons. She had painted their situation clearly; she had begged her friends to intercede with the President to recognize the real debt to Latrobe's genius under which the country lay. She who took at her husband's dictation his queerly doubting letters to Thomas Munroe and perhaps helped him phrase his own appeal to the President, apologetic as it was, had seen to it that a more positive presentation was made to Mr. Madison. Her campaign was magnificently successful. As she tells the story in her memoir later:

Our residence in Pittsburgh was now made very uncomfortable, the spirits of my dear husband sank under his troubles—he lost all energy. The ill usage of Fulton who had actually lived like a brother in our family. . . . But in all our troubles a Merciful Providence never forsook us. I was inspired with an energy that I knew not belonged to me. At this time Peace was declared and well knowing that the Public buildings must be restored, I immediately (unknown to my husband) wrote to the President, to Mr. Dallas, Sec. of State, Gen'l Mason, Mr. C. Ingersoll and one or two others to ask their influence in having Mr. Latrobe reinstated in his former office. To describe my anxiety for a reply to my letters would be impossible—during all this interval I had no money to keep the house but by selling different articles which would raise me a dollar or two—we were obliged to live much upon credit and my husband in a nervous state confined to his chamber. One evening while trying to rouse him, surrounded by our children at the fire, I had a letter handed me, which to my utter surprise contained notes to the amount of $200. It was from my excellent friend Mrs. Barlow with whom I had always corresponded. She was the intimate friend of Fulton and could not believe his treatment of my husband had been the dictates of his own heart. She wrote "depend upon it Fulton is mal entourée." But oh how great was the relief her remittance afforded me! It appeared as from an Almighty hand to interfere for us. The next day I was again relieved by receiving a large Packet with the President's seal, containing a recall for my husband to resume his former situation—never can I forget the transport I felt in going to him as he reclined in deep depression in the easy chair. I presented him the Packet. Behold, I said, what Providence has done for you! and what your poor weak wife has been made the humble instrument in obtaining. He threw himself on my breast and wept like a child—so true it is that women can bear many trials better than men! I received at the same time answers to the several letters I had written to the gentlemen, and of the kindest and most gratifying tenor, all acknowledging that there was "No man in the Country to name but Mr. Latrobe as filling the situation he had hitherto held." Nothing could equal the surprise of my husband on the receipt of this packet, as he did not know of the means I had taken to procure his return. Although much indisposed at the time he wrote an acceptance by the following mail and prepared forthwith to go to Washington alone for the purpose of seeing the State of the Buildings and taking a house for us, leaving me with my children to make the best of our sad affairs in Pittsburgh.

With the recall to Washington, Latrobe's old courage revived. He made a two-week visit to Steubenville for a final inspection of the engine for Bazileel Wells and to suggest various improvements in the cotton and woolen mills there. Immediately on his return (March 22) he wrote a formal acceptance of the Capitol reconstruction commission to John Van Ness, Tench Ringgold, and Richard B. Lee, the commissioners for rebuilding the public buildings in Washington. The next two weeks he spent in winding up as well as he could his Pittsburgh interests—sending Dr. McNeven drawings of the *Buffalo* and the *Harriet,*[23] suggesting that the *Buffalo* be lengthened forty feet to make it suitable for the Mississippi rather than the Ohio trade, and writing several letters to his Steubenville clients. He wrote to Commodore Rogers in Washington (March 23) asking if he might have his old position as Navy Engineer back again, and to Thomas Robertson in Georgetown (March 29) seeking—successfully it appears—to rent Captain Speake's house, "especially as it adjoins Kalorama, the dwelling of our particular friend, Mrs. Barlow." By April 5 he was ready to leave and wrote to Van Ness: "I shall . . . set off tomorrow morning . . . I shall go across the mountains on horseback, & take the stage at Chambersburg . . ." His desperate days at Pittsburgh were over, and save for a brief return in May to fetch the family he never saw the bustling, smoking city again. The best epitaph for this unhappy year is contained in a letter he wrote to Henry on December 31, 1814:

. . . Would to God that I had been early taught that neither love, friendship, sentiment of any kind, not even the enthusiasm of the arts, or of religion can bestow happiness, unless there is an adequacy of some sort, sufficient to keep the enthusiast out of debt. As to myself, it is my duty to you to acknowledge that all my unhappiness is, in its remote causes, to be attributed to my erroneous education. How could a man, whom a short stay at a Moravian school taught to consider wealth & honor as vanity, to trust to providence for

23. According to Hunter, *op. cit.,* the *Buffalo* and the uncompleted freight boat, the *Harriet,* were sold at a sheriff's sale. Both boats were completed and were running profitably in the Cincinnati trade in the spring of 1817. By so little had Latrobe missed his chance of financial security.

daily bread, and whose constant association with German Noblemen till his 20th year gave him the persuasion founded on a habitual mode of thinking—(a thousand times more operative than rational conviction)—that to support yourself by your own industry,—was disgraceful;—how could such a man, deprived of an independent fortune expect to go thro' the world otherwise than I have. That I have indeed been engaged in the same business in Europe which has exchanged ratable property, for frothy reputation in these woods, I should not have wanted the means to live as I unfortunately was educated to live. My industry has indeed been unremitting, my talents sufficient for their employment, but my habits, my habitual sentiments & mode of acting as well as of thinking, have been altogether ruinous. . . . My chivalric honesty has prevented me from amassing a fortune even in this place.—Learn, my dear boy, by my example, & don't talk of unfortunate stars. Remember that among the left overs of self denial which are necessary to virtue, not only the restraint of passion but of benevolence is to be learnt. The latter to my and your disposition may be difficult, but it must be practised, at the expense of pain. *Speak truth* & *keep out of debt,* are precepts which include all the other virtues; the others will follow. But my sermon has lasted too long . . .

Latrobe returned to Washington a financially ruined man, even more deeply in debt than when he had left it so hopefully a year and a half earlier.

CHAPTER

18

Rebuilding of the Capitol: 1815-1817

SO AGAIN, after nearly two years, Latrobe found himself in Washington, engaged to rebuild the Capitol. The commission in itself was a tremendous vindication. He had left the capital city under a cloud, but the anxiety of that earlier period and of the months of defeat in Pittsburgh now dropped from his memory as he plunged into ten days of feverish work, studying the condition of the gutted building, ordering stone, and organizing the labors of almost two hundred workmen whom the three commissioners—Richard Lee, John Peter Van Ness, and Tench Ringgold—had impetuously hired. Though he had arrived in Washington (late in April) still ill and shaky from his nervous breakdown in Pittsburgh, he nevertheless continued to keep going; but perhaps the vital necessity of "keeping going" was the best therapy he could have received. After arranging these preliminaries, he was on horseback again by May 10, bound for Pittsburgh to bring back his family. He arrived there on the twentieth and spent three days (May 22 to 25) at Steubenville, Ohio, making a last inspection of the great cotton and woolen mill he had designed for Henry Orth and Bazileel Wells (more than two hundred people were employed in it). Then back to Pittsburgh for packing, and at last the entire family left the smoky city forever. June 30 saw them in Washington, and the second chapter of Latrobe's work on the Capitol began in earnest.

The British had done a thorough job of demolition. They had fired rockets through the roof; they had kindled fires in every room. On finding that the roof of the House of Representatives resisted their efforts, they had piled up all the furniture and combustible material they could lay their hands on to make a great bonfire in the center of the room, covered it with rocket powder, and lighted it; the terrific heat finally ignited the ceiling ribs, calcined and cracked the marble of floors and the stone of surrounding walls and columns, melted the glass of skylights. Writing graphically to Jefferson of the condition he found, Latrobe tells of picking up lumps of melted glass weighing a pound and more and describes the dangerous condition of the columns—cracked almost through, but still carrying the ghost of the entablature, similarly thinned and cracked yet still supporting the almost undamaged brick vault over the galleries behind.

So grievous had been the destruction that Congress during the previous winter had been puzzled about what to do, but it was agreed that somehow the Capitol must be rebuilt. When an appropriation for the purpose was suggested, a proposal was made to change the site of the structure, felt by many to be too far from Georgetown and even from the President's House. To build anew would hardly cost more than to repair; why not erect a new Capitol on the flat ground near the Potomac? Senator Lewis eloquently and unanswerably supported the idea of keeping it on Capitol Hill, for both sentimental and practical reasons, but when the appropriation came up in the Senate, both Pickering and Webster moved to table it; they were defeated, however, and an appropriation of $500,000 —to be raised by 6 per cent loans from the local banks—was passed on February 16, 1815. This was the first departure from the strict "pay as you go" policy which had controlled in the original building.

Thomas Munroe, still in his old position, made a report on the total cost of the destroyed government buildings up to the time of their destruction: $1,215,111.21½, including $334,334.00½ for the President's House, $457,388.38 for the north wing of the Capitol, and $329,774.92 for the south wing. And, with the help of various contractors, he had made a rough estimate of some $554,000 as the cost of the repair. This estimate was of course absurd. The President's House had been completely gutted; even part of the external wall had fallen. In the Capitol, every stick of wood had perished, along with all the wood-supported floors and roofs, and much of the masonry was so cracked as to make its removal a first necessity. Yet the figure of half a million dollars—a great sum in those days—had become fixed in the Congressional mind, and, as the work went on and the costs inevitably exceeded it, again the accusation of extravagance rang in the architect's ears.

Latrobe was back in Washington with his family by the first of July. Further study of the conditions showed that the job entailed practically a complete rebuilding of the south wing and the western half of the north wing; the eastern half—with the vaulted lobbies, stair halls, Supreme Court room, and Senate chamber—was still structurally sound, though the facing masonry had in most cases calcined away. Latrobe wrote Jefferson (July 12, 1815), describing all this and remarking that the Senate dome, intact and high in the air, made "a most magnificent ruin"; he also explained how he had arranged for the safe demolition of the weakened columns of the House. As Tench Ringgold had suggested, he used cordwood (cheap then because of the wanton cutting down of trees by the British), piling it solidly between the columns to the underside of the entablature. Once this was firmly supported the whole could be taken down stone by stone with perfect safety. Later the cordwood could be sold again at the current prices; it took 500 cords, he wrote, to go halfway around the colonnade.

Meanwhile he had been making his drawings for the new work. Now there was the chance of building a House of Representatives finer than the old, with better lobbies, better committee rooms, and better acoustics, by substituting for the old oval a semicircle, which would use the space more efficiently. Now, too, there was an opportunity to restudy the west side of the north wing, though at this early period Latrobe preferred to let that question wait, for he knew that the completion of the House held priority. He took the plans to President Madison; Madison approved, and Latrobe went ahead.

It is amazing how rapidly the designs were produced, for at this time the architect had no draftsmen on the Capitol work; all the drawings, the details, the notes and calculations came from his own hand, yet the building went on without a hitch. Or almost—for the old Washington difficulties soon reared their heads again: procuring skilled labor, especially stonecutters, and obtaining enough stone. The Potomac freestone quarries were almost exhausted; the stone that was coming from them was coarser and more flawed than that of the beds worked earlier, and Latrobe had to steal many hours from his drafting board for trips of inspection to the quarries. Marble, too, was a problem, and white marble had to be ordered from New York as well as from Philadelphia.

In the meantime the designs for the Exchange in Baltimore—of which more later—were being created, and Latrobe was making periodical visits there to discuss the project with the Exchange authorities and with his Baltimore partner, Godefroy. These trips did not go unnoticed in Washington, and when the rebuilding seemed to drag unduly some saw the reason for the delay in Latrobe's absences rather than in its actual cause—the amount of preparatory razing necessary and the impossibility of getting materials. As yet (through 1815) these criticisms were only a whisper; later they would rise into noisy vituperation. And more labor troubles occurred. The autumn of 1815 was a time of rising prices and many scarcities; at the end of August all the stonecutters struck for higher wages, and, although the strike failed and the masons went back to work, it meant another delay, another worry.[1]

Latrobe and the commissioners had from the beginning faced the problem of what should be done about the necessary sculpture for the new construction. If the Capitol was to be completed rapidly, as much of this work as possible should be ready to install when it was wanted. The slow carving of the Corinthian capitals in the old House certainly would not do, and Latrobe found that it would be much cheaper as well as more expeditious to have the new ones carved in Italy while the building was rising. Accordingly, in August, the dependable Andrei was sent back to Leghorn to make the arrangements for the carving and shipping of the capitals and was asked to bring with him on his return several Italian sculptors for other work. Andrei was gone nine months while the rough work continued, and he brought back with him Carlo Franzoni (Giuseppe's brother), a figure sculptor, and Francisco Iardella, a decorative carver; later another sculptor, Giuseppe Valaperti, arrived and was put to work.

The year 1815 was largely taken up with this preliminary activity. Many drawings were required, and Latrobe himself was also busy with the alterations of Blodgett's Hotel into a temporary capitol and with the Baltimore Exchange and St. John's Church in Washington. He was forced to obtain office assistance and finally engaged a M. de Surville, a well-educated French engineer temporarily in the country. The commissioners refused to pay a draftsman's salary but did add $500 to the architect's pay, with which he could hire what assistance he needed. Deeply apolo-

1. With all his broad sympathy for people, Latrobe never seems to have sympathized with the plight in which labor found itself at this time. Apparently "conditions"—high prices and scarcity—were considered almost as natural phenomena, about which little could be done. The architect, who was anything but rich, had made the revisions in his way of living which these conditions necessitated; why should not labor? That was the basic attitude of the majority of the "best people" and one of the reasons for the slow growth of the labor movement.

getic, Latrobe offered the job to the young Frenchman at "this pittance," and De Surville accepted for a time; later he was replaced by a certain M. Poussin, a friend of Godefroy's. In addition to the pitifully small salary, these draftsmen were provided with a furnished room in the Capitol and the services of a Negro valet.

During the winter of 1815-16, President Madison and Congress had become convinced that the system of handling the work through three commissioners was top-heavy; it was the experience of 1801-2 all over again. Accordingly in April, 1816, a law was passed abolishing the old system and substituting a single commissioner, just as Thomas Munroe had superseded three commissioners twelve years earlier. Latrobe at once wrote Representative Rufus King expressing his approval of the change and suggesting also that in the new arrangement the architect's appointment be made a separate matter (as it had been before) and that the architect's knowledge and responsibility be recognized more definitely. But Congressional suspicion of Latrobe was still violent, and the final arrangements effectively prevented any direct approach by the architect to either Congress or the President; everything had to be funneled through the commissioner. At last, Congress and the Administration thought, they had devised a perfect system for controlling the architect and for preventing extravagance.

President Madison had first nominated as commissioner John Peter Van Ness—a man for whom Latrobe had conceived a great dislike, though he was one of his most opulent clients—but the Senate refused to confirm Van Ness, and in his place Colonel Samuel Lane of the Army, an old friend of James Monroe, the Secretary of State, was appointed and confirmed. At first Latrobe was delighted with the change, describing the colonel in a letter to Henry at New Orleans (May 1, 1816) as "a gentleman of honor & feeling," and for several months the two men got on well enough together in spite of the inevitably mounting costs.

One of the last acts of the old commissioners, who were more sensitive to the demands of the workmen than Latrobe had been, was to limit the working hours of all the Capitol workers to ten hours a day, except the unskilled laborers who were still to be worked from dawn to dark. At once the laborers struck; demolition of the old work ceased, and, Latrobe complains, this forced the loss of "the most important part of a year." Delay again—and in the eyes of Congress and the commissioners the architect was a convenient scapegoat.

Then the Senate made a radical change in its requirements and voted that the new Senate chamber be greatly enlarged over the old dimensions—this despite the fact that the old room still stood, its vault and its structural walls undamaged. Complete demolition of the old brickwork and an entirely new design were now required. Naturally to enlarge the Senate chamber necessitated a revision of the ground floor beneath it, and a new plan had to be evolved which would make use of as much of the existing work as possible and yet permit the enlargement. These changes also entailed a completely new arrangement of the stairs up to the main floor. The old oval Senate stair hall now became a rotunda running up through two floors, with a cupola above through which the light could penetrate down into the center of the building; many of the old walls were preserved and yet new committee rooms and offices were obtained. Despite all these changes, by the end of November, 1816, the new vault over the Supreme Court had been completed and the new Senate chamber walls carried up ten feet above the floor—a remarkable achievement.

The new Supreme Court vault was a triumph both structurally and aesthetically. It followed the umbrella type of the rebuilt vault that had been erected before the fire, although—because the new room was larger than the old—the scale of the lobes was increased. Between these the ribs, decorated with incised moldings, are boldly expressed and at their upper ends are received on a half ring, similarly molded, which borders the top central portion of the vault. The lobes intersect the surrounding wall in simple semicircular lunettes. It is a bold conception of the most complete expressive honesty, entirely unprecedented in shape and detail; the whole is received against the triple-arched composition (along the window wall) retained from the earlier building. Nowhere else perhaps did Latrobe achieve so perfectly that complete expression of the integration of form and structure for which he was always seeking. This vault in the novelty of its forms and its expressive honesty is only paralleled by some of the halls Soane had built and was building in the Bank of England at almost the same time.

In the south wing another question arose, with respect to the material needed for the House of Representatives columns. The freestone that had been used before the fire was no longer available, and diligent search for quarries had failed to find other stone good enough and hard enough. Latrobe's ideals for the building, moreover, suggested a material even finer than the old cut stone; if only a beautiful variegated marble were available! In his travels he had already noticed that marble outcroppings were common in many parts of the Alleghenies and their foothills, and ever since his appointment he had been looking for a supply not too distant from Washington. Finally he found it at Chestnut Hill, in Loudoun County, conveniently close to the Potomac and not far from Harpers Ferry. On his last exploration in April, 1816, he was accompanied by his son John, who has left a vivid picture of how they split a piece of the stone and then with the help of a Negro slave on the plantation polished it on a grindstone; how, when polished, it delighted them with its markings and its variegations of pure white, blue-gray, and black.[2] It was not a true marble but a breccia, a sort of puddingstone; but it was extremely plentiful, dense but workable, susceptible of a high polish, and easily quarried, for large outcroppings came to the surface. Here at last was the perfect material for the columns, which would bring into the great interiors a new and integral richness to delight the eyes of future Congressmen; here was an American material, obtainable at no extra cost, to help make the Capitol the nobly expressive building he had in mind.

But the new quarries had to be opened and developed. The contract for the marble was let early in May, yet the quarrying was a slow business at the start—the cause of another delay that could be laid at the architect's doorstep! And Latrobe, with direct approach to Congress and to the President rendered impossible, was at Lane's mercy. The successful and efficient operation of the system that had been developed depended on sympathetic mutual understanding between commissioner and architect. For several months their accord had continued, but, as the House committee in charge of the public buildings became steadily more demanding and more distressed by what seemed to them unnecessary delays, the pressures on Colonel Lane to place the blame on Latrobe became continually stronger; little by little the sympathy between the two men broke down, and more and more Lane began to treat Latrobe not as a collaborator but as a minor employee.

Another trouble arose when in May, 1816, Congress asked for an estimate of both the cost to complete the two wings and the time that would be required. Latrobe, aware of the danger of estimates founded on mere

---

2. John E. Semmes, *John H. B. Latrobe and His Times, 1803-1891* (Baltimore: Norman, Remington [c1917]).

guesswork, was in a dilemma; he wrote Lane (May 30): "My present opinion is that Congress may possibly occupy the Capitol in December, 1818, should all the circumstances . . . turn out favorably." He went on to describe patiently to the commissioner the processes involved in an architect's work on a large and complex structure, and continued:

If I had the means of making the necessary drawings in detail of both wings, I would not for the moment object to give you the estimate you require. But without them, it is impossible. The drawings which I have made, & which are sufficient to enable me from day to day, with the assistance of Mr. Poussin, to direct the work, I have studied at home, & chiefly at night. Formerly, I had several pupils, Mills, De Mun & Strickland, who, with Mr. Lenthall . . . & such a man as is not to be found, enabled me to prepare all the work at the outset . . . But estimates are now only to be made by guess, founded on experience.[3]

Pressure, pressure, pressure—from Lane, from Congress, from the Baltimore Exchange, from Van Ness and the other Washington clients. The Capitol rising, the Van Ness house beginning, Baltimore clamoring for decisions—and Latrobe, struggling along with one draftsman, drawing, drawing, drawing, night after night, and every day the meetings, less and less pleasant, with the increasingly dictatorial Lane.

By June, 1816, open hostility was never far away. Lane accused Latrobe of filling a letter to him (the one quoted in part above) with irrelevant matter and with disrespect. The future was inevitably shaping. Lane prepared another blow. Latrobe's clerk of the works on the project was Shadrach Davis, who for years had served in that capacity in the Navy Yard before the fire. He was no Lenthall, but he and the architect understood each other; they worked well together, to the great benefit of the

3. Congress and President Monroe had a continuing, irrational, and immovable conviction that Latrobe was extravagant, even though Commissioner Lane, no friend of the architect's, called their attention (March 31, 1817) to the tremendous rise in the price of both labor and materials since the early estimates—absurdly inadequate in themselves—had been made. It did no good. Even after Latrobe's resignation the accusations continued and forced him in 1818 to make long and careful analyses of the building costs, which he sent both to Congress and to Thomas Jefferson, whose continuing good opinion he almost wistfully besought. The analysis, he claimed, proved that actually, making the most liberal allowances for errors or prejudices on his own part, there was a balance of $200,000 in favor of his "extravagance" over construction carried out before his appointment and subsequent to his resignation. See Saul K. Padover, ed., *Thomas Jefferson and the National Capitol, 1783-1818,* with a preface by Harold Ickes, U.S. Department of the Interior, Source Book Series No. 4 (Washington: Government Printing Office, 1946).

Capitol. But, to Lane, Davis was Latrobe's man, for the architect had suggested his appointment. Furthermore Davis brought his questions and his troubles direct to the architect instead of to the commissioner; that was *lèse majesté,* and he would have to go. In the last week of June, without a word to Latrobe, Lane suddenly discharged Davis on the grounds of inefficiency, and Latrobe had no possible redress. Lane had gathered into his own hands another strand of the reins by which single-handed he could rule the project. An unknown Mr. Coombe was appointed in Davis's place. A month afterward (July 27, 1816) Latrobe wrote Isaac Hazlehurst his later estimate of Lane's character:

> . . . as to the Capitol, it goes on but slowly, & while the system under which the public buildings are by law constructed is so very bad a one, despatch and oeconomy are out of the question. . . . Our Commissioner [is] extremely weak & ignorant . . . zealous in performing what he conceives to be his duty, [he] rises before the sun, & watches among the bushes to see whether the laborers & mechanics attend at bell-ringing . . .

In September, much to the architect's distress, Lane decided to send to England for everything the Capitol required that could be brought from there, "in order, as he said himself, to give his friend [George] Boyd, who is going thither as large an order & commission as possible."[4] The Philadelphia *Aurora* attacked this proposal violently. Its editor, Duane, was known to be a friend of Latrobe's; therefore Latrobe must have been responsible for the attack. Boyd wrote to the architect accusing him of instigating the offending editorial, and Latrobe was forced to send him a spirited denial. But Lane now felt he had a new reason to hate Latrobe.

Yet, troubles or no, the work went steadily on. The delightful rotunda that served as a lobby for both the Supreme Court and the Senate was nearing completion; it was for the ring of columns that carried its dome that Latrobe designed his famous tobacco capital (already referred to) and had it modeled and carved by Iardella, the newly arrived Italian sculptor. And the architect had been playing with the ideas to be incorporated in the other sculpture the building was to contain. As in the old House of Representatives, a great eagle was designed for the frieze above the Speaker's desk; it was carved by Valaperti. In addition a monumental clock was desired in the room, and for it Latrobe sketched a sculptured

4. From a letter to Samuel Hazlehurst in Philadelphia, September 5, 1816.

clock case, "the chariot of History," with the dial set into a formalized chariot containing the figure of the Muse of History writing on a tablet. He had sketched the idea as early as the late fall of 1815, but the actual carving was not done until 1818, by Carlo Franzoni, who changed Latrobe's seated figure to a standing one. And the new House, like the old, was to contain a statue of Liberty. This, too, was only completed—by Enrico Causici—after the architect's connection with the Capitol had ceased; it was neither so well conceived nor so well placed as the earlier one had been. Yet today all of this sculptural decoration, the original conception of which had been Latrobe's, still looks down on the wide spaces of Statuary Hall. In the Supreme Court, also, an allegorical relief of Justice (probably by Carlo Franzoni) filled the axial lunette, and Latrobe's original plan for the Senate called for caryatids (later omitted) for the spectators' gallery.

After James Monroe had been elected President in 1816, the Senate and the House could not agree on which chamber should be the site of the inauguration ceremony; they compromised on an outdoor location, in front of the future Capitol steps. Latrobe was called on to design the decorated platform for this first of all the public open-air inaugurations to be held in Washington.

But Monroe's accession proved disastrous for the architect. Madison, it is true, had had little direct association with the new Capitol building, yet he had had the ultimate responsibility. He had readily accepted all Latrobe's suggestions, and for the architect it had been a comfort to know that in the long run the final judgments would be made by an old and fundamentally understanding friend, one who knew and sympathized with his ideals for the building. With Monroe, this spirit was suddenly changed; all Washington felt instantly the new atmosphere of magisterial formality that was the essential quality of the new regime. Monroe was a coldly efficient executive—a man of implacable, hardheaded decisions. To him order, system, and expedition were aims in themselves, almost irrespective of their purpose or even of their results, and everything that got in their way must be rooted out. In addition, the sense of presidential dignity and position must always be maintained; no longer could Latrobe command any such free approach, direct or indirect, as he had enjoyed with the two preceding Presidents. To Monroe, the rapid completion of the Capitol was a first order of business, and he set out bravely and, in the beginning at least, fairly to overcome the difficulties that had arisen.

Latrobe wanted the vault over the Senate to be of brick; Lane had suggested wood, but Monroe supported the architect. There had been trouble and delay in obtaining estimates from the architect. The President ordered the commissioner to see that Latrobe had two more draftsmen to help him. And, aware at first of Lane's ignorance, Monroe set up an unofficial committee—composed of Brigadier General Swift, Colonel Bomford, and the architect—to advise him on Capitol matters. The President and the committee even visited the new marble quarries of the Potomac to find out the truth behind the continuing attacks on the use of the new material; again their decision was in Latrobe's favor—the marble was to be used. For a while the architect's inquiries about the Capitol went to Swift instead of to Lane, and the details of all the marble finish for the Senate chamber were sent to Swift on April 12, 1816. The effect of all this on Lane was naturally to turn him still more violently against the architect.

Colonel Lane, unfortunately, still held the legal approach to the President. He was a little man who had been partially crippled by a musket-ball wound; according to Mrs. Latrobe's account in her unpublished memoir (prejudiced of course by her love for her husband), he liked to have it thought that the injury was a war wound, though actually it had been the result of pure accident. Little by little Lane built up his influence with Monroe. The first sign of it came when the President suddenly reversed himself on the question of brick for the Senate dome and, seconded by Swift and Bomford, ordered Latrobe to make the vault of timber.

At the same time, Lane's influence showed in a similar decision with regard to the House of Representatives. For this chamber Latrobe had designed a daring vault of brick. This was to be kept as light as possible by means of deep coffers built into it, and it was to be covered with stone outside, as in his dome for the Bank of Pennsylvania. The thrust was to be received by heavy iron bands around the spring of the vault. Latrobe's drawing is dated July 25 (probably 1815), and careful details of the room cornice went out to George Blagden, the stonecutter, two weeks or so later. But here, too, he was ordered to make the dome of the lighter material; his dream of a building fireproof throughout was shattered.[5]

---

5. This change in the House dome may have been a wise one; for, although Latrobe's drawing for the masonry dome displays an extraordinary ingenuity in relating the complex form to be covered to the simpler exterior form that he desired, the actual construction it calls for is thin almost to the point of fragility—particularly in the haunches of the brick

Congress in the meanwhile had been fired with enthusiasm for a richly decorated Capitol—an enthusiasm that was the direct result of the seeds Latrobe and Jefferson had sowed. As a result Colonel Trumbull had been commissioned to make four great paintings for the rotunda walls at an agreed price of $32,000 for the four—an unprecedented amount for the support of American art. Some accommodations for these paintings had to be provided, and Latrobe wrote Trumbull (July 11, 1817), sending him a sketch of the type of niche he was designing to receive them. Two months later (October 10) the architect sent him further details: the niches were to be 19 feet long and 14 feet, 7½ inches high; they were to be raised to the height of 5 feet, 7½ inches above the floor, "which should protect them from the touch, and an iron railing at front at 3 foot distance would protect them even from the touch of a cane. There would in this case remain 6 inches on each side for a wooden frame, and a foot may, if required, be put upon the surrounding stone." When he wrote this letter Latrobe had heard but recently of the death of his beloved Henry in New Orleans, and the bust of Trumbull (carved by Cardelli) which he received as a present from the painter was a most welcome symbol of appreciation at a time when a ray of light across the dreary days was singularly moving. The letter continues:

I have now to thank you for the pleasure that is mingled with my sorrow, when I look upon the mild countenance of talent and virtue which your bust presents to me at this moment. I have not deserved so much friendly attention at your hands. You might have distinguished older, more eminent, and richer friends, by such a token of esteem; but you never could have bestowed it where it would have been more gratefully received; and where in fact it would have had more of the character of humanity and consolation. The first smile that has shown through the tears of the mother of my lost son, fell on this mark of your kindness. I shall never cease to value it. . . . I thank you sincerely, though I fear incoherently. . . .

I have to do with a Commissioner and with a very angry President, to whom I have no access because the law forbids it, and who is surrounded

---

vault. If the workmanship could have been impeccable, if the strong hydraulic cement developed two decades later had been available, and if the centerings could have been left in for a long period and removed with the most imaginative care, the dome might have stood, a remarkable monument to its designer's skill. But with bad workmanship, bad mortar, or any other of the accidents to which building at that time was subject, its safety would have been questionable.

by those who having to justify themselves, naturally lay blame upon the absent.

On his arrival the President, misled by I don't know who, expected the Capitol to be finished; of course he was disappointed, and in his first emotion would have ordered my dismissal had he not been prevented by some very disinterested friends. He appointed, however, Gen'l Mason, Colonel Bomford and Mr. George Graham a Commission of enquiry into the conduct of the Capitol. These are honorable and good men; but what a system is that which shutting out from the President all direct and professional information, interposes that of men whom neither leisure or knowledge of the subject qualifies to give it, or to explain difficulties or remove the misrepresentations of ignorance or malice. And under such a system it is expected that Genius shall freely act and display itself. I will do for Cardelli what I can, I fear it will be but little.

This letter reveals the terrifying change in Monroe's attitude toward Latrobe which six months of continual insinuation and open accusation by Lane had brought. Despite the architect's careful estimate in the previous year that it would be December, 1818, at the earliest before the Capitol could be occupied, the President had somehow been given the impression that except for delays attributed to Latrobe the Capitol might have been finished fifteen months earlier and that nevertheless, because of Lane's efficient watchdog tactics, it would be nearly complete when the President returned to Washington in the fall of 1817. This obviously malicious plot worked perfectly. When Monroe arrived and saw the actual state of affairs he was in a towering rage, which no excuses or explanations could divert. In his bluff and military way, he indicated it was *results* he wanted. The results had not been achieved, and (as in the case of Frederick the Great which Latrobe had noted in his book twenty years earlier) the possibility or impossibility of achieving them meant nothing. Who was to blame? Surely not the faithful old soldier Lane, up at dawn every day to watch over the country's interests. It was Latrobe, of course, who was to blame—Latrobe, who had been known to be absent from the job for days! What were drawings, calculations, and all the paraphernalia of professional service in the face of those absences? [6]

---

6. Latrobe's visits to Baltimore in connection with the Exchange had become common subjects of diligently fostered Washington gossip. He lashed back at the gossip in a letter to President Monroe (October 22, 1817): "At the table of Colonel Armistead, at Alexandria, Mr. M. Beverly asserted on the authority of the Commissioner of the public buildings, that

Earlier in the year Robert Goodloe Harper had offered the architect a position in Baltimore at a salary larger than that which he received in Washington, but Latrobe had refused it. He wrote Harper (June 4): "I may be considered to act the part of a mad man, and what is more culpable, of a bad husband and father. But, when you consider, that, loaded with the displeasure of the President, who retains me, as I am told the Commissioner says, from compassion . . . my present resignation would confirm all the President is made to believe, & all that folly & malice & consciousness of wrong [on the part of the commissioner] . . . can invent . . ."

By the autumn the basic disagreements had become common knowledge in Washington. President Monroe was incapable of understanding Latrobe's ideals, the enormous work involved in what was practically the new construction of a great national capitol, or the fact that what had been accomplished in a little over two years was not a cause for censure but rather an astonishing display of speed both of design and of solid construction. Nothing could swerve him from his idea that Latrobe was the villain, and he began making discreet inquiries about a successor.

A month before Latrobe's second letter to Trumbull, William Lee in New York, an old friend of the architect's, wrote to Charles Bulfinch in Boston (September 14, 1817) telling him that a schism had developed, that he thought Latrobe was unjustly disliked in Congress, that either Latrobe or Lane would soon have to resign, and that it looked as if it would be Lane who would be sacrificed. This was obviously meant to prepare Bulfinch, for apparently he was already the chosen successor in case Latrobe and not Lane should resign. Lee's letter is significantly expressive of the feeling about the architect in Washington:

> I am sorry for Latrobe, who is an amiable man, possesses genius, and has a large family, but in addition to the President's not being satisfied with him there is an unaccountable and I think unjust prejudice against him by many members of the Government, Senate and Congress.

---

the work at the Capitol would be much further advanced had it been possible to keep Mr. Latrobe at his duty, but that he was in the habit of going to Baltimore and staying at times *21* days . . . I can neither submit to the vexation and trouble of investigating so unfounded an assertion, nor risk its being repeated to you without contradiction . . . I therefore respectfully request you will read the enclosed account of my absences at Baltimore, a paper which can be judicially verified." The paper showed that the average absence was only four days, and the total only 34½ days in 18 months.

On October 1 Lee wrote Bulfinch again:

. . . either the Commissioner of public buildings or Latrobe must go out . . . As [the Commissioner] has more friends than the architect, he will, I think, be continued. I do not know how it is, but so it is. Latrobe has many enemies; his great fault is in being poor. He is, in my opinion, an amiable, estimable man, full of genius and at the head of his profession. Every carpenter and mason thinks he knows more than Latrobe, and such men have got on so fast last year with the President's house (a mere lathing and plastering job) that they have the audacity to think they ought to have the finishing of the Capitol, a thing they are totally unfit for . . .

While the President was here, you were mentioned in case Latrobe should be forced to retire, and I was happy to find Col. Bomford and others thought such a solution would be judicious . . .[7]

But on October 23 the committee called together to discuss the problem voted that Latrobe should be continued, and he, all unknowing, went on with his work for another six weeks. Nevertheless the finale was inexorably building up. Lane's attacks continued, he had the tougher skin, and apparently President Monroe was unable to appreciate the difficulties under which Latrobe labored, just as he was temperamentally unfitted to understand the personality of the architect. There came a new crisis, a new attack—made by Lane to the President in the architect's presence. Latrobe realized the game was up and on November 20 he submitted his resignation. The details of the affair will be considered in the following chapter, where they belong as part of the story of Latrobe's departure from Washington. He spent much of the remaining weeks of 1817 in completing the drawings for the entire building, and they were all in Monroe's hands before the new year came in.[8]

It is now possible, for these drawings still exist, to assay what Latrobe had accomplished in the twenty-nine months since his arrival in Washington in the spring of 1815. It is an imposing record, and one that, correctly understood, would have impressed even a hostile President. Despite the difficulties of working with unsympathetic commissioners, and especially with Lane, the architect had

7. See Ellen Susan Bulfinch, *The Life and Letters of Charles Bulfinch Architect* (Boston and New York: Houghton Mifflin, 1896).

8. The President's attitude toward Latrobe is shown by the fact that it was not until the architect had departed that he, in his Presidential message of January, 1818, recommended the completion of the entire Capitol.

—Torn down all the damaged work still standing after the fire.

—Developed a completely new and better plan for the south wing.

—Developed a virtually new plan for the north wing, including the larger Senate chamber Congress had requested.

—Developed the plan of the central rotunda and the western or library wing and established the form in which, in all essentials, they were later constructed.

—Built, in spite of constant and unavoidable shortages of labor and materials, a large part of the north and south wings, so that only roofing and finishing remained to be done. Since, because of the changes in the plans, this was no longer a mere repairing or rebuilding but the construction of a new building, as much had been accomplished in two and a half years as had required at least six before the fire.

In other words, during this period, Latrobe had accomplished the design, and in good measure the construction, of one of the great monumental structures of its time. In the light of the primitive building methods then in use, the lack of machines, and dependence on the hand and the eye of mason, sculptor, metalworker, and carpenter, this was an extraordinary performance. It took eleven more years for the whole to be finished under Bulfinch, who except in the details of the western front and the shape of the exterior dome followed substantially the design Latrobe had made. Furthermore, the total amount of building in those eleven years hardly exceeded what Latrobe had accomplished in two and a half. And Congress had called him culpably slow!

Aesthetically the entire structure is essentially Latrobe's. Bulfinch's alterations in the exterior could hardly be called happy. The more delicate western colonnade, in which he followed the precedent of the Boston State House, destroyed the powerful and consistent scale Latrobe's elevation had set, and the substitution of a higher, hemispherical central dome for the lower, monumental, Pantheon-type dome of the Latrobe design gave but an awkward climax to the building. In the interior Bulfinch was more at home, and the first Congressional library he designed was an exquisite and fitting room, strongly composed and gracious in detail. But in the north and south wings he followed Latrobe's drawings, as he did in the entrance portico. And he realized his indebtedness; again and again he expressed to President Monroe and to Congress his admiration of his predecessor's designs.

Today, then, in the central portions of the Capitol—all that part which does not include the present House and Senate wings—it is Latrobe's creation that stands out. It is true that the floor of the House of Representatives was raised a few feet, to the column bases, by Robert Mills in a successful attempt to improve its acoustics, and it is this raised level that exists at present in what—after the House wing was added—has become Statuary Hall. The dignified mahogany furniture and the rich hangings of the Speaker's seat and desk are gone, leaving the room naked and cold; the handsome chandelier no longer gives scale to the space that surrounded it. But in spite of these changes Latrobe's great room still displays its qualities of grandeur and disciplined design.

Across the rotunda, the oval lobby of the Senate—with its ring of tobacco-capped columns supporting an elegantly coffered dome—offers a distinguished approach to the old Senate chamber lobby, dignified and graced by its Ionic columns; and through that in turn one enters the old semicircular Senate chamber itself, a room of great refinement of detail. This was altered for use by the Supreme Court when the Senate was moved into its new wing; now, called the Old Supreme Court, it contains heavy court furniture which effectively destroys the design Latrobe had so perfectly envisioned. The long bench cuts awkwardly across the lovely colonnade of breccia columns, and the true proportion has disappeared. In the Latrobe plan the Vice-President's podium was just in front of and enframed by the central arch; the drawings for the platform and the furniture show a gracious and distinguished simplicity. On either side the columns were visible for their entire height. The original public gallery was over the Vice-President's position, supported by these columns. Later, to increase the area for the public, Bulfinch added a delicate and graceful metal balcony, supported on slim cast-iron columns, which ran around the semicircle; it was effective and beautifully related to Latrobe's patterning of the walls, but it, too, disappeared when the new wings were built and the old Senate became the Supreme Court. Today, then, as we look into this interior, we must imagine the heavy bench removed and must visualize instead the rich curtain-backed Vice-President's desk (enthroned by the arch) and the senators' desks ranged in front in semicircular rows following the curve of the wall; only so can Latrobe's achievement be justly seen.

Beneath it, the old Supreme Court room, later transformed into a court library, retains its ingenious, beautifully detailed, lobed half dome and, along the straight outer wall, the effective triple arch—supported on powerful Doric columns—which Latrobe created and which, in idea at least, parallels the original design made as early as 1806 or 1807. The wall treatment endures untouched, with the gracefully delicate if somewhat empty relief of Justice (probably by Carlo Franzoni) in the axial lunette; yet now the ranged bookcases almost completely hide the controlling concept, and again imagination must take them away and substitute the simple low furnishings of the original Supreme Court chamber.

On paper, the plan looks confused and unduly complicated. This was the inevitable result of changes and alterations over a period of nearly twenty years during which the country grew rapidly and the size of both houses of Congress markedly increased. Yet the visual impressions the visitor receives, if he uses the original entrances, are superb—whether up the great portico stairs and in through the rotunda to either the old House or the old Senate, or through the ground-floor entrances, vestibules, vaulted stairs, and domed lobbies. These views form designed sequences in which each element, however interesting in itself, is but part of a symphonic experience that reaches its resolution only in the climax rooms.

The great rotunda is the least successful part of the whole. How much of this is the fault of Latrobe, how much that of Bulfinch, is difficult to decide. Its great size—ninety feet in diameter—demanded a kind of monumental scale which it does not possess. But between the plan Latrobe had made and the interior as it was built by Bulfinch, there is one important difference. Latrobe designed four great niches on the diagonal axes of the room; in the interior as built they have disappeared—only the great circle, unbroken, remains. Perhaps Bulfinch was skeptical of the strength of these corners of the building in view of the great weight they would have had to carry; perhaps he merely preferred the simpler shape. But the Latrobe niches would have given scale and interest to the whole; as it stands, it is cold, thin, and in spite of the paintings barren.

Latrobe's final drawings show the building throughout to the last partition, and the very fact that they were prepared after his resignation reveals his devotion not only to the ideal he had from the beginning held clear but also to what he felt was the good of his country. In them even the minor north and south entrances to the main floor were made the source of effective grandeur by the use of handsome stone terraces supported on powerful colonnades and reached by broad steps. And the drawings include, at the foot of the hill, the great propylaea Latrobe had designed in 1811; that it was never built was an irremediable loss to Washington.

In this great building, then, Latrobe set the basic tone and established a standard for governmental building which was to persist for generations. His work was so strong an inspiration that it schooled and disciplined many of the superficialities of later Victorian detail, so that Thomas U. Walter, when he added the Senate and House wings and the tremendous cast-iron dome that unifies and climaxes the whole, could not help but emulate the basic classic grandeur which Thornton had dreamed of and Latrobe had brought into being and refined.

Back in 1792 (March 8) Washington had written David Stewart in Philadelphia that "the public buildings in size, form and elegance should look beyond the present day." Of all the architects who worked on the Capitol, it was Latrobe who most faithfully strove to realize this ideal—and the history of the building since he left it at the end of 1817 proves with what essential success.

CHAPTER

19

Final Washington Years: 1815-1817

WHEN the Latrobes returned to Washington, in the midsummer of 1815, it was to a little house that belonged to a Captain Speake. Their new home was half of a double house far out on the hills to the northwest. It was a modest place, fitted better to their poverty than the larger residences they had known in Washington before, but it had many advantages. "We reside on the top of the range of beautiful eminences that surround the cities of Washington, Georgetown, & Alexandria on every side . . . By the aid of a good telescope, my wife sees me ascend Capitol hill, 3 miles distant & can trace me on the whole of my return home," wrote Latrobe to Isaac Hazlehurst (July 27, 1816). Even its distance from the center of the city or from Georgetown was fortunate, for it gave the Latrobes a plausible excuse for not re-entering the social whirl of the capital. No longer could they afford that; no more musical evenings, or large dinner parties, or soirées for forty guests! And the back yard was big enough for a real garden; some, at least, of their food they could raise themselves. But best of all, and the real reason they had chosen the house, was the fact that its yard reached clear back to the boundary of Kalorama. In expectation of their arrival Mrs. Barlow, now a widow, had built a gravel walk from her house directly to theirs and had put in a special gate, usually kept open so that there could be the closest possible touch with their best and kindest Washington friend. It was an ideal location for a simple, quiet life, not too far by horseback or even for a good walker from the scene of Latrobe's chief professional work—the Capitol.

For by now the Latrobes *were* poor, and they had come to accept the fact. Mary Latrobe's bold and almost ruthless selling of their furniture in Pittsburgh while her husband was in Washington had cleared up their Pittsburgh household debts so that they could leave the smoky city without hindrance, but little was left for the new abode. As Latrobe wrote to Bollman (April 19, 1816), in an effort to collect at least some of the money he had advanced for education of the Bollman children, they had only furniture enough to furnish one room sparsely and had no clothes fit for social occasions—hardly, in fact, enough for respectability. In truth their new position meant starting over again, and every penny was important. David, the Latrobe coachman of many years' service, they retained, to be sure, and the ever faithful Kitty McCausland still bore the brunt of the cooking and housekeeping. Little by little, however, their position improved as the government salary started to come in and other professional commissions materialized. Latrobe's mercurial spirits rose and by September 20, 1815, he was writing to Dudley Diggs and offering to help David purchase his wife, if Diggs could bring himself to part with her; David had saved $350, and Latrobe offered Diggs notes for the balance.

Socially, too, despite their poverty, they retained the affection of loyal friends, and a small and intimate circle grew up rapidly around them. Senator Robert Goodloe Harper of Baltimore was a constant visitor when he was in Washington; he seems to have had an almost paternal interest in the little family.[1] Colonel Bomford, of the Engineers, was another close friend; he married Mrs. Barlow's sister Clara, who had been living with her, and thus felt doubly attracted to the Kalorama neighborhood. And Richard Derby of Salem added a touch of spice and elegance. Yet for the most part the Latrobes led a very quiet existence, almost self-sufficient in their little home, though the nearness and the affection of Mrs. Barlow kept them from loneliness.

The problem of the children's education was quickly solved. John and Ben were both sent to Georgetown College, and John remarked later that they were almost the only Protestant students who remained untouched by the Catholic atmosphere. There they received excellent instruction in the fundamentals, supplemented at home by additional training in drawing and music; John was rapidly becoming an excellent archi-

1. After Latrobe's death Harper became the chief adviser and protector of the bereaved family, and on his advice they left New Orleans as quickly as possible and came back to Baltimore. It was in Harper's office that John H. B. Latrobe received his legal training, and it was Harper who launched him on his legal career and introduced him to all that was best in Baltimore society.

tectural draftsman and during the summer of 1817 earned $89 helping his father with drawings for the Capitol. Julia was taught at home by her mother, but she, too, picked up a sensitive and accurate style of drawing; she loved especially, her father wrote to Henry, to draw animals. Indeed, in the atmosphere of intellectual curiosity, wide reading, and artistic sympathy which the Latrobes always contrived to create, no growing children with such a heredity could fail to receive an education of a breadth and a depth no school could offer.

Mrs. Barlow herself had a problem in those years: should she remarry? The example of her sister Clara Baldwin and Colonel Bomford was before her eyes daily; their happiness, perhaps, accentuated her own lonely state. And here was Colonel Bull, eager to make her his wife—a most presentable man, if undistinguished. He was not young; nor, at over sixty, was she, and for a while she was in favor of accepting him. Latrobe wrote to Henry (August 5, 1816) as though the wedding were a certainty. But to many of her friends the match seemed deplorable; the good colonel was no proper spouse for Joel Barlow's widow, they claimed, and perhaps they feared that the prospective bridegroom might have been drawn more by the attractions of Kalorama and a fortune than by the lady herself. At any rate they vociferously disapproved, and Latrobe wrote William Lee (August 25) that "all her friends" were attempting to dissuade her. In this letter Bull is described as "a jovial, sociable and good hearted soul . . . much beloved . . . and is in fact a sensible and pleasant man, a good farmer & manager in general. His only fault is, that like other bulls, he has very notoriously & somewhat publicly—lived on the common. But he is now going to be a good boy . . ." Whether or not it was the result of her friends' advice is uncertain, but no wedding took place. Mrs. Barlow died at Kalorama less than two years later, still a widow.

The Latrobe's first year in their second Washington period ended with a sudden tragedy—the accidental death of the loyal Kitty. It produced a shock of terror and horror that left indelible scars on the plastic minds of John and Ben. Christmas Eve in 1815 was cold. B. H., Mary, and Julia had gone off to church, leaving the two boys and Kitty alone in the house. The boys were upstairs when suddenly they heard a scream from below; they rushed to the kitchen and found Kitty moaning in a chair by the fire, all her clothes burned off and their remains still smoking on the floor. They rushed at once to Kalorama for help, and Mrs.

Barlow's sister hurried back with them down the gravel path; somehow they got Kitty upstairs and into bed and gave her what crude first aid they could just as the others returned, but it was too late and she died that evening. Aside from the harrowing blow itself, Kitty's death was a grievous loss; despite her quirks, her tempers, and her occasional arrogance, for thirteen years she had been the constant and devoted balance wheel that kept their economy—in its humbler aspects—on an even course. With her death another thread that led back to earlier and more prosperous times was cut. Her loss was more than that of a good servant; it was a sort of symbol of the dread words "never more."

Professionally, nevertheless, this second Washington period was the most brilliant Latrobe had ever known. Aside from the extraordinarily rapid designing and rebuilding of the Capitol, and in addition to the continuing work and worry of the New Orleans waterworks, he was engulfed in important architectural commissions. There was a new interest in the erection of the National University in Washington—the first President's earlier dream—and Latrobe made a preliminary plan, placing it at the west end of the Mall. There was St. John's Church. There was the rebuilding of Blodgett's Hotel, to be used for a temporary Capitol if needed. There was a multitude of smaller jobs—a house or an addition for Benjamin Orr, additions to Dr. Herron's Presbyterian Church in Pittsburgh (already mentioned), the Hagerstown courthouse, and St. Paul's Church in Alexandria (a characteristic example of Latrobe's somewhat inept Gothic) among them. And even more important were what the architect called the "three finest houses in Washington"—for Van Ness, Casanove, and Decatur.

The rebuilding of Blodgett's Hotel probably came to Latrobe as the result of Thomas Law's friendship, for Law was the driving force behind the scheme, as he was for anything that would lead to the rapid recovery of the city after the British destruction. Architecturally perhaps it had little importance, yet it was another evidence of the respect in which the designer was held by nearly all those who, like Law, dreamed of a greater and nobler capital city. The same was true of the work for Benjamin Orr, of which no trace is left. St. Paul's in Alexandria still stands, but so many vital changes from the drawings were made in its building—Latrobe did not superintend the work—that for its architect it was a source of irritation and disappointment rather than of pride. Even the major proportions were altered—the height reduced a foot and a half, for instance—and square heads were substituted in the windows for the arches Latrobe had planned. The designer's letters to the rector, the Reverend William Wilmer, were understandably pointed:

> [August 10, 1817:] I have given you the best design which I could find on the foundations for your church . . . I now find from Mr. Bosworth that not only is the whole church lowered eighteen inches, but square windows are put in the flanks. What a confession of ostentatious poverty! The congregation are proud enough to build a handsome front to show the passengers, but too poor to be consistent in the flanks, & too inconsistent in their opinion of their architect, whether of his honesty or skill, I will not pretend to say, to believe that he is capable of judging as correctly respecting the body of a church as of its front . . .

And he takes a wry pleasure in showing that it probably cost the church $354 more to build as they had than it would had they followed his design. The rector's reply failed to mollify Latrobe, and he answered (August 16):

> So you take my objection to the alteration of my design, to have its foundation in the "sensibility of the architect"? which, I confess, it is generally supposed, is far more morbid than that of the professors of any other liberal art or science . . . My object was by strong language first to make an impression that should rescue your building from just criticism, & then to prove that the only plea in favor of the change was not well founded, & that my plan was the most oeconomical . . .

Such were the continuing hardships of the architect; such the wanton disregard of his knowledge and his skill.

Latrobe was more fortunate in the Hagerstown courthouse, another commission of 1817 that he did not supervise. Here his dealings were with General Samuel Ringgold, obviously a man with sufficient experience to realize the benefit to be drawn from accepting professional advice. The result, as shown in an old engraving, was a building of great yet restrained power. It was built of brick, stuccoed, and as in the case of much of Latrobe's later work the detail was reticent; there was nothing to fog the clarity of the scheme. A large central arched entrance dominated the front; it was beautifully related to the quiet windows and doors on either side. Crowning it all was a light, domed cupola—the whole a concept of the greatest simplicity and one endowed with commanding power, dignity, and grace by the beauty of its proportions.

Courtesy Mrs. William F. Bevan

FIGURE 27. Courthouse, Hagerstown, Md. Elevation. Redrawn from an old map, 1850.

Something of the same simplicity distinguishes St. John's Church, on Lafayette Square in Washington, the first private commission Latrobe received after his return. It still stands, although the addition of a long nave, a "Colonial" portico, and a tower creates a whole that gives little idea of the simple geometry of the architect's original building. As he designed it, it was a simple Greek cross in plan; only the added length of a small narthex distinguished the nave arm. A hipped roof covered the central crossing and carried a large but delicately detailed glazed cupola to light the center. Simple arched windows and an arched door accented the sides and front, and Latrobe's favorite eaves treatment—a lightly bracketed gutter rather than a cornice—crowned the plain, undecorated walls.

St. John's is a little masterpiece. As one sees it in the architect's small perspective sketch (owned by the church), with the blackened walls of the fire-gutted President's House in the background, it had a superb and commanding unity. It made no pretensions, yet every dimension was so perfectly related to every other, every part so right, that the whole became much more than the sum of its parts. And the detail, if we may judge by the existing portions, had the same quality of elegant simplicity.

Naturally it was a church of its period; it was light-flooded, open, and airy, with a shallow chancel that brought the altar into the closest possible contact with the worshipers. Such a church was at the opposite pole from the deep-chanceled gloom beloved of the ecclesiologists of the mid-nineteenth century. Definitely a single unit, with the congregation the chief factor to be considered, it was humanist rather than mystical and as such was a perfect expression of its time; Pugin and the Oxford Movement were still far in the future. In the Gothic design for the Cathedral of Baltimore, as in the modest Christ Church in Washington, Latrobe had tried hesitantly to work in a different manner—a manner with which his innate temperament was hardly congenial. Now here, in St. John's, he returned to his more profound feelings (for he was in religion a humanist) and, designing in deep inner harmony with his own true self, created his finest if not his largest church.

He was proud of the building. In a letter to Henry in New Orleans (December 19, 1816) he remarked, with a playfulness that covered a real pride, that he had just completed a church that made many Washingtonians religious who had not been religious before. And he took the occasion to write for the church its dedication hymn,[2] which perhaps marks the high-water level in his verse, just as the building itself ranks high in his architectural design.

At Kalorama too there was more work—chiefly new marble mantels to replace the old wooden ones. But it was the three houses for Casanove, General J. P. Van Ness, and Stephen Decatur that highlight this period. Of the first no evidence has yet been found. The Casanoves were members of a French Huguenot family, long in this country, who had accumulated a sizable fortune in Virginia and lived for many years in Alexandria;[3] for one of them to wish to have a large house in Washington was natural. The house was begun in 1816 and completed in July, 1817; on the fifth of that month Latrobe wrote Mrs. Casanove: "As your house is now finished, I take the liberty to transmit to you my ac-

---

2. See Appendix. For a period Latrobe served as organist and choirmaster, and in recompense for his services he was given a family pew; a little later, as an expression of gratitude for his gift of his architectural services, the vestry voted to give him an inscribed silver goblet worth fifty dollars.

3. The Latrobe papers do not contain any indication of which Casanove the house belonged to. It was probably the Peter Casanove who was mayor of Georgetown in 1795. The Casanove family descended from an Antoine Charles de Casanove, who was sent from Switzerland to the United States by his family to escape the French Revolution. He was for a long period a resident of Alexandria and was the French consul there and the founder of an important banking establishment.

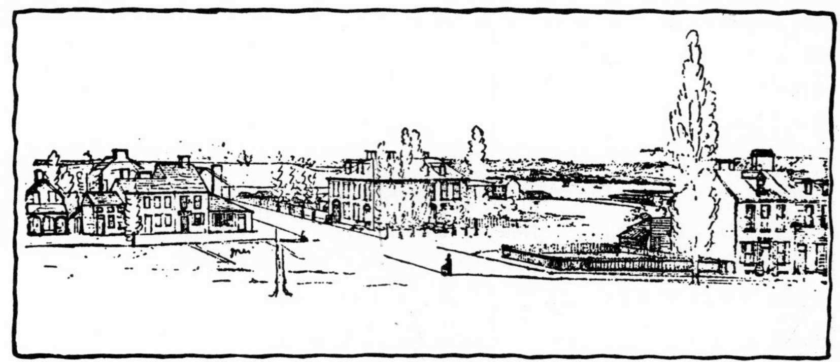

From the Latrobe sketchbooks

FIGURE 28. Pennsylvania Avenue near 20th Street, N.W., Washington, site of the Van Ness House.

count for professional services." This bill was for $307.70, representing the regular 5 per cent commission on the original contract of $5,600.00, plus a few extras. Latrobe liked the house, and he wrote Henry when it was practically complete (June 4, 1817): "My two houses, Mr. Van Ness' and Casanove's are, not to say much, the best in the district." The same letter tells, too, that he is designing a house (40′ by 50′) for Dennis Smith of Washington—the only record of it we have.

Fortunately, however, of the Van Ness house we can speak more definitely; there are photographs and measured drawings of it,[4] and its almost legendary luxury and beauty—as well as the lavish entertainments of which it was the scene—have come down to us in memoirs and letters. General Van Ness, originally of Kinderhook, New York, had married Marcia Burnes in 1802, and with her a fortune. Her father had been one of the largest landowners in the Washington area and had handled his land shrewdly. His early home—the simplest of small frame cottages—stood near Seventeenth Street and New York Avenue Northwest and overlooked the junction of the Washington Canal and the Potomac. He had preserved all through his life this original plot—where the Pan American Building stands today—and out of family piety the

4. It was measured and drawn by Ogden Codman before its destruction. Two plans and an elevation are reproduced in Fiske Kimball, *Domestic Architecture of the Colonial Period and the Early Republic* (New York: Scribner's, 1922), and photographs are shown in Allen C. Clark, "General John Peter Van Ness, a Mayor of the City of Washington, His Wife, Marcia, and Her Father, David Burnes," in *Columbia Historical Society Records,* vol. 22 (1925), pp. 125-204.

little cabin was preserved even after a large and handsome residence had been built beside it. But that "new house," large and lavish as it was, did not satisfy Van Ness, and from 1813 on he was contemplating its replacement with something more convenient, modern, and grand. That he turned to Latrobe for the design shows the light in which the architect was held by the more cultivated in the city, even when his financial fortunes were at their lowest ebb.

Latrobe took the problem with him to Pittsburgh and worked on it spasmodically there in the fall and early winter of 1813; by January of 1814 (as he wrote Van Ness on the seventeenth) the preliminary drawings were complete, though he had had no good opportunity to send them to Washington. Then the matter dropped in the mounting tension of the steamboat imbroglio, to be taken up again when Latrobe returned to Washington in the summer of 1815. The work actually got under way at the beginning of 1816, Van Ness building the gate lodges first. We can follow the progress of the work in Latrobe's correspondence: details are well along in June; on June 25 Latrobe sends interior designs to Mrs. Van Ness; on September 21 he is writing to George Bridport in Philadelphia suggesting that there might be a decorative painting job for him in the house; and on October 15 Latrobe is trying to collect his first bill. Van Ness wanted to delay payment until the house was finished, but the architect refused as he said "to speculate . . . on the completion of the establishment."

In addition to these arguments about the bill there were occasional frictions in the work. The house, as Latrobe remarks in a letter to Isaac Hazlehurst (July 27, 1816), was the largest he had ever designed—and in those days of careful handicraft building it took time to complete such a structure. By midsummer of 1817 the General, anxious to move in, was irked at the delay and accused the architect of inattention. Latrobe replied somewhat testily that since Van Ness was building the house largely with his own workmen, who were responsible only to the owner and not to the architect, he could hardly be blamed for the slow progress. All through 1817 construction went on, but by September the finished plastering was being set, and midwinter saw the completion of the house.

The house was worth waiting for. Its exterior was deceptively simple, with all the restraint and originality of which Latrobe had become such a master. Thin, guttered eaves, supported on pairs of widely spaced

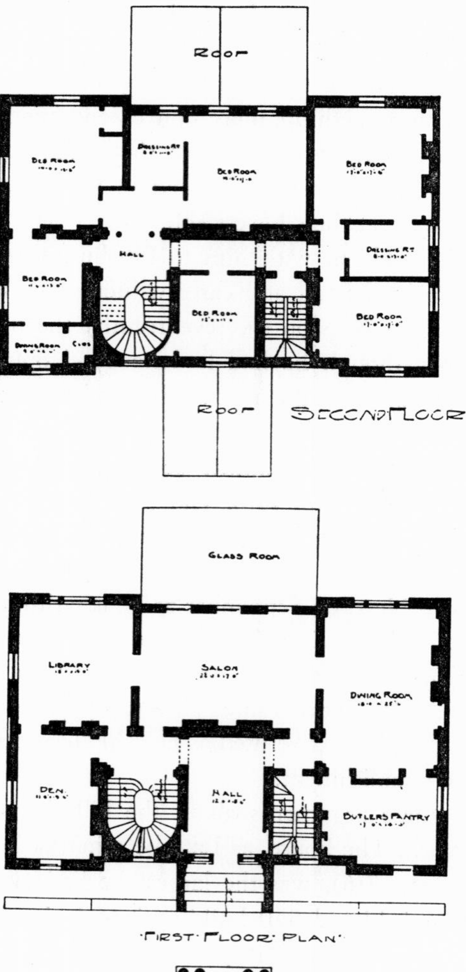

From Kimball, *Domestic Architecture of the American Colonies and the Early Republic*
FIGURE 29. Van Ness House, Washington. Plans.

wooden brackets, replaced the usual cornice. The Greek Doric porch columns carried a simple unmolded architrave and frieze combined, and here too bracketed eaves replaced the conventional Doric cornice. The openings were large, simple, and lovely in proportion. It was this quality of perfectly studied proportion, thoughtful and reticent detail, and large size and great scale that gave to its plain white stucco walls a compelling sense of quiet monumentality. In the center of the south front an ample pedimented loggia opening from the reception room and the great dining room offered lovely views over the garden, the canal, and the Potomac beyond. It was a "great house" in more ways than size alone, for it had a true aristocratic dignity that made it famous. And its size, grandeur, and simple elegance were pointed up by the old Burnes cabin—still carefully cherished by Mrs. Van Ness—which stood close by among the trees.

But the chief glory of the house was within. Here the service elements were most carefully studied, and the functional differentiation of the rooms—each designed for its own special use—was carried to a new height. Across the "back" of the house the grand entertainment suite, ample in size, dignified, and beautifully detailed, commanded a superb view down the Potomac; barges passing up and down the canal which bordered the garden gave interest to the foreground. Upstairs the master's suite, entered from the main hall through its own columned vestibule, looked over the same view and guaranteed privacy; the other bedrooms, some en suite, were planned with equal care. And, we learn from old descriptions, between the dining room and the service areas there were rotating mahogany servers like those Latrobe had used a decade earlier in Adena, the Worthington house in far-off Chillicothe, where they still remain as evidence of the architect's imaginative ingenuity. In Washington they were apparently unique and caused a great stir in society.

The Van Ness house was in many ways its author's domestic masterpiece. Here Latrobe had plenty of money to work with and a client basically sympathetic with his aims, whatever the minor frictions that arose between them. And here plan (both for convenience and for the creation of beautifully ordered interior spaces), exterior design, and detail were wedded together with an almost perfect integration. It is no wonder that in its heyday it was accepted as perhaps the greatest of the Washington private homes.

In the design of a house for Stephen Decatur the problem that Latrobe faced was quite a different one. The Commodore had purchased a lot on Lafayette Square, diagonally across from the front of the President's House and almost directly opposite St. John's Church. It was a relatively small lot, and this meant designing a definitely urban house with a constricted front. Only the Markoe house in Philadelphia had presented the architect with quite that problem. The Decatur house design was begun early in 1817. Before June 4 the working drawings had been finished and sent out to two contractors for bids, and Latrobe on that day forwarded their proposals unopened to the client. He wrote that he supposed they would indicate a cost of about $11,000 and explained that the bids did not include fencing, paving, and stabling, which together might come to from $1,500 to $1,800 more. In addition, the architect suggested that if Decatur expected to rent the house at some time to a foreign minister he should add a lightly built one-story addition at the back for a servants' hall. The bids, Latrobe remarked, did not include papering or the marble mantels for the principal rooms; the mantels, he felt, could be "better procured from Italy."

The house went ahead, and it still stands, its stable now transformed into a naval museum. During its long history, the front was drastically changed by the insertion of fashionable Victorian window heads and the alteration of the door. But fortunately the original drawings exist, and the present owner, Mrs. Truxtun Beale, had the front brought back to its original state under the capable direction of the late Thomas T. Waterman. This architect found that in the actual building there were slight (but only slight) deviations from Latrobe's drawings, so that the house today—which fortunately has been promised to the National Trust for permanent preservation—is substantially as its original architect designed it. It is perhaps less unusual in plan than the Van Ness mansion; but in its scale and the delicacy and rightness of its reticent detail it is winning. The exquisite vestibule and front hall show how brilliantly Latrobe could work even in spaces relatively confined. It is remarkable that the atmosphere of perhaps the country's most important public square comes, at least in part, from three works linked with Latrobe—St. John's Church, the Decatur house, and the front colonnade of the White House which was carried out by Hoban in 1824 on the basis of the design projected by Latrobe as early as 1808.

But these were not the only non-governmental jobs of this busy period. We learn through a letter to Isaac Hazlehurst (July 27, 1816) that Latrobe was also designing "a very large boarding house"—otherwise unidentified. There was "a little monument" for R. G. Harper in Baltimore, on which the architect wished Franzoni to do the sculpture. And, most interesting of all, there was his freely given contribution to the design of the University of Virginia.

By the summer of 1817, Jefferson's daring plan for a university at Charlottesville was approaching realization. The notion he had had for several years of an "academical village" was the controlling idea of the plan, and it had won state acceptance. But before actual construction began Jefferson wished to have more professional advice, and he wrote to both Thornton and Latrobe requesting suggestions for the design of the "pavilions," each of which was to consist of a professor's house and his classroom. Both architects of course were delighted to comply. Thornton sent a design in which the lower floor was an arcade, with a delicate portico above carrying a pediment. It is exquisite in its refinement and its human scale; it has all its author's genius in handling buildings of a domestic nature. Jefferson was deeply pleased with the design, and Pavilion VII (at one time the Colonnade Club) was built in accordance with it. But to Latrobe the problem seemed different. Thornton was thinking, obviously, of the individual buildings. Latrobe, on the other hand, thought of the group as a whole—its large size, its opportunity for monumental composition. To him the pavilions must above all be parts of the whole, and their design must be developed in accordance with it. Especially he felt that the pavilions should be large in scale, to count at the great distances involved. Thus the pavilions he sketched were a far cry from the one Thornton had designed. He used a monumental order running from ground to roof and carried the columns in front of the general line of the plan to count as strong rhythmic verticals in contrast with the long horizontals of the colonnades in front of the students' rooms. Pavilions V, VIII, and X were probably based on the Latrobe sketches, and several of the other pavilions are modifications of this conception. The present group therefore contains ideas deriving from both Thornton's exquisite delicacy and Latrobe's monumental power, and the resultant variety adds living beauty.[5]

Latrobe's thinking about the University of Virginia, however, went beyond the design of the individual pavilions. Studying over the sketch Jefferson had sent, he realized that it lacked focus. The continual alternating rhythm of colonnade and pavilion came to no climax; if built as shown, the group would have charm, perhaps, but no power. And Latrobe felt that this architectural fault was related to a fault in the program—the lack of any single great center where the college as a whole could meet. Accordingly he sent a rough sketch plan showing a large domed building at the center, to contain, he suggests, administration offices below and a public hall above. He had misunderstood Jefferson's

5. See Fiske Kimball, *Thomas Jefferson, Architect . . .* (Cambridge, Mass.: printed for private distribution by the Riverside Press, 1916).

letter, and in his sketch he set the domed building in the middle of the long side of the quadrangle. When he learned his mistake he suggested an entirely different scheme, with different groups of buildings on different terraced levels; later he urged Jefferson to face all the chief rooms south, instead of east or west.

In the fertile but stubborn mind of Jefferson, these suggestions took root. The last two, the breaking up of the group and the change in orientation, he fortunately refused to accept; but the first—the central domed building—was immensely appealing to him. He realized at once its advantages, practical and artistic and symbolical, and at the upper end of his group, between the two rows of pavilions, he placed just such a building, changing its use, however, from public auditorium to library—and just so it was built. Today Jefferson's serene brick cylinder, dome crowned, with its Corinthian portico, looks down the gently sloping lawn with commanding yet gracious power. It pulls together and harmonizes the long row of pavilions and colonnades on either side; it creates an instant unity. Thus Latrobe contributed mightily to this greatest monument of early American education.[6]

He was called on for other projects as well. One was a house for Christopher Hughes, on the corner of Hughes and Forrest streets in Baltimore. Possibly it was a speculative venture, for the architect wrote Hughes (October 26, 1816): "I have now ready . . . three plans of different sizes, in my portfolio to suit different purses and tastes . . ." And there was also the proposed Unitarian Church there, a much more important commission. Dr. George May had applied to Latrobe for a design early in 1817. After completing one scheme, Latrobe had a second almost ready when he learned that Godefroy had been consulted as well and had also prepared a plan. He was in a quandary, for he wanted—and needed—the job, but his professional idealism won out. "It is a rule with me," he wrote Dr. May (April 1, 1817), "never to enter into any competition with the established architects of any city." He continued with an account of the recent controversy that had arisen with Godefroy in connection with the Baltimore Exchange (which will be dealt with later) and added: "But the friendly sentiment I have so long entertained towards Godefroi remains, & my opinion of his talents is unaltered. Now I understand that the vestry has received a design of a church from him.

6. See Fiske Kimball, *op. cit.*

They cannot go wrong in adopting it. . . . Your own feelings will . . . tell you how embarrassed I am between my promise . . . and my determination never to interfere with Mr. Godefroi's interests . . ." Thus it happens that it is Godefroy's beautiful domed Unitarian Church, and not Latrobe's, that remains one of Baltimore's loveliest architectural monuments.

There was some work on a house for William Lee, a good friend—apparently an extensive alteration rather than a new building. And there was the disappointing result of a full and detailed correspondence with Secretary A. J. Dallas. Dallas wanted a large and magnificent house in Washington; this was soon after Latrobe's return there from Pittsburgh in the summer of 1815, and by July 19 the architect had his sketches ready. A certain site had been picked—a lot belonging to Goldsborough—and Latrobe had visited it with Thomas Munroe, the old Capitol commissioner. The house was to be a large one; Latrobe wrote Dallas that anything less than a suite of three entertainment and reception rooms, besides the dining room, "will not furnish space for cards, dancing, & supper." But Dallas did not purchase the lot. Instead, he rented Thomas Law's house—grand, if old-fashioned—and instead of having the architect design a new building Dallas merely asked him to put the Law house in good order for him.

Two other interests occupied Latrobe's mind between 1815 and 1817: the Baltimore Exchange and the New Orleans waterworks. The necessity for an Exchange building had been under consideration in Baltimore at least as early as the spring of 1815, and, through his always thoughtful and admiring friend Robert Goodloe Harper, Latrobe was brought into the picture in the early summer. Since this commission, however, was one of the major reasons for his moving to Baltimore later (in 1818), the whole involved story will be postponed till the ensuing chapter.

The matter of the waterworks, on the other hand, was such a continuous thread through Latrobe's life and worries for so many years—from 1810 till his death—that more consideration of it is necessary here. Under the efficient direction of Henry Latrobe the actual work—stopped during the war years—was resumed, and Henry succeeded in getting an extension of time for the franchise through 1816. The engine house was already nearly complete on its new site. Pipes and materials of all kinds had been accumulated; only the engine and pumps remained to be installed, together with the main supply line. The greater part of the cash required for all this activity came from Henry's profits as a builder and from his father's architectural practice; for the Marks' $40,000 had long since been used up in the project, much of it going into the abortive attempts to build an engine in Philadelphia, Baltimore, Washington, and Pittsburgh—attempts all rendered vain by the War of 1812 and the collapse of the Pittsburgh steamboat plans. Obviously Latrobe wanted to keep control. Obviously, too, thinking of his family, he wanted them to enjoy the largest possible proportion of the immense income he still believed the scheme would bring in. So into it he continued to pour all his ready cash. And the history of New Orleans during the war, as Latrobe wrote Jacob Mark (August 2, 1815), by proving the city impregnable, should double the value of their investment.

Yet the engine constituted a major expenditure that such contributions could never cover, and no engine builder would undertake the work on a speculative basis. Finally, after Jacob Mark had made several vain efforts to obtain an engine, Latrobe wrote to Robert McQueen—"the chief engine builder of New York"—and they came to an agreement; this was in August, 1815.[7] At the same time, Roosevelt, who owned an unused boiler of the necessary size, offered it to the company, thus adding another $2,000 toward the project. But, to raise the $3,000 down payment that McQueen demanded, Latrobe was compelled to go outside and to relinquish some of his own precious stock; he sold a block to his friend and client Benjamin Orr, of Washington, and the proceeds covered the engine payments.

Then, for a while, things ran along smoothly; the drawings for the engine went to New York in mid-October, and Latrobe wrote Mark that construction was under way on December 1. Nothing of import happened in the first part of 1816, except the difficulty of getting an "engine keeper" from the north to go to New Orleans because of fear of yellow fever; but in midsummer came the first serious setback—a rampaging flood. Even nature seemed anxious to delay the project.

Again, on September 28, 1816, came another catastrophe far more severe—a fire that burned a sizable part of the city. It started in David's Assembly Rooms, which Henry had designed and almost finished. Title had not

7. Robert McQueen (or M'Queen, as the name appears consistently in the New York City directory) for many years had an iron-founding company at 72 Duane Street. In 1820-21 the company appears as Iron Founders and Engine Makers, and in the same year Robert M'Queen appears as a civil engineer.

yet passed to the owner; on the contractor, then—Henry Latrobe—fell the entire loss, roughly $12,000. No longer could his father depend on him to take care of the waterworks payroll! Now the need was the other way. Fortunately, so highly was Henry regarded in New Orleans that his credit weathered the catastrophe, and quietly and earnestly he began to rebuild his business. His father helped, too; recalling the design he had made for a lighthouse at the mouth of the Mississippi so long before (in 1806), he tried—successfully—to bring the scheme to life again, this time in his son's name. B. H. had been unable to carry it out because the Treasury Department had insisted on an over-all construction bid, and this he had not been able to obtain. But Henry as an architect-builder right on the spot was ideally fitted to obtain it, and his father sent him not only the plans but all the cost calculations he had made. The result was that Henry obtained the contract and did begin work, though there were already murmurings in New Orleans about the stability of the foundations. Yet the award itself did much to buttress his confidence and his prestige.

Thus 1816 drew to a close and with it the period of the waterworks franchise. There was no cessation of the work, but the architect was uneasily aware of the situation and wrote Henry (July 22, 1817) announcing his intention of asking for another extension of time; the engine and pumps, now complete, were being shipped. Then suddenly, on September 3 (though the father did not learn of the fact for three weeks), Henry, attacked by yellow fever, died, at the age of twenty-four, leaving all his interests in confusion.

Latrobe, at first horror-struck, was bowled over by grief. Then, rousing himself, after informing his friends Jefferson and Harper of the loss, he wrote to John Rogers in New Orleans (who had been sent out to act as foreman) to take charge of Henry's affairs. And he poured out his grief in a long letter to Henry's aunt, Miss Sellon, in England, telling of Henry's charm, brilliance, and courage and of the special sorrow his death brought to his stepmother Mary.[8] Under Rogers the construction of the waterworks went on, slowly and with a much reduced force, for another eighteen months.

It may readily be seen, then, that from the architectural if not the personal point of view these two and a half years were probably the most

8. See Appendix for selections.

creative and productive Latrobe was to know. But the financial picture remained gloomy, with many worrying details.

There was, for instance, the matter of his relation with Robert Fulton's heirs. Mrs. Fulton, he heard, was spreading stories that Latrobe was blackening her husband's name and that he was the source of several paragraphs that had appeared in newspapers in which Fulton had been attacked. At once Latrobe wrote to William Cutting in New York (July 11, 1815) asking him to contradict these rumors; already, a month earlier, he had written Dr. McNeven, of the New York company, that he refused to aid the company in prosecuting Fulton's heirs, that he would give no evidence except the truth, and that he sought no vengeance. He wrote Roosevelt about the matter, urging him to attach the New Orleans boat before she left Pittsburgh, but especially beseeching him to settle the Tustin suit there. Apparently his son-in-law did neither. It was all water over the dam, of course, but it emphasized unhappy memories.

And Eric Bollman turned up again. About the first of December he suddenly appeared. He had returned from England (where he had begun to build up a new career) and, Latrobe says, brought with him to Washington special dispatches from the British government. He claimed, too, to have been instrumental in the achievement of peace between the two countries; as Latrobe wrote Lewis Bollman (December 17, 1815), ". . . among the many motives to peace which operated on the British ministry, the representations of your brother were not the least efficient . . ." Later, in the summer of 1816, when he heard that Bollman was about to leave, he wrote him a polite letter, bringing to his notice again the matter of the $1,000 debt. But it was no use; Bollman might have been charming, but he had a blind spot for his debts. And when he departed from the country, this time for good, he still owed the money.

Then again the speculative fever seized hold of Latrobe. What, he wondered, had happened to the Potomac boat? Surely it was more needed than ever. Had the Fulton heirs sold their interest in it? If they had no more claim on it, why not start on it anew? So again a flurry of notes went out to the investors in the old company, the accounts of which, Latrobe found, were no longer in existence. And eventually, in 1817, Latrobe contracted with a certain Hazlewood Farish of Fredericksburg for the construction of a steamboat of about 150 tons—120 feet long, with a beam of 17′-6″ and a depth of 7′-6″. There was to be, he wrote the contractor, no mast or rigging whatever; it was to be pure steamboat and nothing else. "The arrangement of my boat will be different from any of Fulton's—all of which go faster stern foremost than stem foremost . . ." Later (October 20, 1816) he wrote a memorandum of various boat items: the fastenings were to be "composition" (bronze?); the engine was to be an Ogden engine (like the one he had built for Steubenville); the speed, 6 miles an hour in still water; 20 berths in 2 cabins; a kitchen with complete cooking apparatus; 2 anchors and cables; no movable furniture and no mahogany except locker tops. Delivery was to be in March, 1817. He noted that a certain Flanagan had agreed to do the carpentry work for $32 a ton and that on this basis the boat would probably cost $10,000 and the engine $10,000 more, or a total of $20,000. Yet nothing came of the scheme, and once more valuable energy and time went to the pursuing of will-o'-the-wisps.

The steamboat business left other, and more definite, worries. Mary by her sale of the Latrobe furniture had received enough to cover all the personal bills, so that they had been able to leave Pittsburgh unmolested. Yet what about the unpaid bills on the construction of the *Buffalo* and the *Harriet?* Among the still outstanding claims were sizable ones from Beelen for metal castings and from Beltzhoover for all sorts of materials. Who was to pay these? Fulton was dead and on the face of his correspondence not personally liable. The Ohio Steamboat Navigation Company had liquidated; it, too, had claimed no responsibility beyond the original estimates, which had been far exceeded. There remained only Latrobe, with a government salary and apparently a good practice besides. Obviously, wherever the equity lay, legally he was liable, for the orders had come from him in what according to the strict letter of the law was an illegal assumption of powers he did not possess. The architect of course realized this; all through those years these debts of many hundreds of dollars hung over him. Both Beelen and Beltzhoover were personally friendly and delayed bringing suit for months, but they were businessmen and those were depression years.

And other outstanding debts continued to plague him. There was, for instance, in the Bank of Washington a promissory note to Thomas Law. It had been made on August 9, 1814, apparently to regularize Latrobe's purchase of canal company shares; it had been endorsed to Latrobe's friend and occasional attorney Edward Law, and it was for a sizable sum, $2,750. But now there was no market for canal company shares; the ones he had received as payment for his services and those he had purchased were so much waste paper as far as raising money on them went. He had not been sued on this note yet, but there it lay, a constant threat. If only the waterworks could be completed! Then he could laugh at these threats. So the money that should have been laid aside to cover those past debts was poured anxiously into the New Orleans scheme. With his government salary of $2,500, his salary of $1,500 as one of the city surveyors (Benjamin King was the other), and his fees for professional services, he still had enough to live on and to support the waterworks—but none to save.

Obviously, to judge by his letters, he forced these worries into the back of his mind—and obviously they rankled there, little by little breaking down his confidence. Meanwhile his relations with Colonel Lane, the commissioner in charge of the Capitol, were steadily deteriorating. Lane was a presumptuous little popinjay, who covered his ignorance by a display of more than military arrogance. To him the word architect meant nothing, the difficulties of carrying out a large building meant nothing, the search for worthy materials meant nothing. Latrobe was his draftsman, he believed—almost his servant. He himself was the dictator of the entire work.

The rapid building up of animosity between the two was tragic. Its roots lay in profound temperamental differences as well as in Lane's exaggerated notions of what he was supposed to do. Latrobe was not tactful; he never possessed the art (of which Burr, for example, was such a master) of adjusting his manners or his approach to the character of those with whom he was dealing. He carried to the extreme the British habit of forthright—even brutally forthright—statement; any other system seemed to him insincere. To many Americans, over-sensitive perhaps, this manner of his seemed both arrogant and rude, though no real arrogance was present and no rudeness intended.

In this particular case the same kind of basic misunderstanding was undoubtedly added to by Lane's own feeling of insecurity—his real fear for his job. He had succeeded the three original commissioners (appointed in 1815) because of their incompetence, and he knew full well that there was an informal committee of advisers who watched over the Capitol and reported to the President;[9] he also knew that these men had consistently

9. Letter from Latrobe to Jacob Small in Baltimore (March 21, 1817): ". . . a sort of 'illegal' council has been organized by the President, consisting of Genl Swift, & Col. Bom-

backed Latrobe. Was he, too, to be superseded, as his predecessors had been?

Lane's best defense of his position, as he saw it, lay in asserting his power however and whenever he could. Without consulting the architect, he had (as we have seen) displaced the clerk of the works Latrobe had chosen for the Capitol job, Shadrach Davis. Redoubling his rudenesses, he treated Latrobe more and more like a menial employee. It seems clear that he was trying to oust the architect, whose professional pride and forthright manners—and perhaps even his competence—were continual reminders to the commissioner of his own vulnerability. So all through 1817 matters grew more and more tense, work more and more difficult, and Latrobe suffered deep and rankling humiliation.

Then came the news of his son's death. For a while he pulled himself together, but the shock of it, the apprehension he felt about its effect on the future of the waterworks, the pain (and perhaps a little guilt) brought on by a break with his old friend Godefroy over the design of the Exchange, and especially the continual worry about the debts that were piling up seem for the moment to have completely destroyed his poise, his self-control. The climax came when he was publicly reprimanded by Lane before the President. Something in him snapped; it was too much for his harried nerves to bear. Latrobe leaped at Lane and, as reported years later by his wife, "seized him by the collar, and exclaimed, 'Were you not a cripple I would shake you to atoms, you poor contemptible wretch. Am I to be dictated to by you?' The President said looking at my husband, 'Do you know who I am, Sir?' 'Yes, I do, and ask your pardon, but when I consider my birth, my family, my education, my talents, I am excusable for any outrage after the provocation I have received from that contemptible character.'"[10]

But such an outbreak, in the presence of such an audience, was fatal to further work. Latrobe knew that his loss of temper—and especially his physical attack on Lane, a smaller man, a cripple, and a presidential appointee—made his position impossible. He sought the advice of his best friends, especially Robert Goodloe Harper, and they all advised him to resign. His note of resignation (November 20, 1817) reads:

---

ford of the Engineers & myself, with whom the President consults and then gives the Commissioner his orders . . ."

10. Quoted from Mrs. B. H. Latrobe's memoir of her husband, transcribed by her son John H. B. Latrobe.

My situation as architect to the Capitol has become such as to leave me no choice but between resignation and the sacrifice of all my self respect. Permit me then, Sir, to resign into your hands the office in which I fear I have been the cause to you of much vexation while my only object has been to accomplish your wishes. You have known me more than twenty years. You have borne testimony to my professional skill—and my integrity has never been questioned. You will, I am confident, do me justice, and in time know that never the delay nor the expense of the public works was chargeable to me.

I am aware that much inconvenience may arise from my retiring from my office so suddenly. But I pledge myself to finish drawings and instructions for all the parts of the work that are in hand for a reasonable compensation being made, [which] my circumstances do not permit me to decline.

But petty tyranny did not stop with his resignation. He had offered to continue in the office till December 1, to complete a final set of drawings —plans, elevations, and sections. Yet, as he wrote President Monroe (December 18):

When the commissioner communicated to me the acceptance of my resignation, he told my former clerk, Mr. Blanchard, that he should not admit any, but certain persons whom he named. I was not on the list, and, altho' I had stated that I should attend until the 1st of Dec., chiefly with a view to finish the enclosed and some other drawings, I have been under the necessity of taking them home and compleating them amidst the hurry & inconvenience of my removal. I submit these circumstances as my apology for their not being as perfect as I wish, and for the delay, and shall have the honor to transmit the others in a few days . . .[11]

The very day of his resignation (November 20) Latrobe wrote another significant letter. This was to Robert Mills, informing him of his resignation and suggesting that Mills apply for the job. It was an entirely generous gesture, a final statement of his real feeling for his early pupil and employee. However he might have been irked by Mills's almost stodgy rectitude, however much he might have deplored certain elements in the other's taste, Latrobe knew that, taken all in all, Mills was a real

11. President Monroe realized what a loss to the government Latrobe's resignation was, although he made no effort to get the architect to reconsider. He thought that perhaps *two* architects would be necessary to replace him, and the names of John McComb, Jr., of New York, and Charles Bulfinch of Boston were suggested. Eventually this idea was abandoned and Bulfinch was appointed to bring the Capitol to completion, which was substantially accomplished by him in the years between 1818 and 1830.

architect, thoroughly dependable, and that in suggesting to Mills that he should become his successor he was expressing a hope that the work would fall to the one he considered most worthy to carry it on. The magnanimity of the suggestion must have wiped out any continuing doubts Mills might still have cherished as to where he stood in his master's thoughts.

And also on this same unhappy day, as though he were trying to clear away a number of accumulated jobs in order to start at peace again, he sent to Senator Pope in Frankfort, Kentucky, the designs he had made for a United States arsenal there. The letter that accompanied the drawings is interesting for its picture of early mass manufacture and Latrobe's realization of the enormous advantages in the system of accurate parts production which Eli Whitney had already put in use in Connecticut: ". . . I have submitted the design to Col. Bomford, of the Ordnance Department . . . He approves generally of the plan . . . The shops & buildings are calculated to employ 100 workmen . . . who could turn out 4800 stands of arms p. annum." He then notes that the plan is a development of one he had prepared eighteen years earlier, probably for Harpers Ferry, and mentions that "I had then, in addition to my own knowledge . . . the command of all the information which the War Department could secure." He continues by describing the system by which gun barrels were turned instead of ground, and locks formed by presses instead of being forged, and adds: ". . . the whole labor is so subdivided and distributed that the same work is perpetually performed by the same hand, and that not only the greatest expedition but such extreme accuracy is the result" that the parts are interchangeable. "You will observe that the drawing is adapted to water power . . . But I have also begun a design in which a steam engine is proposed to be employed . . ."

An arsenal of some kind was built in Frankfort, but it perished long ago and was replaced by another building. No evidence of the earlier building's plan and appearance can now be recovered, so that it is impossible to know whether or not the Latrobe drawings were followed. But it is interesting to see Latrobe designing here an early example of a factory with such modern industrial methods as a basis.

With the sudden cessation of the government salary from the Capitol, the architect's position was materially changed. Beelen and Beltzhoover were suing him at last, and there was a small suit by one Talley, a Washington tradesman. For perhaps the first time, Latrobe really examined the total picture of his financial position and found it intolerable. Leaving aside the New Orleans waterworks, the prospects of which were still uncertain, he found that his debts amounted to a terrifying sum. His assets—often uncollectible debts due him—were small, though his future prospects he still felt were bright. Obviously bankruptcy was the only way out, and on December 17 he filed his plea.[12] It was January 5, 1818, before he was formally discharged and the family could leave Washington. Again there were sales of furniture and goods to clear the current bills, and in mid-January the Latrobes departed for Baltimore, their next hope—Baltimore where the Exchange was rising, where the Cathedral was coming to completion, but above all where their dear friends the Harpers lived.

---

12. The schedule of assets and liabilities prepared by Latrobe is in the National Archives. It shows assets of approximately $5,000, but these include such questionable amounts as the old Chesapeake and Delaware Canal notes. The sale of his horses, carriages, and furniture at auction had brought $943.70, but $346.50 of this had been used to satisfy a judgment against him on the suit of Foxton, the Philadelphia plasterer.

He then lists the debts due him, which total $7,729.96, but again there are many the collection of which was problematical, such as $4,226.96 due from the heirs of Robert Fulton and Robert Livingstone on the Pittsburgh affair, and another $1,000 from the heirs of Robert Fulton for work done and payments made in connection with the Potomac Company. Included also is $1,380 owing from J. P. Van Ness for professional services.

He adds a separate list of debts owed to him that he considers uncollectible, including $2,731.32 from Samuel Blydensburg, $1,154.65 from Eric Bollman, $832.48 paid on a note he had endorsed for Teunis Craven, insolvent, and $1,133.20 for bail paid to release Henry Hiort, who, he writes, "absconded and joined the enemy below Richmond."

He lists the creditors who have sued as claiming from him $1,874.50; of this $1,704.50 was for the Pittsburgh boats. The claims of the creditors who have not sued he lists as $5,666.00; the total of all debts for which no suits have been started he estimates at about $8,600.

It all made a good showing on paper—but the assets were chiefly imaginary or uncollectible and the debts all too real.

PART IV: End of the Road

CHAPTER

20

Baltimore Interlude: 1818

THE months in Baltimore were quiet—too quiet, for the depression still held and there was little private building. In many ways, of course, this very quietness must have come as a relief. No more harassing suits, for a while; the Insolvency Act had taken care of these. No more struggles with an unsympathetic Capitol commissioner to lacerate one's nerves. Instead, the steady progression of the Exchange, rising gradually to completion, and the continuing work on the Cathedral. Here at last were two large monuments in which Latrobe's skill could—and did—expand with the fewest of hindrances. The Cathedral especially was a source of deep pleasure. With the old controversies and client changes far in the past, the architect must have felt, as the vaults curved over to enclose the whole superb space, that in this building at least his work of over a decade was finally being crowned with triumph. His dream of imposing space, of restrained richness, was at last a reality; before the beautifully detailed stonework of the exterior and the simple grandeur of the interior—unique for its time—adverse criticism was silent.

Socially, too, Baltimore had much to offer the Latrobes. They had many friends there—William Lorman (for whom in 1816 he had designed a group of stores on Charles and Conewago streets); the Pattersons; Mme Jerome Bonaparte, now a member of their intimate circle; but especially Robert Goodloe Harper, their benevolent and eternally faithful admirer, supporter, and friend. Through him they had rented their house at 11 Lexington Street—small but comfortable, and near his. He was their adviser; he helped them enormously in the setting up of their new home; he showed them ways of economizing. They had reduced their expenditures to the limit, and with their small means the close social circle in which they moved, as in their last years in Washington, was large enough for variety but intimate enough so that they were not tempted toward display. If perhaps it was sometimes galling to the architect's sensitive pride that they could not entertain in their former openhanded manner, it was a much greater satisfaction to know that in so far as the family could arrange it they were living within their means and were surrounded by a group of people who not only loved and admired them but also understood their plight.

With the end of 1817 the polygraph copies of the Latrobe letters cease; in the bankruptcy his polygraph probably went into the creditors' hands. Yet actually the loss of that source material is less important than it might be, for this was essentially a rest period in his life—a time in which, in quiet devotion to his two major Baltimore jobs, he could rebuild his confidence and his health.

Naturally there was other work, but it was all advisory. For instance, he made a report to the city (May 31, 1818) on the handling of Jones Falls—that recalcitrant stream of water which was the source of periodic and destructive floods. After its major fall, the stream wandered sluggishly over nearly flat and marshy land to join the Patapsco, almost bisecting the city with a stretch of derelict swamp. It was the sluggishness of these lower reaches and the lack of adequate outlet to the river that accounted for the flooding whenever spring freshets swept down from the hills at the north and west. Latrobe's report is a complete analysis of the situation. He realized that proper canalization would give the needed outlet to the pent-up waters and would dry the marsh by giving it adequate drainage. The canal, he felt, should divert the water into Herring Creek; this would obviate both the flooding of the city and the silting up of the harbor. His report also considered other suggestions which had already been made—especially the building of elaborate canals above the falls; these, he believed, would entail an unnecessary expense. The city did nothing at that time; but later growth forced action, and at last, long after Latrobe's death, much of what he suggested was carried out. Later still the water course was covered over, and today a network of railroad tracks and a group of railroad stations fill the formerly marshy valley; no longer do spring freshets spread terror in the city.

Latrobe made another interesting report during this period, at the request of the Secretary of the Navy. President Monroe was deeply concerned about the defense of the eastern coast, and especially about Chesapeake Bay, which afforded to a hostile force deep penetration into the country. He knew the disastrous effects that the British command of the bay had had in 1813 and 1814. It was this that had led to the burning of Havre de Grace and the attack on Baltimore, which only a miracle had prevented from being successful. It was this that had led directly to the capture of Washington and the burning of the government buildings. If there had been a great naval base in the bay, perhaps all of these events could have been averted.

Of all the possible sites for such a base, Annapolis seemed the best. It commanded the approaches to both Baltimore and Washington, and the wide and deep Severn River would furnish excellent and protected anchorage for a large fleet. Latrobe was requested to make a survey and report, and this he did. On analysis he realized the advantages offered, yet he also was alert to the difficulties. The harbor was deep and the Severn ample, but at the entrance there was a shallow bar that reached almost across it, and the whole upper end of Chesapeake Bay was relatively shallow beyond this. Latrobe made a complete new survey of the depths available and on that basis gave his approval of the proposal with reservations. The bar was a hindrance, to be sure, but the bottom was soft and dredging would be possible. Undoubtedly his report helped to keep Annapolis in the government's eye as a place for future naval development; as a result, when a full-fledged naval academy was born, it was placed in this strategic location. But the existence of the long dredged channel that makes modern use of the harbor possible and the fact that today the largest ships usually anchor out in the open roadstead of the bay bear mute witness to the hampering problem of the depths of the approaches—a problem to which Latrobe had called attention.

And, however much he had been disliked and distrusted in Washington, the architect's reputation throughout the country still remained high. When in 1818 North Carolina was thinking of embarking on an extensive program of canal building, it was to Latrobe that the governor of the state naturally turned and to him that he offered the position of state engineer. Latrobe refused the appointment, for the Exchange, the Cathedral, and the New Orleans waterworks fully absorbed his time and his energy; but in his long letter of refusal [1] he takes the occasion of presenting a thorough analysis of the state problem in terms of its topography

1. Letter to Governor Joseph Gales, April 16, 1818, in the State Archives, Raleigh. I owe this letter to the generous co-operation of Professor Cecil D. Elliott, School of Design, North Carolina State College, Raleigh, N.C.

and geology. His friend General Stokes had told him that the chief improvement planned was the connection of the Yadkin and Cape Fear rivers—a connection that would furnish easy communication from the uplands to the sea—and to this problem he devotes his letter. He begins by sketching out the basic geology of the river valleys of the eastern United States and the granite ridges that usually divide them. Then he gives the governor long and detailed directions on making the surveys that were prerequisite to any intelligent decision about canal routes; he suggests that such preliminary surveys could be made by land surveyors just as satisfactorily as by an engineer. Then, he says, on the basis of the map which results,

> . . . the sagacity & experience of an engineer can soon determine which of a limited number of courses offers the greatest probability of being practicable—these he then examines with the level in his hand, ascertains all the circumstances of ground, as to its level & composition, balances the advantages of distance, with depth & difficulty of cutting, & using the best of his talent & judgement is enabled first to report generally upon the practicability,—then on the best line of the cut, afterwards on the details of bridges, embankments, locks, or tunnels, & ultimately on the final expense of the work. [He ends by recommending an English engineer, a Mr. Upton,] who on your invitation . . . would immediately come out. Such talents as those which you require are rare, & whoever imports them, deserves well of his country . . .

In his letter he expresses the hope that he may be passing through North Carolina on a proposed visit to New Orleans "in October or November." Apparently no further communication came from North Carolina, however, and when he did leave Baltimore it was by sea.

The Exchange had been the primary magnet to draw the architect to Baltimore.[2] Outside of the United States Capitol it was by far his largest commission. The scheme had long been brewing, for Baltimore merchants had tried in vain to organize an exchange as early as 1793. Then the project lay dormant until early in 1815, when at last an interested group formed a committee and bought a building site; the group was finally

2. For much of the material used in this consideration of the Baltimore Exchange, I am deeply indebted to Mr. Alan Burnham, whose careful studies of the building have been the basis of many of my statements, and to Mr. Richard Borneman, Assistant Curator of the Baltimore Museum of Fine Arts, who has put at my disposal a superb collection of old photographs of the building and transcribed for me important early descriptions, notably that in Fielding Lucas, *Picture of Baltimore* (Baltimore: Lucas, 1832).

organized officially and incorporated by the state legislature a year later. Robert Goodloe Harper was one of the prime movers, and it was through him that Latrobe was approached as soon as the land had been purchased. When the architect returned to Washington from Pittsburgh in mid-June, he at once attacked the problem. He would need a Baltimore representative, and the obvious choice was Maximilian Godefroy—an old friend and also an architect whose taste and skill he admired. When Latrobe wrote (June 15) asking him to become his associate, Godefroy hastened to accept.

The site was a large lot, some 260 by 165 feet, on Water (later Lombard), Second (later East Water), and Gay streets. During the ensuing month the general arrangement was sketched out in a preliminary way, and a program was prepared under the title, "Memorandum Relative to a Project for an Exchange at Baltimore by Messers Godefroi and Latrobe." It provided for a coffeehouse, a reading room, a residence for the manager, the Baltimore customs house, warehouses, counting houses, seven insurance company offices, eight brokers' offices, and, in the center, the "exchange hall" lighted by a dome. On upper floors there were to be meeting rooms (over the customs house) and either exhibition and lecture rooms or additional offices. All these, except the exchange room, would be in two three-story sections running the entire length of the property and creating two large open courts at the ends of the generally H-shaped plan. The bar of the H would contain the exchange hall, entered either directly from the courts or by a monumental passage through the east front along Gay Street.

This memorandum, dated July 16, formalized and described the arrangement shown on a preliminary sketch which Latrobe had sent to Godefroy a week earlier and had forwarded to Harper and to Robert Smith in Baltimore on July 11. Both Harper and Smith, eager to start actual construction, had wondered why the sketch had taken so long. Latrobe explained to Harper in his covering letter: "One of these days has been lost by my thinking it right to send Godefroy . . . a copy of the sketch. I am very well aware that I have not a little embarrassed myself by what you call my chivalric conduct . . ." And he adds that Godefroy is also going to submit a sketch with slightly different details. Robert Smith, it seems, had questioned the desirability of the association of the two architects, and in a letter (also on July 11) Latrobe reassured him, and as to the professional rectitude of his own behavior toward

Godefroy stated: ". . . I would not for the value of ten exchanges appear to carry myself independently of him, or hurt the delicate feelings of a man of so much genius and honor, & whom I so sincerely respect . . ."

But Godefroy and Latrobe were not the only architects interested in the commission. An informal competition was rapidly developing as other eager architects pressed their ideas on the committee. All through the summer of 1815 the struggle went on. Just three days after the "Memorandum" of July 16 had been sent in, Latrobe wrote Godefroy:

> Now the fact is, that Ramée [3] will be the architect, or Mills, and all we are doing is vain. Yet we cannot avoid it, for such is the deplorable state of the arts among the mushrooms of fortune upon whose vile patronage they depend, that we must submit to the only means that exist, to get employment at all & bread for our families. . . . If our friends can outvote Ramée's, that is Parishes, or Mills', that is Gillmore's, then we shall carry it, if our plan was that of Pandemonium or a Panporneion, not else . . . [He goes on to warn of the dangers of such a partnership as theirs.] One thing more . . . It is evident that we two are one in the great principles . . . but difference of education, of habits in the countries and schools in which we have studied, of long practise of mean contrivance on my part, & of grand speculations in design on yours, have totally separated us as to the details of composition in the execution of our art. Yet great as the hindrance . . . that this may afford at first, to the unity of plan, and to agreement in any design, if you can forgive the short and probably dictatorial manner of an old *master carpenter,* I am sure we should be one in every respect . . .

From this it seems that in the first month of their partnership, even before the job had been awarded, disagreements between the two had already begun to arise, and Latrobe here attempts to mollify his impulsive coworker. It is not a happy augury.

All summer the Exchange trustees wrangled. New drawings were asked for and made. On October 22 Latrobe wrote Harper: "I have not the most distant expectation of obtaining it [the job] & Godefroi is in such despair, I do not know whether he is even drawing. He informs me in

---

3. J. J. Ramée, French architect and landscape designer, who had come to New York from Hamburg at the suggestion of the Parish family. He is best known in America for his work on Union College, at Schenectady. In Baltimore he was working on the landscaping of Carrolton, the Denis Smith estate. His competition drawing for the Washington Monument in Baltimore—an exquisite triumphal arch—still exists. He returned to France shortly after the Baltimore Exchange competition had been decided. His son Daniel later became a famous architectural historian.

his letter, that Ramée has spent some time as a guest of Denis Smith, & was drawing his plan at his house . . ." And to Godefroy, trying to encourage him, he wrote the same day: ". . . Let us take our chance, at least, & none ought to be better than yours against Ramée, or mine against Mills . . ."[4]

Even in December the matter was still hanging fire, and on the seventh Latrobe reported to Harper: "I have been busy at the Exchange [and] begun a new set on the plan of 240′ x 150′ . . . [Godefroy] writes despondently [that] a friend of his heard Denis Smith say that he would subscribe $40,000 more to procure Ramée the preference . . ."

Such were the hardships entailed by the then prevalent system of informal competitions.

Eventually, however, the building committee came to an agreement and awarded the commission to Godefroy and Latrobe. The supporters of the brilliant French architect J. J. Ramée and the backers of the dependable Robert Mills were out-argued and outvoted, and Godefroy and Latrobe went seriously to work. But it was February 5, 1816, before Latrobe could write to his brother-in-law Samuel Hazlehurst: "My plan has been so fortunate as to be accepted for the Baltimore Exchange. . . . Mills had nine plans there, Strickland had some, & some Baltimore carpenters had also put in for the premium. Godefroy & myself, for we had joined, had 5 votes, Mills 2, Small 1, the others had none . . ." When the premium ($300) was finally paid, Latrobe wrote that it should be sent to Godefroy—a generous gesture, based on his knowledge of Godefroy's poverty, for Latrobe at that time had at least his government salary to live on.

Meanwhile the partnership was growing more precarious as disagree-

4. Other sections of this letter give a good picture of Latrobe's feelings at that time:

"As to retrospects, I fly them as I do misery of all kinds. I have little more of the Gallican spirit about me, *than you have,* in this respect. When I was younger I understood something of the luxury of *melancholy,*—now, when I brood over my vexations & disappointments, I grow angry, & that is an abominable sensation. I am fool enough to lay awake & groan for hours over the state of France. I have now ceased to read newspapers. Had I a prospect of a long life I should throw all my moral principles to the devil in despair of seeing anything like national or individual improvement of this *monster,* Man.

"But my habits were formed on the dilemma of honor & virtue & how then can I make money, the only substitute for both, unless I had the necessary habits, & were without the unnecessary, & incompatible feelings.—So we must drudge on, till we die & our wives must be satisfied as they are so very romantic that they would never exchange us for Ireland or for Dugan . . ."

ments between Godefroy and Latrobe mounted. Godefroy wanted to use a colonnade along the entire Gay Street front—a scheme embodied in an existing elevation.[5] Latrobe wrote him (March 11, 1816) that the scheme was meaningless because of the slope of Gay Street. And two months later (May 27) Latrobe himself made a beautiful colored perspective of the Gay Street front; he describes it to Harper in a letter of that date as showing "exactly that part of the work to be built first, & hiding the rest by poplars." The description given in this letter precisely matches a preserved perspective which shows the building as it was built. The scheme at that time contemplated leaving the wing ends unfinished, to be completed only when their final use—for banks or for Federal government branches—could be determined.

The use of two of these wings—at the ends of the eastern or Gay Street front—was actually settled during the summer of 1816, largely through Latrobe's negotiations with A. J. Dallas, Secretary of the Treasury.[6] The southern one, on what is now Lombard Street, was to be the United States customs house and the northern one the Baltimore branch of the Bank of the United States. The southwest corner wing had been planned for the post office, and Latrobe made several studies of various possible arrangements; but this scheme was not carried out until half a century after the architect's death. As a result the entire western range of the H, facing Exchange Alley, was omitted in the original construction, thus transforming the H into a broad T.[7]

Originally the scheme had called for the two courts to be colonnaded (several existing sketches show this), not only to provide pleasant sheltered walks for both the public and the users of the building but also to create attractive entrances to the Exchange proper from the north and the south. But, when the negotiations for the post office failed and the western block was omitted, the court colonnades were rendered impossible and the easterly wing designs were simplified accordingly. Soon

5. This and many other drawings dealing with the Exchange are preserved in the Maryland Historical Society.

6. Through Dallas Latrobe trusted that he would also be appointed architect of the Philadelphia customs house. On Dallas's resignation, however, this commission was given to Latrobe's quondam pupil William Strickland.

7. The one-story western wings shown in old photographs were only built in 1871, when the Federal government (which had purchased the entire building in 1857) made extensive alterations and built the western block to accommodate a much enlarged post office.

after the architects had been officially appointed, the general building contract for this reduced plan was awarded to Colonel Jacob Small and the contract for the cut stone to William Steuart,[8] who had furnished large amounts of stone for the United States Capitol. Small was a competent and conscientious contractor, with sufficient architectural knowledge and experience to work sympathetically with the architects, and a warm friendship grew up between him and Latrobe; at one time Latrobe hoped Small's son William would join his office as a student draftsman.[9]

As the work progressed, however, the tensions between Godefroy and Latrobe increased. The obvious intention of the partnership had been that Godefroy should act as the local partner, make the detailed working drawings, and superintend the work to see that it followed the drawings and that its quality was up to the standards required. But to Godefroy any such delimitation of his function seemed ignominious. He was full of suggestions that would change the design, and these he took at once to the Exchange trustees; when, naturally, they were ignored (for all the building contracts had been let), he complained that he was not being sufficiently recognized. Latrobe wrote him (June 5, 1816) protesting his action and trying to smooth his hurt feelings. But it was no use; Godefroy considered that his professional status was at stake.

Of course Godefroy's attitude not merely jeopardized the efficient and economical execution of the building but also tended to confuse the trustees. Latrobe was forced to take action. Evidently during one of his several Baltimore visits at this time he had a conversation with Mrs. Godefroy, hoping through her influence to avoid a disastrous break with her husband; and on June 5 he wrote frankly to John Spear Smith, vividly sketching the situation:

> From what Mrs. Godefroy has been so candid as to say to me, I judge that in his [Godefroy's] view the pecuniary part of the concern is only a secondary consideration. It is the reputation, the immortality, to be acquired in building the Exchange, of that I have robbed him! [The letter continues with the story of how the design was created.] The south front, in its general effect, belongs to Mr. Godefroy . . . the general arrangement is mine, & was approved by Mr. Godefroy. Where he did not approve, I always endeavored . . . to please him . . . The only point [to which] I adhered, because I could not

8. This is the spelling found in Baltimore records of the time.

9. William Small did become an architect; his best-known work is the severely Greek Doric McKim School, designed in association with William Howard and still standing.

do otherwise, after the plan was fixed . . . was to the Venetian windows . . . [the trustees] adopted the design studied by me, which is so arranged that the windows cannot be changed . . . [Godefroy had wished to substitute a continuous row of rectangular openings.] When I forwarded the adopted design . . . I had so minutely studied its execution, as to have calculated the size of the glass . . . [and] the lateral pressure of the arches. I was ready with all this in November . . . Mr. Godefroi had seen & examined with me the general design, &, as I thought, approved it in October. . . .

Here then, is the question . . . is the offer I made to him to make the working drawings if he chose to do so, after I had studied their principles, an affront, to be resented as he has done it . . . because I at the same time explained why I could do it with more ease & to a greater advantage . . . ?

Meanwhile he had written again to Godefroy (May 26):

No two minds ever were formed, that educated in the same school of principles & of practice, they could exactly coincide in the detail of any project . . . Two designs may be mixed as is the case in that which the Trustees have adopted. But, the general plan being fixed, it does not appear to me possible that the details can be the work of us both . . . one or the other must do the whole . . .

Again Latrobe's forthright expressions had an effect quite different from that which he had hoped for. Instead of their showing Godefroy the logical reasons for what had been done and thereby enlisting Godefroy's understanding and co-operation, their very simplicity seemed to Godefroy a brutal ultimatum—a sinister warning for him to get out of the picture entirely. This made any continued collaboration impossible, and Godefroy withdrew, burning with anger, amazed that the trustees of the Exchange upheld Latrobe, and filled with a concentrated bitterness against his former partner that was to last the rest of his life. It was a distressing and tragic experience for both the protagonists—distressing because Latrobe's conduct, earlier and later, proves that the purpose of his letter to Godefroy was to rebuild and not ruthlessly destroy their partnership; tragic because with Godefroy's almost fantastic sense of pride and the supersensitiveness of his always high-strung nerves, and with Latrobe's British habit of bald statement of facts and attitudes, no other end could have been expected.[10]

---

10. See Carolina V. Davison, "Maximilian and Eliza Godefroy," in *Maryland Historical Magazine,* vol. 29, no. 1 (March, 1934), and also Godefroy's own résumé of his work,

As soon as Godefroy withdrew, the trustees authorized a payment to Latrobe of $300, to match that which (at Latrobe's request) had already been made to Godefroy, and on December 5, 1816, a formal contract was made with Latrobe by which he engaged as architect to carry out all the remaining work—details, preparation of documents, supervision, and so forth—for $4,000. From that time on the work progressed smoothly to its eventual completion in the year of the architect's death. Yet the job was not without its effect in complicating the designer's life. One of the greatest criticisms that Lane, the Capitol commissioner, held against Latrobe was his frequent absence from Washington, for to Lane physical presence even when manifestly unnecessary was the only criterion of devoted service. If Godefroy had remained as the local superintending partner at the Exchange, numerous visits by Latrobe would not have been needed. Now, with Godefroy gone, not only was a new load added to Latrobe's correspondence, but his Baltimore visits were multiplied, with the consequence of more attacks by Lane and growing stress in the Capitol work. It was about this time, too, that Latrobe learned that both Godefroy and Mills had been making advances to the Baltimore Cathedral trustees about the completion of the Cathedral, and he was forced to reassert his claim to that work—another episode which turned his thoughts toward the desirability of a Baltimore residence.

The Baltimore Exchange, then, as Latrobe after his removal to Baltimore saw it finally rising to completion, was largely his own. As we have already seen, the small scale of the Gay Street front was at least partly the result of Godefroy's suggestions, but the actual detailing was everywhere Latrobe's. And the major element of the building, the exchange room with its daring brick dome, was entirely his. In the final T plan, this occupied the entire central area. Its chief entrance was from Gay Street, through a passage that separated the customs house on the south from the Bank of the United States on the north. The entire basement, vaulted throughout, was used for offices, store rooms, and the like, and on the upper floors of the Gay Street side there were additional offices. For some years the suite immediately above the Gay Street entrance served as the city hall, until the purchase of the Peale Museum for that purpose.

---

written in Paris in 1836, a translation of which appears in the *Maryland Historical Magazine,* vol. 29, No. 3 (September, 1934). His hatred for Latrobe still burned strong in 1836!

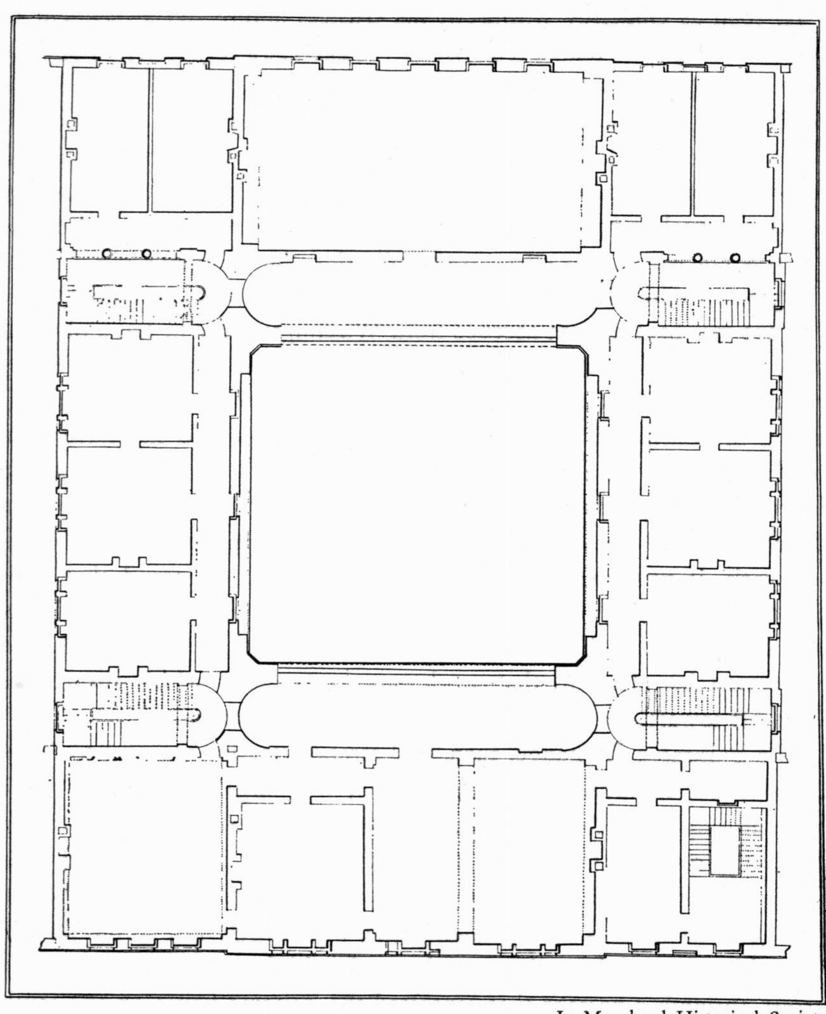

In Maryland Historical Society

FIGURE 30. Baltimore Exchange. Second-floor Plan of Central Section. Latrobe's original drawing.

The Exchange included not only the exchange hall proper, with its necessary rooms for the board and the director, but also the reading room, placed to the west, opposite the chief entrance. Here were kept files of current newspapers from all over the world, books of commercial interest, and all kinds of pertinent records; here were posted notices of vessels arrived or vessels sailing and marine news of importance. From the windows of the high dome there was a good view of Telegraph Hill, where signals were hung to denote the movement of shipping and the arrival of expected ships, so that the news could be almost instantly posted in the reading room. A coffee room, much frequented by merchants and sea captains, was part of the reading-room suite. Existing plans indicate that these rooms were not only ample in size but carefully planned for beauty of shape and the beautiful placing of doors, windows, and fireplaces.

But it was the exchange room itself that was the crowning feature in the whole. It was 53 feet square, with central entrances from Second and Water streets on the north and south respectively and with the chief entrance on the east, from Gay Street. On the east and west sides it was flanked by Ionic colonnades—of six Italian marble columns each—which carried balconies that furnished passage across the area on the second floor. Above these balconies rose semicircular vaults some 50 feet wide, matched on the north and south sides by wall arches of similar size. These four arches carried a pendentive dome, and the four pendentives continued as a single domical surface for some distance above their junctures. The domical surface, in turn, carried a circular balcony that looked inward and down to the Exchange floor far below. A drum, cylindrical on the inside and octagonal without, rested on the pendentive dome and carried above it the dome proper, the crown of which was 115 feet above the floor. Four large windows through the drum on the cardinal points—north, south, east, west—flooded the interior with light and gave people on the high inner circular gallery four superb views over the city and its harbor.

All of this construction was in solid masonry and formed a tour de force of constructional skill as unprecedented in the America of its time as was the interesting interior shape to which it gave rise. The way in which the weights were carried down by heavy piers at the ends of the colonnaded passages on each side, the use of the weight of the drum and upper dome to help buttress the thrusts of the lower pendentive dome, the lightening of the total weights by the large windows and panels of the drum and the deep coffering of the inner surfaces of the dome—these were all brilliantly original. One can but wonder not only at the daring of the designer but also at the impeccable craftsmanship of Jacob Small and his assistants, who, completely untrained in masonry construction

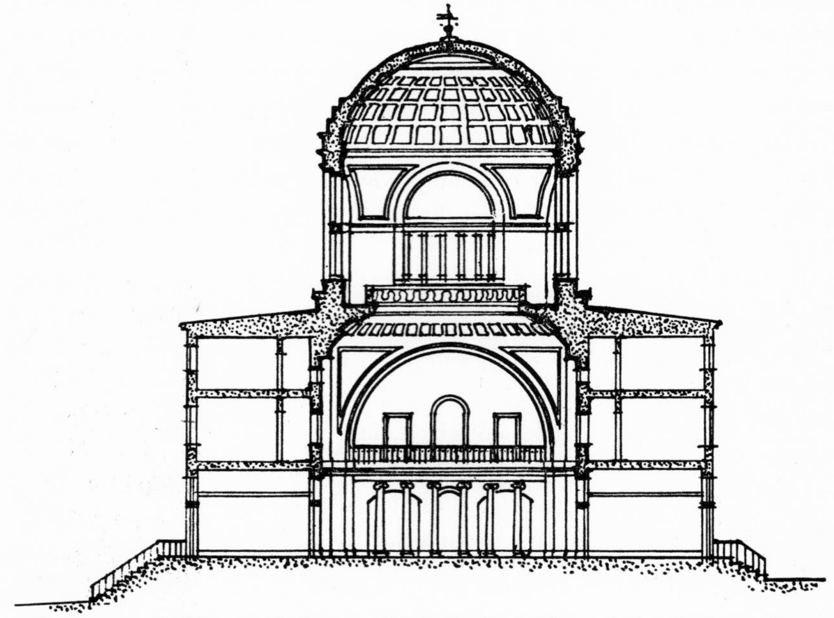

FIGURE 31. Baltimore Exchange. North-South Section of the Exchange Room. Restored by the author.

of such a scale and such complexity, brought it all (under the architect's watchful eye) safely to final completion.

The interior was as rich as its construction was daring. In the lower balconies the Ionic order won instant approval for its purity and grace, and the cast-iron railings were of a Greek Revival type that became common in the country a decade and a half later. The pendentives were paneled in plaster, with symbols of commerce in the four panels, and the domical surface between the pendentives and the upper gallery was enriched and its weight reduced by a row of deep decorated coffers. In the upper dome the spandrels between the windows were deeply paneled too, and at some later date they were richly painted; the coffered surface of the dome itself was climaxed by a large, superbly designed weather vane, operated by the actual vane that swung outside on the dome top. Here, perhaps, Latrobe's imaginative handling of varied but unified interior volumes reached its acme; here his integration of use, construction, and beauty received its most perfect expression.

The simplicity of the exterior served as a striking foil for the interior richness. The walls were of brick stuccoed, with arches, trim, and moldings of cut stone. The first- and second-floor windows were arched, with molded stone archivolts; those above were rectangular. At the ends two-story arched motifs expressed the larger public spaces of the customs house and the bank, and the center of the Gay Street front—the main entrance to the Exchange—projected slightly to give it emphasis. This front contained the three "Venetian windows" (three Palladian motifs each under a single arch) to which Godefroy had taken such violent exception. On either side of the entrance itself stone panels carved with the caduceus of Mercury gave a touch of symbolic richness; above them circular recesses contained marble busts of Washington and Jefferson. Thus the whole long Gay Street front was basically simple and horizontal in feeling, but above and behind it rose the octagonal base of the dome—with its great windows—and the dome itself, the whole crowned by the rich wrought-iron weather vane.

Latrobe saw the virtual completion of the building, though its official opening came only in June, 1820, when he was already in New Orleans.[11]

Another interesting Baltimore project of 1817—one that Latrobe thought would be helped toward realization by his moving to the city—was the Baltimore library. Again Robert Goodloe Harper, a leading figure in the Baltimore Library Company, was the intermediary. The fast-growing city, with ever-increasing ambitions to rival Philadelphia as a cultural center, saw no reason why it could not, like Philadelphia, have an impressive structure to house its library. Thornton had designed the handsome Philadelphia Library; in fact, it was his work on this building that he thought had prepared him to be the architect of the United States Capitol. Now Baltimore had its opportunity to go even farther than had Philadelphia, and Latrobe—Thornton's successor at the Capitol—was an appropriate choice as the architect.

---

11. The later history of this building is complex. The great increase in population and in port business required vast enlargement of the customs house; accordingly, in 1857, the Federal government bought the entire structure, except the bank wing, which after the demise of the Bank of the United States had been taken over by the Merchants' National Bank. Various alterations were made at that time, and the Gay Street entrance (originally the main entrance) was closed. At this time, too, the post office was incorporated in the complex. In 1871 increased population forced a similar enlargement of the post office, and the western one-story block was built to house it. By the beginning of the present century even these enlarged quarters were insufficient, and a new customs house was planned; the old Exchange was finally torn down in 1904, thus bringing to an end what was undoubtedly the most daring vaulted construction as well as one of the most beautiful airy interiors in the United States.

Latrobe received the commission sometime in the spring of 1817. He busied himself at once with the problem, which was particularly congenial to his tastes, and by the beginning of June he had made two designs for it—"one in the Grecian or Roman style of architecture, the other in that usually called Gothic," as he expressed it in the covering letter to Harper sent with the drawings on June 4. The Gothic design has been lost, but the classic drawing still exists in the Maryland Historical Society.

This drawing shows a simple building of excellent proportions. The chief library room, with a gallery around, occupies the larger part of the volume. It is domed and is lighted largely through a glazed cupola. The principal entrance is relatively small (for this was not a public library), but the large simplicity of the wall planes expresses its purpose and prevents its being taken for either a house or a courthouse; its character, in other words, is as appropriate as the interior of its airy reading room would have been welcoming and attractive if built. It may well be compared with the Peale Museum, still standing, which Robert Cary Long, Sr., had designed for Raphael Peale in 1813. The museum composition is more unusual, the library simpler and more elegant; both are interesting examples of early American ideals in the building of "cultural" facilities. It is Baltimore's misfortune that because of the financial stringency of the time the money for the library did not materialize and Latrobe's beautiful design never became a reality.

The attribution of Harper's own Baltimore house is difficult. We know that Latrobe did much work for him, especially at his country home, Oakland, not far from the city, where he designed the stables, the spring house or dairy, and other subsidiary buildings; the dairy is still preserved. No documentary evidence of designs for the city house exists, and even views of the house itself leave the matter uncertain. The "English basement" type of plan was always favored by Latrobe whenever he could get his clients to adopt it, and this is the controlling feature of the Harper residence. Then, too, the Greek Doric porch might have been Latrobe's, as well as the subtle relation of the window heights on the front and the general simple dignity of the whole composition. But the cornices, console supported, of the windows of the main floor do not seem to have the character of Latrobe's own work, and the purely hit-or-miss arrangement of the windows in the flank is definitely non-architectural. Latrobe left Baltimore on a long visit to New Orleans in 1819, then departed permanently in the spring of the next year, and the house was not built until after that. Perhaps the answer to the riddle may be that Latrobe made plans for a house for his patron, and that after the architect's removal from the city the house was eventually built from his plans by a builder who departed from them in many ways.

During 1818, aside from the Exchange and the Cathedral, both approaching completion, Baltimore brought Latrobe disappointingly few prospects. With all the greater eagerness, then, did he plunge into another important project of the day—the great scheme for a new Bank of the United States in Philadelphia. He had been seeking this commission from the moment that news of the proposal first reached his ears in 1816. On August 27 of that year he wrote to both Jonathan Smith, the probable future cashier, and William Jones, the probable future president of the bank, asking their aid; the commission, he said, would "enable me to return to Philadelphia, to my earliest & best friends . . ." A few days later (September 5) in a letter to Samuel Hazlehurst he notes that there is a rumor that Girard's Bank and the Bank of the United States will merge and that the existing building which Blodgett had designed for Girard will be the new bank's home. This, he thinks, "will be a great pity, as it is in every possible respect a miserable building. But, as he [Girard] is said to have subscribed 3 million odd dollars of the stock, he may, I presume, do as he pleases . . . What a change from a captain of a schooner for our father . . ." (For Girard had begun his career, it is said, as a sea captain for the firm of Isaac Hazlehurst.)

The architect also wrote about the project (November 16, 1816) to his friend Dallas, who was about to step down from his position as Secretary of the Treasury. Latrobe solicited a letter from Dallas to the new Secretary, and added: "I am also ambitious enough to look to the design of the Bank of the United States, & have actually amused myself with sketching a building from which I hope I may obtain not less reputation than from the Bank of Pennsylvania . . ." Nothing more was heard about the project for nearly a year. Then, in the autumn of 1817, the government bought the necessary land, and Latrobe wrote at once to Philadelphia friends—to George Harrison, for instance (September 7, 1817): "I have just been informed that the U. States Bank have purchased the whole ground opposite to your house, from 6th Street up to Mr. Powells', & from Chestnut Street to Carpenters Alley . . ." and he seeks Harrison's aid in obtaining the commission for the design.

But the bank directors were not to be pushed into any precipitate choice of an architect. Latrobe's qualifications were of course unique; in addition to his over-all professional brilliance, he had had the largest experience in bank design of any single American architect. His appointment must have been seriously considered, but his resignation from the Capitol job had undoubtedly left him under a cloud; the direct appointment of Latrobe would have stirred up a mare's nest. Obviously, too, for such a magnificent building as the Bank of the United States had in mind, the tapping of all the architectural ability in the entire country was desirable; to achieve that only an open competition would serve.

This competition was advertised in the *Philadelphia Gazette* (May 13, 1818) and the *Gazette of the United States* (July 9, 1818), and a large number of the best architects of the country entered it. Competitors were given till August 1—the time was later extended to August 31—to complete and submit their plans. The program was carefully prepared and much more definite than earlier competition programs had been; it called for an area of 10,000 or 11,000 square feet and for entrance porticoes on both Chestnut and Library streets, and it specified that the design must "offer a chaste imitation of Grecian architecture, in its simplest and least expensive form." With the relatively narrow lot at the disposal of the designers, however, certain general resemblances between the basic schemes submitted were unavoidable. Moreover, the entire system of architectural competition as it was conducted in those days was admirably designed to produce controversies and conflicting claims. There was no anonymity. There was no control over the architects to prevent their going directly to the trustees or the bank officials while the contest was under way. There was no professional adviser to whom competitors could send their questions, and no guarantee that all the competitors had the same information on which to work. Under such a loose system bad feeling was almost guaranteed, and accusations of bad faith were inevitable.

For the competition, Latrobe prepared two superb sets of drawings, still preserved.[12] One set was largely the work of John H. B. Latrobe, now at fifteen already an accomplished draftsman. These drawings show many elements that resemble the executed work—so many that Latrobe claimed the scheme was actually his and that William Strickland, who

12. In the Historical Society of Pennsylvania.

was declared the winner of the competition and became the architect of the building, had stolen his ideas.[13]

The facts are complicated and equivocal. Strickland had had an opportunity of seeing Latrobe's scheme and had asked and received permission to submit a new design. But Latrobe also received a similar permission, for his first scheme (of about 15,000 square feet) exceeded the program requirement by nearly 50 per cent and he wished to restudy the whole and reduce it to the limits set by the program. Strickland's new design might have been affected by his knowledge of what Latrobe was planning. Yet, with the narrow lot available, a large banking room midway between the two entrance porches was almost the only possible solution. Similarly, if two competitors chose to use Greek Doric as the order for the porticoes, the choice of the Parthenon as precedent was natural. Thus the final results of these two competitive designs must, in elevation, have much in common.

Actually, then, what differentiates the designs of Strickland and of Latrobe may be of more significance than what is alike in them. Latrobe's first design is basically an enlargement of his earlier Bank of Pennsylvania. It is essentially a three-part composition—a central cubical block containing a circular domed banking hall, with gabled ends that finish at the two streets in eight-columned Parthenon-type porticoes. Its scale is big, and in his enthusiam for the grandeur he thought the bank required Latrobe allowed his scheme to grow—as we have seen—to dimensions half again as great as the program suggested. Even the restudied smaller scheme is based on the same tripartite division that had governed the first.

Strickland's plan, on the other hand, unifies the whole into one continuous temple-shaped mass, and his banking room is a long rectangle (barrel vaulted, with low side aisles like a basilica) which extends all the way across the building. In both schemes the minor rooms are planned between the banking room and the porches, with the more public offices on the Chestnut Street side and the stockholders' room to the south on

---

13. For the most convincing account of the Latrobe claim, see Fiske Kimball, "The Bank of the United States," in *Architectural Record,* vol. LVIII, no. 6 (December, 1925). For a balanced discussion of the question, see Agnes Addison Gilchrist, *William Strickland, Architect and Engineer, 1788-1854* (Philadelphia: University of Pennsylvania Press, 1950), and "Latrobe vs. Strickland," in *Journal of the American Society of Architectural Historians,* vol. II, no. 3 (July, 1942).

Library Street. Here perhaps both designs show the influence of the Bank of Pennsylvania; this had been standing and in use for eighteen years and was well known. Essentially, the chief differences between the two designs lie in the shape of the banking room and in the fact that Latrobe expresses his scheme in a tripartite division of the exterior and Strickland's design is a single unit. This is such a profound difference architecturally that it is impossible to consider the two designs as anything but two entirely different conceptions.

But Latrobe, in turn, had been permitted to see Strickland's first design, and in describing it in a letter to Captain John Meany (September 23, 1818) [14] he wrote that it was in two stories—a Doric basement with an Ionic temple above—and he felt, naturally enough, that Strickland's change to a single-story Doric scheme was the direct result of the younger man's having seen his old teacher's design. Yet Latrobe submitted no official protest to the bank president, William Jones, and Strickland was appointed the bank's architect. Today we can only say that Strickland *did* change his design after seeing Latrobe's, but that the final structure, both in general scheme and in details, is *not* the scheme Latrobe submitted.

The decision as announced (September 12, 1818) in the *Philadelphia Gazette* read: "The Directors of the United States Bank, have selected the plan, drawn by Mr. Strickland, of this city, to whom they have awarded the first premium—and that Mr. Latrobe's plan has been approved as the next best, to whom they have awarded the second premium." [15] One factor in the judgment deserves special notice. The Bank of the United States in its decision in favor of Strickland was approving the more "classic" of the two designs. Its preference for the architect's unified, temple-like mass, as against Latrobe's freer and more expressive—shall we say more architectural?—triple division of the building, is a definite declaration of strict Greek Revival taste, a prophecy of a movement that was destined to sweep the country. And it is this quality that Strickland emphasized in his description of the design printed in the *Port Folio* in September, 1821.[16]

---

14. Reproduced by Fiske Kimball, in *Pennsylvania Magazine of History and Biography,* July, 1943.

15. According to Agnes Addison Gilchrist, *William Strickland* . . . the other known competitors included Robert Mills, Hugh Bridport, and George Hadfield.

16. See Agnes Addison Gilchrist, *William Strickland* . . . pp. 55-7.

Latrobe felt the disappointment keenly. He believed that he had been cheated out of the greatest building project of its date in the United States. It was a doubly bitter blow—personally as well as professionally—because he could not help believing that his ideas had been pilfered by that ebullient and difficult pupil whom of all his draftsmen he had really loved and admired the most.

Thus another door to fame and fortune in the East was closed; Philadelphia had again rejected him. And, as work on the Exchange and on the Cathedral in Baltimore was drawing to a close and no new local commissions were in sight, there remained for him as a means of livelihood only the New Orleans waterworks. In the year since Henry's death the project had been dragging along under the supervision of Mr. Rogers. The number of employees had been cut to a minimum in order to reduce expenses; but the work had nevertheless reached a point so close to completion that Latrobe felt that his presence was imperative, not only to see that all the completed pumps and the engine were properly installed but also to give to the city—which was becoming restive under the delay—an earnest of good intentions. The undertaking was almost at a standstill; only his presence, he thought, could resurrect it—and with it his one remaining prospect of financial security.

There was, however, a matter that clamored for decision before the architect left Baltimore—the question of the future of his talented son John H. B. Latrobe. His precocious talents as a draftsman were notable; the drawings he had made for the United States Capitol in the summer of 1817 and for the Bank of the United States competition in 1818 were those of a skillful and mature delineator. An architectural future was indicated for him—but where to send him for additional education? According to the usual system he would have to be apprenticed to a practicing architect for several years, or, if his present skill raised him above the apprentice level, he would have to enter an architect's office as a draftsman. But any such solution for John was repugnant to his father. What architect was there in the country in whose taste and skill he could confidently trust? Of Bulfinch in Boston he had little definite knowledge; in any case, his appointment as Latrobe's successor in Washington made him an impossible choice. McComb, in New York, was still half contractor, half architect. There were Mills and Strickland, both his own pupils. But Mills!—we have seen how Latrobe distrusted his taste although he admired his rectitude. And Strickland—could such an undependable whirligig as he had proved, Latrobe thought, be a proper master for his son?

Moreover, Latrobe obviously wished for John a training on a higher intellectual level than this mere practical experience would give. He wanted him to be a gentleman as well as an architect, an artist with a scientific as well as an imaginative background. John had followed his brother Henry into St. Mary's College in Baltimore when the family moved there in January, 1818; but, good as the college was in purely academic subjects, it was no place for a technical education. There was, in those days, but one school in the country where engineering was taught on a high plane—the Military Academy at West Point. And graduation from there would not only guarantee John's social standing but also provide him with a road, if he wished to follow it, to permanent financial security. On all accounts it offered what seemed the perfect solution, both as social preparation and as professional training; it was, Latrobe felt, the ideal approach to architecture.

It would not be difficult to get John the appointment. His technical skills and intellectual precocity were well known, and Latrobe had good friends to help. In August, 1818, John had ended his collegiate career in Baltimore in a blaze of glory, acting the part of Phasaer in Mme de Genlis's *Joseph* and at the end reciting an epilogue written by his father.[17] A month later he left for West Point and entered the Academy. He traveled alone from Baltimore to Clover Hill, then across New Jersey to visit his sister Lydia and her husband, and finally up the Hudson from New York to West Point.

With this problem at last settled, there was little more to hold Latrobe in Baltimore, and in the early winter he took ship for New Orleans.

---

17. Given in Benjamin Henry Boneval Latrobe, *Impressions Respecting New Orleans,* edited with an introduction and notes by Samuel Wilson, Jr. (New York: Columbia University Press, 1951), pp. 108f.

CHAPTER

21

New Orleans: The End

In mid-December, 1818, Latrobe embarked on the brig *Clio,* Captain Wynne, for New Orleans. With him, as one of the passengers, went Elias McMillan, who had been engaged as engine-keeper for the waterworks. The steam engine itself had arrived in Baltimore from New York, but it was too big to be loaded on the little brig and had to be sent on later; actually it had to wait in storage nearly a year.

The *Clio* sailed on December 18. To Latrobe the voyage, in general a pleasant one, was doubly welcome. He liked sea travel; boats and seamanship and navigation always fascinated him and, though he had a bout of seasickness, he found leisure—so rare and so precious in his usually harried life—to rest, to write extensively in his journal, and to fill his sketchbooks with pictures of ships and the ocean and life at sea. Besides Latrobe and McMillan, the passengers included an American merchant, one Gibbon of Petersburg; Samuel Wilson, a mercantile agent from England; a New Orleans shipbuilder named Burton; a young Mr. Reis; and a Dr. Day, who had a dozen slaves along in the steerage and was going out to raise cotton on the Red River. The variety of background and occupation made for interesting talk, and Captain Wynne was not only a good seaman but a genial host.

Their course took them southeast running before a northwest wind, out across the Gulf Stream, then south to the latitude of the Bahamas. On December 22 the sea was amazingly quiet; they were almost becalmed, and a large school of porpoises played round them. Then toward evening a heavy squall introduced a gale from the west, northwest, and north, before which—generally under reefed maintopsail and foresail—they rushed plunging south, except for part of the second day, when because of the breaking sea the captain hove the ship to, under staysails alone. All that night, as Latrobe says, she "rode it out, like a duck." He made two sketches of the storm—one, extraordinarily convincing, of the look of the sea and sky just before the gale struck; the other of the brig scudding ahead in the worst of it. The second is perhaps more conventional in spirit and less impeccably observed, but it is full of dynamic power; it has the sense of drive.

On Christmas the gale moderated rapidly; the passengers, all newly shaven in honor of the day, Latrobe notes, found the "wind gentle, & as I judge from my feelings, temperature about 70°." The next day was equally pleasant; they were getting south, and he remarks on the almost Italian brilliance of the sky over the ocean. Two days later the fact that it was the captain's birthday was the excuse for more celebration—hot rolls, fresh pork (they killed a hog), apple pies, "and a great variety of similar demonstrations of affection." On December 28 they laid their course due west for the Bahamas, and Latrobe got up at first dawn to sight the new land; but so magnificent did he find the starry sky, so brilliant the coming of day, so exciting the final rising of the sun above the horizon that instead of waiting he went below to write a long paragraph dealing with the effect of sun worship on religion.

At eight o'clock Eleuthera was sighted from the maintop; by noon they were drawing in to the southern end of Abaco; in early evening they passed through the strait between the two islands while it was still light, and Latrobe made a brilliant sketch of the extraordinary natural bridge—the Hole in the Wall—at the very end of Abaco Island. He took the occasion, too, during the fascinating cruise down east of the Berry Islands and across the Bahama Banks (December 29 and 30) to make a copy of the ship's chart and carefully mark upon it the *Clio's* course—by which he discovered that in crossing the Gulf Stream they had been set some sixty miles to the north and east of their dead-reckoning position. On the thirtieth they were saddened by the death of a Negro slave, Tom, who was being taken by his owner, a slave dealer named Anderson, to New Orleans for sale. Latrobe himself read the burial service as the body was given to the ocean when they passed from the shallow water of the Bahama Banks to the deeps of Florida Strait.

They skirted the Florida Keys closely to avoid the full strength of the Gulf Stream and by the evening of New Year's Day, 1819, had passed Tortugas and set their course for the Mississippi; but two days of rain and a changeable wind with a heavy sea delayed them, and it was noon of January 5 before they had taken a pilot and crossed the Mississippi bar. It took them five more days to traverse the long 100-mile stretch from Southeast Pass to New Orleans; at one point crew and passengers got ashore to "track"—to help tow the vessel against the current and around "English Bend."

On the morning of January 10 Latrobe awoke to find himself at last arrived; the ship was anchored off the levee, but the fog was so thick that not a trace of the shore could be seen. Instead there came through the murk the noise and hum of the city—"a more incessant, loud, rapid, & various gabble of tongues of all tones than was ever heard at Babel"—a sound, he thought, that could only be likened to what comes from an extensive marsh crowded with frogs of all kinds, "from bull frogs up to whistlers . . ." Little by little, as the morning advanced, the fog cleared and the levee, the ranked ships along it, the low tiled-roof houses, and the thronged market became distinguishable. The brig was warped in to join the line of masts along the levee, and Latrobe's new life in New Orleans began.

Once again, as in Virginia twenty-three years earlier, Latrobe was enthralled with his new environment. Again he was all alert to the new sights, the new sounds, the new ways of living, and his journals for those months [1] give perhaps the most graphic picture we have of the booming New Orleans of that time. To read them is to be there—in the markets, the streets, the hotels and taverns, at the balls and theaters—and to be there in the company of a guide with keen eyes, an inquiring mind, and that special skepticism which maturity often brings. For it is more than the appearances and sounds that he gives us; Latrobe's twenty-three American years had made him keenly aware of the cross currents that eddied through American life. Here was a new kind of America to study. New Orleans seemed, indeed, a symbol of the inclusiveness of the young country, for here were gathered in close chemical interaction the three peoples who had played the chief part in settling this American continent—the

1. Printed complete in Benjamin Henry Boneval Latrobe, *Impressions Respecting New Orleans,* edited with an introduction and notes by Samuel Wilson, Jr. (New York: Columbia University Press, 1951). This chapter is based largely on Latrobe's journals as reprinted in the book, and I have also borrowed heavily from Mr. Wilson's enlightening footnotes. Those who wish a more detailed account will enjoy reading this volume *in toto,* and those interested in Latrobe's sketches will find in it the best reproductions of them that have ever been published.

English, the French, the Spanish. And more besides, for the great river that rolled irresistibly past the city flowed through large areas that were still Indian country, so that many Indians were then part of the New Orleans panorama. The growing wealth of the city, particularly its cotton and its sugar, had also brought settlers and adventurers from Scotland, England, and Germany. New Orleans was at that period the American melting pot as no other city in the country could have been.

And this southern metropolis had another quality that gave it a special character. Here the Anglo-Saxon Americans were the newest 'immigrants," the most recent colonists, almost the intruders, in a city with half a century of French tradition behind it. But already, in 1819, they formed the largest single group; and, as the cotton trade, the Mississippi commerce, and the black soil so fitted for cotton and sugar growing on slave-cultivated plantations drew in daily more and more plantation owners from the Old South and attracted business and professional men from the North, they were becoming increasingly dominant in all the fields of New Orleans life except society and the arts. How would these old and new groups, with backgrounds so various, religions so different, and aims so diverse, interact? What would develop from these cultural conflicts? The city was full of fascinating problems for one with the curiosities and the sensitive vision that Latrobe possessed; all of them crop up for perceptive comment in his journals.

Of course he had a number of acquaintances in the city, yet he was now alone as he had not been for years. At the beginning of his stay he had few intimate friends, and his social engagements were rare enough to leave him extensive evening leisure to think, to read, to write. Moreover, he had come to New Orleans with just one major purpose—to expedite the completion of the waterworks—and when the daily chores were over his mind was free from extraneous worries. Until several months had passed and he had begun to receive new architectural commissions, there was plenty of time for him to set down in his journals almost everything he saw and much of what he thought, as well as to fill his sketchbooks with vivid visual impressions.

The first few weeks he spent in getting adjusted and learning what New Orleans looked like. He walked up and down the market by the levee and sketched the market people—white, colored, and Indian, with their strange costumes, their hooded blanket coats, their occasional slim Empire dresses—or the sailors with broad-brimmed straw hats, striped

Photograph Blakeslee-Lane,
courtesy Mrs. Ferdinand C. Latrobe

PLATE 33

Benjamin Henry Latrobe, *circa* 1800. Portrait by Charles Willson Peale.

Benjamin Henry Latrobe, *circa* 1816. Portrait attributed to Rembrandt Peale.

Courtesy Peale Museum and Avery Library

Front elevation.
Historical Society of Pennsylvania

PLATE 34
Second Bank of the United States, Philadelphia. Latrobe's competition design

Side elevation.

Historical Society of Penns

Section.
Historical Society of Pennsylvania

J. Tanesse, *Plan of the City and Suburbs of New Orleans . . . 1815*

oms House, New Orleans. B. H. Latrobe, archi-

J. Tanesse, *Plan of the City and Suburbs of New Orleans . . . 1815*

Pumping Station, Waterworks, New Orleans. Henry Latrobe, architect.

PLATE 35

e for Suction Pipe, Waterworks, New Orleans. Latrobe's working design.

Courtesy Samuel Wilson, Jr.

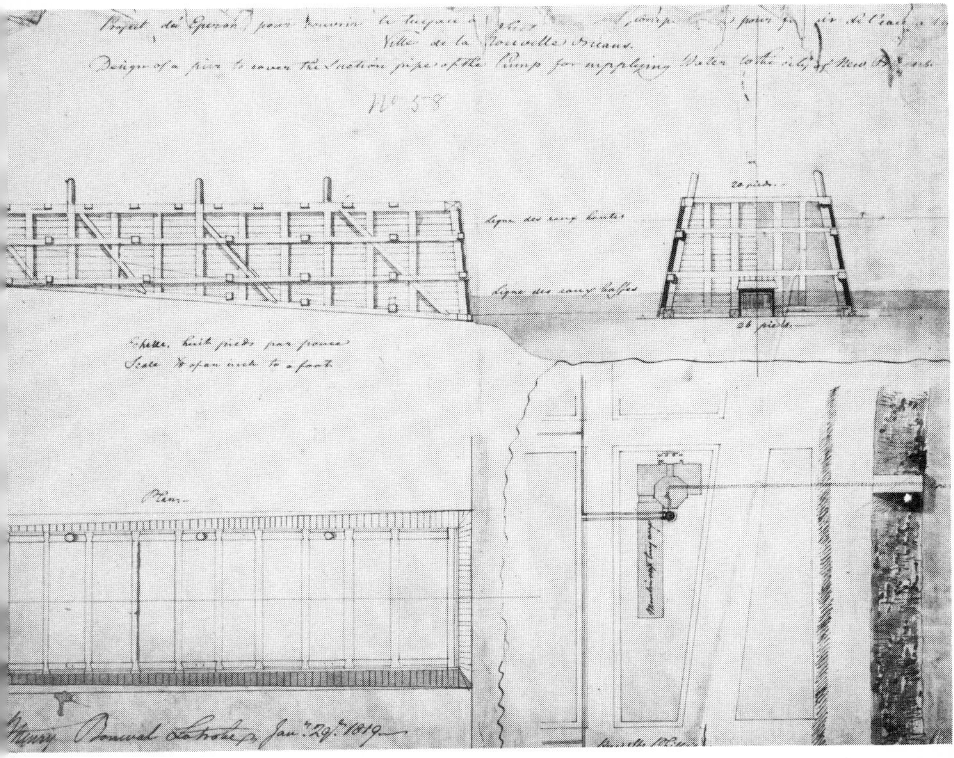

New York Public Library

Cathedral of St. Louis, New Orleans. B. H. Latrobe, architect for the central tower. Drawing by T. K. Wharton, 1845.

PLATE 36

State Bank of Louisiana, New Orleans. B. H. Latrobe, architect.

Photograph Rudolf Hertzberg

Maryland Historical Society

Thomas Jefferson. Pencil portrait by B. H. Latrobe.

View on the Passaic River, New Jersey. Water color. Latrobe Sketchboo

On the Road from Newark to Paterson, New Jersey. Water color. Latrobe Sketchboo

PLATE 38. Characteristic Latrobe Landscapes

New Jersey Roadside. Pen, pencil, and wash. Latrobe Sketchboo

Latrobe Sketchbooks

eakfast on Board the *Eliza,* 1796. Water color.

vo Landscapes and the Face of Washington. Water color.

Latrobe Sketchbooks

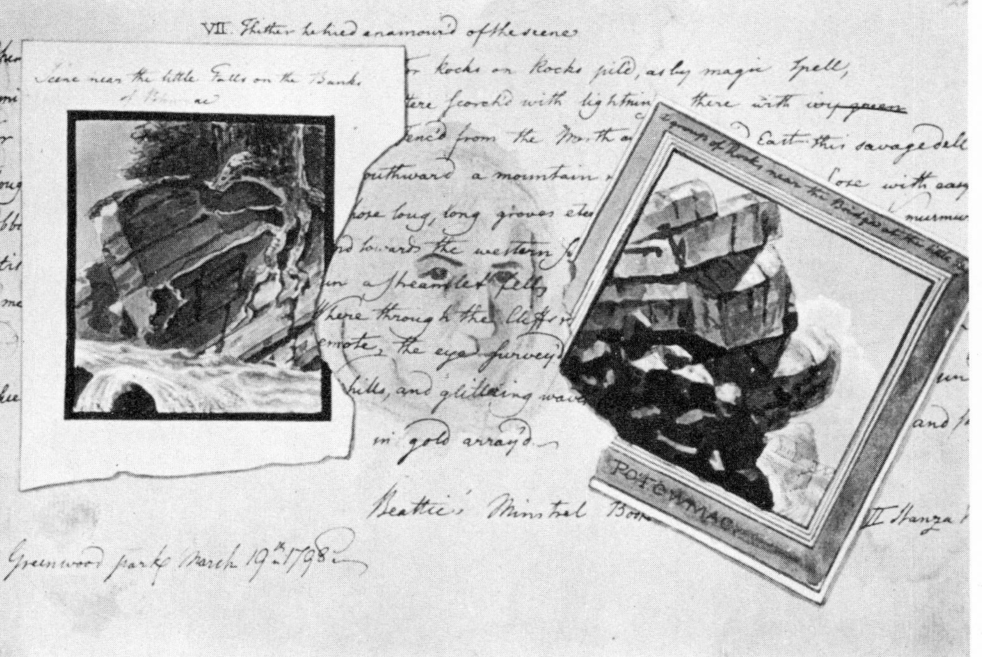

Engine for the Navy Yard, Washington. Latrobe's plan and elevation.

Library of Cong

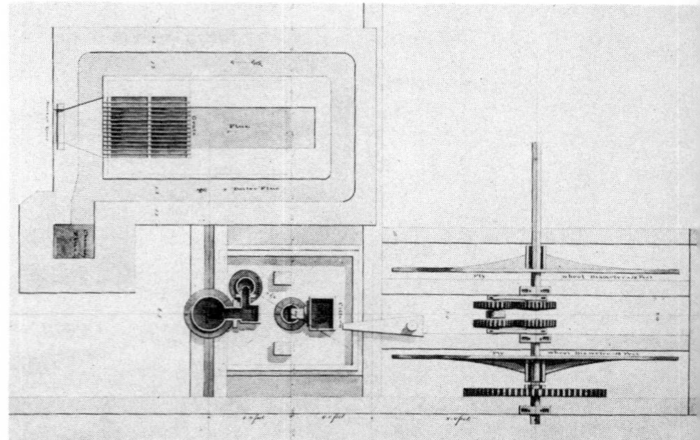

PLATE 40

Washington Canal, Washington. Latrobe's details of a lock.

Library of Congress

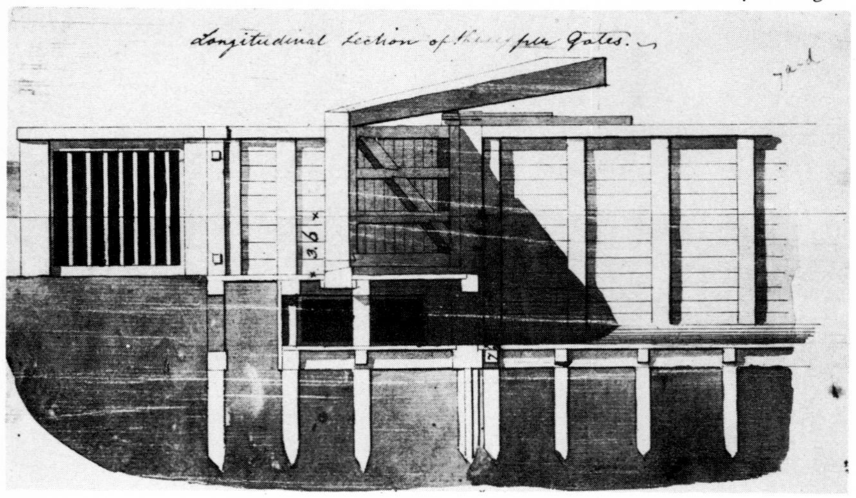

shirts, and close-cut trousers. Even booksellers, he noted, had their places in the market, and their wares—both French and English—"cut no mean appearance." He admired the wide sweep of the public square—the Place d'Armes, with its impressive trio of buildings at the end—the Cabildo (which he called the "Principal"), the Cathedral, and the Presbytère (which he anglicized to Presbytery). Putting up at the Tremoulet hotel, on the square and the levee, he drew its plan, described it at length, and painted a graphic view of the levee in front of it with the crowded masts and the lace of rigging atop the ranked ships. He comments (January 14, 1819): "The growing Americanism of this city is strongly evidenced by the circumstance that Tremoulet's is the only French boarding house in the city, that it is unfashionable, & when he [Tremoulet] removes, for he is going to Havanna, there will be no other opened." But a month later Latrobe found a strong reason for leaving Tremoulet's that had nothing to do with the innkeeper's plans—the shocking cruelty of Mme Tremoulet's treatment of her slaves. This "termagant," as he calls her, he discovered was notorious in the city for her brutality to her servants, and on February 24 he tells of the beating given her best slave, Sophie, because she could not keep up to an impossible schedule—a beating by Mme Tremoulet herself (with her daughter looking on) and then by another slave, Guillaume, until Sophie fainted. "The scene made a noise in the house," Latrobe writes, "& the blood betrayed it. Poor Sophie is ill, & constantly crying. I shall leave the house as soon as convenient to me." Shortly afterward he moved and took lodgings with a Mrs. Kennedy.

This occurrence led him on to write of other instances of similar cruelties—all, it would seem, committed by women—and the memory of those sadistic happenings spoiled, he says, his enjoyment of the great Washington's Birthday ball:

I fancied that I saw a cowskin in every pretty hand gracefully waved in the dance; and admired the comparative awkwardness of look & motion of my countrywomen, whose arms had never been rendered pliant by the exercise of the whip upon the bound and screaming slave. Whatever therefore this community may lose in taste & elegance, & exterior suavity, & acquire of serious & awkward bluntness, & commercial stiffness—may the change be as rapid as possible, if at the same time active humanity is introduced into the deplorable system of slavery which I fear must long, perhaps forever, prevail in this state . . .

Such thoughts forced him the next day to obtain and to study "The Black Code," which was supposed to govern master-slave relations in Louisiana. The code itself, with the exception of a few sections dealing with runaways, was more humane than he had expected, but his keen mind pierced at once to the basic impossibility of enforcing it (February 25):

> But no law of this kind can be fully enforced; the slave cannot possibly be acquainted with all its provisions in his favour . . . & if he fully understood them, the very clause that prohibits his absence from the plantation without a permission from his Master, forecloses his appeal . . . If what Goldsmith says in his Traveler,
>
> "Of all the evils mortal men endure
> How small the number Laws can cause or cure,"
>
> be true among free & equal citizens, how much truer must it be among Masters & Slaves, with whom the appeal to them is almost entirely on one side.

Latrobe was especially interested in the gradual changes in New Orleans life which the influx of Americans was bringing about. With his international background and his own sense of artistic refinement, he could not be blind to the exquisite manners—the gentilities—of the best French society in New Orleans; nor, on the other hand, could he be oblivious of the driving dynamism of the newer American population. Quite early in his stay (January 25) he was troubled by the contrast:

> What is good & bad in the French manners, & opinions must give way, & the American notions of right & wrong, of convenience & inconvenience will take their place.
>
> When this period arrives, it would be folly to say that things are better or worse than they now are. They will be changed, but they will be changed into what is more agreeable to the new population than what now exists. But a man who fancies that he has seen the world on more sides than one cannot help wishing that a *mean,* an *average* character, of society may grow out of the intermixture of the French & American manners.
>
> Such a consummation is perhaps to be more devoutly wished than hoped for . . .

He mentions the diametrically opposed manner in which the French and the Americans observe Sunday, and goes on:

In how far the intermarriage of Americans with French girls will produce a less rigid observation of the gloom of an English Sunday, it is impossible to foresee. For some time an effect will be produced; for I have spent Sunday in a family in which a ci-devant Quaker, and a Presbyterian, who have married two sisters, joined in a very agreeable dance after a little concert.

But the Protestant clergy, he continues, were united in attacking the free gaiety of the French Sunday in New Orleans; soon, he suspects, "Sundays will become as gloomy & ennuyant as elsewhere among us."

Later he notes a similar development in architecture. This comment (February 19) came at the end of a succinct account of New Orleans building ways and short criticisms of the most important buildings. American merchants, he says,

have already begun to introduce the detestable, lop-sided, London house, in which a common passage & stairs acts as a common sewer to all the necessities of the dwelling . . . [and the usual red-brick fronts of the north are rapidly] gaining ground, & the suburb of St. Mary, the American suburb, already exhibits the flat, dingey character of Market Street, in Philadelphia, or Baltimore Street, instead of the motley & picturesque effect of the stuccoed French buildings of the city. We shall introduce many grand & profitable improvements, but they will take the place of much elegance, ease, & some convenience.[2]

Naturally the architect visited the scene of the Battle of New Orleans, where Henry had distinguished himself and where the danger of foreign invasion had been scotched for a century. He was first taken out to it in February by Vincent Nolte,[3] whose close friend he had become and

---

2. As matters proved, however, the French and regional character of the architecture of New Orleans had more tenacity than he counted on. The soil, the climate, and the general pace of life soon convinced the newly arrived Americans that no mere copying of the plans and appearance of northern homes could be a proper environment for them here, and gradually a new vernacular developed, entirely regional in its character and in surprising harmony with the earlier French structures.

3. Vincent Nolte, fifteen years younger than Latrobe, was the New Orleans agent of the Parish family of New York, Philadelphia, and Baltimore, and indirectly of the great firm of Henry Hope of Amsterdam, one of the world's largest international bankers. Born in Leghorn and brought up to speak English, Italian, and French more than German, his father's native tongue, he had come to New Orleans in 1806 to further a fantastic and largely successful scheme by means of which Napoleon could get the use of the vast Spanish treasures in Mexico despite the American embargo and English control of the ocean. He had become an American citizen and was a large dealer in cotton and one of

who had been a fellow soldier with Henry in the battle. On his return home Latrobe not only described the scene but drew a careful plan that showed the old redoubt at the Mississippi bank, the ruins of the battery that his son had designed and built, and the line of the long entrenchment facing a broad field. Up this field—without a shelter—Pakenham's seasoned troops marched in close order against the withering fire of the Americans under General Andrew Jackson, only to fall in windrows in one of the most decisive defeats ever suffered by British regulars. In his sketchbook, Latrobe made a graphic pencil sketch showing the situation, carefully noting the colors and textures as if to make a finished water color from it; but time evidently pressed and the water color was never made.

He was interested, too, in the religious politics of New Orleans. His old friend Father William Dubourg, formerly the Sulpician head of St. Mary's College in Baltimore, had been appointed Administrator Apostolic of the Roman Catholic district of Louisiana in 1812 and later had been made Bishop; but almost at once he got into a serious controversy with Father Antoine (the Capuchin Fra Francis Antonio Ildefonso Moreno y Arze de Sedella), who was the chief preacher in the Cathedral. The natives of New Orleans rallied around the beloved Friar, and twice when Dubourg attempted to preach his words were drowned out by sneezing, coughing, foot-scraping, and confusion. Father Antoine was suspended, and during the Battle of New Orleans Abbé Dubourg gained a temporary popularity by leading the women of the city and the Ursuline nuns in prayers for victory during the battle and later organizing a religious parade into the Cathedral, where a Te Deum service was sung in thanksgiving for the victory. This popular approval was short-lived, however, and in 1819 Father Antoine still refused to accept Dubourg's authority. The parish was in an anomalous state; its services went on as usual, and Father Antoine continued to serve despite his official removal. Dubourg and his superior, Archbishop Marischal of Baltimore, feeling

---

the leading merchants of the city. In 1822 he left New Orleans and spent the rest of his life, with gradually decaying fortunes, in Europe, especially in Trieste. He left a fascinating if often incorrect autobiography, *Fifty Years in Both Hemispheres,* written in German but first published in an English translation in New York in 1854; it served as the basis for much of Hervey Allen's *Anthony Adverse.* Nolte was an interesting, vital person with an acquisitive mind and an extraordinary background, and it tells something of both men that Latrobe and he seemed quickly to have formed an intimate friendship.

that the problem was insoluble, took the wise course of doing nothing; then Bishop Dubourg went up the Mississippi to St. Louis, which he made his headquarters and where he established his cathedral. Latrobe tells the story with verve; he is doubly interested because of his old friendship for Dubourg and because it was such a significant expression of the cross currents of power—French, Spanish, and American—which ran through the community.

In the journals there are many notes on the Indians. Latrobe, like so many of his compatriots then and later, was deeply puzzled by the problem they presented. He was aware of their virtues, but he was also conscious of their faults. In many ways his attitude seems to have been colored by the views his early friend Volney had expressed in his *Tableau du climat et du sol des États-unis d'Amérique* (referred to in Chapter 5), a book for which Latrobe had a boundless admiration. He comes back to the problem several times. For example (March 9, 1819), he discusses Indian courage before torture or inevitable death and compares it unfavorably with that shown by a Freemason, Ley—tortured by the Inquisition in Spain—since Ley had the alternative of avoiding the torture, but there was no alternative whatsoever in the case of the Indians. He was especially incensed by the romanticizing of the Indians by Chateaubriand—"the disgrace of eloquence and of talents," as Latrobe describes him—and by the Americans who were following his lead. Latrobe knew the Indians' cruelty; he had, he confessed, a family prejudice that dated back to the Indian massacres of Moravian colonies during the French and Indian War. In an attempt to sum up the question (March 6, 1819) he lists the Indian virtues in general: courage, hospitality, love of truth, love of freedom, and—in the case of the Choctaws at least—chastity and honesty; on the other side he places their chief faults: ferocity, cruelty to their captives, idleness and common theft, and ill treatment of their women. He points out that hospitality exists everywhere where food cannot be bought or sold and concludes with a sweeping assertion that "the sum of human happiness would be greater in the *same* space if the Indians did not exist." Apparently he was completely blind to the cruelties and ferocities—on the part of the whites—which would inevitably result when the country as a whole adopted the same notion.

The state of the fine arts in New Orleans was perhaps Latrobe's chief interest. Besides his architectural comments, some of which have already been cited, he showed his curiosity about the pageantry of funerals, noted the lack of good music in the Cathedral, was intrigued by the singing, playing, and dancing of the Negroes, especially on their Sunday holidays, and carefully observed and sketched their homemade instruments—one of which, a guitar-like example with a crude carved figure of a sitting man at the end of the fingerboard, he thought must have been imported from Africa. He went to the theater. Here in New Orleans the great French classics of Molière and Racine often held the stage; they stimulated him to ponder the entire relationship of realism and make-believe in dramatic productions, as well as the necessity (perhaps best satisfied by verse) of getting the audience to accept a major convention at the very start in order that they may later accept the entire fabric of the drama. He even examined afresh the problems of French dramatic verse writing and noted the extreme freedoms in rhyme that Molière allowed himself when he was writing informal conversations.

While he was in New Orleans, a certain local woman painter, Mme Plantou, put on exhibition a large allegorical picture, "The Peace of Ghent." [4] It was popularly admired, and it is indeed a remarkably polished composition of great complexity, carried out with considerable finesse; parts of it, Latrobe notes, "have very extraordinary merit." Yet it left him cold. It was full of Greek gods and goddesses, personified countries, classic architecture, and classic costume. Its message—the triumph of America over England—could only be understood by those with a comprehensive knowledge of classic mythology, and the architect is forced to the conclusion that "an allegorical picture stands as much in need of an interpreter as an Indian talk." But even that does not suffice him; he analyzes the whole question of allegory in contemporary art and finds it an extremely difficult field, where only the simplest symbolisms are possible. As an example he cites an occasion when Dr. Thornton at a large party had described the allegorical group of sculpture he wanted to have erected in the center of the Capitol in Washington. Latrobe, who was present, immediately gave what he thought the group as described would mean to someone coming upon it without prior knowledge; of course he found in it a meaning quite different from what Thornton had intended—a meaning much closer to ordinary life. And the entire party, Latrobe says, broke into laughter at Dr. Thornton's expense.

---

4. An engraving from it is reproduced in *Impressions Respecting New Orleans.*

But perhaps the greatest value of the copious notes which poured from Latrobe's pen as he sat at his desk in New Orleans lies in the fact that they allow us to see deep into the inmost recesses of his feelings about life and about religion. Humanist that he was, he was always deeply religious and intensely curious about religious customs and usages. His thorough Moravian education had given his mind a basic direction it never lost. And religion in New Orleans was a fascinating spectacle in which a traditional Catholicism—freighted with local peculiarities—was challenged by the dominant Protestantism of the growing American population. In the beginning, it seems, Latrobe was slightly shocked by the purely secular character of a New Orleans Sunday; his background, his training, and his membership in the Episcopal Church all seemed to put him on the "American" side of the controversy. But then he began to think of the historical reasons behind the growing Protestant intolerance. Recoil from the excesses of the French Revolution was the principal motive force, but, as he says (January 25, 1819):

> The holy alliance, of Greek, Roman, Lutheran, & Calvanistic sovereigns, who before the battle of Waterloo, most piously consigned each other, as far as religious belief went, to eternal damnation, has given authority of high effect to this fashion. For my part, the effect of this impious farce upon my own mind is to make me retire, with the more humility into my own heart & seek there a temple, unprofaned by external dictation.

He is forced by this line of thought to go farther—and here again he proves himself a son of the Enlightenment and even a predecessor of Pragmatism: "How wonderfully the whole course of human events would be changed if everything were considered as of *no* importance that has not an operative effect." As dreadful examples of the contrary opinion he cites all sorts of schisms which had arisen in churches he knew because of minor or even meaningless innovations, such as the introduction of an organ or the adoption of the Isaac Watt version of the Psalms.

He goes back over his own experience (February 28) to examine the roots of his own beliefs. When he was sixteen he heard a sermon at Nimtoch, in Silesia, on "Indifferentism," in which the preacher claimed that passionate belief, however heretical, was more praiseworthy than what he called the great modern heresy—soul-destroying indifferentism. The sermon made a profound impression on the young Latrobe. He notes that one of his best friends at that time was an ex-Jesuit, ostensibly a Catholic but actually a confirmed deist. Since then the architect had been much troubled by the sermon, but further knowledge and experience had only confirmed his original deistic, indifferentist concepts.

"It is singular," he writes (February 28), "that we Christians have cut so many throats, reciprocally, about doctrines, & prayers, & creeds . . . I know of no church that professes the true *Christian indifferentism* in the pulpit excepting the American Episcopal Church. . . . I therefore in professing myself a member of that church, claim connection with it chiefly on account of the liberality of its practise." And the next day he adds a note about the growing tolerance in New Orleans; a new Presbyterian church was being built, and the congregation had applied for a contribution from the city council. "These heretics would have been burned a few years ago," he remarks, "& would run some risk now, had Ferdinand the Beloved still possession of the place."

A week later (March 7) he adds a significant note about an address made years earlier by a certain Dr. Watson, Bishop of Landaff. The address—in a clipping he had preserved—stated that Christianity was "not a speculative business" and that salvation could not depend upon what other people had decided. Latrobe adds his own statement: "It would be indeed a monstrous belief that happiness after this life could depend on any decision of the Doctors of the Sorbonne, Louvain, Salamanca, or even of Oxford."

He brings the same quiet rationalism to the problem of burial. The cemeteries of New Orleans, with their aboveground tombs, were striking features in the city. What was their meaning? How could any good cause—now or hereafter—be served by this preservation of the body after death? He points out the irrationality of the "Christian" belief; surely, to Omnipotence, resurrection of the body would come as easily from ashes as from burial decay and skeletons. And—again ahead of his time—he brings forward the tremendous advantages of cremation. From every rational point of view—the health of cities and the value of open spaces in them—burning would be better than burial. Emotionally too, he felt, the preservation of the ashes in urns would be vastly superior to the cult of cemeteries.

With the development of such opinions on religious dogmas and practices, it was inevitable that Latrobe's attitude toward Sunday observance should change. He notes the change (February 21, 1819) and says it was speeded by a conversation with Thomas Urquhart, an old inhabitant and the president of the Louisiana Bank.[5] "The Sabbath is made for man, and not man for the Sabbath," Christ said, and Latrobe can find no justification anywhere in the Bible for the strictness of the usual Protestant custom. Recreation, per se, is not evil. The slaves especially need the recreation that Sunday permits them. And a certain amount of necessary work is unavoidable. From any sympathetic, human point of view, Latrobe finds, there is much to be said for the freest possible enjoyment of the one leisure day of the week.

As winter wore into spring, the architect's business increased, and in the summer his journal was set aside. At the waterworks the old wooden pipes that had been accumulated by Henry and left to dry out were by now almost all rotted and unusable, for water in them was their only means of preservation. Latrobe had foreseen this possibility and had brought with him a pipe-boring machine, which had to be erected on a firm foundation and set to work. This boring machine was set up in a new long narrow wing which was added to the original engine house that Henry had built—an octagonal building on the levee at a spot that was later included in the French market; it faced downstream and was entered through a four-columned portico, flanked by low wings for offices and the engine-keeper's quarters. The building of the pipe mill and the installation of the engine itself, which finally arrived from Baltimore late in March, kept Latrobe extremely busy all through the summer. Now, with the engine almost completely installed, the future of the waterworks at last looked bright.

But there was another problem on his mind—the Mississippi lighthouse. He had made the original design for it in 1805 and 1806; this design had been revised by Henry in 1816, and on that basis construction had started. Latrobe was asked to inspect the work, for rumors had reached Washington of bad cracks and unequal settlement in it. He made the trip from New Orleans on the steamboat *Alabama,* leaving on April 10 and returning on April 14, 1819. On the way they stopped at the Balize (the old pilot town near the Mississippi mouth), of which the architect had made a striking water color on his arrival in January. Across the river from it and up a short bayou was Franks Island. the

5. The Louisiana Bank was a totally different organization from the Louisiana State Bank, for which Latrobe was to design a new building in the following year.

site of the lighthouse. Latrobe made a plan of the site. The foundation of the lighthouse was complete, and he found the island covered with temporary buildings; but, noting also that the shores—five or six feet high—were subject to erosion by the surf, he recommended the piling of the entire perimeter as well as the construction of a suitable wharf.[6]

A more important commission also came in the late spring—the design of the central façade tower of the Cathedral. Two architects—Latrobe and Buisson—had prepared designs, and Latrobe was awarded the commission on May 29, 1819. The committee noted that the architect would make no contract but would supervise and direct the work for a 10 per cent commission. Later, however, because of difficulty in getting proposals from building contractors, he was forced to serve in that capacity himself.[7] The chief reason for Latrobe's receiving the job, as noted in the council action, was that "the steeple represented on his drawings harmonizes perfectly with the kind of architecture according to which the parish church was built." This must have been to him a welcome vindication of his architectural taste and tact.[8]

By the end of September Latrobe felt that he had accomplished all he could on this first visit to the city. He came to the conclusion, too, that his immediate future lay no longer in Baltimore or Philadelphia but in New Orleans. Here he had been welcomed by the best and the most powerful, here almost for the first time his international background could have its freest expression. The Cathedral tower, he believed, was but the beginning of a busy practice which the growth of the city would give him. Before he left, therefore, he bought a house, paying half the price down, with the rest on mortgage. The house was small, but it had a delightful and well-planted garden and yard; it was conveniently situated, too—close to the river bank and a mile and a half south of the bustling market. These arrangements made, he took passage north on the brig *Emma* for New York, sailing on September 19 at noon. Captain

6. The complete report, now in the Records of the U.S. Coast Guard in the National Archives, is given as Appendix A in *Impressions Respecting New Orleans.*

7. Did this difficulty possibly arise because Latrobe was still considered an outsider? See *Impressions Respecting New Orleans,* p. 164, note.

8. Latrobe's central tower consisted of a cubical belfry stage, cornice crowned, carrying a tall slim cylindrical element pierced with round-arched openings, and the whole was capped by a spire to harmonize with the caps of the two flanking turrets. The present façade is from a rebuilding of a much later date.

Bartlett Shepard was in command, and there were but two other passengers.

Again the voyage was an agreeable one—"never," writes Latrobe, "for 12 hours together so rough as to have rendered it unpleasant to write, draw or read." Yet he seemed profoundly tired; perhaps the hot, damp summer weather of New Orleans had sapped his energy. In all the three weeks of the trip he made but two extensive notes. These have a kind of minatory significance, as though his unconscious intuition was already aware of the dangers as well as the opportunities awaiting him in the South; the notes deal with mosquitoes (September 29) and with yellow fever (October 7). Latrobe had carefully observed the mosquitoes; he identifies four different types, including the deadly species with the striped legs (though he was not fully aware of their deadliness), notes how mosquitoes breed in standing water even withindoors, and describes the mosquito nets in use—including one that would completely surround a writing table and chair. But he sees the insects more as a nuisance than as a scourge. Of yellow fever he is respectful but unafraid. He notes that most of his workmen on the waterworks had been attacked—some mildly, some severely—and says: "The sober lived; the drunken died with few exceptions." Even Dr. Rice, whom he had engaged to care for his employees, had a slight attack. But, as the journal states, there were many recoveries, though the treatment given by different physicians varied. Latrobe had already seen yellow fever carry away his former partner, Robert Alexander, and his dear son Henry. Was he consciously exorcizing a real dread in thus emphasizing the cases that recovered?

The *Emma* beat in past Sandy Hook on October 10, anchored overnight in Sandy Hook Bay, and on the eleventh sailed up to Quarantine. There the architect received permission to land; he set out immediately for Philadelphia and Baltimore, where he arrived on the fourteenth. He remained in Baltimore till the first days of December, winding up his affairs there and making drawings "for every possible want of the Exchange & Cathedral." Meanwhile the family started packing up, for their departure was imminent. Latrobe had decided that the best and cheapest way to go was to travel overland to Wheeling in the late winter and thus be ready for the first steamboat down the river in the spring.

But before they left there were friends and relatives to see and to bid farewell, and the family all went off to the north, arriving at hospitable

Clover Hill on December 5. There Mary and Julia remained, while B. H. Latrobe and his son Ben proceeded to New York and to West Point. Arriving in the metropolis on the eighth, they spent but one day in the city and were at the Military Academy on the tenth. During their short stay at West Point, John had the pleasure of seeing his father captivate the professors and his own classmates with his brilliant talk, wide knowledge, and wit;[9] it left the son in a glow. And the architect had the equal pleasure of finding his son well, happy, liked, and standing high in his class. As Latrobe stood looking out over the Hudson and the tumbled precipitous hills through which at that point it has carved its winding course, he thought of the whole picture of the past as Volney and he had imagined it—the wonderful way in which the hills had been rounded and the river valley cleaved through them. The magnificent view impressed him deeply and he tried, that evening, to set his vision down in verse—some of the most compelling he had ever written.[10] It was a memorable two days.

From West Point Ben and his father returned to New York, where they lingered more than a week; here they had the opportunity of seeing again their beloved Lydia and her mercurial husband, Nicholas Roosevelt. This was a great delight to the senior Latrobe, but what chiefly held him was business in connection with the New Orleans waterworks—probably conferences with the Marks and the settling of their complicated accounts, besides last arrangements with Robert McQueen, the engine builder. The business done, father and son left New York on December 21 for Clover Hill, and the architect went to Philadelphia briefly (till the twenty-seventh) to see a number of his old friends there. It must have been a moving visit—Philadelphia, the scene of his first successes, of his happy marriage, of such great hopes and expectations—Philadelphia, the home of his best friends, yet the city that found nothing for him to do, that had almost cast him out. Now he was saying good-by to it for a long time to come. As he saw again the handsome pump house he had designed for Centre Square and passed on Chestnut Street the fronts of the Waln and Markoe houses (both already given over to commercial uses), as he saw Strickland's bank rising and, closer

---

9. See John E. Semmes, *John H. B. Latrobe and His Times, 1803-1891* (Baltimore: Norman, Remington [c1917]).

10. Printed complete in *Impressions Respecting New Orleans.*

to the Delaware, the red-brick Gothic front of his own Bank of Philadelphia, as on Second Street he contemplated the pure shapes and gracious detail of the Bank of Pennsylvania, his earliest triumph and always his favorite among his works—as all the memories which these sights aroused flooded over him—he must have been filled with a sense both of achievement and of regret. Then back to Baltimore, on December 28, for two weeks and a little more of final packing and last farewells. Eventually on January 15, 1820, the little caravan set out.

This was a different kind of trip from their journey to Pittsburgh, now almost seven years in the past. No longer did they have their own beautifully designed traveling coach, their own horses, and faithful David to drive them; the coach and horses had gone to their creditors two years earlier, in Washington, and David had passed out of their lives. Now, like so many other travelers westward, they were forced to hire a huge covered wagon—probably a Conestoga wagon—and into its interior, filled with furniture and bedding, they fitted themselves as best they could. It was tiring and cold and uncomfortable. They still, however, had servants—a man, Johnson, who was to prove a jewel; a boy, Frank; and their new Pennsylvania German cook, Grunevelt.[11] At overnight stops Johnson and Frank and the dog Mars slept in the wagon, the family and Grunevelt at the inns; but the inns along the way were generally foul and uncomfortable.

As they slowly worked westward it grew colder and colder, heavy snow robed the mountain slopes in white, the road was difficult with drifts; more and more it became a rugged experience—and on the way Latrobe, after the emotions he had been through, suffered another excruciating attack of his old "hemicrania." It was a slow, grueling trek; the stages are listed in the journal—16 miles to Reistertown, then 22 to Edwards, 15 to Gettysburg, 25 to Chambersburg, 21 to McConnelstown, and 34 to Bedford.

But the discomforts of the first three days proved their wagon too uncomfortable for them to dream of making the whole trip in it; they had to find some other way, even if it cost more money. So at Gettysburg they left the wagon; it drove on with their goods and Johnson and Grunevelt, while the family hired a sleigh for $15 to take them to Cham-

11. Latrobe spells her name "Grunwald"; his wife uses the "Grunevelt" which I have adopted.

bersburg, where they stayed over a day to rest. Then on again in other hired sleighs; this was better traveling! They could see the gorgeous mountain scenery through which their route took them; they could go at a pace that was swift enough to gain them restful mornings or long afternoons at their various stops. At once their spirits rose. And the inns, too, seemed much cleaner, the food better, as they traveled on west. Latrobe took the occasion to make some superb sketches of the snowy hillsides and the road curving along the bank of a river. What a joy to him his delight in scenery, his ability to set it down in color!

They reached Washington, Pennsylvania, on January 27—via Somerset, Mount Pleasant, and Williamsport—and put up at Morris's tavern there, "The Globe," to await their wagon, now left far behind. Since the weather was still very cold and all the creeks were frozen, with no chance of a steamer down the river for some time to come, they decided to stay for a fortnight. So on January 31, when their wagon arrived, they hired rooms and furnished them with their own things—"the deficiency," Latrobe notes in his journal, "being kindly made up by our friends and relatives, Mr. Parker Campbell's & Mr. Reede's family." And here they remained for just over two weeks—a pleasant winter vacation.

The Latrobes liked the town of Washington; they found food cheap, and they strove to give the children a feeling of continuity by setting up a "school." Every morning Julia and Ben had lessons from their father in Italian, Latin, and drawing. In the afternoons the architect sketched when the weather allowed; in the journal there is a detail of the old cupola of the Washington courthouse, a diagrammatic view of the town, and a rough sketch of one of the stone-arched bridges—he calls them "very handsome"—which carried the National Road over the winding creeks. "Upon the whole," he writes, "the road does honor to the nation & is a *great* work." It was good to be able to say this, for Latrobe for a time had been chairman of the National Road Commission, and Henry had once acted as surveyor for it.

At last, in mid-February, the weather began to moderate; the February thaw had come. On the seventeenth they gave up their rooms and set out again on the hilly road to Wheeling, thirty-two miles away. They arrived as darkness fell and put up temporarily at Simm's tavern, which they found dirty; the next day they moved to Sprig's, a pleasanter inn, where they remained until February 20, when they boarded the steamboat *Columbus* the night before she sailed.

As the paddle wheels, beating the yellow river to foam, drove them down the Ohio to Marietta, Latrobe, watching the brown snow-streaked hills flow by, must again have been filled with excitement and regret, and the terrible twenty months in Pittsburgh, while he strove to finish the *Buffalo* and the *Harriet,* must have come crowding into his mind. He had seen the *Vesuvius* leave triumphantly and had been filled with enthusiastic admiration; now he, too, was a passenger on a downriver steamboat, and every puff of the exhaust set reverberating a painful nostalgia for what might have been. But he was not one to sentimentalize his past or dwell on its failures, and not a word of it all goes into the journal; perhaps the very baldness of the account he writes is in itself significant.

They reached Marietta on the afternoon of the day they sailed, but here they lay over for three days, for a paddle-wheel drive shaft had broken; this proved but the first of a series of mechanical failures that dogged their trip. Latrobe sketched Marietta, visited its ancient fortifications, pictured the grotesque facelike rocks of a near-by bluff, and noted and described a severe thunder squall and gale followed by a serene night. Later, at Maysville, he wrote at greater length about the Marietta antiquities, and particularly about the discovery of the silver and copper mountings of a sword and scabbard—probably, Latrobe thought, in the grave of some wandering Spanish or French adventurer. Once more, repaired, the *Columbus* got under way and reached the Kentucky town of Maysville (formerly known as Limestone) on February 26.[12] Again radical repairs were necessary, for at this point one of the boilers had burst.

The whole trip, in fact, was a succession of accidents, while what should have been an eight-day voyage lengthened out into five weeks. To the two elder Latrobes the delays were torture; anxiety about the waterworks filled their minds, and here were days upon days of needless delay. The sooner their arrival in New Orleans the earlier would be the completion of the works and the flow of dollars—reward of so much patience, work, contriving—and ultimately the security they sought. Now the drive shaft broke a second time; the wedges that held the wheels

12. The *Columbus,* one of the two largest steamboats afloat on the western waters at the time, was a new vessel just completed in 1819. It was 440 tons and had a Boulton & Watt engine imported from England. See Louis C. Hunter and Beatrice Jones Hunter, *Steamboats on the Western Waters . . .* in Studies in Economic History (Cambridge, Mass.: Harvard University Press, 1949).

together failed repeatedly and had to be replaced; an engineer by mistake let all the water out of the boiler, so that the fire had to be extinguished and they passed a restless night at anchor (March 1, 1820) under the battering of a northwest gale. And there were still more delays—a week at Cincinnati; another at Louisville when the *Columbus* went up the Kentucky River for freight.

Yet these pauses brought variety. Mary Latrobe was particularly pleased with Cincinnati, thrilled at the respect her husband commanded, and delighted with the cultural richness of the life there; her pleasure is a comment on the restricted existence to which their poverty had limited her for the last three years. "We had tickets of admission to Lectures on Geology which we attended twice," she wrote to her friend Catherine Smith in Baltimore, "and even went to their Little theatre one evening; and as I have for several years lived in retirement I confess I was much amused, particularly at the many happy faces around me." At Louisville they were extravagantly feted; their letters of introduction from Henry Clay and Luke Tiernan brought them a royal welcome. But, as Mary writes Catherine, "we were entertained with a sort of ostentatious grandeur that made us think less favorably of the place then any we had been at." Apparently Louisville was conscious of its own present and growing importance and aimed to impress the fact on its visitors.

Once again on their way, they passed Shawneetown, where they went ashore on a Sunday (March 26) to savor the quality of a new town built entirely of logs. Two days later, in the evening under a brilliant moon, they at last emerged from the Ohio into the Mississippi, and Julia was so impressed that she wrote to John at West Point, "I went to bed almost wondering how I ever got there." And she added, "How often have I wished for you, my dearest brother, on this journey, which had not Papa's business been so pressing would have been very pleasant . . . We have the most *sneaking, pitiful, smooth-tongued, softly, money-making, scrapping, vulgar, illiterate* fellow for a Captain that you can imagine, who almost starves us . . .[13]

On the Mississippi they made better time and at length came to Natchez, where again they spent a day. The riverside area was filthy and wicked, a confusion of muddy streets, grog shops, and gambling halls;

---

13. This vivid letter, as well as Mrs. Latrobe's to Catherine Smith, is quoted entire in the Appendix of *Impressions Respecting New Orleans.*

but on the bluff behind and above was the town proper, where great houses were rising one after another and in the finest of all (now known as Auburn, designed in 1812 by the New Englander Levi Weeks) lived an old and dear friend, Mrs. Harding—loosely identified by Julia as "a cousin of Aunt Betsy's and a daughter of Dr. Abercrombie." Her home, luxuriously and beautifully furnished, was already one of the show places of the region and gave the Latrobes an opportunity of seeing gracious southern luxury on the hilltop as contrasted with the squalor and dirt of the foreshore. When Natchez had been left behind, the *Columbus* was on her home stretch; down she slipped past plantation after plantation—drawn out almost like a continuous village, Julia thought, and she wrote about seeing real oranges on trees—until finally, on April 3 or 4 (the letters use both dates!) New Orleans appeared around a bend. Joining the long parade of ships at the levee, they made fast. They had arrived.

Latrobe was eagerly awaited; people crowded aboard to greet the family, and two of the waterworks employees at once brought the waterworks barge alongside to pick up the baggage. Mary, who had feared that New Orleans would be "a vile hole" like Natchez, was agreeably surprised. Alert to the quality of it all, she noted the oranges for sale, the vegetables in the market, the breadth of the levee, the old Spanish houses, the Ursuline Convent, and the Place d'Armes; so anxious, indeed, was she to see her new home that she refused to wait for a carriage and with husband and children walked the mile and a half to their house. It was a raised cottage of a familiar New Orleans type, with five large rooms, galleries at front and rear, and a walled cool-room beneath. Mary was especially pleased with the large and luxuriant walled garden with its roses, jasmine, myrtles, and oleanders, its figs, and its hedge of bearing orange trees. Soon the rooms would be freshly papered and their own furniture put in place, and she would write to Catherine Smith, "If a kind Providence blesses us with health I shall be quite satisfied to remain here a year or two." The New Orleans venture was beginning auspiciously.

With two jobs under way—the Cathedral tower and the waterworks—there were plenty of questions that needed immediate answers, and Latrobe was at once submerged in a maelstrom of activity. The waterworks, now so near completion, demanded close supervision—nothing must interfere with its success. The Cathedral tower, almost finished, was bringing in welcome cash to pay the waterworks wages, for other funds were getting dangerously low and the unexpectedly long trip had been expensive. Another commission—which seemed the herald of more architectural work in the future—now came in from the Louisiana State Bank (a different institution from the Louisiana Bank). These projects kept Latrobe extremely busy all through the late spring and the summer of 1820, and he found time to write but one passage in his journal (referred to below). For the bank he designed a handsome building, reticent in detail and excellently planned, with its ground-floor banking quarters all vaulted in masonry. On a site more constricted than those of his two banks in Philadelphia, it was naturally smaller than either but, especially in the curved shape of the banking room, had a certain family resemblance to the Bank of Pennsylvania.[14]

Meanwhile, as the summer advanced, the level of the Mississippi gradually fell; then, as the damp heat increased, yellow fever broke out again and little by little spread its deadly mantle over the city. Was it the increasing number of funerals which daily passed the Cathedral doors that led Latrobe to make in his last journal note (August 10) a comment on New Orleans funerals and their cost? He was aware of the growing epidemic; in a letter about it to Robert Goodloe Harper (August 27) he noted the deaths of Peter V. Ogden (whom he calls "Burr's Ogden") and William Sampson, a brilliant young editor from New York. He must have been acutely conscious of the fact that almost three years earlier his own son had fallen a victim. The disease, as many noted at the time, seemed to strike uncannily at the young, the brilliant, the visitors from the North.

Soon, as the river fell, it was discovered that the waterworks suction pipe had to be extended much farther out into the bed of the river than the original plans had called for. The lowness of the river which disclosed the necessity also furnished the opportunity for the extension, and on August 26 (the day before he wrote Harper) the City Council passed a resolution granting Latrobe permission to use the city chain gang for three days to complete the digging. One can see the architect—now so

14. The bank was built from Latrobe's designs after his death, and it still stands as one of the distinguished monuments of the city. The roof as originally built was a flat roof, and the present dormer window and the balls on the parapet (which seem inharmonious with the rest of the building) date from the much later period when the roof was raised to its present shape.

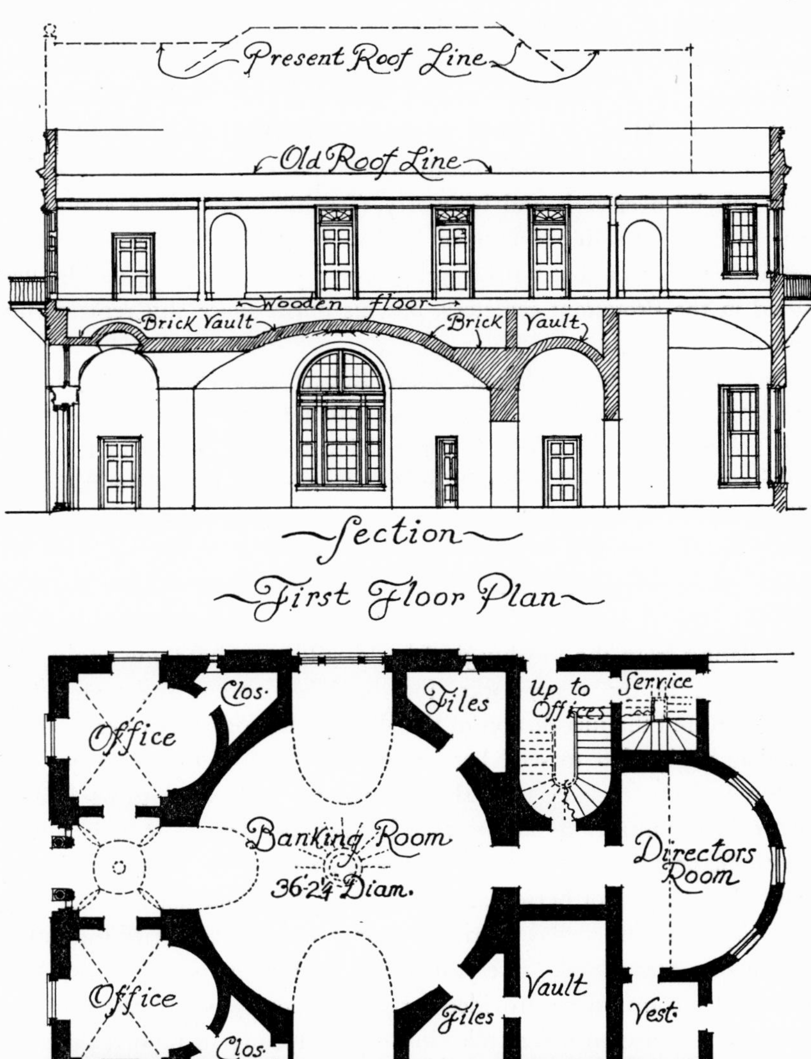

In Library of Congress

FIGURE 32. State Bank of Louisiana, New Orleans. Plan and Section. Redrawn from Historic American Buildings Survey.

close to his goal—actively engaged down by the river bank, directing the gang, slapping vainly at the clouds of mosquitoes which haunted the damp shore. Then suddenly one day, feeling ill, he hurried home, took to his bed—as Henry had probably done. On September 3, exactly three years after his talented son's death, Benjamin Henry Boneval Latrobe, worn out by overwork and by worry (for his means were almost exhausted) and probably enervated by the summer's heat, succumbed—one more victim of that terrible yellow-fever year. The next day he was buried in the Protestant cemetery, but his burial place still remains unknown.[15]

Mary, out of her desolation, wrote Robert Goodloe Harper sixteen days later, describing her heartbreaking situation and asking for advice.[16] The Talcotts took the family in for the first stricken days. Then, to add to the anxiety, Julia fell sick with yellow fever; fortunately she had only a light case and, still strong, recovered. Nolte and Talcott, aware of the family poverty, each gave Mrs. Latrobe a hundred dollars to take care of immediate necessities. Edward Livingston, too, came to offer his services—but with the ominous statement that heavy claims against her husband, dating from the Pittsburgh debacle, still hung over any equity she might have in the waterworks, for the Washington bankruptcy had merely covered the jurisdiction of the Washington court. All her advisers joined in urging her to send her furniture back east at once—even Livingston had the decency to wish that pathetic little asset to be free of seizure in any litigation—and to take her family north as soon as steamboat traffic opened. The furniture she sent on the ship *Tennessee,* as she wrote Harper, but for herself and her family she could not face the long sea voyage, and she feared hurricanes, for it was the height of the hurricane season. She added, "Everything I behold reminds me of my loss. All the little comforts he provided for me are hourly before my eyes and I am only recalled to my recollection by the feeling in how responsible a situation I am placed as regards my children . . ."

So the bereaved family returned to Baltimore to start life anew, with John, who had resigned from the Military Academy when he heard of his father's death, as its new head. They started practically destitute;

15. Originally it may have been marked, but the area of the cemetery has been so reduced (at least one street has been cut through it) that the actual site of Latrobe's remains cannot be established today.

16. This letter is given entire in the Appendix to *Impressions Respecting New Orleans.*

the last of Latrobe's cash had gone into the waterworks. The city took over the waterworks and completed them; they remained in use till 1840, when a new and larger plant, designed by Albert Stein, was completed. Yet from it the family received not one cent, for, having no money to put into the last little necessary elements, they were forced to decline the succession.[17] Again, as in the case of the Philadelphia water-

---

17. A schedule of the stock ownership at the beginning of the summer of 1819 is as follows:

New Orleans Water Company, 1819

Names of the Stockholders	*Shares*	*Amount*	*Paid*
The Corporation of New Orleans	12 at 500	$ 6,000	$ 6,000
B. H. B. Latrobe	60 do.	30,000	
E. E. Parker	20 do.	10,000	10,000
Michel Fortier	1	500	500
Méricult	1	500	500
David Talcott	2	1,000	1,000
Talcott & Bowers	2	1,000	1,000
Ursulines	1	500	500
Laurent Millaudon	3	1,500	1,500
E. B. Caldwell, of Washington	1	500	500
Fred. C. Graf, of Baltimore	16	8,000	8,000
Justus Hoppe, of Do.	1	500	300
Meyers & Brantz	2	1,000	1,000
J. Mark, of New York	10	5,000	5,000
Noha Talcott, Do.	2	1,000	1,000
N. G. Rosevelt, Do.	3	1,500	1,500
V^t Rilling	1	500	300
A. Coulter	1	500	100
J. Thompson	1	500	100
A. Davizac	1	500	500
Planter's Bank	2	1,000	200
H^ri Devigne	1	500	500
McLanahan & Bogart	1	500	100
	145	$72,500	$40,100
Shares, subscribed by Mess^r Orr & Graf, to be sold in New Orleans	95		
	240		

There are about 10 Shares to which the title is subject to discussion } *B. Henry Bon^l Latrobe*
June 17, 1819

The sale of the waterworks (June 14, 1821) was the result of a suit by Benjamin Orr—the Orr mentioned in the list as holding jointly with Graff 95 shares to be sold in New Orleans. The city bought the entire enterprise at the purely nominal price of $10,100. Since in the list Latrobe's 60 shares were down as unpaid, despite his tremendous invest-

works and the Washington Canal, Latrobe's work was in actuality an outright gift not only of his labor but of thousands of dollars besides. Of all his engineering work, only the Chesapeake and Delaware Canal ever brought him more than renown; on this contract, after the canal company was resuscitated in the 1820's, some six hundred dollars were paid to Mary Latrobe to cover the arrears that had been due her husband. Such was the financial reward of one who literally gave his all for the improvement and the beautification of the country he had adopted and loved so wholeheartedly.

Yet the tragic irony of Latrobe's death should not obscure the triumphant richness of his life—rich in friends, in family, in the joy of creative work. From whatever abyss of despair, he always emerged—chastened though victorious—to pursue his unique destiny in the country's growth to maturity and to enrich it with further fruits of his indomitable idealism and his creativity—fruits which were to add flavor to America for a long time to come.

---

ments in time and actual cash, his heirs could hope for little or no recovery. Edward Livingston's threat to Mrs. Latrobe that he would attach any recovery the family might make from the sale to cover Latrobe's debts for the Ohio steamboats is quite in character; the picture drawn of him by Vincent Nolte in his *Fifty Years in Two Hemispheres* (cited in an earlier footnote) is that of a shrewd, grasping, and completely selfish opportunist.

CHAPTER

22

Latrobe as Artist

That Latrobe as an architect was a creative genius should now be clear. Perhaps an attempt to codify some of his revolutionary contributions and to relate them to the art movements of his time will still further demonstrate his significance.

In his work we have seen the early influence of the Prussian classic revival in Silesia and, later in England, the effect on him of the conflicting tendencies in the work of Adam and of Dance and Soane. But on his arrival in the United States in 1796 he found an architectural scene even more confusing than that of the country he had just left. On one side were the continuing English colonial traditions so strongly entrenched in the work of most country builders and many carpenters' companies. Confronting these was the dominant classicism so strongly upheld by Jefferson—a movement popular among the intelligentsia but still limited in its acceptance. Also, as a third movement, there was a marked nationalistic trend, largely centered in New England, which aimed to produce a native American architecture by radical modifications in what was fundamentally an Adam type of design; the three great leaders in this development were Bulfinch, McIntire, and Asher Benjamin.

The classic movement, started by Jefferson and firmly entrenched in Virginia and the region of the new capital, had been reinforced by the work of Thornton, Hallet, and Hadfield, each standing for a different type of expression—Thornton still in many ways basically Palladian and working in the vein of Sir William Chambers, Hallet striving to introduce the brilliant and logical classicism of the French academic tradition, and Hadfield distinguished by a new and fundamental restraint. Jefferson himself was architecturally uncertain, basing his details almost entirely on Palladio, swayed by a passion for ancient Roman forms, full of striking imagination in essentially pictorial or sculptural composition, yet like many self-trained designers weak in the fundamental architectural concept of the relation of structure and materials to design.

Into this chaos the work of Latrobe came as a revelation. It was restrained and geometric in much of its composition; it was naturally classic in detail and turned always to Greek precedent for inspiration; but in addition it invariably demonstrated that Latrobe thought of architecture in an entirely different way from those around him. To him, architecture meant not only well-planned and well-built structures, well composed from the aesthetic point of view, but also, and pre-eminently, such a complete integration of the three basic aspects of architectural design—functional planning, construction, and beauty—that he could never think of effect as separate from plan or of either as a consideration apart from the materials and the structural methods used to produce the effect. This at once gave his buildings a practical rightness, a reality, and a variety that were rare in the United States. It led him inevitably to experiments in different types of construction—particularly in the use of vaults as controlling elements in design—which raised the best of his work to a plane far above the merely decorative or the merely useful. And these experiments led, in turn, to interior shapes of a new and expressive kind—we need only cite the lobed dome of the Old Supreme Court in the United States Capitol or the interior of the exchange room in the Baltimore Exchange. In England Soane's development proceeded in the same general direction and occasionally produced effects perhaps more brilliant. But in the United States for two decades, say from 1805 to 1825, it was only the pupils of Latrobe and those who came directly or indirectly under his influence—like John Haviland—who sought for a similar integration. To this vision all of Latrobe's detail was adjusted. It was this that made him always prefer the simple to the complex, that led him to the progressive stripping of inessential details from his exteriors, and that accounted for his early enthusiasm for the primitive Greek Doric which he used so crudely in many of his early designs but so brilliantly—with magnificently controlled modifications—in the ground floor of the Capitol.

Along with this compelling ideal of use, structure, and beauty as a single design principle, and not as three separate steps, went another search—a search for forms that were *expressive*. This can be seen, for

From the Latrobe sketchbooks

FIGURE 33. A Classic Group at Mount Vernon.

instance, in the tobacco and corn capitals in the United States Capitol; but in more subtle ways it is evident everywhere, from the extreme elegance achieved in the assembly room he designed for Richmond to the quiet simplicity of the Van Ness house and of St. John's Church in Washington or the stark power of the lower pumping station for the Philadelphia waterworks. None of these developments were mere accidents; all were the result of conscious thought and conscious effort on Latrobe's part. In other words, as an architect he was a creative artist, consistent in his aims and fired by a passion for his controlling ideals.

His creativeness naturally spilled over into many other fields. He wrote verse, sometimes of considerable power; his notes contain literary criticism and philosophical and psychological speculations of marked originality. The breadth and depth of his education lent itself to this variety; he was perhaps among the last architects who really attempted in their own lives and thoughts to realize the old Italian Renaissance concept of the universal genius. The drawings in which he expressed his architecture and even his engineering are themselves proof of this. In England the tradition of architectural and engineering delineation in the last decades of the eighteenth century was magnificent, and some of the quality in the Latrobe drawings undoubtedly comes from the engineering education he received from Smeaton, coupled of course with the more technical facility in architectural drafting which he developed by himself and which was furthered and refined by his three or four years of work under Cockerell. But Latrobe's drawings go even farther than those of his masters; each one apparently was seen by him, almost unconsciously, as a work of art in itself. Even the designs for the settling basin of the Philadelphia waterworks have a beauty of color, a pleasantness of over-all composition, and especially a quality of graphic legibility which make them remarkable. The same type of imaginative visualization appears in the long map of the Susquehanna, where from mere indications one can imagine almost perfectly the rocks, the river banks, the areas of placid flow or of hurried and foaming rapids.

And again and again in the Latrobe drawings one feels his unconscious desire to leap over the border of architectural presentation into the realm of pure painting. He liked to draw people, drew them well, and had a sense of character; apparently he seized every opportunity offered by an architectural perspective—or sometimes even by a strictly geometric elevation or section—to introduce figures, as in his drawings for the Richmond theater, his perspective for the New York City Hall competition, and a number of his Capitol perspectives. Similarly, full of a love for nature, he made the surroundings of his buildings as graphically expressive of their neighborhood as he could. This is particularly true of his drawings for buildings in Virginia, where in addition to indications of the topography there is often a striking expression of dramatic and appropriate atmosphere. A forceful example may be seen in the perspective of the Richmond penitentiary, where a dark cloud sweeping up over the walls of a building still brilliantly illuminated by the sun not only suggests how the building will be seen on such a day as is frequent in that latitude but also gives exactly the correct psychological coloration of both gloom and hope.

Besides his strictly architectural presentations, Latrobe left a series of sketchbooks containing hundreds of drawings and water colors of European and American scenery. The standard of these is so universally high and the beauty he achieved in many of them so surprising that some examination of the forces behind them is warranted.

From the Latrobe sketchbooks

FIGURE 34. Profile of Edmund Randolph.

The architect, as we have seen, had been an enthusiastic draftsman and sketcher from childhood, and without a doubt in his Continental years he had exercised his talents extensively. Although occasionally there are hints of the rather dry style current in German drawings and topographical sketches of the 1780's and of the nascent romanticism which was rapidly developing there—as, for instance, in the drawings of Friedrich Gilly (1772-1800) [1]—naturally most of his existing work bears a

1. Nevertheless there are strong parallels between the work of Gilly and that of Latrobe, although it is doubtful whether the two men ever met. Both illustrate the power of the early Prussian classic revival as a liberating and creative force in architectural design. This parallelism extends even to certain details of landscape indication—as, for instance, in a method used for indicating masses of foliage, which both laid in with a rather wet brush and at the edges used a rapid to-and-fro movement to give a broken and light-filled outline. Latrobe, as we have seen, was acquainted with the publications of Friedrich's

strong English character, for the style he uses in his American painting undoubtedly matured during his later English years.

In early English water-color painting, the decade from 1785 to 1795 was a climax period. During this time the foundations were laid for much of the extraordinary development seen in the art of men like Cotman and Turner. Latrobe's work resembles that of neither, but a comparative examination does show a frequent and remarkable parallelism to the water colors of Thomas Girtin (1775-1802)—so much so indeed that there are some Girtin sketches that might occur in a Latrobe sketchbook and in respect to treatment arouse only the slightest doubt as to their author. They show the same quiet drama, the same feeling for light and shade, for foliage, for sky and clouds. Yet Girtin was a younger man than Latrobe, and it is noteworthy that this parallelism is most noticeable in some of Girtin's work dated after Latrobe had left England forever. One is therefore forced back to a consideration of the influences under which the style of both men developed.

Girtin was a pupil of Edward Dayes (1763-1804), a man known more for the engravings made from his sketches than for his water colors themselves, and one whose influence seems to have been greater as a teacher than as an original artist. To judge by the engravings, the actual work Dayes produced had few particular characteristics—it was a sort of generalized, rather softened, slightly romanticised realism, with foliage much conventionalized and picturesque accents almost artificially inserted. This was as far from the Latrobe tendency as it was from the later creative work of Girtin, so that any direct personal influence from Dayes seems unlikely. Furthermore, in 1805, after both Dayes and Girtin had died and a decade after Latrobe had crossed the Atlantic, Dayes's widow published a book containing a number of his essays on painting, several of which deal with landscape,[2] and a comparison of this text with Latrobe's treatise on landscape painting (1798-9) prepared for Miss Susanna Catharine Spotswood (see page 83) reveals strongly the difference in approach. Dayes's whole effort seems to have been to develop a standardized production—conventional to the last degree—and the stu-

---

father, David Gilly. See Alste Oncken, *Friedrich Gilly, 1772-1800* (Berlin: Deutsche Verein für Kunstwissenschaft, 1935) and Alfred Rietdorf, *Gilly, Wiederburt der Architektur* (Berlin: von Hugo [1940]).

2. *The Works of the late Edward Dayes . . . Instructions for Drawing and Painting Landscapes . . .* (London: Mrs. Dayes [etc.], 1805).

dent is urged again and again to simplify, to soften, and to modify actuality until it meets the correct level of gentility. He has definite rules for how colors should be applied (working always from cool to warm), and to him the painting of skies—to which he devotes considerable attention—becomes a mere routine for obtaining conventional values and acceptable accents. Latrobe's treatise is almost the complete opposite of this; he seems to be directing his pupil not to the conventional society woman's "pretty picture" of the time but rather to the most acute observation of those specific local characteristics which constitute the dominant character of any landscape, whether that character fits into the usual formula or not. To him sketching was a means not only to representation but, perhaps even more important, to increased discrimination and greater accuracy in the vision itself. Sketches, he feels, must gain their chief value from expressive realism, and his own work universally expresses this aim. It is something of the same feeling in Girtin that accounts for much of the resemblance between his paintings and Latrobe's.

Behind the work of Dayes and Girtin, and to a certain degree that of Turner, lies that of another English water-colorist of great importance, John R. Cozens (1752-99?),[3] who, traveling widely in Europe during some of the same years that Latrobe spent abroad, painted many scenes in which an unconventional and expressive approach is magnificently stressed. The water colors Cozens made are not mere topographical sketches but vivid attempts to create works of imaginative art in which composition, light and shade, and color all combine to express character. In them may be seen some of the technical methods in the handling of the medium which Latrobe used, especially in the indication of foliage and the accurate but expressive drawing of the branchings and anatomy of trees, the handling of rocks, and so on. In these matters the work of Cozens is far removed from the conventional representation of earlier water-colorists—Gainsborough, for example—in which the aims and the manner led straight back to the work of Claude Lorraine and Poussin; Cozens's water colors contain in themselves prophecies of the extraordinary future developments that Cotman and Turner were to make. It is probable that Latrobe knew these water colors, for willy-

3. *The Drawings and Sketches of John Robert Cozens,* vol. 23 of the Walpole Society (Topsfield, Mass.: Wayside Press, 1935).

nilly they seem to have exerted a considerable influence on him. Yet here too the differences are pronounced, for Cozens took wide liberties with his subject matter which were abhorrent to Latrobe's sense of what landscape painting should be. The architect may even have met Cozens in Italy on the Bay of Naples, for a passage in his treatise on landscape painting tells the story of an artist who was working definitely in the Cozens manner:

> A young painter of my acquaintance, whose talent for landscape was of the first class, whose genius was universal, but who labored under that common disease of men of superior abilities, indolence, joined a party on an excursion around the bay of Naples. . . . But he was wholly impracticable & would do anything but paint. A young gentleman who had been also of the party quarrelled with him rather too seriously upon the subject, and it was with difficulty I accommodated matters. When we were alone, I told him, that I thought him, myself, to blame, in missing so good an opportunity of showing his abilities. "Sir," said he, "you are mistaken. I did not choose to exhibit upon the stage to the motley crew we had, but I have here 20 of the most enchanting scenes in the world." He pulled out his sketch book. It was full of pen and ink drawings something in this style [referring to three very rough pen-and-ink sketches by Latrobe of Vesuvius ("The Devil Smoking a Pipe to a North Wind," "Old Nick as Usual," and "Smokibus"); and he goes on to say that a week later he saw the finished water colors and they were magnificent]. But since my first emotions of admiration had subsided, I discovered the grossest errors in the geology of his pictures. Islands, mountains, & palaces were shifted about by his magic pencil at random, & the productions of his luxuriant fancy sold at high prices for "Views in the bay of Naples taken on the spot."—This is not fair. It is to me, I think, a considerable advantage to be a very indifferent painter. I shall never be an eminent one, but I hope always to be correct, & I advise you to follow the same rule.

Latrobe's vision, then, was personal and his ideals were often at variance with those of the fashionable English water-colorists, although his manner naturally had been affected by their work. He seems almost to have anticipated the ideal of accurate delineation which Ruskin so patiently upheld, although in Latrobe's finished sketches there is also a sense of the picture as a picture that far surpasses that in most of Ruskin's own drawings. In leafing through the sketchbooks and the treatise on landscape painting, one is often astonished at the way in which this feeling for the scene itself—and not only the appearance but the life of it—makes the architect's work prophetic of various developments of a much later time. He loved the sea and had an amazing sense of the motion of waves and the shape and feeling of ships; the best of his marines, small though they are, in their presentation of the mood of the weather and the actual rhythms of the waves are far in advance of, say, the naval scenes of Birch, his American contemporary. Similarly, the beautiful accuracy and exquisite rendering of his drawings of plants and occasionally of animals—as, for instance, in his remarkable sketch of a chipmunk—seem almost to parallel the work of Audubon. Other sketches, in their care and accuracy in presenting significant detail, seem anticipations—in vision at least—of the Hudson River School, just as the architect's grasp of and delight in the basic romance of the American landscape seem to parallel the ideals of the later painters of that school. Sometimes this realism is of an even more modern type, as in his broad spreading view of New Jersey between Newark and Paterson, where the qualities of the rail fence, the rough bifurcated road, the wide fields on either side, and the distant woods and mountains have almost the fresh atmosphere of such plein-air French painters of the mid-nineteenth century as Daubigny or Rousseau. And one has only to compare the Latrobe sketches with the contemporary American sketchbook of Charles Fraser to realize that in the Latrobe drawings there is evidence of a quality of competence, imagination, and sureness of aim of a totally different order from the naïve charm of the Charleston artist.[4]

It is not the purpose here to overstress the artistic importance of the water colors Latrobe has left us. He never claimed to be a great creative painter, yet these strange anticipations have their own significance in illustrating not only the quality of Latrobe's own genius but also the variety of artistic influences that were playing on the imagination of a sensitive architect in the early years of the nineteenth century.

Among his drawings and paintings there is a small group in which totally different influences seem to be at work and an altogether different effect is produced. Thus in the Spotswood volumes, at the end of a description of the siege of Yorktown, there is a moving vignette of a woman weeping over a dead soldier. In the relaxed recumbent figure of the soldier and in the pose and the simplified treatment of the mourner

---

4. Charles Fraser, *A Charleston Sketch Book, 1796-1806* . . . with an introduction and notes by Alice R. Huger Smith (Charleston, S.C.: Carolina Art Association [c1940]).

In Virginia State Library

FIGURE 35. "Taste, Anno 1620." From Latrobe's illustrated manuscript book, "An Essay in Landscape."

there is almost that complete domination of emotion over subject matter of which one is so conscious in the work of Blake. Even the figures are drawn with a kind of Blakean expressiveness, and something of the same quality of Blake-like brooding—or, in certain cases, of Blake-like emotional violence—underlies a group of imaginative paintings made in Richmond in 1797, which express the loneliness that after a year of excitement had finally overpowered the architect. One picture especially has won from nearly all who have seen it the instant expression, "How like Blake!" It represents an old man clothed in white sitting in a cave in the foreground; a low moon casts bright reflections on the distant stormy water, and the ghosts of a boy and a girl are borne past in flying clouds. The sky is dark and the clouds only break close to the horizon to allow the rising moon to appear. Blake (1757-1827) was seven years older than Latrobe, and it is possible (although hardly probable) that Latrobe met him in London or attended his exhibition of 1793. But Blake's name is never mentioned in the existing Latrobe papers, and the social circles in which the architect moved would hardly have brought the two into any intimate contact. Perhaps it was merely the fact that both were living at the same time and under the same influences which produced these occasional surprising similarities.

There was, however, another artist in London of whose work Latrobe could scarcely have remained ignorant—Henry Fuseli, whose genius after a century of neglect we are only now beginning to realize. He was a friend of and a sympathizer with Blake, and his painting (like Blake's) though admired by a small and vocal group was violently attacked by others. The powerful figures, the erratic compositions, the strident emotionalism, and the occasional grandeur of Fuseli's productions were admirably fitted to appeal to and influence young Latrobe, and it is in them perhaps rather than in the work of Blake that we are likely to find the influence behind Latrobe's own visionary paintings. This is rendered all the more probable when we consider the pencil technique of such a drawing as Latrobe's portrait of Jefferson, which is similar to the technique used in some of the Fuseli drawings and quite different from that seen in the pencil sketches of Gainsborough, Reynolds, or Lawrence. And occasionally there are even more striking resemblances to Fuseli. For example, the title page Latrobe made for his "Designs of Buildings in Virginia" has as its main decorative element a flying figure representing, the architect explains, the genius of architecture. She carries a model of the Bank of Pennsylvania and is leaving the rocks of Richmond for Philadelphia. Latrobe credits the idea for this figure to Flaxman, but in pose, treatment, and especially the drawing and modeling of the wings it is much closer to the winged figure in Fuseli's "Spirit of Night" than to the colder and more stereotyped imaginings of Flaxman; if it is based on Flaxman, it is Flaxman deeply modified by Fuseli. There is no more evidence that Latrobe had known Fuseli than that he had met Blake; yet much would have drawn the men together, for Fuseli—Swiss born, German trained, and completely cosmopolitan in outlook—had a background not too unlike that of the architect, and both, moreover, were on the same side in the great political divisions of their time.[5]

Among the architect's sketches a small group reflects still another trend—the vision and aim of what today is termed *trompe-l'oeil* painting. In France at the time occasional popular paintings of a somewhat similar type appeared, and a few English examples survive.[6] But Latrobe's

5. See Paul Ganz, *The Drawings of Henry Fuseli,* translated by F. B. Aikin-Sneath, with a foreword by John Piper (New York: Chanticleer Press, 1949).

6. I am grateful to Mr. Henry-Russell Hitchcock, Director of the Smith College Art Gallery, for pointing out to me these precedents.

sketches in this vein seem unique in the American painting of that period; they almost presage the attitude of Harnett or Peto eighty years later. He paints, for instance, a view of the breakfast table of the ship *Eliza*. Drawn in perspective there is a tray divided with strips to prevent the plates, cups, and "silver" from sliding; this is superposed on a group of objects shown almost in straight elevation, as though the tray itself were a sketch dropped on a crowded table, and the playing cards, letters, and printed matter which appear beneath the tray are each drawn with such extraordinary and painstaking accuracy that we can read the letters and the print. In another example in the sketchbook, two little landscapes are superposed in a similar way on the manuscript of a poem and a piece of printed matter; the edges of the landscapes are represented as torn and rough, and in this case another element is added—a ghostly head of George Washington, whose eyes look out at the observer in an oddly magic way between the two views. What was behind these original and vivid sketches? He may have seen French or perhaps even English examples, although the dominant tendency of English water-color painting was almost diametrically opposed to such work. They do not seem imitative; the vision behind them is intensely personal. Instead, they appear to have risen spontaneously from a mind nourished, however unconsciously, by all the streams of feeling that eddied through the world in Latrobe's time. He seems to have been one of those individuals who act as a kind of funnel into which life pours its random chemicals—with the result that they come out in a single and definite stream of new and unexpected compounds.

Latrobe's ideal of accuracy, which he so strongly stresses in the treatise on landscape painting addressed to Miss Spotswood, makes the sketches he has left the most authentic existing presentations of the America of his time. With him we visit Hors du Monde, the Skipwith plantation; we view the eroded clay cliffs of the York River; we see the log-cabin mansion of Colonel Blackburn; we call on Washington and meet the family; we travel the long miles north to New York, or west along the Juniata, or through the wintry Appalachians. In early Washington we observe the half-built Capitol and note the look of Pennsylvania Avenue at Twentieth Street. At Lancaster, Pennsylvania, a vivid sketch shows the courthouse (then the state capitol). And under his guidance we chuff-chuff down the Ohio and the Mississippi on a steamboat and are finally introduced to New Orleans. En route we have seen innkeepers, have looked on as barefoot gentlemen played billiards in a country tavern, have attended the court at Richmond; we have had all kinds of views, serious and comic, of people met along the way. As a record these sketches are unique, and yet that is not their only value, for the more they are studied the more we realize that here a creative mind was at work—a creative sensitivity and a creative hand—which under other circumstances might have made Latrobe a distinguished painter. Instead, his true originality—his mastery of color, drawing, and composition and, especially, the creative and daring imagination which all appear at one time or another in his paintings—was directed to his chosen profession, architecture. And it was these very qualities in their architectural guise that made him the great designer he was.

CHAPTER

23

Latrobe as Engineer

In the last decade of the eighteenth century the engineering profession in England was making tremendous strides, though by today's standards it was still unformed and tentative. Engineering design was still largely empirical and a matter of unchallenged rules of thumb, for the mathematical and scientific foundation on which modern engineering is based was then in its infancy. There was no professional school of engineering in the British Isles; in France the École Politechnique was founded only in 1795, but from an even earlier period it was French treatises on hydraulics that were chiefly influential in English design. On the other hand, English practice was highly developed, and in canals, harborworks, factories, and bridges the years from 1780 to 1800 laid the foundation for many important subsequent developments.

The typical engineering training in England at that time came largely from practice or apprenticeship with established engineers; its worth depended on whatever personal training the master might see fit to give. And it was apparently just such a training that Latrobe received from Smeaton in the years immediately preceding his entry into the architectural profession. There is evidence that he worked with Smeaton on certain "scouring works" [1] in the Fen district; his later distrust of such a method of keeping channels clear in America was founded on that experience. He also worked, as we have seen, on the Basingstoke Canal under the famous engineer William Jessup, and just before he left England he himself was engaged in the planning and design of the Chelmsford Canal. It was this equipment and experience which the architect

1. A system of narrowing or directing tidal channels by wing dams or jetties in such a way that the accelerated current would prevent the deposit of silt and hence preserve the original depth or even increase it.

brought with him to the United States and which justified his calling himself an engineer.

In those days the term engineer was used in the broadest possible sense. Its province included harborworks, canals, bridges, roads, and some techniques of building construction; it also embraced the design and use of steam engines and of all sorts of other mechanical aids to life, such as heating systems and all the machines required by an emergent industrialization. In all these fields save one—the application of steam to navigation—England was far ahead of America, and the difference in background and in materials available had produced in the United States an attitude toward engineering problems quite different from that in England. The locally trained American engineers were often brilliant improvisers and at times showed an extraordinary structural intuition, but when they began their work they were almost totally self-taught and without technical training or experience. A characteristic example of their constructions may be seen in the wharves of Norfolk which so interested Latrobe on his arrival there in 1796.

There was another profound difference in the problems which the two countries presented—a difference so deeply based that it has persisted in some fields even to the present day. This concerns the matter of permanence. In the United States low investments, short amortization periods, and expectation of frequent renewal often controlled engineering design, whereas in the England that Latrobe knew construction was designed for permanence and low upkeep. This basic difference in engineering attitudes controlled general plans, details, and the choice of materials. Latrobe recognized it as an unsolved problem in his own practice, and he strove to reach the correct balance between the permanent and dignified construction to which his English training and tradition directed him and the lighter, cheaper improvisations that frequently served for design in the early United States. But the American point of view was essentially foreign to his nature; again and again, in trying to adopt it, his fundamental aims were thwarted and the results were necessarily compromises.

Still another major difference between English and American building customs lay in the availability and cheapness of wood, for in the new country this was still a period when the cutting off of forests to provide agricultural land was a social gain. Although Latrobe expressed admiration for certain American wooden bridges and such inventions as the wharves of Norfolk, he himself always sought wherever possible to use stone or brick for major structural elements. The tendency of wood to rot when carelessly used—a tendency he knew all too well from his experience at the United States Capitol and in the President's House—at times even led him to misunderstand and underrate its true value. Thus his refusal to use wooden logs laid in the foundation trenches beneath the walls of his customs house in New Orleans was one cause of its ultimate collapse. Where American engineers thought in terms of years, Latrobe thought in terms of decades; and it was this difference between American and English building ways and ideals that often made his career as an engineer a frustrating experience. Nevertheless what he did accomplish in spite of these handicaps is extraordinary, and there is hardly a field of engineering which he did not cultivate.

There was in the United States one more difficulty he was forced to surmount—a general suspicion of theory as theory, a fundamental doubt of the value of professional advice. The Americans had accomplished so much through their improvising that they were skeptical of any other approach to a problem. In 1799, for example, when Latrobe was being attacked for his design for the Philadelphia waterworks, the author of an answer [2] to the architect's second publication concerning the enterprise makes one of the counts in his indictment the fact that Latrobe quotes Belidor (author of *Architecture hydraulique*) and other European engineers.

Yet the public works which the new and growing country required inevitably created a demand for trained engineers which at the beginning could only be filled by men with foreign training. In introducing engineering improvements into this country, for example, many of the French engineer officers of the Revolutionary army, with their excellent engineering training in the royal military schools of France, played an important part. And, in addition to Latrobe, the talented English engineer Weston, although only for a relatively short time a resident of the United States, gave a tremendous impetus to the improvement of canal building and construction.[3] Often these men found themselves in the rather anomalous

2. *Remarks on a Second Publication of B. Henry Latrobe, engineer, Said to be Printed by Order of the Committee of the Councils: and Distributed among the Members of the Legislature* [Philadelphia], 1799.

3. William Weston came to the United States in 1792 to direct the Schuylkill and Susquehanna Canal. Two years later he made the surveys for the Middlesex Canal and

position of being forced to work for clients who, grudgingly accepting the need for their services, at the same time fundamentally suspected both their motives and their methods.

Latrobe's engineering commissions were many. His survey and report on the navigation of the Appomattox, as well as one on the work already accomplished on the Dismal Swamp Canal, apparently had little if any effect in either case on what was done then or later; but his much more important commission on the Susquehanna navigation scheme—on which, characteristically enough, his chief surveyor was a Frenchman, Hauducour—did result in actual improvements to the river channel and won him such official approval as to lead to his appointment as engineer of the Chesapeake and Delaware Canal. In this, as we have seen, another difficulty arose: the fact that his judgment of the correct route—a judgment later followed in the canal construction after his death—could not be accepted because of the opposing financial interests of the stockholders. Similarly, when later he was working on the construction of the Washington Canal, his recommendation that the locks and walls of the canal should be masonry lined could find only one supporter among the directors, Latrobe's own friend Dr. Frederick May. The wooden locks—his beautiful drawing for one of them exists in the Library of Congress—produced (as he had foreseen) endless trouble and expense in repair and replacement. In July, 1811, for instance, as he wrote Fulton (July 31), a heavy storm broke down one of the wooden locks, and by 1816 they had all collapsed. Sometimes it seemed as though there were only three demands which the architect had to fulfill: "Do it fast, do it cheap, and do it in a way that is profitable to me" (whoever the "me" might be). This was the inevitable result of the fact that these public works were chiefly constructed as private speculations and not, as in England, largely under government direction and with considerable government investment.

In canal building, therefore, Latrobe had little opportunity to contrib-

---

the following year proceeded to New York in connection with the Western Navigation, working especially in the area between Oneida Lake and the Mohawk River. He built there the masonry locks at Little Falls, which were probably the first masonry canal locks in the United States. In 1799 he made a report on the New York City water supply, recommending the use of water from Westchester. Soon after this he returned to England. In 1813 the commissioners for the New York Western Navigation, after Latrobe's refusal of the job, sent to Weston in England and offered him the position of chief engineer, which he too refused.

ute the best of what he was capable of. Only such a great state-supported enterprise as the New York Western Navigation could have furnished him that, and this commission (as we have seen) it was impossible for him to accept. In much the same way, his contributions to harbor design and harbor building were limited. We have observed that he was consulted and paid for advice in connection with the navigation of the Delaware and that he was a consultant for the Washington Bridge. It was in connection with the latter that he expressed doubts about the permanent efficacy of scouring by means of wing dams, realizing fully that although they prevent shoaling in one place they build up shoals in others; and he stated that when they were improving the Susquehanna he always took care to see that current was preserved in other places besides the channel, in order to carry away the silt. His report of 1816 on the availability of Annapolis as a naval base is another interesting example of the swiftness and the sanity of his judgment in evaluating navigation possibilities.

The anomalous position in which engineers found themselves in those years is well shown by the large number of instances in which, despite the widespread suspicions, Latrobe's advice or professional services were solicited in connection with canals. At least three times—in 1806, 1808, and 1811—the New York Western Navigation sought his services; in 1811 and again in 1818 North Carolina urged him to assume charge of all its canal developments; in 1812 he was offered the job of engineer for the proposed Roanoke-James canal; and in 1815 he was asked to help with the Beaufort canal. He could accept none of these offers, but the fact that they came to him reveals that the need for advice was great enough to overcome the general distrust of the engineer. It is perhaps fortunate that conditions rendered it impossible for him to seize those opportunities, for—except in the case of the New York Western Navigation—if he had undertaken the work he would probably have been subjected to the same frustrating round of objections, criticism, and refusal to accept his advice that came to him on the Chesapeake and Delaware and the Washington canals.

Latrobe's skill as an engineer was recognized not only in such navigation projects but also in his appointment as one of the commissioners for the National Road and the fact that he was chairman of the commissioners of the Baltimore-Washington turnpike. Here his job was less the detailed design of the road and the bridges involved than the larger problems of the actual choice of the route to be followed. In the already mentioned letter to the governor of North Carolina respecting canals he included a vivid description of the method an engineer uses in making these larger major decisions, and the same kind of judgment is required in the choice of an economic route for an important highway, particularly where the terrain is rough and confused. Incidentally, his son Henry Latrobe worked as a surveyor on a stretch of the National Road in Maryland. Latrobe's practicality in dealing with large problems like these comes to light when in describing the bridges for the National Road which had been built near Washington, Pennsylvania, he writes (February 1, 1820):

> Upon the whole, however, the road does honor to the nation & is a *great* work. From Alexandria, a small town just rising at the distance of 15 miles from Wheeling, the road descends into the valley of Wheeling Creek. The creek winds from [the] side of a very narrow glen, and the road crosses it many times on very handsome bridges, constructed much more with a view to appearance, and at a much greater expense than with skill or judgment. One single arch would in all cases have given sufficient bent for the largest freshets. But the superintendent Jopil Thompson, has conceived that three arches of smaller span would be more picturesque. This is the general design of most of them. They are all of hewn stone of a yellowish color, and add greatly to the beauty of the landscape.

At the same time, as we see here, his practical knowledge did not blind him to aesthetic values.

All in all, then, we cannot say that the actual achievements of Latrobe in this particular field are either numerous or in themselves significant. Nevertheless they did have their importance in the United States of the time, for they kept alive in the minds of those who could understand and appreciate them the tremendous advantages of trained professional judgment. This may be seen especially in what was undoubtedly the most important engineering function he performed—his advice to Secretary Gallatin in connection with the controversial bill for canals and roads. In this he revealed a far-flung imagination as to the real future needs of the country and projected a series of canals that formed a coherent network to serve them. The soundness of his vision is sufficiently proved by the number of canals built later along the routes and at approximately the positions he envisaged. Though the bill was not passed, the whole scheme was a daring leap forward and its proposals were never forgotten.

The second great engineering branch in which Latrobe was deeply interested comprises what today would be called mechanical engineering.

We do not know where he had picked up his knowledge of steam engines and their potentialities. It appears, however, that his father was acquainted with Matthew Boulton (1728-1809), the great English steam-engine manufacturer, for the architect wrote (February 14, 1814) a letter to Professor Cooper (already cited) telling how his father had heard Boulton's story of Newcomen's discovery. There is no other evidence of any particular interest in steam power on the part of the young architect before he came to the United States, and although he undoubtedly brought with him a general understanding of the subject it seems probable that his specific knowledge was picked up largely from Nicholas Roosevelt.

In any case he was an apt pupil, and either from books or from experience—or more probably from both—he had learned the requisite sizes for engine parts and a great deal concerning the relation of fuel consumption to the power produced. He designed and detailed many engines, and they worked. Yet his knowledge was almost entirely empiric, and boiler sizes at least were at that time still most uncertain; one of the chief criticisms of the Philadelphia waterworks was the fact that the boiler of the lower engine was ill adjusted to the demands placed upon it, with a resultant unevenness in the power delivered.[4]

It was undoubtedly this empiric and rule-of-thumb method of engine design which blinded him to the advantages of the high-pressure engine designed by Oliver Evans and thus brought about the long-continued controversy between the two men. Toward the beginning of the nineteenth century Evans had the only steam-engine factory in Philadelphia and was building automatic flourmills powered by his own engines; he had also, in 1805, produced a steam-power dredging machine, erected on a small scow and so designed that the whole could become either a self-propelled steamboat afloat or—by applying wheels to the scow and connecting them with the engine—an automobile on shore. In that year this "eruktor amphibolis" of his ran under its own power completely around

4. Many of the "extras" required to complete the Philadelphia waterworks that so enraged Thomas Cope were the result of the fact that this was a pioneering enterprise, using engines of a size and power before unknown in the United States. With only empiric standards to work with, it was impossible for any engineer to foresee every contingency. In one sense both Latrobe and Roosevelt were "out of their depth"; they had to discover and improvise as the project developed. But the engineer's basic design was sound—the system worked.

Centre Square in Philadelphia before descending to the river and its more humdrum occupation of keeping the channel clear. And Latrobe also knew the type of engines made with oscillating horizontal cylinders, such as French was building; of these he had an equal and a better-founded suspicion.

Yet the architect, less daring, found in the quiet dependability of the Boulton & Watt engines, especially when improved by the new valve system of Ogden, a completely satisfactory source of power, and to him Evans seemed almost a quack. This conservatism was so contrary to his general nature that one can only account for his attitude as the result, first, of some personal prejudice and, second, of the superficiality that arose out of his empiric approach to the whole problem. He did, it is true, at an early period run a smoke pipe through his boiler, producing a sort of embryonic fire-tube boiler, and according to a letter to James Smallman (July 2, 1813) he added to the Navy Yard engine a pipe through the firebox, through which all the boiler-feed water was forced so that it was boiling before it entered the boiler and "the saving of fuel & increase in steam was very great." Roosevelt and he together had increased the efficiency of the typical Boulton & Watt engine by doubling the air pump. But beyond these he made no innovations. The value of his contribution in this phase of engineering lies chiefly in his continual and enthusiastic support of steam as a source of power not only for boats but for factories of all kinds, as well as in the fact that by building and selling engines himself he aided the rapid spread of steam power all over the country.

His interest in this field was colossal, and from 1799 almost to the end of his life he was in close touch with it. At the Philadelphia waterworks he proved conclusively that steam power was reliable enough even in its then imperfect state to furnish a city with the water it needed, and the successful completion of the New Orleans waterworks shortly after his death offered further evidence. In 1810 he introduced a steam engine at the Washington Navy Yard to drive a sawmill, a forge (both the blower and a hammer), and a blockmill. He was spasmodically in correspondence with many clients interested in steam engines, advising them about the design of their mills and enumerating the advantages of steam power; for a short period he was manufacturing steam engines; and, to his cost, in his disastrous association with Fulton he played a part in the revolutionary introduction of steam navigation to the great rivers of the West.

Though he was not an inventor but rather a mediator and adapter, in the history of the industrialization of the country he deserves a place.

But Latrobe's concern with industrialization was not limited to the use of steam power. In the general field of mechanics he was both inventive and ingenious.[5] His correspondence with Eric Bollman is full of reflections of their mutual interest in this great area. He devises and sketches for him various types of corn kiln for drying grain. A long letter (June 21, 1809) in which he warns Bollman of the dangers inherent in the over-rapid mechanization of American industry and some of the technical questions involved is especially interesting because it reveals so completely the architect's own difficulties—difficulties which perhaps at that time made him unduly skeptical. He writes:

You say I am a croaker.—As to manufacturing establishments I certainly am.—The success of manufacturing depends on the division of labor, or the performance of it by machinery. If labor is divided, it is necessary to the perfection of the ultimate state of the article produced, that each intermediate state should be perfect,—that is, that the work should be done by persons long habituated to one *single operation* & *none other*. Such persons cannot be collected in America but by much expense of money & time. Thus we see that paper manufacture has been a long time arriving at a state in which the competition is of good workmen in each department for employ, and not of the masters for workmen.—

As for manufactories carried on by machinery, ——— [illegible] is generally necessary to establish them, and except in the cotton business in which workmen capable of erecting the different machines are beginning to be numerous, I know of no branch in which the proprietor is not at the mercy of his workmen.—On this account I rein in my natural bent to manufactories, and endeavor to tie down my very soul to the drudgery of my profession, which I understand thoroughly and in which no one can improve upon me.—

---

5. J. Leander Bishop, *A History of American Manufactures from 1608 to 1860 . . .* 3 vols. (Philadelphia: Edward Young & Co.; London: Sampson Low & Co., 1864), contains a wealth of material dealing with the development and use of power and the achievements of early American industrialists and engineers. It is especially valuable on the economic background of the period and hence on the difficulties under which engineers were often forced to work.

Charles B. Stuart, C.E., *Lives and Works of Civil and Military Engineers of America* (New York: Van Nostrand, 1871), is valuable evidence of the inchoate condition of American engineering in the first half of the nineteenth century. There are many interesting accounts of engineers, but the material is entirely without documentation.

[Bollman apparently had inquired about a certain Voight or Vogt as a possible caster of steel, and Latrobe goes on:] As to cast steel—if the *casting* is the matter, there can be nothing very important in his discovery. Steel has been perfectly melted in England from time immemorial, & cast steel is one of our constant importations. The Perkinses [6] whom we had at the rolling works, were masters of that business, but could do nothing for want of crucibles.—But the *welding* of cast steel & generally, the working it into a variety of cutting tools is a matter of difficulty.—A New Englander by the name of Pettibone, whom I well know, who is a smith himself, and has worked in that business, till ill health obliged him to desist,—has a patent for welding cast steel, and working it, which he sells the use of to states or individuals. It is a very valuable discovery. I have seen one of his axes chop a file in two without injury to the axe.—The U States have encouraged & employed him but yet he is very poor,—tho' modest, & of regular habits. . . .

As to rolling bar iron from the pig, it has been many years in practice in England, and is now carried on, on an immense scale by Mr. Crashaw in Wales, who has a wheel (I am told but hardly believe it) of 90 feet diameter. Foxhall attempted it & *he says,* practiced it at the Delaware works at Morrisville. . . . I know how the thing is done but have no time to describe it tonight. The iron however is inferior for most purposes to that which has been forged by the hammer.—

This letter also discloses the embryonic state of industrial development in the United States as well as Latrobe's keen interest in the problem—which, although he strove to "rein it in," drove him nevertheless into many unprofitable schemes.

In fact, his association with all sorts of industrial developments was extensive, embracing as it did almost the entire gamut from ironworking to weaving and spinning machinery. Thus Roosevelt and he together designed the rolling and slitting mill attached to the lower engine of the Philadelphia waterworks, and it was operated successfully for several years; characteristically enough, too, it was one of the major sources of Latrobe's financial embarrassment, as we have seen. Blydensburg's power loom fascinated him for two years, from 1810 to 1812; it is interesting to note that it was not until 1814 that the Appleton-Moody power loom was put in successful operation in Waltham, Massachusetts. Again Latrobe's prophetic realization of the importance of such a machine led merely to

6. Probably the Parkyns brothers, who came to the United States in 1802 and were valuable employees in the rolling and slitting mill attached to the waterworks in Philadelphia. They had had extensive English experience in metalwork.

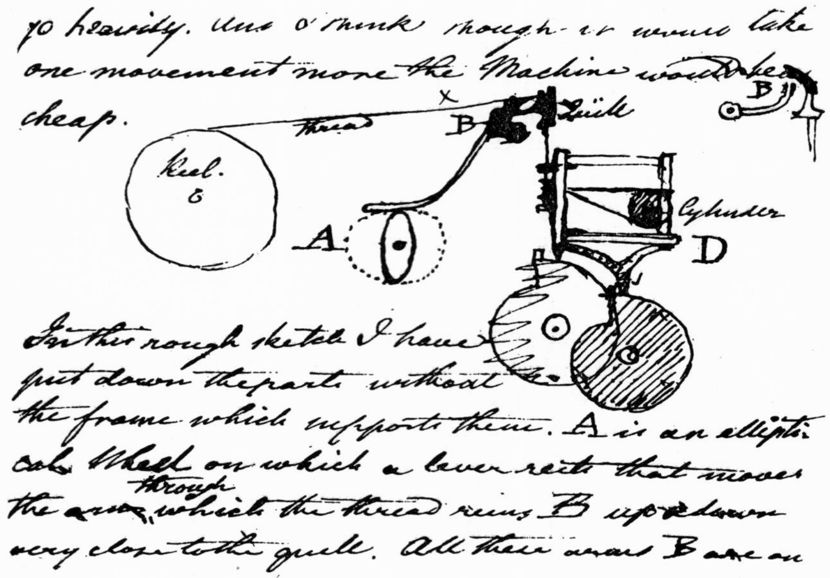
so heavily. And I think though it would take one movement more the Machine would be cheap.

In this rough sketch I have put down the parts without the frame which supports them. A is an elliptical Wheel on which a lever rests that moves the arm through which the thread runs B up & down very close to the quill. All these arms B are on

From the Latrobe letter books

FIGURE 36. Improved Quilling Machine, invented by Latrobe. From Latrobe's letter to Henry Orth, April 5, 1815.

financial loss on his part. In the Steubenville textile factories of Bazileel Wells and Henry Orth he not only furnished the engine but invented a new type of quilling machine, with which Mr. Orth was deeply pleased.[7] Latrobe invented or developed a new kind of door lock, working on suggestions made by his uncle John Antes in England, and in a colorful letter to Colonel Lane (September 14, 1816) he described how several years earlier in Virginia he had had a set of them made by a mulatto smith; these had proved completely satisfactory and were still in perfect condition.

And he was unselfishly interested in the inventions of other men. He wrote Nicholas King (April 10, 1810) asking his help in obtaining a patent on a new kind of steering engine designed by James Smallman, the builder of the Navy Yard engine, and he did everything he could to promote the employment of a Mr. Rose as director of the Navy Yard blockmill. Becoming interested in the Pettibone hot-air furnace, he suggested (August 10, 1817) installing it in the new Capitol. The new technique of

7. See letter of March 27, 1815, to Henry Orth at Steubenville.

mass manufacture by the use of interchangeable parts each produced by a special workman—a method that had been developed chiefly in the munitions industry and largely by Eli Whitney—also fascinated him, and in 1817 he designed an arsenal for Frankfort, Kentucky, specially planned to house this new process. In fact, hardly a suggestion made in those birth years of American industry failed to receive his attention or his support, and like all the early industrialists and inventors he harped on the necessity of developing as rapidly as possible a body of trained workmen to handle the new devices.

Naturally railroads also aroused his interest. Railways of a sort had been in use, particularly in mines, for at least a century and a half before Latrobe's arrival in the United States, although the applicability of the system to ordinary road transportation had scarcely been projected; their chief function had been to carry heavy weights for relatively short distances. To Latrobe their possibilities seemed much greater; as Gallatin wrote to James Nicholson in 1826 after the architect's death: "Latrobe, 18 years ago, suggested to me wooden railroads, as a substitute to common turnpikes, in the sands and swamps of the southern states, where no stones could be had, where timber costs little or nothing . . ." The architect also suggested the use of railroads to supplement the New York Western Navigation.[8] As we have seen, he tried to form a company to build a railroad from the Virginia coal mines to Amthill on the James River. There is evidence, too, that in the government quarry at Acquia an actual railroad of some sort, designed by Latrobe, was put into service. It was probably in connection with this that the architect wrote (May 11, 1805) to Joshua Gilpin asking him to return his "drawing, ever so slight a sketch, with dimensions, of the railwaggons, now in use in England . . ." and he used such railroads in the construction work of the Chesapeake and Delaware Canal, as he wrote Gilpin the same year (August 19): "At the post road I have introduced the railwaggons I used in England. They answer most perfectly and do very great execution . . ." Yet of the application of steam to the railroad there is no indication whatsoever in his papers, although steam engines had been used experimentally in England from as early as 1802.

One of the most difficult problems in large buildings in those years was the question of heating, for fireplaces were too inefficient in large

8. I owe these references (the first) to Mr. Wayne Andrews, of the New-York Historical Society, and (the second) to Mr. Van Wyck Brooks.

rooms to raise the temperature to the level that the growing standards of comfort required. Latrobe was faced with this question early in the Capitol, and for the House of Representatives he designed a system (like the Roman hypocaust) in which the smoke and hot gases from a furnace were conveyed in a large duct under the gallery floor. The duct, curving back and forth, occupied almost the whole area, so that the entire floor became a radiating surface. Unfortunately the system did not work as well as he had hoped, probably because the heated area was not on the floor of the House where the heat was most necessary but several feet above in the gallery, and all the convection currents which it set up—as well as the direct radiation which it produced—were directed away from that portion of the House where the representatives sat. Latrobe himself tried to find other reasons why the system did not function—the wetness of the masonry, the lack of proper ventilation, and so forth—but eventually he found it had to be changed and in 1808 he suggested the use of a steam system to replace it.

This was not his first suggestion of the sort, for already he had recommended it (in 1805) in connection with the anatomical theater of the University of Pennsylvania Medical School. Here he had said that the best way of heating would be by steam conveyed through pipes of tin around the exterior walls of the room. And in the old Senate room of the Capitol before it was replaced he had suggested a similar system, which apparently was installed although there is no evidence of the actual details of the installation. In any case these systems were not designed to take care of the total heat requirement, for numerous fireplaces were always included in addition. Hot air also played its part in heating the Capitol, as we have seen. For rooms of medium size Latrobe preferred stoves to fireplaces, and many decorative stoves of German and Dutch manufacture were used, although sometimes ordinary iron-plate stoves would be surrounded and covered by some sort of ornamental composition—usually an urn on a pedestal.

Another engineering aspect of construction engaged his attention—the problem of acoustics—and J. H. Parker invited him to write an article on the subject for the encyclopedia he was contemplating. The article, complete and proofread by 1812 (although the encyclopedia[9] was not

9. *The Edinburg Encyclopaedia,* edited by Sir David Brewster, 1st American ed., with the addition of articles relative to the institutions of the American continent (Philadelphia: Joseph & Edward Parker, 1832), Latrobe's article on Acoustics, vol. 1, pp. 104-24.

actually published for another twenty years), is a fascinating document. It reveals that Latrobe had a wide acquaintance with European theory on the subject and that as an accomplished amateur musician he had a considerable knowledge of the special acoustic qualities of various types of musical instruments as well as of the experiments for their improvement which had been carried on, especially in France. An excellent general outline of the basic theory of sound and its transmission and reflection is followed by a section on the acoustics of buildings which shows both the strengths and the weaknesses of his knowledge.

The problems of sound refraction and reverberation time were still unappreciated. It was of course well known that some materials reflected and others absorbed sound, and that the secret of why some rooms were good for hearing lay in the proper balance of sound-reflecting and sound-absorbent surfaces; but there was no quantitative way of calculating this, and the planning of rooms for acoustic satisfaction was still largely a matter of experiment, intuition, and convention. Since the importance of mere room size as a factor was little realized, Latrobe's experiences in design for these purposes were sometimes disappointing. The first House of Representatives, for example, was a room filled with echoes and reverberations. The architect claimed that he had foreseen this and that heavy curtains between the columns were part of his original design; their installation later largely remedied the condition.

In the second House of Representatives, designed after the fire, Latrobe thought he had definitely improved matters by changing the plan from an oval to a semicircle. His much smaller Senate chamber and Supreme Court room had both been semicircular rooms and completely satisfactory, and there was a general feeling among architects that the semicircle was the best acoustic form for an audience chamber because it brought the seats in the outer rows closer and within approximately equal distances from the speaker. Yet the new House, when it was completed by Bulfinch from his predecessor's design, was even more unsatisfactory than the earlier one; although curtains again helped, the speaking was still marred by intrusive echoes. In designing the room the architect had made one serious error. The fact that the level of the sound source—the speaker's throat—was approximately on the same level as the spring of the vault caused the sounds to be fired back in the most disconcerting manner. Various attempts were made to improve the condition. A textile ceiling was stretched across the room at the level of the entablature; this killed the echoes, to be sure, but it also reduced the intensity of the sound to such a degree that the ordinary voice was inaudible. One suggestion offered was that a transparent glass ceiling be put across at this same level, but the expense would have been prohibitive. Robert Mills finally solved the problem in a brilliantly simple way, merely by raising the floor some four feet to the height of the column bases, and this at once seems to have done away with all the unpleasant echoes and still preserved the necessary voice reinforcement. The whole episode is expressive of the difficulties involved in working with the queer combination of knowledge and guesswork, of science and rule of thumb, which controlled a great deal of engineering in those days.

But as an architect Latrobe's chief engineering problems and those with which he had the greatest success were the techniques involved in actual building construction. In these his knowledge was extensive, his experience wide, his imagination daring, and his achievement remarkable. Here was a field in which he was thoroughly at home—and one, moreover, in which engineering imagination was a vital factor in architectural effect. Yet in that area too the same lack of quantitative analysis and quantitative theory can occasionally be seen. This is the real reason for the failure of the foundations of both the New Orleans customs house and the Mississippi lighthouse—in the latter Henry apparently followed in part the basic scheme his father had originally set. B. H. Latrobe had no such personal experience of New Orleans conditions as that with which he approached his other work, and the theoretical basis for that type of construction was not yet sufficiently sound to allow him to improvise successfully; in the case of the customs house, for example, the omission of the logs in the bottom of the trenches produced fragmentary and unequal settling.

Except for small wooden spans over the Washington Canal, Latrobe built few bridges in the United States. Nevertheless his knowledge of such construction was great and he acted as consultant to bridge companies in several cases. Thus he made a design for a Schuylkill bridge in Philadelphia as early as 1798, and although his design was not adopted it had a striking influence upon the structure as it was actually built. He was familiar, too, with chain suspension bridges; he never designed one himself, but he realized their strength and economy and hoped (as he wrote James Greenleaf on January 9, 1813) for their wide use throughout the country. But the two greatest monuments of his skill as a bridge designer are, first, an estimate (November 10, 1804) for a bridge from New York to Long Island across Blackwells Island for Nicholas Roosevelt, and, second, an application (February 21, 1806) for a patent on bridge construction.

The Blackwells Island bridge is completely described in his letter to Roosevelt enclosing the estimate.[10] It reveals a thorough appreciation of the possible difficulties and it uses the experience gained in the Philadelphia waterworks as a means of establishing the cost of coffer dams and pumping. It also indicates a knowledge of the use of caissons to be sunk as means of forming bridge foundations and suggests that the superstructure may consist of arches of wood, stone, or iron. Since the major expense lay in the erection of the foundations and the piers, Latrobe decided to base his estimate for the superstructure on the most expensive of the three types, stone. The widest arches were to be 120 feet in span, with a crown 80 feet above the water. This height, he said, would permit the largest warships to pass through by merely lowering their topgallant masts. The final estimate for the bridge itself without the approaches amounted to $950,000—a sum manifestly beyond the economic resources of the city at the time.

His patent on bridge construction was requested in a letter from Philadelphia (February 21, 1806) to Thornton, the Commissioner of Patents:

> It has been about 15 years ago [1791] since I first built a bridge on this principle . . . When it was proposed to erect a bridge across the Schuylkill in this city, I offered a plan to the company, which was rejected on the ostensible ground—that they did not wish to try experiments. I now find that the information . . . in my report, in the hands of an officer of the company, is going to be used for the erection of two bridges near this city . . . I therefore wish to secure my property in the discovery . . .

The patent specifications call for a bridge to be built on two or more arched ribs, with longitudinal segmental vaults connecting the arches and forming the base for the road. These vaults are to be supported on web walls built on the main arches, and in the patent specifications the architect suggests that the walls may be pierced or themselves arcaded to form light and open spandrels. The thrusts generated by the longitudinal vaults are to be taken care of by tie rods of iron or timber built across the bridge between the ribs and spaced as necessary. In this way, the designer felt,

10. See Appendix for complete text.

the weight of a masonry bridge could be enormously reduced, the amount of stone cut to a fraction of that required in a continuous-arch bridge, and the cost thereby markedly lessened. The system seems never to have been employed in important structures in the United States, although bridges with open spandrels over continuous vaults were occasionally used not only in this country but also in England, France, and China. In fact, the entire scheme may be a further development of French concepts. The one great difficulty involved in such a bridge would be the placing and permanence of the tie rods and the anchors they would require, but with the light weight of the ordinary traffic to be carried at that time there is no reason why bridges of that type should not have proved both successful and economical. (Since the greater number of the early records of the Patent Office have perished, there is no way of knowing whether or not Latrobe's application was granted.)

But the architect's major contribution to structural engineering lay in his use and development of the vault as a major element in American architecture. From the very beginning of his practice he conceived that any important public building he designed should be, as far as it was within his power to make it, a fire-resistant structure vaulted in masonry. His was not the first large-scale use of vaults in the United States (the Philadelphia jail vaults were pre-Revolutionary), but it was the first important architectural use in which the form of the vaults themselves became a controlling element in the design. The Richmond penitentiary, which he designed as early as 1797, was almost completely vaulted in masonry. And the Bank of Pennsylvania (1798-1800) had vaulting as the very basis of its design; its 45-foot brick dome was at the time an unprecedented achievement. Vaulting established many of the room shapes and sizes in the United States Capitol, and domes are the chief motifs in the Baltimore Cathedral interior. Latrobe considered it a great tragedy when in 1816-17 he was forced to substitute timber ceilings for the masonry domes he had planned for the House of Representatives and the Senate in the rebuilt Capitol. The climax of his vault design came in the Baltimore Exchange.

Before Latrobe's arrival in the country, vaults had been used chiefly for bridges and occasional foundations or cellars and had usually been simple barrel or tunnel vaults. There was as yet little tradition of vault building and there were few masons trained in the special skills necessary. This was the major difficulty which the architect faced, and in the circumstances it is remarkable that he succeeded as well as he did. Vaults designed by him did fall in at least three cases, but only in one case was it because of bad design; in the others it was the result of imperfect or unskillful construction methods and carelessness in removing the centering—as demonstrated by the fact that the vaults of the Treasury and Post Office "fireproofs" in the wings of the President's House, after their collapse, were rebuilt successfully according to the architect's original design. The one great exception was the vaulting of the Supreme Court which fell in September, 1808, and in this case the failure, obviously one of design, was due to a change in scheme made at the suggestion of John Lenthall—a change made in search of economy but one Latrobe should never have countenanced. In view of the fact that all Latrobe's vaults were built with lime mortar, the record seems extraordinary, and the architect's training of the masons who erected these elaborate elements—often deeply coffered—is as remarkable a proof of his skill as the creation of the shapes themselves. In all his domical vaults the thrusts are resisted by iron bands built around them at the spring, and this is probably one reason for Latrobe's love of the segmental rather than the hemispherical form.

It was in his last vaulted structure, the Baltimore Exchange, that he achieved his most daring and ingenious dome. Here on a 50-foot square he first built four arches and on them placed four pendentives. The piers were light for the weight they carried, but they were apparently sufficient, for they stood undamaged until the final razing of the building; and the thrusts of the major arches were well taken care of by the almost Roman manner of planning. Continuing up as a partial dome to support a circular interior balcony, the pendentive surfaces were lightened with a row of coffers; above them and weighting their haunches a drum was carried, octagonal outside and cylindrical within, which in turn carried the final deeply coffered dome, with a decorative weather vane at its crown. The ingenious plan of the drum established the greatest weight at the eight corners of the octagon, the walls of which were lightened on the four cardinal sides by wide, arched windows; on the diagonal sides the heavier weights were well supported by the pendentives. The crown of this upper dome was a full 115 feet above the floor, and the resulting superbly airy interior had an interest completely integral with the brilliant constructional forms that made it possible.

All these achievements came from a man working with none of the codified, quantitative standards that are a commonplace today. Like all the engineering of the time, they were based chiefly on experience and intuition. It is not strange, therefore, that occasionally structural failures resulted, as they had so frequently in medieval days when men were building vaults on a similar basis. The Supreme Court vault fell; as designed, the vault for the rebuilt House of Representatives might have fallen if it had been constructed; and, in 1818, when Bulfinch began to remove the centering under a large thin dome over the Capitol's north wing—a dome which supported and brought together around the cupola all the various chimney stacks from the rooms beneath—the vault deformed to such a degree as to reveal fundamental instability. Bulfinch claimed this occurred because its loading was unequal and he therefore removed the light dome completely and substituted a brick cone to support the lantern.

Yet these few failures, important as they are, were perhaps inevitable for a man of Latrobe's daring, working in a technique he himself had developed, in a country where such vaults were almost unknown and where there was very little definite information available in published works. Against his failures one must place his major achievement of introducing a brand-new structural method into the United States and making it not merely a means of spanning voids but also a major element in architectural design. Today we often forget that for a period of twenty years the country had developed a vital tradition of skillful masonry vaulting alike in bridges and in buildings. This was largely the result of the work of Latrobe's followers, many of whom he had trained—Strickland, Mills, other later Greek Revival architects, and the early railroad engineers—who after the invention and development of hydraulic cements, had gone on to remarkable achievements comparable with the best European structures. It is in the work of Latrobe, and his alone, that this vital architectural movement had its birth.

In all this engineering work the architect was faced, as he was in his architectural design, by the fundamental American suspicion of expert advice—a suspicion supported by the extraordinary accomplishments of the self-trained and improvising native American contractors. Thus in writing to Richard Peters of Philadelphia (January 10, 1808) he says:

> I cannot leave . . . without thanking you sincerely for the pamphlet on the [Schuylkill] bridge . . . The work is a great one & does honor to the

perseverance, public spirit, & talents of the directors, especially of your excellent father . . . tho' I have mentally quarrelled with him for setting an example of *lay* success, so injurious to my profession.

And in a letter to Henry Ormond of Baltimore (November 29, 1808) he expresses a gloomy view of the prospects of the profession; Ormond had wished to join Latrobe's office as an apprentice to become an architect and civil engineer, and the architect writes him frankly of the difficulties involved:

I believe I am the first who, in our own country, has endeavored & partly succeeded, to place the profession of architect and civil engineer on that footing of responsibility which it occupies in Europe. But I have not so far succeeded as to make it an eligible profession for one who has the education & the feelings of a gentleman . . . The best in all our great cities is in the hands of mechanics who disgrace the art but possess the public confidence, and under the false appearance of oeconomy have infinitely the advantage in this degrading competition. With them the struggle will be long & harassing. . . . Fascinating and honorable as is the profession, it is not lucrative . . .

Evidently Ormond was frightened away and did not go on with his plan to become an architect.

Even when Latrobe had been definitely appointed the engineer of various projects, he was forced again and again to write his clients severe letters to support his professional position. To his friend Dr. Frederick May, for example, in connection with the Washington Canal he wrote (August 14, 1812):

In May, 1811, I was ordered to cause a bridge to be built at the intersection of Maryland Avenue & of the canal . . . David Tweedy was employed in the work . . . In August 1812 he states . . . after several applications to the company for his money . . . he has been referred by you to the corporation of Washington city for payment . . . There is nothing in which my interests as a professional man, &, in fact the interests of my employers, are so much engaged, as that full credit should be given to my official accounts; and that whenever I, as engineer, engage or assume payment for the company, the company should make good my assumptions. . . . In order to exhaust the drift & intentions of your letter, that if my resignation depends on my adopting any other set of moral principles than those I have mentioned above, I beg that this letter may be considered as my resignation.

The letter seems to have been efficacious, for Latrobe did not resign.

In his letter to Thomas More at Brookville, Maryland (January 20, 1811), already cited in connection with the Washington Bridge, he sketches vividly—in support of his own claims to competence—the development of engineering in this country, and he notes that on the Middlesex[11] (Massachusetts) and Connecticut canals no European engineer was consulted but that Weston,

an engineer of reputation in England [was sent for from England] to lay out the Susquehanna & Schuylkill, & Delaware & Schuylkill canals & afterwards [was] employed in the Western Navigation for the State of New York. . . . The Potomac canal is the work of Colonel Gilpin & other Americans. The Richmond canal & that of the Appomattox are also the works of men who had never seen a canal before, excepting . . . I was consulted before the latter was begun . . . The Santee canal indeed is the work of a German, Colonel Leuf . . . Immediately after the revolution . . . a number of French pretenders to knowledge as architects & engineers were the fashion long enough to do mischief . . . [He then notes that because of this fact and the antipathy which had arisen against anything French, his own French name had been a great barrier to his success.] It is impossible for me to believe that education, observance & experience are unnecessary . . . yet . . . witness the pendulum mills, the New England tilt hammer & other projects adopted at once under my nose at the navy yard at a useless expense of 4-$5000, while I vainly labored for 5 years to erect a steam engine at . . . $6000, which already earns . . . $80 p. day . . . & scarce any thanks.

Similarly, in a letter to Volney in Paris (July 28, 1811), with respect to his own position he notes:

Your anxiety about me, & regret that I have not yet made my fortune is very flattering & honorable to me. . . . You forget that I am an Engineer in America, that I am neither a mechanic nor a merchant, nor a planter of cotton, rice or tobacco; for you know it as well as I do, that with us the labor of the hand has precedence over that of the mind; that an engineer is considered only as an overseer of men that dig, and an architect as one that watches others that hew stone & wood . . . The service of a republic is always a slavery of the most inexorable kind, under a mistress who does not even give to her hirelings civil language. This kind of treatment extends from her first political characters to her menials . . .

11. Latrobe is incorrect in his statement about the Middlesex Canal, for which William Weston made the surveys.

Herein, then, lies the essential reason for the tragedy in Latrobe's career, the reason why one whose professional knowledge and experience and whose imagination and professional ideals were so far in advance of those of his competitors—whose contribution both to the architectural development and the structural and engineering evolution of his country was so incalculably great—died nearly destitute and almost forgotten.

APPENDIX

1. Road Directions, Virginia Style *

The soil between Major Eggleston's & Chinquopin is so full of mica that after the rain of last night the clear sun of this morning was reflected from the road in ten thousand sparkles as brilliant as Diamonds. It is a circumstance so constantly before the eyes of the inhabitants that nobody remarks it; but a more beautiful & magnificent road for the chariot of a Mythological deity could not be laid out by the warmest imagination of a poet. Flat Creek winds among these hills to the extent, I am told, of 40 miles above its junction with Appomattox. It deserves the name it bears, & if it was a little straighter, it appears to me that it would be already navigable for Batteaux [sic]. The rains of last week had considerably swelled its water, & General Meade's milldam, situated upon it, was blown up night before last. The fault was owing in a great measure to its imperfect construction. Indeed the millers & millwrights of this country are as remarkably deficient in their knowledge of that part of their business as they are perfect & ingenious in their contrivance of their internal millworks.

I was in hopes of getting by 12 o'clock to Colonel Skipwith's. At Chinquopin church I struck into the woods and pursued the *direct road* without suffering any *fork to the right or left to puzzle me,* according to the advice of an old man whom I met *near Chinquopin.* The road indeed was straight enough. I rode without fear till I fancied I must have much exceeded the 7 miles of distance I had to travel. I then turned into a plantation, the *third* opening only, which I had met with in these eternal woods.—A negro man came to the gate, who in a long speech bewailed my having missed the *proper turning to the right* in this infallibly straight road. It was about 4 miles behind me. The day was excessively sultry and

* From the Latrobe manuscript journal of 1796.

my horse appeared as tired as his rider.—Nothing however could be done but go back, & I got nearly the following direction.

"I am right sorry, Masser, you are so far out in this hot day, it is very bad indeed, Masser. You must if you please turn right round to your right hand which was your left hand you see when you were coming here, Masser; I say, you turn right round to your right hand, which was your left hand, and then you go on I'd go on about 2 miles & a half, Masser, it's very bad indeed to have so far to ride back again in so hot a day & your horse tired and all,—but when you have got back again 2 miles or 2½ miles you will see a plantation and that plantation is Dicky Hoe's, that's on your right hand now as you're going back but it was on your left hand when you were coming here, you see, Masser. The plantation is Dicky Hoe's on your right hand, right handy to the road, and there is a house with two brick chimnies on it; but it is not one house, it only looks like one house with two brick chimnies but it is two houses and is only built like one house, but it is really two houses, you will see it right handy to the road a little way off with two brick chimnies on your right hand which was your left hand when you were coming here, and so you ride by Dicky Hoe's plantation with the house with two brick chimnies which is two houses you know, and then you ride on and come to another plantation about a mile further which plantation is on your left hand which was your right hand when you came here,—right handy to the road."—"Well," said I, "I know it, and then I get again into the wood, & how then when I am in the wood past the plantation & house?"—"Why then, Masser," says the negro, "when you have passed the plantation on your left hand which was your right hand when you came here, right handy to the road, you go along till you come into the wood and ride about 100 yards,—no, Masser, you don't ride 100 yards, only 50 yards,—but I think Masser you had better ride about 150 yards and then it will be all plain to you, for you'll see a fork on your right hand which was your left when you came here, turn down there.—"

—*"Now I know all about it,"* cried I fatigued, "good morning my good fellow & thank you, thank you many times."—I rode off in full trot & when he was out of sight he was still [calling] out to me about my right hand which was my left.—As soon however as I got out of the wood I saw the house with the two brick chimnies on my left instead of my right, & presently the next house was on my right instead of my left.—I therefore tied up my horse, got over the fence, & at the house got a direction *in good German* to the mill from which I was then only two miles distant . . .

2. Art, Manners, and Morality *

[Latrobe had noted that one of his woman friends, probably a Mrs. Wood, had objected to the language Shakespeare uses in *Othello* as fundamentally indecent.]

By degrees however the field of discussion enlarged itself. I found it necessary to attempt the proof that Shakespeare did not so much violate the decency of the manners of his age as the ladies of the correct delicacy of Virginia may suppose.

The Merry Wives of Windsor was written in the days of Queen Elizabeth. The Bible was translated in the reign of James the 1st, perhaps twenty years after. I mean no disrespect to that Book when I say that the translators, who were men of great piety & learning, & in such a work, published for the correction of morals & manners, would no doubt be as cautious as was necessary, not to give offence to delicacy—have every where used language consonent to the original no doubt,—but highly repugnant to our present ideas of delicacy.—They certainly might have avoided it, by circumlocution, or a different arrangement of expression; for it happens, that every language with which I am acquainted is on no subject more ductile than when common expressions are to be rendered equivocably allusive to indelicacy; or natural functions, unfit to be *plainly mentioned,* are to be *intelligibly* hinted.—How little care has been taken to soften the necessary mention of these things by the translators of the Bible Leviticus & Ezekiel can fully show. The fact is, I believe,—that the manners of the time admitted all the freedom they took, & no one was offended thereby. I was proceeding to quote Beaumont & Fletcher, Dryden, Congreve,—but Mrs. Wood very properly observed that during the reign of Charles II & sometime afterwards the stage partook of the profligacy of the manners of the court, & she might have added that even to the moral authors of *that day,* whose delicacy of expression when they necessarily mentioned indelicate subjects is always conspicuous, the stage appeared to use a most unjustifiable licence of language, &

* From the Latrobe manuscript journals, May 22, 1797.

that it was thought highly disreputable for a young modest Woman to appear at the theatre.

Delicacy, however, admits of many degrees, and is subject to fashion. Xenophon tells us, that a persian lost his character entirely, & became almost infamous if he were heard to cough or seemed to spit. They did not, I presume, chew tobacco. In Virginia this seems ridiculous. The Hindoos never use a right hand for any *indelicate* purpose. It would be profaned & rendered unfit for feeding themselves or for performing any honorable function were they accidentally to make a mistake in this respect. And yet their modest Women, and no women are more scrupulously so, publicly worship their Priapus, *Lingam,*—the grossest of all emblems of the fertilizing powers of the deity. Every married woman wears the *Taly,* a small representation of the same deity. The dress of the Greek Ladies would appear *loose* to a modern belle. A Prostitute would scarce dare to wear it publicly. That of the men was very little short of nakedness. I need say nothing of their naked statues, for we moderns equal them in our apathy at beholding them although in Virginia the infant state of the Arts renders them rare. The Egyptians were not less modest than the Greeks in their morals, & yet the Worship of Priapus was a thing of course. As to the Romans, the delicacy of their Matrons, & the pudicitia of the young women has been held up as an example to the modern World,—& yet the rites of Venus, & many other parts of their divine Worship would appear shocking to us. It may be taken for granted, I think, that the *best* comic poets of every Nation, though they may extend the licence of language to the utmost limits, will not go beyond it in any gross degree. Many have called Horace an impudently licentious poet.—I think it might be proved that the Romans did not think him so,—and Virgil was never suspected by them of licentiousness. His *modesty* has been even praised . . . [Latrobe goes on to quote many lines and phrases from Roman poets each more outspoken than the one preceding in its physiological or erotic references.] I did not,—of course, —insult Mrs. W. with all this indelicate Latin, but *generally* stated what I knew & believed of the manners of the ancients,—& as I have no books, I even now quote scantily & perhaps incorrectly.

I believe it might be easily proved that many things said, done & written as we think, licentiously & indelicately among them,—had no effect upon the moral character of the people; because the *fashion* of delicacy was different.

In order to make out my point, which had grown into the general assertion, *that though much of the moral character of every nation depends upon its manners, it is in a much less degree than should be imagined.*—I then had recourse to what I had myself seen of the manners of different Europaean nations. A very modest Italian girl called her old uncle & guardian an old *buggeroni:* the expression she perhaps did not understand,—I mention it merely as having struck me,—I may say shocked me, in the mouth of a young lady,—whose modesty was not affec[ta]tion. . . . An Italian lady at the table of Sir Wm Hamilton, where french happened to be spoken, of the Buffalo cows, and addressing herself to a Gentleman, said, *N'est il pas bien une circonstance tres singuliere, qu'elles ont leur petite incommodité chaque mois, comme nous autres.* Mrs. Hart—Lady Hamilton, could scarcely keep her chair. The Italians felt nothing.—I disbelieve the fact, by the bye.)—

The French ladies are known to receive visitors in bed in their dressing rooms. I never heard of an instance in which these visits had produced infidelity or even the slightest indelicacy beyond the fashion. In London there is more attention to external decorum, but, I am well convinced, not a whit less real licentiousness. . . . In france the toilet and the bedchamber are open to all visitors. They cannot therefore become places of assignation. And if an assignation be intended, there is no corner of the earth that does not furnish convenient retreats for lovers.

But I can appeal to the experience of almost any one who is past thirty as to a very great Change that has taken place in the fashion of delicacy among ourselves. Look at your Mother's picture, & ask yourself whether you would expose to any painter what is there exhibited. [Latrobe continues by comparing the costume of 1750, with its tight lacing, unnatural silhouette, and exposed bosom, to the fashions of 1800, loose and natural but with the bosom modestly covered, and he comes to the conclusion that each would appear indecent to the wearers of the other.]

In this way we might carry our reasonings almost to any length, and at last be tempted to conclude that *indelicacy* as far as it is free from vice is an artificial idea, and that delicacy is a *relative* not a *positive* virtue. . . .

We are children of habit herein as in almost every thing else.—You tell me, & I agree with you most cordially,—that the virginian ladies are *delicate* in the highest degree. This I discover'd very soon after my arrival among them. I prefer their manners without exception to those of the Women of any country I was ever in. Were I to chuse a Wife by manners I would chuse a Virginian, and yet let me tell you there are things done & seen in Virginia which would shock the delicacy of a bold Englishwoman, a free Frenchwoman, & a wanton Italian. What do you think, Madam, of the naked little boys & girls running about every plantation. What do you think of the Girls & Women, waiting upon your daughters in presence of Gentlemen with their bosoms uncovered. What think you of the known promiscuous intercourse of your servants, the perpetual pregnancies of your young servant girls, fully exhibited to your children, who will know, that marriage exists not among them?

Oh but who minds the blacks; you surely are aware of the difference between them and the whites. Our Girls never think of these things; they appear to them as a different race, neither objects of desire, nor actuated by the same *refined* passions with themselves!—

You are right, Madam! Poor wretched Blacks! You are indeed degraded; not even considered as better for virtue, or worse for vice! Outcasts of the moral, as of the political world! Your *loves* on a level with those of the dogs and cats,—denied protection to your affections, and deemed incapable of that sentiment, which, refining sexual desire into love, melts soul into soul with a union not less rapturous than the embrace of wedded & *virtuous sensuality*.—

You are certainly right: our Girls never think of these things.—Neither do the frenchwomen think any thing of toilet visits, the Bostonians of bundling, the Kentish peasants of pregnancies previous to marriage, the Hindoos of the Worship of Lingam, or the Mundingo & Dahomy negroes of assemblies of the Naked of both sexes.—

3. Dr. Sellon's Death and the Reading of His Will *

[In midsummer, 1790, Dr. Sellon had a serious paralytic stroke in his house at Halsden Green.] He was senseless. It happened that *all* his married daughters and daughters in law were in a situation which rendered violent grief extremely dangerous, but nothing could move them from the Chamber of their dying friend. D[r] Potter who attended, was so affected as to be unable to administer those medical applications which

* From the Latrobe manuscript journals, April 15, 1797.

were advised by himself, and in fact I became the only active nurse, and exerted myself for near 24 hours incessantly to recall departing life by friction & various other means. In the mean time all the Ladies were in tears, & his two eldest sons sat in silent grief upon the side of the Bed. The youngest was in Ireland & Mr. Smith did not choose to attend. Mrs. Sellon seemed totally torpid evidently overpowered by the weight of her grief. I prevailed upon most of the married Ladies to lie down alternately for a few hours.—They all met again in the Chamber very early on the second morning and a few moments afterwards Dr. Sellon expired without a groan.—I removed Lydia from the scene as soon as possible into the garden and succeeded in moderating the expression of her grief. On my return to the bed-chamber, I found every one dissolved in tears; loud lamentations filled the room, the men were as intemperate as the women, they were embracing, vowing eternal and indissoluble affection, & invoking the departing spirit of their father to witness the attachment of his Children to one another, and their dutiful veneration for their mother.—It was a little overdone, but as they were all beings of warm imaginations, I am sure it was sincere. I had been talking philosophy in the garden, & was not wound up to the key in which the rest were performing. I kept Lydia out of the room, & by degrees broke up the party and cleared the Chamber. . . .

I was most exceedingly moved by the romantic attachment that seemed to have melted all the contrarieties of their characters into one mass of strongly cemented affection. Late in the evening I accidentally heard Patty [one of Lydia's sisters] half whisper and half cry to her brother John who sat in the next chair,—"My dearest Jack, when is our dearest father's will to be read?" "Tomorrow morning," said he.

We shall have a quarrell in the course of tomorrow, said I, to Lydia.—

How could she think of the Will, said she. Let us go to town immediately, I would not stay to hear it.

The curricle [their only method of travel] however was returned.

We went to bed early. Before breakfast I was out in the fields with Lydia. At eight we returned and John gave notice that after breakfast the will would be read. This will had been drawn without any consultation with any of the family but Mr John Sellon the barrister, & was upon the whole a most equitable and elegant production. It had been signed only a few days before Dr Sellon's last illness, and its contents were unknown to any but John.

The Ladies were in a corner whispering guesses at the probable disposal of their father's effects.

Lydia was shocked, and I wished to get away, pleading her ill health; but Mrs White [a sister of Lydia] *would* stay, & had sent away my carriage meaning to take us home in her coach.

Dr White had got drunk the evening before & was very unwell and not quite sober. Wm Sellon had the principal part of the personal estate in his possession and was uneasy lest unpleasant arrangements might be made to take the money out of his hands.

Mr Smith [Lydia's brother-in-law] had just arrived and was angry at his wife's evident fatigue and indisposition.

Mrs White was vexed at her husband and fretful. Mrs John Sellon was frightened lest she might have caught a fever, or be overset in going home, and her fears were soon encreased to a panic by a slight thunderstorm.

Mrs William Sellon looked ill & began to broad hem a piece of muslin.

Poor Mrs Sellon wept silently.

There was no kissing, no embracing, no vows, no protestations, an air of suspended discontent reigned throughout the company.

Breakfast was at last got over and we adjourned to ye drawing room.

"In the name of God, Amen,—I William Sellon of the parish of Clerkenwell,—" &c, &c.

All the chairs moved three inches nearer into the middle of the room, except mine and Lydia's which moved six inches back,—

"do give and bequeath,"—

Two more inches advance in the position of the chairs,—

"unto John Sellon . . ." [The details of the will then follow.]

As these different articles were read the Chairs gradually retreated till they were all close to the wall.

Silence reigned for some minutes when John Sellon had done reading.

"I should like to know who drew that Will," said Mrs White, "and why I am worse off than my Sisters."—

"You are much better off," said Martha, "than we who may starve if the estate fail; I think you cannot complain. Our father has been very considerate."

"I am sure I cannot tell how to pay 10,000 out of my business," said William, "without becoming a bankrupt."

"And I am sure,—" said Aunt Fraser, "the Chapel will not pay all these annuities & Latrobe's settlement into the bargain which is as good as a bond debt."—

"I will then give up my settlement," said Lydia.—

"That you shan't, my dear,—" said her mother.—

"Don't be a fool girl," said Smith, "but I am sure my wife has charity enough to provide for poor Mrs White by sharing with her, her revenue of 50 pounds Sterling pr annum. Don't cry, Mrs White, I'll find you bread & butter. There's a dear love!—"

"Pray hold your tongue you brute," replied Mrs White.

"Ladies!" said Doctor White, "suppose you say no more about it now, but let us have a glass of wine together and then go home."—

"I wish I were safe home," said Mrs John S., "the roads are very bad & dangerous."—

"It was an odd whim," said Mrs White, "of our father's to give Latrobe that settlement & rob the rest of his Children."—

"I cannot hear my wife's father called a robber even by a Lady," said I. "You will therefore be so good as to say you were mistaken."

Lydia left the room.

"Don't talk nonsense," said Dr White [to his wife], "you are eaten up with the sin of covetousness. Latrobe, come & drink a glass of wine with me."—I did so, Mrs Sellon left us.

John Sellon then *commanded* in a very elegant & pertinent little speech silence upon the subject of the will, & recommended separation.

The Coach drew up. Dr White pushed me & my wife in, got in himself, and then pulled his wife in after him.

This was very distressing to me and I was beginning to make some sort of an apology to Mrs White for getting in first,—but she only answered that her father might as well have left her £1,000 besides her share of the Residue, for she should certainly have given it to her Sisters.—As for me, it was a shame that I should enjoy my £1,000 on such better terms than any of the rest.

The fact is that I lost about 400 by the arrangement, though my security was certainly excellent. I had even to pay for my wife's wedding cloaths after her father's death, no provision having been made by the will for that debt, and *Lydia* having ordered them.—

This most equitable Will thus separated a family, before proverbially affectionate. Whenever they afterwards met there was the greatest show of attachment, sincere, no doubt, for the time, but it was daily growing colder when I left them.

4. Letter to Mary Latrobe Describing a Dinner with Jefferson *

Washington City Novr 30th 1802

My dearest Mary,

Yesterday I wrote to you a long letter for which you will have to pay treble postage, but if you value my letters, as I do yours you will not complain. I had dined with the president: his invitation was to meet a small party of friends,—& accordingly I found only 3 besides myself.—I was introduced to them all, but their names were pronounced in so slovenly a way by Capt. Lewis, the President's secretary,—that I only half understood them & had in ten minutes forgotten them entirely, for my head was full of a previous conversation on the Drydocks. Their names are however of no consequence: they were all men of science,—one of them had a broad Scotch accent & seemed lately arrived.—The conversation turned on the best construction of arches,—on the properties of different species of Limestone,—on cements generally,—on the difference between the French and English habits of living as far as they affect the arrangement of their houses,—on several new experiments upon the properties of light,—on Dr. Priestley,—on the subject of emigration,—on the culture of the time,—on the dishonesty of Peter Legoux & his impudence,—on the domestic manners of Paris, & the orthography of the English & French Languages,—by this time the President became very entertaining & told among others the following anecdote of a Friend, Dorcas.—

A number of English, & some french Ladies with their husbands were assembled at Dr. Franklin's,—who spoke wretched French. Dorcas whose proficiency was not much greater, undertook on several points to set him to rights, & had become very ridiculous by some of her corrections. At that moment Temple Franklin entered, & in one of his freaks of assurance kissed the Lady who stood nearest to the door,—& then went round the room saluting each of them;—& last of all he kissed Mrs. Jay.—Mrs. Jay unused to such gallantry blushed so deeply that Dr. Franklin observ-

* In the possession of the Latrobe family.

ing it, asked why she blushed.—Mrs. M. [Dorcas] immediately answered, "Parc'qu'il a *lui* baissé *la derriere,"* instead of *la derniere.* Poor Dorcas might as well have used the broad English phrase of Moll Turner,—as to the feelings of Mrs. Jay, or the entertainment of the French Men.

Yesterday night I wrote thus far, I was then absolutely driven by the cold into bed, for as it was the first day of the Races, every body had gone out, & there was no Wood split.—This is one of my grievances,—for the wood comes home in long logs & must be cut up by the Servants. —The races have brought hundreds to this city, and among the rest Judge & Mrs. Washington who called upon me for ten minutes,—& appeared, & I am sure were so unfeignedly glad to see me, that I have not felt so much pleasure since I left home.—You are absolutely bespoke for Mount Vernon, & no denial is to be taken.—Several other of my Virginia acquaintance are here & have called, but I have not [been] out of my room,—not even to spend the evening with Judge Washington as I was invited to do, or with Chevalier d'Yrujo as I also ought to have done,—for it rained violently all the evening & night, & I was glad of the excuse,—for I cannot afford the time, and as to amusement I find none in any party.—I did not receive a letter from you yesterday,—for no mail arrived but today expect a few lines with certainty. You ought to have received a letter from me daily,—for I have not once missed,—nor do I intend it. Would to God I could return to you on the day you mention,—Monday,—but you forget that that is the *day* on which at *soonest* I can leave this Place,—for it is the day on which Congress opens, & of course I must stay till then. Then there are *three days of travelling* to be got over before I can again embrace you. I shall not be able to say with certainty what day I can return till *Saturday* next. God keep you my best beloved wife. Take care of yourself & of your dear infant, & believe me unalterably

Yours,

B. Henry Latrobe

5. Report and Estimate on the New York–Long Island Bridge *

N. I. Roosevelt, Esq.

Wilmington, Nov[r] 10th 1804

My dear Sir,

After all the conversations I have had with you on the situation which you deem the most eligible for the construction of a bridge to connect New York Island with Long Island;—and with all the information you have given me as to the depth of water, the strength of the tide, and the nature of the bottom between Blackwell's Island and the opposite shores, I can only give you a general opinion on the practicability and expense of a work, which will require great patience, and considerable liberality of wealth in the projectors, and all the science, perseverance, & courage in the Engineer, which perhaps any similar work ever demanded.

That,—as a *work of art* it is practicable, may indeed at once be asserted. The depth of the water, the length of each part of the bridge, and the rapidity of the current are difficulties, which singly & perhaps in combination have been successfully overcome in similar undertakings in Europe, & certainly works have been erected in which much more formidable obstacles presented themselves singly. The impracticability,—if it exist, is in the expense, and of this it is your wish that I should give you some idea.—

The expense of a Bridge at Blackwell's Island, from the bottom to the springing of the arches, will not be considerably lessened or increased by any species of superstructure which may be adopted. The same piers must be built to support stone, Iron, or Wooden arches,—and the expense of the abutments of a wooden bridge compared with those required for a stone structure, will produce but a small saving, in comparison of the whole expense.—

To estimate, or even guess at the expense of a work of this kind, experience is necessary. Europaean experience, however, is not of much use in respect to estimating the expense; the circumstances under which public works can be there undertaken & built being very widely different.—In America, I have been engaged in one work of similar construction, but

---

* From the Latrobe letter books.

much inferior magnitude, I mean the river Wall of the Basin in the Schuylkill at Philadelphia. When this wall was built the depth at high water was 15 feet, though it has since considerably diminished. The foundation of the Wall at the South end was laid 12 feet below the bed of the river, by the removal of all the loose rocks and gravel. The expense of this wall, including that of the Cofferdam, and of the machinery for piles & drainage was 4$87 p perch,—or very nearly 20 cents p cube foot.

Near the Basin have been constructed the piers of the Schuylkill bridge, —one of which is a work very similar both in the difficulty of construction & size to those which will be required in the Sound at New York. This work however has rather been a school in which experience has been acquired by those who had never before seen or undertaken any similar [work], than a work begun & carried on with system & knowledge. In many instances therefore it has been unnecessarily expensive, & would probably have failed altogether, but for the extraordinary natural talents, perseverance, & integrity of the Stonemason, Thos Vickers, who had before been employed in the Waterworks of Philadelphia and is now engaged by the Chesapeake & Delaware Canal company. I have taken some pains to procure the best information respecting the expense of these Coffredams, & pumping, and also the repair of the damages by accident, which ought not to have occurred,—much more than 10 Dollars p perch, or about 40 Cents p cubic foot. But lest this estimate may be too favorable, which is more probable than the contrary, 50 Cents p foot is certainly a very ample allowance.

Now if the bottom, in the Sound, have a lining of 3 or 4 feet of mud or gravel, the same mode of constructing a Coffredam, or one nearly similar, may be used which was employed in the Schuylkill, and then,—the price of 50 Cents p foot cubic, would be a very good datum on which to reason as to the probable expense of the piers of your proposed bridge.—But if either the rapidity of the current or the nature of the bottom render it necessary to sink Cassoons [caissons],—though this method may prove much cheaper,—yet it is also liable to more expensive accidents.—Upon the whole however, when it is considered, that in constructing your bridge you will probably begin by collecting the best talents, especially the most experienced workmen, which you can command,—and not adopt the propositions of men without instruction, merely because they are men of reputation for *natural* genius, you may escape much of the expense incurred at the Schuylkill bridge;—which, notwithstanding the ineligible system adopted,—is a great & noble work, & should operate to encourage similar undertakings in the United States, by exhibiting an instance of perseverance,—public spirit overcoming the most formidable difficulties in the finances of the company, as well as the nature of the work.—It appears also that in the supply of stone, and lime, & of Timber your advantages are superior to those of the Schuylkill bridge company,—and a reduction of expense may also be calculated from thence.

What I have stated above furnishes the ground of the estimate I shall offer to you; of a work which after all is dependent on unforeseen events both as to time, and the expense of its construction.—

Whether the bridge be of wood, or Iron, or of Stone I would not on any account advise the construction of Arches above 120 feet in Span. A less Span would in every case be better, though a much larger would be practicable. But then the risks are greater in value, than the saving of one or two piers.

I will suppose the bridge to be thus constructed. Between the N. York shore & Blackwell's Island you state the distance to be by estimation 700 ft. I suppose it may be contracted in its waterway to 540 feet.—Over this part let the Bridge be of 5 Arches.—

	ft
Center Arch	120
Two next arches, on each side, 110 f each	220
Two Land arches—@ 100 ea.	200
	540
Four piers—at 20 ea.	80
Leaving between the abutments ashore	620 feet

The width of the bridge should not, on any principles of permanence, convenience, or beauty to [sic] be less than 50 feet wide, including the parapet Walls.—This would make the piers about 80 feet long. The largest ship of war may pass under an arch of 80 feet above the water, (if I recall right) by lowering her topgallant masts. Now if the piers be carried up 20 feet above the Water line at high Water, and the arches be semicircular, there will be 80 feet under the Center arch and 70 feet under the two Land arches and such a bridge would offer no material obstruction to the Navigation.

2. Between Blackwell's Island and Long Island.—

The distance between Blackwell's Island & Long Island, you state to be 1400 feet by estimation;—that the deepest Water is near Blackwell's, & that shallower Water extends a considerable distance from the Long Island shore,—which is also less elevated than the shore of N. York Island.—I will therefore suppose, that from Blackwell's Island towards Long Island, there be constructed 5 Arches exactly similar to those on the opposite side,—that the last of these abut on a pier of 30 feet in width and that from thence a series of smaller arches say, of 60 feet span lead to the Long Island shore.

The Waterway would then be contracted to *1080 feet.*

5 Arches as on the other side, ...	540
9 Arches of 60 feet span	540
Waterway	1,080
4 piers of 20 feet	80
1 do—of 30 feet	30
8 do—of 12 feet	96
Distance between the abutments	1,286

On this general plan of a bridge the estimate will proceed thus:

The 8 principal piers, suppose the average depth of water to be 30 feet, will be 50 feet high—

height leng. wide piers cubic f^t cts $

50 × 80 × 20—80,000 cubic f^t × 8—640,000 @ 50 320,000

wid leng. high

One pier 30 × 80 × 35—84,000 cubic f^t— @ 50^{cts}.............. 42,000

Eight lesser piers on the Long I. side, say in 15 feet

high piers

35 × 80 × 12—33,600 Cub. f^t × 8—267,800 @ 40 ^{cts}........ 107,520

4 Butments, equal in expense to 4 lesser piers 84,000

Brought forward 553,520

With common good luck as to the seasons, & the bottom, this ought to be a very ample estimate of the piers.—I will now suppose a stone superstructure. Of course a wooden bridge will be much below it in expense. Anyone acquainted with such subjects may analyze the following heads of estimate.—

1. Centering for 3 large Arches, & 3 small arches	75,000
2. Solid Stone work in all the Arches, which may be executed at 6$25 p perch or 25^{cts} nearly p cube feet, 720,000 cube ft	180,000
3. Flank walls, parapets, spandrels, wings, 280,000 cube f^{t} at 25^{cts} cub. f^{t}	70,000
4. Stairs, and Wharfwalls 42,000 @ 40 ^{cts}	16,800
	895,320
Add for incidents 10 p Cent	89,532
	984,852

I have no doubt whatsoever that,—if the leading features of the work be as I have stated them the expense will be about 950,000 Dollars & no more.—

But in order to proceed on safer grounds, I must request you will send to me as soon as possible the following points of information—

1. A survey of Blackwell's Island, and of the opposite shores,—showing the nature & elevation of the soil on each side.

2. The soundings across the two channels in all places supposed to be at all eligible. These soundings may be taken with the common log line between Flood & Ebb, in two or three places up & down stream in each 600 feet, & in distances not exceeding 25 feet across the stream.—

3. The nature of the bottom,—particularly observing whether it be encumbered with large masses of loose rocks,—stating also whether and where covered with mud or sand. The best bottom for such an undertaking is rock covered with 6 to 10 feet of mud.

4. The price of Quarry stone, (I presume granite) on the spot,—of Newark freestone,—of Lime, and whether the stone of the Island & shores will bear rough hammering at a moderate expense.—

With this information I shall be able to correct the above estimate. Whenever I receive it I will pay as early attention to the subject as my present engagement will permit.

I am with true respect

Yours truly

B. Henry Latrobe

6. References to the Plan and Sections of the Town of New-castle *

1. Plan of the Town.

In this Plan is laid down every description of Houses which stood at the time the survey of the Town was made for the regulations of the Streets, with the division of the lots.—NB. as these divisions of the lots were not laid down from actual measurement no reference must be had to them for the purpose of ascertaining limits.

The names written upon the plan are not in all cases those of the proprietors but in many,—of the tenants.

The dotted lines represent the proposed extension of certain Streets, and the introduction of others for the enlargement of the Town. Though these streets are drawn parallel with the others I would not recommend them to be so laid out; if in process of time the Commissioners should find it necessary to extend the boundary of the town, for the following reasons: During the unhealthy months of the year—that is from July to October the prevailing winds are from the South West—It is a general and true observation that the Eastern shores of our Rivers are less healthy than the Western, most probably because the SW wind blows from the Water upon the former, & from the Land upon the latter. It is therefore best to place a town upon the shore of a river which is to windward of the River when the South West wind blows.

The North-west winds in the United States in the Winter and the North East at all seasons are the most unpleasant, and the latter the most unwholesome of our winds. Every house and every town ought therefore to be so constructed & placed as to be as well as possible protected against them.

Next to the Winds, the *Sun* in our Climate most influences the health and the pleasantness of our Towns & houses—A house built with its front to the East & West is therefore both in Summer & Winter a disagreeable habitation. Exposed to the NW & NE winds, it is also heated to its center by the ascending & by the declining Sun.

From these simple facts it is evident that we have in America only *one*

* Original manuscript in the Historical Society of Delaware.

good aspect—the *South*—Next to the South is the North aspect, for though equally exposed to the North West & North East winds with the East & West faces, it escapes in a great degree the effects of the Sun looking into and heating the deep recesses of our chambers.

From the preceding facts which are too simple and too well known to be doubted, it results that to place a house to face the SW & NE or the SE & NW is to court every possible inconvenience which can result from the effect of the Sun & wind in our climate. The NW & NE winds blow directly upon two of the sides & the South West which is by far the pleasantest breeze is confined to one single front. In Summer the Sun rising on the North East front looks into the SE & NW at a low angle in its ascent & descent, and sets on the NW front, driving,—as we see in many instances, the inhabitants from one part of the building to the other for shelter in the course of every day.

With these facts before us, it would seem surprising that the majority perhaps of our American towns & houses are actually built so as to face the SW or NE. The influence this circumstance has upon our manners & our health is much more extensive & powerful than we are aware of, and may be guessed at even from the enquiry into what will be the difference of attention to business of a man who in summer inhabits a cool dwelling, every apartment in which has its appropriate & permanent distinction, & of one who is driven from his front into his back & from his East into his West rooms in the course of every day, without finding himself perfectly at ease in any of them.—

What in regard to aspect is true of houses is also so of towns—a town the streets of which run in parallel lines pointing to the SW & NW cannot possibly have a single well placed house in it. The reason why so egregious an error has been committed in the plan of most of our towns and of our many cities destined to be very populous, is, on this side of the Allegheny, & South of New York, the general course of the rivers on which they are situated & which is almost universally SW or SE—It has not been considered that streets diverging from the Water render every part of the town quite as, if not more, accessible from the wharves than streets at right angles with them. The only inconvenience that can arise from such an arrangement of the streets is, that a few houses will not have rectangular corners. The houses on the street next to the river will have a bad aspect, because convenience will require that they should run parallel with the river. But all others may be placed parallel to, or at right angles with the meridian, and it is surely better to sacrifice the form of half a dozen houses in a part of the town in which form is of little or no consequence, than to ruin the aspect of all the houses in the town.

[?] next to SW or SE position the E & W fronts is the worst—it ought to be considered in planning a town in what manner it may be so arranged as to increase the S & N fronts as much as possible in proportion to the number of houses that look to the East & West. This can only be done by laying down the streets that run E & West and the houses in [sic] which front N & W, at such distances from each other that there shall be only sufficient depth for roomy accommodations backwards & for a spacious alley between them & to remove those streets that run N & South as far from each other as convenience will permit, that is, not more than 500 f[t]. It is evident that by this means there will be much less room for houses looking East & West than for those that front N & South—

7. Letter to Robert Mills with Regard to the Profession of Architecture *

Mr. Rob[t] Mills, Ph[a]

Washington, July 12th 1806

My dear friend:

Every new proof of your talents, your excellent disposition, & of the respect you acquire wherever you are known gives me the truest pleasure. In this point of view, I have derived real satisfaction from the correspondence you have communicated to me. The letter of the Governor of S. Carolina does both him and you honor; and accustomed as I have been to receive & place a *true* value upon the polite & flattering things which Men of education & of the world so well know how to say and to write,—I cannot but consider his letter to you as an exception to the general rule,—and as a deserved testimony to your merit by a man of true discernment.—

You will however permit me to make a few remarks, both on your own conduct on entering into the practice of a liberal profession and upon that of the Gentlemen who have hitherto, or who may in future reap the advantage of your talents.

* From Latrobe's letter books.

The profession of architecture has been hitherto in the hands of two sorts of men. The first,—of those, who from travelling or from books have acquired some knowledge of the theory of the art,—but know nothing of its practice:—the second—of those who know nothing but the practice,—and whose early life being spent in labor, & in the habits of a laborious life,—have had no opportunity of acquiring the theory. The complaisance of these two sets of men to each other, renders it difficult for the Architect to get in between them, for the Building mechanic find[s] his account in the ignorance of the *Gentleman-architect;*—as the latter does in the submissive deportment which interest dictates to the former.—

It is therefore with sincere regret that I have observed your talents and information thrown into a sort of scramble between the two parties,—in the designs of the churches you have given to the congregations at Charleston. You remember the faults I pointed out to you at an early period of your studies in my office especially in the round church.—You corrected them. Your design had besides very great & intrinsic merits of its own.—What has been the event.—Of all those who have contributed their ideas to that church you have been considered as the most ignorant. You have not even been permitted to correct your own errors, and in other points you have been overruled so far as to have [been] obliged to admit into your plan absolute absurdities,—such as, for instance the Gallery within the cupola, which may probably be the cause why within an interior circle of a certain diameter in the Center of the Church the preacher's voice is said to be not perfectly heard.—

Such a situation is degrading and would not be submitted to by any other member of a liberal Profession, & scarcely by a Mechanic whose necessities were not greater than his pride.—In our country indeed the profession of an Architect is in a great measure new. The building artisans, especially the Carpenters have been sufficiently informed to get through the business & supply the orders of a young country. Out of this state of infancy we are now emerging,—& it is necessary that those who have devoted their best Years & a very considerable expenditure to the attainment of that variety of knowledge which an Architect ought to possess,—should take their legitimate rank themselves, or not venture into that Ocean of contact with all above & all below them into which a mistaken complaisance will throw them, but adopt some other profession sanctioned by the habits & opinions of the country.—

It will be answered,—"If you are paid for your designs & directions, he that expends his money on the building has an undoubted right to build what he pleases."—If you are paid!!—I ask in the first place are you paid? —*No!* The custom of all Europe has decided that 5 p Cent on the cost of a building, with all personal expenses incurred, shall be the pay of the Architect.—This is just as much as is charged by a Merchant for the transaction of business,—expedited often in a few minutes by the labor of a Clerk:—while the Architect must watch the daily progress of the work perhaps for Years, pay all his Clerk hire, & repay to himself the expense of an education greatly more costly than that of a merchant.—But it was not my intention to enter at present into the question of *compensation,* for in your case, I believe that you have neither asked nor received anything but have given your advice, pour l'amour de dieu.—The question is in how far you ought to permit yourself to be overruled in your opinion by your employers,—and in order to answer it,—I have neither leisure, nor inclination to go into a methodical disquisition,—but shall in a desultory manner proceed to the end of my letter which as it is dictated only by friendship, will not be received by you, as a regular treatise of the *Ethics* of our profession,—but as a proof of my good will.—

If the most distinguished lawyer of our city,—Mr. Rawle for instance, or Mr. Wm L. Smith of South Carolina, were consulted as to the division, settlement, or alienation of a large Estate,—he would be informed by the parties concerned,—*what it was, that they actual*[*ly*] *wanted,*—the titles would be put into his hands, the shares, as to their amount and locality perhaps, exactly defined,—& the drafting of the instrument then would be committed to him.—As soon as the *draft* of the instrument were prepared, the parties would be called together, its nature, obligations, covenants, & general tendencies would be fully explained. In examining this draft, it would very probably occur, that some intelligent person would discover that the intention of the parties had been mistaken,—that the operation of the arrangement would be different perhaps than was expected, or that improvements in the settlements might be made. The lawyer consulted would not hesitate, to redraw, to change his disposition, untill all parties were satisfied.—But if on hearing the deed read,—any one of the party were to attempt to correct the technical phraseology, —the *terms* of the conveyance,—or to produce the opinions of the physician next door, or of the planter five miles off,—or of some wonderfully ingenious young Lady, or some person of surprizing *natural legal* talents from the backwoods, as to the form of the deed, its construction, or its alteration,—you would certainly hear no more from Mr. Rawle or Mr. Smith, excepting as to the amount of his charge for trouble already incurred.

In exactly this situation is an architect who is consulted on a public work.—He should be first informed *what it is that is wanted,*—what expense might be contemplated by his design,—what are the particular views of the persons who have the management of the money devoted to the Work.—

There will be on the part of a sensible & good tempered Man,—no objection to any reasonable extent of revision, or rerevision of a first design. Enlargement, contraction, alteration of arrangement, of construction & of decoration may be made by a Man of talents in almost infinite variety, & suggestions from unprofessional Men politely & kindly made are always acceptable.—But no honest man will for a moment listen to the proposal that he shall lend his name to the contrivances of Whim or of ignorance, —or under the pretence of a cheap, give to the public a bad work.—there is, as in most proverbs, a vast deal of good sense in the old Latin proverb . . . in sua arte credendum. We allow full faith to our plainest mechanics in their particular callings. No man thinks himself capable of instructing his shoemaker, or his tailor. Indeed we swallow what the physician orders with our eyes shut, & sign the deed the Lawyer lays before us with very little enquiry.—But every gentleman can build a house, a prison or a city.—This appears extraordinary;—for when a Gentleman sets about the work, he has the interests of all those he employs in array against his fortune, without any protection in his own knowledge. The mechanical arts employed in the erection of a capital building are more than 20. Of these every architect has a competent knowledge, so as to judge of the quality as well as of the value, & the *amount* of the work, but it is at least 20 to one, against the *Gentleman* who trusts only himself, that he will lose 5 p Cent at least.

Then as to the arrangement. Every architect who has been regularly educated knows what has been done before in the same line. This knowledge he necessarily acquires in the office in which he studies not only from the books, and designs which he finds there, but in the instructions, & *actual practice* of his principal, provided he [be] a man of intelligence, candor, and of business.

You are, on the subject of the difference between the professional & regular mode of conducting your works, as well as small buildings,—and the desultory guessing manner in which they are otherwise managed,—too well informed by experience, to render it necessary for me to proceed further on this head.—I will now give you with my accustomed frankness, my opinion of the conduct you should pursue in respect to the proposed peni[tent]iary house.—

1. In the first place,—*do nothing gratuitously.* The state of Carolina are infinitely better able to pay you well, [than] you are to subscribe your time & your talents,—which is your subsistence towards the *annual revenue* of the State:—for this is the actual effect of gratuitous professional services.—As far as you have hitherto promoted the very laudable design of the Government by exhibiting the practicability of such a building as will be necessary, if the penitentiary law be enacted you have done well. For many people despair of the *end,* unless they see the *means.* But further you ought not to go without a very clear understanding as to what is to be the reward of your labor.—You know too well the course of my professional transactions to suppose that this advice is the result of a mercenary disposition. The gratuitous services on a very great scale which I have given to *unendowed* public institutions for the promotion of religious, or litterary objects are well known to you, for you have had your share of the labors. But when a rich state is about to execute a project, from which great public benefit is expected to result, compensation to those who assist in effecting that object is a thing so much of course,—that all I have said would appear superfluous,—if the example of the *donation* of time & talent, & expense had not in many instances been set by yourself. Some years ago I resided in Virginia. [Here he narrates the account of his financially disastrous experience as architect of the Virginia penitentiary—an account already cited on page 125. He continues:] My subsequent experience of what is to be expected from public bodies has not differed from that which I gained from Virginia.—You must take it for granted that no *liberality,* that is, *voluntary reward* is ever to be expected from a public body. Individuals, responsible only to themselves in the expenditure of their money, are often generous,—& reward handsomely, independently of stipulation; but a number of the same individuals, meeting as guardians of the public money, feel in the first place, the necessity of pleasing their constituents,—& in the second that

of involving themselves in no unnecessary responsibility.—And if at a public board, one or more individuals are willing at all hazards to act as they would in their own case, it is ten to one but they are a minority.

To balance this want of liberality in public boards, they have this advantage to offer over individual employment,—that when a bargain is made, for a salary, or a commission, it is always rigidly adhered to,—provided it be in writing, & *clearly expressed,* for every ambiguity will always be interpreted for the public, and against the individual.—

In settling what shall be your compensation,—on the presumption of your being employed, I would by all means advise you, to prefer a salary to a commission. It will be both more certain to you, & more satisfactory to your employers.—

2. Take care that before the work begin, the plan is *perfectly understood,* and stipulate that no alteration, but by mutual discussion & agreement shall be made.—

3. Stipulate for the following points,—all of which are most essential:—

No workman shall be employed to whom you object.—

No workman shall be allowed to apply to the *board,* or *individual* to whom the state may delegate the management of the erection of the Work but through you.—

No account shall be paid, unsanctioned by your signature.—

With these powers you will have the mastery of all the operation, and you may do then justice to yourself & to the public, and as no money will pass through your hands,—you will not labor under the temptation, the power, nor the suspicion of violating any point of *pecuniary morality,* —that virtue, which like chastity in women, is in the general opinion supposed to be superior to all others, & almost to render them unnecessary.

4. I fear you have already committed one blunder,—that of leaving your drawings in the hands of the public.—Of the honor, & the gentlemanly feeling of the Governor, far be [it] from me to suggest the slightest suspicion. But his very admiration of your design will produce its exhibition, and as the *principles* of the plan, are the great merit of it,—and these strike at *one view,* you have armed all those who see it, or who hear it described with the weapons of competition against you.—But this is not now to be remedied.

My time will not permit me to say more to you at present. In the conduct of the work should my experience be of any service to you, you will know how freely you may use it.—

May every happiness, & success attend you.

B. Henry Latrobe

8. A Comparison of Alexander Hamilton and Aaron Burr *

You are no doubt acquainted with the individual characters of the late General Hamilton and Colonel Burr. They had been rivals from their youth,—in war, in love, and in politics. Both possessed superior talents and inordinate ambition. Their characters were so similar, and their abilities so equal, that the difference between them appears to have existed rather in their dispositions than in their talents.

Mr. Hamilton had more apparent frankness and candor, with less actual benevolence; Colonel Burr, more discretion and command of himself, with the most generous and liberal mind. Of Colonel Burr, numerous proofs of the most disinterested benevolence are known. He has educated at his own expence, to letters and to the arts, several young men who are now useful to themselves and the public. Not a single instance of munificence is known to Hamilton. As individuals, Burr undoubtedly is infinitely more amiable than Hamilton was, and he is less a hypocrite. Hamilton tho' an insatiable libertine, talked of religion and order; and went to church from the bed of the wife of his friend. He was shot on the very spot where his son had fallen in a duel, to which his father advised him; and when brought home wounded, sent for a Bishop to administer the sacrament to him to prepare him for death. The papers he left behind breathe piety and resignation; and his object was accomplished, for at his death he was canonized. Burr, on the contrary, pretended to no religion, and indulged in amorous excesses without disguise; but, he carried unhappiness into no man's family. Seduction was no part of his plan of pleasure, and yet he was abused for his libertinism more than Hamilton; for he was not a Federalist, and in this respect, no hypocrite. It is singular that both Hamilton and Burr were little of stature, and both inordinately addicted to the same vice.

* From a letter to Philip Mazzei (December 19, 1806) in the Latrobe letter books.

9. Letter to Henry Baldwin on Latrobe's Connection with the Early Development of Steamboats *

Henry Baldwin Esqr

Pittsburg Octr 10th 1814

Dear Sir,

I do not at all regret, that my engaging you *generally,* on my arrival here, in the causes which might arise between Mr. Fulton, or the Ohio Steamboat company & others, deprive me, as you inform me, of your counsel in the situation in which I find myself with those parties.—I have that confidence in your integrity, that I should be very willing to submit the whole case to your single decision, and I cannot give you a stronger proof of my sincerity in this respect, than by laying before you all I have to say on the whole subject of my connexion with Mr. Fulton from the beginning. The narrative may I fear be tedious, but I will endeavor to avoid unnecessary prolixity.—

In the Year 1798, Chancellor Livingston, Mr. John Stevens, & Mr. Roosevelt were engaged in the attempt to navigate the River Hudson, & its neighboring Waters by machinery driven by Steam. I was a witness to their attempts, although I was not on board at the time, I have reason to believe that their boat which I saw & examined at Laurel hill on the Passaick did go to New York in the time limited by the act of the State of New York for the purpose of entitling the parties to a monopoly of the navigation of the Hudson.—

About this time, or a little after, Chancellor Livingston was sent out as Ambassador to France from the U. States. I saw him in Philadelphia just before he left the city, and he requested me to give all my exertions to his friends to compleat the project in which he had been engaged.—But I had other pursuits, & the many failures of the Steamboats discouraged in me all hopes of their success.

In 1808, I think, (perhaps later) I saw Mr. Fulton at Washington. Mr. Roosevelt was also there, & was soon after married to my daughter. A suit against Mr. Roosevelt, on the part of the U. States, for money formerly advanced to him to a great amount, had at that time exceedingly

* From Latrobe's letter books.

depressed the circumstances, & credit of Mr. Roosevelt. Against the influence of the Chancellor Livingston who was then connected with Fulton in the steamboat navigation of the North river with their wealth, it was in vain to contend, under the circumstances of Mr. Roosevelt's doubtful fortunes. He consulted me on the subject, & after showing me his grounds of a claim in the Chancellor's share of the concern, I undertook to speak to Mr. Fulton, & to endeavor to procure for him such advantages, as it might be practicable to obtain by negociation.

With Mr. Fulton's conduct on this difficult occasion I have every possible reason to be satisfied. The grounds on which I was able to urge Mr. Roosevelts claim, were not the best which he might have produced. With his real title to a share in the whole Patent, I was not made acquainted untill July 1813 when I saw him at New York, when he laid the correspondence of himself with the Chancellor before me which passed in the Year 1798-9; & in which he Roosevelt had urged the Chancellor to employ,—instead of all his other contrivances, the very wheels over the side which are the sole foundation, & peculiarity of Mr. Fulton's claim to exclusive privileges;—as far as the application of the principles of his system to practice, are concerned. It is not my intention to deny the claim of an original invention of this application to Mr. Fulton. He has I believed proved, that in a letter to Bolton & Watt of a prior date the same mode of navigation had been suggested by him; but it does not appear that he ever put it into practice untill his connexion with Chancellor Livingston at Paris: and before an impartial Jury, it would hardly be decided that Mr. Roosevelt had not any claim to a share in the Chancellors profits of any project, which he had rejected with contempt when connected with Roosevelt, but which he had adopted in connexion with Fulton & thereby amassed great wealth. At all events Mr. Roosevelt could have entered a caveat as to the patent & supported his prior claim before a commission appointed under the patent law, by the Secretary of State.

I have collected the whole of the merits of Mr. Roosevelt's case here, altho' at the period of which I am speaking I was very imperfectly acquainted with it. I knew however enough to induce Mr. Fulton to take them into consideration, & after much negotiation it was at last arranged, that Mr. Roosevelt should establish a Navigation by Steamboats on the Western Waters, & share with Livingston & Fulton the profits arising from the Patent, on the condition that he should raise a company or companies for the purpose of carrying it into effect. Mr. Roosevelt found it difficult to collect subscriptions on his own credit, under the circumstances of his suit with the U. States, and Mr. Fulton stepped forward with readiness, & effect, and the subscription was filled. The boat was built at Pittsburg, to which place Mr. Roosevelt & his family removed. The subscription however proved insufficient, and Mr. Fulton again exerted himself, to raise the sum which was deficient, so that at last the New Orleans steam boat went down the river, & untill the loss of the Vessel last Summer not only produced enough to pay all the debts contracted in building her together with the advance on her nominal capital but to yield the stockholders & patentees very handsome dividends.—

In the meantime, irreconciliable disagreement arose between Mr. Fulton & Mr. Roosevelt. It originated, I believe, in the inability of Mr. Roosevelt to fill his subscriptions, and the exertions Mr. Fulton had to make to compleat it: it was afterwards encreased by the call for monies beyond the Capital, to finish the boat, in which Mr. Fulton fancied he saw bad management or waste. But all this could have been explained & justified had not personal irritation preceeded the embarrassments of the concern. The Newspapers were filled with accounts of Mr. *Roosevelt's* boat, & Mr. *Roosevelt's* successful navigation, & Mr. *Roosevelts* dinners on board, without a word said of Mess[rs] Livingston & Fulton. In these puffs I am convinced, by my knowledge of Mr. Roosevelts temper & character that he had no hand. He was on the river when they were published. They were the indiscreet effusions of the wonder & pleasure of his friends,—but certainly they could not be expected to please the patentees. Another very justifiable cause of complaint against him, was, that neither letters nor accounts were received directly from him, altho' he was heard of from others along the whole line of the Mississippi.— These causes of irritation arose to such a highth, that persons were set out to supercede Mr. Roosevelt in the agency & management of the boat;—who, as Mr. R. says, executed their trust with very little delicacy either towards him or his family. Mr. Roosevelt also has assured me that he wrote by every possible conveyance, & transmitted his accounts regularly; but that as his voyage was performed while the whole country was convulsed by Earthquakes, & the navigation of the river altered & rendered dangerous, & while the inhabitants were alarmed & in some places dispersed, it is possible that his letters were lost.—

On his return, new & greater causes of dissention arose: his accounts were objected to & the balance claimed by him detained, to the great distress of his family.

It was necessary that I should give this account of the dispute between the Patentees & Mr. Roosevelt, because, in it, originated my own connexion with them; at the period of which I am now arrived.—

My personal intimacy with Mr. Fulton, & the Share I had in introducing Mr. Roosevelt into connexion with him, made me acquainted with the whole progress of the dispute in all its details, and as matters were represented to me, I thought justice was entirely on the side of Mr. Fulton. My correspondence with Mr. R. would clearly prove with what zeal I entered into the cause against him; nor were my opinions altered untill I saw the whole of his proceeding, & accounts in connexion at New York in July 1813. I then became thoroughly satisfied that he had acted, *throughout,* the part of an honest & zealous agent of the company but also that he had committed the great errors of forgetting that he had to do with a Committee of Merchants, who would admit not even the most probable & justifiable charge unless formally executed, that he had depended more on the weight of character & the influence of gentlemanly feelings than on the dry proofs of the counting house system, & that at all events he had not been very scrupulous in guarding his own interests in detail. But it was also very evident that if he had wronged anybody it was not the Company.—

It is now necessary to state that from the first introduction of Mr. Roosevelt to Mr. Fulton, the latter always stated to me, that the connexion was bottomed on his friendship for *me* & my family, & that his friendship which I believe was very sincere on his part, & I am sure was as sincerely returned on mine led him to all the concessions which he made, in ultimately permitting the accts of Mr. Roosevelt to pass, & the balance then claimed to be paid him.—His friendship for me and my family is also expressly stated to be the consideration; for which the grant of one third of the Patentees profits were settled on his wife Lydia Roosevelt, my daughter, and her heirs,—in lieu of the grant to himself.

Of the zeal with which I have endeavored to serve Mr. Fulton, I will not say any thing. I have no objection to his claims of gratitude from me, for I have in fact received essential favors from him, of the value of which I shall always be sensible, & from which I should have derived essential benefits had the state of the country permitted it.—But in respect to the grant of one third of the Patentees profit on the navigation between Pittsburg & Louisville, I owe him nothing, for I hold it in right of Mr. Roosevelt,—with whom Mr. Fulton positively declared he would never again be connected. I therefore was permitted to step into his place, with the additional grant of one half of the patent right on either the Cumberland or Tennessee on certain conditions.—For the latter I fairly acknowledge my obligation.—

In July 1813 I arrived in New York to make my ultimate arrangements with Mr. Fulton. I received from him drawings of the boat which I now possess, & which I have followed scrupulously, *as I engaged to do* in all the material parts, varying only where the details were not expressed, or former experience on these waters had pointed out improvements without greater expense. I made minute enquiries into the probable cost of such a boat from Mr. Roosevelt. I learned that wages, fuel, board & lodging, timbers, in fact every article which could influence the cost, but Bar Iron were cheaper in Pittsburg than in New York. I knew that Mr. Fulton had contracted to build a boat not much less than that which I was to build, & had estimated it, finished at New York at from 21 to 24000 $, & that he had permitted the Company to proceed & advance money upon the Estimate for which he himself was responsible. I was also persuaded by him, that Mr. Roosevelt had been more lavish in his expenditures than was at all necessary, & that 25,000 $ would with tolerable economy be amply sufficient to finish the boat he directed to be built. I was unavoidably ignorant on the subject of the expense of Steamboats, the only experience in that department being in possession of Mr. Fulton himself.

I returned to Washington in Augt 1813, & sent out my Shipwright & other workmen. I followed them as soon as I could sell my furniture, & arrange my affairs & was in Pittsburg, after a dreadful Journey, the latter part of October.

My first operations were, to lay in lumber, to make contracts for Iron, to find a Scite on which to build to hire Shops & workmen. Unfortunately I was taken seriously & dangerously ill in November & was confined to my room for near a month. On my recovery in December, I collected the castings provided for me by order of Mr. Fulton in the foundery of Mr. Beelen, & the Brasses cast by Meltenberger. I then began to suspect from the amount of the cost of these articles that I should find my Capital deficient;—but it was now too late to alter by diminishing the size of the boat.—My next great disappointment was this: that I could not in any way use the Shops & tools of the Mississippi Company: that no useful Shops could be hired, & that I must build others. I found it would be economy to set about this latter operation immediately, & in the beginning of January I had built the Shops which have been the subject of so much obloquy—but without which the boat & Engine if built at all would have been built at much greater cost.—On the 16th of Nov. I had already given notice that I had purchased timber for Shops, to which no objection was made, in any letter I received. From that day to Decr 12th I was incapable of writing.

In January 1814, every article in which I was interested took a sudden rise, & on the 20th of January I wrote to Mr. Fulton as follows:

"What are we agents to do in the abominable rise of Iron & every thing else necessary to build the boat? Today I gave 86 $ for an Anvil at 40^{cts} p pound. I want 4 Anchors for my boat & freight boat, & must pay 25^{cts} p pd for them. Bar Iron is at 695 $, Plate Iron 300 $, . . . I have not received it."

Feb^{r} 17th I wrote, "I am gradually obliged to provide every thing de novo, necessary to build the Engine except patterns for which I have paid Livingston 500 $." Feb^{r} 22^{d}: "I have been most egregiously disappointed in finding the Shops of the Mississippi company scarce of any use to me beyond the example of what to follow or to avoid which they afford."

On the 4th of March Mr. Fulton wrote to me that I must not be surprised if he protested any further drafts. I had then drawn for 22,807.54 $.

On the 15 & 21st of March I wrote to Mr. Fulton at very great length, and gave him most ample explanations on the expenditure necessary to compleat the boat. The letters are too long to be copied, but the general result is this, that the boats could not cost much less than 45,000 $, but that by the sale of the shops, tools, & other property of the Company their price might perhaps be reduced to 35,000 $.—In these letters I proved, incontestably, by comparison with other boats, that the same tonnage, & other expenses & the same Engine would necessarily amount to that sum.—

On the 20th of April, among much other matter I informed him that I had undertaken business in my profession advantageously. I mention this because he attributed afterwards the failure of my funds to this circumstance whereas on the contrary, my private business supported the boat.

May 1st I proposed 40 more shares to the stock & still insisted that the expense must be *35,000* at least, independently of incidents, shops, tools, &c. This letter of the 1st of May appears to me to have been sufficient to have satisfied any reasonable man of my fair conduct & open exposition of my proceedings. May 14th 1814—I announced the launch of the boat & explained why I had ventured the risk of her receiving the small & reparable injury which I described, & which has since been repaired, & advised of my drafting 2500 $ which Mr. Fulton suffered to be protested, —but which the company afterwards paid.

May 17th. I wrote that having received notice from Mr. Beelen that Mr. Fulton had suffered the drafts of his brother in law Mr. Livingston to be noted, I was in the utmost anxiety respecting my own funds, and urged him to raise money on my Shares of the patent right, to compleat the boat, for which I sent him a power of Attorney.

My letters of the 20th & 22[d] enclosed accounts which are justificatory of my expenditures.

On the 24th I sent a general report to Mr. Fulton of all my proceedings from the commencement of the work, and drafted to the Stockholders the report which you have seen containing all I can even now say on the subject, and as you have read it, I need not further notice it here.

My correspondence from this period is so voluminous that I can only give a general summary of its contents. I had sent monthly general statements of my expenditures. Mr. Fulton complained of want of detail! and I sent him a perfect copy of my day book which I have since brought up to the 1st of Sept[r].

I justified my expenses in the minutest detail, and by a comparison with the expenditures of the Mississippi boats which he approved.—Mr. Fulton sent me estimates of what *ought* to be the cost of the boat, I sent him accounts of what it actually was.—Mr. Fulton became angry reproached me with benefits conferred on me & my family & left my arguments unnoticed. I restrained my feelings & endeavored to give him no offence.—He accused me of speculating, & I stated all my private transactions. Of the only speculation I had made in Nov[r] 1813 I had given him a most minute account then. At last he turned me over to the company, and our correspondence ceased.—

July 9th. I acknowledged in a letter to Dr. Neven the receipt of 3000 remitted to me, & reported the state of the Works. July 24th. I acknowledged the rec[t] of 500 $ more. That money is the last which I have received, & makes the total stand thus:

Drafts on New York	34,231.55	
producing nett proceeds		34,000
Payments by Stockholders in Pittsburg		2,500
Cash remitted by the Company		3,500
		40,000

A draft of 300 $ was protested & paid by a remittance which I made from hence.

On the 1st of Sept[r] I had ascertained clearly that the command of from 6 to 7,000 would enable me to start the boat in a month or five weeks time, & I called the Stockholders together with a view to raise that sum. To encourage them to this exertion, I proposed to secure them by all the property I possessed in the Shops, the boat, & the patent. But I failed in my attempt. Of this failure I apprized the Company, & the answer to my letter was an order to me to deliver the boat & all the property of the Company into the hands of the Agents of the Mississippi company, & a dismissal from my agency.—To the injustice of this proceeding Mr. Fulton added the insult of sending me the letter open by Mail.

I had now to consider what I owed to myself & to the workmen who on the faith of my encouragement had permitted their hard earned Wages to remain in the hands of the Company.—The boat was already attached by a Man whose account for timber I could not possibly sanction, & had refused to pay, & for a small sum by a person in Pittsburg.— The Law of Pennsylvania giving to all persons concerned in the building of houses & Vessels & their outfit, a lien on the same, occurred to me & on consulting counsel I resolved to have recourse to it immediately.— As soon as I had done so, I wrote to the Secretary of the Company, stating that I was ready to settle the business amicably unless treated in an hostile manner.

Having thus stated to you the whole case, I offer to you a perusal of the whole correspondence, & a minute inspection of all my books: or I propose that the whole case shall be submitted to three Merchants or other respectable Men of this town, who have no interest in the boat, & I will abide their decision. I will explain my ideas more fully, as to the course which it should take. The demands against the boat consist of

1. Wages,—2. the claim of persons for Materials, principally, of Mr. Cowan, Mr. Beelen, Mr. Meltenberger, Mr. Boyle Irwine, Mess[rs] Stackpole & Whiting & a few others,—3. of myself for monies advanced &c &c.

1. The first will probably have to be paid in Cash. 2. For the second may be obtained a credit sufficient to enable the boat to proceed, and to earn money to pay them. On the third head every possible facility will be given, provided I am respectfully treated.—I am under personal responsibility for the company to the amount of 600 $ which must be paid.—

I have written this letter with a view to conciliation.—But I shall certainly not quit the ground I have taken without good advice, if I am treated as a culprit.—

Very respectfully Y[rs]

B. H. Latrobe

10. Selections from a Letter to Miss M. Sellon (November 15, 1817) on Henry Latrobe's Death *

. . . On his arrival in Philadelphia he was only 7 years old. I had been, after a widowhood of 7 years nearly, married to Miss Mary Elizabeth Hazlehurst, the only daughter of one of the first merchants, and most respectable men on this side of the Atlantic. One of the conditions which she made with me, was that I should as soon as possible put Lydia and Henry into her hands. Accordingly, about five months after our marriage they arrived. . . . With such a stepmother, no apprehensions of neglect or severity could find room, and in fact, from the first hour of their meeting, little Henry attached himself to her with peculiar fondness, while the approaches of Lydia were much more cold and tardy. From that moment an affection grew up between Henry & his new mother, that had more of freedom & less of the constraint of duty, than might possibly have subsisted between a mother and a child. The great feature, next to her benevolence, of my wife's character is an undaunted firmness in the practice of what she deems right. She is in the highest sense of the word, *a woman of honor*. I have had great occasion to observe this feature of her character in the difference of her conduct towards her adopted & her own children. To the latter, acting without deliberation, she is as we all are, sometimes hasty, & always unceremoni-

* From Latrobe's letter books.

ous, while to Lydia & Henry she mixed the truest affection, with much more consideration of their own wishes & feelings. . . . For I may truly say, that in losing Henry, she has lost what I cannot replace,—the confidant of all her vexations, & the depository of all her secrets; the correspondent to whom she laid open her whole heart without restraint of discretion, without apprehension of the grave lectures of a husband on the imprudence of her wit, and of her satire on the puppets that surround us. With him she scolded, she wept, & she laughed & railed without restraint, and her correspondence with Henry in New Orleans, while it would do honor to the first pens of the age, was, in the course of our numerous vexations of the last four years, a never failing refuge to her in her most moody dispositions, & under her severest trials. . . . Henry & Lydia came to America in October, 1800. [Latrobe then tells how Henry, sent to a boarding school, caught the headmaster in a mistake in grammar and how, after a discussion had ensued, he refused to go back after the holidays.]

During this period as he was walking with one of my pupils, a boy much older than himself, he observed a little boy of about 4 years old, playing in a boat in the Schuylkill, a very rapid stream, between which & the Delaware Philadelphia is built. The chick fell out of the boat into the river, & Henry then just 9 years old, ran & getting into another small boat, caught him by the head, just as he approached a floating bridge at that time the principal one across the Schuylkill. The body of the child was sucked under the bridge but Henry held him fast, kept his head above water and calling loudly for assistance, his companion (Strickland, now the principal architect in Philadelphia) lost all presence of mind & by jumping in and out of [the] boat, had nearly filled it with water & drowned both children, before spectators from the shore could relieve them. It was on Sunday, & the shores were crowded with people among whom was the President of the Humane Society, Dr. Glentworth . . . [Henry told his sister, but enjoined her silence] & we did not know anything of the matter untill a medal had been voted to him, & a certificate was sent home, handsomely framed & displayed, recording the fact. This certificate has ever since hung up in our nursery, an invaluable evidence, of what we have lost . . .

[Henry was then sent to the academy of Mr. Desfeuilles at Germantown, until he was twelve, then to St. Mary's at Baltimore. There was no attempt there to convert the pupils. The boy was a decurion in charge of ten other pupils. Next he entered the University of Pennsylvania and assisted Dr. Thornton in his chemical experiments. Later he was awarded a scholarship in St. Mary's and returned there to take his bachelor's degree at sixteen. His valedictory address dealt with education for a free citizenry; its delivery was too much for him and he broke down near the end and fled the stage in tears.

[Latrobe continues with the tale of how Henry had taken over Mr. Lenthall's work at the Capitol at the age of seventeen; how he had invented a machine for blowing away into a designed receptacle the sawdust from the Navy Yard sawmill; and how he had served as superintendent of one of the difficult sections of the National Road—all prior to his departure for New Orleans.]

11. Criticism of Tom Moore's Verse *

I have been reading Moore's epistles, odes, & other poems.—In my opinion,—he is, since the death of Darwin the greatest of living poets:—Superior, as the poet of the passions, to any other in any language that I have ever read.—And as a serious satyrist [sic] he exhibits talents equal to our best poets *en ce genre*. What a pity, that, associating with violent party men, he should have immortalized the Billingsgate slanders of opposite politicians against the present ruling party and the present president. No man is so good, or so bad as his friends and his enemies paint him. Moore, received nothing but civilities in this country.—He had no business with its party politics as he was a mere bird of passage.—His hatred of republican forms of government, and his admiration of everything British was the natural result of early associations and habits. No one, if he thought these subjects fit company for his other more elegant poems could find fault with his treating them as he pleased. But he ought to have respected himself too much to have given the sanction of his immortal verse to personalties [sic], of which every political party will be ashamed as soon as the time is passed, during which they can influence an election.

As *far* as I am willing to go in respect to the *lusciousness* of Anacreatic poetry, I must yet say, that I stop short many miles of Thomas Moore.—

* From Latrobe's manuscript journals; this passage apparently dates from the late autumn of 1806.

Some years ago, I wrote a little Memorandum, in which *delicacy* as the result of *manners,* and as depending wholly on them, was considered. But no manners whatever can authorize, the public exhibition of sensual connection,—or the poetry that describes it;—because,—to treat the subject in the *driest* & most philosophical manner possible;—the *natural* monopoly of the individuals of the other sex,—by the individuals of our sex,—requires *privacy* as its security.—This engenders, in the first instance, *that,* which grows, with the improvement of the social state, into what is called delicacy,—the limits of which will be nearly in proportion to the state of refinement existing in a community.—

Mr. Moore has in some of his poems, particularly in his *Senses,* gone beyond all *modest* limits. Such a poem I believe has as yet never appeared in any work claiming a place among books, not liable to be taken into cognizance by the *Society for the suppression of vice & immorality.*— It is more dangerously immodest, than Capt[n] Morris's plenipotentiary because more slily seductive, and less disgusting.—

I brought the book with me, as an amusement, on my journey. Having lent it to Mr. Galatin where I have spent the evening, the conversation on its merits produced the follow[g] extemporaneous criticism.—

To Thomas Moore.

Taste, science, genius, all are thine
Spoild child of fancy,—minion of the nine!
When with soft sweep thy fingers touch the lyre
The chillest bosom throbs with warm desire;
When loud, thy forceful hand provokes the string
When Britain is thy theme, and Britain's king,
So burns the patriot flame in ev'ry line
E'en list'ning foes forgive the king that's *thine.*
But he who hears the lay thy muse inspires
While virtue reddens, and chaste love expires
Or hears thee 'gainst a newborn nation rave
Thy king could neither conquer nor enslave—
Laments, that with the love of kissing curst
Of all the kissing thou must do the worst
And press the mouth that so divinely sings
On lips of Harlots, and on feet of kings.

And yet, who would not be Mr. Moore with his feelings, his genius, his certain immortality, and his chance that riper Years will correct him into the first poet of the age!

12. Hymn for the Dedication of St. John's, Washington *

Tune, the Catholic hymn called in the New England books Hotham.

1. God of power, God of love!
Earth thy footstool heaven thy throne,—
From the realms of bliss above,
Bow thine ear in mercy down!
Thou who dwell'st in endless space
Fill the house we now prepare
With thy presence & thy grace!
Hear oh hear thy people's pray'r!

2. Vainly human pow'r essays,
Vainly toils the artist's skill,
Worthily a shrine to raise
Which Thy Majesty may fill.
But where in Thy sacred name
Two or three assembled are,
They may thy sure promise claim
Thou wilt hear their humble pray'r.

3. Once where o'er this favor'd land,
Savage wilds, & darkness spread,
Fostered now by thy kind hand
Cheerful dwellings rear their head;
Where once frown'd the tangled wood,
Fertile fields & meadows smile;
Where the stake of torture stood,
Rises now thy Church's pile.

4. Where the arrow's vengefull flight,
Sex, nor age, nor childhood spar'd,
Fraud was skill, and pow'r was right
There thy Gospel's voice is heard!
Heard alas! Too oft in vain!
Still with mild, prevailing force,
Spreads its love-diffusing reign,
Nor shall aught impede its course.

5. When the hostile firebrand's flash
Reddened, late, the midnight air
And the falling Column's crash
Drown'd the shriek of wild depair
Thou, whose nod the Storms obey
Midst the wreck of blazing domes,
Bad'st the foe his fury stay,
And respect our private homes.

6. For these wonders of thy grace
See us bow the grateful knee,
And in this thy holy place,
Consecrate ourselves to thee.
And when in this Temple's bound
To thy Altar we repair,
Breathe thy healing presence round,
Hear! oh hear thy people's prayer.

* From Benjamin Henry Boneval Latrobe, *Impressions Respecting New Orleans,* edited with an introduction and notes by Samuel Wilson, Jr. (New York: Columbia University Press, 1951).

MAJOR SOURCES

Letter books of B. H. Latrobe, 1804-17, in the possession of the Latrobe family.

Manuscript journals of B. H. Latrobe, in the possession of the Latrobe family and in the Maryland Historical Society.

Latrobe drawings and some letters, in the Library of Congress; this is the largest collection of Latrobe drawings, including much valuable miscellaneous material and many drawings dealing with the Capitol, the Marine Hospital, and the President's House as well as with other government projects.

Latrobe drawings in the Historical Society of Pennsylvania, especially those dealing with the Philadelphia waterworks, the Bank of Pennsylvania, and the competition for the Bank of the United States.

Latrobe drawings and sketches in his sketchbooks, in the possession of the Latrobe family.

Latrobe drawings and sketches in the Maryland Historical Society, especially those of the Susquehanna survey and the Baltimore Exchange.

Latrobe drawings of the Baltimore Cathedral, in the archives of the Roman Catholic Diocese of Baltimore.

The Jefferson Papers, in the Library of Congress.

The Lenthall Papers, in the Library of Congress.

The Livingston Papers, in the New-York Historical Society.

The Fulton Papers, in the Gilbert H. Montague Collection, New York Public Library.

Drawings and documents by or dealing with Latrobe, in several departments of the National Archives.

Scattered examples of Latrobe's drawings, in the Historical Society of Delaware and in various private hands, including St. John's Church, Washington; Mrs. Truxtun Beale, Washington; and Bishop H. St. George Tucker, Richmond.

INDEX

(*illustration pages in italics*)